# Problems from Reid

# Problems from Reid

James Van Cleve

OXFORD
UNIVERSITY PRESS

# OXFORD
## UNIVERSITY PRESS

Oxford University Press is a department of the University of Oxford. It furthers the University's
objective of excellence in research, scholarship, and education by publishing worldwide. Oxford is a
registered trade mark of Oxford University Press in the UK and in certain other countries

Published in the United States of America by
Oxford University Press
198 Madison Avenue, New York, NY 10016,
United States of America

Library of Congress Cataloging-in-Publication Data
Van Cleve, James.
Problems from Reid / James Van Cleve.
p.   cm.
ISBN 978–0–19–985703–6 (hardback)
1.  Reid, Thomas, 1710–1796. I. Title.
B1537.V36 2015
192—dc23
2014043487

1  3  5  7  9  8  6  4  2

Typeset in Arno

Printed on EB 45# Glat 400

Printed by Edwards Brothers

For Claudia, the love of my life

# CONTENTS

# PREFACE

I feel fortunate to have been reared in an academic environment rich in Reid. As an undergraduate at the University of Iowa, I took a canon-busting course on Hume and Reid from Phillip Cummins, learning early on that there was an alternative to the Humean path that ends in a coal pit. As a graduate student at the University of Rochester, I studied with Keith Lehrer, who was then at work on his groundbreaking book on Reid. Lehrer did not actually teach Reid during those years, but we all knew he was working on something big. At Brown University, I became a colleague of Roderick Chisholm. Chisholm did not teach Reid, either—Chisholm never taught any other philosopher, but simply tackled philosophical problems head-on. Nonetheless, many of Reid's insights live on in Chisholm's work. Finally, when I moved to the University of Southern California, I became a colleague of Gideon Yaffe, an expert in Reid's theory of action as well as most things Reidian. I am grateful to them all.

I did not undertake a really systematic study of Reid until I began teaching graduate seminars on Reid, first at Brown in the mid-1990s and later at the University of Southern California. These seminars fueled my first articles on Reid, and I thank the students in them for the stimulation they provided.

I attended conferences on Reid at the University of Aberdeen in 1998, 2000, and 2004, as well as a tercentennial conference on Reid in 2010 in Aberdeen and Glasgow. I am grateful to the organizers and the other participants for these valuable occasions.

In the summer of 2000, I taught a Summer Seminar for College Teachers entitled "Reid on Perception, Knowledge, and Action," funded by the National Endowment for the Humanities. The participants, many of whom have gone on to make valuable contributions to Reid scholarship, were Terence Cuneo, Jack Lyons, Jennifer McKitrick, Ryan Nichols, Michael Pakaluk, Patrick Rysiew, Jack Sanders, Ed Slowik, Paul Tidman, William Tolhurst, John Wingard, John P. Wright, and Gideon Yaffe. I thank them all for what I learned from them.

I wrote several chapters of this book and rewrote several others under the vaulted glass and towering pines of the National Humanities Center, where I was William C. and Ida Friday Fellow for 2011-12. I was also supported that year by a grant from the National Endowment for the Humanities and a subsidy from USC. I thank both the NHC and the NEH for taking me in and supporting my work a second time. I thank the Center's Marianne Wason for helping me with diagrams for the book.

Finally, I would like to thank all those (in addition to those already mentioned) who have made helpful suggestions about one or another part of this book. They include David Bennett, Todd Buras, Panayot Butchvarov, Tim Chambers, Rebecca Copenhaver, Lorne Falkenstein, Marina Folescu, Brian Glenney, Christopher Hill, Janet Levin, Tran Nguyen, Kenny Pearce, Lewis Powell, Baron Reed, Ernest Sosa, Claudia Strauss, Dale Tuggy, and Kadri Vihvelin. Thanks also to Rex Welshon for his expert hand in preparing the index.

# ACKNOWLEDGMENTS

I am grateful to the following publishers and journals for permission to use or adapt material from previously published articles:

Van Cleve, James. "Reid on the First Principles of Contingent Truths." *Reid Studies*, 3 (1999), 3–30.

Van Cleve, James. "Thomas Reid's Geometry of Visibles." *Philosophical Review*, 111 (2002), 373–416.

Van Cleve, James. "Lehrer, Reid, and the First of All Principles." In *The Epistemology of Keith Lehrer*, edited by Erik Olsson (Dordrecht, Holland: Kluwer Academic Publishers, 2003), 155–72.

Van Cleve, James. "Reid versus Berkeley on the Inverted Retinal Image." *Philosophical Topics*, 31 (2003), 425–55.

Van Cleve, James. "Reid's Theory of Perception." In *The Cambridge Companion to Reid*, edited by Terence Cuneo and René van Woudenberg (Cambridge: Cambridge University Press, 2004), 101–33.

Van Cleve, James. "Reid's Answer to Molyneux's Question." *The Monist*, 90 (2007), 251–70.

Van Cleve, James. "Reid on Single and Double Vision: Mechanics and Morals." *Journal of Scottish Philosophy*, 6 (2008), 1–20.

Van Cleve, James. "Reid's Response to the Skeptic." In *The Oxford Handbook of Skepticism*, edited by John Greco (Oxford: Oxford University Press, 2008), 286–309.

Van Cleve, James. "Reid on the Real Foundation of the Primary-Secondary Quality Distinction." In *Primary and Secondary Qualities: The Historical and Ongoing Debate*, edited by Larry Nolan (Oxford: Oxford University Press, 2011), 274–303.

Van Cleve, James. "Four Questions about Acquired Perception." Forthcoming in *Mind, Knowledge, and Action: Essays in Honor of Reid's Tercentenary*, edited by T. Buras and R. Copenhaver (Oxford: Oxford University Press).

Van Cleve, James. "Berkeley, Reid, and Sinha on Molyneux's Question." In *Sensory Integration and the Unity of Consciousness*, edited by Christopher Hill and David Bennett (Cambridge, MA: MIT Press, 2015).

# INTRODUCTION

Thomas Reid (1710–1796) was the founder of the Scottish common sense school of philosophy. A contemporary and critic of his countryman Hume, Reid is best known for his trenchant opposition to skepticism and the "way of ideas"—the assumption that what is immediately present to the mind is never an external thing, but only an internal image, sense datum, or idea. His contributions to epistemology and the theory of action have increasingly attracted attention during the last several decades, and I look forward to the day when the "big seven" of modern philosophy courses is expanded to the big eight: Descartes, Spinoza, Leibniz, Locke, Berkeley, Hume, Kant, and Reid.

After being educated at Marischal College in Aberdeen, Reid served for fifteen years as a parish minister in nearby New Machar. In 1752 he was appointed professor at King's College in Aberdeen, where he taught mathematics, physics, and philosophy among other subjects. During the years 1758–64 he took part in the meetings of the Aberdeen Philosophical Society, a group whose agenda was set in good part by the works of Hume. As Reid said in a letter to Hume, "If you write no more . . . I am afraid we shall be at a loss for Subjects" (IHM 265). Many manuscripts of material he presented to the society survive, sounding themes he later expounded in his books.

In 1764 he published the first of his three books, *An Inquiry into the Human Mind on the Principles of Common Sense*, in which he systematically set forth his account of how we arrive at knowledge by means of the various senses and gave his reasons for opposing the reigning theory of ideas as intermediaries in all cognition. In the same year he accepted the chair in moral philosophy at the University of Glasgow, recently vacated by Adam Smith. He lectured there for sixteen more years, resigning in 1780 to prepare his last two books, *Essays on the Intellectual Powers of Man* (1785), devoted to the contribution of perception, memory, reason, and other cognitive powers to human knowledge, and *Essays on the Active Powers of Man* (1788), devoted to the nature of action, will, freedom, and morality.

As was said above, Reid is famous for his critique of the assumption that what is directly present to the mind is never anything but an idea. He was one of the first of the early modern thinkers to question this assumption, which was dominant in the philosophy of his day and still prevalent in our own. He pointed out some of the disastrous consequences to which it leads, exposed some of the misconceptions underlying it, and developed some of the philosophical resources needed for avoiding it. In its place, he espoused direct realism, the common sense view that we perceive stars and trees directly, not just by way of their mental representatives. As direct realism was a major theme for Reid, so it will be a major theme in this book; it is discussed at greatest length in chapter 3, but also makes its appearance in chapters 5, 6, 10, and 12.

The various chapters of this book cover the following topics and contributions by Reid as well:

Chapter 1: Reid's distinction between sensation and perception, now standard in psychology texts; his early version of the adverbial theory of sensation; his threefold analysis of perception in terms of conception, belief, and immediacy.

Chapter 2: Reid's nativist or innatist account of the provenance of certain important concepts, including active power and the self, which he offers as an antidote to the empiricism of Hume; his argument that not even the concept of spatial extension can be derived in the way empiricists prescribe.

Chapter 3: how to characterize Reid's direct realism and how to respond to four important arguments against it.

Chapter 4: Reid's way of drawing the primary-secondary quality distinction, according to which in knowing the shape of a thing, we know how it is intrinsically, whereas in knowing the color of a thing we know only what sensations it gives us—a version of the distinction not vulnerable to Berkeley's criticisms.

Chapter 5: Reid's account of the phenomenon of acquired perception, in which perception is enriched by learning: owing to past associations of object or quality A with object or quality B, one automatically takes B to be present when one perceives A, resulting in a state that *almost* (but according to me, not quite) amounts to perceiving B.

Chapter 6: the true basis of Reid's claim that the visual field is governed by laws other than Euclid's; whether this claim gives him the honor of having discovered non-Euclidean geometry before the mathematicians, and whether it compromises his direct realism.

Chapter 7: a nativist solution to the conundrum of the inverted retinal image— why do we see the world right side up despite having a retinal image of it that is upside down?—differing from the leading solutions of his day (including Berkeley's learning-based solution) and confirmed by contemporary cognitive science.

Chapter 8: an affirmative answer to Molyneux's question—would a man born blind and made to see recognize by sight alone objects he formerly knew only by touch?—challenging the better known negative answers of Locke and Berkeley.

Chapter 9: Reid's account of memory, according to which memory is direct acquaintance with things past, just as perception is direct acquaintance with things in the external world; his critique of the Lockean theory that personal identity is constituted by memory links.

Chapter 10: an answer to the question of how there can be cognitive relations to objects that do not exist, as in imagination and hallucination—an answer that refuses to invoke ideas as stand-ins and anticipates Meinong's theory of nonexistent objects, as well as opening up a new strategy for defending direct realism.

Chapter 11: an epistemology that gives pride of place to first principles (propositions evident without argument), taking the domain of such principles to extend beyond the current contents of our minds (to which Descartes had confined them) and letting them include propositions about the physical world and the past as well.

Chapter 12: a response to philosophical skepticism powered by epistemological externalism (the view that knowledge-making factors need not themselves be known), which permits us to know that our cognitive faculties are reliable through the use of those very faculties.

Chapter 13: a comparison of my interpretation of Reid's epistemology with that of Keith Lehrer.

Chapter 14: the distinction between event causation and agent causation and an analysis of human action according to which actions are events caused or constituted by volitions, which are themselves caused by agents.

Chapter 15: Reid's deployment of the notion of agent causation to slip between the horns of the fundamental dilemma for human freedom—either arbitrary uncaused acts of will or deterministic causal chains stretching back to dinosaur days; whether Reid's view succumbs to infinite regress.

Chapter 16: a theory of morality according to which moral approvals and disapprovals do not express mere feelings as in Hume but embody genuine knowledge that certain actions are right and others wrong.

It is gratifying to expound the views of a philosopher I find so often to be in the right. Though I express misgivings about Reid's views in chapters 2, 6, and 10, I am largely sympathetic to the views discussed in the remaining chapters, and I defend them to the extent that I can.

References to Reid's works will be given in the text using abbreviations in the following style: IHM 2.3:27 for *An Inquiry into the Human Mind on the Principles of Common Sense*, chapter 2, section 3, page 27; EIP 6.5:480 for *Essays on the Intellectual Powers of Man*, essay 6, chapter 5, page 480; EAP 5.7:350 for *Essays on the Active Powers of Man*, essay 5, chapter 7, page 350; COR 206 for page 206 in *The Correspondence of Thomas Reid*, generally with date and correspondent noted as well. Page numbers pertain to the Edinburgh University Press editions of Reid's works listed in the bibliography; essay, chapter, and section numbers pertain to Reid's works in any edition. IHM citations with a page number and no section number refer to unpublished manuscripts included in the Edinburgh edition of the *Inquiry*.

# 1

## SENSATION AND PERCEPTION

The external senses have a double province; to make us feel, and to make us perceive. They furnish us with a variety of sensations, some pleasant, others painful, and others indifferent; at the same time they give us a conception, and an invincible belief of the existence of external objects. . . . This conception and belief which Nature produces by means of the senses, we call *perception*. The feeling which goes along with the perception, we call *sensation*. (Thomas Reid, *EIP 2.18:210*)

Perception bulks large in Reid's writings. Nearly all of the *Inquiry into the Human Mind* is devoted to it, with chapters allotted to each of the senses of Smelling, Hearing, Tasting, Touch, and Seeing. In the *Essays on the Intellectual Powers of Man*, by far the longest essay is Essay II, "Of the Powers We Have by Means of Our External Senses." In this chapter, I expound Reid's views on the distinction between sensation and perception and discuss the two main components into which he analyzes perception, namely, conception and belief. Subsequent chapters take up other topics connected with perception, including Reid's defense of direct realism, his treatment of the distinction between primary and secondary qualities, and his account of the phenomenon of acquired perception.

## A. EXPLANATIONS OF TERMS

Reid devotes the first chapter of the *Intellectual Powers* to explaining how he uses key terms. This does not always involve defining them, since some terms are best explained simply by pointing out examples of things to which they apply. As a saying cited by Reid's editor Sir William Hamilton has it, "a view of the thing itself is its best definition" (Hamilton, 220a).[1] I give a brief rundown here of several of the terms that are important in this book, retaining Reid's numbering from EIP 1.

1. "By the *mind* of a man, we understand that in him which thinks, remembers, reasons, wills" (EIP 1.1:20). Reid is an unabashed dualist, taking for granted that a mind is a substance distinct from anything material, but few if any of his important views on other topics depend on this assumption.

2. By an *operation* of the mind, Reid understands "every mode of thinking of which we are conscious" (EIP 1.1:20). Examples are sensing, perceiving, remembering, hoping, and willing. Reid also uses the term *act* in this connection, systematically distinguishing between acts of the mind and their objects (for example, conceiving and the thing conceived, either of which might be called by the term *conception*).

3. A *faculty* is an original power of the mind, that is, a power that is innate rather than acquired. Reid does not mean to reify faculties; to say that someone has the faculty to V simply means that he is innately able to V.

4. To be *in the mind* is to have the mind as its subject, as operations and faculties do; everything that is not a mind or in a mind is *external*.

5. *Thinking* is a term Reid generally uses in broad Cartesian fashion to cover all operations of the mind—not just intellection, but also perceiving, remembering, imagining, and so on (EIP 1.1:22; see also 2.14:179, lines 22–23).

6. *Perception* is an operation about which much more is said below. Suffice it for now to say that Reid reserves the term for awareness of *external* things. He excoriates Hume for corrupting the English language by using "perception" as the all-purpose word for mental acts and their objects (EIP 1.1:23).

7. "*Consciousness* is a word used by Philosophers, to signify that immediate knowledge which we have . . . of all the present operations of our minds" (EIP1.1:24). "Consciousness" is thus Reid's word for what Locke calls inner sense (EIP 6.1:420) and what we now call introspection. We need to add this caveat, however: consciousness for Reid, unlike introspection, is something that automatically accompanies any thinking at all, not something that requires any special exercise on our part.[2]

8. *Conceiving* is another term important enough to be the subject of its own section below. Suffice it for now to say that conceiving is "the same thing which Logicians call simple apprehension," which is "an act of the mind by which

---

[1] Sir William Hamilton (1788–1856) edited Reid's collected works and added his own copious notes, to the frequent annoyance and occasional enlightenment of generations of readers.
[2] See EIP 3.5:268–69 for Reid's distinction between consciousness and reflection.

nothing is affirmed or denied, and which therefore can neither be true nor false" (EIP 1.1:24).[3]

9. The paragraph bearing this number introduces no new term, but records Reid's conviction that nearly all operations of the mind involve a subject-act-object structure. "The mind that perceives, the object perceived, and the operation of perceiving that object, are distinct things, and are distinguished in the structure of all languages" (EIP 1.1:26). So it is as well with remembering, conceiving, and nearly all other operations.

10. *Ideas* are items posited by philosophers to serve as the immediate objects of all thought. Reid is the great foe of ideas. It is important to realize, however, that he is opposed to ideas only in the philosophical and not in the popular sense of the term. In the popular sense, "to have an idea of any thing, is to conceive it" (EIP 1.1:27). Reid is giving here what Russell would call a contextual definition—he does not define "idea" (which he thinks is a term with no referent), but only the longer expression "to have an idea." In everyday parlance, people do undoubtedly have ideas of things, but this is only to say that they think of them.[4]

In the philosophical sense of the term, an idea is not an act of thinking, but an object of the act (EIP 1.1:28). Moreover, it is not an external object like the sun or moon, but an internal object, existing only in the mind. Whereas Reid and the vulgar think of a cognitive situation as having three components—a subject or mind that thinks, an act or operation of thinking, and an external object of that act—philosophers add a fourth object, an idea, which they think is the only immediate object of one's cognition (EIP 1.1:26 and 31). It is ideas as "fourth things" that Reid regards as fictions. He wryly remarks that once ideas are admitted, they tend to take over, driving the first three types of object out of existence (EIP 2.12:163; see also IHM 2.6:33–34).

---

[3] I find puzzling Reid's view (expressed here and elsewhere, e.g., EIP 4.1:296) that where there is no affirmation or denial, there can be no truth or falsehood. I could understand him if by "affirming" and "denying" he meant what Locke and the Port Royalists do, namely, operations that form affirmative or negative propositions—for in that case, where there is no affirmation or denial there would be no proposition (Owen 2003). But what Reid seems to mean by "affirming" and "denying" is believing and disbelieving, respectively, and he allows that there can be bare conception of a proposition that is neither affirmed nor denied. Such conceptions could be called true or false according to whether the proposition is true or false.

[4] Reid employs a similar contextualist strategy at EIP 4.2:322: "an image in the mind is only a periphrasis for imagination." That is, to have an image of something (in the innocent popular sense) is simply to imagine it. Compare also IHM:314: "*having an idea* is merely that figure of speech which Critics call a *pleonasm*, as if I should say, *I have a remembrance*, for *I remember*."

11. *Impression* is a term that for Reid has a purely physical meaning. Broadly, he takes an impression to be a change in a body produced by an external cause, as when a cannon ball dents a wall. More narrowly, he takes an impression to be a change in our sensory surfaces produced by an external cause in the causal chain leading up to perception. The striking of a retina by a ray of light would count as an impression (EIP 1.1:34–36).

Reid faults Hume for misusing the term *impression*. As already noted, Hume uses *perception* as the most general term for items of the mind's furniture, so that even a twinge of nausea and the belief in tomorrow's sunrise count as perceptions. He then uses "impression" for any sufficiently lively perception (EIP 1.1:32–34). Reid offers forceful criticisms of Hume's attempt to distinguish between impressions and other mental acts or objects simply in terms of force and vivacity at EIP 3.7:289 and IHM 6.24:197–98.

12. *Sensation* is another term important enough to receive its own section below.

There are two further terms, *causation* and *suggestion*, that merit preliminary explication despite not being on Reid's list in EIP 1.1.

*Causation.* In Reid's view, causation in the proper sense of the term is exercised only by *agents*, conscious beings with will and intelligence. What is commonly referred to as causation, such as the causation of thunder by lightning, is really only the lawful succession of one type of event by another, not causation in the strict sense of the term. Yet Reid is happy to speak with the vulgar, saying that lightning causes thunder and that sound waves cause impressions on eardrums. I shall follow Reid in this regard. When it is necessary to distinguish lawful succession from genuine causation, I shall refer to the former as *physical* or *event* causation and the latter as *efficient* or *agent* causation. This distinction is discussed at greater length in chapter 14.

*Suggestion.* Berkeley uses this term for the process by which one idea automatically brings to mind another, as when a certain sound makes us think of a passing coach or a visible cue makes us think of a tangible shape. Reid takes over the term along with the Berkeleyan paradigms of its application, but he adds an important twist. Whereas Berkeley thought all relations of suggestion are the product of experiential learning or association, Reid allows for innate, original, or natural relations of suggestion (IHM 2.7:38). As we shall see, a substantial part of his philosophy consists of pointing out cases in which certain sensory or conscious cues innately suggest other things to us. To cite just three cases, certain tactile sensations suggest hard, external bodies, memories suggest past events, and thoughts suggest a thinker.

## B. SENSATION VERSUS PERCEPTION

A sensation is an event that occurs in a sentient subject when he smells a rose or tastes a fig. It lacks figure and extension and other qualities of bodies, being entirely mental. Reid calls sensations "principles of belief," by which he means that when we have a sensation, we cannot help believing that it exists, that a subject of it exists (ourselves), and that some external object (for example, some quality in the rose) is the cause of it.

J. J. Gibson credits Reid with being the first thinker to draw the distinction between sensation and perception, which is now standard in psychology textbooks.[5] It is not always drawn in the same way, but the following glossary entries are typical: sensation is "the initial process of detecting and encoding environmental energy," caused by stimulation of a sensory organ; perception is "the process of organizing and interpreting sensations into meaningful experiences," involving judgment and other higher-level operations (Schiffman 1976: 522 and 518).

Here is how Reid draws the distinction in the *Inquiry*:

> Thus, *I feel a pain; I see a tree*: the first denoteth a sensation, the last a perception. The grammatical analysis of both expressions is the same: for both consist of an active verb and an object. But, if we attend to the things signified by these expressions, we shall find that in the first, the distinction between the act and the object is not real but grammatical; in the second, the distinction is not only grammatical, but real.
>
> The form of the expression, *I feel pain*, might seem to imply, that the feeling is something distinct from the pain felt; yet, in reality, there is no distinction. As *thinking a thought* is an expression which could signify no more than *thinking*, so *feeling a pain* signifies no more than *being pained*. What we have said of pain is applicable to every other mere sensation. (IHM 6.20:167–68)

When I see a tree, there is an object (the tree itself) apart from my act of seeing, but when I have a sensation, there is no object apart from the act of sensing. As he says in his explications of words, "Sensation is a name given by philosophers to an act of mind, which may be distinguished from all others by this, that it hath no object distinct from the act itself" (EIP 1.1:36).

"It hath no object distinct from the act itself." Is that because an act of sensing has *itself* for its object? Or is it because it has *no* object? My answer on Reid's

---

[5] Reid is credited with this distinction by Price (1932:22), Gibson (1966 I:319), and Pastore (1971:114) among others. Some find an earlier version of the distinction in Malebranche. If Reid did not originate the distinction, he at least established it (Boring [1929] 1950:206).

behalf, defended at length in section G below, is that sensations are objectless. If that is correct, sensations are distinguished from all other acts of the mind in being *nonintentional*. Other acts of the mind—perceiving, remembering, hoping, and so on—are *intentional* as that term is used in medieval and contemporary philosophy.[6] That is to say, they have "ofness" or "aboutness"; they are directed at some object. Sensations, by contrast, are devoid of intentionality; they are not directed at any object at all.

If we take Reid to hold that sensations are objectless, he is a precursor of what is now known as the adverbial theory of sensation, which gained great currency through the work of C. J. Ducasse (1942) and R. M. Chisholm (1957:115–25).[7] In this theory, to have a sensation of red is not to sense some*thing* but is simply to sense some*how*. It is to sense *redly*, as Chisholm says. The logical form of a sensation statement is not subject-act-object or *aRb*, but simply *Fa*. As Ducasse says, sensing is more like dancing a waltz than eating a cake: its nominal object does not denote anything apart from the dancing or sensing of it. As Reid says, when I have a pain, there is not a pain that I have or stand in a relation to; I am simply pained. Moreover, pain is the model for all other sensations. "What we have said of pain may be applied to every other sensation" (EIP 1.1:37).

Ganson (2008:247) identifies four traits of Reidian sensations (denoted by the variable "x") that it will be useful to list here, along with citations of passages in which Reid attributes the traits to pains or other sensations:

> *Trustworthiness*: x necessarily exists if you feel it. (EIP 2.18:214; 2.22:243; IHM 2.3:27)

> *Disclosedness*: x necessarily is felt by you if it exists. (EIP 1.1:37; 2.16:94; 2.22:243; IHM 2.3:27; 5.6:64; COR 113)

> *Unmistakability*: x necessarily is F if it is felt as being F. (EIP 1.1:37; 2.16:197; 2.18:214; 2.22:243)

> *Transparency*: x necessarily is felt as being F if it is F. (EIP 2.16:194; IHM 175–76; Brookes 258; COR 113)

The first two properties are converses of each other, as are the second two. The difference between the pairs is that the first two are concerned with the *existence* of

---

[6] "Intentional" is derived from the Latin verb "intendo," which means *to aim*, as with a bow and arrow.

[7] Among those who attribute an adverbial theory of sensation to Reid are Chisholm (1957:117, n.1) and Lehrer (1989:15). For others, see Buras 2005, notes 12 and 14.

sensations, while the second two are concerned with their *character*. In the second two, it is to be understood that "F" is restricted to intrinsic features, such as the acridness of a smell, rather than extrinsic properties, such as simultaneity with a solar flare. The first three of the four properties are affirmed in the following passage:

> For we are conscious of all our sensations, and they can neither be any other in their nature, nor greater or less in their degree than we feel them. It is impossible that a man should be in pain, when he does not feel pain; and when he feels pain, it is impossible that his pain should not be real, and in its degree what it is felt to be. (EIP 2.22:243)

The four properties will be important below when we discuss in detail whether sensations have themselves as their objects.[8]

The four properties of sensations must be distinguished from four structurally similar properties sometimes claimed for *beliefs* about sensations—that sensations necessarily exist if they are believed to exist, necessarily are believed to exist if they exist, are necessarily F if they are believed to be F, and are necessarily believed to be F if they are F. The first and the third of these are sometimes expressed by saying that our beliefs about our sensations are *infallible*, the second and the fourth by saying that in regard to our sensations we are *omniscient*.[9] It may be that Reid ascribes infallibility and omniscience to our beliefs about our sensations as well as ascribing the four Ganson properties to sensations themselves. I return to this matter later.[10]

As I said above, there is more than one way of drawing the sensation-perception distinction. I tabulate some of them in Table 1.1. The fourth column gives the name of someone who accepts the way of drawing the distinction proposed in a given row; the third column indicates whether Reid would accept the proposed way of drawing the distinction as aligned with his own way (in some rows, for reasons yet to be discussed).

---

[8] Ganson says the four properties do not hold of perceptions. I do not think they are even *defined* for perceptions, since perceptions are not felt.

[9] For precise definitions of these terms, see Alston 1971. Hume writes, "Since all . . . sensations of the mind are known to us by consciousness, they must necessarily appear in every particular what they are, and be what they appear" (THN 1.4.2). There may be a way of understanding "appear" so that Hume is saying that sensations have unmistakability and transparency. On the other hand, Alston interprets "appearing F" as being believed to be F, thus ascribing to Hume the doctrine that we enjoy both infallibility and omniscience with respect to our sensations (228).

[10] To anticipate section F, I believe Reid would say we enjoy omniscience about our sensations only when we are attending to them.

**Table 1.1**

| Sensation | Perception | Reid? | Who else? |
|---|---|---|---|
| Unintentional; has no object | Intentional; has an (external) object | Yes | Kant (CPR, A320/B376) |
| Correlates with surface stimulation; peripherally aroused | Correlates with brain processes; a function of central states | Probably | William James, many psychologists |
| Is acquaintance with objects or qualities | Is knowledge-about or knowledge that something is the case | No, since sensation has no object (and see box below) | James (1890, vol. 1, 221) |
| Does not have as its content a proposition about an external object | Has as its content a proposition about an external object | Yes, if belief is an ingredient in perception, but not if it is a mere concomitant | Peacocke (1983, chapter 1) |
| Confined to one sense modality | May be multi-modal | Yes | Morgan (1977, 110) |

## C. REID'S THREEFOLD ACCOUNT OF PERCEPTION

Reid's official characterization of perception in the *Intellectual Powers* identifies three elements in it—conception, belief, and immediacy:

> If, therefore, we attend to that act of our mind which we call the perception of an external object of sense, we shall find in it these three things. *First,* Some conception or notion of the object perceived. *Secondly,* A strong and irresistible conviction of its present existence. And *thirdly,* That this conviction and belief are immediate, and not the effect of reasoning. (EIP 2.5:96)

These three elements are already singled out by Reid in the *Inquiry*:

> I know this also, that the perception of an object implies both a conception of its form, and a belief of its present existence. I know moreover, that this belief is not the effect of argumentation and reasoning; it is the immediate effect of my constitution. (IHM 6.20:168)

He mentions the same three elements again and again in the *Intellectual Powers*.[11]

The "immediacy" that Reid mentions here is characterized in a psychological way: the perceiver does not arrive at the belief by inference but transitions to it spontaneously on the appropriate occasions. We shall see later, however, that there is also an epistemic dimension to the immediacy of the beliefs involved in perception. The beliefs are not only taken up without using any other beliefs as premises, but they are also *evident* or *justified* without depending on the support of any other beliefs.

The reader may be surprised to learn that Reid's threefold account makes no mention of sensation. Although Reid holds that sensations generally serve as the *triggers* for the conception and belief involved in perception, he does not usually list them as *ingredients* in perception.[12] There are two assignable reasons for this. First, Reid thinks it possible that there should be beings in whom perception occurs in the absence of sensation (IHM 6.21:174–76; EIP 2.20:227; COR:112, letter 61).[13] Second, he holds that there is one variety of human perception that actually *does* occur without any characteristic sensation—namely, the perception of visible form (IHM 6.8:99–101 and 6.21:176). A good example of perception without sensation from contemporary psychology is afforded by the Kanizsa triangle, a figure in which a triangle is perceived even though there are no sensations corresponding to its sides (see Figure 1.1):

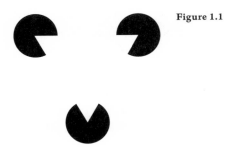

Figure 1.1

Is the threefold account in terms of conception, belief, and immediacy meant to be any sort of *definition* or *analysis* of perception? This question decomposes into

---

[11] See, for example, EIP 2.16:199, 2.17:210, 2.18:211, 2.20:226–27, and 3.1:253. The first three of these passages mention conception and immediate belief; the fourth and fifth mention conception and belief.

[12] He does sometimes say that sensations are ingredients in perceptions (e.g., at EIP 2.16:197), but he more often says that perceptions are *accompanied* by sensations or have sensations *corresponding* to them—see, e.g., EIP 1.1:37 and 2.16:194.

[13] The possibility Reid affirms here is conceptual or metaphysical possibility, not physical possibility. In the passage at EIP 2.20:227, he allows that sensations and perceptions (except in the case of visible figure) are "conjoined in our nature by the will of heaven." That is all that can be meant in his philosophy by a physically necessary connection.

two others. First, are the three conditions meant to be jointly sufficient as well as individually necessary for perception? And second, even if the conditions are necessary and sufficient, are they so for conceptual reasons or merely causal reasons?

As for the first question, Reid sometimes cites further conditions besides his standard three as necessary for perception. One condition is that the object of perception must be an external object that really exists and is contemporaneous with the act of perceiving it (EIP 1.1:22–23, 2.20:232, 4.1:311).[14] This condition distinguishes perception from memory (in which the object is past) and consciousness (in which the object is something mental rather than something external). Another condition is that there must be a causal chain connecting the object with the perception of it—a process starting with the object, typically running through some medium and some organ of sense, and culminating with the conception and belief in the object (IHM 6.21, especially 174, and EIP 2.2:76).

As for the second question, I think it may well be that some of the conditions on Reid's threefold list (for example, belief) are included not because they are *analytical ingredients* of perception, but because they are *inevitable effects* of it. Reid does not always pay much heed to this distinction.[15]

Indeed, I think it possible that Reid thinks of perception as a *primitive* operation, not susceptible of any analysis at all. There are places where he says as much: "I am conscious of this act of my mind [perception], and I can reflect upon it," he says, "but it is too simple to admit of an analysis" (IHM 6.20:168). If that is so, his listing of the conditions always found along with perception should be thought of in just those terms—conditions always found along with it.

Let us consider belief as a case in point. Shortly after giving the threefold account quoted above, Reid qualifies the claim that perception always involves belief by saying that if a perception is "faint and indistinct" (as in the case of a ship just beginning to appear on the horizon), there may be doubt about the existence of its object—a doubt that gives way to belief as the perception becomes distinct (EIP 2.5:97). Here he is *explaining* the existence of a belief by the existence of a perception—a procedure that would be nonsense if perception included belief by

---

[14] Reid is actually vexingly inconsistent about whether the object perceived must exist. He usually insists that perception must be employed about an existing object (as at EIP 4.1:310–11), but occasionally admits cases of hallucinatory perception in which there is no existing object (as in the perception of pain in an amputated limb at EIP 2.18:214).

[15] For example, he says in one place that belief is part of the "meaning" of seeing a chair (EIP 2.20:232), but in another place that every man feels that belief is an "immediate consequence" of perception (EIP 2.15:193). And at EIP 6.1:409, he says this: "The man who perceives an object, believes that it exists . . . nor is it in his power to avoid such judgment. . . . Whether judgment ought to be called a necessary concomitant of these operations, or rather a part or ingredient of them, I do not dispute."

definition. Consider also this: "My belief is carried along by perception, as irresistibly as my body by the earth" (IHM 6.20:169). That remark certainly suggests that the relationship between perception and belief is causation rather than containment.

## D. THE CONCEPTION IN PERCEPTION

What is the nature of the *conception* that Reid lists as the first element in perception? Contemporary readers are likely to think of Kant when they encounter this term. They are likely to connect "conception" with *concepts*, and to think that when Reid talks of conception, he is talking about subsuming something under a concept—classifying an object in some way, thinking of it as being of a certain sort, or judging it to be so and so. ("The only use the understanding can make of these concepts," Kant says, "is to judge by means of them" [(1787) 1929: A68/B93].) If so, the conception involved in perception would be nothing not already involved in the belief component; it would simply be a matter of possessing and deploying the concepts that enter into the belief. Forming a conception of an object would be entertaining some proposition about it, and the belief component of perception would consist in affirming that proposition. Reid's account of perception would make perception simply a matter of forming non-inferential beliefs about objects, as in the contemporary accounts of perception advanced by Armstrong (1968) and Pitcher (1971).

It would be wrong, however, to conclude that Reid holds a pure belief theory of perception (or even a theory of perception as non-inferential belief accompanied by sensation) and more fundamentally wrong to think that Reidian conception has anything essentially to do with concepts. As Alston and Wolterstorff have forcefully pointed out, if we are to understand Reid, we must set aside our Kantian lenses (Alston 1989a, Wolterstorff 2001:9–12). We must pay full heed to Reid's own official explanation of what he means by "conception," which occurs in EIP 4.1, "Of Conception, or Simple Apprehension in General." There we learn that conception is the most basic operation of the mind, presupposed in all others. It is "that operation of the understanding, which the Logicians call simple apprehension," and which they define as "the bare conception of a thing, without any judgment or belief about it" (EIP 4.1:295). To avoid the verbal circle in defining conception in terms of simple apprehension and simple apprehension in terms of bare conception, we could restate the definition of simple apprehension as "the bare *apprehension* of a thing, without any judgment or belief about it."[16] Reid goes on to characterize judgment

---

[16] In appendix B, I argue that Reid should have defined his terms as follows: Conception of x = Df apprehension of x with no belief as *ingredient*; bare conception of x = Df apprehension of x with no belief about x as *accompaniment*.

(or belief—he tends to use these terms interchangeably) as involving affirmation or denial. Given just this much, it could be his view that simple apprehension is always an act with propositional content, but an act in which the propositional content is simply entertained without being affirmed or denied. His further discussion makes clear, however, that simple apprehension may have nonpropositional as well as propositional objects:

> Judgment can be expressed by a proposition only, and a proposition is a complete sentence; but simple apprehension may be expressed by a word or words, which make no complete sentence. (EIP 6.1:408)

> [When the words 'I conceive' are followed by a noun] the thing conceived may be no proposition, but a simple term only, as a pyramid, an obelisk. (EIP 1.1:25; cf. 1.7:65)

He also tells us that the objects of simple apprehension expressed by words or subsentential phrases include both individuals and universals (EIP 6.1:302 and 305).

Reid mentions two ways in which we may obtain conceptions of individuals (EIP 6.1:303). If I have never seen Westminster Bridge, I may conceive of it by means of a description it satisfies, for example, *a bridge from Westminster over the Thames*. This mode of conception is similar to what Russell calls knowledge by description, and it does involve concepts. But if an object is present to my senses, I need no such description in order to conceive of it; I need only mentally point it out. This mode of conception is similar to what Russell calls knowledge by acquaintance, and it is more akin to Kantian intuition than to Kantian conceptualization.[17] It is a mode of conception of which we may say *there are no concepts in conception*.

Since I am assimilating one variety of Reidian conception to Russellian acquaintance, let me remind the reader of Russell's views. Russell distinguishes between knowledge of *truths* (for which the French have *savoir* and the Germans *wissen*) and knowledge of *things* (for which the French have *connaitre* and the Germans *kennen*). Knowledge of things further divides into knowledge by description and knowledge by acquaintance. Knowledge by description presupposes knowledge of truths (for example, knowing anything about an individual under the description *the president of the United States in 2015* presupposes knowing that there is one and only one president of the United States in 2015). Knowledge

---

[17] See the discussion of conceptual apprehension (apprehension of an object by means of a singular concept that it satisfies) and apprehension by acquaintance in Wolterstorff 2001, Chapter 1, especially pp. 9–22. Wolterstorff proposes that "having in mind" is the best short explication of what Reid means by "conception."

by acquaintance does *not* presuppose any knowledge of truths. Russell further characterizes acquaintance as follows:

> I say that I am *acquainted* with an object when I have a direct cognitive relation to that object, i.e. when I am directly aware of the object itself. When I speak of a cognitive relation here, I do not mean the sort of relation which constitutes judgment, but the sort which constitutes presentation. In fact, I think the relation of subject and object which I call acquaintance is simply the converse of the relation of object and subject which constitutes presentation. (1910:108)

I liken the variety of Reidian conception we are now discussing to Russellian acquaintance primarily because it is presentational rather than judgmental. Further similarities between Reid and Russell are (i) that both individuals and universals are among the possible objects of conception or acquaintance, and (ii) that conception or acquaintance is presupposed by every other cognitive relation ([1912] 1999:32–35, and [1913] 1992:5). There are also differences, however. The chief ones are (i) that Russell thinks we can be acquainted only with what exists (since relations require existent relata), whereas Reid thinks we can conceive of the nonexistent, and (ii) that Russell thinks the only individuals we are acquainted with are sense data (and possibly the self), whereas Reid thinks we can be acquainted with external objects. But these are differences in doctrine, not definition. Nothing in the very concept of acquaintance prevents one from holding, as Reid does, that we have acquaintance with external things and nonexistent things.[18]

In any case, Reid's taxonomy of the operations of the mind explicitly leaves room for acts of apprehension whereby an object is presented to the mind without any conceptualization or judgment. Should the conception that is an element in perception be understood in this way? I believe the answer is yes, for three reasons.[19]

First, Reid tells us that the conception involved in perception can be *more or less distinct*. We see an object more distinctly at a small than a great distance and more distinctly on a clear than a foggy day (EIP 2.5:96–97). Can the merely conceptual apprehension of an object be subject to this sort of variation? One conceptual apprehension can involve descriptions or concepts that are more determinate than those

---

[18] John Grote, who introduced into English philosophy the distinction between knowledge by acquaintance and knowledge by description that Russell took over, held that objects of acquaintance include ordinary objects in the external world, such as the sun. See Martens 2010.

[19] At any rate, our perception of primary qualities involves conception of the acquaintance variety. As discussed below in chapter 5, the same may not be true of our perception of secondary qualities.

involved in another (*the seagull over there* versus *the bird-like thing over there*), but I do not think greater distinctness of conception can be *analyzed* as greater conceptual determinacy. Rather, it is the former that makes the latter possible.

Second, Reid tells us in a number of places that perception is a *ground of belief*. He seems to mean this in both a genetic and a normative sense: if I see a tree, that induces me to believe in the tree and gives me evidence for my belief. Both of these claims seem to presuppose that seeing a tree (or some component of the seeing) is distinct from the belief I form about it. If the real core of perception is conception, and if conception is a nonconceptual and therefore nondoxastic act, we have as required something distinct from belief that can serve as a ground of it (in both senses).

Third and most important, unless the conception involved in perception were some sort of knowledge by acquaintance, Reid's threefold account of perception would be *enormously implausible*. He would be unable to distinguish the belief I form when my friend cries "Look out! There's a snake ahead!" from the perception I form when I see the snake myself. After all, my belief involves a descriptive conception of the snake and is formed as immediately as any beliefs ever are. If the conception in perception need only be knowledge by description, my total cognitive situation as regards the snake has all three of the standard Reidian elements in perception—but it is not perception!

I shall assume, then, that the conception involved in Reidian perception is some sort of apprehension or acquaintance that is not constituted by conceptualization or judgment. I shall sometimes call relations of this sort A-relations.

I close this section by saying more about an alternative way of thinking about Reidian perception, broached in the previous section. As noted there, it *may* be Reid's view that perception is a simple, unanalyzable operation, in which case it would have conception as a by-product rather than an ingredient. This view is suggested by his saying that our conceptions of sensible things, like sounds and colors, must derive from previous perceptions of them (EIP 4.3:327; 6.1:416) and, more generally, that any object we conceive of must be decomposable into "things with which we were before acquainted by some other original power of the mind" (EIP 4.1:308–9). It is probable, he tells us, that sensation and perception are the first operations of the mind (EIP 4.3:327). If so, the perceptions that give us our first conceptions cannot have conceptions as ingredients. I shall nonetheless often write in this book as though perception has conception as an ingredient. If Reid's real view is that perception is an unanalyzable act with conception as a concomitant, it will not much matter for our purposes. The important point to take away is that Reidian perception either *contains* an A-relation (if it is analyzable in terms of conception) or *is* an A-relation (if it is not analyzable at all).

In contemporary epistemology and philosophy of mind, countenancing the existence of A-relations puts one in a small minority. *All* cognitive relations, according to contemporary orthodoxy, are relations with propositional contents. I have therefore included in this book five appendices, A through E, arguing for or defending the existence of A-relations.

## E. PERCEPTION AND BELIEF

The second element Reid says he always finds in or along with the perception of an object is "a strong and irresistible conviction and belief of its present existence" (EIP 2.5:96). ("Of" is the preposition he generally uses in connection with "belief.") What is the nature of this belief? What is its content? And why does Reid think it is always there in any case of perception?

As to the nature of belief, Reid thinks belief is one of those operations that is difficult or impossible to define, but whose nature everyone understands simply by being aware of instances of it in his own mind. (See EIP 1.1:19–20.) He offers trenchant criticisms of Hume's attempt to analyze belief in terms of the forcefulness and vivacity of ideas (IHM 2.5:30 and 6.24:197–98).

As to the content of the belief that is involved in perception, here are several representative passages:

> Smell, taste, and hearing give us "certain sensations, and a conviction that these sensations are occasioned by some external object." (EIP 2.21:235)

> The sensations produced in me by an ivory ball in my hand are "followed by the conception and belief, that there is in my hand a hard smooth body of a spherical figure." (EIP 2.21:237)

> By sight, "we perceive visible objects to have extension in two dimensions, to have visible figure and magnitude, and a certain distance from one another." (IHM 2.21:236)

> "I perceive a tree that grows before my window. . . . The perception of an object implies both a conception of its form, and a belief of *its* present existence." (IHM 6.20:168, emphasis added)

As one can gather from these and other passages, the belief involved in perception is sometimes said to be a *de dicto* belief with an existential proposition as its content and is at other times said to be a *de re* belief about a certain object to the effect that *it* exists. What is believed *about* the object is said sometimes simply to be that it exists and other times to be that it has some sensible property (which on normal assumptions would imply that it exists). Reid does not seem to have a settled and uniform view about the contents of the belief component of perception.

As to the involvement of belief in *all* perception, Reid's official view on this issue seems to be wrong—despite the common saying, seeing is not always believing. Suppose I am having a vivid (and veridical) perception of a snake wriggling on the floor but have been assured by a trusted friend that I have swallowed a pill that induces hallucinations of just this sort. Might I not suspend belief in the existence of the snake, even though I am actually perceiving one? Reid himself occasionally offers examples somewhat along these lines. He speaks of persons with phantom limbs who still have perceptions of pains in their toes, even though they know their foot has been amputated (EIP 2.18:214).[20] It seems doubtful that such persons *believe* that there is pain in their toes. He also reports the following about himself:

> I have amused myself with such observations [of objects seen double] for more than thirty years; and in every case wherein I saw the object double at first, I see it so to this day, notwithstanding the constant experience of its being single. (IHM 6.17:156; cf. 6.4:85)

Presumably, he does not believe there are two objects in these cases.

In light of such counterexamples, how might Reid's view be qualified or corrected? I shall mention three possibilities without taking a stand on which is best.

First, the subject really *does* believe that there is a snake on the floor, a pain in the toe, or a second object, despite also believing that these things are not really there. In other words, the subject has contradictory beliefs, one induced by perception and the other by background knowledge. Though perhaps not out of the question, this seems implausible.[21]

Second, the subject does not have a belief in the snake, but a *strong disposition or inclination* to believe in one, which has been inhibited in this case by background knowledge about the hallucinogen. This idea is discussed in Armstrong 1968.[22]

Third, the subject does not believe in the snake, but has an experience that *represents* a snake as being there. This is the line taken by Peacocke in a critical emendation of Reid (1983, chapter 1). He notes that a person familiar with a *trompe l'oeuil*

---

[20] Reid's example is not perfectly parallel to mine, since the pain perception is not veridical.

[21] A similar explanation is offered in Armstrong 1972 of a mother's disbelief in her son's death in the war, despite having learned of it from a government messenger.

[22] Armstrong is not expounding Reid, but refining his own theory of perception as the acquisition of beliefs about the environment by means of the senses. It is incumbent on him, therefore, to discuss the phenomenon of "perception without belief," which he tries to handle in terms of inclinations to believe and states that would be beliefs but for the presence of inhibiting beliefs.

painting, say of a window on a wall, will continue to have an experience that represents the wall as containing a window even though he no longer believes a window is there (6).

Peacocke's chapter is an influential document in the now widely held representational or intentional theory of perception, according to which perception does not necessarily involve outright belief but does involve an experience that represents things in the world as being a certain way. Perception is belief-like in having propositional contents just as beliefs do, but it need not involve the subject's endorsing the contents or taking them to be true. It is as though something in your perception *tells you* that there is a window in the wall, even if you know better than to believe what you are told.

The intentional theory is typically held by its contemporary advocates in a stronger form: not only do perceptual states have intentional content, but their intentional content completely determines their phenomenal or qualitative character, or what it is like to be in them. In other words, phenomenal character supervenes on intentional or propositional content in such a way that two experiential states cannot be alike in propositional content without also being alike in phenomenal character (Byrne 2001). I do not believe that Reid is an intentionalist in this sense. Insofar as attendant sensations contribute to the phenomenal character of perceptual states, there is an aspect of phenomenal character that is not determined by propositional content. And insofar as conception is not reducible to states with propositional content (as argued in the previous section), there is another element in perception that may contribute to its phenomenal character without being determined by propositional content. See appendix E for more on this issue.

Peacocke himself is not an intentionalist in the stronger sense (an "extreme perceptual theorist," in his terms). He argues that the character of perceptual experience cannot be exhaustively determined by its propositional content, citing three features of perceptual experiences that he believes must belong to the sensational rather than the intentional side of experiences. Thus far, his views are quite Reidian in spirit. Ironically, though, his three chosen features—differences in apparent magnitude, differences in visual depth, and the underlying samenesses across shifts of aspect, as when one sees a wireframe cube now with one face and now another foremost—are all *spatial* features.[23] In Reid's own philosophy (as discussed in chapter 2) sensation is devoid of any spatial features.

To distinguish intentionalism from another view discussed in chapter 10 and called by the same name, I henceforth call the view we have just discussed *propositionalism*.

---

[23] See Byrne 2001 for critical discussion of Peacocke's three features, but see also appendix K for a more dramatic case of differences in apparent depth that challenge intentionalism.

# F. CONSCIOUSNESS AND ATTENTION

A good entrée to the present topic is provided by an apparent inconsistency in Reid's philosophy pointed out by Duggan (1970:xvii):

1. When we have a sensation, we believe that we have it.
2. Many of our sensations go unnoticed.
3. If we believe we have a sensation, it is not unnoticed.

Proposition 3 is supplied by Duggan rather than Reid (xxii), but it is hard to deny. The other two propositions are definitely to be found in Reid. We get proposition 1 in IHM 2.3, where Reid tells us that sensation is a "natural principle of belief," meaning that if we have a sensation (a smell, for instance), "it is necessarily accompanied by a belief in its present existence" (27). We get proposition 2 in many places, including the following:

> We are so accustomed to use the sensation as a sign, and to pass immediately to the hardness signified, that, as far as appears, it was never made an object of thought, either by the vulgar or by philosophers; nor has it a name in any language. (IHM 5.2:56)

He goes on to say that the sensation is a fugitive, hiding in the shadow of the external quality it signifies (56). There is much more in the same vein, including the following:

> Feelings of touch . . . pass through the mind instantaneously, and serve only to introduce the notion and belief of external things, which by our constitution are connected with them. . . . The mind immediately passes to the thing signified, without making the least reflection upon the sign, or observing that there was any such thing. (IHM 2.5:63; see also 6.2:81–82)

There certainly does look at first sight to be an inconsistency here, but when we read a little further in Reid, it becomes apparent how he would resolve it. The first proposition is true only with a qualification: if we have a sensation *and attend to it*, we believe that we have it. But we frequently do not attend to our sensations, which is why proposition 2 is true.

Attention is a factor whose presence or absence can make an enormous difference for Reid. When we are *not* attending to an aspect of our mental lives, we can be well-nigh oblivious to it. A good example is afforded by what Reid has to say about double vision. Hold a finger in front of your face while focusing your eyes on some more distant object, say a candle on a shelf. While continuing to *focus* on the candle, *attend* to your finger. You will see the finger double, perhaps one copy of it on either side of the candle. Reid makes the following observation about this phenomenon:

> You may find a man that can say with a good conscience, that he never saw things double all his life; yet this very man, put in the situation above mentioned, with his finger between him and the candle, and desired to attend to the appearance of the object which he does not look at, will, upon the first trial, see the candle double, when he looks at his finger; and his finger double, when he looks at the candle. Does he now see otherwise than he saw before? No, surely; but he now attends to what he never attended to before. The same double appearance of an object has been a thousand times presented to his eye before now; but he did not attend to it; and so it is as little an object of his reflection and memory, as if it had never happened. (IHM 6.13:134)

Two philosophers who are otherwise admirers of Reid, Taylor and Duggan, find this passage shocking. They call it "an outrage against the common sense which it was the general purpose of his philosophy to confirm" (1958:171). I think it should be regarded instead as illustrating a phenomenon that is surprising at first, but easily accepted once several instances of it have been pointed out: "that the mind may not attend to, and thereby, in some sort, not perceive objects that strike the senses" (IHM 6.13:135).[24]

On the other hand, when we *are* attending to sensations or sensory appearances, we can know them perfectly:

> If we can only acquire the habit of attending to our sensations, we may know them perfectly. (IHM 6.21:176)

> I concluded that I might know perfectly what my Sensations are. (Brookes IHM:258)

This point is important for Reid's methodology of the mind; he holds that attentive reflection is our main source of information about mental phenomena (EIP 1.5:59).

---

[24] If the man who "can say with a good conscience" that he has never seen double positively believes that he has never seen double, he is not infallible about sensory appearances; if he merely fails to believe that he has seen double, he is not omniscient about them. Doctrines of infallibility and omniscience can be maintained with plausibility only in regard to what we are attending to.

In this connection, it may be useful to note how Reid regiments the language of consciousness, attention, and reflection:

> The difference between consciousness and reflection, is like to the difference between a superficial view of an object which presents itself to the eye, while we are engaged about something else, and that attentive examination which we give to an object when we are wholly employed in surveying it. Attention is a voluntary act ... but consciousness is involuntary. (EIP 1.5:59; see also EIP 6.5:472)

As this passage intimates, if we are not attending to something, it does not follow that we are not conscious of it. Reid makes the point explicit elsewhere: "We are conscious of many things to which we give little or no attention" (EIP 1.2:42).

This last claim is controversial within contemporary cognitive science and philosophy of mind. On the anti-Reidian side, some equate consciousness with attention, or at least hold that attention is a necessary condition for consciousness (Mack 2002, Noe 2004).[25] On the pro-Reidian side, others argue that we are conscious of many things to which we do not attend (Koch 2004:163–37, Tye 2004, Hill and Bennett 2008). Two classical experiments may be cited in this regard. In one (Broadbent 1958), subjects made to hear two streams of speech when they could only attend to one were aware of properties of the unattended stream (for instance, that it was a male voice). In another (Sperling 1960, summarized in Tye 2004), subjects were briefly presented with three rows of four letters; after the letters were extinguished from the screen but before they had faded from immediate sensory memory, the subjects were asked to tell what they had seen. Subjects told to report as many letters as they could from the entire array could get at most a third of them before the array faded from sensory memory altogether. Subjects told to direct their attention to a specified row (indicated by a tone just after the display was extinguished) could get at least three of the four letters in the attended row. This suggests that they were conscious of the entire array before they directed their attention to it. As Tye puts it, "The letters to which the subjects are not attending appear in ways that *would* have enabled the subjects to identify them, *had* their atttention been directed differently" (513).

---

[25] What Mack actually says is that there is no *seeing* without attention, but assuming that you are not conscious of a visible object if you do not see it, it follows that there is no consciousness of unattended visible objects.

## G. ARE SENSATIONS SELF-REFLEXIVE?

In explicating his terms, Reid defines *sensation* as "an act of mind, which may be distinguished from all others by this, that it hath no object distinct from the act itself" (EIP 1.1:36). Does that statement mean a sensation has *no* object, or that it is its *own* object? In other words, are sensations nonintentional states, or are they intentional states directed upon themselves? Buras (2005) and Hossack (2008) defend the latter option (sensations as self-reflexive); Ganson (2008) and I prefer the former option (sensations as objectless, as in the adverbial theory of them). There is textual and philosophical evidence on both sides of the question, but on balance I believe it favors the "no object" view.

*Textual evidence.* I consider first several single-sentence passages that seem to favor one or the other of the answers. In a discussion of Locke's use of the word "perception," Reid says this:

> When I am pained with the gout, it is not proper to say I perceive the pain; I feel it; or am conscious of it: It is not an object of perception, but of sensation and of consciousness. (EIP 2.9:136)[26]

That says that pains may be objects of sensations. If sensations have no objects distinct from themselves, it follows that some sensations have themselves as objects. I do not place great weight on this passage, however, as Reid's main point is that "perceive" is not the right verb to use with sensations. Moreover, "object of sensation" could be just a way of saying "something sensed," and even an adverbialist can say that pains are something sensed (as dances are something danced).

Here are two more passages that favor Buras:

> Sensation implies the present existence of its object. (IHM 2.3:29)

> The powers of sensation, of perception, of memory, and of consciousness, are all employed solely about objects that do exist, or have existed. (EIP 4.1:311)

In context, the first sentence could perhaps be taken as a restatement of a point several lines earlier: "sensation compels my belief of the present existence of the smell." I have no answer to the second.

Now for passages on the other side. Here are two that favor the "no object" view.

> Feeling, in the sense in which it is equivalent to sensation, "has no object." (EIP 1.1:38)

---

[26] Thanks to Lewis Powell for bringing this passage to my attention.

[Hunger has two ingredients, an uneasy sensation and a desire for food.] The last, from its nature, must have an object; the first has no object. (EIP 2.16:196)

Buras maintains that in each of these, "no object" should really be understood as "no object distinct from itself," leaving open the reflexive view (228). But the next passage is not so easily accommodated:

As *thinking a thought* is an expression which could signify no more than *thinking*, so *feeling a pain* signifies no more than *being pained*. (IHM 6.20:168)

If in the face of this passage Buras says that pain is a sensation that feels itself, should he not also say that thoughts think themselves? Yet surely it is *we* who do the thinking and feeling, not the thoughts and feelings themselves. (For confirmation, see EIP 2.9:132, where Reid says that thought and its object are always two different things.)

As no clear victor emerges from the battle of the one-liners, I turn to two syllogisms Buras constructs from the texts in favor of his view. The first is

1. "Conception enters as an ingredient in every operation of the mind" (EIP 4.1:295–96).
2. Conception always has an object—"he that conceives, must conceive something" (EIP 4.1:311).
3. Therefore, every operation of the mind has an object.[27]

If we add to 3 Reid's express view that a sensation has no object distinct from itself, it follows that a sensation must have itself as object.

This argument I find inconclusive for a reason noted by Ganson (2008:250): Reid may not intend the first premise in a strict sense. He tells us that he is sometimes indifferent in his use of the terms "ingredient" and "concomitant":

Whether judgment ought to be called a necessary concomitant of these operations [perception, memory, consciousness], or rather a part or ingredient of them, I do not dispute. (EIP 6.1:409; see also COR 108)

---

[27] As Lewis Powell has pointed out to me, the inference to 3 presupposes that if an ingredient of an act has a certain object, so does the act itself. This I find plausible, but perhaps not undeniable. Hunger has the desire of food as an ingredient alongside an uneasy sensation, but does hunger have food as its object?

As a case in point, he calls sensations "ingredients" of perception at EIP 2.16:197, even though his official view is that sensations *accompany* perception. In the sentence quoted as the first premise above, then, he may only mean that every operation of the mind either has conception as an ingredient *or is accompanied by some act of conception*. In that case, we could only conclude that every operation of the mind either has an object or is accompanied by some operation that has an object. Sensations might be accompanied by acts of consciousness taking the sensations as objects without taking themselves as objects.

Buras also offers the following variant on the syllogism above:

1. "Thinking is a very general word, which includes all the operations of our minds" (EIP 1.1:22).
2. "Thought cannot be without an object" (EIP 2.9:132).
3. Therefore, every operation of the mind has an object.

As before, if we add that a sensation has no object distinct from itself, it follows that a sensation must have itself as object.

This argument, too, I find inconclusive. The complete sentence from which Buras extracts his second premise is this: "It is true, thought cannot be without an object; for every man when he thinks must think of something; but the object he thinks of is one thing, his thought of that object is another thing." So if "thought" in this sentence is used in the broad sense in which it covers sensations, Reid is *denying* that sensations are their own objects. He is saying there is always a distinction between the object of an operation and the operation that has that object. On the other hand, if (as seems likely) Reid is here using "thought" in a more restrictive intellectual sense, then his claim that thought cannot be without an object does not imply that sensations cannot be without objects.

The straight textual evidence we have considered so far is indecisive, every passage being either answerable or opposed by a passage on the other side. So let us turn to philosophical arguments that Reid's views are better served by one side or the other.

*Explaining the properties of sensations.* As noted above, Ganson ascribes to Reidian sensations the four properties of trustworthiness, disclosedness, unmistakability, and transparency. He holds further that these properties are best explained on a no-object view of sensations. Consider first trustworthiness and disclosedness. If sensing has no object, in a sense implying that the feeling of pain just is the pain,[28] then of course there cannot be the feeling without the pain or the pain without the

---

[28] "Feeling of pain" should be construed on the model of "city of Detroit."

feeling. Where there is identity between x and y, you cannot have x without y or y without x. The necessary coextensiveness of pain with the feeling of it has been explained.

The problem with this argument is that explanations of necessities by identities are not the prerogative solely of the no-object view.[29] Reflexivists such as Hossack also believe in an identity principle—sensations *are* their objects—but in their case the identity holds between an intentional act and itself, not between a nonintentional state and itself. Moreover, Hossack appeals to this identity to explain why you cannot have the act without the object or the object without the act: they are one and the same. In my opinion, neither Ganson's argument nor Hossack's is conclusive, since their shared explanandum (the necessary coextensiveness of pain with the feeling of it) is compatible with either of their explanations.

Consider now the second pair of properties, unmistakability and transparency. What is it about the no-object view that is supposed to explain why a sensation must be F if it is felt as F and felt as F if it is F? I confess that I do not quite understand Ganson's thinking at this point.[30] In any case, I would raise a dilemma for his argument.

What does it mean to say that a sensation is "felt as F"? On the one hand, "felt as F" could be a representational notion, akin to being believed to be F. In that case, the conclusion could not be that feelings are nonintentional—they would represent themselves as having properties.[31] On the other hand, "felt as F" could be just another way of saying "is F." In that case, it would of course be true that sensations are F iff they are felt as being F, but it would be a tautology, not needing explanation by any special property of sensations.

---

[29] Ganson (2008) acknowledges this point and seeks to meet it on pp. 255–56. He claims that the reflexivist will have a hard time saying what makes one sensation different in kind from another unless he appeals to different manners of representing, which opens up the possibility of misrepresentation, thus forsaking unmistakability and transparency. I believe with Hossack, however, that difference in kind could be explained by differing qualia without invoking differing manners of representation.

[30] Pursuing Ducasse's dance analogy, we could say that you dance gracefully if and only if your dance is graceful. In the analogy, though, it is hard to see where the idea of mistake or its opposite even comes in to play.

[31] In a typical remark, Reid says this: "The sensation is nothing else, nor has any other qualities than what I feel it to have. Its *esse* is *sentiri*, and nothing can be in it that is not felt" (IHM:258). What is this "feeling to have?" At EIP 1.1:25, Reid tells us that verbs in the infinitive mood are typically used to express judgments, as in "I conceive x to be F." Could it be that in the passage at issue Reid is really giving voice (though confusedly) to a doctrine of infallibility and omniscience regarding beliefs about sensations, rather than a doctrine of unmistakability and transparency regarding sensations themselves? If so, he is not giving us the materials for a Ganson-style argument.

*The infinite regress of conscious states.* A philosophical argument on the other side of the reflexivity issue has been pressed by Buras (2005). He maintains that we need self-reflexive states to avoid an infinite regress of higher-order mental states that would otherwise threaten to arise, given Reid's other assumptions. His argument would not show that sensations in particular must be self-reflexive, but it would show that *some* mental states must be self-reflexive, opening the door for the view that sensations are among them.

The specter of an infinite regress of conscious states was already pointed out by Aristotle. As the following argument shows, four premises are sufficient to generate such a regress.

1. There are conscious states.
2. If a state is conscious, that is because some other state takes it as object.
3. If S1 is conscious because S2 takes it as object, S2 is conscious.
4. S1 and S2 cannot be conscious in virtue of taking each other as objects.[32]
5. Therefore, there is an infinite regress of conscious states.

Historically, there are two main ways of avoiding the regress. One way is to deny premise 3, saying that a state may be conscious in virtue of being apprehended by a state that is *not* conscious. This is the line taken by contemporary higher-order monitoring theorists of consciousness, including Armstrong (1980) and Rosenthal (1986);[33] it was also the line taken by Leibniz, who sought thereby to avoid a regress he took to be implied by the views of Locke.[34] The other way is to deny premise 2 by holding that a state may take *itself* as object. This line was advocated by Aristotle and Brentano, and it is the view Buras and Hossack attribute to Reid.[35]

Brentano's version of the reflexive way out merits brief description. According to Brentano, perceptions of external things are conscious states that are conscious in virtue of being apprehended by themselves. One and the same state may have both a *primary* object, such as a tree or the sun, and a *secondary* object, namely, itself. Brentano cites Aristotle as a precursor, quoting a passage in *De Anima* in which Aristotle says that by sight we are aware both of an external object and of seeing itself

[32] Nor can we have a larger circle in which S1 is conscious because it is apprehended by S2, S2 because it is apprehended by S3, and S3 (or Sn) because it is apprehended by S1.

[33] Armstrong analyzes consciousness in terms of higher-order perceptions, Rosenthal in terms of higher-order thoughts.

[34] See Coventry and Kriegel 2008 for a discussion of the views of Leibniz and Locke, including the suggestion that Locke may have held a reflexive view rather than the regress-engendering view Leibniz attributed to him.

[35] See Kriegel 2003 for a defense of the Aristotle-Brentano view.

(Brentano [1874] 1973:127). The situation may be depicted by an arrow with two heads, one pointing at an object in the external world and the other bending back upon its own shaft (Figure 1.2):

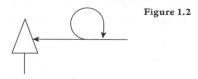

**Figure 1.2**

If Reidian sensations were self-reflexive, their diagram would contain only the bent-back arrowhead, since sensations do not have any object distinct from themselves.

Reid appears to take a line similar to Brentano's in a passage in a 1748 manuscript:

> I cannot imagine there is any thing more in perceiving that I perceive a Star than in perceiving a Star Simply otherwise there might be perceptions of perceptions in Infinitum.[36]

However, he never repeats this remark in his published work or returns to the problem it is meant to solve.

Why, then, attribute the reflexivist view to Reid? The case for doing so is (i) that he would surely want to avoid the regress affirmed in 5, and (ii) that he explicitly affirms or would likely affirm all the premises leading to 5 except for 2. He does not explicitly affirm 4, but 4 is perhaps obvious enough to go without saying. Nor does he explicitly affirm 3, but 3 is arguably a corollary of his frequently voiced view that (*pace* Leibniz) all mental states are attended with consciousness (see, for example, EIP 1.1:20, 1.5:58, and 2.15:191).[37] That leaves only premise 2 as a candidate for denial, and if one denies premise 2, the most obvious alternative to it is that some states take themselves as objects.[38]

---

[36] Lehrer called attention to this passage (from 2131/6/I/18 in the Birkwood Collection in the Aberdeen University Library) in Lehrer 1986. It is now included in the supplementary manuscripts section of the Brookes edition of IHM at p. 317.

[37] The other assumption needed to arrive at the corollary is that S1 can be rendered conscious by being the object of S2 only if S2 is mental—which is true if any state with an object is mental.

[38] Self-reflexive states are not the only alternative to 2, however. A complete treatment of the topic would have to consider two other possibilities: that a state can be conscious in virtue of taking an external object (as in first-order representation theories, discussed in Copenhaver 2007), and that a state's being conscious is not a relational property at all, but some sort of intrinsic glow.

Before we conclude that Reid held, or ought to have held, a reflexive view, we ought to pay heed to metaphysical difficulties that the reflexive view faces itself—arguably including an infinite regress at least as bad as the one we have just considered.

Hossack raises the following as a potential objection to the view that Reidian sensations are self-reflexive or conscious of themselves. Suppose e1, a sensation of pain, is represented as in Kim's theory of events as the pair <pain, S>, S being the subject and pain his property of hurting. Suppose e2, the consciousness of the pain, is represented as the triple <K,S,e1>, K being the consciousness relation. The objection is that you cannot identify e1 and e2 because you cannot identify a pair with a triple or an instance of a monadic property with an instance of a dyadic one. Hossack replies that Reid can get around this objection because he holds that sensations have qualia. The more fine-grained representation of e2 is therefore <K,S,<q,e1>>, where q is a quale of the pain event. Hossack says we *can* identify e1 with e2 construed in the latter way (58). I do not see what he has gained by this maneuver, however, since we are still identifying a pair with a triple.

Moreover, Hossack's notation brings out another problem with the reflexive view. If e1 = <K,S,<q,e1>>, then an event (namely, e1) is a constituent of itself. Since we can substitute for "e1" on the right side of that last equation in accordance with the equation itself, we also have it that e1 is a constituent of a constituent of itself.[39] This may be repeated ad infinitum. Hossack is willing to take this consequence in stride; he says there is no reason that the constituency relation needs to be well founded (55, 59). I think myself that we should think twice about a stratagem for avoiding an infinite "upward" regress of conscious states that works only by begetting an infinite "inward" regress of conscious states. Further problems of infinity and reflexivity are discussed in appendix F.

We should hesitate to ascribe a reflexivity view to Reid not only because such a view would generate regress problems of its own, but also because various features of his thought positively preclude it. Lehrer has identified three such features (1986). These features do not necessarily imply that there can be *no* reflexive mental states in Reid, but they do imply that it cannot be true generally that the consciousness of an operation is identical with that operation. First, Reid cites the faculty of consciousness as a separate original power of the mind alongside perception, memory, and the rest. Why should consciousness be a separate faculty if it has no operations unique to itself, but all its operations are identical with operations of another faculty? Second, Reid says that one ingredient in an act of consciousness is the

---

[39] Actually, e1 was already a constituent of a constituent of itself—it was a member of a pair that was a member of a triple that is identical with e1. The substitution I have just mentioned in the text shows that e1 is a constituent of a constituent of a constituent of a constituent of itself—each substitution reveals two more layers of constituency, and there is no bottoming out.

belief that its object exists (EIP 2.20:227 and 228). This claim would give rise to an infinite regress of belief—unless beliefs themselves could be self-reflexive, which is implausible. Third, Reid notes that consciousness is involuntary. But many mental operations are voluntary; therefore, there are many mental operations that cannot be identical with consciousness of themselves.

*Two more textual arguments.* I end this section by presenting two more arguments against a reflexivist interpretation of Reid, which so far as I know have not previously been discussed.

First, there is this telling passage:

> *Most* of the operations of the mind, from their very nature, must have objects to which they are directed, and about which they are employed. He that perceives, must perceive something. . . . What we have said of perceiving, is equally applicable to *most* operations of the mind. (EIP 1.1:26, emphasis added; see also COR 108)

Why would Reid say "most" unless he envisioned exceptions? And what exception could there be but sensations? None, given that Reid tells us that all acts *except* sensations *do* have objects distinct from themselves.

Second, there is the following passage from Reid's EIP chapter on Arnauld:

> It is true, that consciousness always goes along with perception; but they are different operations of the mind, and they have their different objects. Consciousness is not perception, nor is the object of consciousness the object of perception. *The same may be said of every operation of mind that has an object.* (EIP 2.13:170, emphasis added)

Arnauld held that perceptions have themselves as objects along with their primary objects, as in the view of Aristotle and Brentano. It is clear that in the quoted passage, Reid is repudiating this aspect of Arnauld's views; he does not think perceptions are self-reflexive, even if sensations are. But if self-reflexivity is to be ruled out in the case of perceptions, why would it be any less problematic in the case of sensations?

Indeed, it is clear from the sentence I have italicized that Reid means to make a more general point. Let us suppose (as we certainly may for Reid) that some sensation S is the object of some act of consciousness C:

1. $S = O(C)$.

If sensations have objects, the passage quoted above implies that the object of consciousness is never the object of sensation. ("Consciousness is not sensation, nor is the object of consciousness the object of sensation," we could say.)

2. $O(C) \neq O(S)$.

Therefore,

3. $S \neq O(S)$.

Otherwise, by 1 and the transitivity of identity, we would have $O(C) = O(S)$, contradicting 2.

Conclusion 3 may be reached by a slightly different route. The italicized sentence tells us that if an act A has an object O, then $O(C(A)) \neq O(A)$. $O(C(A))$ is of course none other than A. So $A \neq O(A)$, for any act that has an object at all. Therefore, if sensations have objects, they do not have themselves as objects: $O(S) \neq S$. When we combine this result with Reid's oft-repeated claim that sensations have no objects distinct from themselves, it follows that sensations have no objects at all.

# 2

## REID'S NATIVISM

A third class of natural signs comprehends those which, though we never before had any notion or conception of the thing signified, do suggest it or conjure it up, as it were, by a natural kind of magic. (Thomas Reid, *IHM 5.3:60*)

## A. REID'S NATIVISM

Though united by soil and temperament with the British Empiricists, Reid rejects their central tenet: that all concepts are derived from experience. He believes that there are many important concepts, including those of substance, body, self, and power, that we possess and legitimately deploy despite not having got them from experience. In one good sense of the term, he holds these concepts to be *innate*. He does not hold that they have been with us from birth, but rather that they arise within us in accordance with innate laws of our constitution (IHM 5.7:72). Certain types of sensory stimulation may be necessary before these concepts arise within the human mind, but they could never have been derived or abstracted from those stimulations alone. Reid could easily have penned the following famous sentence from Kant: "But though all our knowledge begins with experience, it does not follow that it all arises out of experience" (CPR, B1).[1]

---

[1] The rest of Kant's paragraph could also have been written by Reid: "For it may well be that even our empirical knowledge is made up of what we receive through impressions and of what our own faculty of knowledge (sensible impressions serving merely as the occasion) supplies from itself.

The sense in which Reid believes that some of our concepts and conceptions are innate is the sense Hume articulates in a footnote in Section II of the *Enquiry Concerning Human Understanding*:

> It is probable that no more was meant by those, who denied innate ideas, than that all ideas were copies of our impressions.... For what is meant by *innate*? ... If by innate be meant, contemporary to our birth, the dispute seems to be frivolous.... But admitting these terms, *impressions* and *ideas*, in the sense above explained, and understanding by *innate*, what is original or copied from no precedent perception, then may we assert that all our impressions are innate, and our ideas not innate. (EHU 2:22)

Reid believes that some of our concepts are innate in precisely the sense in which Hume denies that any are: they are copied from no precedent impression.

Hume was quick to spot this implication of Reid's views. After being sent a partial draft of Reid's *Inquiry* through the mediation of Hugh Blair, Hume wrote to Blair (July 4, 1762) that "if I comprehend the Author's Doctrine, which, I own, I can hitherto do but imperfectly, it leads us back to innate Ideas" (IHM:256).

To combat the Humean principle that all our ideas or conceptions are copies of impressions or sensations, Reid offers a thought experiment he calls his *experimentum crucis*, in which he cites two conceptions he thinks we indisputably possess, but which lack a proper Humean birthright in our sensations.[2] The first is the conception of *hardness*, the second that of *extension*. He introduces the experiment concerning extension in the following words:

> To put this matter in another light, it may be proper to try, whether from sensation alone we can collect any notion of extension, figure, motion, and space. (IHM 5.6:65)

He then asks us to consider a blind man deprived of all the notions he formerly had through touch and tasked with acquiring them anew. Could he do it just by attending to his tactile sensations and exercising his powers of reasoning upon them? Reid's answer is *no*. He asks us to imagine the subject's being given a progressively richer diet of sensations, beginning with the prick of a pin and advancing to the sensations accompanying the pressing of a blunt object against his arm, the dragging

---

If our faculty of knowledge makes any such addition, it may be that we are not in a position to distinguish it from the raw material, until with long practice of attention we have become skilled in separating it" (CPR, B1–2).

[2] IHM 5.6 and 5.7; the term "experimentum crucis" is introduced at IHM 5.7:70.

of a fingertip across his face, his unsuccessfully trying to move his limbs, and his actual moving them. Reid asks at each stage whether any of the sensations would convey to the blind man the notion of extension if he had lacked it before, and his answer is always no—the conception of extension is not derivable from tactile sensations. But all of us, including the blind, do somehow have it. Reid's conclusion is that our conception of extension must be innate—not in the sense that we have it from birth, but in the sense that we form it as a hardwired response to certain sensations from which it could never have been derived by any process of abstraction or ratiocination.[3]

Once he has established that we have some conceptions not derived from our sensations, Reid thinks the way is open for admitting that we have others, too. Among them are the notion of a *self*, considered as a "haver" of sensations rather than a bundle of them, the notion of *body*, considered as something outside us in space and neither resembling nor depending on any operations of the mind, and the notion of *power*, considered as causal efficacy in a sense going beyond constant conjunction. For more on Reid's opposition to Hume on the notion of power, see chapter 14, section A.

In the remaining sections of this chapter, I discuss Reid's notion of natural signs as a further articulation of his nativism, review the *experimentum crucis* and various critical responses to it, ask what sort of issue Reid is really raising in the experiment, and consider whether Reid's nativism offers any leverage against the external-world skeptic.

## B. NATURAL SIGNS

The positive import of Reid's nativism can be spelled out further by restating it in terms of his threefold classification of natural signs, which he offers in sections 4.2 and 5.3 of the *Inquiry*. Reid first divides signs into the artificial and the natural. In the case of artificial signs, the connection between sign and thing signified is established by compact or convention, as with the words of human language and their denotata. In the case of natural signs, the connection between sign and thing signified is established by nature, as with smoke and fire and other cases of effect and cause. Reid then further divides natural signs into three important classes. In the first class, the connection between sign and thing signified is "established by nature, but discovered only by experience" (IHM 5.3:59), as in the example of smoke and fire already given. In the second class, the connection is "not only established by

---

[3] For discussion of the senses in which various furnishings of the mind are and are not innate for Reid, see Falkenstein 2004.

nature, but discovered to us by a natural principle, without reasoning or experience" (IHM 5.3:60). Belief in the connection is hardwired into us, so there is no need to learn it. Reid thinks that certain features of the human countenance are signs in this way of thoughts and other mental states; an infant in any culture is innately disposed to read a smile on its mother's face as a sign of approval without having to learn this connection through experience.[4] Unless there were a basic repertoire of natural signs of this second class, Reid believes, the signification of artificial signs could never be agreed upon or learned.[5] Finally, in the third class are those signs "which, though we never before had any notion or conception of the thing signified, do suggest it, or conjure it up, as it were, by a natural kind of magic" (IHM 5.3:60). Not only is the *connection* between sign and thing signified innately programmed into our constitution (as with signs of the second class), but the very *notion* of the thing signified is innate, in the sense that it is not derivable by abstraction from any of our sensations or inner experiences.[6] Reid's nativism may now be expressed by saying that the tactile sensations to which we respond with conceptions of extended bodies are natural signs of the third class.

Reid's threefold classification may be displayed in the diagram on the next page (Figure 2.1).[7]

Let me clarify two points of terminology. First, "belief in a connection" need not be a matter of believing the general proposition that whenever X is present, Y is present; it could just be a matter of believing in Y whenever you are presented with X. Second, the "experience" referred to in the final divide includes sensation and other mental states, but not perception. If "experience" included perception, Reid would

---

[4] Certain facial expressions "have the same signification in all climates and in all nations" (IHM 6.24:191). On this point, Reid is confirmed by contemporary research such as that of Ekman et al. (1969). A smile's a smile the world around.

[5] The argument here is that artificial language requires compact or agreement (for example, to use "water" as a sign of this kind of stuff here), and agreements can be established only through the use of signs. Therefore, "there must be a natural language before any artificial language can be invented" (IHM 4.2:51). For example, there must be facial features that are naturally understood as assent when someone proposes to use an artificial sign in a certain way.

Note that by "natural language" Reid does not mean the totality of natural signs, but just the natural signs of the second class, in which the thing signified is some aspect of the mental state of another person.

[6] Thus "innate" means somewhat different things as applied to connections and as applied to notions.

[7] The table offered in Nichols 2007 on p. 88 gives the impression that Reid distinguishes *four* classes of natural signs, but I believe that two of the four in his table—the habitual and the experiential—are really the same. If there is a distinction between them, it would lie in whether we have acquired the habit of making an automatic transition in thought from X to Y in addition to having learned by experience that X and Y are correlated. In any case, the habitual and the experiential would both be subclasses of Class I natural signs.

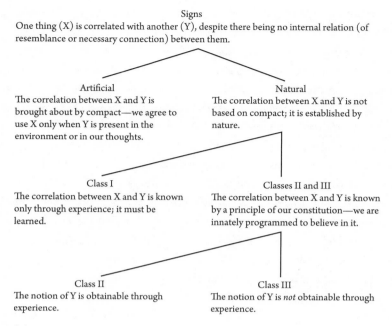

**Signs**
One thing (X) is correlated with another (Y), despite there being no internal relation (of resemblance or necessary connection) between them.

**Artificial**
The correlation between X and Y is brought about by compact—we agree to use X only when Y is present in the environment or in our thoughts.

**Natural**
The correlation between X and Y is not based on compact; it is established by nature.

**Class I**
The correlation between X and Y is known only through experience; it must be learned.

**Classes II and III**
The correlation between X and Y is known by a principle of our constitution—we are innately programmed to believe in it.

**Class II**
The notion of Y is obtainable through experience.

**Class III**
The notion of Y is *not* obtainable through experience.

**Figure 2.1**

say that *of course* we can get the notion of extended bodies from tactile perception. But that happens only because, thanks to our hardwiring, perception involves responding to our sensations with conceptions that could never have been afforded by the sensations alone.

Jonathan Ichakawa has posed to me an interesting puzzle about Reid's classification of signs: how can there be Class II natural signs that are not also Class III natural signs? In other words, if there is an innate connection between X and Y, would that not make the conception of Y innate? Suppose a child has never felt anger before and now sees his father's furrowed face: will the child not now attain a conception of anger, despite never having experienced it before?

To this question, I believe Reid could make either of two answers. The first answer is that with Class II signs, there are *two* possible avenues to our first conception of the thing signified: experience and hardwired connections. We could get the conception of anger from our own experience of it, or we could get it as a hardwired response to certain facial expressions. But with Class III signs, there is only *one* avenue: the *only* way to get the conception of hardness or of a mind is by courtesy of its magical connection with certain sensations. This answer is permitted by the way I labeled the nodes in Figure 2.1: the conception of a Class II significatum is obtainable through experience (but perhaps also as an innate response to certain stimuli), while the conception of a Class III significatum is *not* obtainable through experience.

The second answer affirms that notions signified by Class II signs are obtainable only through experience and goes on to solve Ichakawa's puzzle by positing an interesting kind of cognitive architecture. Until the infant knows from the inside what it is to be happy or angry, he has no conception of these emotions, and no awareness of another's facial expressions will give it to him. But once the infant *does* have conceptions of these emotions from his own case, the sight of a smile or a frown *will* signify them to him. The child's wiring diagram is such that the connection between X and Y is not activated until the child has independently arrived at the conception of Y.

Reid's recognition of Class II and III natural signs marks a major departure from Berkeley. In his *Theory of Vision*, whenever he establishes that there is no necessary connection (discoverable by reason) between a sign and what it signifies, Berkeley concludes straightaway that the connection between the two must be learned by experience. For example, because there is no necessary connection between the sensation of turning our eyes and the distance to the object our eyes are converging upon, Berkeley concludes that the connection must be learned by experience (NTV, sec. 17). Reid is always prepared to entertain the nativist alternative that the connection is hardwired into us, and he often endorses it. He is right to take the nativist alternative seriously, since it seems in principle that any correlation we learn about by experience could have been one that we were innately programmed to believe in.[8]

## C. THE *EXPERIMENTUM CRUCIS*

Many of the consequences of Hume's philosophy that Reid deems disastrous stem from his adherence to the empiricist principle that there is no idea not copied from a previous impression or sensation. To avoid these consequences, Reid tackles the empiricist principle head-on. His strategy, as noted above, is to consider an idea that he knows Hume would concede we possess—the idea of *extension* (along with other ideas like motion that presuppose it)—and to contend that there is no way this uncontroversial idea could have been extracted from our sensations or impressions.

Reid frames the issue as follows:

> This I would therefore humbly propose as an *experimentum crucis*, by which the ideal system must stand or fall; and it brings the matter to a short issue: Extension, figure, motion, may, any one, or all of them, be taken for the subject of this experiment. Either

---

[8] An interesting case in point is noted in Grandi 2003. In his published writings, Reid agrees with Berkeley that we come to judge of depth by sight only after learning correlations between depth as gauged by touch and various visual cues. In earlier unpublished manuscripts, however (such as AUL MS 2131/8/II/21, fol.2v and 3r), he entertains the possibility that the connections between visual cues and spatial depth are innate.

they are ideas of sensation, or they are not. If any one of them can be shown to be an idea of sensation, or to have the least resemblance to any sensation, I lay my hand upon my mouth, and give up all pretence to reconcile reason to common sense in this matter, and must suffer the ideal skepticism to triumph. But if, on the other hand, they are not ideas of sensation, nor like to any sensation, then the ideal system is a rope of sand, and all the laboured arguments of the skeptical philosophy against a material world, and against the existence of every thing but impressions and ideas, proceed upon a false hypothesis. (IHM 5.7:70)

What, then, is the *experimentum crucis*? Here is how he introduces it in 5.6:

To put this matter in another light, it may be proper to try, whether from sensation alone we can collect any notion of extension, figure, motion, and space. (65)

He notes that since a blind man can acquire these notions, they are presumably obtainable from tactile sensations if they are obtainable from sensations at all. He therefore proposes to leave aside the sense of sight and

suppose a blind man, by some strange distemper, to have lost all the experience and habits and notions he had got by touch; not to have the least conception of the existence, figure, dimensions, or extension, either of his own body, or of any other; but to have all his knowledge of external things to acquire anew, by means of sensation, and the power of reason, which we suppose to remain entire. (IHM 6.5:65)

There is one condition of the experiment that Reid does not make explicit, but that must be presupposed if his procedure is to make any sense. To appreciate the need for this condition, let us jump ahead to the conclusions Reid draws from the experiment. Negatively, he contends that the blind man could not, by any process of abstraction or ratiocination, "collect" the notion of extension from his tactile sensations. The sensations are merely the occasions for conceiving of extension; there is no internal connection (of resemblance or necessitation) between any sensation or complex of sensations and any quality involving extension (such as figure or motion) that would enable him to do so. Positively, he contends that the notion of extension is one we acquire only by means of Class III natural signs—in other words, by innate suggestion relations or natural magic. We are hardwired to respond to tactile sensations by conceiving of and believing in extended objects, but extension is not to be found in the sensations themselves. Nor, of course, is it to be found in their objects, since sensations do not have objects.

We may now identify the unstated condition of the experiment. The blind man has no notion of extension, but must attain it anew, and for this purpose he is given two things: tactile sensations and the power of reason. Would these suffice? If he were constructed as Reid thinks the rest of us are—that is, if it were a law of his constitution that tactile sensations trigger the conception of extension—the answer would obviously be *yes*. So for purposes of Reid's thought experiment, we must suppose that *all hardwiring has been stripped away*. That is the unstated condition. If the blind man can collect the notion of extension from his sensations, it will have to be because there is some internal relation between the two.

We may now proceed with the experiment. It consists of six phases, which I indicate by numbers in brackets. For each phase, I either quote or summarize Reid's comment on it and then give my own criticism of his comment.

[1] Suppose him first to be pricked with a pin; this will, no doubt, give a smart sensation: he feels pain; but what can he infer from it? Nothing surely with regard to the existence or figure of a pin. . . . Common sense may lead him to think that this pain has a cause; but whether this cause is body or spirit, extended or unextended, figured or not figured, he cannot possibly, from any principles he is supposed to have, form the least conjecture. Having had formerly no notion of body or of extension, the prick of a pin can give him none. (65)

The prick of a pin will not do the trick, avers Reid. I am inclined to accuse him of an *ignoratio elenchi* right at the first phase.[9] The question is not whether I can *know* that something extended is causing my sharp sensation, but whether I can obtain the *idea or notion* of extension from the sensation. Perhaps Reid is right that I cannot, but if so, it is not for the reason he gives.

[2] Suppose, next, a body not pointed but blunt, is applied to his body with a force gradually increased until it bruises him. (IHM 5.6:65–66)

What this phase adds is extension in the cause along with increasing intensity.[10] Reid's comment is that a tumor within one's body could produce an exactly similar sensation without authorizing any inference to anything extended and external. I suspect here the same *ignoratio* as in his reply to [1]. I also wonder what Reid gains

---

[9] Reid's corresponding move in the hardness version of the *experimentum crucis* is to point out that the sensations now caused in us by hard bodies might just as well have been caused by soft bodies or vibrating bodies (IHM 5.4:62 and 5.5:64).
[10] Nichols notes that we add a temporal dimension as well (2007:79) but that may not be the key variable.

by noting that the cause might be within one's body—if the subject inferred such a cause, he would still be conceiving of something extended.

[3] Suppose, thirdly, that the body applied to him touches a larger or a lesser part of his body. (66)

Reid replies that one could know how long an object touching one's body was only if one knew the distance from one of the bodily parts touched to another, but that would presuppose already having "some previous notion of the dimensions and figure of his own body, to serve him as a measure." But with what right is *measure* introduced into the question at all? Just so long as you have the idea of two points being separated, no matter by how much, you have the idea of extension.

[4] Suppose, again, that a body is drawn along his hands or face, while they are at rest. (IHM 5.6:66).

Reid allows that tracing a finger along the subject's face will give him a new feeling—of succession, presumably[11]—"but how it should convey a notion of space or motion, to one who had none before, I cannot conceive." I note here that if Reid concedes that the subject could get the notion of succession, his strategy of reply to phases one and two is shown to be too strong. Recall that in those phases, he questioned whether the subject could infer an extended cause from his sensations. Well, the external cause of two successive sensations (or of a feeling of successiveness) might for all one knows be two simultaneous physical events with different time lags to their effects. So there can be no infallible inference to successiveness in the external cause of the sensations; but might the subject nonetheless get the notion of successiveness from the sensations? If so, he might equally get the notion of an extended cause from sensations that do not permit an infallible inference to it.

[5] Let us next suppose, that he makes some instinctive effort to move his head or his hand; but that no motion follows, either on account of external resistance, or of palsy. (IHM 5.6:66)

Can this effort convey the notion of space and motion to one who never had it before? Reid answers, "Surely it cannot."

[6] Last of all, let us suppose, that he moves a limb by instinct. . . . He has here a new sensation, which accompanies the flexure of joints, and the swelling of muscles. (66)

---

[11] Reid seems indifferent in this paragraph to the distinction between a succession of feelings and a feeling of succession.

What is added in this phase are kinesthetic and perhaps also proprioceptive sensations. Reid's only apposite comment is that an embryo in the womb probably has similar sensations, but without any idea of space or motion.

On reviewing Reid's grounds for dismissing various candidate sensations, we see that they come down to one or another of two claims: that extension in the cause of the sensation cannot be deduced from the sensation, which I have argued to be irrelevant, and that the sensation in question would not give the notion of extension to one who did not have it already, which is bare assertion. It is disappointing that an experiment on which Reid is prepared to stake so much should be supported by so little.

Moreover, it may be objected that there are significant variations in the experiment that Reid failed to consider. The simplest may be this: we give our subject *two* pricks of a pin simultaneously, separated by several inches along his forearm. He will experience the pricks as being separated, and where there is spatial separation, there must be extension (at least in one dimension). As Reid says in a manuscript, "Shew me once how by any or all of these feelings we get an idea of length and the difficulty is over" (AUL MS 2131/8/II/21, 2–3, quoted in Nichols 2007:104). The two simultaneous pricks ought to give him the notion of extension as readily as two successive sensations would give him the notion of succession. What would Reid say to this?

An answer emerges, I believe, in other passages where Reid discusses the localization of sensations. He would say that the proposed strategy works only if something inherent in sensations conveys to the mind their locations (or to speak more properly, given Reid's belief that sensations are purely mental, the locations of their bodily causes). Reid holds that a sensation "from its own nature" conveys nothing about location (IHM 6.12:125.)[12] We speak of our pains and other sensations as having locations only because by our constitution some of our sensations have annexed to them beliefs about the location of their causes. Perhaps the last physical link in the chain of causes leading to the sensation carries information about earlier links and prompts a belief about the location of the first link. Applying this point to the objection about the two pinpricks, Reid's reply would be that when we strip away all hardwiring (as we are supposed to do in the *experimentum crucis*), we also strip away beliefs about location. So the subject of our experiment would not feel the pricks as separated. If they were qualitatively alike, perhaps he would feel them as one; if they were qualitatively different, perhaps he would feel them as two in the

---

[12] There is a tradition in psychology, stemming especially from Lotze, that posits "local signs" in our sensations. These are intrinsic nonspatial features of the sensations of one sense that do not inherently suggest location, but which do correlate with location as gleaned by another sense. Local signs in our tactile sensations would not be available to the subject of Reid's *experimentum crucis* because he has no *other* sensory avenue for learning about location.

way that one discerns two notes within a chord as two. He would not experience them as spatially separated.

Byrne has raised an apt objection to Reid's view on the localization of sensations (2001:227–30). If localization is just a matter of annexed belief, how can Reid account for the phenomenon of pains in a phantom limb? As Reid himself points out (EIP 2.18:214), a man may feel pain that seems to come from a limb he knows is no longer there, so presumably he does not believe that the cause of the pain lies in the limb. In reply, perhaps Reid could say that the man has an *inclination* to believe the pain comes from his leg, but that this inclination gets overridden by his knowledge that the leg is gone. Or perhaps he could say, with contemporary philosophers like Peacocke, that what the man has annexed to his pain is an attitude that *represents* the pain as coming from his leg without being a *belief* that the pain comes from his leg. For more on this issue, see appendix E.[13]

A second variation on the *experimentum crucis* that Reid failed to consider is to give the subject sensations of *color*. Reid chooses a blind person as his subject because he is convinced that blind persons do somehow acquire the notion of extension, which shows that color sensations cannot be necessary for this purpose. But might they nonetheless be sufficient? Here is what I think Reid would say in reply: The sensations we get through sight are of color alone. They are caused by physical impressions on the retina, which by a law of our constitution make us perceive an object at a certain place in the visual field—in the direction of a line from the stimulated point of the retina through the center of the eye and out into ambient space. (This law, sometimes called the law of visible direction, is discussed in greater detail in chapter 7.) If there were no such law, and if we were given *only* the color sensations, they would suggest nothing to us of location, extension, or any sort of manifold. Thus once again, for a being stripped of the hardwiring possessed by normal human beings, sensations would convey nothing of extension.[14]

---

[13] The account of localization just sketched goes some way toward answering the following question: if tactile sensations inherently suggest nothing of location or extension, why do we feel an object in our hand as a ball rather than a block? Reid might answer that each physical impression causing a tactile sensation "knows" where it came from and conveys this information to us in the form of a concomitant belief or representation. The totality of representations of the positions of the parts of an object could amount to a representation of its shape. But to my mind, a puzzle still remains: why do we *feel* an object as round, as opposed to merely believing or representing that a round object is causing our sensations?

[14] I am at a loss to imagine the phenomenological state Reid must attribute to beings in whom the law of visible direction is inoperative. I would see red, but I would not see a red patch, nor even a red point à la Hume, since a Humean point at least has location. See Falkenstein 2000 for more on Reid's views on the localization of color.

The elements of Reid's psychophysics I have brought in to defend his thought experiment might prompt a procedural objection, brought to my attention by Gideon Yaffe. How does Reid know that it is only by dint of contingent hardwiring that tactile sensations and color sensations convey information about location? Isn't that exactly what the experiment is supposed to establish—that sensations in their own intrinsic nature convey nothing of location, or anything else that could give us the notion of extension?

If the charge is circularity, I do not believe that Reid is guilty of it. The injunction to ignore hardwired external connections *is* the injunction to look at the sensations themselves and see what they convey by their intrinsic nature. The problem posed by Yaffe's query is rather that it may be hard to know whether a feature we attribute to our sensations belongs to them intrinsically or is instead one we are programmed to conceive of and believe in on the occasion of the sensations. Berkeley claims that we misattribute certain spatial features to our visual data because after long association of the visual data with tactile data, the features of the two are "most closely twisted, blended, and incorporated together" (NTV 51).[15] When the linkage is the product not of past association but of our native constitution (as Reid says it is with tactile sensations and conceptions of spatial features), how much more difficult must it be to sort things out? Reid is committed, however, to its being possible in principle.

## D. RESPONSES TO THE *EXPERIMENTUM CRUCIS*

Though I know of few writers who have responded explicitly to Reid's thought experiment, there are a number of classical authors who have taken positions implicitly at variance with his. The question is: from what sensations, if any, do we get our notion of space or extension? A distinct but related question is, from what experiences do we get our notion of external or mind-independent objects? Some of the authors discussed in this section treat the questions in tandem.

*Berkeley.* DeRose (1989) argues that Reid has too limited a view of which tactile sensations might plausibly be thought give rise to concepts of extension and figure. He attributes to Berkeley a sophisticated sensationalism, according to which to think of a thing of a certain shape is to entertain a battery of conditionals about what tactile sensations would ensue if we took this or that action, for instance, moving our hands in a certain way. He suggests that knowledge of sufficiently many action-sensation conditionals might give us the concept of a line or a sphere.

---

[15] Reid makes a similar point in the paragraph about the apothecary at IHM 1.2:14.

I set aside the objection that to be able to think of the motions mentioned in the antecedents of action-sensation conditionals is already to have the concept of extension. I ask instead whether the various sensations that ensue upon the actions are localized or not.[16] If they are, DeRose's suggestion adds nothing to the two-pricks case discussed above. If they are not, there is no reason to think that experiencing or imagining a systematic train of them would give one the concept of extension, any more than a sequence of smells or tones would do.

*Adam Smith.* In a youthful essay on the senses (probably preceding Hume's *Treatise* of 1739), Adam Smith proposes that touch alone among the senses gives us the ideas of externality or mind-dependence and extension (1980).[17] He says that the objects of touch always present themselves as resisting the bodily part that perceives them, which gives us the idea of objects independent of us. The power or quality of resistance he calls solidity, and he takes solidity to imply both externality and three-dimensionality.[18] By discerning the limits of a solid body, we arrive at the notions of extension and figure. Similar views are advocated by a latter-day Smith, A. D. Smith, who holds that one important source of our notion of objects independent of us is the *Anstoss*, or experience of resistance to our pullings and pushings.[19]

Reid peremptorily dismisses the feeling of resistance as the source of our idea of extension in phase 5, as we have seen. Could it be the source, though, of our idea of externality, as Smith contends? The connection is not obvious to me. When I cannot call something to mind, I do not think any alien force is withholding it from me; I simply attribute my failure to my own inability to think of it.

*Condillac.* A thought experiment strikingly like Reid's was carried on at book length by Condillac in his *Treatise on the Sensations* of 1754—ten years before

---

[16] The question of whether the sensations are localized is relevant also to the issue of whether genuine spatial concepts must be concepts anchored in simultaneous representations (Evans 1985). I say that knowing what it feels like to trace a wire with your finger suffices for your having a spatial concept if and only if you are aware that what you feel at one instant is in a different place from what you felt at an earlier instant. The successiveness of the feelings need not keep them from delivering a spatial concept, provided there is location in their content.

[17] For a good account of Smith's views, see Glenney 2011.

[18] Smith takes it that solidity and three-dimensionality are mutually entailing, but I cannot see that there is entailment in either direction. On the one hand, if a detached two-dimensional surface could exist at all, why could it not be strong enough to resist penetration? On the other hand, why could there not be eight points of light forming the vertices of a three-dimensional but intangible cube?

[19] There are three types of experience that A. D. Smith holds to be individually sufficient (and the disjunction of which he holds to be necessary) for the presentation of ostensibly mind-independent objects: phenomenal spatiality (that is, three-dimensionality and spatial separation from the self), variation in our experience as we move in relation to an object, and the *Anstoss*. See 2001, chapter 6.

Reid's *Inquiry*.[20] Condillac imagines a statue given sentience one sense at a time, starting with smell and progressing through hearing, taste, sight, and touch. With the first four senses alone, Condillac maintains, the statue would have no notion of space or of external bodies. It would not know that it has a body, and it would not attribute its sensory states to outside causes. It would simply regard itself as "a savorous, sonorous, and colored smell" ([1754] 1982:220).[21]

When the statue acquires touch—"the Only Sense that Judges External Objects on Its Own"—the situation dramatically changes. Not just any sensations of touch will give the notion of extension and of external bodies; for example, moving the statue's arm or touching its head and feet simultaneously will not give the statue these notions (2.2:226–27). But there is one set of tactile sensations that Condillac thinks will do the job—the sensations the statue gets when its hand touches its own breast. Condillac defines impenetrability as the property of a body by which it excludes all others from the place it occupies and solidity as the sensation that informs us of impenetrability. When the statue touches its own chest, "its hand and its chest will be distinguishable by the sensation of solidity that they send mutually and that places them necessarily outside of each other" (2.5.3:234). Thus does the statue come to know that it has a body. When it draws its finger continuously along its arm, it will now form the idea of extension, and when it goes on to touch a foreign body, in which it "does not feel itself modified" as it does in its own chest, it will form the notion of external bodies (234–35).

What would Reid say to all this? He considers the case of a finger being drawn along the subject's arm in phase 4 of his experiment, but not the case of the *subject's* tracing a path along his arm with his *own* finger. In an unpublished manuscript, however, he considers the case in which the subject explores his own face with his hand (AUL MS 2131/8/II/21, 2–3, discussed in Grandi 2003, Grandi 2008b, and Nichols 2007:101–7). He claims that it would be the "work of years" to arrive at a notion of the shape of one's face in this way, but that is beside the point—the issue is simply whether he could attain the notion of extension. Here, too, Reid's answer is negative—the feelings obtained in this way "seem to me not to convey the least Idea of Space"—but he offers nothing in support of his verdict.

There is one thing we can be sure that Reid would have asked Condillac: how is it that the sensations Condillac calls sensations of solidity inform us of impenetrability and extension? What are these sensations like, and how do they do the job? If

---

[20] It is tempting to speculate with Nichols that Reid must have read Condillac, though he never mentions him (2007:97n.)

[21] Condillac does apparently think that seeing an array of colors would give one the idea of extension, but not of extension outside oneself or of size and shape. See ([1754] 1982, 1.11.8–9:216–19).

they give the notions of impenetrability and extension only because they function as Class III natural signs of these qualities, Reid can stand his ground.

*Hume.* According to Hume, any extended expanse is made up either of minima visibilia or minima tangibilia, the smallest possible visible or tangible items. Most Hume scholars agree that Hume's minima (perhaps unlike Berkeley's) are unextended (Raynor 1980). But whether themselves extended or not, minima set alongside one another make up larger extended expanses. In our awareness of such expanses, it may be claimed, we have the origin of our notion of extension. Indeed, Hume says so explicitly: the impressions from which I get the idea of extension are

> the impressions of colour'd points, disposed in a certain manner. . . . The table before me is alone sufficient by its view to give me the idea of extension. (THN 1.2.3:34, reversing Hume's order of sentences)

For this reason, Falkenstein classifies Hume as an *intuitionist* about visual and tangible location and extension (2000a).[22]

Why, then, did Reid think Hume could not account for our notion of extension? Perhaps it was because he too readily equated Hume's term "impression" with his own term "sensation." A Reidian sensation is both extensionless and positionless, so no notion of extension can be derived from it by nonmagical means. But Humean impressions of sight and touch have position, and in the aggregate if not individually, they have extension. The notion of extension is there for the taking in the apprehension of such impressions.

*In the apprehension of them*: on that score, if not on the original terms of his thought experiment, Reid could fault Hume. What is it to apprehend an impression, or be conscious of it? Whenever any apprehending goes on for Reid, three items are involved: a subject, an act, and an object. But as he notes, it is often unclear whether Humean impressions are acts or objects, since Hume systematically conflates these categories (EIP 1.1:26; 3.7:286). Insofar as impressions are extended, they are presumably objects. But then in virtue of what do they get apprehended, if there are no subjects or acts? What do you have to add to the *esse* of an impression to get its *percipi?* The best Hume can muster is this: an impression is apprehended when it belongs to a self, that is, when it is bundled together with other impressions rather

---

[22] Falkenstein proposes intuitionism as a third view alongside nativism and empirism, the two standard "isms" about the genesis of spatial perception ever since Helmholtz distinguished them in the nineteenth century. Nativists about a mode of spatial perception hold that it occurs at birth or upon maturation without any need for learning; empirists hold that it arises only through learning. For more on this distinction, see Hatfield 1990:271–80.

than roaming around on its own. So Reid could reply to Hume as follows: "Yes, you have sketched an account whereby one could attain a conception of extension—an account rather like my own, in which there is an original awareness of extended items or arrays out there in the world, not derived from sensations in my sense of the term; but you have given no plausible account of what this awareness itself could possibly amount to." Admittedly, that would be an *ad hominem* objection to Hume, in the sense that it discredits Hume's total package of views without necessarily affecting his view on the issue at hand.

In the previous paragraph, I imply that Reid, like Hume, is an intuitionist in Falkenstein's sense: we get the notion of extension by perceiving extended objects. Yet I have also been calling Reid a nativist: certain aspatial sensations innately trigger in us the conception of extension. Can he hold both views? There seems to be no inconsistency in doing so, but there may be redundancy. If we perceive the object, why do we need the hardwired response? If we have the response, why do we need the object? If we have them both, why are they in agreement? Perhaps a Kant or a Helmholtz would jibe at Reid's position as an implausible case of pre-established harmony.[23] This is one of the places where I am not confident I understand Reid's philosophy.

*William James.* Here are the opening sentences of the chapter on the perception of space in James's *Principles of Psychology*:

> *In the sensations of hearing, touch, sight, and pain we are accustomed to distinguish from among other elements the element of voluminousness.* We call the reverberations of a thunderstorm more voluminous than the squeaking of a slate-pencil; the entrance into a warm bath gives our skin a more massive feeling than the prick of a pin. . . . Some tastes and smells appear less extensive than complex flavors, like that of roast meat or plum pudding, on the one hand, or heavy odors like musk or tuberose, on the other. The epithet *sharp* given to the acid class would seem to show that to the popular mind there is something narrow and, as it were, streaky, in the impression they make, other flavors and odors being bigger and rounder. . . . *Now my first thesis is that this element* [extensity or roominess as he calls it], *discernible in each and every sensation, though more developed in some than in others, is the original sensation of space.* ([1890] 1950:134–35)

On the question of whether our sensations convey any notion of extensity, it seems at first that no two philosophers could be more opposed than Reid and James. On

---

[23] See Kant CPR, B167–68 and Hatfield 1990:191.

further reflection, however, it appears that there may be no genuine disagreement between them. The sensory experiences to which James refers—hearing thunder and smelling roast beef—are classified as sensations in his book because they are cases of acquaintance rather than knowledge-about. But in Reid's book, if they are cases of acquaintance, they are already cases of perception and not mere sensation. From Reid's point of view, James is really saying that we find certain *sounds* voluminous and certain *smells* sharp—it is the object and not our sensing of it that has spatial features. For present purposes, Reid need not disagree.[24]

There is a complication: I say it is the object, not the act, that is roomy, but James, like Hume, makes no distinction between act and object. That makes me wonder what the acquaintance supposedly involved in sensations can be for James, and it suggests that Reid's reply to James would echo his reply to Hume on the apprehension of manifolds of minima.

## E. *WOULDS, COULDS,* OR *SHOULDS*?

Rather than engage in further debate at this point about whether Reid or his opponents are right on the question of whether any sensations give us the notion of extension, I believe it behooves us instead to step back and ask what sort of question Reid is asking. Is it a question about *woulds, coulds,* or *shoulds*?

Is Reid asking whether a blind man, given the prescribed diet of sensations, actually *would* form the notion of extension? If so, who knows? And why are we trying to answer a question like that in the philosophy classroom? Such, at any rate, is the impatient response of some of my students to Reid's question (along with other questions of the same ilk, such Molyneux's Question, discussed in chapter 8). They are empirical questions, and philosophers should not attempt to answer them.

If the question really is a question about what conceptions the blind man would or would not attain,[25] the students are no doubt right. But I suggest that the question is not about *woulds*, but about *coulds* or *shoulds*. The issues are either modal or normative, and as such they are properly resolvable after all by armchair methods.

Let us consider first the modal alternative. Is Reid asking a question about what the blind man *could* do? Not if we state it just like that, for there are entirely too

---

[24] He does disagree when he gives his analysis of secondary qualities, which are not perceived as spatial items but simply as dispositions to produce sensations in us.

[25] If we find ourselves responding to Reid's experiment by saying the blind man "would not" get the notion of extension from sensation, I think we really mean that it is not the case that he would. "If P, it would not be the case that Q" is sometimes colloquial for "It is not the case that if P, it would be the case that Q." The negated conditional is equivalent to "Even if P, it might not be the case that Q" rather than "If P, it would definitely not be the case that Q."

many things that the blind man *could* do. The question is now easily answerable a priori, but with an answer other than the one Reid intended. Plainly, it could be that the blind man forms the conception of extension after being subjected to the sensory regimen of Reid's experiment—what would prevent it? He might do so randomly, or because he is struck by lightning just as the final sensation is induced.

We may reinforce this line of thought by using David Lewis's "patchwork principle" about possibilities: "If it is possible that X happen intrinsically in a spatiotemporal region, and if it is likewise possible that Y happen in a region, then also it is possible that both X and Y happen in two distinct but adjacent regions" (1983:77). The argument employing this principle would run as follows: a region is possible in which the blind man undergoes Reid's sensory regimen; a region is also possible in which the blind man forms the conception of extension; therefore, by the patchwork principle, a connected region is possible in which the blind man does the first of these things followed by the second.

If Reid's question is to be a question about what the blind man *could* do, it must be interpreted as a question about what he could extract from his sensations using only certain circumscribed methods—for example, inspection, abstraction, and ratiocination. Even then, the patchwork principle would imply that the blind man could do the specified things and get the conception of extension in the next moment. The patchwork argument would *not* imply, however that he could get that conception as the *necessary upshot* of doing those things. So it looks as though our initial question about *could* gives way to a question about *must*: is it necessary that anyone who performs operation O upon sensation S will obtain conception C? That question is still a modal question, and as such it is amenable to a priori adjudication. As we are construing things now, Reid's experiment would refute a claim of necessity, and that is something within the traditional competence of thought experiments.

If Reid's experiment is meant to refute a claim of necessity, however, we have to ask whether his principal opponent, Hume, is committed to a claim of necessity. Must Hume claim that it is necessary that anyone who performs certain operations on his tactile sensations will form the conception of extension? Perhaps not; he might regard the sensations and the conception (or the impressions and the idea, in his parlance) as distinct existences, between which there is no necessary connection. Perhaps the most he would say is that someone who underwent the sensations and did not form the conception would suffer from some cognitive abnormality.

This brings us to the third way of construing Reid's question—as a question about *shoulds*, or at any rate a question under the broad umbrella of the normative. I am not sure how best to put the matter, but perhaps the moral of Reid's thought experiment is something like this: there would be nothing irrational about a person who was given tactile sensations and employed his reason about them but was not led thereby to form the conception of extension. He would not be like a person who fails to see the validity of an obvious inference or like a person who fails to see a similarity that is manifestly before him. In short, he would not be a person who fails to do something that (given the materials at his disposal) he ought (in some cognitive sense) to do.[26]

That Reid's question in the *experimentum crucis* is a normative question seems correct to me, but recognizing this fact does not give us any new leverage in answering it. The answers to normative questions supervene on the answers to non-normative questions, questions about what is in some sense natural or matter-of-factual. If a man is a good man, that is presumably in virtue of his performing certain deeds or having certain traits of character—Nelson Mandela was a good man because he was patient, courageous, and a force for peace. If a belief is justified, that is presumably in virtue of its reliable manner of formation or its inferential relations to other beliefs the subject holds or its relation to experiences the subject is having. If a concept is justifiably acquired or pressed into play on the occasion of the subject's having certain experiences, that is presumably in virtue of some natural relation between the experiences and the concept, some relation that can be specified in non-normative terms.[27] What might that relation be in the *experimentum crucis*?

I do not see what the answer can be except that the concept is somehow *on display* in the experiences. It is no accident that Hume so often uses the language of *resemblance* in talking about the relation between ideas (concepts) and impressions,[28] and that Reid puts his negative thesis in the *experimentum crucis* by saying there is no resemblance between any sensation and any attribute implying extension.

But now we have come full circle. We started with the question of whether a blind man could obtain the notion of extension from his sensations, and we recognized at a certain point that the question has a normative dimension: Would it be reasonable to form the notion in response to the sensations? Would there be something wrong with you if you did not? But any reasonableness or lack thereof in the subject's response to his sensations must be a function of the obtaining of other relations, such as resemblance. Is extension to be found in tactile sensations? All we can do is look and see.

---

[26] In chapter 8, I discuss a parallel construal of the Molyneux question as normative.

[27] Here I must confess my puzzlement about another aspect of the *experimentum crucis*. I understand how the *application* of a concept to something, or the belief that it is instantiated, can be justified or not, but I do not understand how the *formation* of a concept on a certain occasion can be justified or not.

[28] On this score, there is an important difference between the empiricisms of Hume and Locke; see chapter 14, section A.

Scrutinize the sensations you get when you press your hand against a tabletop. You conceive of something hard and extended; but are the sensations themselves hard or extended? Pay close attention, says Reid, and you will see that the answer is no.[29] I am by no means certain myself that I am able to isolate the sensations Reid wants us to inspect. There is something elusive about them. When I attend to my visual or tactile experiences, I am not able to discriminate within them any elements about which I can confidently say, "*This* is the sensation proper, and it is utterly devoid of extension."

There is a widely held doctrine in contemporary philosophy of mind that could be used to explain why Reid's thought experiment is so difficult—namely, the doctrine of the transparency of sensations, as espoused by Harman (1990) and others. Proponents of this doctrine typically make two points: first, they say that when we attend to our sensations, we never notice any of their intrinsic features; second, they say that what our sensations reveal to us is not their own qualities, but those of the objects they represent. Both of these points are anti-Reidian, the first because Reid thinks we can know our sensations perfectly and the second because Reid holds that sensations are nonrepresentational. If transparency is the explanation of the difficulty of Reid's thought experiment, it is a subversive one.

## F. NATIVISM AS AN ANTIDOTE TO SKEPTICISM

Reid and some of his commentators, including Morgan (1977), Daniels (1974), and DeRose (1989), think his nativism affords an answer to skepticism. Does it really? I answer that it affords an answer to skepticism of one variety, but not another. We need to distinguish semantic skepticism, or skepticism about understanding, from epistemological skepticism, or skepticism about knowledge. Semantic skepticism entails epistemological skepticism (since we cannot know what we cannot understand), but not conversely. Reid's nativism is relevant to semantic skepticism only.

The main tenets of semantic skepticism are contained in the following syllogism, which Reid attributes to Berkeley and Hume:

---

[29] There is actually an odd disparity in the reasons Reid gives for his doctrine of "no resemblance" between sensations and external things. Sometimes he presents it as though it were the result of careful introspection: attend to your sensations carefully enough, and you will see that they resemble nothing in the external world (IHM 6.6:92; EIP 2.17:209 lines 10–18). At other times he presents it as though it were a matter of a priori ontology: sensations are mind-dependent, traits of external objects are not, and no resemblance can span such fundamentally different types of being (IHM 6.6:94; EIP 2.17:209 lines 31–38). At EIP 2.17:203, he presents both considerations seamlessly in the same paragraph.

1. We can have no conception of any thing but what resembles some sensation or idea in our minds.
2. The sensations and ideas in our minds can resemble nothing but the sensations and ideas in other minds.
3. Therefore, we can have no conception of an inanimate substance, such as matter is conceived to be, or of any of its qualities.

The conclusion and both premises may be found in exactly these words among lines 4–12 of IHM 5.8:75. The argument is reprised at IHM 7:212, where Reid says that according to the ideal system, bodies are either reducible to ideas, in which case they have no existence outside the mind, or not reducible to ideas, in which case "they are words without any meaning." Hence the propriety of the label "semantic skepticism."

If this argument were correct in both its premises, it would follow that we cannot even *conceive* of a world beyond our sensations, let alone have knowledge of it. Reid thinks the second premise is correct, and he credits Berkeley with having established it (IHM 5.8:75). But he thinks the first premise—which states in Reid's language Hume's principle that all our ideas are copied from precedent impressions—is demonstrably false. That is the intended moral of the *experimentum crucis*. "That we have clear and distinct conceptions of extension, figure, motion, and other attributes of body, which are neither sensations, nor like any sensation, is a fact of which we may be as certain, as that we have sensations" (IHM 5.8:76).[30]

Reid's reply to Berkeley and Hume has an echo in our own time in the response of Edward Craig to the positivist semantics of Schlick and Dummett (Craig 1982). According to Schlick, if a term is not definable by means of terms whose meaning can be conveyed ostensively—by displaying their referents within the content of our sensory experience—we cannot understand it. According to Dummett, if a sentence does not express a verifiable state of affairs—one lying wholly within the scope of what one can observe—it could never be learned. Nor, even if it could be learned, could teacher and learner know that they were using their terms with the

---

[30] An argument similar to the argument Reid attributes to Berkeley is also attributed to Berkeley by John Campbell (2002): (1) all concepts we possess are "made available" by experience (the principle of "the explanatory role of experience"); (2) experience cannot make available concepts of mind-independent objects; therefore (3) we do not possess concepts of mind-independent objects. If an experience can "make available" a concept only by resembling it, Reid would deny premise (1). Campbell chooses instead to deny premise (2), claiming that an experience can make available the concept of a mind-independent object simply by incorporating a mind-independent object as a constituent, as happens on his own "relational conception of experience." For critical discussion of Campbell's views, see Van Cleve 2006a.

same meaning. Schlick and Dummett, having executed the "linguistic turn," are transposing what Hume says about the provenance of concepts into doctrines about the understanding of language.

Craig seeks to get around such positivist strictures on the limits of understanding by invoking something strikingly similar to Reid's nativism. Here are Craig's proposals:

> Suppose for a moment that there are some human beliefs not equivalent in content to any construction out of observables or what is experienceable. Then these beliefs may enter into the process of language learning, for all that has yet been shown to the contrary. For the learner might, when faced with the ostended object, form beliefs about it beyond what he experienced or observed; why should he not then take the words he hears to be the expression of that belief, and so come to ascribe to them a meaning not admissible according to Schlick's semantic theory? (543)

> Suppose that all human beings, when faced with certain sense data, naturally form beliefs which go beyond sense data, in the sense of not being reducible to complex beliefs about them. Then our learner will come to hold such beliefs. In accordance with the hypothesis [that learners attribute to others in the same circumstances the beliefs they form themselves], he will impute similar beliefs to his teachers, and they to him, and both sides will be right, even though the states of belief, about which the assumption is confidently made, are unobservable to anyone but their subject. (557)

These suggestions have a remarkably Reidian ring. Craig's first supposition is that humans are so constituted as to form certain conceptions and beliefs in response to sensory data that go beyond anything simply to be found in the data themselves. That is exactly what Reid says about the concept of body in relation to tactile sensations. His second supposition is that human beings take others to form the same beliefs that they themselves do under the same circumstances. Though not explicit in Reid, that is certainly Reidian in spirit. Combining the two suppositions, Craig concludes that there is no reason that human beings should not come to understand language describing matters going beyond the sensory given and, moreover, to understand it in the same way as their fellows.[31]

Reid's nativism can thus serve as an antidote to one form of skepticism—skepticism about understanding. But skepticism about knowledge remains untouched.

---

[31] But can we *know* that we understand language in the same way as our fellows? To secure that result, we may need to supplement Craig's proposals with an externalist theory of knowledge, such as I discuss in chapter 12.

Unfortunately, the distinction between semantic and epistemological skepticism is sometimes missed. Morgan says that making an idea innate protects it from skepticism, and that "to the extent we can show that an idea is innate, we can trust it" (1977:111 and 125). I say to the contrary that if to "trust" a concept means to believe justifiably that it is instantiated, nativism does nothing to make our concepts more trustworthy. Indeed, for a thinker like Kant, showing that a certain conception is nonempirical, an "offspring of my own brain," only exacerbates the question of its legitimate application; it raises the demand for what Kant called a "transcendental deduction" of it. See Van Cleve 1999:32–33.

Epistemological skepticism remains to be reckoned with; it is the topic of chapter 12.

# 3

## DIRECT REALISM VERSUS THE WAY OF IDEAS

I think there is some merit in what you are pleased to call *my Philosophy*; but I think it lies chiefly in having called in question the common theory of *Ideas* or *Images of things in the mind* being the only objects of thought. (Thomas Reid, letter to James Gregory, August 20, 1790)

His merit lay in the independence of thought required to free himself from this assumption [that the immediate objects of the mind in perception are its own ideas], question it, and hunt it home. (Henry Sidgwick, 1895 lecture)

Almost alone among the great modern philosophers, Reid sought to uphold a direct realist theory of perception.[1] He repudiated the "way of ideas," whose central assumption is that what is immediately present to the mind is never an external thing, but only an internal image, sense datum, or (to use the most common eighteenth-century term) *idea*.[2] Ideas were conceived of as mental entities that exist only as long as there is awareness of them. Some proponents of the theory of ideas (such as Descartes and Locke) were realists, holding that physical objects outside the mind are the causes of the ideas existing within the mind. Others (such as Berkeley

---

[1] The main thinker other than Reid with a claim to this distinction is Arnauld, whose credentials I examine in appendix H.

[2] The epithet "way of ideas" was used disparagingly by Sergeant and Stillingfleet as a description of the philosophy of Locke in their works of 1697. (Thanks to Kenny Pearce for the reference to Sergeant.) I do not know of a place where Reid himself uses the phrase; he usually says "the theory of ideas" or "the ideal theory." The classic exploration of the way of ideas in connection with Locke is Yolton 1956.

and Hume) were idealists or phenomenalists, questioning the existence of a world outside the mind and believing that the things we call physical objects are simply bundles of ideas. In either case, the theory of ideas cuts us off from direct perception of the external world, either because there is no external world to be perceived or because our perception of it is indirect—not strictly perception at all, in Reid's view, but only an inference based on what we do perceive, namely, ideas. Reid was convinced to the contrary that external things exist and that we perceive them directly (or "immediately," to use his own term). What this claim means and why Reid thinks it true are the topics of this chapter.

## A. THE WAY OF IDEAS

Reid devotes seven chapters of the *Intellectual Powers* to tracing the history of philosophy from the ancient Greeks up to his contemporaries, finding nearly every thinker he mentions to have held some version of the theory of ideas. He pauses in chapter 2.14, "Reflections on the Common Theory of Ideas," to deliver his criticisms of the theory under five heads.

Reid's first reflection is that the theory of ideas is opposed to the ordinary person's conviction that she perceives external things themselves, directly or immediately:

> [The theory of ideas] is directly contrary to the universal sense of men who have not been instructed in philosophy. When we see the sun or moon, we have no doubt that the very objects which we immediately see, are very far distant from us, and from one another. . . . How are we astonished when the Philosopher informs us, that we are mistaken in all this; that the sun and moon which we see, are not, as we imagine, many miles distant from us, and from each other, but that they are in our own mind; that they had no existence before we saw them, and will have none when we cease to perceive and to think of them; because the objects we perceive are only ideas in our own minds. (EIP 2.14:172)

Reid's second reflection is that the theory is supported by no good arguments:

> The authors who have treated of ideas, have generally taken their existence for granted, as a thing that could not be called in question; and such arguments as they have mentioned . . . to prove it, seem too weak to support the conclusion. (EIP 2.14:174)

In sections B, C, D, and E, I discuss two arguments for the existence of ideas Reid singles out for scrutiny and two more arguments he ought to have considered but didn't.

Reid's third reflection is that philosophers are strangely divided in their opinions about the nature of ideas:

> Philosophers, notwithstanding their unanimity as to the existence of ideas, hardly agree in any one thing else concerning them. (EIP 2.14:184)

Reid claims this disagreement does not befit entities that are supposed to be the things we know best of all. He cites disputes as to whether ideas exist in minds or in brains; if in minds, whether our own or God's; whether they are all adventitious or some of them innate; and whether they are all individual or some of them general. In fairness to his opponents, it should be said that these issues are not all ones we should expect to settle simply by inspecting the ideas of their theory.

Reid's fourth reflection is that ideas are explanatorily redundant:

> Ideas do not make any of the operations of the mind to be better understood, although it was probably with that view that they have been first invented, and afterwards so generally received. (EIP 2.14:184)

Ideas are supposed to explain how we manage to perceive or apprehend what is distant, what is past, and what does not exist at all, but in fact they are no help in this regard. ʕIdeas are of no use in explaining the intentionality or aboutness of mental operations because such explanations inevitably *presuppose* intentionality.ʔIn the first place, ideas can represent objects for us only if the ideas are interpreted (like the symbols in a book) as standing for the objects, but that presupposes precisely the ability of the interpreter to have the object in mind.[3] In the second place, ideas themselves would have to be objects of perception or some kind of awareness, but that again presupposes intentionality:

> It is as difficult to conceive how the mind perceives images in the brain, as, how it perceives things more distant. If any man will shew how the mind may perceive images in the brain, I will undertake to shew how it may perceive the most distant objects: for if we give eyes to the mind, to perceive what is transacted at home in its dark chamber, why may we not make these eyes a little longer-sighted? (IHM. 6.12:121)

Reid's fifth and final point against the theory of ideas is that it runs counter to the common sense of mankind:

> The natural and necessary consequences of it furnish a just prejudice against it to every man who pays a due regard to the common sense of mankind. (EIP 2.14:185)

---

[3] This point is developed in Lehrer 1989:13–14 and taken up in Nichols 2007:56–62. In Reid's own writings it is most explicit in *Philosophical Orations* (his Aberdeen commencement addresses), 62.

One such consequence is skepticism about the external world. If we do not simply *see* external objects, it becomes necessary to prove their existence by arguments, but the arguments philosophers have offered to this end are all problematic, leaving us in danger of losing the material world. Another consequence, as developed by Hume, is that the mind itself must be reduced to a series of ideas. Reid tells us that although he subscribed to the theory of ideas in his youth, Hume's philosophy convinced him (by making its inevitable consequences manifest) that it must be rejected (EIP 2.10:142).

The dialectical progression associated with the way of ideas may be illustrated in a series of four cartoons. The first cartoon illustrates the view of common sense. Ordinary perceptual situations involve a subject, an act of awareness, and an external object. The subject need only open his eyes, and the arrow of awareness will fly out into the external world and make contact with a stone or a tree, as in Figure 3.1.

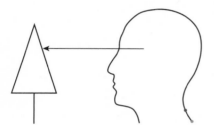

**Figure 3.1**

The arguments to be discussed shortly persuade many philosophers that the arrow of awareness cannot reach all the way into the external world. It is stopped short by an idea, from which we then infer the existence of a corresponding external object. Such is the view Reid attributes to Descartes, Locke, and nearly the entire pantheon of philosophers who preceded him. It may be illustrated as in Figure 3.2.

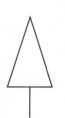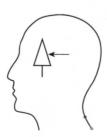

**Figure 3.2**

One need only inspect the picture to have misgivings about it. If we are aware only of the idea, how do we know that the external object resembles it? More radically, how do we know that the external object exists at all? The theory of ideas has skepticism built in to it. In Berkeley's philosophy, material things or things existing outside the mind are claimed to be not merely unknowable, but impossible. We thus arrive at Figure 3.3.

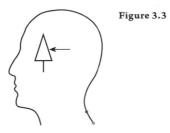

Figure 3.3

Finally, Hume takes the final step, eliminating the self as anything beyond a collection of ideas, giving us Figure 3.4.[4]

Figure 3.4

As Reid trenchantly remarks, once ideas are admitted as "fourth things" in addition to subjects, acts, and objects, they tend to take over, crowding out all else (EIP 2.12:163). Reid's claim to fame is that he allows us to stop with Figure 3.1—at least if we can resist the four arguments now to be considered.

## B. FIRST ARGUMENT FOR THE WAY OF IDEAS: NO ACTION AT A DISTANCE

In EIP 2.14, Reid identifies and criticizes two arguments for the way of ideas. The first, which might be dubbed the "no action at a distance" argument, is intimated in the following striking passage from Malebranche:

> We see the sun, the stars, and an infinity of objects external to us; and it is not likely that the soul should leave the body to stroll about the heavens, as it were, in order to behold all these objects. Thus, it does not see them by themselves, and our mind's immediate object when

---

[4] It is contested among Hume scholars whether the arrow should be erased. I tend to think that it should be—that for Hume there is nothing more to the *percipi* of an idea than its *esse*, or at any rate its being bundled together with other ideas. See THN 1.4.2:206–208. But see Ainslie 2008 for a view of Humean perceptions as "packages" of act and object.

it sees the sun, for example, is not the sun, but something that is intimately joined to our soul, and this is what I call an idea. (Malebranche 1992:27; quoted by Reid at EIP 2.7:108)

Reid names as proponents of this argument Malebranche, Clarke, and Porterfield. The argument is more popular than this list might suggest, being present as well in Berkeley, Descartes, and Russell.[5]

The argument may be set out in full as follows:

1. Nothing can act or be acted upon where it is not (the words of Clarke and Porterfield).
2. When we perceive objects, we act upon them or they upon us.
3. Therefore, we perceive objects only if they are where we are—smack up against our minds.
4. The only such objects are ideas.
5. Therefore, we perceive only ideas.

For now let us not worry about reaching the positive conclusion in step 5, but only about reaching the negative conclusion in step 3—that we perceive nothing remote from us.

It appears at first that Reid's response is to deny premise 2. That premise "ought not to be admitted," he says, for "there appears no reason for asserting, that, in perception, either the object acts upon the mind, or the mind upon the object" (EIP 2.14:176–77).

This response may come as a surprise, as it seems to contradict contemporary wisdom as enshrined in the causal theory of perception. Moreover, it seems to contradict Reid's own views as expressed elsewhere:

There is therefore sufficient reason to conclude, that, in perception, the object produces some change in the organ; that the organ produces some change upon the nerve; and that the nerve produces some change in the brain. (EIP 2.2:75)

Note also the following, which makes it clear that in Reid's view the causal chain involved in perception extends even into the mind:

In perception there are impressions upon the organs of sense, the nerves, and brain, which, by the laws of our nature, are followed by certain operations of mind. (EIP 2.1:71)

[5] Berkeley, First Dialogue, 1949:186 or 1975:177; Descartes, letter to Hyperaspistes, 1991, vol. 3:193. The argument is discussed under the name "the space-gap argument" in Quinton 1973:197–98, where it is attributed to Case and Russell.

To be sure, he denies on the same page that bodily impressions are *efficient* causes of perceptions, but he admits on page 87 that bodily impressions are constantly conjoined with perceptions. So impressions and perceptions are causally connected as much as any two events ever are in his philosophy. For more in this vein, see IHM 6.21, "Of the process of nature in perception."

There are two ways to understand Reid so that he is not guilty of inconsistency. The first is to take it that the causation Reid denies in EIP 2.14 is *agent* causation, whereas the causation he affirms in 2.1 and 2.2 is *event* causation. Reid holds that efficient causation, or causation in the strict sense of the term, is exercised only by conscious agents, whereas physical events are causes only in a Humean sense—they are events followed by other events in accordance with the laws of nature. (I discuss this distinction at greater length in chapter 14.) That Reid has agent causation in mind in 2.14 is suggested by the sentence preceding his denial of premise 2:

> When we say that one being acts upon another, we mean that some power or force is exerted by the agent, which produces, or has a tendency to produce, a change in the thing acted upon. If this be the meaning of the phrase, as I conceive it is, there appears no reason for asserting, that, in perception, either the object acts upon the mind, or the mind upon the object. (176–77)

Denying 2 with agent causation as the meaning of "acting" had better not be Reid's only response to the argument, however, since his opponent could simply reaffirm both premises with event causation as the intended variety of causation.

The second way to absolve Reid of contradiction is to distinguish between *immediate* causation (causation with no intervening links) and *mediated* causation. He would thus be denying in 2.14 that external objects are immediate causes of my perceptions while affirming in 2.1–2 that they may be remote causes by way of the intervening media, organ, nerves, and so on.

Not only does the mediate-immediate distinction absolve Reid of inconsistency, but it sets up a decisive reply to the argument he is criticizing. The first premise of the "no action at a distance" argument is plausible only if it asserts there is no *immediate* action or causation at a distance. After all, lighting a fuse here can cause the explosion of a keg way over there, provided there is an intervening series of contiguous causal links. When philosophers of Reid's day decried "action at a distance," such as was believed to be involved in Newton's theory of gravity, they were objecting to it because Newton posited no intervening causal chain. When Reid grants the first premise himself, he says explicitly that immediate action at a distance is what the premise rules out (though there is a muddying reference to agents as well):

> That nothing can act immediately where it is not, I think must be admitted; for I agree with Sir Isaac Newton, that power without substance is inconceivable. It is a consequence of this, that nothing can be acted upon immediately where the agent is not present. (EIP 2.14:176).

If immediate action at a distance is what the first premise rules out, then immediate action at a distance between objects and minds must be what the second premise says perception requires. But in that case, the second premise is highly questionable, and it is no longer any surprise that Reid denies it.[6]

Sir William Hamilton also took Reid's denial of 2 to be a denial of immediate causation between object and perception. In several footnotes to 2.14, he complains against Reid that there *is* an immediate causal relation between the proper object of vision and our perception of it, the proper object of vision in his opinion being not the wall, but the light that reaches us from the wall (Hamilton:299–303). It is clear, then, that Hamilton endorses the argument through step 3, denying only that the argument reaches all the way to ideas. If nothing else, Hamilton shows us that Reid was not tilting at a straw man.

We may sum up the verdict on the "no action at a distance" argument with a threefold separation of cases. If "action" means *agent* causation, the first premise may be true, but the second is false. If it means *immediate event* causation, the first premise may again be true, but the second is false. If it means *mediate event* causation, the second premise is now true, but the first is false. Under no construal of action do both premises come out true. This is what Reid could and should have said in response to the "no action at a distance" argument, and I believe it is also what he actually did say.

Though the "no action at a distance" argument is unsound, it may serve as the opening wedge for a more general argument against direct perception of external objects. If x is remote from the perceiver, then (given the finite speed of light) it is possible that x fails to exist when the experience supposedly "of" x occurs. This possibility is exploited in Malebranche's Master Argument, discussed below in section E.

---

[6] Denying the second premise under the immediacy construal seems also to be Quinton's response to the argument. He denies that the object of perception must be contiguous to the perception, presumably because he denies that the object of perception must be the immediate cause of the perception.

# C. SECOND ARGUMENT FOR THE WAY OF IDEAS: HUME'S TABLE ARGUMENT

Another argument for the way of ideas exploits the phenomenon of perceptual relativity. Hume claimed in his *Enquiry Concerning Human Understanding* that the "universal and primary opinion of all men" that they perceive external objects directly is "destroyed by the slightest philosophy, which teaches us, that nothing can ever be present to the mind but an image or perception." He elaborates as follows:

> The table, which we see, seems to diminish as we remove further from it; but the real table, which exists independent of us, suffers no alteration. It was therefore nothing but its image which was present to the mind. (EHU 12:152)

Recast somewhat, Hume's slight bit of philosophy takes the form of the following syllogism:

1. What I see diminishes in magnitude as I retreat from it.
2. The table itself does not diminish in magnitude as I retreat from it.
3. Therefore, what I see is not the table itself (but only an image or idea).

Reid contends that Hume's premises are true only if we restate them as follows (EIP 2.14:180–82):

1. What I see diminishes in *apparent* magnitude as I retreat from it.
2. The table itself does not diminish in *real* magnitude as I retreat from it.
3. Therefore, what I see is not the table (but only an image or idea).

Here Reid is appropriating for his own purposes Berkeley's distinction between visible and tangible magnitude or, in Reid's terms, apparent and real magnitude. As Reid develops the distinction, the real magnitude of an object (such as the edge of a table) is an intrinsic property of it, measured in inches or feet, whereas the apparent magnitude of an object is a relation between the object and a perceiver, measured by the angle the object subtends at the perceiver's eye.[7] It is easy to see that apparent magnitude varies with the distance between object and perceiver (objects subtending smaller angles when farther away) while real magnitude does not. Once we record these facts correctly as in Reid's version of the syllogism, we see that the

---

[7] Reid's terminology is taken from the astronomy of the day. The apparent magnitude of a star is the angle it subtends at the viewer's eye or telescope; there is no connotation of "mere appearance."

conclusion no longer follows. "I admit both the premises in this syllogism, but I deny the conclusion. The syllogism has what the logicians call two middle terms" (EIP 2.14:182).

Reid adds a second criticism of the argument that, in my opinion, is not cogent, or at any rate not adequate by itself to avoid Hume's conclusion. He notes that by the laws of geometry, it is necessary that the real table must seem to diminish as we move away from it:

> How then can this apparent diminution be an argument that it is not the real table? When that which must happen to the real table, as we remove farther from it, does actually happen to the table we see, it is absurd to conclude from this, that it is not the real table we see. (EIP 2.14:182–83).

Although it invokes a good Bayesian point—if H entails E, E cannot disconfirm H—Reid's second response is not sufficient by itself to dispose of Hume's argument. To see why not, suppose the table's appearing smaller as we retreat from it were not a change in its dyadic relational properties (as on Reid's view) but a matter of its presenting to us a succession of items that are progressively smaller in their intrinsic magnitude. In that case, we *would* have to conclude that it is not the real table we see, since the intrinsic magnitude of the real table is constant. So it is not enough for Reid's purposes to observe that the apparent diminution of the table is just what we should expect; it is essential as well that he insist on an irreducibly relational analysis of apparent magnitude.[8]

To reinforce the present point, it is helpful to jump ahead to the theory of sense data, the twentieth-century successor to the theory of ideas. Consider a tilted coin that looks elliptical to the viewer. How can that happen if the coin itself is round? C. D. Broad, one of the principal proponents of the sense-datum theory, answered as follows: "If, in fact, nothing elliptical is before my mind, it is very hard to understand why the penny should seem elliptical rather than of any other shape" ([1923] 1959:240). More generally, we can say that when a physical object appears to a viewer as F (where "F" denotes a sensible characteristic such as color or shape), it does so by presenting the viewer with an item that really *is* F. If the physical object is not itself F (like the coin, which is not elliptical), then the F item must be other than the physical object. "Sense data" is the name for such items. Sense data were typically thought to be items existing only in the perceiver's mind, and they were held to be incapable of appearing F without actually being F—otherwise, there would be need of yet further sense data to explain the apparent properties of the original sense data.

---

[8] For more on the inadequacy of Reid's second criticism, though not directed specifically at Reid, see Broad (1923) 1959:234–6.

If a sense-datum philosopher analyzes "x looks F to S" as "x presents S with an F sense datum," he will naturally also analyze "x looks *more* F than y" as "x presents S with a sense datum that is more F than the sense datum presented to S by y." "The table appears smaller from here than it did from close up" will thus get analyzed as "the sense data I am presented with by the table from here are smaller than the sense data I was presented with by the table when I was close up." It follows that the items I am presented with are items distinct from the table, for the table was assumed to be constant in size.[9]

In Reid's view, what I apprehend about the table as I move away from it is a relational fact about it—how large it looks from here, as determined by the angle it subtends. Moreover, the table's looking so big to me is a dyadic fact involving just the table and me or my point of view. It is not, as in the sense-datum theory, a triadic fact involving the table, the perceiver, and a sense datum as an intervening item with a certain intrinsic size.

I have heard it objected that from a phenomenological point of view, size *is* intrinsic; in registering size, you do not seem to yourself to be detecting a relation. This may be granted, I think, without detriment to Reid's position. Sometimes perceivers can apprehend a relational state of affairs without explicitly representing all the terms or relata of the relation (Dokic 2010). They may simply *occupy* one of the relata without representing it, as happens when one perceives the simultaneity of two events without representing one's own frame of reference (which, if Einsteinian relativity theory is correct, is required as a third term).[10]

Hume's table argument can be given as readily in terms of shape as size: what I see varies in shape as I move around (being rectangular from above, trapezoidal from the end, and so on); the table itself does not vary in shape as I move around; therefore, what I see is not the table. Reid can make essentially the same reply as before, distinguishing between real and visible figure: what stays constant is real figure, an intrinsic property of the table; what varies as I move around is visible figure, construed as a relation of the table to the eye; therefore, Hume's conclusion does not follow. In this connection, some contemporary philosophers employ notions of perspectival or relational appearance properties very like Reid's notions of

---

[9] In logical strictness, what follows is that not *all* the items I am presented with are identical with the table; it could be that *one* of them is. But I doubt that anyone would seriously think that there is some privileged distance at which I am presented with the table itself, all other distances yielding mere sense data.

[10] Another example: the weight of an object is a relation between the object and a planet, but it presents itself as a one-place property to a person who stands on the planet and hefts the object.

apparent magnitude and visible figure; see Huemer (2001), Noe (2004), and Hill and Bennett (2008).[11]

Other contemporary philosophers prefer a different response to Hume's table argument, refusing to concede to Hume that there is any sense in which a table looks smaller from a distance and trapezoidal from the end. Ryle, for example, insists that a round plate viewed obliquely still looks round, not elliptical (1949:216). To support such contentions, some writers appeal to what psychologists call *object constancy*: an object of known constant shape, size, and color will appear to be constant in these respects despite variation in perspective and lighting. In my view, appeals to such constancies are weak for two reasons. First, if it is made clear that the question concerns how things look in a *phenomenal* sense, not a *doxastic* sense (= what shape do you *believe* the object to have?), many subjects will report that a tilted plate *does* look elliptical.[12] Second, there are experiments indicating that shape constancy is in any case not perfect; apparent shape is actually a compromise between known objective shape and angular or perspectival shape (Thouless 1931, discussed in Hill and Bennett 2008 and Wagner 2006). Even if the table looks only *slightly* smaller from a distance (or the plate only slightly elliptical from an angle—not as elliptical as geometry would dictate), Hume's table argument has its initial premise.

Reid knew about the so-called perceptual constancies of size, shape, and color. He calls attention to them in IHM 6.3, "Of the visible appearances of objects." He says, for example, that the apparent figure of a book must vary with every change in position, but that a man with no notion of perspective will affirm that it has remained the same. His explanation is that the man

> hath learned to make allowance for the variety of visible figure arising from the difference of position, and to draw the proper conclusions from it. But he draws these conclusions so readily and habitually, as to lose sight of the premises: and therefore where he hath made the same conclusion, he conceives the visible appearance must have been the same. (EIP 6.4:84)

In other words, how the book appears really does change, but the man overlooks it, being more concerned with the real shape, which he knows to be constant.

[11] Huemer renames Reid's distinction between real and apparent magnitude as linear versus angular size and uses it in his own way to get around Hume's table argument. He also shows how an analogous strategy may be used against other versions of the argument from perceptual relativity, such as Berkeley's argument about the lukewarm water that feels warm to a hand previously placed in cold water and cool to a hand previously placed in hot water. See Huemer 2001:119–24.

[12] For another example, watch a tennis match on television filmed from a vantage point above and behind the baseline. Whether others see the court as rectangular, they best can tell. As for me, it obviously and inescapably looks trapezoidal, despite my knowledge that it is rectangular.

In sum, the best response to Hume's table argument is not Ryle's but Reid's. We should admit that the table varies in apparent size and shape as our perspective changes, but then go on to construe this variation as change in the relational properties of the table rather than in intrinsic properties of any intervening entities. When we do so, it no longer follows that we do not see the table.

## D. THIRD ARGUMENT FOR THE WAY OF IDEAS: DOUBLE VISION

Hold a finger in front of your face while focusing your eyes on some more distant object, say a candle on a shelf. While continuing to *focus* on the candle, *attend* to your finger. You will see the finger double, perhaps one copy of it on either side of the candle. Now switch, focusing on the finger while attending to the candle. You will see the finger single and the candle double. Reid offers an explanation of this phenomenon in terms of what is now known as the law of corresponding retinal points; for the details, see IHM 6.13, appendix R, or Van Cleve 2008. My concern here is not with the mechanics of double vision, but with an argument it affords against direct realism.

Hume gives just one argument against direct realism in the entire *Enquiry*, the table argument; he likewise gives just one argument against direct realism in the entire *Treatise*, the double vision argument. Here it is:

> When we press one eye with a finger, we immediately perceive all the objects to become double, and one half of them to be remov'd from their common and natural position. But as we do not attribute a continu'd existence to both these perceptions, and as they are both of the same nature, we clearly perceive, that all our perceptions [i.e., all the things we perceive] are dependent on our organs, and the disposition of our nerves and animal spirits. (T 1.4.2:210–11)

In his customary phrase, the things we perceive do not have a "continu'd and distinct existence," but are only mind-dependent ideas.

It is remarkable that Reid never addresses this argument. As a student of the *Treatise* he would have known of it, and as an early cognitive scientist, he was quite interested in double vision, devoting seven sections of the *Inquiry* to the topic (IHM 6.13–19). As described two paragraphs back, he gives a safer and more reliable method than Hume for inducing double vision, not requiring you to poke yourself in the eye. Yet he never takes up the question of how direct realists should respond to Hume's argument. In this section, I set out the argument in step-by-step fashion and canvass possible replies on Reid's behalf. Here is the argument as I reconstruct it:

When you attend to your finger while focusing on something in the distance,

1. You see two fingery objects.
2. There are not two (existent) physical fingers before you. Therefore,
3. a. You see at least one fingery thing that is not an (existent) physical finger.
   b. It is a mental finger—a fingery image or sense datum existing in your mind.
4. The other fingery object you see is (as Hume says) "of the same nature" as the mental finger (i.e., is phenomenologically just like it). Indeed, every finger you have ever seen is "of the same nature" as the mental finger
5. Items that are phenomenologically just alike have the same ontological status.
   (To tweak an old slogan from biology, ontology recapitulates phenomenology.)
6. Therefore, every finger you have ever seen has been a merely mental finger. Generalizing, you have never seen any objects in the physical world, but only mental images of them.

When I speak of "seeing" in this argument, I mean *direct* seeing—being acquainted with the thing itself and not merely with some intermediary from which you infer its existence. Like Reid, I think nothing but direct seeing is worthy of the name.[13]

Let us consider which steps in this argument might be challenged, working our way up from the bottom.

We should not balk at generalizing the conclusion in step 6. There is no plausibility in the thought that direct realism fails for fingers, but manages to work somehow for toes.

Step 5 in the argument is denied by the philosophers nowadays known as disjunctivists.[14] Suppose we feel compelled by the first half of the argument to say that at least one of the things you see in a case of double vision is a mental finger. Must we therefore say that the other fingery object you see (or the single fingery object in a case of single vision) is likewise a mental object? Disjunctivists say no. Even if everything about the experiences of two objects is just the same qualitatively or from the inside, that does not mean that we must give the two experiences the same

---

[13] "Astronomers see new extra-solar planet," proclaims a headline, but the story reveals that what they really observed were perturbations in neighboring bodies, which they explained by hypothesizing the existence of the planet. Reid would challenge the headline writer's use of "see." I return to this point in section I.

[14] An early expression of disjunctivism is McDowell 1982. The doctrine is so called because it affirms that veridical experience and hallucinatory experience have nothing in common but such disjunctive characterizations as "either seeing a real external finger or seeing a mental finger." For more on disjunctivism, see Van Cleve 2004 and Byrne and Logue 2008.

ontological assay.[15] One of the experiences may have a mental finger for its object while the other has a flesh and blood finger for its object; same phenomenology, different ontology.

I criticize disjunctivism in chapter 10, section D. For now, I simply record my conviction that it is not the best way out of the predicament posed by double vision, nor Reid's way out, and move on.

Step 4 in the argument says that the second finger in a case of double vision is phenomenologically indistinguishable from the first. This, too, has been challenged. Merleau-Ponty cites a wealth of examples to show that in typical cases of hallucination, the victim is able to distinguish hallucinatory experiences from their veridical counterparts.[16] Can we say the same about the experiences of the two fingery objects in double vision?

It does generally seem to me that one of the two fingery objects looks more *substantial* than the other. In corroboration of this, the reader may wish to try the following "touch test," proposed to me by Brian Glenney: Induce double vision by Reid's method—hold up a finger and focus afar while attending near. Ask yourself which finger looks more substantial; then try to touch the tip of each finger in turn with a pencil. I find that when I try to touch the more substantial finger, I successfully make contact: I feel the pencil with my finger, and I seem to see two pencils touching two fingers. But when I try to touch the less substantial finger, I make no tangible contact, and I seem to see a pencil waving right through the space visually occupied by the finger. I take this to confirm that one of the fingery objects really does look more substantial than the other. If it did not, how could I reliably produce as desired either the experience of touching a pencil to a finger or the experience of passing a pencil right through a finger?

We could deny step 4, then, and insist that phenomenology does enable us to distinguish the fingers—one is flesh, the other phantom. I would be uneasy, however, if we could stop the argument nowhere but at step 4. Even if hallucinated objects and second objects in double vision are *in fact* typically less substantial or vivid than veridically seen objects, it seems to me *possible* that a hallucinated or doubled object should duplicate a perceived object in all phenomenological respects. With suitable adjustments in the other premises, one could still argue that the objects of veridical

---

[15] Note that premise 5 might take either of two forms, depending on the argumentative context: (i) objects phenomenologically alike must have the same ontological status, or (ii) experiences phenomenologically alike must be given the same ontological analysis. The second is perhaps on firmer ground.

[16] Merleau-Ponty 1962:334–45, especially 334 and 339. Thanks to Rebecca Copenhaver for bringing this passage to my attention.

perception must belong to the same ontological category as whatever objects are needed to account for these possible cases.[17]

We come next to premise 3, which I have split into two parts. Part (a)—you see at least one thing that is not an existent physical finger—follows from 1 and 2, so it cannot be denied unless we are prepared to deny one of them as well.[18] But part (b)—you see at least one thing that is a mental finger—does *not* follow from 1 and 2 alone. It follows from them only with the help of the assumption that anything you see must be an *existing* thing.[19] This assumption is denied by Alexius Meinong and his followers

Meinong is famous for holding that the totality of objects includes objects that do not exist. This doctrine would enable him to allow that in double vision you see at least one fingery thing that is not an existing physical finger without having to say that it is an *existing mental* finger—an image or sense datum. Instead, it is a *nonexisting physical* finger. This, at any rate, is the sort of thing that some Meinongian philosophers say about cases of hallucination. When Macbeth hallucinated his dagger, there was indeed an object that he was aware of—a dagger, located at some point in physical space before him—but unlike a veridically seen dagger, it was a dagger that did not exist.

Reid himself is sometimes seen as a precursor of Meinong, at least as regards the objects of conception. He tells us that one of the features of conception is this:

> It is not employed solely about things which have existence. I can conceive a winged horse or a centaur, as easily and as distinctly as I can conceive a man whom I have seen. (EIP 4.1:310)

Reid's Meinongian views have been brought into his theory of perception by Phillip Cummins (1974). According to Cummins, perception itself, in virtue of having conception as its core ingredient, inherits the distinctive Meinongian property of conception: it may have nonexistent objects. If that is right, it is possible to hold that what you see in a case of veridical vision and what you see in a case of doubled or distorted vision is the same thing—a finger, say, or a bent stick—but in the veridical case it exists and in the nonveridical case it does not. There is no need to posit special mental objects in the nonveridical case.

---

[17] See Smith 2002: 194 for a version of the argument from hallucination that takes off from the premise that "for any veridical perception, it is possible that there should be a hallucination with exactly the same subjective character."

[18] Here is a formalization of 1 and 2 under which it is clear that 3a follows from them: $\exists x \exists y(Fx \,\&\, Sx \,\&\, Fy \,\&\, Sy \,\&\, x \neq y)$; $\sim\exists x \exists y(Px \,\&\, Py \,\&\, x \neq y)$; therefore, $\exists z(Fz \,\&\, Sz \,\&\, \sim Pz)$. As the formalization shows, I take "seeing an F" to imply $\exists x Fx$, but not necessarily to imply $\exists x(Fx \,\&\, x \text{ exists in the perceiver's environment})$.

[19] Also needed is the assumption that objects of vision are either physical or mental.

The Meinongian approach to perception, double vision, and hallucination merits serious consideration, but it will be easier to appreciate after we have considered the Meinongian approach to the objects of *conception*, which I defer to chapter 10.

The next step to be considered is step 2: when you see one upraised finger double, there are not two existing physical fingers standing before you. When this step is properly understood, there are few who would seriously suggest denying it.[20]

That brings us at last to step 1: when you see your finger double, you see two fingery objects. That may seem obvious, but there are philosophers who would find it the most questionable step of all.

To motivate the denial of premise 1, let us consider an argument against direct realism to which the argument from double vision may instructively be assimilated— the argument from illusion, one version of which runs thus:

1. When I view a sheet of white paper under red lights, what I see is pinkish.
2. The sheet of paper is not pinkish.
3. Therefore, what I see under the red lights is not the sheet of paper (but only a pinkish sense datum, etc.: the argument continues roughly as in 3b through 6).

Here many philosophers will want to deny the first premise. It is not true that what I see *is* pinkish; rather, what I see (= the sheet of paper) only *looks* pinkish. Moreover, the paper can look pinkish without there having to be before my mind a proper object of visual awareness that really is pinkish, like a classical sense datum.

How is looking pinkish to be analyzed, if not in terms of the classical sense-datum analysis? There are two main options, drawing on two theories introduced in chapter 1. Adverbial theorists say that an object looks F when it causes the subject to sense F-ly, where sensing F-ly is a monadic state of the subject rather than a relation to an inner sensory object. Propositional theorists say that an object looks F when it causes a subject to represent the object as being F (or to represent there being something that is F), where representing is a state with propositional content (whether singular or merely existential). Theorists of either persuasion typically go on to say that the core component of seeing an object is its looking some way to you.

If either of these options is a satisfactory response to the argument from illusion, it may be adapted against the argument from double vision. Just as you can see a white

---

[20] The only exceptions I know of are the American New Realists, who would say both of the fingery objects you see are externally existing physical and finger-shaped objects, even if at most one of them is a flesh and blood finger. For further discussion, see Sinclair (1944) 1973 and Van Cleve 2008.

sheet of paper that looks pink without having to see anything that really is pink, so you can see a single finger that looks double without having to see two of anything.

The adverbial theory and the propositional theory would both need further development as applied to appearances of unity or duplicity. What does it mean to say that someone is sensing two-ishly or representing an object as being two? We can make some headway with this problem by swapping it for another, given the equivalence recognized by Reid between seeing an object as single or double and seeing it as being in one place or two. (See IHM 6.13:135, 6.14:138, 6.18:157–58, 6.19:166, and the passage from an undated manuscript at IHM 329–30.) Under this equivalence, what we would need from the adverbialist is an account of what it is to sense an object "here-ishly" or "there-ishly," and what we would need from the propositionalist is an account of what propositional content is involved in representing an object as being at a certain place or places.[21]

Would either the adverbial or the propositional strategy have been open to Reid? Copenhaver interprets Reid as a propositionalist (2007), but I have raised doubts about this in appendix E. I have attributed an adverbial theory of sensation to Reid in chapter 1, section G, but Reid's adverbialism about sensation is not enough for present purposes. That is because Reid thinks sheer sensation never presents us with an extended expanse or an object at a certain location, as discussed in chapter 2. He thinks it is only *conception* that presents us with objects having spatial attributes. To account for double vision, then, we would need an adverbial account not just of sensation but also of conception. I say more about the prospects for this in chapter 10.

I have canvassed several responses to the argument from double vision, including disjunctivism, Meinongism, propositionalism, and adverbialism. I postpone any further choice among them to chapter 10. For now, I simply offer a consideration that convinces me that there must be *something* wrong with the argument, even if it does not conclusively show what.

Psychologists have experimented with displacing lenses—lenses that make a spoon or a fork appear to be a foot to the right of where it really is, so that a subject not yet accustomed to the lenses will reach in the wrong place to pick it up. The standard argument from illusion, when applied to such cases, would have it that what the subject sees is not the spoon, since the spoon is at one place and what he sees is at another. I have not the slightest temptation to agree. What I see is not some

---

[21] In his 2001, Michael Huemer offers a reply to the argument from double vision in which he assimilates double vision to illusion, denies the first premise in the argument as I have presented it here, and adopts an intentionalist (= propositionalist) theory of appearing (130–31). He observes (n. 8, 146) that the intentionalist should not assign to double vision the impossible content "there is a single finger that is both here and there." However, it is not quite clear to me what intentional content Huemer *would* assign to it.

pseudo-spoon located in a different place from the real spoon; it is the real spoon, located at one spot on the table but appearing a foot to the right. That it appears to the right of where it is does not mean that it is not the spoon itself that I see.

Now vary the experiment by giving me lenses that make the spoon appear simultaneously to the right and to the left of where it really is—in other words, give me double vision. If the first experiment does not compel me to renounce direct perception, then neither should the second. Direct realism can withstand the challenge of double vision.

## E. FOURTH ARGUMENT FOR THE WAY OF IDEAS: MALEBRANCHE'S MASTER ARGUMENT

Reid devotes a chapter of the *Intellectual Powers* (EIP 2.7) to Malebranche, citing him as a proponent of the theory of ideas notable for holding (i) that the ideas we are presented with are not private to our own minds, but dwell in the mind of God, and (ii) that in consequence of our seeing only ideas, we have no evidence for the existence of a material world except for God's assurance in scripture. Unfortunately, Reid does not discuss the most powerful of Malebranche's arguments for adopting the theory of ideas—the argument I call Malebranche's Master Argument.

The argument is given in the following passages from the *Dialogues on Metaphysics*:

> Now, the circle I perceive has properties which no other shape has. Hence, the circle exists at the time I think of it, since nothing has no properties and one nothing cannot differ from some other nothing. . . . All these ideas have some reality at the time I think of them. Since nothing has no properties and these do, you are in no doubt about that. ([1688] 1992:151–52)

> Now, on the supposition that the world was annihilated and that God nonetheless produced the same traces in our brains or, rather, presented the same ideas to our minds which are produced in the presence of objects, we should see the same beauties. Hence, the beauties we see are not material beauties . . . for the supposed annihilation of matter does not carry with it the annihilation of the beauties we see when we look at the objects surrounding us. . . . I maintain that a Chinese who has never been in the room can, in his own country, see everything I see when I look at your room provided—which is by no means impossible—his brain is moved in the same way mine is when I now consider it. Is it not true that people with a high fever and people who sleep see chimeras of all sorts that never were? ([1688] 1992:153)

> I tell you again, Aristes, your room is not, strictly speaking, visible. It is not really your room which I see when I look at it, since I could very well see what I am now seeing even though God had destroyed [your room]. ([1688] 1992:153).

A short preliminary reconstruction of the argument is the following:

1. There are situations in which I see *something* (that is, an existing thing), but not a material thing.
2. Therefore, there are situations in which I am seeing an *immaterial* existent—an idea.

Examples of such situations are seeing chimeras in a fever or a dream.

What warrants Malebranche in saying that in such situations I am seeing some *existing* thing? His answer invokes the Cartesian slogan "nothing has no properties." In English, that slogan has a nice ambiguity; it could mean "no thing is propertiless" or it could mean "no property is thingless." Descartes intends the principle in the latter way, as shown by his invocation of it to secure knowledge of the existence of substances (as in the inference *cogito, ergo sum*):

> We can, however, easily come to know a substance by one of its attributes, in virtue of the common notion that nothingness possesses no attributes, that is to say, no properties or qualities. Thus, if we perceive the presence of some attribute, we can infer that there must also be present an existing thing or substance to which it may be attributed. (PP I.52; see also PP I.11 and Second Replies definition 5).[22]

Malebranche uses the principle in a similar way. His thought is that when one hallucinates a dagger, one is aware of properties such as silveriness and slenderness, and these properties cannot belong to nothing. One sees a silvery *something*. Moreover, Malebranche takes the principle to imply something more he thinks goes without saying—that whenever we are aware of any property, there is an *existing* thing that has it. For him, the Cartesian slogan rolls together the two theses that if a property is presented to us, there is a thing that has it, and that if a thing has a property, it exists.

The latter thesis—that to have properties a thing must exist—puts Malebranche squarely at odds with Meinong and arguably also with Reid, as noted in the previous section. Along with holding that the totality of objects includes objects that do not exist, Meinong holds that nonexisting objects may have properties; as his slogan has it, a thing's possessing properties (its *Sosein*) is independent of its existence (its *Sein*). I allow Malebranche his anti-Meinongian principle for now, but I revisit it in chapter 10.

[22] I surmise that Cottingham, Stoothoff, and Murdoch use "nothingness" rather than "nothing" in their translation precisely because "nothing possesses no attributes" has the ambiguity I noted, and they want to head off the erroneous first reading of it. The Latin is *nihili nulla sint attributa, nullaeve proprietates aut qualitates*, in which "nihili" is the dative of "nihil." It might therefore have been translated as "there are no attributes, properties, or qualities that pertain to nothing." (Thanks here to John Monfasani.)

One shortcoming of the 1–2 argument above is that it implies nothing about what I see in normal or veridical situations. Perhaps when I am having an experience as of a room that no longer exists, I must merely be seeing roomlike ideas, but if the room has *not* been annihilated, why may I not be seeing it *then*? If Malebranche is to reach the conclusion that in *all* perceptual situations, we perceive only ideas, he needs some way of extending the argument.

One way to extend it would be to add the premise that if a hallucinatory experience has an idea as its object, so must a phenomenologically similar veridical experience. This premise, sometimes called the common factor principle, is intuitively plausible but is disputed by disjunctivists.

I prefer another way of extending the argument, which I think is nearer to what Malebranche had in mind. Here is Malebranche's Master Argument as I construe it:

1. If an experience e is a seeing of o, then, necessarily, if e occurs, o exists.
2. For any experience e and any material object m, it is possible that e occurs and m does not exist. In other words, it is *not* necessary that if e occurs, m exists.
3. Therefore, *no* experience is a seeing of a material object (but only of an idea).

This argument validly reaches the more general conclusion Malebranche desires— at least up to the parentheses. I consider presently what would justify the addition of "but only of an idea."

First, though, we need to be clear about the logic of the argument. The first premise is meant to involve necessity *de re*, not necessity *de dicto*. It should not be confused with

1.' Necessarily, if an experience e is a seeing of o, then if e occurs, o exists.

That premise could be true just because the arguer has endowed "sees" with success grammar. But with that premise, the argument would not be valid. It would be comparable to the following patently invalid argument: necessarily, if one person is married to another, then if the first exists, so does the second; for any distinct human persons x and y, it is possible that x exists and y does not; therefore, no human persons are married. If you place the word "necessarily" inside the quantifier, though, as I have done in the first premise, the resulting argument is valid, being a simple case of modus tollens.[23]

---

[23] Some of my readers have voiced the suspicion that the argument contains an equivocation— that the first premise is true only if words like "seeing" and "experiencing" have success grammar, whereas the second premise is true only if such words do *not* have success grammar. I reject both halves of this suggestion. In the first place, the reason for thinking the first premise true has

Malebranche clearly affirms the conclusion and the second premise of the argument. Here are two expressions of the second premise:

The supposed annihilation of matter does not carry with it the annihilation of the beauties we see. (153)

I tell you again, Aristes, your room is not, strictly speaking, visible. It is not really your room which I see when I look at it, since I could very well see what I am now seeing even though God had destroyed it [the room]. (153)

I do not find a place where he explicitly affirms the first premise, but I ascribe it to him because it makes his argument valid.

The first premise is also required, though not explicitly stated, in a number of related arguments against direct realism. Consider the insidious time-lag argument, popularized by Russell:

Though you see the sun now, the physical object to be inferred from your seeing existed eight minutes ago; if, in the intervening minutes, the sun had gone out, you would still be seeing exactly what you are seeing. We cannot therefore identify the physical sun with what we see. (1948:204)

The earliest statement of the time-lag argument I know of is due to Leibniz:[24]

For strictly we see only the image, and are affected only by rays. And since rays of light need time (however little), it is possible that the object should be destroyed during this interval and no longer exist when the ray reaches the eye; and that which is not cannot be the present object of sight. ([1765] 1981:135)

---

nothing to do with success grammar. The idea is rather that an experience, whether veridical or not, cannot even be *ostensibly* of an object x unless x exists and is a constituent of the experience. That is another reason that the first premise has to be formulated using necessity *de re* rather than necessity *de dicto*. In the second place, if we did endow "experience" with success grammar, we would not thereby make the second premise false. To suppose the second premise false is to suppose its negation true: *some experience e and some material object m are such that necessarily, if e occurs, m exists.* But the italicized statement would not be true just because we are stipulating that all experiences are veridical. To think otherwise is to commit a *de dicto/de re* confusion. It is necessary that if e is a veridical experience of m and e occurs, then m exists; but it does not follow that if e is a veridical experience of m, then necessarily, if e occurs, m exists.

[24] Thanks to Stephen Puryear for bringing Leibniz's statement of the argument to my attention.

The argument of Leibniz and Russell is invalid as it stands.[25] To be valid, it needs to be supplemented by the premise that the *sheer possibility* that the sun has ceased to exist by the time I experience it makes my experience not strictly an experience of *it*. Without that premise, we could only conclude that in those cases in which the object *has* ceased to exist, we are not perceiving it.[26] With the premise, we have exactly what we need for Malebranche's Master Argument, which may be regarded as a generalization of the more familiar arguments from burned-out stars, doubled fingers, and hallucinated daggers.

The negative part of Malebranche's conclusion is that we never see material things; the positive part is that we see ideas. What entitles Malebranche to the positive part—how does his argument require ideas to be the objects of perception, or even allow this? Proponents of ideas or sense data do generally think of them as entities whose existence is guaranteed by the acts by which they are apprehended—they are somehow built into those acts—and in that case they would satisfy the demands of premise 1. But how can ideas be like that? According to Hume's "distinct existences" principle, which I regard as a maxim of sound philosophizing, if x and y are distinct entities, it is always possible for x to exist without y.[27] So how can ideas, if they are distinct from the acts by which they are apprehended, be such that their existence is necessitated by the occurrence of those acts? A case can be made that the only objects of awareness permitted by premise 1 are what Ducasse called "internal accusatives," related to mental acts as a smile is related to the smiling of it. That would in effect get rid of objects of perception or sensation in favor of adverbially modified acts, as in Arnauld's theory of perception rather than Malebranche's. I doubt, therefore, that the Master Argument can do all that Malebranche wants from it in his own philosophy.[28]

---

[25] The same is true of most contemporary versions of the time-lag argument I have seen, including those presented by Huemer (2001:131–32) and LeMorvan (2004:223).

[26] It is sometimes replied to the time-lag argument that we may see a distant star "as it was." That is all right so long as the star still exists. But if seeing x "as it was" implies seeing x, and if seeing x implies that x exists to be seen, then it is not all right to say that we see a now- extinguished star "as it was."

[27] I interpret the distinctness as mereological: entities are distinct when they have no part in common. For two among dozens of expressions of Hume's principle, see T 1.3.6:86–87 and 1.4.5:233.

[28] One of Malebranche's distinctive theses may help him meet the objection that not even ideas can satisfy the demands of premise 1. He holds that the ideas we are aware of are not our own private ideas, but ideas existing eternally in the mind of God. "Ideas have an eternal and necessary existence" ([1688] 1992:151); they are not things that perish in the blink of an eye, but things that are "eternal, immutable, necessary, in short, divine" ([1688] 1992:154). If ideas are necessary existents, their existence would be necessitated by our perception of them—if only in the "paradox of strict implication" sense in which the existence of a necessary being is necessitated by the existence of anything else whatever. I doubt, however, that the paradox of strict implication was any part of Malebranche's own basis for saying we see all things in God.

Nonetheless, his negative conclusion that we never perceive material things is troubling enough as far as Reid is concerned. How, then, should we respond to Malebranche? One of the beauties of his argument is that it has only two premises, so there are only two broad strategies: deny the first or deny the second.

The second premise is

2. For any experience e and any material object m, it is not necessary that if e occurs, m exists.

A contemporary view that denies this premise is the so-called relational view of experience, advocated under this name by John Campbell (2002). According to Campbell, a veridical experience of a certain object incorporates that very object in such a way that nothing could be that experience unless it had that object as a constituent. Thus some experiences *do* necessitate the existence of certain material objects.[29]

What, then, of hallucinatory experiences, such as the experience of a room that has been annihilated? It has no material object as a constituent, yet may be indistinguishable in its phenomenal character from a veridical experience of the room. Perhaps Campbell could allow that it derives its phenomenal character from having a certain idea as a constituent.[30] But he would deny that there is any constituent common to the veridical and the hallucinatory experience: the hallucinatory experience contains no room as a constituent, and the veridical experience contains no idea as a constituent. The two experiences have in common only that each is describable by the disjunctive phrase "either a veridical experience of a room or a hallucinatory experience as of a room." For better or worse, a proponent of a relational view like Campbell's is almost bound to be a disjunctivist.

The other premise in the Master Argument is

1. If an experience e is a seeing of o, then, necessarily, if e occurs, o exists.

---

[29] Note that Campbell is not merely saying that it is necessary that if an experience of o is veridical, o exists. That could be accepted as a necessary truth *de dicto* by those who do not espouse a relational view of experience. He is saying that if an experience of o is veridical, that experience is *de re* necessarily such that it could not occur unless o exists. See note 23 (on an alleged equivocation).

[30] Or from being adverbially modified in a certain way, or by being related to a certain Meinongian object, or ... But however Campbell grounds the phenomenal character of the hallucination, he would deny that the same ground is present in the veridical experience.

Several theories deny this premise, holding that in the right setting, an experience e can be a seeing of o even though the occurrence of e does not entail the existence of o.[31] What the theories have in common is that they are *conjunctivist* theories—theories according to which the veridical experience of an apple can be analyzed as the conjunction of two conditions, an intrinsic condition specifying the apple-ish character of the experience and an extrinsic condition saying that the apple exists and causes the first condition to obtain.[32] How the first condition is spelled out will depend on the resources of the theory—the experience might be an adverbially modified state, a state with a certain propositional content, or a relation to a Meinongian object. Common to all the theories is the thought that the two conditions are independent—the experience specified in the first clause can occur apple or no apple, but is veridical only if there is an apple.

At this point, we are left with four ways of responding to Malebranche's Master Argument: disjunctivism, adverbialism, propositionalism, and Meinongism. These are the same four strategies we canvassed as responses to the argument from double vision. I defer choice among the strategies to chapter 10. For the time being, I leave behind the arguments against direct realism and turn to its content. What exactly does Reid's direct realism affirm?

## F. THREE FORMS OF DIRECT REALISM

Reid is clearly a realist, that is, one who holds that there are physical things existing outside the mind. As I understand his philosophy, he is also a *direct* realist in each of three senses: he is an *epistemological* direct realist, a *perceptual* direct realist, and a *presentational* direct realist. These claims are progressively more controversial.

The first form of direct realism is

*Epistemological direct realism (EDR)*: Some beliefs about physical things are epistemically basic. The warrant they have for a subject does not derive from the warrant of any other propositions the subject believes; they are justified apart from any reasons the subject has for believing them.

---

[31] I am discussing Malebranche's argument and possible responses to it under the assumption that perception has singular content—that one may have an experience not merely as of an F, but as of a certain individual o. I believe the same issues arise, though, even if perception is held to have nothing but general contents.

[32] I take the term "conjunctivist" from Johnston 2004:114–15, but I use it in a somewhat broader sense than he does.

It is amply clear that Reid is a direct realist in this sense. Here is just one of many passages one could cite:

> If the word axiom be put to signify every truth which is known immediately without being deduced from any antecedent truth, then the existence of the objects of sense may be called an axiom. (EIP2.20:231)

Where I have said "direct," Reid usually uses the term "immediate"; I shall generally use the two terms interchangeably.[33] In chapter 11, I expound Reid's epistemological direct realism in greater detail.

The second form of direct realism is

> *Perceptual direct realism (PDR)*: Physical things are perceived directly, in a sense to be further elucidated below. It amounts roughly to this: they are perceived without any perceived intermediaries.

It is also clear that Reid is a perceptual direct realist, or at least that he intends to be one. Here is one of many passages one could quote on this score:

> When we see the sun or moon, we have no doubt that the very objects which we immediately see are very far distant from us, and from one another. . . . But how are we astonished when the philosopher informs us that we are mistaken in all this . . . because the objects we perceive are only ideas in our own minds. (EIP 2.24:172).

The first two forms of direct realism are independent of each other. It would be possible to hold that although we perceive physical objects directly, beliefs about them are not epistemically basic, but need to be supported by background information, for example, about the conditions of observation or the proper functioning of one's senses. Conversely, it would be possible to hold that beliefs about physical objects are basic despite the fact that we do *not* perceive them directly (advocated as a possibility in Greco 1995). But in Reid's mind, the two forms of direct realism are closely linked. He observes, "It was this theory of ideas [the paradigm of an indirect theory of perception] that led Descartes, and those that followed him, to think it necessary to prove, by philosophical arguments, the existence of material objects" (EIP 2.14:186). In other words, if you are not a perceptual direct realist, you cannot be an epistemological direct realist. He also makes the converse claim: that if a

---

[33] When Reid uses the term "direct," it is usually to contrast "direct notions" with "relative notions." This distinction is discussed in chapter 4.

philosopher holds that the existence of external objects requires proof, it must be because he is of the opinion that we do not perceive external objects, but only the ideas of them (EIP 2.7:106). In other words, if you are not an epistemological direct realist, you cannot be a perceptual direct realist.[34]

The third form of direct realism is

> *Presentational direct realism*: Not only are physical things perceived directly, but our perception of them is a matter of their being presented to us, or of our being acquainted with them in a Russellian sense.

Alston further describes this view as follows:

> In perception an external object is directly "presented" to our awareness; it is "given" to consciousness. We are immediately aware of it, as contrasted with just thinking about it, forming a concept of it, or believing something about it. . . . This is "knowledge by acquaintance" rather than "knowledge by description." (Alston 1989:36)

Presentational direct realism entails perceptual direct realism, but not conversely; it is possible to be a perceptual direct realist without being a presentational direct realist. Armstrong and Chisholm are both perceptual direct realists, because both hold that we perceive physical things without perceiving sense data or suchlike intermediaries, but neither is a presentational direct realist, because neither thinks perception involves a relation of acquaintance. Armstrong analyzes perception as a kind of noninferential belief (1968, chapter 10), Chisholm analyzes it as a kind of propositional "taking" in response to appropriately caused sensation (1957:3, 77, and 148–49) and neither countenances acquaintance or any other A-relation—an irreducible cognitive relation with nonpropositional objects. Reid does countenance such a relation as one of the species of conception (as I argued in chapter 1), but it has been questioned whether he thinks we stand in this relation to external things. Thus, it is controversial whether he is a presentational direct realist.

Before we can settle that question, we need to settle whether Reid is a perceptual direct realist. To do that, we need the promised further elucidation of "direct

---

[34] It is possible, however, that Reid is not here advancing the conditional ~EDR → ~PDR, but is instead advancing an abductive argument using the converse conditional ~PDR → ~EDR. That idea-theorists hold the antecedent would be the best explanation of their holding the consequent.

perception." I use the following definition proposed by George Pappas as a point of departure:

> A person S *directly perceives* an object O at a time t = df (1) S perceives O at t, and (2) it is false that: S would perceive O at t only if S were to perceive R at t, where R ≠ O, and where R is not a part of O. (Pappas 1989:156)[35]

Pappas says that clause (2) is meant to capture the idea of "non-dependence on perceived intermediaries"—I do not perceive something directly if I perceive it only by perceiving something distinct from it. More accurately (as the further proviso brings out), I do not perceive something directly if I perceive it only by perceiving something else that is not a *part* of it. If I perceive an elephant only by perceiving one side of it, I still perceive the elephant directly. But if I perceive Hume's table only by perceiving an image of it (which is not part of it, but something existing only in my mind), I do not perceive the table directly. Indeed, Reid would say that in that case I do not perceive the table at all. By banishing images, ideas, and other such perceived intermediaries, he hoped to clear the way for direct perception of external things.

## G. DO SENSATIONS OBSTRUCT DIRECT PERCEPTION?

It is abundantly clear that Reid has banished *one* type of objectionable intermediary in perception, namely, ideas. But many of his readers, from Sir William Hamilton to the present day, have thought that sensations play a role in Reid's theory analogous to ideas, and that in the end Reid is an indirect realist despite his best intentions.[36] I consider here several ways in which sensations might be thought to make trouble for perceptual direct realism.

---

[35] To simplify exposition, I have omitted the following condition, which Pappas includes in clause (2): "and where R is not a constituent or group of constituents of O." I surmise that Pappas includes this condition so that a philosopher like Berkeley may qualify as believing in direct perception of everyday objects: I perceive the cherry only by perceiving something distinct from it (e.g., a certain tartness or redness), but since the redness is a constituent in the congeries that constitutes the cherry, I still qualify as perceiving the cherry directly. I have also omitted the clause "nor is O [a part] of R," which I surmise is included to deal with the "background" problem discussed below.

[36] According to Galen Strawson (1990), "the question of whether [Reid] is really a 'direct realist' about perception, or whether he is really some kind of indirect realist, has been seen as the central question of Reid scholarship ever since Hamilton."

Hamilton distinguishes two varieties of indirect realism or "Representationism," as he calls it: Nonegoistic Representationism, in which the representation is an entity in its own right or *tertium quid*, intervening between the subject and the external object, and Egoistic Representationism, in which the representation is a modification of the subject's own mind. He holds that

We must first be clear on the fact that by giving an adverbial analysis of sensations, Reid has pulled the rug out from under *one* argument for indirect realism. Suppose a mountain looks blue as I approach it from a distance and green from up close. On a subject-act-object theory of sensations, this would be a matter of the mountain's presenting me first with blue and then with green sensory objects. Since the mountain itself does not change from blue to green, these objects must be other than the mountain—they must be sense data or ideas. But on an adverbial theory, the change in how the mountain appears to me is simply a matter of its causing me first to sense bluely and then greenly. There are no sense data that come between the mountain and me.

Nonetheless, sensations may be thought to be objectionable intermediaries in perception not because they *have* objects, but because they *are* objects of the mind's awareness.[37] Such are the concerns we must now address.

John Immerwahr (1978) has proposed that there is a significant difference in Reid's views about the relation of sensation to perception as we move from the *Inquiry* to the *Intellectual Powers*. In the *Inquiry*, Reid holds that in the causal chain culminating in perception, sensations serve as links between physical impressions (for instance, retinal impressions) and perceptions (Figure 3.5):

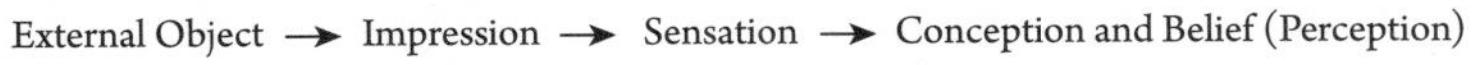

External Object ⟶ Impression ⟶ Sensation ⟶ Conception and Belief (Perception)

**Figure 3.5**

In the *Intellectual Powers*, by contrast, the picture according to Immerwahr is this (Figure 3.6):

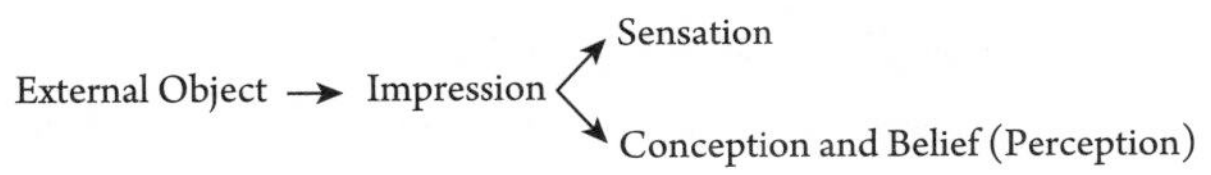

External Object ⟶ Impression ⟨ Sensation / Conception and Belief (Perception)     **Figure 3.6**

---

Reid, though forceful in his criticisms of the first variety of Representationism, unwittingly falls under the category of Egoistic Representationism with his doctrine of sensations. For more, see Supplementary Dissertation C, "On the Various Theories of External Perception," appended to his edition of Reid's *Philosophical Works*.

For contemporary advocacy of the view that Reid's sensations play a role analogous to ideas, see Chappell 1989:49–64.

[37] Perhaps this distinction aligns with Hamilton's (in the preceding note) between the two forms of Representationism.

Here sensations are effects of impressions produced in parallel with perceptions rather than being intervening links. Immerwahr thinks this difference makes Reid an indirect realist in the *Inquiry*, but a direct realist in the *Intellectual Powers*.

Immerwahr's view is subject to two criticisms. First, as he himself notes, the difference he alleges between the *Inquiry* and the *Intellectual Powers* does not amount to a clean break. There are a good many passages in the *Intellectual Powers* that reaffirm the *Inquiry*'s model of the relation of sensation to perception (EIP 2.16:312, 2.17:204, 2.19:223–24, 2.21:237, and 6.5:486). Second, the fact that sensations come between impressions and perceptions in the first of the causal chains depicted above would not jeopardize direct perception if sensations (like impressions) were merely *causal* intermediaries in the perceptual process. The crucial question (if we operate with the Pappas definition above) is whether sensations are *perceived* intermediaries.

In this connection, some think it relevant that according to Reid, we seldom *attend* to our sensations. They pass largely unnoticed. Here are three representative passages:

> But it is one thing to have the sensation and another thing to attend to it, and make it a distinct object of reflection. The first is very easy; the last, in most cases, extremely difficult. We are so accustomed to use the sensation as a sign, and to pass immediately to the hardness signified, that, as far as appears, it was never made an object of thought, either by the vulgar or by philosophers; nor has it a name in any language. There is no sensation more distinct, or more frequent; yet it is never attended to, but passes through the mind instantaneously, and serves only to introduce that quality in bodies, which, by a law of our constitution, it suggests. (IHM 5.2:56)

> When a primary quality is perceived, the sensation immediately leads our thought to the quality signified by it, and is itself forgot. We have no occasion afterwards to reflect upon it; and so we come to be as little acquainted with it as if we had never felt it. (EIP 2:17:204)

> There are many phenomena of a similar nature [to seeing double], which shew, that the mind may not attend to, and thereby, in some sort, not perceive objects that strike the senses. . . . I have been assured, by persons of the best skill in music, that in hearing a tune upon the harpsichord, when they give attention to the treble, they do not hear the bass. (IHM 6.13:135)

Reid says similar things about sensations belonging to other sense modalities and about visible figure—the shape of a body actually presented to the eye at a given vantage point. It requires the skill of a painter to discern the colors and shapes that are really before the mind, our attention normally being focused instead on the features of the external scene that the presented features signify (IHM 6.3:82–83).

Could our normal inattention to our sensations be what keeps everyday perception direct?[38] The idea would be that if we do not notice our sensations—if "in some sort" we do not perceive them—then it cannot be that we perceive external things only by perceiving sensations.

It seems to me, however, that what we do or do not pay attention to can hardly be the key to direct perception. Suppose I spend the morning painting a landscape and the afternoon playing tennis. Do I perceive indirectly in the morning when I am attending to the "looks" of things and directly in the afternoon when I am intent on hitting the ball? That seems to me an unlikely shift. Let us inquire, therefore, whether there is a sense in which we perceive physical things directly even on occasions when we *are* attending to the accompanying sensations.

For this purpose, we need to work our way to a revised definition of direct perception. Here is Pappas's definition again, slightly reworded:

S directly perceives O at t = df (1) S perceives O at t, and (2) it is false that S would perceive O only if there were an item R distinct from O such that (a) R is not part of O and (b) S perceives R.[39]

I believe there are two difficulties with this definition as it stands: in one way it is too strict and in another way too lax.

To see that the definition is too strict, suppose two objects A and B are inseparably connected in such a way that one never enters my field of view unless the other does as well. Then I would never perceive one without perceiving the other, but it seems that I might still perceive each of them directly. Or suppose I can never perceive an object without perceiving a bit of background (though no particular bit);

---

[38] Nichols (2007, chapter 7) offers a variation on this theme: since we attend to the sensational signs of secondary qualities but not to the sensational signs of primary qualities, we have direct perceptions of primary qualities, but not of secondary qualities.

[39] Pappas's original wording does not make it explicit how the quantifier governing "R" in clause (2) should be placed. One possibility is "it is false that there is an item R distinct from O such that (a) R is not part of O and (b) S would perceive O only if S perceived R." But this version of clause (2) would be satisfied if my perception of O depended on perceiving some sense datum or other but not any particular one, thus letting a sense-datum theory count as a theory of direct perception. I have therefore favored the version in the text, in which the quantifier is moved inside the consequent of the conditional in (2).

then my perception of the object will depend on there being something else that I perceive, yet it seems I might still perceive both background and object directly.[40]

Perhaps we can avoid this first difficulty if we turn to a definition of direct perception offered by Frank Jackson. Jackson's definition is similar in spirit to Pappas's, but importantly different in one way:

> S directly perceives x at t = df (1) S perceives x at t, and (2) there is no object y distinct from x such that S perceives x *in virtue of* perceiving y. (Jackson 1977, chapter 1, especially 19–20)

Jackson is operating with the same basic idea as Pappas: you see directly those things that you do not see by (or in virtue of) perceiving other things. But unlike Pappas, Jackson does not try to capture the "in virtue of" relation in terms of counterfactual dependence. Jackson's definition thereby avoids the difficulty raised above. Even if I never see A without seeing its inseparable companion B (or a bit of A's environment), it seems wrong to say that I see A *in virtue of* seeing B.[41]

Unfortunately, there is still the "too lax" problem, which affects Jackson's definition as well as Pappas's. Both definitions characterize direct perception as perception that does not depend on (or occur in virtue of) *perceived* intermediaries. Well, consider the following view: "When we perceive any object, the object causes certain ideas or sense data to arise in our minds; our awareness of these sense data then leads us to infer the existence of the object." That is a textbook case of indirect perception as depicted in Figure 3.2, but a proponent of the view could insist that perception is not indirect by Pappas's or Jackson's definition. We do not *perceive* sense data, since for one thing they do not cause any further sense data to arise in us. Our relation to sense data is not perceiving, but something else.[42]

---

[40] The trouble here is that the extraneous item I perceive is not an item of the sort to which a direct realist would object—it is not an image, sense datum, or the like. One might think to avoid the difficulty, then, simply by modifying Pappas's second clause to read thus: it is false that S would perceive O only if there were a *mental* item R that S perceived. That would allow that direct perception may depend on the perception of physical background. Unfortunately, however, it would also allow one to perceive the president directly by seeing his physical image on a TV screen or hearing a recording of his voice—probably an unwanted consequence.

[41] But why exactly is it wrong? Is it because one perceives A in virtue of perceiving B only if *necessarily*, any case of perceiving B would be a case of perceiving A? If so, not even a paradigm case of indirect perception, such as perceiving a physical object by perceiving a sense datum, would count as indirect, since perceiving a sense datum is not enough by itself to constitute perceiving a physical object.

[42] Ayer proposes that we *perceive* physical things by *sensing* sense data ([1940] 1969:24 and 58). Reid himself insists that the verb "perceive" is properly used only in regard to extra-mental things (EIP 1.1:22).

The view just sketched is an indirect view of perception nonetheless. The sense data it posits are objectionable intermediaries precisely because they are *objects* to which the subject stands in some sort of *cognitive* relation—apprehension, awareness, acquaintance, or what have you. So it seems to me that in Pappas's or Jackson's definition, we should replace the final occurrence of "perceive" in the definiens by some more general cognitive verb, such as "is acquainted with."[43] If we do this in Jackson's definition, we arrive at the following:

> S directly perceives x at t = df (1) S perceives x at t, and (2) there is no object y wholly distinct from x such that S perceives x in virtue of being acquainted with y.[44]

Let us now return to the question of whether sensations obstruct direct perception.

According to Buras, who appeals specifically to Jackson's definition together with his own view that Reidian sensations are self-reflexive, the answer is *yes* (2003). We perceive bodies or their qualities only if we have sensations that serve as signs of them, and given that sensations are self-reflexive, we have sensations only if we are acquainted with them (by means of those very sensations). Therefore, we perceive bodies only if we are acquainted with sensations, contradicting the supposition that we perceive bodies directly.[45]

It seems to me, however, that sensations do not obstruct direct perception, even if we are in some sense acquainted with them. There are three reasons for this. In the first place, sensations are not *objects* at all. Though they may be "objects of awareness," they are not objects ontologically speaking. They are not individual things, but states of a subject—manners in which a subject is affected. (See EIP 2.16:199.) So when Reid speaks of awareness of sensations, the awareness in question is really the apprehension of a *fact* about oneself—that one is sensing in a certain way—rather than acquaintance with any object. Perception is not rendered indirect just because it involves apprehension of some fact about oneself. Consider the view (espoused in various forms by Descartes, Arnauld, and Kant) that perception necessarily involves apperception—that you cannot perceive O without being aware that you perceive O. That view should not debar one from being an upholder of direct perception, even if the thinkers just mentioned fail to uphold it for other reasons.

---

[43] I assume here that acquaintance is a genus of which perception is a species, *pace* Chisholm and Armstrong (as discussed in section F).

[44] By "wholly distinct from" I mean "having no part in common with." I insert "wholly" to allow that one may perceive an elephant directly by perceiving just one side of it (*pace* Jackson: 19–20).

[45] Actually, given the definition of "in virtue of" Buras cites on p. 49, it is not at all obvious to me that we perceive qualities in virtue of apprehending sensations. According to that definition, perceiving quality Q would have to be *analyzed as* (and therefore presumably equivalent to) apprehending sensation s, but there is more to perceiving a quality than apprehending a sensation.

A second reason for holding that sensations do not obstruct direct perception is that even if sensations are objects of acquaintance, one does not perceive physical objects *in virtue of* being acquainted with one's sensations. I hesitate to rest my case on this consideration, however, lest a sense-datum theorist maintain that one does not perceive physical objects (solely) in virtue of being acquainted with sense data.[46]

The third and strongest reason for holding that sensations do not obstruct direct perception emerges below in section I.

## H. IS REID A PRESENTATIONAL DIRECT REALIST?

Having argued that Reid's account of the role of sensations in perception does not stand in the way of his being a perceptual direct realist, I turn now to the question of whether he is a presentational direct realist. Recall that a presentational direct realist holds not only that we perceive physical objects directly, but also that our perceiving them is a matter of their being presented to us or, equivalently, our being acquainted with them. In arguing in chapter 1 that the "conception" involved in Reidian perception is a form of acquaintance, I have in effect already argued that Reid is a presentational direct realist. However, two prominent contemporary interpreters of Reid argue otherwise, so we need to consider what they say.

Alston and Wolterstorff deserve credit for bringing it to our attention that Reid's scheme of things includes a relation of acquaintance, but both of them deny that Reid's views allow him to say that we stand in this relation to external things. Here is Alston's argument on this score:

> Most crucially, if the conception involved in perception is the direct awareness of [i.e., acquaintance with] an external object, how is that object presented to that awareness? There would seem to be no alternative to holding that it is presented as exhibiting "sensible" or "phenomenal" qualities—colors, shapes, heat and cold . . . and so on. . . . But this construal is not open to Reid. For, as noted earlier, he places all the qualitative distinctness of perceptual consciousness (except for visual extension) in the sensations,

---

[46] Nor do I altogether dismiss this consideration, since it may be necessary in explaining why another apparent obstacle to direct perception is specious. Consider the view that one never perceives an external object without being acquainted with oneself. (Reid does not hold this view, for he thinks that we have only a relative and not a direct notion of the self—in effect, that knowledge of the self is knowledge by description rather than knowledge by acquaintance. See IHM 2.7:36–38 and 2.10:42–43.) Even if we add that a self is an object, such a view does not seem to compromise direct perception. Why not? One possible answer would be that one does not perceive physical objects simply in virtue of being acquainted with oneself.

which he takes to involve no awareness of any object other than itself. What it is natural to refer to as an awareness of colors, warmth, and odours (or of objects as colored, warm, and odorous) Reid construes as *modes* of feeling (awareness), as ways of being aware, directed on to no object beyond themselves. (Alston 1989:44–45)

If I understand this difficult argument correctly, it may be compressed into two premises and a conclusion as follows:

1. If the conception involved in perception is direct awareness of (acquaintance with) an external object, it is an awareness in which the object is presented as having some color or shape or other sensible quality—an awareness in which these very qualities are presented to us.
2. For Reid, all the sensible qualities of objects are "drained away" into sensations—they are modes of sensing rather than qualities objects are presented as having. Thus in Reid's view, the consequent of (1) is false.
3. Therefore, the conception involved in Reidian perception is not acquaintance with external objects.

My reply to this argument is that the second premise is false. Alston is ignoring what Reid has to say about the distinction between primary and secondary qualities, our topic in chapter 4. Even if it were right to say that Reid drains colors and odors away from objects,[47] it would be wrong to say that seen shapes or felt hardnesses are drained away. These are not modes of sensing, but qualities of external objects of which we have a clear conception that owes nothing to sensation. So there is nothing in Reid's view to prohibit him from saying that (in the case of the primary qualities, at least) our perception is a form of acquaintance.

Another argument against interpreting Reid as a presentational direct realist has been advanced by Wolterstorff. He sums up Reid's "standard schema" for perception thus:

> S perceives external object O *if and only if* O affects one's sensory organs in such a way as to cause in S a sensory experience which is a sign (indicator) of O, which sensation in turn causes in S an apprehension of O, and an immediate belief about O whose predicative content is or implies that O exists as an entity in S's environment. (2001:103)

---

[47] In fact, it is not right, for Reid thinks color and fragrance exist in the rose as powers to produce certain sensations in us. But colors and fragrances in this dispositional sense arguably do not count as sensible objects of acquaintance, in which case they do not constitute an exception to Alston's claim that the consequent of premise 1 is false.

So far, so good. He then poses the question, "Does Reid think of the conception that is ingredient in perception on the standard schema as apprehension by acquaintance or as apprehension by singular concept?" (144) His answer is twofold. There is one type of perception noted by Reid that is an exception to the standard schema, because it is not mediated by sensation—namely, the perception of visible figure, which is prompted by physical impressions (patterns on the retina) rather than mental sensations.[48] In the perception of visible figure, we *do* have conception of the acquaintance variety with external objects. But in all other cases of perception—those mediated by sensation, as in the standard schema—our conception of external objects is *not* of the acquaintance variety. We apprehend the object only by means of some singular concept, such as *the object or quality that is producing this sensation in me* or (Wolterstorff's example) *the hardness of the object I'm touching.*

Wolterstorff attributes this position to Reid because he thinks it is the only tenable position for Reid to take in light of the following "no double information" argument:

> On this view [that there is acquaintance with external objects or qualities], there would, in fact, be a superfluity of information. . . . If awareness of primary qualities involved acquaintance with those qualities, there would be too much information. My acquaintance with the primary quality yields me information about it; but the sensory experience [i.e., sensation] is also supposed to function as a source of information about the primary quality. Something seems definitely wrong here. Given acquaintance with primary qualities, the sensory experience seems otiose; given the sensory experience, acquaintance with primary qualities seems otiose. . . . I submit that if perception consisted in acquaintance with the object perceived, there would also be "no necessity, no use" for [a sensation serving as] a *sign* of the object. (148–49)

Drawing on this passage and a few other explanatory remarks in its vicinity, I reconstruct Wolterstorff's argument as follows:

1. There are not *two* sources of information in perception.
2. Therefore, either sensations are not a source of information or acquaintance with external objects is not source of information (from 1).
3. If sensations evoke conception and belief, they are a source of information.
4. Sensations evoke conception and belief (a premise from Reid).
5. Therefore, sensations are a source of information (from 3 and 4).

---

[48] This is the majority view among Reid scholars, though disputed by Yaffe. See Yaffe 2003a and b and Falkenstein and Grandi 2003 for discussion.

6. Therefore, acquaintance with external objects is *not* a source of information (from 2 and 5).
7. If there were acquaintance with external objects, it would be a source of information about them (22).
8. Therefore, there is no acquaintance with external objects (from 6 and 7).

There must be *something* wrong with this argument, or else it could be turned against Wolterstorff's own view. He maintains that in our perception of visible figure, we *do* have acquaintance with external things. But a "no double information" argument parallel to the one above could be used to argue with equal force against acquaintance with visible figures. To arrive at the parallel argument, simply replace every occurrence of "sensations" by "physical impressions" and every occurrence of "external objects" by "visible figures." The resulting conclusion is that there is no acquaintance with visible figures, which contradicts Wolterstorff's own view.

What, then, is wrong with the argument? Let us draw a distinction between two kinds of information source, the autonomous and the dependent. An *autonomous* source carries information simply in virtue of its own intrinsic nature, without benefit of any contingent principles of interpretation or conception and belief formation. Acquaintance is an autonomous source of information about its objects; in being acquainted by touch with a marble in my hand, I thereby acquire information about the shape and hardness of the marble. (The acquaintance caries information in analog form regardless of whether it is also digitalized in beliefs; see appendix D.) But sensation is not an autonomous source of information about external things or qualities. If we were not hardwired to form certain conceptions and beliefs on the occasion of our sensations, our sensations would tell us nothing about the external world. They are *dependent* sources of information—sources that work by activating autonomous sources, with which they are only contingently linked.[49]

With this distinction in mind, I would counter the "no double information" argument with a dilemma. If we classify a state of mind as a genuine source of information only if it is an autonomous source, then premise 3 is false. Sensation is not an autonomous source of information, even if it invokes conception and belief. On the other hand, if we allow dependent sources to qualify as

[49] On a related note, Copenhaver (2004) maintains that the mediation of perception by sensations is compatible with direct realism so long as the relation between sensations and what they signify is an external relation, not supervening on intrinsic features of the relata. Her version of direct realism is not presentational, however. She would say that one who is programmed to believe in fire upon smelling smoke perceives fire directly, since the relation between smoke sensations and fire is external, whereas I would not say this. These differences between us will come to the fore in chapter 5 (on acquired perception).

information sources, then premise 1 is false. There are indeed two sources of information in perception, one of them autonomous (acquaintance) and the other dependent (sensation).

The distinction between autonomous and dependent sources calls for several further comments. (i) It is arguably a necessary truth that if there are dependent sources of information, there are also independent sources, on pain of circle or regress. But it is a further point to maintain that independent sources must be autonomous in the sense I have defined—carrying information in virtue of their intrinsic nature. (ii) The thought—which is a very Reidian thought—that there are sources that carry information by their intrinsic nature runs counter to much contemporary philosophy of mind. It is opposed to the idea that a state carries information only in virtue of nomological correlations between it and external things or properties. (See Putnam 1981 for a statement of contemporary orthodoxy.) In Reid's view, if our conceptions of primary qualities were not reliably correlated with instances of those qualities, our perceptions would be "fallacious." But they would still carry information, even if it be misinformation. Nomological correlation is not necessary for the carrying of information. (iii) By the same token, the thought that sensations on their own are *not* sources of information about external objects is opposed to the idea that nomological correlations between states and external objects are *sufficient* to make the states carriers of information. Reid affirms that there are such correlations, as well as nomological correlations between sensations and conceptions, but denies that the correlations give sensations any informative power unless the correlated conceptions already have it. This last point receives confirmation from Reid's account of the primary-secondary quality distinction, discussed in chapter 4. Our conceptions of the primary qualities of things give us information about how the things are in themselves, but they do not do so in virtue of nomic correlations between the conceptions and the qualities. If such correlations were the whole story, our conceptions of secondary qualities would tell us as much about the objects bearing the qualities as do our conceptions of primary qualities—but they do not.

The arguments to the contrary of Alston and Wolterstorff having been set aside, I reaffirm that Reid is a presentational direct realist.

## I. ALL PERCEPTION IS DIRECT PERCEPTION

I have been working so far with a distinction between direct and indirect perception that amounts roughly to this: you perceive something indirectly when you perceive it by perceiving (or otherwise apprehending) something else; you perceive something directly when you perceive it, but *not* by apprehending anything else. We should now stop and ask the following question: could there really be such a thing as indirect perception? I am not asking whether the theory-of-ideas assay of the perceptual situation could be correct. I am asking the following question instead: *assuming* that assay to be correct, would our cognitive relation to external things properly be classified as perception? In other words, is what you do when you "perceive one thing by apprehending another" really *perceiving*? Could *both* clauses in the following definition of indirect perception (which is the complement of the revised Jacksonian definition of direct perception) ever be satisfied?

> S indirectly perceives x at t = df (1) S perceives x at t, and (2) there is an object y wholly distinct from x such that S perceives x in virtue of being acquainted with y.

I believe Reid's answer is *no*. When you move a stone by moving a stick that presses against the stone, you really do move the stone. But when you perceive a table by perceiving or apprehending something else that is not even a part of it, you are not really perceiving the table at all:

> A body in motion may move another that was at rest, by the medium of a third body that is interposed. This is easily understood; but . . . to think of any object by a medium, seems to be words without a meaning. (EIP 2.9:134)

A little later on the same page he concludes:

> I apprehend, therefore, that if Philosophers will maintain that ideas in the mind are the only *immediate* objects of thought, they will be forced to grant that they are the *sole* objects of thought. (EIP 2.9:134, emphasis added; see also EIP 6.3:437, lines 35–37.)

Since Reid takes "thinking" to be "a very general word, which includes all the operations of our minds" (EIP 1.1:22), what he says here implies that there is no such thing as a mediate object of perception.

Reid has another point to make against the propriety of the phrase "mediate object of perception" (or "indirect object of perception," in my equivalent usage). He asks,

> Whether, according to the opinion of Philosophers [who embrace the theory of ideas], we perceive the images or ideas only, and infer the existence and qualities of the external object from what we perceive in the image? Or, whether we really perceive the external object as well as its image? (EIP 2.7:105)

And he answers,

> If the last be their meaning, it would follow, that, in every instance of perception, there
> is a double object perceived: That I perceive, for instance, one sun in the heavens, and
> another in my own mind. But I do not find that they affirm this; and, as it contradicts
> the experience of all mankind, I will not impute it to them. (EIP 2.7:106)

Reid's view, then, in which I concur, is that "indirect perception" is an oxymoron—if
we perceive something at all, we perceive it directly.[50] He confirms this when he remarks, "Every object of thought, therefore, is an immediate object of thought, and
the word immediate, joined to objects of thought, seems to be a mere expletive" (EIP
6.3:437). If this is right, the definitions from Pappas and Jackson cited above could
have stopped with the first clause: S perceives x directly iff S perceives x, period![51]

The preceding reflections suggest to me that we should change our tack in discussing whether such things as sensations and visible figures "get in the way" of
direct perception. We have been asking: is our cognitive relation to various intermediaries such as to preclude direct perception? Is it a matter of being acquainted
with some object that serves as a mere sign of the thing to be perceived? We have
been assuming that an answer of yes would imply that our perception of the thing
signified is not direct. But this now seems wrongheaded. We should ask instead: are
we acquainted with the thing signified? If we are *not*, then no acquaintance with anything else can count as perceiving the thing signified, however indirectly. If we *are*,
then no acquaintance with anything else can stand in the way of our perceiving the
thing signified as directly as you like. In short, what is important in securing direct
perception is not *downgrading* our cognitive relation to the sign, but *upgrading* our
cognitive relation to the thing signified.

Acquaintance with a sign would exclude acquaintance with the thing signified
only through a "no double object" argument. But double objects may be admissible
in certain cases. Consider the following passage:

> There is a sense in which a thing may be said to be perceived by a medium. Thus any
> kind of sign may be said to be the medium by which I perceive or understand the

---

[50] I am happy to have as my ally on this point Walter Hopp: "Being conscious of A through the
presentational consciousness of some distinct object B is precisely not a presentational consciousness of A. It is not *perception*" (2011:150).

[51] My proposal is at odds with the contention of O'Callaghan 2007, chapter 10, that one can hear
one of FDR's speeches by hearing a recording of it in some dusty archive. One's hearing of the
speech according to O'Callaghan is mediated and indirect, but counts as hearing the original for
all that.

thing signified. The sign, by custom, or compact, or perhaps by nature, introduces the thought of the thing signified. But here the thing signified, when it is introduced to the thought, is an object of thought no less immediate than the sign was before: And there are here two objects of thought, one succeeding another, which we have shown is not the case with respect to an idea, and the object it represents. (EIP 2.9:134)

To those who wish to ascribe perceptual or presentational direct realism to Reid, the first two sentences may look like apostasy. They imply that if sensations are signs whereby external objects are perceived—as they are for Reid—then external objects are perceived by the medium of sensations. Reid even allows in the fourth sentence that the sign itself may be an immediate object of thought. But the passage as a whole tells us that notwithstanding all that, the thing signified may still be an *immediate* object of perception or thought.[52] It may be perceived *in propria persona* and not just by proxy.

Reid makes this point in the abstract. Can we offer a concrete example of the sort of situation that might serve in his philosophy as an example of it?

It is easy enough in the case of objects of thought in the narrow sense of "thought." I think of bagipes and am thereby led to think of kilts. The bagpipes are in this instance the "medium" whereby I think of kilts, but for all that has been said, both types of object are immediate objects of thought.

Can we think of parallel examples in the case of perception? We can easily imagine contrived examples. Suppose I am so constituted that I can see a certain type of bird only if its chirp first alerts me where to look; surely I can still see the bird directly. Real-life examples are harder to come by, in good part because the signs we use in perception are usually ignored and quickly forgotten. But perhaps the perception by sight of three-dimensional objects via the medium of two-dimensional visible figures affords an example of the sort we want. When I look at a wireframe box, what I see in the first instance according to Reid is a visible figure consisting of various polygons, but my mind is swiftly led to conceive of and believe in a three-dimensional cube. If my conception of the cube is an instance of being acquainted with it and not merely of thinking about it, we have here a case in which the direct perception of one thing is cued by the perception of another.

---

[52] Buras notes that in this passage, Reid is in effect denying definitions of directness such as Jackson's (2003:61). That would be true if "in virtue of" meant "in consequence of."

We shall be better placed to appreciate this example after chapters 5 (on acquired perception) and 6 (on the geometry of visibles). For now, I simply ask the reader to keep in mind the possibility that the sensational or visual signs employed in perception may serve as stepping stones to direct perception rather than barriers to it.[53]

[53] The psychologist Irvin Rock offers two further possible examples of seeing one thing by seeing another that do not, in my opinion, jeopardize direct perception (1997). (i) The apparent lightness of a surface is determined by the ratio of its luminance to that of surfaces *perceived* to be adjacent to it—not to that of surfaces retinally adjacent to it but perceived to be separated in depth from the original. (ii) When presented with an array as of a square overlapping one quarter of a circle, one sees a three-quarter circle before one sees (amodally) a complete circle occluded by a square. For my purposes, both of these examples are somewhat questionable—the first because it involves perceptions of two properties of one thing rather than perceptions of two things, the second because the status of amodal perception as perception is debatable. Suppose, however, that the examples are both accepted as cases in which the perception of one thing depends on and is determined by the perception of another. In that case, Rock says, they would be cases in which perception is not direct in J. J. Gibson's sense—determined by the proximal stimulus alone. Be it so; they would still be cases in which perception is direct in the sense I am promoting in the text.

# 4

## PRIMARY AND SECONDARY QUALITIES

The distinction betwixt primary and secondary qualities hath had several revolutions. Democritus and Epicurus, and their followers, maintained it. Aristotle and the Peripatetics abolished it. Des Cartes, Malebranche, and Locke, revived it, and were thought to have put it in a very clear light. But Bishop Berkeley again discarded this distinction, by such proofs as must be convincing to those that hold the received doctrine of ideas. Yet, after all, there appears to be a real foundation for it in the principles of our nature. (Thomas Reid, *IHM* 5.4:62)

Every student of philosophy knows how to draw up the lists of primary and secondary qualities: on the left go extension, size, shape or figure, solidity, motion or rest, and number; on the right go color, sound, scent, taste, heat and cold. But what is the principle of the distinction? Does it have to do with objective versus subjective? Categorical versus dispositional? Intrinsic versus extrinsic? Or several or none of these? And does the distinction stand up to the criticisms that Berkeley and others have made of it? In this chapter, I expound Reid's answers to these questions.

## A. REID'S RELATION TO LOCKE AND BERKELEY

Though the term *secondary quality* was introduced by Boyle, the distinction between primary and secondary qualities comes down to us mainly through Locke and Berkeley. Here is how Locke defines secondary qualities:

> [Secondary qualities are] such *Qualities*, which in truth are nothing in the Objects themselves, but Powers to produce various Sensations in us by their *primary Qualities*, i.e. by the Bulk, Figure, Texture, and Motion of their insensible parts. (ECHU 2.8.10)

It is clear from this passage that what Locke understands by a secondary quality is something quite definitely in the object. Locke scholars may disagree about whether this something is a dispositional property or its categorical basis—an interpretive issue we shall shortly encounter in connection with Reid as well—but in either case, secondary qualities reside in external objects.[1]

When Berkeley came to present Locke's teaching on primary and secondary qualities, he did not adhere to Locke's own understanding of what a secondary quality is. Here is how Berkeley has Hylas present the distinction in the *Three Dialogues*:

> You must know sensible qualities are by philosophers divided into *primary* and *secondary*. The former are extension, figure, solidity, gravity, motion, and rest. And these they hold exist really in bodies. The latter are those above enumerated [colors, sounds, tastes, etc.]; or briefly, all sensible qualities beside the primary, which they assert are only so many sensations or ideas existing nowhere but in the mind. (DHP, First Dialogue, 1975:178)

As Hylas uses the term, a secondary quality is a quality that exists nowhere but in the mind. This divergence in usage—secondary qualities as properties (if only dispositional ones) in external objects versus secondary qualities as properties existing only in the mind—persists down to the present day. Unfortunately, there is not only divergence from one writer to another, but sometimes even divergence from one passage to another in the same writer.[2] Students do well not to be confused by this.

Despite their divergence in terminology, we can identify an important thesis on which Locke and Berkeley agree. If by *red* we mean the occurrent, sensuous,

---

[1] Students sometimes stumble on Locke's comma, taking him to say that secondary qualities are "nothing in objects themselves." But that reading conflicts with the rest of the sentence, which says that secondary qualities are powers, which can hardly be anywhere but in the object. On this point, see Mackie 1976:12, or McCann 1994:63.

[2] Hume and Putnam may be mentioned as classical and contemporary cases in point. Hume compares his account of moral virtues and vices to the account of secondary qualities given by the modern philosophy. He says his philosophy "defines virtue to be *whatever mental action or quality gives to a spectator the pleasing sentiment of approbation*; and vice the contrary" (EPM:289). That definition puts virtue and vice in the action contemplated, not in the spectator. But he also says this: "When you pronounce any action or character to be vicious, you mean nothing, but that from the constitution of your nature you have a feeling or sentiment of blame from the contemplation of it. Vice and virtue, therefore, may be compar'd to sounds, colours, heat and cold, which, according to modern philosophy, are not qualities in objects, but perceptions in the mind" (THN 3.1.1:469). That comparison puts virtues and secondary qualities in the mind.

The same double usage occurs in Putnam 1987. Putnam characterizes secondary qualities both as "dispositions to affect us in certain ways" (8), which puts them in objects, and as properties that are "merely 'appearance,' or merely something we 'project' onto the object" (9), which puts them in minds.

aesthetically significant quality that most of us initially mean by the term (as opposed, say, to the power of objects to reflect light of certain wavelengths and absorb the rest), then redness is not in external objects, but only in minds. It is a feature of sensations or ideas only, as Hylas says. This is the thesis that Locke states in terms of resemblance:

> The ideas of primary qualities of bodies are resemblances of them, and their patterns do really exist in the bodies themselves; but the ideas produced in us by these secondary qualities have no resemblance of them at all. (ECHU:2.8.15)[3]

Locke is saying that colors, tastes, and so on—"the ideas produced in us by these secondary qualities"—do not resemble any properties in the objects that cause them.

We can also identify significant points on which Locke and Berkeley disagree. For Locke, there certainly are primary qualities in objects, and they do resemble the ideas "of" them in our minds. For Berkeley, by contrast, all qualities reside in the mind alone, and nothing in the mind resembles anything outside it.

Reid agrees with Locke on some of the foregoing points and with Berkeley on others. In agreement with Locke and in opposition to Berkeley, he maintains that there are indeed objects outside the mind, and that they are invested with the primary qualities. In agreement with Berkeley and in opposition to Locke, he maintains that ideas or sensations do not resemble external things in respect of primary qualities any more than they do in respect of secondary qualities.

Reid's resistance to Locke's positive resemblance thesis comes out most strongly in the *experimentum crucis*—the thought experiment, discussed in chapter 2, by which he seeks to show that we have a clear conception of extension (which is presupposed by size, shape, motion, and the other primary qualities) that we could not have derived from our sensations. The interesting implication of the experiment for present purposes is that there is *no resemblance* between our sensations and extended objects. If there were, the subject of the experiment *could* get the conception of extension by reflection on his sensations.

To summarize this section, the basis of the primary/secondary quality distinction for Reid cannot be that primary qualities reside in objects and secondary qualities do not (as Berkeley's Hylas has it), since *both* sets of qualities reside in objects. Nor can it be that primary qualities resemble their associated ideas or sensations and secondary qualities do not (as Locke has it), since in *neither* case is there any resemblance. So what, if anything, is the basis for the distinction?

---

[3] Ideas "of" primary qualities are not necessarily intentional states; they may simply be ideas produced in us by primary qualities, in parallel with Locke's language in the second half of the sentence.

## B. THE REAL FOUNDATION: EPISTEMOLOGICAL
## OR METAPHYSICAL?

Reid gives his own account of the primary/secondary quality distinction in the following passage from the chapter in the *Intellectual Powers* devoted to the distinction:

> Is there a just foundation for this distinction? Is there anything common to the primary which belongs not to the secondary? And what is it?
>
> I answer, That there appears to me to be a real foundation for the distinction; and it is this: That our senses give us a direct and a distinct notion of the primary qualities, and inform us what they are in themselves: But of the secondary qualities, our senses give us only a relative and obscure notion. They inform us only, that they are qualities that affect us in a certain manner, that is, produce in us a certain sensation; but as to what they are in themselves, our senses leave us in the dark. (EIP 2.17:201)

A few paragraphs later, he gives a reprise:

> Thus I think it appears, that there is a real foundation for the distinction of primary from secondary qualities; and that they are distinguished by this, that of the primary we have by our senses a direct and distinct notion; but of the secondary only a relative notion, which must, because it is only relative, be obscure; they are conceived only as the unknown causes or occasion of certain sensations with which we are well acquainted. (EIP 2.17:202)

So there we have it: our notions of primary qualities are *direct* and *distinct*, whereas our notions of secondary qualities are *relative* and *obscure*.

"Direct" is the opposite of "relative." Reid explains what he means by "relative" as follows:

> A relative notion of a thing, is, strictly speaking, no notion of the thing at all, but only of some relation which it bears to something else. (EIP 2.17, 201)

> This [the notion of gravity as whatever causes one body to be drawn toward another] is a relative notion, and it must be obscure, because it gives no conception of what the thing is, but of what relation it bears to something else. (EIP 2.17:202)

An example of a relative notion would be the notion conveyed by the description "the object Descartes was thinking of on the day he died"; clearly, such a description leaves us in the dark about what the object was or what it was like. Reid cites as further examples the terms "astringent" and "narcotic," which signify qualities known only by their effects on animal bodies (IHM 6.5:88).

Examples of direct notions are our notions of the various shapes and the notion of hardness, which Reid defines as the firm adhesion of the parts of a body so as to make it resistant to change of shape (IHM 5.4:61–62). When we know a thing to be hard or square, we do know what it is like in itself, not merely how it is related to something else.

"Distinct" is the opposite of "obscure." It appears to have been Reid's view when he wrote the EIP chapter on secondary qualities that relative notions are ipso facto obscure: when we know only what relation a thing bears to something else, we have no distinct notion of it, but "only a relative notion, *which must, because it is only relative*, be obscure" [emphasis added].[4]

According to Reid's official account of the difference between primary and secondary qualities, then, our notions of the former are direct and distinct while our notions of the latter are relative and obscure. This account may well prompt the following thought:

> Reid's distinction between primary and secondary qualities is merely epistemological, not metaphysical. The two types of quality differ not in their own natures, but in the types of access we have to them.

This is the understanding of Reid advocated in Lehrer 1978 and McKitrick 2002 (186), and there is undeniably support for it in Reid's text. But I believe it is also possible to interpret Reid in such a way that his distinction between primary and secondary qualities is rooted in the nature of the qualities themselves after all: primary qualities are *intrinsic* and secondaries *extrinsic*. In the next two sections, I explore what can be said for and against these two interpretations.

## C. DISPOSITIONS OR BASES?

The question of whether Reid's foundation for the distinction is epistemological or metaphysical is closely aligned with another question: does Reid think of secondary

---

[4] By the time he wrote the *Essays on the Active Powers of the Human Mind*, however, he had come around to the position that some relative notions are distinct, not obscure. He says that the relative notion we form of a chiliagon by considering its relations to polygons of a greater or lesser number of sides is distinct—indeed, more distinct than the direct conception of a chiliagon we obtain when we see or imagine one (EAP 1.1:11). I discuss this example further in chapter 14, section A.

qualities as *dispositions* in objects, or does he think of them as the *causal bases* of dispositions? As explained below, the "disposition" answer suggests a metaphysical foundation for the distinction, whereas the "base" answer suggests a merely epistemological one.

Where contemporary philosophers use the term *disposition*, Reid more often uses the terms *power* and (with no pejorative intent) *occult quality*.[5] I shall generally use the contemporary term.

Dispositions are often defined by subjunctive conditionals. To say that the glass is fragile is to say that if it were struck, it would break; to say that sugar is soluble is to say that if it were placed in water, it would dissolve; and so on. Schematically, to say that x has a certain disposition (to exhibit manifestation M in circumstances C) is to say that if x were placed in C, it would exhibit M. A definition of the color red fitting this schema might look like this:

x is red = df if x were placed in view of a normal human observer in daylight, the observer would receive red* sensations.

By "red* sensations," I refer to the type of sensations you get when something looks red to you—a type I could define ostensively by putting you in the right circumstances and letting you see what happens.[6] I use "red*" rather than "red" in the definiens for two reasons: (i) I do not want to give the appearance of a circular definition, and (ii) in Reid's view, sensations and external things are not red in the same sense (else we would have an instance of the resemblance thesis he so strenuously opposes).

The *causal base* of a disposition is the categorical property (if any) in virtue of which the disposition is possessed—in other words, it is some nondispositional property of the object such that it is a causal law that objects with that property exhibit M in C. The basis of the fragility of glass is presumably some aspect of its molecular structure, its pattern of bonding or whatnot; the basis of an object's looking red (i.e., producing red* sensations in observers) might be whatever properties of its surface make it reflect light of certain wavelengths while absorbing light of other wavelengths. Philosophers debate the question of whether all dispositions must have categorical bases; I shall simply assume here that the answer is yes.[7]

---

[5] See, for example, IHM 6.5:88 and EIP 2.18:216. We do have "disposition" at EIP 2.17:204.

[6] My device of starring does much the same work as Peacocke's device of priming predicates in Peacocke 1983, chapter 2; I prefer it only for typographical reasons.

[7] In Van Cleve 1995, appendix 1, I argue for an answer of *yes* with one qualification: although *universal* dispositions (those possessed by everything) need not have categorical bases, dispositions possessed by some things but not others must have them.

Now we may pose the issue of this section: are Reidian secondary qualities dispositions to produce sensations, or are they the bases of such dispositions?[8] Bases, say McKitrick and Wolterstorff; dispositions, say Yaffe and I.[9] This question is related to the epistemological versus metaphysical issue in a clear-cut way. If secondary qualities are bases, they may simply be (as in Locke's view they explicitly are) combinations of primary qualities, in which case, of course, they would be the same in nature as primary qualities. Secondary qualities would differ from primary qualities only in our mode of access to them (via their effects). But if secondary qualities are dispositions, they will differ metaphysically from primary qualities—they will be relational or extrinsic properties, in a sense to be explicated below, whereas primary qualities are intrinsic.

The textual evidence on the disposition versus base issue pulls in both directions. Reid sometimes says that secondary qualities are powers, suggesting a dispositional account, as in the following two passages:

> Colour is not a sensation, but a secondary quality of bodies, in the sense we have already explained; that it is a certain power or virtue in bodies, that in fair day-light exhibits to the eye an appearance, which is very familiar to us. (IHM 6.5:87; see also IHM 2.9:43, line 3)

> Upon the whole, Mr Locke, in making secondary qualities to be powers in bodies to excite certain sensations in us, has given a just and distinct analysis of what our senses discover concerning them. (EIP 2.17:209–10)

---

[8] The question "disposition or base?" is short-circuited by those philosophers who *identify* dispositions with their bases, as D. M. Armstrong professes to do. There are objections to such an identity view, however. For one, the same disposition may have different bases in different objects and cannot be identical with them all. (For this objection along with two others, see Prior, Pargetter, and Jackson 1982.) Conversely, two dispositions (e.g., a disposition to produce certain tactile sensations and a disposition to produce certain auditory sensations) can have the same base in vibrations of a certain sort.

In some of Armstrong's own elucidations of his so-called identity view, it appears that he really holds something else. In Armstrong 1996, he spells out his view thus: what it is for x to be brittle is for it to have a categorical property P such that x's having P and its being struck entails (with the help of the laws of nature) that x shatters. That makes dispositions supervenient on categorical properties without being identical with them.

[9] For the view that Reidian secondary qualities are bases, see McKitrick 2002, Wolterstorff 2001:112–13 (where it is said that this is Reid's "dominant tendency") and Maund 2008. For the view that Reidian secondary qualities are dispositional (and relational) properties, see Yaffe 2008.

However, his more frequent formula is that secondary qualities are *unknown causes of known effects*. Here is a sampling of passages:

> The qualities in bodies which we call *heat* and *cold*, are unknown. They are only conceived by us, as unknown causes or occasions of the sensations to which we give the same names. (IHM 5.1:54)

> That idea [a term Reid uses here interchangeably with "sensation"] which we have called *the appearance of colour*, suggests the conception and belief of some unknown quality in the body, which occasions the idea; and it is to this quality, and not to the idea, that we give the name of *colour*. (IHM 6.4:86)

> But of the secondary qualities, our senses . . . inform us only, that they are qualities that affect us in a certain manner, that is, produce in us a certain sensation. (EIP, 2.17:201)

> Smell in the rose is an unknown quality or modification, which is the cause or occasion of a sensation which I know well. . . . The same reasoning will apply to every secondary quality. (EIP 2.17:202)

Characterizing secondary qualities as "unknown causes" suggests that secondary qualities are bases rather than dispositions for two reasons: it is bases, not dispositions, that do the causing,[10] and it is bases that are unknown.[11]

The second of these points has been pressed by Wolterstorff: "If green were a disposition in things to cause certain sensations under certain conditions and not the physical basis of that disposition, we would know what it was" (2001:112). This argument is presumably to be spelled out as follows:

1. If green were a disposition in things to cause certain sensations in us, we would know what green is (for we know what that disposition is).[12]
2. According to Reid, we do *not* know what green is—it is an unknown quality.
3. Therefore, Reid's view implies that green is not a disposition, but its base—for it is the base of which we are ignorant.

---

[10] See Prior, Pargetter, and Jackson 1982 for an argument that dispositions are causally impotent.

[11] A related point is that if Reid were thinking of secondary qualities as dispositions, it would be more natural for him to speak of the property *of* causing such-and-such sensations rather than the property *that* causes them.

[12] Compare what Reid says about gravity at EIP 2.17:201–2: when the word is used to signify the tendency of bodies toward the earth (as opposed to the cause of this tendency), we know perfectly what it is.

Call this the argument from ignorance.

It seems to me that this argument cannot be decisive, since it may be countered by an equally good argument from knowledge. If we do not know *what* green is, then we do not know of anything *that* it is green. This is an instance of the general principle that you know x to be F only if you know what it is to be F. But it is clear that for Reid, we *do* often know of things that they are green. Hence, we must know what it is for them to be green, contrary to premise 2 in the argument from ignorance.[13]

I said above that the textual evidence on the disposition versus base issue pulls both ways. Here is a passage that makes trouble for the base view and favors the disposition view:

> [Sensations belonging to secondary qualities] are not only signs of the object perceived, but they bear a capital part in the notion we form of it. We conceive it only as that which occasions such a sensation, and therefore cannot reflect upon it without thinking of the sensation which it occasions. (EIP 2.17:204; see also IHM 6.4:86, lines 31–36)

Call this the "capital part" thesis. The thesis is clearly true if secondary qualities are dispositions, defined in the manner above. The definiens in each dispositional definition of a secondary quality makes reference to a type of sensation, and for that reason, we could not conceive of the property without conceiving of the sensation. But the thesis is not so clearly true, and indeed seems false, if secondary qualities are bases. The base might be a primary quality with which we are in fact acquainted (perhaps without knowing that it is the base), and in that case we would be able to conceive of it without conceiving of any sensation. People who do not know that motion is the base of the disposition to produce heat sensations (and even those who do) may conceive of motion without conceiving of heat sensations.

The argument I have just given may raise suspicions. An instance of it would be the following:

1. I cannot conceive of heat without conceiving of heat sensations. (The "capital part" thesis)

---

[13] Reid's own attitude to the argument I have just given is difficult to make out. At EIP 203–4, he seems to repudiate its general principle (that you know something is F only if you know what it is to be F): "Our feeling informs us that the fire is hot; but it does not inform us what that heat of the fire is." Yet before the paragraph is over, he acknowledges that "if we had not some notion of what is meant by the heat of fire, and by an inebriating quality, we could affirm nothing of either with understanding." (Compare also EAP 1.4:25–26.) He seeks to reconcile this remark with the preceding one by saying that our notion of heat is merely relative—what we know in knowing the fire to be hot is that it contains some cause of our heat sensations, but not what this cause is. I argue below that his reconciliation is best effected by taking the notion of heat to be dispositional.

2. I can conceive of motion without conceiving of heat sensations.

3. Therefore, heat is not motion.

We know nowadays that heat is a form of motion, so must there not be something wrong with the argument?

The validity of the argument ought to be conceded by anyone who adopts an intensional criterion for the identity of properties, and premise 2 seems beyond question. The controversial part is premise 1. Contemporary readers who know their Kripke would say that if we characterize heat by the formula "Heat is the cause of heat sensations," we are not giving the *meaning* of "heat," but fixing its reference. We are not saying that "heat" is synonymous with "whatever causes heat sensations," but are saying instead something that amounts to this: there is a property P that causes heat sensations, and heat is *that property P*. If motion turns out to be the cause of heat sensations, it would then follow that heat is motion.[14] The first premise and the conclusion of the argument above would both be false.

The argument is therefore contentious. What matters for our interpretive purposes, however, is whether Reid would have accepted its first premise. I believe he would have. When he affirms his "capital part" thesis, I do not believe he is merely expressing a deficiency in human knowledge—that in our ignorance of the causes of certain types of sensations, we can only refer to them indirectly as whatever properties cause the sensations. I believe he is affirming an essential link between the concept of heat and heat sensations, the concept of color and color sensations, and so on. In Lehrer's terms, he is saying that sensations are "semantic constituents" of secondary-quality concepts (1989:27); in McDowell's terms, he is saying that secondary qualities are "essentially phenomenal qualities," that is, "qualities that could not be adequately conceived except in terms of how their possessors would look" (McDowell [1985] 1997:203).[15]

We have now reviewed two sets of passages in Reid that seem to pull in opposite directions on the present issue—the "unknown cause" passages, which suggest that secondary qualities are causal bases, and the "capital part" passages, which suggest that secondary qualities are dispositions essentially defined in terms of certain sorts of sensations. Is there any way to accommodate them all? Perhaps not, if we must

[14] Galileo was one of the first to conjecture that molecular motions are the cause of heat sensations. It is of interest that he states his conjecture by saying that motion is the cause of *heat*. In other words, he identifies heat with the sensations and not with their cause. This shows just how much the semantics of "heat" has changed between Galileo's day and our own. See Frova and Marenzana 1998:409.

[15] McDowell goes on to say that if in light of improved microphysical knowledge of the causal base of redness, we began to ascribe the microphysical quality to objects that look red to us, we would no longer be ascribing redness to them.

remain true to their letter; but perhaps so, if we may hazard a guess as to their intent or spirit. In what follows, I take up an idea mentioned by McKitrick, though not attributed by her to Reid.

McKitrick points out that some philosophers analyze dispositions along the following lines (67–68):

> X has disposition D to produce manifestation M in circumstances C iff there is some property P such that (X has P & P would cause M in C).

A disposition as defined by a definition in this style is a *second-order* property—the property of having some property that satisfies a certain condition.[16] If redness were a disposition in this sense, it would be the property of having some property P that causes red* sensations in humans (in the specified circumstances). It would not be whatever *specific* property causes red* sensations—perhaps there is more than one—but the property of having *some property or other* that causes red* sensations. Properties that are dispositional in this sense are also dispositional in the "bare" sense discussed earlier (defined in terms of subjunctive conditionals), but the converse is not necessarily true—the bare sense leaves it open whether there is a causal base and the second-order sense does not.

McKitrick does not ascribe to Reid the view that secondary qualities are dispositions on the second-order property model—she thinks secondary qualities for Reid are bases.[17] But I think the second-order view may be just what we need to accommodate some of the things Reid says. Look again at this passage:

> That idea [sensation] which we have called *the appearance of colour*, suggests the conception and belief of some unknown quality in the body, which occasions the idea; and it is to this quality, and not to the idea, that we give the name of *colour*. (IHM 6.4; 86)

How should we characterize the "belief of some unknown quality in the body" that occasions the sensation? There are two possibilities. One is

(1) We believe there is a property P such that (P is in the object & P causes such-and-such sensations in us)

---

[16] This notion of a second-order property should not be confused with another that also goes by the name "second-order property," namely, a property had by first-order properties rather than individuals. Second-order properties in the current sense may be had by individuals; they are called second-order because in the specification of them we quantify over other properties.

[17] Her view is actually more complicated than this, as she ascribes to Reid the supposedly Armstrongian view that dispositions and bases are identical. In my view, this leaves her hard pressed to handle Wolterstorff's observation that dispositions are known and bases are not, as well as the objections mentioned in n. 8

and the other is

(2) There is a property P such that we believe (P is in the object & P causes such-and-such sensations in us)

The second formula cannot be right, precisely because the quality that causes red* sensations is unknown to us; until we have discovered which quality it is, we do not really believe of any property that *it* is the cause of our sensations. What we believe is better captured by the first formula—we believe that some property or other is in the object and causes red*sensations. Now if that is what we *believe* when we believe an object is red, it would be natural to say as well that that is what it *is* for an object to be red: namely, to have some property P that causes red* sensations in us. That would make redness a disposition as dispositions are construed on the second-order property model.

To be sure, Reid says that we give the name of color to the property that does the causing. But that is because he is operating with just two alternatives: is redness the cause in the object, or is it the effect in us? His main concern is to reject the second alternative—he wants to locate secondary qualities in objects. Given just those two alternatives, he plainly prefers the former. But were he apprised of three alternatives—the effect in us, the specific cause of this effect, or the property of containing some cause or other of this effect—I believe he would opt for the third. That would nicely accommodate the following passage, which is the *Inquiry*'s version of the "capital part" thesis:

> [The notion of color] is really in some sort compounded. It involves an unknown cause, and a known effect. . . . But as the cause is unknown, we can form no distinct conception of it, but by its relation to the known effect. (IHM 6.4:86)

The second-order conception involves both elements Reid requires—it involves the known sensory effect by referring to it directly, and it involves the unknown cause by existentially quantifying over it. But it does not identify secondary qualities with unknown causes.

So let us adopt the hypothesis that secondary qualities are dispositions to produce certain sorts of sensations in us and see if that gives us a metaphysical foundation for the primary/secondary quality distinction. I believe it does. This will be so regardless of whether we think of dispositions as defined simply by conditionals or as defined in terms of second-order properties.

## D. INTRINSIC OR EXTRINSIC?

If secondary qualities are dispositions rather than their bases, then there is at least one important metaphysical difference between primary and secondary qualities: primary qualities are *intrinsic* properties of their bearers, while secondary qualities are not.

To establish this point, it is necessary first to take some care with the notion of an intrinsic property. Intrinsic properties are often contrasted with relational properties, and relational properties are sometimes explicated as properties whose exemplification requires the existence of something else beyond the thing having it.[18] Kant gave a famous test for whether a property P is intrinsic in this sense:

> *Kant's test*: A property P is intrinsic iff it would be possible for an object that was all alone in the universe to have P.[19]

Although dispositional properties are often regarded as being relational or extrinsic, a little thought shows they are intrinsic by Kant's test. Take a typical disposition, for example, the disposition of sugar to dissolve in water. Is water solubility a relation to water? No, for a given sugar cube would presumably still be water soluble even if all water were removed from the universe.

There is another sense, however, in which dispositional properties *are* correctly thought of as extrinsic rather than intrinsic. This sense is brought out by another test:

> *Moore's test*: A kind of [property] is intrinsic if and only if, when anything possesses it, that same thing or anything exactly like it would *necessarily* or *must* always, under all circumstances, possess it in exactly the same degree. (Moore [1922] 1968:265)[20]

I maintain that being such as to dissolve in water and being such as to give human beings who view it red* sensations are not intrinsic properties by Moore's test. An object that is *just like* one of the red objects in our world (having the same surface structure, reflectancy, etc.) could be situated in another possible world where it was no longer red. This could happen if the neural constitution of humans in that world were such that they did not get red* sensations upon viewing it or if human beings were the same, but the laws of nature connecting causes with effects were different.

---

[18] By "beyond x" I mean not merely *distinct* from x, but *discrete* from x, i.e., having no part in common with x. Otherwise, any property that implied having proper parts, such as being square, would count as relational, which is not what is intended.

[19] Kant invokes this test in "Concerning the Ultimate Ground of the Differentiation of Directions in Space" to show that the property of being a right hand is not a relational property involving other material things ([1768] 2003). For discussion, see Van Cleve 1987.

[20] Moore actually stated this just as a criterion for when *values* are intrinsic, but the criterion may be extended to properties in general. That in effect is what David Lewis has done with his suggestion that an intrinsic property is one that can never differ between two duplicates; see 1986a:59–63.

I am obviously presupposing here that the laws of nature are contingent—that they could have been different from what they are.[21] This is an assumption with which Reid agrees; he notes in many places that for laws of nature, no other reason can be given but that they are the will of our Maker. It is also the view of Hume, who holds that there are no necessary connections between distinct existences, and of Locke, who says that God must "superadd" the power to produce certain sensations in us to its physical basis in bodies.[22]

Let us now return to what Reid says about the real foundation of the distinction between primary and secondary qualities—namely, that our senses inform us what the primary qualities are in themselves, but leave us in the dark about the secondary qualities, telling us only how they affect us. I would put the point thus: in knowing that an object is square, we know something about how it is intrinsically, or as Reid puts it, how it is in itself. We do not merely know something about how it would interact with our sensory apparatus. By contrast, in knowing that an object is red, we do not know anything about how it is in itself. We only know that it is such as to produce a certain kind of sensation in us, which is something an object could do even if it were intrinsically quite different. An object's being red is not a fact about how the object is in itself. This is not an epistemic point, but a point about the natures of the properties known; it concerns the informational contents of *x is square* and *x is red*. Reid's thesis about the difference between primary and secondary qualities is a metaphysical thesis about the nature of what is known, not a thesis about our manner of knowing it.

## E. FIXED OR VARIABLE?

I turn now to an interesting issue raised by McKitrick: whether Reid's way of drawing the primary/secondary quality distinction makes it relative to individuals and times. Might the same quality be secondary for one individual and primary for another, or secondary at one time and primary at another?

On McKitrick's understanding of Reid, it may seem initially that the answer is *yes*. According to her,

> Both [primary and secondary] qualities are causal bases of dispositions to cause sensations. . . . Reid's account of the foundation of the distinction is that the sensations caused by primary qualities suggest or signify [for us] something about the intrinsic

[21] For a defense of this position against contemporary views that oppose it, see Schaffer 2004. In Schaffer's terms, I am a *quiddistic contingentist*.

[22] For a good discussion of Locke's views on this issue, see Langton 2000.

nature of those qualities, while the sensations caused by secondary qualities signify only some unknown cause of that sensation. . . . On this picture, the only difference between primary and secondary qualities is "in the head," not in the properties. There is no metaphysical difference in the properties, only a difference in our epistemic access to them. (77–78)

Her account suggests that if our heads change in the right way, the status of a given quality as primary or secondary would also change. Suppose that heat sensations prompt us to believe that some quality of an external object is causing our sensations, but we have no idea of what this cause is—we conceive of it *only* as the cause of our sensations. Suppose further that as science progresses, we come to know exactly what property of hot objects causes heat sensations in us,[23] and that we teach ourselves and our offspring to respond to the sensations by attributing that property. Would heat not then have become a primary quality for us?

Before we answer this question, let us note that if the primary/secondary quality distinction must be relativized to individuals and times, it must also be relativized in a further way not noted by McKitrick—to types of sensations. The fully relativized notion would be something like this:

Q is a {primary, secondary} quality relative to S, t, and K iff (i) Q causes K sensations or impressions in S at t, and (ii) S is disposed at t to respond to K sensations by deploying a {direct, relative} conception of Q.

To see why we need the reference to K as well as to S and t, suppose that molecular motions at certain energy levels are the cause of heat sensations in us, and suppose (as in a figure of Locke's) that we are endowed with microscopical eyes, enabling us to see those very motions. If the relationship between motion and heat sensations is subtle enough, we may not realize that the motions we see (and form direct conceptions of as prompted by our visual impressions) are the cause of our heat sensations. We will respond to our heat sensations by conceiving the state of motion that causes them merely as "whatever causes heat sensations," and we will respond to our visual impressions by forming a direct conception of this very state of motion.

---

[23] Reid envisioned this possibility. McKitrick cites EIP 2.17:204: "The nature of secondary qualities is a proper subject of philosophical disquisition; and in this, philosophy has made some progress. It has been discovered, that the sensation of smell is occasioned by the effluvia of bodies; that of sound by their vibration. The disposition of bodies to reflect a particular kind of light occasions the sensation of colour. Very curious discoveries have been made of the nature of heat, and an ample field of discovery in these subjects remains."

In this circumstance, motion would be a primary quality relative to visual impressions and a secondary quality relative to heat sensations.

Now let us return to McKitrick's question. In the situation envisioned two paragraphs back, would heat have become a primary quality for us (relative to heat sensations) owing to the advance in our knowledge? Her answer is *no*. She points out that on Reid's understanding of primary qualities, they are qualities of which our senses *naturally* or *by our original constitution* give us a direct notion.[24] So if we discover what quality in objects causes our heat sensations and teach ourselves to respond to our sensations by forming a direct conception of this quality, it will not yet be the case that heat has become for us a primary quality. For it to be a primary quality, heat sensations would have to prompt us to form a direct conception of their external cause as part of our native endowment.[25]

But let us take her scenario one step further. Suppose we do not merely *train* ourselves to respond to heat sensations with a direct conception of their cause, but somehow *evolve* into creatures who so respond as part of their native constitution. In that case, heat would indeed have become a primary quality for our descendants. McKitrick concludes that although Reid's primary/secondary distinction need not be relativized to individual perceivers and times, it must be relativized to species (81).

That conclusion would be correct if the primary/secondary quality distinction were merely epistemological, as McKitrick believes. But what if primary qualities are intrinsic and secondary qualities are extrinsic, as I have proposed? In that case, there could be no such thing as a secondary quality's becoming primary because

---

[24] At IHM 6.4:61, Reid contrasts secondary qualities with primary qualities by saying that of the secondary "we know no more *naturally*, than that they are adapted to raise certain sensations in us." On the next page, he says that our conceptions and beliefs in primary qualities "are invariably connected with the corresponding sensations, by an *original* principle of human nature." (Both emphases are mine.)

[25] McKitrick connects this point with Reid's distinction between original and acquired perception. We have acquired perception of a feature F when we form perceptual beliefs about the presence of F only because we have learned a correlation between F and other features perceived originally. For example, we do not, in Reid's view, have original perception of three-dimensional shape by sight, but only by touch. Once we have learned correlations between two-dimensional visual cues (shading, etc.) and three-dimensional shape (as gauged by touch), we automatically respond to the cues by conceiving of and believing in the three-dimensional shape of the object. In the case of learning to respond to heat sensations by conceiving of molecular motion, McKitrick would say that this is only acquired perception, not original perception. I add this: whether it would even count as acquired perception depends on whether the microstate that causes heat sensations is directly accessible to us through some other sense modality or whether it is something we learn about only through the hypothetico-deductive method. I return to this point in section E of chapter 5.

there is no such thing as an extrinsic property's becoming intrinsic. Nor is there any such thing as a change in the opposite direction.[26]

## F. FOUR VIEWS THAT CONFLICT WITH REID'S

To bring the contours of Reid's views about primary and secondary qualities into sharper relief, I now discuss four significant views that are opposed to his (and therefore ruled out if he is right). The four oppositions hold up regardless of whether I am correct in contending that Reid's foundation for the primary/secondary quality distinction is metaphysical.

*Naïve Realism: Sensuous Color Is in the Object.* Reid, the self-proclaimed champion of common sense, seldom admits to holding any views at odds with those of the plain man or woman. He thinks that the central tenet of modern philosophers about the secondary qualities, with which he agrees, is not at variance with common sense, but appears to be so only because of the philosophers' misleading use of ambiguous terms. In particular, he thinks that secondary quality terms are systematically ambiguous, the same term, "heat" for instance, being used both as the name for a type of sensation and as the name of a power in objects to produce that sensation in us. When philosophers deny that there is heat in the fire, they are only denying that the fire has any sensations, which the vulgar deny as well. When the vulgar affirm that there is heat in the fire, they are only affirming that there is some quality in the fire that causes heat sensations in us, which the philosophers admit as well. So it is with color and the other secondary qualities—the apparent dispute between philosophy and common sense is only verbal:

> One of the most remarkable paradoxes of modern philosophy . . . is, in reality, when examined to the bottom, nothing else but an abuse of words. . . . When philosophers affirm that colour is not in bodies, but in the mind; and the vulgar affirm, that colour

---

[26] What *might* be possible on Reid's view, however, is that a property should pass from primary to *nonprimary* or vice versa. I have not aligned the primary/secondary distinction completely with the intrinsic/extrinsic distinction. Powers to produce changes in other insentient things—what Locke scholars sometimes call tertiary qualities—are extrinsic properties without being secondary qualities. There is also room in Reid's scheme for the converse combination of intrinsic properties that are not primary qualities. To qualify as primary in Reid's view, a quality must not only be intrinsic, but must also be such as to produce sensations that natively trigger in us a direct conception of the property. If so, a property could gain or lose its status as primary in consequence of a change in the native sensory or cognitive endowment of human beings. If hardness ceased to produce any sensations in us, or if the sensations it did produce ceased to elicit in us a direct conception of hardness, hardness would no longer count as a primary quality in Reid's sense.

is not in the mind, but is a quality of bodies; there is no difference between them about things, but only about the meaning of a word. (IHM 6.5:88; the same point is made again at EIP 2.17:205–6)[27]

It seems to me, however, that there is something the person in the street believes and Reid denies, along with the philosophers.[28] It is this: there is *sensuous color* in external objects. Call this naïve realism about color.[29] A good emblem for naïve realism (as I once heard George Pappas say) is the "cover the earth" logo of the Sherwin-Williams paint company, in which red paint pours out of a tilted bucket and coats the globe. Despite the fact (as it seems to me) that naïve realism is what most of us believe most of the time, it is not an easy view to pin down for a philosophical audience. It is not enough to characterize the view simply by saying that objects really are red, for there are meanings of that formula under which Lockean dispositionalists and Australian materialists would both assent to it (along with Reid himself, depending on which of these camps we assimilate him to). Yes, says Locke, objects are red, for they have the power to give us red* sensations. Yes, says the Australian materialist, objects are red, because their microstructure is such that they absorb light of most wavelengths while reflecting light of wavelengths in the 760-to-647 nanometer range. But I do not believe that either of those things is what a child or a poet believes in believing that a rose is red. How shall we characterize the property that is attributed to objects by the naïve and the romantic? It is a property that has no dependence on sentient minds; it is categorical, not dispositional; it is intrinsic; its nature is manifest to those who know nothing of physics; its nature is not manifest to those who know a lot of physics but have never experienced it. The various sophisticated philosophers' versions of red do not have all these characteristics.[30]

I am not yet saying that Reid is *wrong* to exclude sensuous color from external objects. I am only saying that he is wrong to think that in so excluding it, his views are compatible with common sense. On this point, I agree with Lorne Falkenstein, who has observed that "Reid is really *denying* that visible figures are 'coloured' in the truly common sense of the term" (2000:322).

---

[27] Reid holds in his published work that color terms are the one exception to the systematic ambiguity of secondary-quality terms. He says that color terms are never used to refer to sensations, but only to the external qualities that cause them (IHM 6.4:85–87).

[28] Reid admits as much in an unpublished manuscript of unknown date, but presumably earlier than the *Inquiry*: "Color is imagined to be in the body by the vulgar but not by philosophers." (Aberdeen University Library MS 2131/8/VI/3).

[29] I distinguish naïve realism from direct realism, the view that external things are directly perceived. I take Reid to be a direct realist, but not a naïve realist.

[30] Naïve realism is not the prerogative of the vulgar alone. It has been defended by able philosophers, including John Campbell (1994) and Peter Unger (2006, especially chapter IV).

*Mill, Putnam, and Langton: All Properties Are Secondary Qualities.* I turn now to a view at the other end of the spectrum from naïve common sense: the view that *all* properties of external things, or at least all properties we know of, are secondary qualities in the Lockean sense—powers to produce sensations in us. Mill, Putnam, and Langton have all attributed versions of this thesis to Kant, as well as favorably entertaining it themselves.

Here is Putnam's version:

> I suggest that (as a first approximation) the way to read Kant is as saying that what Locke said about secondary qualities is true of *all* qualities. . . . If *all properties are secondary*, what follows? It follows that *everything* we say about an object is of the form: it is such as to affect *us* in such-and-such a way. *Nothing at all* we say about any object describes the object as it is "in itself," independently of its effect on *us*. (1981:59 and 61; see also 63)

Putnam is apparently attributing to Kant the thesis that the only properties *there are* in external things are powers to affect us in certain ways. This raises two interesting issues that I cannot pursue here. If one thinks of powers to affect us as relations, the question arises of whether all properties of things can be relational. If one thinks of powers to affect us as dispositions, the question arises of whether all properties of a thing can be dispositions, or whether instead the dispositions must have some categorical basis. I have discussed both issues elsewhere (1995).

A somewhat less extreme view, making a claim not about *all* the properties of external things but just the ones we *know of,* is expounded by Mill under the label "the relativity of knowledge":

> That all the attributes which we ascribe to objects, consist in their having the power of exciting one or another variety of sensation in our minds; that to us the properties of an object have this and no other meaning. . . . This is the doctrine of the Relativity of Knowledge to the knowing mind. (1865, vol. 1:16)

Mill attributes this doctrine to a number of philosophers, including Kant. We may distinguish two versions of it: one according to which the only properties we can *know objects to have* are powers to produce sensations in us, and another according to which the only properties of external things we can even *form any conception of* are powers to produce sensations in us. Mill's language somewhat more strongly suggests the second.[31]

---

[31] For a contemporary incarnation of Mill's doctrine, see Foster 1982:63.

Reid's views are clearly at odds with Putnam's thesis and both versions of Mill's. Squareness and hardness, according to him, are intrinsic properties of objects in the sense we have discussed above; they are not merely dispositions to give us sensations.[32] They are also properties that we can easily conceive of and know objects to possess.[33]

Why would anyone hold that we cannot have any knowledge of the intrinsic properties of things? Rae Langton has given an answer (1998). She reconstructs what she takes to be one of the central arguments of Kant's *Critique of Pure Reason* as follows:

> *Receptivity*: Human knowledge depends on sensibility, and sensibility is receptive: we can have knowledge of an object only insofar as it affects us. We have knowledge only of those properties of things in virtue of which they enter into causal relations with us.

> *Irreducibility*: The relations and relational properties of substances (which include their powers to affect us) are not reducible to the intrinsic properties of things. The causal relations between things are not necessitated by their intrinsic properties. *Therefore,*

> *Humility*: We have no knowledge of the intrinsic properties of things.

Langton explains that by an intrinsic property she means "a property something can have, no matter what else exists—and no matter what the laws are" (119). The first clause—"no matter what exists"—says in effect that intrinsic properties must pass Kant's test; the second—"no matter what the laws are"—implies they must

---

[32] Actually, there is a potential difficulty in the classification of hardness as intrinsic. Reid says our conception of hardness is "as clear and distinct . . . as of any thing whatsoever" (IHM 5.4:61), and he defines hardness thus: "When the parts of a body adhere so firmly, that it cannot easily be made to change its figure, we call it *hard*; when its parts are easily displaced we call it *soft*" (IHM 5.2:55). Is hardness in this sense an intrinsic property by Moore's test? It is not clear to me that it is. Consider an object that is hard in our world and a duplicate of it in another world with different laws of attraction and motion. The object in the second world might have parts that easily slide past each other, making it not hard per Reid's definition and thereby making hardness not intrinsic by Moore's test. Perhaps that is a problem for the test.

[33] One qualification is called for. What I can know *immediately* through vision is that an object is visibly elliptical, i.e., that it looks elliptical from a certain angle or to a viewer situated at a certain place in relation to it. This is a relational property of the object, not an intrinsic property of it. It is founded on an intrinsic property, however: the object's being round, together with its lying obliquely to my line of sight. I can have *mediate* knowledge (which eventually becomes acquired perception) of the object's roundness by inference from what I know immediately through sight, and I can verify this knowledge by the immediate knowledge I have through touch. For Reid's discussions of these matters, see IHM 6.3 and 6.7 as well as his various discussions of acquired perception.

pass Moore's. Langton takes the Irreducibility premise to be true because she believes (as I do) that a thing with the same intrinsic properties as a given thing need not have the same powers as the original if placed in a setting with different laws.

Strikingly, Reid accepts both premises of Langton's Kantian argument, but rejects the conclusion. Human beings are so constituted, Reid tells us, that they achieve knowledge of the world around them only because objects affect their sense organs, giving rise to physical impressions, which in turn give rise to mental sensations, which are the occasions for perception (IHM 6.21:174). This is Receptivity. Moreover, of the laws whereby this sequence of operations takes place, we can give no explanation except that they are the will of God: "Who knows but their connection may be arbitrary, and owing to the will of our Maker?" (IHM 6.21:176). This clearly implies that laws of nature are contingent, and thus implies as much of the Irreducibility premise as is needed in Langton's argument. Yet Reid is far from accepting Humility. When we know something is square, we know how it is in itself and not merely how it affects our sensibility. So Reid would have cited the primary qualities as exceptions to Kantian Humility.

If Reid's position is tenable, Langton's argument is unsound. And indeed, further inspection reveals that the argument is invalid. It would be valid only if supplemented by another premise, such as the following: a causal relation holds between two things in virtue of certain of their properties only if it is *necessary* that any two things with those properties are causally related. For short, there is causation only where there is necessitation. This is a premise that Reid (siding for once with Hume) would deny—as would I. We can be affected by things in virtue of their intrinsic properties even if those properties do not necessarily have the effects they do.[34]

*Berkeley and Hume: No Object Could Have the Primary Qualities Exclusively.* An issue raised by Berkeley and Hume for "the modern philosophy" is this: *could* an object have the primary qualities exclusively, without having any properties from the list of secondaries?[35] Finding it inconceivable that an object should have the primaries without any secondaries, Berkeley and Hume both say *no*. Reid says *yes*.

---

[34] I discuss Langton's argument at greater length and consider further ways of making it valid in Van Cleve 2002b and 2011.

[35] Ironically, two of the issues raised by the thesis that all properties are secondary—could all properties be relational, and could all properties be dispositional?—are thought by some writers to arise for the thesis that all properties are *primary*. J. J. C. Smart notes, "All the properties which science ascribes to physical objects [mass, charge, spin, even shape insofar as it is defined in terms of length] seem to be purely relational" (1963:72), and he equates the question "Can a thing have the primary qualities alone?" with the question "Can a thing have relational properties only?" (73–74). Simon Blackburn, who like Smart is trying to clear the way for the view that objects have only the properties that science ascribes to them, sees his task as defending the possibility that all properties of objects are dispositional (1990).

Let us be clear about the issue Berkeley and Hume are raising. As we have seen above, secondary qualities are identified by some authors with dispositions in objects to produce sensations in us and by others with the bases of such dispositions. Berkeley and Hume are not asking whether an object could have primary qualities but no power to produce sensations in us. The answer to that question, if I am right about the contingency of laws, is obviously *yes*. Nor are they asking whether an object could have primary qualities without having those qualities that are in fact the bases of powers to produce sensations. Given that the causal bases of such powers *are* primary qualities—as Locke explicitly says—the answer to that question is obviously *no*. What Berkeley and Hume are asking is a question of which the following is a more concrete instance: could an object have a shape without having any *sensuous* color or texture to fill in its boundaries and differentiate it from its surroundings? To that question, their answer is *no*.

In the rest of this section, let it be understood that "color" without qualification means "sensuous color" in the sense of the term I have tried to indicate above.[36] Let it further be understood that we are talking of *seen* objects, for which tangible properties would not suffice as their sensuous "filling."

If shape without color can neither be nor be conceived, as Berkeley and Hume maintain, what follows? Three interesting lines of argument open up. The first is an argument for naïve realism: there is no shape without color; there is shape in external things; therefore, there is color in external things. The second is Berkeley's argument for extending idealism to shapes: there is no shape without color; there is no color except in minds; therefore, there is no shape without minds.[37] The third is Hume's twist on Berkeley: we cannot conceive of an object with extension or figure but no color; color exists only in internal impressions; therefore (since we cannot conceive of external things if we do not conceive of them as extended), we cannot conceive of external things.[38]

---

[36] With this exception: sensuous color for Berkeley and Hume is not independent of minds.

[37] Here is how Berkeley states the argument in the *Principles of Human Knowledge*, section 10: "For my own part, I see evidently that it is not in my power to frame an idea of a body extended and moved, but I must withal give it some colour or other sensible quality which is acknowledged to exist only in the mind. In short, extension, figure, and motion, abstracted from all other qualities, are inconceivable. Where therefore the other sensible qualities are, there must these be also, to wit, in the mind and nowhere else."

[38] Hume's argument at THN 1.4.4:228–29 is actually more complicated, running as follows: it is impossible to conceive of a body as extended without conceiving of it as either colored or solid; color is excluded from bodies by the modern philosophy; the idea of solidity is the idea of being impenetrable by other bodies and therefore presupposes an antecedent conception of what bodies are; therefore, the modern philosophy leaves us no just conception of bodies. Since we are concerned at present only with what sensuous properties *visible* extension must have, we can work with the simpler argument I use in the text.

Reid disputes the conclusions of all three arguments. He holds that we *do* have a conception of external things, that they *are* endowed with shape, and that they are *not* endowed with sensuous color. Since he accepts the minor premise in each argument, it is incumbent on him to deny the major—that there can neither be, nor be conceived, shape without color. That is exactly what he implicitly does in his discussion of visible figure in section 5.8 of the *Inquiry*. Curiously, however, he does not there connect the discussion with the issues I am raising now, nor mention Berkeley and Hume as his antagonists.[39]

In IHM 5.8, Reid argues that it would be possible to see shape without seeing any color. As we are presently constituted, he says, the stimulation of a point on one of our retinas (which Reid calls the "material impression" involved in vision) has two effects: it makes us see a point of the object at a certain location (along the straight line from the point of stimulation running through the center of the eye and out into the environment), and it gives us a sensation of color. The stimulation of many retinal points simultaneously makes us see an array of object points at various locations, and that is just what it is to see figure. (Visible figure is determined by the location of all the points in an object with respect to the eye.) Now if it had pleased our Maker, Reid says, our eyes might have been so framed that retinal stimulations had the first of these effects without having the second—the perception of figure without any sensation of color.[40] Contrary to Berkeley and Hume, then, it would be possible to see shape without seeing any color.[41] This takes away their reason for saying there could not *be* an object with shape but no color.

---

[39] He does take explicit exception to Berkeley and Hume on the shape-color issue in a discourse delivered before the Aberdeen Philosophical Society, but never published: "I think both Berkly & Hume affirm that there can be no idea of visible space without colour. I am of a contrary opinion & think I have a distinct conception of visible extension without colour" (IHM:277).

[40] This possibility was disputed by Reid's disciple Dugald Stewart and by his critic John Fearn, both of whom held color sensations to be essential for the perception of shape; see Grandi 2014 for discussion.

Reid also argues for the converse possibility of an eye in which retinal stimulations give us color sensations but do not make us see points at any locations. In that case one would see color without perceiving extension or figure. He thinks this is actually or nearly what happens in those who suffer from severe cataracts—"such persons see things as one does through a glass of broken gelly" (IHM 6.8:100). If he means to show that one could perceive color without extension, I demur. Does not the cataract sufferer perceive blurry extension?

[41] In an unpublished manuscript, Reid gives the following as an example of an object with visible figure but no color: "That Visible figure can be without colour I think evident by supposing the whole field of Vision of one uniform Colour excepting one Triangle perfectly black or without Colour. We should have as distinct an Idea of this Triangular Space as if it was coloured" (IHM:324). The example is suspect for two reasons. First, it is arguable that black is a color (Sorensen 2008:268). Second, the example is consistent with the claim that nothing can be seen as having a figure unless *something* (perhaps its boundary or background) has a color.

On the question whether there could *be* objects with shape but no color, I side with Reid. There is nothing inconceivable in the idea of a hexagonal pane of perfectly clear glass. What seems more doubtful to me is his contention that one could *see* an object as shaped without seeing any color in it or its surroundings. That is what Reid says we would do if endowed with the eye he imagines; it is even arguably what we do on Reid's view as we are constituted now.

Reid allows that under our present constitution, color is always "joined with" figure in our perception of figure (IHM 5.8:101, lines 10–13). But we must note what this being "joined with" amounts to. It certainly does not mean that sensuous color is spread out over objects or is co-located with any of the object's surface points. The closest things we can get to instantiators of sensuous color in Reid's philosophy are color sensations, but it would be a category mistake on his view to think that color sensations take up any area or are located at any point. What can be spread over an area is only some primary quality that causes the sensations in us. So that which Berkeley and Hume regard as impossible—seeing an object with figure but no sensuous color—is not only possible on Reid's view, but actual; it happens whenever we see at all.[42]

Without sensuous color, I do not see what satisfactory account Reid can give of seeing boundaries. What happens, on his account, when I see a wall painted green on the left side of a central line and red on the right? (i) Concerning the locations on the left side of the line, I have the perception-induced beliefs "there is something *there* and something *there* and something *there*," and similarly for locations on the right. (What are the *somethings*? That is going to be the nub of my difficulty.) (ii) The retinal stimulations that cause beliefs with respect to environmental locations also cause color sensations; points of the retina stimulated by light from the left side of the wall cause green* sensations and points stimulated by light from the right side cause red* sensations. (iii) I believe that the sensations are caused by properties instantiated in my environment in various parts of the wall.

Conditions (i)–(iii) cannot be the whole story, however. They are not sufficient to distinguish seeing green on the left and red on the right from seeing things the other way around (with no reversal of actual wall color), for all three conditions are satisfied in both cases. What must we add?

On Reid's view, the following condition will also be satisfied: (iv) I believe, concerning the various locations on the left, "something *there* is causing green* sensations in me," and concerning the various locations on the right, "something *there* is

---

[42] Some contemporary "error theories" of color have it that we mistakenly paint objects with colors or project colors onto them. The error itself (if we take the description of it literally) is an impossibility on Reid's view, as it is contrary to the nature of color sensations to be projected onto any surface.

causing red* sensations in me." I have qualms about whether Reid is entitled to say this.[43] Assuming that he is, however, I wish to raise the question whether (iv) would be sufficient for perceiving boundaries.

My question is whether a perceptible boundary can be created for me just by the fact that I believe objects on one side to cause aspatial F-sensations and objects on the other to cause aspatial G-sensations. Recall that color sensations are no more spatial for Reid than olfactory sensations. Suppose I were blindfolded and placed before a tangle of honeysuckle on the left and a heap of pine mulch on the right. If I believed that the sweet scent had its cause on the left and the pungent smell had its cause on the right, would that create a perceptible boundary for me? I doubt that it would, and the same doubt carries over to color sensations. While agreeing with Reid, then, that the world might be a locus of primary qualities without being a locus of sensuous colors, I cannot believe that we could ever *see* objects in a world like that.

*Smart, Armstrong, and Harman: We Do Not Know what Sensations Are Like Intrinsically.* The last anti-Reidian view I shall consider is that we do not know what our sensations are like intrinsically. This might be held on the basis of any of the following successively stronger doctrines, all sometimes advanced under the banner "the transparency of sensations":

— that we seldom, if ever, notice our sensations;
— that even in attending to our sensations, we are aware only of their relational features, not their intrinsic features;
— that sensations do not even *have* any intrinsic features.

Views along one or another of these lines have been put forward by many contemporary philosophers, including Smart, Armstrong, and Harman. The motive, in many cases, is to make the world safe for materialism—if we are not aware of any intrinsic features of our sensations, then we cannot claim that sensations have features that no brain state could have.[44]

---

[43] The qualms arise from a suspicion that Reid faces some sort of binding problem. What can enable the believer to place the causes of aspatial sensations in various locations? Perhaps Reid can solve the problem with material impressions, which (unlike sensations) carry spatial information, and which might be able to inject the sensations they cause into the contents of beliefs about locations.

[44] Such was the motive for Smart's thesis of "topic-neutrality," a version of transparency in the early days of identity-theory materialism. According to Smart, we can conceptualize our experiences only by descriptions along the lines of "it's like what goes on in me when I see ripe tomatoes" (Smart 1959).

Reid himself goes part way with the first of the three transparency doctrines. It is a recurrent theme of his philosophy that there is a broad range of sensations that we seldom notice, as it requires a special effort to do so. He compares sensations to "the words of a language, wherein we do not attend to the sound, but to the sense" (IHM 2.9:43) He often says things like this:

We are so accustomed to use the sensation [of hardness] as a sign, and to pass imme-diately to the hardness signified, that, as far as appears, it was never made an object of thought, either by the vulgar or by philosophers. . . . There is no sensation more distinct, or more frequent; yet it is never attended to, but passes through the mind instantaneously, and serves only to introduce that quality in bodies, which, by a law of our constitution, it suggests. (IHM 5.2:56)

But Reid would have opposed the bolder form of the first transparency doctrine, which says we are *never* aware of our sensations. His analogy with the words of a lan-guage implies as much, for there is nothing to prevent our attending to the sounds that express the various senses. Moreover, in the case of sensations associated with secondary qualities, we are bound to be aware of them, as we know from the "capital part" thesis: we can conceive of the qualities only by reference to the sensations.[45] Finally, even in the case of sensations associated with primary qualities, which normally make our thoughts leap immediately to the qualities they signify, we can know what they are like by careful attention. We *must* be able to do this to carry out his *expermimentum crucis*, which teaches us that tactile sensations are nothing like the extension, hardness, and other primary qualities they signify.

Those who hold the middle transparency doctrine listed above hold that the only features of our sensations or experiences we are aware of are their relational features—typically, their intentional features or their causal relations (the first of which some philosophers try to reduce to the second). Thus Harman:

When Eloise sees a tree before her . . . [she does not] experience any features of any-thing as intrinsic features of her experiences. . . . She is aware only of the intentional or relational features of her experience, not of its intrinsic nonintentional features. ([1990] 1997:667)

---

[45] We do not always attend to them, though. Reid was one of the first authors to emphasize the various perceptual constancies. He notes that a plain person who is not a painter will perceive an object that is moved farther away or into the shade as remaining constant in color, though the various color appearances or sensations have certainly changed. See IHM 6.3:83.

And Armstrong:

> A perception of something green will involve a green-sensitive element, that is to say, something which, in a normal environment, is characteristically brought into existence by green things. (1998:273)

> A green-sensitive element within need not be green, nor is it introspected as something green, nor indeed is it introspected as having any quality at all. It is introspected simply as something having sophisticated causal relationships to green things. (1998:275)

Reid would say that Armstrong has things backward. Rather than being able to characterize our sensations only by reference to their causes—say, green things— we can characterize green things only by reference to the sensations they cause in us. As for the sensations themselves, we do know what they are like intrinsically. If our notions of them were only relative—a matter of how they are related to something else—we would not have distinct notions of them, but we do: "Upon reflection I find, that I have a distinct notion of the sensation which [that quality in a rose I call its smell] produces in my mind" (EIP 2.17:202). Reid even goes so far as to say we know our sensations *perfectly*: "The sensations of heat and cold are perfectly known; for they neither are, nor can be, any thing else than what we feel them to be" (IHM 5.1:54).

The final transparency doctrine listed above was espoused by Moore, from whom contemporary writers have taken the term "transparency," but often without realizing how radical his view really was. The sensation of blue, says Moore, "seems, if I may use a metaphor, to be transparent—we look through it and see nothing but the blue" ([1903] 1922:20). His point is not just that we are unaware of the intrinsic nature of the sensation, but that the sensation itself *has* no intrinsic nature: everything it is, it owes to its object. Sensory consciousness is like a clear pane of glass through which we view objects, the glass differing from one episode of consciousness to the next only in what lies on the other side.[46] Reid's view cannot be like this, for he holds that sensations do not *have* objects; they are simply modifications of the mind. Sensing bluely and sensing greenly differ intrinsically rather than in their relation to anything beyond themselves.

An especially unsettling mix of un-Reidian views would arise if we combined the thesis of Mill, Putnam, and Langton with that of Smart, Armstrong, and Harman: we know nothing intrinsic about external things (but only that they are related to

---

[46] I have developed this interpretation of Moore at greater length in Van Cleve 2015.

mental states in certain ways), nor anything intrinsic about mental states (but only that they are related to external things in certain ways). That would mean we have no knowledge of the intrinsic properties of *anything*—knowledge of the relational features of some things would always dissolve away into knowledge of the relational features of yet other things, with nothing to anchor the system.[47] Needless to say, Reid would oppose this combination even more strenuously than he opposes each element separately.

---

[47] If I am not mistaken, this is the real upshot of Langton's Kantian argument from Receptivity, for knowledge of our own mental states presumably depends, just as much as our knowledge of external things does, on our being affected by them.

# 5

## ACQUIRED PERCEPTION

It must be a dull man indeed whose appetite will not be whet by the possibility of perceiving the world directly in the terms of the conceptual framework of modern physical theory. (Paul Churchland, *Scientific Realism and the Plasticity of Mind*)

What treatment then do those philosophers deserve, who would deprive these noble and delightful scenes of all reality? How should those principles be entertained, that lead us to think all the visible beauty of the creation a false imaginary glare? (George Berkeley, *Three Dialogues between Hylas and Philonous*)

Learning cannot increase what one sees. (Roy Sorensen, *Seeing Dark Things*)

"Acquired perception" is the name Reid gives to a cognitive phenomenon that arises through three steps that may be characterized schematically as follows: (i) On the occasion of sensation S, I form (in accordance with my native constitution) a conception of and a belief in the presence of some external object or quality A. This much is *original* perception. (ii) As time goes by, I find that my perceptions of A are always or nearly always accompanied by perceptions (perhaps belonging to another sense) of some other object or quality, B. I develop the habit of thinking that B is present on occasions when I perceive A—even if I have not yet perceived B. (iii) Eventually, the association between A and B becomes so strong that on the occasion of perceiving A, I automatically conceive of and believe in B without making any inference. I now have *acquired* perception of the quality B. Reid's own exposition of these matters is concentrated in IHM 6.20–24 and EIP 2.21–22.

Reid's favorite examples of acquired perception are the perception of distance and three-dimensional figure by sight. Reid agrees with Berkeley that what is given originally to sight is only a two-dimensional array in which objects are displayed as having locations along the left-right and up-down axes, but not along the near-far axis. "Outness" and three-dimensional shapes, such as being cubical or spherical, are given originally only to touch. I think Berkeley and Reid are both wrong about this, owing mostly to stereopsis, a mechanism not known in their time—see appendix L. In this chapter, though, I go along with them for the sake of being able to work with their examples. In Reid's view, we come to learn by experience that certain sensations connected with adjusting the "trim" of the eye and certain patterns of light and shadow are signs of distance and three-dimensional convexity. Eventually, we automatically conceive of and believe in a globe when we see an appropriately shaded disk. It is almost as though we *see* the convexity of the globe:

> It is experience that teaches me that the variation of colour is an effect of spherical convexity, and of the distribution of light and shade. But so rapid is the progress of the thought, from the effect to the cause, that we attend only to the last, and can hardly be persuaded that we do not immediately see the three dimensions of the sphere. (EIP 2.12:236)

Other examples of acquired perception are hearing the size of a bell (EIP 2.14:182) and seeing the weight of a sheep (IHM 6.20:172).

In this chapter, I take up the following four questions: (1) Is acquired perception really *perception*? (2) Are secondary qualities objects of original perception or of acquired perception only? (3) Does acquired perception involve any alteration in the content of our original perceptions? Finally, (4) are there any limits in principle to what might one day become an object of acquired perception for us? Before we get to these questions, however, it is necessary to say a little more about the mechanics of acquired perception.

## A. THE MECHANICS OF ACQUIRED PERCEPTION

Reid first draws the distinction between original and acquired perception in the *Inquiry* in the following passage:

> Our perceptions are of two kinds: some are natural and original, others acquired, and the fruit of experience. When I perceive that this is the taste of cyder, that of brandy; that this is the smell of an apple, that of an orange; that this is the noise of thunder, that the ringing of bells; this the sound of a coach passing, that the voice of such a friend; these perceptions and others of the same kind, are not original, they are acquired. But the perception which I have by touch, of the hardness and softness of bodies, of their extension, figure, and motion, is not acquired, it is original. (IHM 6.20:171)

The distinction is further elaborated in the chapter of the *Intellectual Powers* entitled "Of the improvement of the senses" (2.21), where it is illustrated by Reid's favorite example of it—the acquired visual perception of three-dimensional figures on the basis of originally perceived two-dimensional signs.

In what way are acquired perceptions "the fruit of experience"? There are two models to consider, an inference model and an association model. In the inference model, after being exposed to many cases of B conjoined with A (for instance, spherical shape with a certain pattern of shading), we form in accordance with induction the general belief that anything that looks like *this* is a sphere. On subsequent occasions of something's looking that way, we draw the inference "It looks like *this*, and things that look like *this* are spheres; therefore, it is a sphere." After several such occasions, the inference becomes fully automated: when we see something that looks the right way, we believe forthwith that it is a sphere, no longer passing through a major premise of the form "All As are Bs" or combining it with a minor premise of the form "o is an A" to conclude "o is a B." We simply leap to the belief that o is a B. We now have an acquired perception that the thing we are perceiving is a B.

In the association model, we go through the same history of experiencing As in conjunction with Bs as above, but we never form the explicit general belief that As are Bs (or if we do, we do not use it as a premise in an inference). We simply form an association between As and Bs, which eventually becomes strong enough that on the occasion of perceiving an A, we instantly believe that it is a B. We again have an acquired perception that the thing we are perceiving is a B.

In either model, we have acquired perception only when the transition from A-perceptions to B-beliefs has become fully automatic and no longer (if it ever was) a matter of inference. The difference is that in the association model, we do not go through an inferential phase on our way to acquiring the acquired perception; in the inference model, we do. We might put the matter thus: the inference model posits a phase in which the subject has a belief in a constant conjunction, symbolizable as "S believes $(x)(Ax \rightarrow Bx)$"; the association model posits no more than a constant conjunction of beliefs, symbolizable as "$(x)(S$ believes $Ax \rightarrow S$ believes $Bx)$."

Which model did Reid intend? I do not think he cared; so long as the product is right, the process does not matter. His indifference is shown in his indiscriminate use of two different formulations of the inductive principle underlying our ability to form acquired perceptions:

> When we have found two things to have been constantly conjoined in the course of nature, the appearance of one of them is immediately followed by the conception and belief of the other. (IHM 6.24:196, lines 1–3; see also 197, lines 9–11)

Thus, if a certain degree of cold freezes water to-day, and has been known to do so in all time past, we have no doubt but the same degree of cold will freeze water to-morrow, or a year hence. (IHM 6.24:196, lines 10–12; see also 197, lines 6–8)

In the first formulation, the inductive principle is said to produce in our minds a constant conjunction of beliefs; in the second, it is said to produce belief in a constant conjunction. Here and elsewhere, Reid uses the two formulations interchangeably.

I end this section by commenting on the relation of Reid's account of acquired perception to ideas in three other writers—Berkeley, Helmholtz, and Ryan Nichols.

*Berkeley.* Reid is indebted to Berkeley for many examples of acquired perception, which Berkeley often describes using the term "suggestion." Suggestion is the automatic triggering of conception and belief in one thing by the sensation or perception of another, as when a blush suggests shame or a word suggests its denotatum. In the following passage, Berkeley explicitly distinguishes suggestion from inference:

> To perceive is one thing; to judge is another. So likewise to be suggested is one thing, and to be inferred another. Things are suggested and perceived by sense. We make judgments and inferences by the understanding. (TVV 42 1975:293)

Reid's notion of acquired perception and Berkeley's notion of suggestion are related as follows: A suggests B to person S iff whenever S experiences A, S has an acquired perception of B for which A serves as the sign.

*Helmholtz.* Whereas Berkeley says that certain of our perceptions are based on suggestion, not inference, Helmholtz says that they are based on *unconscious* inference. Is there a disagreement between them? Robert Schwartz (1994:87–88) notes that the "psychological reality" of the major premise "All As are Bs" in what Helmholtz calls inference may simply consist in the disposition of A ideas to trigger B ideas—what I have called a constant conjunction of beliefs. In that case, the difference between Helmholtz and Berkeley would be merely verbal.

*Nichols.* Ryan Nichols distinguishes two types of acquired perception in Reid: *inferential* perception (really an oxymoron, given that there is no reasoning in perception), in which one makes a conscious inductive inference from some perceived quality A to a further quality B, and *habituated* perception, in which the perception of a thing as being A makes one automatically believe it to be B, owing to the subject's previous history of inferential perceptions that a thing is B based on its being A (2007:233–34). If these two types are exhaustive, it follows that all acquired perception is built on previous inference. However, despite this implication, I do not believe Nichols intends to force an inferential model on Reid. On page 235, he seems to want to keep the possibility of an associationist model open.

## B. IS ACQUIRED PERCEPTION REALLY PERCEPTION?

Acquired perception is a powerful means of gaining information through the senses, but is it really *perception*? We cannot let the issue be decided by Reid's name for the phenomenon. A toy gun is not a gun, and artificial teeth are not teeth. By contrast, a toy block is a block, and artificial illumination is illumination.[1] My question is whether acquired perception is like artificial illumination or artificial teeth.

Berkeley's answer to this question is clear and explicit:

> In short, those things alone are actually and strictly perceived by any sense, which would have been perceived, in case that same sense had then been first conferred on us. (DHP, 1975:194 or 1948:204)

By this criterion, what we perceive only with the help of learning we do not strictly perceive at all. Had we just now been given sight without any opportunity to learn correlations between the visible and the tangible, sight would afford us no clue of distance or three-dimensional shape. Berkeley unhesitatingly concludes that these properties are not strictly perceived by sight.[2]

Reid's answer to our question is more equivocal. After describing several apparent instances of acquired perception—for example, a farmer's apprehension that his neighbor's cattle have broken loose, based on the down-trodden state of his corn—he remarks,

> These are instances of common understanding, which dwells so near to perception, that it is difficult to trace the line which divides the one from the other. (IHM 6.20:173)[3]

---

[1] Thanks to Roy Sorensen (personal communication) for these examples.

[2] To be sure, Berkeley has a broad sense of "perceive" in which we may be said to perceive anything that is suggested to our imagination by a sensible cue, including the shame in another's soul when it is suggested by a blush and even God when we are made to think of him by the word "God." But things perceived in this broad sense are not *immediately* perceived, and Berkeley insists that only things immediately perceived are sensible things, or things perceived by the senses. "By *sensible things* I mean those only which are perceived by sense, and that in truth the senses perceive nothing which they do not perceive immediately" (DHP, 1975:164 or 1948:174).

[3] In Reid's examples in this paragraph, the various facts "perceived" are all facts about the recent past. Elsewhere, he says perception always has a present object (EIP 1.1:23, lines 1–9) For this reason, I am not sure whether he would regard these instances of quasi-perceptual "common understanding" as cases of acquired perception.

In another passage, he describes a case in which he at first mistook a nearby seagull on a foggy beach for a man on horseback half a mile off. (Fog throws off our acquired perceptions of distance). He observes,

> The mistake made on this occasion, and the correction of it, are both so sudden, that we are at a loss whether to call them by the name of *judgment*, or by that of *simple perception*. (IHM 6.22:183)

In yet another passage, he calls the whole question I am raising a verbal one:

> [When a kind of judgment becomes habitual] it very much resembles the original perceptions of our sense, and may not improperly be called *acquired perception*. Whether we call it judgment or acquired perception is a verbal difference. (EIP 2.14:182)

Even if Reid refused to answer my question, is there an answer he *ought* to have given in light of his other commitments? Rebecca Copenhaver has forcefully argued that Reidian acquired perception in no way falls short of genuine perception (2010). I offer five arguments to the contrary.

*First argument: acquired perception is not immediate.* One of the hallmarks of perception for Reid is that it is *immediate*. Here is his official threefold account of perception again:

> If, therefore, we attend to that act of our mind which we call the perception of an external object of sense, we shall find in it these three things. *First*, Some conception or notion of the object perceived. *Secondly*, A strong and irresistible conviction and belief of its present existence. And, *thirdly*, That this conviction and belief are immediate, and not the effect of reasoning. (EIP 2.5:96, and repeated elsewhere)

If it turns out that acquired perception is not immediate in the requisite sense, we will have the materials for the following syllogism:

1. All genuine perception is immediate perception.
2. No acquired perception is immediate perception.
3. Therefore, no acquired perception is genuine perception.

What, then, is the requisite sense? What all does Reid mean by calling perception (or the belief involved therein) *immediate*?

Much of the time, Reid simply means that no reasoning or inference is involved, psychologically speaking. There is no marshaling of premises and drawing of conclusions. If this is all he ever means by immediacy, the syllogism above would have a false minor premise. As discussed in the preceding section, even if inference is part of the process by which acquired perception is developed, once the habit is fully acquired, the inference is no longer there. The transition from sensory sign to perceptual belief in the thing signified has become fully automated, and no vestiges of reasoning remain.

Nonetheless, there is another sense in which it is arguable that genuine perception is immediate for Reid and acquired perception not. Genuine perception is immediate in an *epistemic* sense: deliverances of perception are *immediately justified*, that is, justified without deriving their justification from any other beliefs. In Reid's favored terminology, deliverances of perception are first principles. But acquired perceptions do not seem to be like that. Even though my perceptual belief that the bell I am hearing is large is psychologically noninferential, it is justified only because on many past occasions when I heard similar sounds, I knew by sight or touch that they came from a large bell.[4] Had I not been justified on those sundry occasions in what I believed about the source of the sound, I would not be justified now. Thus my current belief is not epistemically immediate.

On this point, I agree with Nichols:

> Habituated perceptual beliefs . . . depend for their justification upon other perceptual beliefs upstream in the belief-forming and habit-forming processes. In this sense, habituated perceptual beliefs could not serve as basic beliefs in a foundationalist theory of the structure of empirical knowledge. (2007:237)[5]

However, Nichols and I do not agree on the other premise in the argument from immediacy—that *all* genuine perception is epistemically immediate. He maintains that Reid is an epistemic direct realist—one who holds that the deliverances of perception are epistemically basic or immediately justified—*only* as regards the

---

[4] What I mean by "perceptual belief" in this sentence is the belief that is an ingredient in perception in Reid's threefold account. I am departing from the terminology of Copenhaver, who uses "perceptual belief" for a further belief based on the perception.

[5] For further reinforcement of this point, see Pollock's discussion (1974:60–64) of "the principle of implicit reasons," according to which our justification for believing things may derive from general propositions that we may never have articulated and the supporting instances for which we no longer specifically recall, provided our past observation of the instances played a causal role in generating our present belief.

Abelard Podgorski has pointed out to me that in holding that the justification of acquired perceptual beliefs depends on justification one possessed in the past, I am implicitly rejecting the principle that justification supervenes on one's current intrinsic state. That is all right with me, since for reasons given in Huemer 1999, we must reject that principle anyway to have an adequate theory of memory knowledge.

deliverances of original perception. In the inconsistent triad {*all perception is imme-diate perception, acquired perception is not immediate perception, acquired perception is perception*}, we both accept the second proposition, but he chooses to deny the first and I the third. Since the matter is controversial, I do not rest my case on the argu-ment from immediacy.

*Second argument: I do not perceive my upstairs wife.* In previous work, I advanced the following example as a conundrum for Reid's theory of perception:

> I return home and see my wife's car keys on the counter, whereupon I automatically conceive of her and believe that she is home. Since she is upstairs, I do not perceive her, but it seems that I fulfill all the conditions for [acquired] perception. (Van Cleve 2004a:127)

This example can be made the basis of the following argument:

1. I have an acquired perception of my wife on the occasion of seeing her keys.
2. In fact, I do not perceive her on that occasion.
3. Therefore, not all cases of acquired perception are cases of perception.

Some friends and interpreters of Reid have taken exception to the first premise. Nichols opposes it on the ground that the example is out of character with Reid's other examples of acquired perception (2007:232),[6] and Copenhaver opposes it on the ground that my wife does not enter into the content of my car-key perception in the way she holds to be required for bona fide acquired perception (2010:305–6).[7] Yet it seems to me that my critics must concede that the example contains all the ingredients that Reid ever lists as necessary for acquired perception. I do have a con-ception of my wife, I do believe in her present and nearby existence, my conception and belief have been produced in me by the past association between seeing her keys and subsequently seeing her in the flesh, and my conception and belief now arise in me as automatically as the conception and belief in any other case of acquired

---

[6] See Reid's examples at IHM, p. 173, however, for examples not far removed from my own.

[7] Copenhaver develops a threefold distinction among beliefs *ingredient* in perception, beliefs for-med on the *basis* of perception, and beliefs *inferred* from perception (2010:287–89). She regards the belief that one's spouse is home as a belief belonging to the middle category—a belief formed on the basis of perceiving the keys (304–6). However, she also explicitly argues that beliefs that initially belong to categories two or three may migrate (in the development of acquired percep-tion) into category one—they may become perceptual contents or beliefs ingredient in percep-tion, as happens when someone becomes expert at spotting counterfeit coins. I should like to know from Copenhaver what, if anything according to her, keeps belief in my upstairs wife from becoming a perceptual content

perception.[8] If this is *not* a case of acquired perception, it must be because there are conditions of acquired perception that are yet to be articulated.

One additional condition to propose on Reid's behalf might be this: in acquired perception, the signifying item and the signified item must be *qualities of the same object*. This would rule out perceiving my wife by perceiving her keys, since my wife is not a quality of the keys.[9] It would also rule out kindred cases such as seeing the fire behind the ridge by seeing the smoke produced by it.

Even with that condition in play, however, it will be possible to generate examples of acquired perception that we may well hesitate to classify as perception. A color-blind motorist can see that a traffic light is red by seeing that the illuminated light is the one in the top position. Here the signifying quality (place) and the signified quality (color) are qualities of the same object, so our motorist satisfies our latest condition for having an acquired perception of the color of the light. But does he perceive the redness of the light? No, for he is colorblind.[10]

The car-key example in my 2004a was not meant in the first instance to be a counterexample to "all acquired perception is perception" as a Reidian thesis. It could not be a counterexample to that, since the reasons for thinking that the example satisfies all the conditions for having an acquired perception of my wife—that I conceive of her and so on—are also reasons for thinking that the example satisfies all Reid's conditions for having a perception of her *simpliciter*. The example is instead a counterexample to Reid's account of perception at large, indicating that his standard threefold account either leaves out some crucial ingredient in perception or else fails to make explicit some way in which one of the included ingredients is to be understood. My suggestion in 2004a (which I reaffirm here) was that Reid should be understood thus: the conception that is involved in perception must be *conception of the acquaintance variety*. It must not merely be conception of something by

---

[8] What of Reid's requirement that the belief that is an ingredient in perception be *irresistible*? If that rules out acquired perception of my upstairs wife, it also rules out many of Reid's own examples of acquired perception—for instance, that this is the handwriting of such-and-such a friend (IHM 6.20:172). Perhaps I can resist believing that my wife is home by supposing she has been kidnapped, but so likewise can I resist believing that this is her handwriting by supposing it to be a clever forgery.

[9] Someone could run around the proposed restriction by saying my keys have a "wife-is-home-y" quality about them. Being such that my wife is home is a property of the keys—albeit a "Cambridge property"—signified by their being on the counter. If the requirement that signifying qualities and signified qualities must belong to the same object is to do the work desired of it, then, we will have to require as well that Cambridge properties not be among the signified qualities.

[10] If you doubt that the colorblind person can *conceive* of redness, assume that he once had normal vision and acquired the ability to conceive of redness at that time. Not all colorblindness is congenital.

means of some description it satisfies. That is why I do not perceive my wife on the occasion of seeing her keys: though I may conceive of her under some description, I am not acquainted with her in any way, shape, or form.

Instead of acquaintance, why not appeal to the epistemic immediacy discussed above, saying that genuine perception must be epistemically immediate and my acquired perception of my wife is not? That seems right to me, but it cannot be the full story. Epistemic properties supervene on nonepistemic properties, and we would have to say what the relevant nonepistemic properties are. Perhaps genuine perception is epistemically immediate precisely because it incorporates acquaintance.

I went on to suggest in 2004a (and I urge again now) that with the acquaintance requirement on perception, few cases of acquired perception qualify as perception. Thus even if the car-key example does not underwrite the simple 1–2–3 argument above, it does serve in the end to motivate the claim that not all acquired perception is perception.

*Third argument: I do not perceive by sight the heat of the poker.* One of the remarkable features of acquired perception is that it enables us to jump across sensory modalities, perceiving by one sense qualities that were originally given only to another. As Reid tells us,

> We learn to perceive, by one sense, what originally could have been perceived only by another, by finding a connection between the objects of the different senses. (EIP 2.21:236)

> [By means of acquired perception] we often discover by one sense things which are properly and naturally the objects of another. Thus I can say without impropriety, I hear a drum, I hear a great bell, or I hear a small bell; though it is certain that the figure or size of the sounding body is not originally an object of hearing. (EIP 2.14:182)

Berkeley gives another example of the same phenomenon—seeing the heat of a red-hot bar of iron when the heat of the iron is "suggested to the imagination by the colour and figure, which are properly perceived by that sense" (DHP, 1975:194 or 1948:204).[11]

Using this example to explicate what Berkeley means by "immediate" when he says we do not perceive distance immediately, George Pitcher writes as follows:

> A person, when he views a red, glowing poker that has just been taken from a roaring furnace . . . sees *that* the poker is very hot, but he does not really see the heat itself. . . .

---

[11] Berkeley actually speaks of "being said to see a red-hot iron bar," but it is clear from the context that he means to discuss the sense in which one sees the heat of the bar, not just the sense in which one sees a bar that is hot.

Just so, Berkeley tells us, a person can see that something is located at such-and-such a distance from him; but he cannot see the distance.... To say that we do not literally see the heat of the poker ... is to say that the visual manifold of which we are aware when we see a hot poker does not contain any heat in it. Similarly, to say that we do not literally see the distance of objects is to say that the visual manifold of which we are aware when we see them does not contain distance. (1977:7–8)

Pitcher is endorsing Berkeley's own view as quoted earlier—that we actually and strictly perceive by any sense only those things we would perceive if that same sense had then been first conferred on us.

Drawing on examples of this sort, we may now construct another argument for the thesis that not all acquired perception is perception:

1. There are some properties that are proper to a given sense, as heat is to touch: they cannot be strictly perceived by any other sense.
2. We sometimes have acquired perceptions through one sense of qualities proper to another.
3. Therefore, we sometimes have acquired perceptions that are not strictly perceptions.

This argument seems intuitively compelling to me, and I let it stand without further comment on its merits.

I take this opportunity to discuss another issue prompted by Pitcher—the relationship between the original/acquired distinction and a further distinction invoked in Pitcher's remarks. Pitcher is willing to allow that we see *that* the poker is hot, but not that we see the heat itself. Implicit here is a distinction between *propositional* perception and *objectual* perception. Propositional perception is perception *that p*, for example, perception that O is F. Objectual perception is perception simply *of O* (an object) or of *the Fness of O* (a quality of an object), where these do not resolve into propositional perception.[12]

With this distinction in mind, let's look again at a passage from Reid:

Our perceptions are of two kinds: some are natural and original, others acquired, and the fruit of experience. When I perceive that this is the taste of cyder, that of brandy;

---

[12] Some people use "S sees the Fness of O" as a stylistic variant of "S sees that O is F" (as in "Tom saw the hopelessness of his situation.") In addition, some philosophers allow that "S sees O" is a permissible locution, but only if it is analyzable as "∃F(S sees that O is F)." What I mean by objectual perception is perception of O (or the Fness of O) that is not equivalent, whether by stylistic variance or philosophical analysis, to anything propositional.

that this is the smell of an apple, that of an orange; that this is the noise of thunder, that the ringing of bells; this the sound of a coach passing, that the voice of such a friend; these perceptions and others of the same kind, are not original, they are acquired. But the perception which I have by touch, of the hardness and softness of bodies, of their extension, figure, and motion, is not acquired, it is original. (IHM 6.20:171)

It is striking that every one of Reid's examples of acquired perception in this passage is a case of propositional perception, while each of his examples of original perception is a case of objectual perception. Are the two distinctions aligned in Reid's thought—is every case of original perception a case of objectual perception and every case of acquired perception a case of propositional perception?[13]

The answer to the first question is *no*. Reid's language indicates that there may be propositional perception in regard to the objects of original perception—for example, "we perceive visible objects to have extension in two dimensions" (EIP 6.21:236), and I may perceive "that there is in my hand a hard smooth body of a spherical figure" (EIP 6.21:237). Of course, we may also have objectual perceptions of the objects and qualities that are constituents of those propositions.

The answer to the second question is harder to determine. There are passages in which Reid does use objectual locutions to refer to acquired perceptions—for example, hearing the size of a bell (EIP 2.14:182) and seeing the weight of a sheep (IHM 6.20:172).[14] But insofar as people sometimes use objectual locutions as stylistic variants of propositional ones, these passages do not settle the question. Reid might speak of the butcher's seeing the weight of the sheep even if he thinks that strictly speaking, the butcher only sees *that* the sheep weighs so much.[15] So the answer to the second question is not clear.

It is a thesis worthy of consideration that whereas genuine perception may take either an objectual or a propositional form, acquired perception may take a

[13] Reid probably meant the distinction between original and acquired perception to be exhaustive, but he overlooked an intermediate case. Suppose that some years after my birth, someone programs my brain so that upon smelling a certain scent, I automatically believe that there are oranges nearby. The resulting perception would be neither original (because it does not arise in me by my native constitution) nor acquired (because it is not acquired by experience).

[14] He actually says the butcher "knows by sight" the weight of his sheep, but in the other examples in the same paragraph, he uses "perceives by his eye" and "sees" as though all three were equivalent.

[15] Compare this remark from an unpublished manuscript from 1758: "In this case [in which the place of a coach is suggested by the sound it makes] it is not proper to say I hear the place of it but I perceive it to be in such a place by the Sound" (IHM:327).

propositional form only.[16] If the thesis were true, it would give us one more reason for thinking that acquired perception is not genuine perception.

*Fourth argument: errors in acquired perception are not errors of the senses.* Perhaps the best case for thinking acquired perception is not perception in Reid's opinion is to be found in EIP 2.22, "Of the fallacy of the senses." The purpose of this chapter is to refute the opinion of those philosophers who maintain that the senses are systematically fallacious, or at any rate, that they often deceive us. Reid admits that the senses *sometimes* deceive us, his leading example being the case of phantom pain felt in a limb no longer possessed (EIP 2.18:214 and 2.22:251). But he maintains that *most* so-called fallacies of the senses are not fallacies of the senses at all; they are errors, but not errors of the senses proper.

Reid distinguishes four classes of alleged errors of the senses, of which only the fourth class contains errors of the senses properly so called (such as pain felt in a phantom limb). The first class is described (and dismissed) in the following paragraph:

> Many things called deceptions of the senses are only conclusions rashly drawn from the testimony of the senses. . . . Thus, when a man has taken a counterfeit guinea for a true one, he says his senses deceived him; but he lays the blame where it ought not to be laid: For we may ask him, Did your sense give a false testimony of the colour, or of the figure, or of the impression? No. But this is all that they testified, and this they testified truly: From these premises you concluded that it was a true guinea, but this conclusion does not follow. (EIP 2.22:244)

Note that the only qualities Reid mentions here as being testified to by the senses are color, figure, and impression. These are all on the list of original objects of perception.[17] In other nearby places, he uses interchangeably the expressions "what our senses testify" and "what we perceive."[18] So it is tempting to generalize from the guinea example to the

---

[16] A. D. Smith quotes Merleau-Ponty as saying that we hear the solidity of the cobbles in the sound of a carriage that is passing over them (2002:144). He notes that this is a case of what Reid would classify as acquired perception, and he says that Merleau-Ponty's claim is true only in the sense that we hear *that* the cobbles are solid. I take Smith to be affirming my thesis.

[17] Color and figure are objects of original perception by sight. I am not sure what he means by "impression." Perhaps he means the pattern impressed on the coin, which would be an original object of sight in two dimensions and of touch in three, or perhaps he means its heft, which would be an original object of touch.

[18] For example, at EIP 6.22:246, he says "Our senses testify only the change of situation of one body in relation to other bodies" and restates this one sentence later as "It is only the relative motions of bodies that we perceive."

Note that Reid's reason for denying that there are errors of the senses is not the same as that of Descartes, who says in Meditation Three that sensations cannot be in error because they do not tell us anything. Reidian original perceptions do tell us something.

claim that the only objects we strictly perceive are the objects we originally perceive. Putting it the other way around, acquired perception is not perception strictly speaking.

The second class of alleged errors of the senses are errors we make in our acquired perceptions. Reid tells us that if acquired perception could be resolved into some form of reasoning, this class would reduce to the first class along with the false guinea, but since he thinks acquired perception "results from some part of our constitution distinct from reason," he makes it a class of its own (EIP 2.22:247). In any case, Reid maintains "that the errors of acquired perception are not properly fallacies of our senses" (EIP 2.22:247). For example, if I am deceived by a clever painter into believing that a flat patch on canvas is really a sphere, I am in error, but my error lies not in original but in acquired perception. The objects of original perception—the light and colors—are distributed just as my senses say they are.

What Reid unequivocally affirms here is that *errors in acquired perception are not errors of the senses*. This provides the take-off point for the following argument:

1. No error in acquired perception is an error of the senses (premise).
2. If every acquired perception is an exercise of the senses, then every error in acquired perception is an error (in an exercise) of the senses. (This is a logical truth; compare DeMorgan's "If every horse is an animal, then every head of a horse is a head of an animal.")
3. Therefore, not every acquired perception is an exercise of the senses (from 1 and 2).
4. Every genuine perception is an exercise of the senses (premise).
5. Therefore, not every acquired perception is a genuine perception (from 3 and 4).

That argument seems to me decisive. However, as noted above, Copenhaver stands on the opposite side of the issue, holding that acquired perception *is* in all cases perception. She has sought to defuse the textual argument based on premise 1 above by proposing that "error of sense" is a technical term for Reid. She takes it to refer specifically to errors in original perception. This proposal apparently keeps the door open for saying that errors in acquired perception, though not errors of sense in the technical sense, can nonetheless be cases of misperception, as required by her view. However, her proposal does nothing to block the argument as I have stated it. The premises are 1, 2, and 4, and her proposal leaves all of them standing.[19]

---

[19] Perhaps one could maintain that if "error of sense" has a technical meaning in Reid, one cannot drop the parenthetical expression in my premise 2, shortening "error in an exercise of the senses" to "error of the senses." I need take no stand on that. I can stay with the longer formulation of premise 2, under which it is a logical truth. And I can rewrite premise 1 as "No error in acquired perception is an error in an exercise of the senses" to make it engage with premise 2. It is clear from his remarks at EIP 2.22:247 that Reid would assert 1 in either the longer or the shorter version.

The question of whether acquired perception is genuine perception has been reincarnated in contemporary philosophy of mind as the question of whether so-called higher-level properties (properties such as being a pine tree or being an apple, which are not on Reid's list of objects of original perception) can be *represented* in perception. That is, can such properties belong to the contents of perception proper and not just to the contents of beliefs formed on the basis of perception? Susanna Siegel (2006) offers the following test question as a diagnostic for determining one's stand: if you are taken in by a bowl of wax fruit, is your error an error in perception or an error in accompanying belief? If your visual experience represents only colors and shapes, you have made an error in belief; if it represents apples and pears, you have made an error in perception.[20] It seems to me that in his discussion of the fake apple made of turf, Reid has given as explicit an answer as one could like to Siegel's question: your error is an error in belief, not in perception (EIP 2.22:245).

*Fifth argument: speak with the vulgar, but think with the learned.* For my final argument, I let Reid speak for himself:

> Acquired perception is not properly the testimony of those senses which God hath given us, but a conclusion drawn from what the senses testify. . . . The appearance of the sign immediately produces the belief of its usual attendant, and *we think we perceive* the one as well as the other. [emphasis added]
>
> That such conclusions are formed even in infancy, no man can doubt; nor is it less certain that they are confounded with the natural and immediate perceptions of sense, and in all languages are called by the same name. We are therefore authorized by language to call them perception, and must often do so, or speak unintelligibly. But philosophy teaches us in this, as in many other instances, to distinguish things which the vulgar confound. I have therefore given the name of acquired perception to such conclusions, to distinguish them from what is naturally, originally, and immediately testified by our senses. (EIP 2.22:247)

Gone now is the equivocating of the passages cited above. Reid all but says that in calling acquired perception "perception," we are speaking with the vulgar. When we think with the learned, we acknowledge that acquired perception is not perception proper.[21]

---

[20] In this context, Copenhaver remarks, "It is precisely because we are perceptually sensitive to such features as 'being a tomato' and 'being a quarter' that we may be misled by wax vegetables and counterfeits." I do not see why that is so. Even if the content of my perception were limited to colors and shapes, could it not still mislead me into believing falsely that there is a tomato in the bowl?

[21] Compare EAP 3.3:208, where Reid says that to make himself understood by the vulgar, the Copernican philosopher will happily say that the sun rises and sets.

## C. ARE SECONDARY QUALITIES OBJECTS OF ACQUIRED PERCEPTION ONLY?

As discussed in the previous chapter, Reid upholds the distinction between primary and secondary qualities, but he rejects two traditional ways of drawing it. *Pace* Locke, it is not true that primary qualities resemble our sensations while secondaries do not; *pace* Berkeley's Hylas, it is not true that primary qualities are mind-independent while secondaries are not. Both sets of qualities are mind-independent, and neither set resembles anything in our minds. But in Reid's view, there is a basis for drawing the distinction nonetheless:

> Our senses give us a direct and a distinct notion of the primary qualities, and inform us what they are in themselves: But of the secondary qualities, our senses give us only a relative and obscure notion. They inform us only, that they are qualities that . . . produce in us a certain sensation. (EIP 2.17:201)

Some commentators, including Lehrer and Smith (1985:27–28), Lehrer (1989: 36–37), Nichols (2007:224), and Buras (2009:348ff.) attribute to Reid the thesis that all perception of secondary qualities is acquired perception.[22] One piece of evidence for their attribution is the following passage:

> Three of our senses, to wit, smell, taste, and hearing, originally give us only certain sensations, and a conviction that these sensations are occasioned by some external object. We give a name to that quality of the object by which it is fitted to produce such a sensation, and connect that quality with the object, and with its other qualities.
>
> Thus we learn, that a certain sensation of smell is produced by a rose; and that quality in the rose, by which it is fitted to produce this sensation, we call the smell of the rose. Here it is evident that the sensation is original. The perception, that the rose has that quality, which we call its smell, is acquired. In like manner, we learn all those qualities in bodies, which we call their smell, their taste, their sound. (EIP 2.21:235)

Reid does indeed seem to say here that at least *three* classes of secondary qualities—smells, tastes, and sounds—are perceived only via acquired perception. But are we entitled to generalize this claim to *all* secondary qualities?

---

[22] Incidentally, I disagree with the contention in Lehrer and Smith 1985 that secondary quality perception depends for Reid on the inductive principle. Induction is applicable only when we have past knowledge of items of both the types that induction connects, but this is not true in the case of sensations and secondary qualities. What secondary quality perception depends on is the causal principle, not the inductive principle.

I think not. The outstanding exception is *color*, which Reid certainly regards as a secondary quality (EIP 2.17:201) and which he lists among the original objects of sight in the *Inquiry*: "By [sight] we perceive originally the visible figure and colour of bodies only, and their visible place" (IHM 6.20:171). Confounding the issue, however, is the fact, noted by Nichols (224), that Reid omits color when he comes to list the original objects of sight in the *Intellectual Powers*:

> By [sight] we perceive visible objects to have extension in two dimensions, to have visible figure and magnitude, and a certain angular distance from one another. These I conceive are the original perceptions of sight. (EIP 2.21:236)

Does this signal any change of view on his part?

Again, I think not. For one thing, it is quite possible that Reid's pronoun "these" in the sentence quoted is meant to refer back not just to the qualities mentioned in the previous sentence, but to color, which was mentioned in the sentence just before that.[23] For another and more decisive thing, Reid clearly implies later on the same page that color is originally perceived. Speaking of a sphere that we now know (by acquired perception) to be three-dimensional, he says "The eye originally could only perceive two dimensions, and a gradual variation of colour on the different sides of the object" (EIP 2.21:236, lines 26–28; see also lines 36–37 on the same page).

So there is at least one secondary quality, color, that we perceive originally.[24] Are there others? I advance the following conjecture: if our senses enable us to *localize* a secondary quality (as they do in the case of colors, textures, and temperatures), we may have original perceptions regarding it. To see what lies behind the conjecture, look back at the quotation about the rose. By our original constitution, when we smell a rose, we know that some quality of some external object is causing our sensation—we just do not know

---

[23] Here is the sentence: "By sight, we learn to distinguish objects by their colour, in the same manner as by their sound, taste, and smell." What makes the matter ambiguous is that sound, taste, and smell are also mentioned in the same breath.

[24] Buras maintains that perception of *all* secondary qualities is acquired because we must learn that the cause of sensations of a given type lies in an *external* object, even if we believe innately that sensations have *some* cause (2009). In support of this contention, he cites the *experimentum crucis* of IHM 5.6, where Reid says the subject of the experiment would have no idea whether the cause of his sensations lay in body or spirit. Yes—but that subject is not one of us; his hardwiring has been stripped away. Human beings *do* believe by their original constitution that their sensations have not only causes, but external causes. Witness: "Three of our senses, to wit, smell, taste, and hearing, originally give us only certain sensations, and a conviction that these sensations are occasioned by some external object" (EIP 2.21:235). "In smelling, and in hearing, we have a sensation or impression upon the mind, which, by our constitution, we conceive to be a sign of something external" (IHM 6.8:99).

what object or where. It takes repeated experience and induction to let us know that the quality (i.e., the cause of the fragrant sensations we are getting) resides in a rose. At that point, we have acquired perception: we can perceive by smell that a rose is in the room, even if we have not yet seen or touched it. With color, we do not need to go through any such process to learn where the external cause of our sensation lies. That is because the same retinal excitations that give us sensations of color also make us believe that the cause of them lies in a certain direction. According to a law of vision Reid formulates, we always see any point of an object as lying along the line passing from the retinal point stimulated by it back through the center of the eye and into ambient space. (See IHM 6.12:122–23 for Reid's statement of the law and chapter 7 below for further discussion of it.) Owing to this law, we have an innate ability to localize the distal causes of our color sensations. We have no such innate ability to localize the causes of our olfactory sensations.[25]

Are there any other secondary-quality sensations that should be grouped with color rather than smell in this regard? Yes: heat and cold. When we feel a surface to be warm or cold, we do not merely have a certain sensation and believe it to have an external quality somewhere as its cause; we know that the cause is right here, at the ends of our fingertips. The same is true of rough and smooth, if they count as secondary qualities.[26]

Apart from the matter of localization, there is another way in which I think Lehrer, Smith, and the others may be too hasty in declaring secondary qualities to be objects of acquired perception only. What Reid gives as an example of acquired perception in regard to smell is "the perception, that the rose has that quality, which we call its smell." That leaves open the possibility that we have an original perception to the effect that *some* quality exists that is causing our sensation or, more colloquially, that a certain scent is in the air. Perhaps (though it seems a stretch) one could even be said to have an objectual perception of the scent or quality itself, without knowing where it resides. In one or both of these latter two ways, there could be original perceptions of all secondary qualities, including those that are not innately localized.

That is a welcome result for me, since it provides a way out of an inconsistency in Reid that might threaten to arise on my interpretation otherwise. According

---

[25] Some animals, such as wide-nostriled mushroom-hunting pigs, do have the ability to localize smells. As what Reid regards as matter of contingent fact, humans have no such ability.

[26] I am not sure whether they do. They supervene, of course, on primary qualities—the hardness of an object and its figure at a fine level of resolution. But I do not think our senses give us any very determinate notion of the configuration responsible for the roughness or smoothness we feel, and that fact would make textures secondary qualities in Reid's scheme.

One more example of a localized secondary quality may be mentioned: *pain*. In its principal sense, pain is a sensation, but there is also a sense in which we perceive pain as some unknown disorder in our toe causing the sensation (IHM 6.21:175).

to Lehrer, Smith, and the others, (1) secondary qualities are objects of acquired perception only. According to me, (2) acquired perception is not perception. Yet according to Reid himself, (3) secondary qualities are objects of perception—after all, EIP 2.17 is entitled "Of the Objects of Perception; and first, of primary and secondary Qualities." The problem is that (1), (2), and (3) form an inconsistent triad; at least they do so if (2) is read strongly as "*no* acquired perception is perception." Some of my arguments in section B above establish only the weaker thesis that *not all* acquired perception is perception, and if I retreated to that thesis, the inconsistency would be averted. But even with the stronger version of (2), inconsistency would be averted if, as I propose in this section, Reid does not embrace (1).

A deeper potential contradiction about secondary qualities is identified and addressed below in section F.

## D. DOES ACQUIRED PERCEPTION ALTER THE CONTENT OF OUR ORIGINAL PERCEPTIONS?

Originally, I perceive a sphere only as a variegated disk and a certain type of bird only as a slow flutter of gray and white. Subsequently, I have the acquired perception of the disk as a sphere and the moving patches of color as a mockingbird. Do my original perceptions survive as ingredients in the enriched perception? Or are they transformed into or superseded by something else?[27]

As a preliminary to determining Reid's answer to this question, let us consider Locke's answer, which he presents under the heading "Ideas of Sensation often changed by the Judgment":

> *The Ideas we receive by sensation, are often* in grown People *alter'd by the Judgment*, without our taking notice of it. When we set before our Eyes a round Globe, of any uniform colour . . . 'tis certain, that the *Idea* thereby imprinted in our Mind, is of a flat Circle variously shadow'd, with several degrees of Light and Brightness coming to our Eyes. But we having by use been accustomed to perceive, what kind of appearance convex Bodies are wont to make in us; . . . the Judgment presently, by an habitual custom, alters the Appearances into their Causes: So that from that, which truly is variety of shadow or colour, collecting the Figure, it makes it pass for a mark of Figure, and frames to its self the perception of a convex Figure, and an uniform Colour; when the

---

[27] They survive, say Titchener and the structural psychologists of the early twentieth century. They are superseded, say Köhler and the Gestalt psychologists. The debate is reprised in Firth 1949 and Lewis 1966, Lewis siding with the structuralists and Firth with the Gestalt school.

Idea we receive from thence, is only a Plain variously colour'd, as is evident in Painting. (ECHU 2.9.8–10:145)[28]

That seems to be an unequivocal answer to our question—sensation is altered by learning and judgment. But does Locke really mean it? I think not. In the first place, there can hardly be any question of a two-dimensional object somehow morphing into a three-dimensional object. Dimension is a topological invariant; if the original cue does not survive, that must be because it is replaced, not altered. In the second place, not even the talk of replacement accurately expresses Locke's view if such talk is taken literally. Scrolling ahead to Locke's more careful statement of what he is getting at, we read:

[The judging of shape from shadow] is performed so constantly, and so quick, that we take that for the Perception of our Sensation, which is an *Idea* formed by our Judgment; so that one, *viz*. that of Sensation, serves only to excite the other, and is scarce taken notice of it self; as a Man who reads or hears with attention and understanding, takes little notice of the Characters, or Sounds, but of the *Ideas*, that are excited in him by them. (146)

And therefore 'tis not so strange, that our Mind should often change the *Idea* of its Sensation into that of its Judgment, and make one serve only to excite the other, without our taking notice of it. (147)

Although Locke uses the language of "changing" one more time, the surrounding commentary makes clear that it is not to be taken literally. The original cues are "scarce taken notice of," but like the letters on a page, they are still there.

Turning now to Reid, we find that his view of the matter is substantially the same as Locke's:

It is experience that teaches me that the variation of colour is an effect of spherical convexity, and of the distribution of light and shade. So rapid is the progress of the thought, from the effect to the cause, that we attend only to the last, and can hardly be persuaded that we do not immediately see the three dimensions of the sphere. (EIP 6.21:236)

He even uses the same example of words or characters, comparing sensory cues to "the words of a language, wherein we do not attend to the sound, but to the sense" (IHM 2.9:43 and elsewhere). It appears, then, that the objects of original perception

---

[28] Interestingly, Locke's discussion of this issue is the context in which he poses and answers Molyneux's question. Locke's answer is *no*: the newly sighted person would not recognize what he saw as a globe or a cube because he would not yet have connected the two-dimensional objects he sees with the three-dimensional objects he knows by touch.

are still present in richer states of acquired perception. It is just that we do not attend to them.

Yet there are passages in which Reid tantalizes us by pulling us in the opposite direction:

> Nay, it may be observed, that, in this case, the acquired perception *in a manner* effaces the original one; for the sphere is seen to be of one uniform colour, though originally there would have appeared a gradual variation of colour. (EIP 6.21:236, emphasis added)

> There are many phaenomena of a similar nature [to double vision due to lack of focus], which shew, that the mind may not attend to, and thereby, *in some sort*, not perceive objects that strike the senses. (IHM 6.13:135, emphasis added)

> Custom, by a kind of legerdemain, withdraws gradually these original and proper objects of sight, and substitutes in their place objects of touch, which have length, breadth, and thickness, and a determinate distance from the eye. (IHM 6.20:167)

What are to we make of these passages?

For a potentially illuminating parallel, we may consider the recently much investigated topic of inattentional blindness (Mack and Rock 1998). I invite any readers who are unfamiliar with this phenomenon to seek out a demonstration of it, easily available on the Internet, before reading on.[29]

In one famous demonstration, subjects are asked to view a video of two interspersed teams passing basketballs back and forth. They are asked to count how many times the ball changes hands among members of the white-shirted team. With their minds thus occupied, over 50 percent of subjects do not notice what they are amazed to see on a replay: that someone wearing a gorilla suit has strolled right through the midst of the basketball players and thumped his chest. This is an example of the "blindness" we sometimes have to objects to which we do not attend.

My suggestion is that once a cue has become a sign for us in the acquired perception of something else, we often become inattentionally blind to it. Of course, this proposal may simply be a case of *obscurum per obscurius*, replacing one imponderable question by another. Did I see the gorilla or not? It was right there before my eyes; yet in some sense I was oblivious to it.

Reid's answer, I believe, is that we are still aware of the cues—even though they are "in a manner" effaced and even though "in some sort" we do not perceive them. It is a measure of the perplexingness of the phenomenon that Reid uses such equivocal language, but I believe we can construct a respectable Reidian case that we are still conscious of the cues.

---

[29] Try youtube.com/watch?v = vJG698U2Mvo&feature=player_embedded.

One argument that awareness of the cues remains is physiological. The cue or sign in acquired perception may be either a sensation or something originally perceived (EIP 621:237). Suppose it is a sensation. For Reid, connections between physical impressions and mental sensations are part of our original constitution and are therefore not undoable by learning or shifts in attention. If we have the same stimulus again, we shall have the same sensation again. (This is a principle that was made famous by Helmholtz a century later.) The physical causes of sensations to which we no longer attend are still there, and therefore the sensations are still there. Moreover, we never have a sensation according to Reid without being conscious of it (IHM 6.21:175, last three lines). It follows that sensational signs we no longer attend to, even if we are in some sense blind to them, are still there before our consciousness.[30]

The same argument can be extended to cover cases in which the sign is something originally perceived. This is because Reid holds (i) that the laws connecting sensations with original perceptions are as much a part of our constitution as laws connecting physical impressions with sensations (IHM 6.21:174), and (ii) that there is no such thing as an unconscious perception (EIP 2.15:191). Cues in the external world to which we no longer attend are therefore still consciously perceived. Reid explicitly allows for this when he says, "We are conscious of many things to which we give little or no attention" (EIP 1.2:42).[31]

My suggestion, then, is that the legerdemain that "withdraws" the original objects of sight withdraws them only from attention, not from existence or consciousness.[32] The attentive eye can catch the magician's hand.

---

[30] Yaffe (2009) challenges my assumption that Reid makes use of the premise that sensations supervene on physical states of organs. However, he thinks Reid has reasons independent of that assumption for holding that we can be conscious of items to which we do not attend. The latter proposition is all I need to sustain my claim that one's original cues survive in acquired perception.

[31] Russell endorses a Reidian position (1913:9): "Thus the question we have to consider is whether *attention* constitutes experience, or whether things not attended to are also experienced. It seems we must admit things to which we do not attend, for attention is a selection among objects that are 'before the mind,' and therefore presupposes a larger field, constituted in some less exclusive manner, out of which attention chooses what it wants." For further arguments in support of the claim that we can be aware of items to which we do not attend, see Koch 2004:163–37, Tye 2004, and Hill and Bennett 2008.

[32] In a passage I have been unable to track down, Quine says there is a type of "transitivity of conditioning" whereby if C is conditioned to B and B to A, C is conditioned to A. This principle might be used to argue that when an originally perceived quality B becomes a sign of an object of acquired perception C, B drops out of the picture, C now being cued directly by the sensation A. Quine is right if he means that the relation of being directly *or indirectly* conditioned to another thing is transitive, but wrong if he means that in such cases the intermediate cue drops out, leaving C conditioned to A *directly*.

# E. COULD *ANYTHING* BECOME AN OBJECT
# OF ACQUIRED PERCEPTION?

Acquired perception far outstrips original perception and greatly enlarges our cognitive faculties. As Reid notes,

> The acquired perceptions are many more than the original. . . . We learn to perceive by the eye, almost every thing which we can perceive by touch. (IHM 6.20:171)

But are there any limits on the class of objects to which our acquired perceptions might one day extend?

A good foil to Reid's stance on this issue is the view of Paul Churchland, a proponent of the radical plasticity of perception (1979). According to Churchland, we could come to perceive anything that causally interacts with our sensory systems, given only scientific progress and enlightened education.

Churchland identifies two conditions for perceiving a property $\varphi$: (i) we must have sensations that are caused by $\varphi$ and reliably indicate its presence, and (ii) we must respond noninferentially to those sensations with the belief that something is $\varphi$, that is, with a belief deploying a term or concept that means $\varphi$ (14). Reid would agree that these conditions are in most cases necessary for perception. Perception of an object is typically mediated by sensations nomically correlated with it,[33] and perception always involves psychologically noninferential beliefs in response to these sensations.

Churchland goes on to offer a holistic conceptual-role account of what it is for a belief containing a given concept to be about one property rather than another. In a nutshell, "The meaning of a term (or the identity of a concept) is not determined by the intrinsic quality of whatever sensation happens to prompt its observational use, but by the network of assumptions/beliefs/principles in which it figures" (15). Reid would agree with the negative part of this thesis, holding that the beliefs that figure in perception are not about the sensations that prompt them, but about external qualities. He would disagree with the positive part, maintaining that which qualities a belief is about is a primitive intentional property of the belief rather than something determined by the web of theoretical connections to which the belief belongs. However, that difference between Reid and Churchland is not the key difference for present purposes.

---

[33] The one exception Reid mentions is the perception of visible figure, which he thinks is directly cued by retinal impressions rather than by sensations (IHM 6.21:176).

If the points in the previous two paragraphs are correct, Churchland says, "the possibility of a dramatic modification and expansion of the domain of human perceptual consciousness—without modification of our sense organs—becomes quite real" (15). He invites us to imagine an advanced scientific society in which children are taught to respond noninferentially to their sensations with terms from the best theories of the day. Where we respond with "loud noise," they are taught to respond with "large amplitude atmospheric compression waves"; where we respond with "red," they are taught to respond with "selectively reflects electromagnetic waves at $0.63 \times 1^{-6}$ m," and so on. These children

> do not sit on the beach and listen to the steady roar of the pounding surf. They sit on the beach and listen to the aperiodic atmospheric compression waves produced as the coherent energy of the ocean waves is audibly redistributed in the chaotic turbulence of the shallows. . . . They do not observe the western sky redden as the sun sets. They observe the wavelength distribution of incoming solar radiation shift towards the longer wavelengths. . . . They do not observe the dew forming on every surface. . . . [T]hey observe the accretion of reassociated atmospheric $H_2O$ molecules as their kinetic energy is lost to the now more quiescent aggregates with which they collide. (29–30)

"O brave new world!" expostulates Jerry Fodor in reaction to these lines, "that has such children in it" (1984).

Reid's views do not afford such a dramatic extension of our perceptual horizons. Setting aside the question of whether acquired perception is perception, the main point is that Reid does not let us get even as far as acquired perception of such things as the accretion of $H_2O$ molecules. For Reid, we can come to have acquired perceptions only of properties that we already perceive in some fashion to begin with. This is because the mechanism by which acquired perceptions are acquired is induction, and as Hume taught, we can learn by induction that a correlation holds between two properties only if we have perceived the properties independently. So we cannot have acquired perceptions of esoteric properties or entities that we first come to know about through the postulational methods of science.

The key methodological question dividing Reid and Churchland now comes to the fore: whether explanatory postulation (also known as abduction or the method of hypothesis) is a legitimate method alongside enumerative induction in scientific inquiry. Reid takes a strongly disapproving line on what he calls hypotheses (see EIP 1.3:47–52). By a hypothesis he means a proposition whose only recommendation to our belief is that it would, if true, explain other things that we know to be true, but whose truth is not open to confirmation by any more direct method. An example is the Indian philosopher's hypothesis of a great elephant supporting the earth on its back, offered to explain why the earth does not hurtle downward—"His elephant was a hypothesis, and our hypotheses are elephants" (IHM 6.19:163). By what Reid takes to be proper Newtonian method, we may invoke a proposition to explain phenomena only if it is supported by induction from the phenomena themselves—either the phenomena to be explained or other related phenomena. His strictures thus rule out of play explanatory assumptions about entities that are never observed.

Reid's prohibition of hypotheses would be faulted by some for putting a straightjacket on scientific inquiry. However, the point I am about to make does not depend on his blanket proscription of hypotheses. It only depends on his disallowing hypothetical reasoning as a mechanism of acquired perception.

Here is one of Reid's key claims about acquired perception:

> In acquired perception, the sign may be either a sensation, or something originally perceived. The thing signified, is *something, which, by experience, has been found connected with that sign.* (EIP 6.21:237; emphasis added).

Note the implications of the italicized words: the finding *by experience* of a connection between sign S and feature X requires that we perceive X.[34] So acquired perception of X requires prior perception of X, and if the prior perception were always itself acquired, there would be an impossible infinite regress. (Compare the regress involved in the supposition that there are indirect flights to Toronto, making a stop on the way, but no direct flights to Toronto from anywhere.) Therefore, we can have acquired perceptions only of those features that are original objects of perception for some sense. We now perceive the convexity of the ball by sight, but only because we previously perceived it by touch.[35]

---

[34] Compare EIP 6.6:508: "Experience can show a connection between a sign, and the thing signified by it, in those cases only, where both the sign and thing signified are perceived." The requirement that the thing signified have been previously perceived does not hold for natural signs of the third class, but it does hold for all those cases in which the connection between sign and thing signified is known by experience.

[35] Three supplementary remarks: (1) Nothing I say here rules out the possibility that perception is many layered, S serving as the sign for the acquired perception of X, which serves in turn as the sign for the acquired perception of Y. Two-dimensional cues are the signs for the acquired perception of three-dimensional shape, which might in turn become the sign for the acquired perception of a ship or a barn. (2) Instead of saying any object of AP must be an object of OP for some sense, one should probably say that any object of AP must be a constellation of properties—a Lockean "nominal essence"—each of which is an object of OP for some sense. (3) If one wanted to allow (as I suspect that Reid would not) that acquired perceptions may be acquired by testimony as well as by personal experience, one should say that we can have AP only of objects of which *someone* has had OP.

For Reid, then, it is not the case that we can come to perceive new things under the sun. We can only develop new sensory routes to the same old things. Reid's world is not as brave or new as Churchland's.

And yet alongside Reid's conservativism about what we may *come* to perceive, there is a radicalism about what we *might have been* able to perceive, even given our present sensory organs. That is because he holds that the links between what sensations we receive and what conceptions and beliefs we form in response to them are contingent:

> Perhaps we might have been so made, as to taste with our fingers, to smell with our ears, and to hear by the nose. . . . We might perhaps have been made of such a constitution, as to have our present perceptions connected with other sensations. (IHM 6.21:176).

It is in the spirit of Reid's view to affirm the converse as well—that we might have been so constituted as to have our present sensations connected with other perceptions, including perceptions of properties of which we now have no notion. The very sensations that are the occasions of our perceiving redness might have been lawfully correlated with hardness, or some property altogether unknown to us, and they might have induced us to conceive of and believe in that property. In that case, we would have perceived a property undreamt of by us now. Had it pleased our Maker, we might have been constituted so as to perceive a vastly different realm of things from what we perceive now on the same sensory occasions.

## F. IS REID INCONSISTENT ABOUT THE REQUISITES OF PERCEPTION?

I end this chapter by discussing three inconsistencies that threaten to arise in Reid's philosophy on my interpretation of him. I leave it to others to decide whether the fault lies in his philosophy or in my interpretation of it.

To begin with, there is the following inconsistent tetrad, taking off from the proposition I used to distinguish Reid from Churchland:

1. We can have acquired perception only of things of which we also have original perception.
2. All perception of secondary qualities is acquired perception.
3. We come to have acquired perception by sight of the coldness of the distant mountain and the hotness of the glowing poker.
4. Hotness and coldness are secondary qualities.

1 and 3 imply that there is original perception of hotness, while 2 and 4 imply to the contrary that all perception of hotness is acquired perception.

If my conjecture about localization is correct, we can avoid the inconsistency of 1–4 by denying 2: hotness and coldness are secondary qualities of which we *do* have original perception. However, that strategy would leave standing the following simpler contradiction:

1. We can have acquired perception only of things of which we also have original perception.
2. There is acquired perception of some secondary qualities (e.g., smells) that are never objects of original perception.

Here one could deny 2, for reasons brought forth in section 2. We do have original perception of the sheer existence of smell qualities, even if we do not have original perceptions of which objects they proceed from.[36]

The third inconsistency is more vexing. In section D of chapter 1 and section B of this chapter, I advance the suggestion that we have genuine Reidian perception only of those objects and qualities with which we are *acquainted*. Following Russell, I characterize acquaintance as a relation to an object (or quality) rather than to a proposition and as a relation that is direct rather than being mediated by some description, such as *the woman I married* or *the quality that causes this sensation in me*.[37] This characterization permits us to say (what Russell himself did not say) that we are acquainted with physical things or at least with some of their qualities. My suggestion above is that it is for want of acquaintance with my wife that I do not see her when I see her keys, even though I do think of her. The problem I want to air is this: by the acquaintance standard, it seems that I do not perceive secondary qualities, for according to Reid, I only conceive of them under descriptions such as *the quality that causes this sensation of color in me*.[38] I have no conception of what red things are like in themselves, but only a relative notion of them, a notion of their relation to other things. Yet Reid says we *do* perceive secondary qualities. In brief:

---

[36] This position is tenable only if the content of perception can be a bare existential proposition— that *there is* a quality causing such-and-such a sensation in me. The thesis that the contents of perception are existential propositions is affirmed by a number of contemporary philosophers, including Searle (1983).

[37] Such descriptions express what Reid calls "relative notions." "A relative notion of a thing, is, strictly speaking, no notion of the thing at all, but only of some relation which it bears to something else" (EIP 2.17:201).

[38] Or perhaps (as I suggested in chapter 4) *the property of having some property that causes this sensation in me*.

1. We perceive only those qualities with which we are acquainted.
2. We are not acquainted with secondary qualities (since we have only "relative notions" of them.)
3. We do perceive secondary qualities.

Since Reid definitely affirms 2 and 3, there is a presumption against my attributing or even recommending 1 to him. Nonetheless, I believe there is good reason all things considered for doing so. Reid should have affirmed 1 and denied 3.

Reid should have affirmed 1 because otherwise he is hard put to distinguish perception from various things that are not perception. How, for example, is he to distinguish perception from belief formed on the basis of testimony? Reid is a non-inferentialist about knowledge from testimony; according to his "principle of credulity," when we hear someone say *p*, we believe *p* forthwith without any reasoning (IHM 6.24:194; see Van Cleve 2006b for further discussion). Yet believing on the say-so of a fellow traveler that there is a washed-out bridge around the next bend is not perceiving the bridge, nor even perceiving that there is one.[39] What is the missing ingredient, if not acquaintance?

Reid should have denied 3, that we perceive secondary qualities, because in affirming it he is guilty of an inconsistency of sorts.[40] It is not that he affirms *p* and ~*p*, but rather that his reason for saying we perceive secondary qualities is a reason he holds to be insufficient for perception in other cases. The reason for saying that we perceive secondary qualities is that on the occasion of certain sensations, we have by our constitution a conception of and a belief in some property in the object as the cause of our sensations. The conception is merely a relative one. The question I am raising is whether conceiving of and believing in some external quality or object is sufficient for perception of it *if the conception is merely a relative notion*, not a direct one such as would be afforded by acquaintance. There are several instances in which Reid either hints at or delivers outright an answer of *no*.

First, though equivocally, *bodies*. It is a first principle, Reid says, that motion, hardness, and other qualities cannot exist without a substance or body to which they belong (EIP 1.2:43). We cannot perceive these qualities without believing in a body as the subject of them. Our notion of the body is relative—we conceive of it only as that to which the qualities belong (EIP 2.19:218–19 and EAP 1.1:10). The question is, does Reid think we perceive bodies? On the one hand, he declares that

[39] If I am alerted to the broken bridge by a shouted warning and you by a written sign, do I perceive it by hearing and you by sight? Or do we each have amodal perceptions? If we turn back before we reach the bridge, have we nonetheless both perceived it?

[40] There is the same inconsistency in his saying in EIP 2.18 that we perceive what Locke scholars call tertiary qualities—powers of objects to affect other external objects, such as corrosiveness.

"All the things which we immediately perceive by our senses . . . are things which must be in something else as their subject"—that is, they are qualities (EIP 1.2:43). Moreover, his official lists of the objects of perception never mention anything but qualities (EIP 2.17–18). On the other hand, he gives plenty of examples in which bodies are among the things we perceive—I see trees (IHM 6.20:167–68), the sun and the moon (EIP 2.14:172), billiard balls (EIP 2.19:217), and so on. Reid seems to have no settled position on this issue.[41]

Second, *minds*—our own and others. The title of one of the sections of the *Inquiry* (IHM 2.7) is "The conception of a sentient being or mind, is suggested by our constitution." As Reid further explains, a sensation suggests to us not only the conception of and belief in some external cause of it, but also of a subject for it—our own mind. Yet in several places he denies that we perceive minds:

> Though we have an immediate knowledge of the existence of thought in ourselves by consciousness, yet we have no immediate knowledge of a mind. The mind is not an immediate object either of sense or of consciousness. (EIP 6.6:508)

> The understanding of another man is no immediate object of sight, or of any other faculty which God hath given me; and unless I can conclude its existence from tokens that are visible, I have no evidence that there is understanding in any man. (EIP 6.6:512)

> But neither mind, nor any of its qualities or powers, is an immediate object of perception to man. (EIP 8.4:603)

Reid does not issue this denial simply because he reserves the term "perception" for a relation we have to external things. He says we do not even have *consciousness* of minds.[42]

Third, the *imperceptible parts* of things:

> There is a limit beyond which we cannot perceive any division of a body. The parts become too small to be perceived by our sense; but we cannot believe that it becomes then incapable of being farther divided. . . . We carry on the division and subdivision in our thought far beyond the reach of our senses. (EIP 2.19:219)

---

[41] The most thorough discussion of the issue I know of is Folescu 2013, reprised in Folescu 2015. Folescu holds that Reid's best view is that we perceive bodies as well as qualities.

[42] I must acknowledge that there are passages one could cite on the other side, including this one: "The involuntary signs of the passions and dispositions of the mind, in the voice, features, and action . . . are so many openings into the souls of our fellow-men, by which their sentiments become visible to the eye" (EAP 3.2.6:141). I suspect, though, that Reid is here using the language of perception in the figurative way he describes at EIP 1.1:23.

This passage is not decisive, since Reid does not say we believe by our constitution in parts beyond what we perceive—only that we cannot believe there are *not* such parts.

Fourth, *absolute motion*. At EIP 2.22:245–46, Reid tells us that our senses testify only to relative and not to absolute motions of bodies. "When one body seems to remove from another, we can infer with certainty that there is absolute motion, but whether in the one or the other, or partly in both, is not discerned by sense." This passage also fails to be decisive, since Reid does not say we immediately conceive of and believe in the absolute motion, but only that we can infer it with certainty.

Fifth, *absolute space*. When we perceive something extended by sight or touch, we are "necessarily led to conceive space, though space be of itself no object of sense" (EIP 2.22:245; see also EIP 2.19:221). If the previous two passages were not decisive, this one is: space is something we conceive of and immediately believe in without having any perception of it.

Sixth, there is one final consideration that clinches the point that Reid should not hold that conception via relative notions is sufficient for perception. As noted above, whenever we have a sensation of color, sound, or smell, we believe by our nature that there is some external cause of it. But the point is not confined to these sensations: whenever we perceive *any* event, we believe by our nature that there is some cause of it.[43] "By a like natural principle it is, that a beginning of existence, or any change in nature, suggests to us the notion of a cause, and compels our belief of its existence" (IHM 2.7:38). We cannot perceive any change without forming some conception of and immediate belief in a cause of that change, if only by means of the highly general and relative conception "whatever it is that causes the change I am perceiving." Therefore, if Reid held that anything we conceive of and believe in by our constitution (even through a relative notion) is something we thereby perceive, he would be committed to the view that *we never perceive any event without perceiving its cause*. And that I take to be absurd.[44]

---

[43] My claim here is not *we believe that for any item x, (if we perceive x, there is a cause of x)*, but rather *for any item x, (if we perceive x, we believe there is a cause of x)*. This is in line with Reid's observation that many first principles "force their assent in particular instances, more powerfully than when they are turned into a general proposition" (EIP 6.5:482).

[44] It might be objected to what I have just argued (i) that Reid does not say we always believe in an *external* or environmental cause for any change we perceive, and (ii) that as Reid uses "perception," only external things or events can be perceived. I make two replies. First, so long as the cause of the change we perceive *is* an object or event in our environment (as opposed, say, to God acting directly), it will follow on the relative-notions-are-good-enough view that we perceive it, since it satisfies the conception we form of it. Second, even if we do not always believe in external causes for changes we perceive, we (or some other beings) *might* have been so constituted as to have such beliefs. To say that beings so constituted would perceive the cause of every change they perceive is still an absurdity, discrediting the relative-notions-are-good-enough view. A view that implies that some absurdity is possible is as bad as a view that implies that the absurdity is actual.

The conclusion I draw is that Reid ought to hold, and does in places actually hold, that direct perception requires direct notions. All perception is direct perception; therefore, there is no perception of that of which we have only a relative notion. And that means there is no perception of secondary qualities.

Why, then, does Reid list secondary qualities among the objects of perception, despite holding that we have only a relative conception of them? I cannot help suspecting that like most of us, he often falls into a naïve realism according to which colors, sounds, and smells are not mere powers to affect us, but intrinsic properties of things whose natures are revealed to us—that we inhabit a world "splashed with color, ringing with sound, charged with odor" (Jessop 1966:104). A naïve realist *can* legitimately claim to perceive secondary qualities. But in his official philosophy, Reid is not a naïve realist.

# 6

## THE GEOMETRY OF VISIBLES

The name of Reid ought to head the roll on which will be inscribed the names of Lobatschewsky, Riemann, and other investigators. (Sir James Cockle, *Presidential Address, 1888*)

With [Reid's *Inquiry into the Human Mind*], the study of visual space *per se* began. (Mark Wagner, *The Geometries of Visual Space*)

In a brief but remarkable section of the *Inquiry*, Reid argues that the visual field is governed by principles other than the familiar theorems of Euclid—theorems we would nowadays classify as Riemannian. On the strength of this section, he has been credited by Daniels (1974),[1] Angell (1974), and others with discovering non-Euclidean geometry over half a century before the mathematicians—sixty years before Lobachevsky and ninety years before Riemann.[2] I believe that Reid does indeed have a fair claim to have discovered a non-Euclidean geometry. However, the

---

[1] For Daniels, there is no doubt that Reid did establish that the visual field is non-Euclidean; the question is only how Reid could have done what he did working (as Daniels believed) in isolation from the mathematical practice of the day. Using Reid's unpublished manuscripts, Paul Wood has shown that Reid was not isolated from relevant mathematical practice—he taught Euclid's Elements as part of his duties at Aberdeen, was in contact with the leading Scottish geometers of the day, and was preoccupied for several decades of his life with proving Euclid's parallel postulate from other propositions with a greater degree of self-evidence (1998). Wood does not address my main question here: what is the real basis of the geometry of visibles?

[2] Sir James Cockle gives priority to Reid over Lobachevsky and Riemann in a presidential address delivered to the London Mathematical Society on November 8, 1888 ("On the Confluences and Bifurcations of Certain Theories"). My epigraph is taken from his address.

real basis of Reid's geometry of visibles is subtle and easy to misidentify. My main aim in this chapter is to make clear what the real basis is, separating it from several fallacious or irrelevant considerations on which Reid may seem to be relying. A secondary aim is to air the worry that Reid's case for his geometry can succeed only at the cost of compromising his direct realism.

Reid holds that Euclidean geometry is indeed the correct geometry for the objects we touch and the space containing them. But it is not the correct geometry for the immediate objects of sight:

> When the geometrician draws a diagram with the most perfect accuracy; when he keeps his eye fixed upon it, while he goes through a long process of reasoning, and demonstrates the relations of the several parts of his figure; he does not consider, that the visible figure presented to his eye, is only the representative of a tangible figure, upon which all his attention is fixed; he does not consider that these two figures have really different properties; and that what he demonstrates to be true of the one, is not true of the other. (IHM 6.8:102–3)

He goes on to say, "This perhaps will seem so great a paradox, even to mathematicians, as to require a demonstration before it can be believed" (103).

Reid's case for the non-Euclidean geometry of visibles has two parts. First, he argues that because depth is not perceived, every visible figure has the same geometrical properties as some spherical figure, that is, some figure drawn on the surface of a sphere. Second, he points out that the geometrical properties of spherical figures are not the properties familiar to us from Euclidean plane geometry—for example, spherical triangles always have an angle sum greater than 180 degrees. The properties of figures on the sphere are in fact precisely those of the corresponding figures in Riemannian double elliptical geometry. Putting the two parts together, we get the result that the geometry of visibles is not Euclidean, but Riemannian.

I now examine the two parts of Reid's case, beginning with the geometry of the sphere. Readers who wish to form their own independent understanding of Reid's case should read IHM 6.9 before proceeding.

## A. THE PROPERTIES OF SPHERICAL FIGURES

Reid offers as a "small specimen of the geometry of visibles" a numbered list of twelve propositions, each "not less true nor less evident [with regard to visible figure and space] than the propositions of Euclid, with regard to tangible figures" (IHM 6.9:105). I comment on several of these propositions below, noting how they come out true if the terms "right line" and "straight line" (which Reid uses interchange-ably) are taken to denote great circles of the sphere (or segments of such circles).

1. *Every right line being produced, will at last return into itself.* Trace the equator (or any other great circle on the globe) and you will eventually return to the point from which you started.

5. *Any two right lines being produced, will meet in two points, and mutually bisect each other.* Any two lines of longitude intersect each other at the poles; similarly, any other great circles on the globe intersect each other at two opposite points. Thus, no two straight lines are parallel to each other if parallels are defined in Euclid's fashion as lines that do not intersect. This proposition denies Euclid's parallel postulate in the Playfair version of it, which says that through any point outside a given line there is exactly one line parallel to the original line.

6. *If two lines be parallel, that is, every where equally distant from each other, they cannot both be straight.* If parallels are defined in terms of equidistance, there are still no parallel straight lines on the sphere. Consider, for example, the equator and any other line of latitude. They are everywhere equidistant, but the line of latitude (being a lesser circle) does not count as straight.

10. *Of every right-lined triangle, the three angles taken together, are greater than two right angles.* Consider a triangle composed of a stretch of the equator as base and segments of two lines of longitude meeting at the North Pole as its legs. There are two right angles at the base, to which we must add the angle at the pole, which may be anything from just over zero degrees to just under 360 degrees. Triangles so composed may have angle sums ranging from just over 180 to just under 540 degrees. Triangles containing no right angles must also have angle sums exceeding 180 degrees (for example, there can be equilateral triangles with each angle equal to 61 degrees).

11. *The angles of a right-lined triangle, may all be right angles, or all obtuse angles.* The "all right angles" case has been covered above: take two lines of longitude that make right angles with the equator and with each other at the North Pole. For the "all obtuse angles" case, consider a short segment of the equator as base and two legs each making obtuse angles with it. In a flat plane legs making obtuse angles with the base would never meet, but on the sphere they may wrap around and meet in an obtuse angle on the other side.

If the foregoing propositions are merely taken to hold of "right lines" interpreted as great circles on the sphere and of figures composed of segments of such lines, there is nothing inherently counter-Euclidean about them. In fact, they all belong to the Euclidean geometry of the sphere—a body of truths that was known and used by the Greek astronomers who believed that the stars were embedded in a great sphere rotating around the earth. But if the propositions are taken to hold of genuinely straight lines and figures composed of them, we do get a non-Euclidean geometry; it is one of the geometries that now bear the name of Riemann.[3]

## B. DEPTH IS NOT PERCEIVED

I turn now to the other half of Reid's case—that every visible figure has the same relevant geometrical properties as some spherical figure. Reid's reason for thinking so is bound up with the Berkeleian claim that depth is not perceived by the eye:

> Supposing the eye placed in the centre of a sphere, every great circle of the sphere will have the same appearance to the eye as if it was a straight line. For the curvature of the eye being turned directly toward the eye, is not perceived by it. And for the same reason, any line which is drawn in the plane of a great circle of the sphere, whether it be in reality straight or curve, will appear straight to the eye. (IHM 6.9:103)

The middle sentence is reminiscent of what Berkeley says in the second paragraph of the *New Theory of Vision*—the only argument he gives in that work for its central presupposition that distance is not perceived by sight:

> It is, I think, agreed by all that distance, of itself and immediately, cannot be seen. For, distance being a line directed endwise to the eye, it projects only one point in the fund of the eye, which point remains invariably the same, whether the distance be longer or shorter. (NTV 2)

---

[3] In particular, it is double elliptical geometry. In elliptical geometries there are no lines parallel to a given line; in hyperbolic geometries there are many. Double elliptical geometries are called double because any two straight lines intersect in two points, as noted in Reid's Proposition 5. Riemann also investigated single elliptical geometries, in which any two straight lines intersect in a single point. To convert the sphere into a model of single elliptical geometry, one may identify antipodal points, as proposed by Felix Klein (Peil 2006).

Some readers may wonder how Reid could have declared in his published work that visual space is governed by a geometry in which the parallel postulate fails, yet tried so hard in his unpublished manuscripts to prove that the parallel postulate follows from Euclid's other postulates (see note 1 of this chapter). I learned the answer from Grandi 2005. Reid did indeed propound a geometry without parallels for visual space, and he did indeed believe for all his life that the parallel postulate ought to be derivable from Euclid's other axioms. But one of those axioms, the incidence axiom that says two points determine a line, does not hold in Reid's spherical model for visual space. Hence he could have believed that the parallel postulate fails in visual space.

Grandi points out that Reid did not know that it is possible for the parallel postulate to fail even in a geometry in which the incidence axiom holds; hence his futile attempts to prove the parallel postulate from Euclid's other postulates.

Lateral distance (distance in two dimensions) is perceivable by the eye: the distance between the endpoints of a line viewed broadside is proportional to the angle subtended by that line at the eye. But outward distance (distance out from the eye in three dimensional space, or what Berkeley calls "outness") is not. Whether a point is near or far along a line extending outward from the eye, it will produce the same impression, from which Berkeley and Reid both conclude that the eye is incapable of any depth discrimination. That is why a straight line and a line whose curvature is purely outward from the eye will appear exactly the same. All this is reflected in Reid's definition of "position of objects with regard to the eye:"

> Objects that lie in the same right line drawn from the centre of the eye, have the same position, however different their distances from the eye may be: but objects which lie in different right lines drawn from the eye's centre, have a different position; and this difference of position is greater or less in proportion to the angle made at the eye by the right lines mentioned (IHM 6.7:96).

As I said in chapter 5, I believe that Berkeley and Reid are wrong in holding that depth is not immediately perceived; my reasons are set forth in appendices J and K. In this chapter, however, I assume for the sake of argument that Berkeley and Reid are correct. It is of great interest to see if the rest of what Reid says about the geometry of visibles is sound if we grant him his starting point.

The alleged consequence of the unperceivability of depth that will be important for us is this: *every visible triangle is indistinguishable from some spherical triangle*. For any triangle that I see, there is a corresponding triangle composed of segments of great circles centered on my eye; the sides of this spherical triangle share endpoints with the sides of the original triangle, but curve out away from my eye. Since this outward curvature is undetectable by the eye, the spherical triangle presents exactly the same appearance to the eye as the original triangle. In this sense, the two are indistinguishable.

To forestall confusion, let me note three points about the relation I am calling "indistinguishability." First, when I call two figures "indistinguishable," I mean that one is capable of exactly occluding the other from view, or that one could be substituted for the other without making any perceptible difference in their spatial properties. A sufficient condition for the indistinguishability of two lines or figures in this sense is that corresponding points of them occupy the same visual position in Reid's sense (i.e., they lie on the same outward line from the center of the eye), as when one figure does exactly occlude another.[4] Second, there is a sense in which a perfectly straight line and a line containing minute side-to-side deviations too small for an eye of limited acuity to see may be called indistinguishable. As is well known, indistinguishability in this sense is not a transitive relation. But this is not the sense of indistinguishability that figures in Reid's argument. The unseen deviations from straightness Reid is talking about lie in the outward dimension that is unseen even by an eye of unlimited acuity. Indistinguishability as it figures in Reid's argument *is* a transitive relation. Third, Reid tell us that "as the real figure of a body consists in the situation of its several parts with regard to one another, so its visible figure consists in the position of its several parts with regard to the eye" (IHM 6.7:96). In other words, the visible figure of any object is determined by the totality of directions in which its various points lie from the eye. Since the same lines of direction may pass from my eye to every point on a tilted circle and to every point on an ellipse placed orthogonally to my line of sight, the tilted circle and the ellipse (when appropriately placed) have or present the same visible figure; they are visually indistinguishable. More generally, objects with very different real figures may be visually indistinguishable (as we shall see later in the case of objects that differ more dramatically than a circle and an ellipse).

## C. THE ARGUMENT FROM INDISTINGUISHABILITY

Two fundamental facts from which Reid derives his geometry—the properties of spherical figures and the eye's inability to distinguish visible figures from spherical figures—are now before us. They come together in the following paragraph, to which Reid attaches the numeral "5," and which is set forth as though it constitutes the core of his argument for the geometry of visibles:

> 5. Hence it is evident, that every visible right-lined triangle, will coincide in all its parts with some spherical triangle. The sides of the one will appear equal to the sides of the other, and the angles of the one to the angles of the other, each to each; and therefore the whole of the one triangle will appear equal to the whole of the other. In a word, to the eye they will be one and the same, and have the same mathematical properties.

---

[4] Note that my definition says x and y are indistinguishable if one of them could occlude the other—not that *either* could occlude the other. That is, the definiens is the disjunction "x could occlude y or y could occlude x," not the conjunction "x could occlude y & y could occlude x." This allows that figures of different sizes can be indistinguishable—the smaller could (exactly) occlude the larger from a given point of view though not vice versa. Figures of different *colors* may also be indistinguishable in the purely spatial sense that is at issue here.

The properties therefore of visible right-lined triangles, are not the same with the properties of plain [Reid's variant spelling of "plane"] triangles, but are the same with those of spherical triangles (IHM 6.9:104).

The context makes clear that when Reid says that every visible triangle "coincides in all its parts" with some spherical triangle, the relation he has in mind is not *real* coincidence, but the relation he elsewhere calls coincidence *to the eye*. In other words, it is the relation of indistinguishability, or so I assume. Let us use *having an angle sum greater than two right angles* as a specimen property possessed by spherical but not by plane triangles. It then appears that the argument of paragraph 5—which I henceforth call *the argument from indistinguishability*—may be set out as follows:

1. Every visible triangle is visibly indistinguishable from some spherical triangle.
2. Spherical triangles have angle sums greater than two right angles.
3. Therefore, every visible triangle has an angle sum greater than two right angles.

If *that* is Reid's argument, however, it commits an alarming fallacy. It has the same form as the following argument:

1. Every visible straight line is visibly indistinguishable from some squiggly line. (Reid implies as much when he says, "Any line which is drawn in the plane of a great circle of the sphere, whether it be in reality straight or curve, will appear straight to the eye [placed at the centre of the sphere]" (IHM 6.9:103)).
2. Squiggly lines contain squiggles.
3. Therefore, every visible straight line contains squiggles.

That should make the fallacy obvious enough. To dramatize the difficulty with the argument, however, I now present two more counterexamples to it. (These examples may be overkill for present purposes, but they will be useful for other purposes below.)

The first counterexample is an argument that stands on all fours with the original, but shows that every visible triangle has an angle sum of *less* than 180 degrees (as happens in Lobachevskian or hyperbolic geometry). Let lines of direction be drawn from my eye to every point of a plane triangle that I see, and let there be interposed between this triangle and my eye a saddle-shaped surface of the kind used to model Lobachevskian geometry. The lines of direction will intercept this surface in a triangle one side of which curves outward and two sides of which curve inward in relation to the eye. This inward or outward curvature being invisible to the eye, the saddle triangle will be visibly as indistinguishable from the plane triangle as any of the spherical triangles that are projections of the plane triangle in Reid's scheme. Yet the saddle triangle has an angle sum of less than 180 degrees. By the argument of paragraph 5 as we are presently understanding it, it should therefore follow that the visible triangle in this situation has an angle sum of less than 180 degrees.[5]

I have just shown that if the original argument from indistinguishability proves visible triangles to be Riemannian, another application of the argument proves them to be Lobachevskian. I show next that a further application of the argument proves the visual field as a whole to be *neither* Riemannian *nor* Lobachevskian. Euclidean, Riemannian, and Lobachevskian spaces are all members of the family of *homoloidal* spaces—spaces of constant curvature, in which figures can be moved around without distortion. What I am going to show, then, is that the argument from indistinguishability proves space to be nonhomoloidal.

Take a sphere and at one or more points on its surface "pinch up" a bit of it to form a peak or a spike. On each of the peaks, let two straight lines cross at the apex to form four equal angles. By Euclid's definition of a right angle, the angles formed at such intersections will all be right angles, since all are equal to one another.[6] But these angles will clearly be narrower than right angles formed by lines intersecting at smooth places on the sphere. Hence we get a violation of Euclid's Postulate 4, which says that all right angles are equal. Since this is precisely the postulate that affirms that space is homoloidal, the spiky sphere is a nonhomoloidal space.

The next thing to notice is that the substitution of a spiky sphere centered on the eye for the normal sphere that Reid employs in his exposition of the geometry of visibles would occasion no difference in the visible figures presented to the eye. For example, two straight lines that bisect each other will present the same appearance to the eye whether they meet at a smooth place or at peak. If they meet at a peak they will be receding from the eye as they approach the peak, but this recession will be as undetectable as the curvature possessed by lines crossing at a smooth place on the sphere. More generally, projections on a sphere and projections on a spiky sphere will present exactly similar visible figures to the eye. To see this, consider lines of direction from the eye to every point in some object, and consider surfaces of varying orientation or curvature intercepted by these lines. The real figures of the

---

[5] Tom Banchoff has pointed out to me that at least one side of the projection of a triangle on a saddle surface will fail to be a geodesic, in which case the projected figure is not really a triangle. It is nonetheless a *figure* indistinguishable from the original and having an angle sum of less than 180 degrees, so it stands as a counterexample to the argument from indistinguishability.

[6] "When a straight line set up on a straight line makes the adjacent angles equal to one another, each of the equal angles is *right*." This is definition 10 in Book I of Euclid's *Elements* as translated in Heath 1956, vol. 1:153.

intercepts may vary considerably, but the visible figures of all will be the same—because in varying the intercepting surface, we do not alter the directions of the lines from the eye.

Reid tells us that "the whole surface of the sphere will represent the whole of visible space . . . since every visible point coincides with some point of the surface of the sphere" (IHM 6.9:104). But in just the same way, every visible point coincides to the eye with some point on the surface of a spiky sphere. If it were legitimate, then, to conclude that visible space has the geometrical properties of the sphere representing it, it would be equally legitimate to conclude that visible space has the geometrical properties of the spiky sphere representing it. But the sphere and the spiky sphere have incompatible geometries, one being homoloidal and the other not.

The argument of paragraph 5, as I am now construing it, is seriously deficient, and it is hard to believe that Reid would have offered so patent a fallacy. Our task in the next four sections is to find a better argument for the geometry of visibles.

## D. VISIBLES AS SENSE DATA

The fallacy apparently present in paragraph 5 is the assumption that anything visually indistinguishable from an F thing is itself an F thing. Without this assumption, the argument is invalid, yet the assumption seems plainly false. The first proposal I wish to explore is that the assumption, though not correct in general, *works for the special entities Reid calls visibles*. Well, then, what sorts of entities must visibles be, if they are to play the necessary role in Reid's reasoning? One natural suggestion is that they are phenomenal entities akin to classical sense data.

To introduce this possibility, I quote from Strawson's discussion of Kant on phenomenal geometry:

> The straight lines which are the objects of pure intuition . . . are not physical objects, or physical edges, which, when we see them, look straight. They are rather just the looks themselves which physical things have when, and in so far as, they look straight. (1966:282)[7]

Strawson's "looks" are a special kind of phenomenal object, presumably satisfying the central axiom in the theory of sense data: if a physical object looks F to a

---

[7] Ironically, Strawson invokes phenomenal objects to secure a domain in which Euclidean geometry holds even if the geometry of the physical world is non-Euclidean. For Reid it is the other way around—physical geometry is Euclidean, visual geometry non-Euclidean.

perceiver, it does so by presenting the perceiver with a sense datum that really *is* F. Sense data themselves are the immediate objects of perception, and they have all (and perhaps only) the properties they appear to have.[8]

Alas, there are two things wrong with trying to salvage the geometry of visibles with "looks," construed as a special kind of phenomenal object. The first, as the reader will immediately surmise, is that the introduction of such objects threatens to jeopardize Reid's direct realism. We would perceive external things (if we perceive them at all) only by directly apprehending sense data. The second is that the introduction of such objects, contrary to what one may at first suspect, does not suffice to make the argument from indistinguishability valid after all.

On the first point, note how out of character the introduction of special phenomenal objects would be with Reid's response to Hume's argument about the table. In assessing that argument, Reid said that if an object looks so big to an eye placed here, that is a fundamental dyadic relation between the object and the eye. It does not unfold into a triadic relation of Object's presenting Item to Eye. But under the current proposal, Reid would be saying that if a line looks straight to the eye, it does so by presenting to the eye an item that really is straight. That, of course, is the classic sense datum move. It is at odds with a theory of direct perception, because it implies that when a curved straw looks straight, I see the straw only by seeing something that really is straight, and that something must be other than the straw.

The second point is that even if we do construe Reid's visibles as sense data, that is not enough to save him from the fallacy above. The fallacy was embodied in the following principle, which is evidently what must be added to the argument from indistinguishability to make it valid: if x is visibly indistinguishable from y and y is F, then x is F, too. The supposedly saving sense-datum suggestion would be that the following qualified version of the principle is true: if x *is a visual sense datum* visibly indistinguishable from y and y is F, then x is F, too. But the qualified principle turns out to be as false as the original. This may be seen by adapting an example already used above: a straight sense datum may be visibly indistinguishable from a physical line that contains squiggles without containing squiggles itself. So not even our modified principle is true,[9] and it remains fallacious to assume that visible triangles

---

[8] Classical sense-datum theory always assumed that sense data have *all* the properties they appear to have, but did not necessarily assume that sense data have *only* the properties they appear to have. See Broad (1923) 1959:244–45.

[9] What would be true is this: if x and y are *both* sense data and x is visibly indistinguishable from y, then if y is F, so is x. But the spherical figures that play the role of y in Reid's argument are not sense data.

indistinguishable from physical triangles drawn on a sphere would have the same geometrical properties as the spherical triangles.

## E. COINCIDENCE AS IDENTITY

Suppose we take literally (as I initially refused to do) Reid's claim in paragraph 5 that every visible triangle *coincides in all its parts* with some spherical triangle.[10] He would then be implying that every visible triangle is *identical with* some spherical triangle. The resulting argument would avoid the fallacy we have been discussing, for properties not transferred by indistinguishability are indisputably transferred by identity.

1.' Every visible triangle coincides in all its parts with, and is thus identical with, some spherical triangle.
2. Spherical triangles have angle sums greater than two right angles.
3. Therefore, every visible triangle has an angle sum greater than two right angles.

If real coincidence falls short of identity, as with the statue and the clay, it is nonetheless a strong enough relation to transfer all geometrical properties, so the argument would still reach the desired conclusion.

There are three reasons, however, for not construing Reid's argument as an argument from identity or real coincidence.

First, I think it is clear that the argument just presented is not the argument Reid intended to give. As I mentioned above, it is clear from the context that the "coincidence" he speaks of in the first sentence of paragraph 5 is not real coincidence, but the relation he elsewhere calls coincidence *to the eye* or apparent coincidence. A plane figure and a spherical figure may be coincident in this sense without being identical or even congruent.

Second, the identity interpretation of Reid's argument raises the question of why visible figures should be identified with projections on the *sphere*, rather than with equivalent (i.e., indistinguishable to the eye) projections on some other surface. I pointed out above that there are projections on surfaces other than the sphere (e.g., the saddle and the spiky sphere) that yield visible figures indistinguishable from those yielded by projections on the sphere. So what justifies the choice of the sphere, and why identify visible figures with spherical figures in particular?

---

[10] I thank Ed Minar for asking me to consider this possibility further.

Daniels mentions two considerations in favor of the sphere. The first is that "the eye sees all points in its visual field (as if they were) equidistant" (8). As he explains further:

> Seeing no depth differences between visible points is just like seeing all visible points equidistant from the eye. But this is equivalent to projecting visible points onto an arbitrary sphere. (11)[11]

It is true, of course, that the locus of all points equidistant from a given point is a sphere. But that the eye sees all points "as if" equidistant confers no privilege on the sphere as the surface of projection. The sense in which the eye sees all points as equidistant is simply this: if all points seen by the eye were replaced by points equidistant from the eye but retaining the same visual position as before, everything would look the same. But it is equally true that if all points seen by the eye were replaced by points on the surface of a *spiky* sphere but retaining the same visual position as before, everything would look the same. So the eye sees all points "as if" placed on a spiky sphere, which could with equal right have been chosen as the surface of projection.

Daniels also notes that the anatomy of the human eye—in particular, its being roughly spherical—seems to have been a motivating consideration in Reid's singling out of the sphere (10). He says that this consideration makes the choice of a sphere natural and even inevitable, given that any other surface "would violate the symmetry considerations based on the anatomy of the eye" (11). But I doubt that such anatomical considerations can have had anything to do with Reid's choice. For one thing, he thinks the geometry of visibles is *exactly* the geometry of the sphere, whereas the shape of the eye is only *approximately* round. For another, he would have realized that a camera obscura "sees" the same visibles as the eye despite having nothing spherical in its anatomy. I return to this point in section H.

I come now to the third difficulty with the identity interpretation of Reid's argument. Let us grant that there is a good reason for choosing the sphere as the surface of projection (as I shall in fact propose before we are done). It would still not serve Reid's cause to identify visible figures with spherical figures—at least not if we wish to credit him with discovering a non-Euclidean geometry. With the argument from identity, rather than getting a non-Euclidean geometry of straight lines, we would get instead a Euclidean geometry of curved lines.[12] No one credits the ancient Greek

---

[11] Graham Nerlich also suggests that Reid chooses the sphere because it models the eye's inability to see depth (1994:119–20).

[12] This danger is pointed out by Daniels (11–12).

astronomers who worked out the geometry of figures on the celestial sphere with being the first discoverers of non-Euclidean geometry.

## F. ANGELL'S APPROACH

In 1974, R. B. Angell published an essay entitled "The Geometry of Visibles," worked out independently of Reid, but given its title in honor of Reid's priority. Like Reid, Angell believes that the visual field has a Riemannian (or double elliptical) geometry, and he thinks so for reasons having in good part to do with the fact that the eye does not perceive depth. But Angell makes his case using a strategy different from the strategy I have so far imputed to Reid. Whereas Reid may seem to assign properties to visible figures by letting them inherit properties from spherical figures with which they are indistinguishable, Angell assigns properties to visible figures *directly*, by measurement or in some cases by simple inspection. He thereby avoids the non sequitur that is involved in the argument from indistinguishability. I shall nonetheless raise two difficulties for Angell's approach: that it can succeed only at the cost of an objectionable reification of visibles, and that even with the reification granted, there is reason to question his claims about what can be verified about visible figures by inspection or measurement.

Here is how Angell identifies the domain of visibles about which his geometry is supposed to be true:

> Visibles or visual objects are not the same as what would ordinarily be denoted by "an object which is visible." Thus, I might say that a certain tree was an object which was visible to me at a certain time; the "object which is visible" in this case is a physical, three-dimensional object, a tree. I might say of the tree that I judged it to be about seventy feet tall.... But I might also say that the tree *appears* to be no larger than my thumb *appears* when held at arm's length. The *appearances* thus compared and found equal are the visual objects, or visibles, in our present sense. (89–90)

Angell thus believes that when the tree and my thumb appear to be of the same length, there exist a tree-appearance and a thumb-appearance that *are* of the same length. That is the classical sense-datum move. It is of a piece with saying that as I retreat from the table, I see appearances that are successively smaller—even though the table itself "suffers no alteration." If that is true, I do not see the table itself, and direct realism is lost.

But let us grant for now the reification of visibles and see why Angell thinks their geometry is non-Euclidean. He lists a number of non-Euclidean theorems that he claims may be verified by careful measurement of visibles or in some cases by simple inspection of them. Here are two of the propositions supposedly verifiable by inspection, along with Angell's commentary on them:

> *Every pair of straight lines intersects at two points.* Imagine standing in the middle of a straight railroad track on a vast plane. The *visual* lines associated with the two rails are demonstrably visually straight in every segment—they appear perfectly straight, not curved, visually. Yet these visually straight lines meet at two points which are opposite each other on the horizon, and they enclose a substantial region on the visual field. (95)

> *Two straight lines, cut by a third straight line perpendicular to both, always intersect.* The two rails, both appearing visually straight, are cut by the straight edge of the railroad tie at our feet, and this tie is perpendicular visually, to both of them; yet the two visual rails intersect twice. (95)

Angell's second example gives us in the bargain triangles with angle sums greater than 180 degrees: two base angles with 90 degrees each at our feet (where the rails cross the tie), and an apex angle with some positive magnitude at the horizon (where the rails appear to converge).

Now the striking thing about the example of the railroad track is that the purportedly non-Euclidean configuration it involves is never given in a single view. There is an appearance composed of two straight rail-appearances meeting at the horizon; there is also an appearance of two straight rail-appearances making right angles with a tie-appearance; but these appearances are never combined in a single view. As developed so far, Angell's geometry is a geometry of appearances that never appear.

It would be all right if the appearances of which Angell's geometry holds do not *appear*, just so long as they nonetheless *exist*. So he needs a principle assuring us that certain total appearances exist even though nothing more than various alleged parts of them are ever given to us at once. He recognizes the need for some such principle in the following passing remark: "We will therefore speak of a person's total visual field as that expanse which includes all possible continuous extensions of lines or regions in his momentary visual field" (91). But how exactly would we formulate a principle that guarantees the existence of a more-than-180-degree triangle composed of the appearance of right angles I get if I look at my feet and the appearance of an apex angle I get if I look toward the horizon? It would have to be a principle allowing us to identify extensions of the lines that meet at the horizon with extensions of the lines that cross the tie at our feet. I am skeptical whether there is any acceptable principle that will fill the bill.

Another purported example of an appearance that is inspectably non-Euclidean is described by J. R. Lucas, whom Angell quotes:

> Let the reader look up at the four corners of the ceiling of his room, and judge what the apparent angle at each corner is; that is, at what angle the two lines where the walls meet the ceiling appear to him to intersect each other. If the reader imagines sketching each corner in turn, he will soon convince himself that all the angles are more than right angles, some considerably so. And yet the ceiling appears to be a quadrilateral. From which it would seem that the geometry of appearance is non-Euclidean. And so it is. (Lucas 1969:6, quoted at Angell 115 with the omission of the final sentence)

It is, of course, a theorem in Riemannian geometry that quadrilaterals contain more than four right angles, since every quadrilateral is composed of two triangles, and the triangles contain more than 180 degrees each. The question is whether the visual field really contains such quadrilaterals. Lucas's ceiling, like Angell's tie-and-track triangle, is evidently one of those appearances that never appears (in toto).

Angell is on safer ground, it seems to me, insofar as he rests his case on the measurement of visible figures that we *can* take in at a single view—for example, triangles and quadrilaterals that take up only a small portion of the visual field. Such figures are not noticeably non-Euclidean. As Reid points out, any figures small enough to be seen "distinctly and at one view" are approximately ("very nearly, although not strictly and mathematically") Euclidean (IHM 6.9:106). That is part of his explanation of why the alleged non-Euclidean character of visibles is so easy to overlook. But if inspection will not tell us that small figures are non-Euclidean, Angell tells us, careful measurement will. To measure a visible angle, fix a protractor in front of your eyes with its angles aligned with the angle in the visible; do that for each of the angles in a visible triangle and you will obtain a sum greater than 180 degrees.

Is he right about this? I find myself that I cannot measure small visible figures with any precision. Too much depends on how I hold the protractor or how I cock my head—problems that do not affect the measurement of stable lines on paper— and I seldom get the same result twice. So far as I can tell by measurement, visible triangles might contain 180 degrees, or 175 or 185.

Let me recapitulate the three most important results of sections C through F. First, Reid's argument (or the only one we have so far identified, the argument from indistinguishability) for the non-Euclidean character of visibles rests on a fallacy— the fallacy of transferring properties from spherical figures to any figures indistinguishable from them. Second, Angell's argument does not rest on the same fallacy, but it is still problematic. It must rest either on dubious claims about the existence of figures that are never given in one view or on dubious claims about the results of measuring the properties of figures that are given in one view. Third, even if these claims were correct, Angell's approach yields a non-Euclidean geometry only if we reify visibles in a way that jeopardizes direct realism.

## G. THE ARGUMENT OF PARAGRAPH 4

Can we find a better argument for Reid's geometry of visibles than any we have considered so far? I believe we can. Reid's paragraph 5, on which I have so far concentrated the search, is meant to follow in part from paragraph 4. Let us back up one paragraph and see whether we can find anything there that bolsters Reid's case.[13]

Here is paragraph 4, with labels inserted to mark its conclusion (C), its two main premises (P1 and P2), and one auxiliary premise (A1):

(C) That the visible angle comprehended under two visible right lines, is equal to the spherical angle comprehended under the two great circles which are the representatives of these visible lines. For since (A1) the visible lines appear to coincide with the great circles, (P1) the visible angle comprehended under the former, must be equal to the visible angle comprehended under the latter. But (P2) the visible angle comprehended under the two great circles, when seen from the centre, is of the same magnitude with the spherical angle which they really comprehend, as mathematicians know; therefore (C) the visible angle made by any two visible lines, is equal to the spherical angle made by the two great circles of the sphere which are their representatives. (IHM 6.9:104)

Letting "line" and "great circle" be short (as Reid often intends them) for "line segment" and "great circle segment," the main argument of this paragraph may be set out as follows:

P1. The visible angle made by any two visible straight lines = the visible angle made by the two great circles representing these lines. (When visible angles are spoken of, they are always angles as seen from a certain point of view. I often leave it implicit, as Reid does, that the point of view is the center of the sphere containing the great circle representatives.)

P2. The visible angle made by two great circles (when seen from the center of the sphere containing them) = the real angle made by these great circles.

---

[13] I am indebted to Tim Chambers for helping me get clear on the role of paragraph 4 in Reid's overall argument.

C: The visible angle made by any two visible straight lines = the real angle made by the two great circles representing them.[14]

The conclusion follows from the premises by the transitivity of equality. The questions we need to address are these: Why are the premises true? And how does the conclusion contribute to Reid's overall argument?

*Why is P1 true?* Reid gives us half of the answer, namely A1: any two visible straight lines appear to coincide with two great circles. (As Reid does, I often let 'line' and 'circle' be short for 'line segment' and 'circle segment'.) The other half of the answer, which Reid thought obvious enough to go unstated, is A2: if the angle-making lines 1 and 2 appear to coincide respectively with the angle-making lines 3 and 4, then the visible angle made by 1 and 2 is equal to the visible angle made by 3 and 4. A1 and A2 seem entirely unobjectionable, and the two together yield Reid's P1.

*Why is P2 true?* Reid gives no argument for P2; he simply says that it is something that "mathematicians know." What exactly did he have in mind? I am not sure, but I conjecture that he would have approved of the following argument:

A3. The real angle made by two great circles (X) = the plane angle made by lines tangent to them at their point of intersection (Y). (This premise is true by standard mathematical convention. In general, one measures the angle between curves by measuring the angle between lines tangent to the curves at their point of intersection and lying in the same plane with them.)

A4. The visible angle made by two great circles (Z) = the visible angle made by their tangents (W). (This follows from A2 and something very like Reid's A1: the great circles appear to coincide with their tangents.)

A5. The visible angle made by two such tangents (W) = the plane angle made by ("really comprehended by") the tangents (Y). (This is true given our assumption that the tangents are viewed from the center of the sphere containing the great circles, since in that case one's line of sight will be orthogonal to the plane of the tangents.)

P2. The visible angle made by two great circles (Z) = the real angle made by these great circles ("the spherical angle which they really comprehend") (X).

As before, the conclusion follows from the premises by the transitivity of equality. I have inserted the letters X, Y, Z, and W to make the transitivity easier to track.

---

[14] A visible straight line does not have a *unique* great circle representative, since a circle of any radius would do. The word "the" in the formulation of P1 and C should therefore really be replaced by "any," which could be done without harm to the argument.

For further light on why P2 is true, I now present an alternative argument for it. In this argument, as in the one just given, we need to consider two kinds of angle— visible angle, or the angle between two lines as seen from a certain point of view, and real angle, or what Reid calls "the angle really comprehended" by two lines. (Perhaps we should speak instead of the *real magnitude* of an angle and its *visible magnitude* from a certain point of view, but for brevity I shall often speak simply of real and visible angle.) The visible angle made by two lines AB and BC as seen from e may be equated with (or measured by) a certain *dihedral* angle—namely, the angle made by the two planes eBA and eBC.[15] The visible angle made by two curved lines may be equated with the dihedral angle of the planes containing them. The real angle made by two lines, if they are straight, is simply the plane angle made by them; if they are curved, it may be equated with the plane angle made by the two lines tangent to the curves at their point of intersection and lying in the same planes as the curves. (This is a general-ization of the mathematical convention referred to above in justification of A3.) If we adopt the further convention that straight lines are identical with their own tangents, we may save words by saying that the real angle of two lines is their tangent angle. Thus visible angle equals dihedral angle and real angle equals tangent angle. Now in the case of angles between segments of great circles seen from the center of the sphere, the dihedral angle and the tangent angle are the same. Hence the visible angle of two such segments and their real angle are the same—which is just what Reid's P2 says.[16]

*How does conclusion C help?* How does conclusion C contribute to the overall case for the geometry of visibles? I believe it does so by making possible the following argument. First, for every visible triangle, there is a spherical triangle that is indis-tinguishable from it—a triangle whose sides and angles coincide visually with the sides and angles of the visible triangle. This is what Reid recapitulates in the open-ing sentences of paragraph 5. Second, each visible angle made by lines in the visible triangle is equal to the real angle made by the great circle representatives of these lines in the spherical triangle. This is conclusion C from paragraph 4. Third, as we know from the geometry of the sphere, the angles in a spherical triangle always add

---

[15] For this suggestion I am indebted to Gideon Yaffe. It implies that the visible angles in a triangle as seen from point e are equal to the angles between the walls of the pyramid having that triangle as base and point e as its apex.

[16] In a manuscript at the Aberdeen University Library ("Of the Doctrine of the Sphere," 2131/5/II/36), I find that Reid defines the angle made by great circles as the dihedral angle made by the planes containing them: "The angles [in a spherical triangle] are measured by the inclination of the planes of the great circles under which the angles are comprehended." This definition would yield by a more direct route yet the equality of visible angle with real angle for spherical figures. The manuscript is undated, but it appears to consist of notes for Reid's lectures at Aberdeen, which would have been delivered prior to the publication of the *Inquiry* in 1764. Thanks to Sabina Tropea for directing my attention to this and several other relevant manuscripts.

up to more than 180 degrees. Put these three premises together and it follows that the visible angles in any visible triangle add up to more than 180 degrees. Q.E.D.

Alternatively, as I find more perspicuous, we could make the overall argument using P1 and P2 from paragraph 4 rather than C:

1. Every visible triangle is indistinguishable from some spherical triangle, and therefore (by P1) has its visible angles equal to the visible angles in the spherical triangle.
2. The visible angles in a spherical triangle equal its real angles (from P2).
3. The real angles in a spherical triangle add up to more than 180 degrees.
4. Therefore, the visible angles in a visible triangle add up to more than 180 degrees.

With that argument, we have apparently arrived at last at a valid argument for a non-Euclidean geometry of visibles.

## H. THE REAL BASIS OF THE GEOMETRY OF VISIBLES

We are now in a position to understand the true basis of the geometry of visibles, disentangling it from several fallacies and irrelevancies.

*Not an argument from indistinguishability.* Contrary to the impression given by paragraph 5, Reid is not giving the argument from indistinguishability. He is not saying that visible triangles have the geometric properties of spherical triangles because they are indistinguishable from spherical triangles. That would be fallacious for all the reasons belabored above—that visible triangles are also indistinguishable from plane triangles, saddle triangles, and triangles drawn on all manner of exotic surfaces.

*In what sense spherical figures represent visible figures.* What may lead the reader astray on the previous point is that Reid says that visible figures have the geometrical properties of the spherical figures that represent them.[17] If the reader supposes that a visible figure may be represented by any figure indistinguishable from it, it may then appear that Reid is giving the argument from indistinguishability. But in fact, for a figure x to represent a visible figure y, it is not sufficient that x be indistinguishable from y. (Spherical triangles are indistinguishable from visible triangles,

---

[17] Reid uses "represent" in two disparate senses: spherical figures represent (i.e., model the properties of) visible figures, and visible figures represent (i.e., signify or suggest to the mind) tangible figures. For instances of the first usage, see IHM 6.9:104, throughout. For instances of the second usage, see IHM 6.8:103, lines 1–3, and 6.9:105, lines 36–40. My remark in the text concerns how to understand "represent" in the first sense.

but so are appropriately chosen plane triangles, saddle triangles, and so on.) There is a further necessary condition on representation: figure x represents visible figure y only if the *apparent* magnitudes of angles in y are equal to the *real* magnitudes of angles in x.[18] This further condition is satisfied by spherical figures (as Reid's argument in paragraph 4 shows), but not by figures on the other surfaces of projection I have discussed. For example, it is not satisfied by figures on the spiky sphere. Two lines that bisect each other at a peak on the spiky sphere will make apparent angles (for an eye looking up from the center) equal to right angles, but they will make real angles very much narrower than right angles.

Perhaps surprisingly, not even plane figures meet the further necessary condition on representation. Consider a 90–90–90 triangle on the globe, consisting of one quarter of the equator and legs running from its endpoints up to the North Pole. Connect the vertices of this triangle by three really straight lines. To the eye looking out from the center of the sphere, the resulting plane triangle will be indistinguishable from the original spherical triangle (in the sense that one perfectly occludes the other), but it will be a 60–60–60 triangle rather than a 90–90–90 triangle. Reid's claim, implied in the argument of paragraph 4, is that the visible triangle presented to the eye by either of these indistinguishable real triangles will have apparent angle magnitudes equal to the real angle magnitudes in the spherical triangle and *not* to those in the plane triangle. The visible triangle will have apparent angle magnitudes of 90 degrees at each vertex, hard to imagine though this be. See appendix N for further discussion of whether Reid's geometry contains unimaginable elements.

How can the visible angles in the visible presented by the 60–60–60 plane triangle not have 60 degrees? The answer is that when one views any of the 60-degree angles from the position of the central eye, one will be viewing it obliquely rather than head-on, and in that case it will appear to have more than 60 degrees. This of

---

[18] Actually, it may be that Reid himself operates with a weaker notion of representation that does not incorporate this condition. He concludes that a visible straight line may be represented by a great circle merely from the fact that the two coincide to the eye, or have corresponding points in the same visual position (IHM 6.9:103, line 27, through 104, line 6). He similarly concludes that "the whole surface of the sphere will represent the whole of visible space" from the fact that "every visible point coincides with some point on the surface of the sphere, and has the same visible place" (IHM 6.9:104, lines 31–33). In these inferences, he is apparently taking indistinguishability as a sufficient condition of representation. In that case, my proposed additional condition should come in not as a component condition of the premise "x represents y," but as an auxiliary condition for inferring from this premise to "y has the same relevant geometrical properties as x." The upshot would be this: we should not say that visible figures have the geometrical properties of *any* figures representing them, but only that they have the properties of *spherical* figures representing them. By insisting on the additional condition (as a separate premise if not part of the meaning of "represents"), Reid arrives at an argument free from the flaws of the argument from indistinguishability.

course is why the angles in Lucas's ceiling appear from the center of the room to be obtuse, even though a carpenter's square would fit snugly in each corner.

*What is special about the sphere?* Now we can say what is special about the sphere as a surface of projection. That spherical figures are indistinguishable from visible figures confers no special privilege on them as representatives, for the same is true of appropriately chosen plane figures, saddle figures, and so on. But spherical figures are different from the other figures in this respect: among figures indistinguishable from a given visible figure, *spherical figures alone have their real angle magnitudes equal to the apparent magnitudes of the angles in the visible.*

It might be thought that there are plane angles that will represent the angles in any visible just as well as spherical triangles. If I trace the angle made by two edges of my ceiling on a flat sheet of plastic held normal to my line of sight, I will obtain a plane angle that meets both conditions of representation—it is visually coincident with the visible angle and its real magnitude equals the apparent magnitude of the visible angle. True enough. But if you compute the angle sum of the visible ceiling by adding up the angles in their planar representatives, you will get more than 360 degrees, just as Reid says. So this exception, if it is one, does not lead to un-Reidian results. Moreover, we do not really have an exception here to the italicized claim in the preceding paragraph. There is no *one* figure that can contain all four representative planar angles. If we want a *single* figure (as opposed to a system of four uncombinable plane angles) to represent the properties of a visible quadrilateral, the most obvious candidate is a spherical figure. (Are spherical figures the *only* candidates? I address that question in appendix M.)

*Angell and Lucas revisited.* I complained above against Lucas that no ceiling ever appears in a single view as a quadrilateral having four obtuse angles, and I questioned whether we are entitled to assume the existence of non-Euclidean appearances if they never appear.[19] I also questioned whether figures small enough to be seen in one view are measurably non-Euclidean, as Angell contends. Reid can sidestep both objections, for he need not claim that visible figures are either inspectably or measurably non-Euclidean.

Regarding the first objection, Reid would concede that no figures that appear to the eye are ever noticeably non-Euclidean. He notes that when a triangle "is so small as to be seen distinctly at one view, and is placed directly before the eye, . . . its three

---

[19] Note, by the way, that my complaint against Lucas can be made against an inference of Reid's. In paragraph 5 he says. "The sides of the one will appear equal to the sides of the other, and the angles of the one to the angles of the other, each to each; and therefore the whole of the one triangle will appear equal to the whole of the other." If the whole of the one triangle never appeared at all, the premises of this inference would be true and the conclusion false. Fortunately, however, Reid does not need to affirm the conclusion of this inference, as I am about to explain in the text.

angles will be so nearly equal to two right angles, that the sense cannot discern the difference" (IHM 6.11:118–19, eliding several lines; see also IHM 6.9:106). Regarding the second objection, Reid need not claim that we could discover visible figures to be non-Euclidean by measurement. His case for the non-Euclidean character of visibles is the argument we have set forth in the previous section, drawing on the combined resources of paragraphs 4 and 5. The argument is a theoretical argument showing that the angles in any visible triangle are not "strictly and mathematically" equal to the angles in any Euclidean plane triangle, but are equal to the angles in a spherical triangle instead. It is an argument that applies to any visible triangle, even if the triangle is too big to be seen at once, too small to be noticeably non-Euclidean, or too evanescent to be accurately measured.

*The relevance of the spherical eye.* Contrary to the impression formed by some of his commentators (e.g., Daniels 1974:10–11 and Pastore 1971:114), Reid's case for the geometry of visibles has nothing to do with the roundness of the human eye. I supported this contention above by noting that a camera obscura "sees" the same things we do without having any spherical component. We are now in a position to go into this point more deeply.

What is it that the camera "sees"? Nothing, of course, if we take "seeing" literally. But let us assume for expository purposes that the camera obeys a variant of the law of visible direction, which Reid takes to govern human vision. Reid says that any point in an object is seen in the direction of a straight line running from the point of retinal stimulation back through the center of the eye and into the environment.[20] The variant for a camera obscura would be that it "sees" any point in the direction of a straight line drawn from the image of the point on its rear wall back through the pinhole. Under this assumption, the visible figure of what the camera sees will be unaffected by the curvature of its rear wall—it will be the same regardless of whether the surface on which the image is cast is flat, hemispherical, or curved like a funhouse mirror. That is because the directions of all lines from image points through the pinhole will be unaffected by these variations—and Reid tells us that visible figure is uniquely determined by the totality of all such directions (which in the case of the eye pass through its center rather than through the camera's pinhole).

Of course, the *real* figure of the *image* will vary with the curvature of the surface on which it is cast: a quadrilateral projected on a flat retina or camera wall will

---

[20] Reid puts it thus: "Every point of the object is seen in the direction of a right line passing from the picture of that point on the *retina* through the centre of the eye" (IHM 6.12:122–23). In chapter 7, I explain how Reid uses this law to solve the puzzle of how we see objects erect by means of inverted retinal images.

have an angle sum of 360 degrees while one projected on a hemispherical surface will have an angle sum greater than 360 degrees. But the real figure in the rear of the camera is not what the camera sees, and the image painted on the retina is not what we see. Reid is at pains more than once to point out that we do not see retinal impressions.[21]

The relevance of retinal contour to visible figure seems to be just this: because of the happy accident that the retina is roughly hemispherical, it is correct for Reid to observe that the projection on a sphere that determines visible figure "is the same [species of] figure with that which is projected upon the *tunica retina* in vision" (IHM 6.7:95). If the retina were flat, Reid could not make this claim, for the real angles in the retinal image would not equal the apparent angles in the visible figure or the real angles in its spherical projection. But he could still make the same case for the geometry of visibles, for whether the retinal image is flat or curved, it will determine (in accordance with the law of visible direction) the same visible figure.[22]

*The geometry of visibles is the geometry of the single point of view.* This idea is implicit in the explanation I give above of why the sphere is special, but let me now be more explicit about it. If you view each of your ceiling corners from directly beneath it, you will see each corner as a right angle. The sum of the visible angles in your ceiling, *as seen successively from these four points of view,* will be 360 degrees. But if you insist on viewing all four corners from the *same* point of view, you will you come up with a sum of visible angles *greater* than 360 degrees. If the single viewpoint is near the center of the room, all four angles will appear obtuse. If the single viewpoint is directly beneath one of the corners, that corner and the two adjacent corners will appear as right angles, but the diagonally opposite corner will appear obtuse. Wherever you position yourself, so long as you confine yourself to a single viewpoint, the sum of the visible angles is bound to exceed four right angles. (Note that I am saying "single viewpoint" rather than "single view"—it may be necessary for the eye to rotate in order to take in all four angles of the ceiling.)[23]

---

[21] "We have reason to believe, that the rays of light make some impression upon the *retina*; but we are not conscious of this impression" (IHM 6.8:100). "Nor is there any probability that the mind perceives the pictures upon the *retina*. These pictures are no more objects of our perception, than the brain is, or the optic nerve" (IHM 6.12:121).

[22] I do have to convict Reid of one mistake, however. He says that what a blind man needs in order to determine the visible figure of a body is its projection on a sphere, "for it is the same figure with that which is projected upon the *tunica retina* in vision" (IHM 6.7:95). If I am right, Reid's "for" should merely be an "and."

[23] Question: If the eye may be allowed to rotate, why did I complain above that Angell's tie-and-track triangle is never given in a single view? Answer: Insofar as Angell's argument is a phenomenological one, inviting us simply to "read off" the non-Euclidean character of what is before our eyes, it is important that we have some assurance that there actually are such figures as the

*What happens if we add a second eye?* What happens to the geometry of visibles if we add a second eye? This is a question to which I cannot do justice here, but I wish to mark out two issues for further investigation: whether a second eye alters the geometry of visibles by enabling us to perceive depth, and how the concepts of visual geometry are to be defined if there are two eyes or viewpoints rather than one.

The most powerful mechanism of depth perception is retinal disparity, which of course requires two eyes and which was unknown to Reid.[24] If the eye (or rather, the eyes) can perceive depth after all, is Reid's case for the geometry of visibles undermined?

Reid himself certainly connects the geometry of visibles with the unperceivability of depth. In his numbered list of "evident principles" underlying the geometry of visibles, the unperceivability of depth is at the top: "For the curvature of the circle being turned directly toward the eye, is not perceived by it" (IHM 6.9:103). Moreover, in a manuscript version of the geometry of visibles, he tells us this: "Now if it is allowed that an Idomenian [one of Reid's fictional creatures endowed with sight but not touch] can have no notion of distance or proximity betwixt himself & what he sees, I think after careful examination, their Geometry must be such as Apodemus hath described it."[25] In other words, it must be the non-Euclidean geometry that Reid himself has described; he repeats this claim when he retells the story of the Idomenians at the end of *Inquiry* 6.9. Finally, it is a key premise in the argument for the geometry of visibles as I have reconstructed it that any visible straight line appears to coincide with (or is visibly indistinguishable from) a great circle centered on the eye. This is assumption A1 underlying both of the main premises P1 and P2 in the argument of paragraph 4, and Reid rests it squarely on the unperceivability of depth.

---

tie-and-track triangle. We cannot have such assurance if the triangle is not presented in a single view. Reid is not open to this challenge, since he has a theoretical argument applying to triangles of any size. We can take a small triangle, of whose existence we are assured because we see it, and apply Reid's argument to show that it has an angle sum exceeding 180 degrees.

[24] In IHM 6.22 Reid identifies five types of depth cue, which according to him enable an acquired perception of depth even though we have no original perception of depth. Of his five, the first four are monocular and the fifth—the angle of convergence between the eyes—is binocular, but useful only at short distances. Reid evidently did not know about retinal disparity, the discovery of which is generally credited to Wheatstone, inventor of the stereoscope, in 1838. However, Reid's theory of corresponding retinal points, which he uses in IHM 6.13 to explain why we see single with two eyes, is an important ingredient in the retinal disparity explanation of depth perception. On the connection between corresponding points and retinal disparity, see Hochberg 1978:55–60.

[25] IHM 275. This is from one of Reid's Discourses delivered before the Aberdeen Philosophical Society, dated June 14, 1758. As far as I know, this Discourse is the first extant version of Reid's geometry of visibles.

And yet it is not obvious to me exactly how Reid's argument would be undermined if we grant that depth *can* be perceived. There are two main ways of taking the question of whether depth is perceived by sight. One is epistemological: do we *know* through vision how far out things are? The other is phenomenological: do things *look* to be more or less distant? Suppose first that depth is perceived in an epistemological sense. Suppose, for example, that as in Abbott's Flatland, an ever-present fog makes more distant objects appear dimmer, in proportion to their distance (Abbott [1884] 1994, section 6). We would then be in a position to know that a line curving away from us really was curved (or to interpret it as being a curved line), even though it had the same appearance as a straight line. Would that affect Reid's case for the geometry of visibles? I think not. Reid would still be able to maintain that the visible triangle presented to us by three such lines of varying brightness or dimness has the angle sum of a spherical triangle.

Suppose next that depth is perceived in a phenomenological sense, as H. H. Price famously claimed when he said that tomatoes look bulgy (Price 1932:3 and 218–21). Would that undermine Reid's argument? The key question is whether a straight line can still perfectly occlude an outwardly curved line and thus be indistinguishable from it, as claimed in assumption A1. If an outwardly curved segment of a great circle is seen as straight by an eye lying in the plane of that great circle, it will be seen as curved by an eye displaced a bit from that plane. How will the outwardly curved line be seen by a visual system employing two eyes—as distinguishable from a straight line (contradicting Reid) or not? I am not sure. It is worthy of note that our binocular sense of depth does not undo various key claims Reid bases on his monocular assumptions—for example, that right angles seen obliquely look acute or obtuse.

However we resolve the issue of how Reid's argument depends on the unperceivability of depth, there is another way in which adding a second eye threatens to undermine his case. Visible figure, visible magnitude (of lines), and visible angle are all defined by reference to a point of view. The visible angle made by lines AB and AC is relative to a point e; we have equated it with the dihedral angle made by the planes eAB and eAC. How are we even to define such notions if there are *two* viewpoints, $e_1$ and $e_2$? Although I do not believe this difficulty is insuperable, I lack the space to address it here.[26]

---

[26] Essentially the same problem arises for the classical definition of the visible magnitude of a line as the angle it subtends at the eye: how are we to adapt this definition given that there are two eyes? Psychologists resort to the artifice of the "Cyclopean eye," the midpoint between the two eyes, defining visible magnitude as the angle subtended at this midpoint.

*Postscript.* In this chapter, I develop Reid's case for the geometry of visibles almost exactly as I do in Van Cleve 2002a. I now have second thoughts about the soundness of his case, prompted by Falkenstein, forthcoming. I discuss Falkenstein's critique of Reid in appendix O.

## I. DOES THE GEOMETRY OF VISIBLES JEOPARDIZE DIRECT REALISM?

Angell's way of developing the geometry of visibles explicitly involves positing visibles as entities akin to sense data. Does Reid's argument for the geometry of visibles involve a similar commitment? I now offer a prima facie case for answering *yes*.

Here, slightly reworded, is the reconstruction of Reid's argument we reached at the end of section G:

1. Visible triangles are indistinguishable from spherical triangles. In particular, for every visible triangle v seen from e, there is a spherical triangle centered on e such that the apparent magnitudes of angles in v are equal to the apparent magnitudes of angles in s.
2. In a spherical triangle, the apparent magnitudes of the angles (as seen from the center of the sphere) are equal to their real magnitudes.
3. The real magnitudes of the angles of a spherical triangle sum to more than 180 degrees.
4. Therefore, every visible triangle has apparent angle magnitudes that sum to more than 180 degrees.[27]

The first of these premises is what Reid takes to follow from the unperceivability of depth, the second is what he establishes in paragraph 4, and the third is geometrical fact already known to the ancient Greeks. The conclusion implies that visible figures are governed by a non-Euclidean geometry.

---

[27] One must take some care in stating 4, in which there is some danger of scope ambiguity. The point is not that visible triangles appear to have angle sums of more than 180 degrees, in which case they would "look non-Euclidean." Rather, they have sums of apparent angles that exceed 180 degrees. Formally, the difference is that between "v appears to have angle magnitudes x, y, and z such that x + y + z > 180 degrees" and "there are magnitudes x, y, and z such that (i) x + y + z > 180 degrees and (ii) v appears to have angles of those magnitudes x, y, and z." Premise 4 does not assert the former, but at most the latter. Even the latter may be in a certain way too strong, suggesting as it does that visible triangles appear to have angles of certain numerical magnitudes. It is rather that visible triangles have angles that appear equal to the angles in a spherical triangle with certain numerical magnitudes. Compare: a line may appear to be the same in length as a line that is two inches long without appearing to be two inches long.

Or does it? It is arguable that to obtain a genuinely non-Euclidean geometry of visibles, we must add one more premise:

5. Visible triangles *are what they appear to be* in relevant geometrical respects. If a visible triangle has angles of certain apparent magnitudes, its angles really are of those magnitudes.

With that premise aboard, we may take one more step:

6. Therefore, every visible triangle has angles whose real magnitudes sum to more than 180 degrees.

The rub, of course, is that premise 5 is none other than the sense-datum move. It implies, for example, that if a visible triangle appears to have one of its angles obtuse, that angle really is obtuse.

Why think the sense-datum move essential to Reid's case? For an answer, listen to a direct realist who resists the move: "That triangular piece of wood over there, which I am now directly seeing and which *I* call a visible, does indeed appear, when seen from a single vantage point, to have angle values that exceed 180 degrees. But it doesn't really have such values; nor is there anything else, a 'visible' in *your* sense, intervening between it and me, that really has such values." In short, without the sense-datum move, the argument stops at step 4, and in that case we do not get any entities that have non-Euclidean properties. We only get entities that *appear* to have non-Euclidean properties.[28]

To obtain entities that really *do* have non-Euclidean properties, we must reify visible angles. But if we do that, a version of Hume's table argument against direct realism may be reinstated. When I view a rectangular tabletop from an oblique perspective at one end, its two nearer angles appear acute and its two farther angles appear obtuse. If I reify visible angles, I will say that what I see contains two angles that *are* acute and two that *are* obtuse. But then what I see cannot be the tabletop, for all of *its* angles are right angles.

## J. WHAT ARE VISIBLES?

"Figure" can be either an object word, as in "he drew a figure on the blackboard," or a property word, as in "these two objects have the same figure." Reid uses it both ways, but more often in the object way, and visible figures in the object sense are what he generally means by "visibles."

But what exactly *are* visibles? As Reid frames the question himself, "To what category of beings does visible figure then belong?" (IHM 6.8:98). The question proves

---

[28] Remember the caveat in the preceding note about this claim is to be understood.

to be a perplexing one, capable of eliciting at least four possible answers: visible figures might be taken to be mental entities, physical entities, abstract entities, or non-existent Meinongian entities.

Some readers have entertained the suspicion that visible figures are mental entities. Cummins, for instance, says that by introducing visible figure as something distinct from tangible figure, Reid "came perilously close to reintroducing ideas of sense" (1974:n. 56). But this is a suggestion Reid repudiates. Visible figure cannot be an impression or an idea, he tells us, because "it may be long or short, broad or narrow, triangular, quadrangular, or circular: and therefore unless ideas and impressions are extended and figured, it cannot belong to that category" (IHM 6.8:98). Instead, "The visible figure of bodies is a real and external object to the eye" (IHM 6.8: 101).[29]

When I suggested in the preceding section that visibles are like sense data insofar as they satisfy the "x looks F $\rightarrow$ x is F" formula that governs sense data, I was not thereby implying that they are mental. Sense data are not necessarily mental entities; they were not construed as such by Moore, Russell, and other classical sense-datum theorists. And Frank Jackson, the most notable exponent of sense data in recent decades, explicitly holds that they exist at various distances from the perceiver, rather than being located in a special private space (Jackson 1977:102–3).[30]

If visible figures are external objects, what sort of external objects are they? In one place, Reid seems to identify visible figures with the projections on a sphere we have discussed above:

> Now I require no more knowledge in a blind man, in order to his being able to determine the visible figure of bodies, than that he can project the outline of a given body, upon the surface of a hollow sphere, whose centre is in the eye. This projection is the visible figure he wants. (IHM 6.7:95).[31]

[29] In light of Reid's insistence that visible figure is real and external, what he says about the visible figures of the Idomenians is quite mystifying. Lacking any notion of the third dimension because they lack the sense of touch, the Idomenians can conceive of visible figures neither as plane (i.e., uncurved through the third dimension) nor as curved. Therefore, Reid says, their visible figures *are* neither plane nor curved (IHM 6.9:108). But what could authorize that inference besides the assumption that the *esse* of visible figures is *concipi*? And how could that assumption be true of visible figures if they are real figures external to the mind?

[30] Despite holding that they exist at a distance from the perceiver, Jackson holds that sense data are mental entities.

[31] The sentence continues as follows: "for it is the same figure with that which is projected upon the *tunica retina* in vision." I find that some students take this sentence to imply that visible figures

In most places, however, Reid refrains from *identifying* visible figures with projections on a sphere, using the language of representation rather than the language of identity. For example, he says "every visible figure is represented by that part of the surface of the sphere, on which it might be projected, the eye being at the centre" (IHM 6.9:104). And in the section that explicitly raises the question where visible figure belongs in the system of categories, he gives this coy answer: "A projection of the sphere . . . is a representative in the very same sense as visible figure is, and wherever they have their lodging in the categories, they will be found to dwell next door to them" (IHM 6.8:99).

Reid does not explain his refusal to identify visible figures with projections on a sphere, but there are at least two good reasons for it (already familiar to us from section E). First, though we have now seen why Reid chooses the sphere as his surface of projection, how could he nonarbitrarily identify visible figures with projections on a sphere of one size rather than another? Projections on spheres with the same center but different radii will all represent the same visible figure, but will be numerically different arrays of points. Second, if visible figures are identical with projections on a sphere, they are really curved. The geometry of visibles would simply be the Euclidean geometry of the sphere, and there would be nothing non-Euclidean about Reid's geometry.

These reasons for not identifying visible figures with projections on a sphere are in fact reasons for not identifying visible figures with any particular physical arrays of points whatsoever. If they were arrays of points external to the mind, just where would they be? Not, it seems, at one distance rather than another. Indeed, Reid goes so far as to say, "visible figure hath no distance from the eye" (IHM, 6.23:188). Moreover, if visible figures were points in physical space, would their geometry not by Reid's own account be Euclidean?

This brings us to the third suggestion, which is that visible figures are not concrete arrays of points but abstract equivalence classes. Daniels suggests that Reid's visible points are really classes of points having the same visible position (chapter 1); by extension, visible figures would be classes of arrays of points all possessing the same visible figure in the property sense. But this suggestion has its difficulties, too. Reid insists that visible figure is something extended—that is why he takes it to be nonmental. But classes, as abstract objects, are no more extended than mental

---

are figures on the retina in particular; such may also be the assumption of Pastore (115). But when Reid says that visible figure is the "same figure" as that projected on the retina, I think the sameness he is talking about is just sameness of type, not sameness of token. He tells us unequivocally that visible figure is an "external object to the eye" (IHM 6.8:101); he also tells us that we do not see retinal images.

entities. Moreover, Reid emphasizes that visible figures are "the immediate objects of sight"—they are things seen (IHM 6.8:102 and IHM 6.9:105). But I doubt that we ever see classes. In short, equivalence classes are neither figures nor things visible, and that makes them poor candidates to be visible figures.

The last possibility I wish to mention is that visible figures are nonexistent objects, perhaps of a Meinongian sort (as hinted in Falkenstein 2000).[32] It is an important part of Reid's theory of conception (examined in chapter 10) that we may conceive of objects that do not exist at all, and that provides a possible fourth status for visibles within his system—they are nonexistent intentional objects. But this proposal runs against the whole tenor of Reid's discourse about visibles, which strongly suggests that they are existing things.

## K. DIRECT REALISM AND SEEING WHAT WE TOUCH

Berkeley notoriously held that the realms of vision and touch are totally disparate. In explicit opposition to Berkeley, Reid affirms that we see and touch the same things: "When I hold my walking-cane upright in my hand, and look at it, I take it for granted, that I see and handle the same individual object. . . . I conceive the horizon as a fixed object both of sight and touch" (IHM 6.11:119). It is not clear that Reid is entitled to this affirmation, however, for it appears to be at odds with what he says about the geometry of visibles. Discussion of this inconsistency will once again highlight the worry that the geometry of visibles is inconsistent with direct realism.

Before I turn to the main inconsistency, I dismiss a superficial one. Reid tells us in several places that whereas tangible objects are three-dimensional, visible objects are merely two-dimensional (IHM 6.9:106–8 and 6.23:188). So how can we see and touch the same things? This difficulty is easily resolved. Reid could still hold that visible objects are *parts* of tangible objects, in the way that a two-dimensional square face is part of a three-dimensional cube, and that we see parts of the very objects we touch. This would fit well with what he says about visible and tangible space:

> When I use the names of tangible and visible space, I do not mean to adopt Bishop Berkeley's opinion, so far as to think that they are really different things, and altogether unlike. I take them to be different conceptions of the same thing; the one very partial, and the other more complete; but both distinct and just, as far as they reach. (EIP 2.19:222–23)

---

[32] "Though Reid does not come out and say it in so many words, he would appear to be forced to admit that our beliefs in visible figures are beliefs in something that does not actually exist in the external world, though they serve as signs for the things that do so exist" (Falkenstein 2000, n. 38).

Now for the deeper inconsistency, which is not as easily removed. Reid apparently affirms each of the propositions in the following inconsistent triad:

1. I sometimes see and touch the same things.
2. The geometry of what I touch is Euclidean.
3. The geometry of what I see is non-Euclidean.

If the objects of sight and touch are governed by different geometries, we are evidently precluded even from saying that I see *parts* of what I touch. The surface of a triangular slab of wood has an angle sum of 180 degrees; any visible triangle has an angle sum of more than 180 degrees; therefore, no visible triangle can ever be the facing surface of a slab of wood or of any other tangible object. By extension, scarcely anything I ever see is the facing surface of anything tangible.[33]

We could get around this inconsistency by distinguishing a broader from a narrower sense of "seeing." What I see in the narrow sense are just the visibles; what I see in the broader sense includes as well things that are suggested to the mind by visibles, that is, things of which the mind automatically conceives upon being presented with the visible signs of them (compare IHM 6.8:101–2). Our triad would then look like this:

1. I sometimes see (in our new broader sense) things that I touch.
2. The geometry of what I touch is Euclidean.
3. The geometry of visibles (of things I see in the narrower sense) is non-Euclidean.

No inconsistency there. The problem with this suggestion (or so it may seem) is that it removes the inconsistency only at the cost of abandoning a direct realism of vision. Seeing in the broader sense—the seeing of tables and trees that is mediated by visibles—is arguably not direct seeing *if the visibles themselves are what we immediately see.* And that is what Reid tells us:

[In the geometry that mathematicians have been developing for two thousand years] not a single proposition do we find with regard to the figure and extension which are the immediate objects of sight. (IHM: 6.8:102)

Those figures and that extension which are the immediate objects of sight, are not the figures and the extension about which common geometry is employed. (IHM 6.9:105)

---

[33] There are a few exceptions. For all the argument shows, the visible item I see when I look at a circular tabletop head on may be identical with the tabletop.

Reid evidently closes off the option of saying that visibles function as signs in vision without being seen.[34] It would seem to follow that tables and trees are at best mediate objects of sight—that we do not see them directly.

I am not suggesting that Reid lapses back into the way of ideas. His visibles are clearly not ideas or mental entities of any sort—whatever they are, they are supposed to be external to the mind. Nonetheless, he is committed to saying that my seeing the table in front of me depends on my seeing something else that is not even *part* of the table—an object whose geometrical properties are incompatible with those of the table and any of its parts. So he fails to be a direct realist in the Pappas and Jackson sense.

He does indeed. But recall that chapter 3 ended with the suggestion that we should employ a more liberal standard of direct perception than the Pappas-Jackson standard. Perceiving x by means of perceiving y can still count as direct perception of x if you *really do* perceive x. I consider in section M below whether by the more liberal standard, there is direct visual perception of three-dimensional objects.

## L. VISIBLE FIGURE AS A RELATIVIZED PROPERTY OF ORDINARY OBJECTS

In the hope of reconciling Reid's geometry of visibles with direct realism, I now present one more conception of what visibles and visible figure might be.

Recall that Angell distinguished between *visibles* or visual objects in his sense and *objects that are visible*. That may have struck the reader as a surprising distinction, and the suggestion I wish to make now is that we repudiate it. Visibles simply *are* objects that are visible; they include tables, trees, and all the furniture of the earth. Visible figure is a property of such objects—not an intrinsic property, like real figure, but a relational property (or perhaps better, a relativized property), possessed only in relation to a point of view.[35] "As the real figure of a body consists

---

[34] Other language Reid uses for our cognitive relation to visible figures includes the following: they are "presented to the mind by vision" (IHM 6.9:105, line 33); they are "presented to [the mathematician's] eye" (IHM 6.9:105, lines 37–38); they are among "the perceptions which we have purely by sight" (IHM 6.9:106, lines 26–27). Of course, he tells us repeatedly that we seldom, and only with difficulty, *attend* to visible figures, but they are nonetheless there before the mind.

[35] For discussion of visible figure as a relational property, see Nichols 2002. For discussion of the distinction between relational and relativized properties (though I was there somewhat dubious about it), see Van Cleve 1999:248. In a nutshell, the distinction is this: as a relational property, visible figure would be a dyadic relation between an object and a point of view; as a relativized property, it would be a monadic property of objects possessed by them in relation to some points of view but not others.

in the position of its several parts with regard to one another," Reid tells us, "so its visible figure consists in the position of its several parts with regard to the eye" (IHM 6.7:96). Since all that is relevant about the eye is its location, we may as well say "with regard to a point of view." Elaborating Reid's distinction further, we may say that objects have certain shape properties in themselves (that is, absolutely or nonperspectivally) and other shape properties relative to various points of view. For example, the mouth of a bucket may be round in itself or absolutely, but elliptical to varying degrees from various oblique points of view. A line may be curved absolutely (because there is a dimension of space through which it curves) and yet straight to the eye (if the absolute curvature is turned away from the eye). An angle may be a right angle in itself (or have 90 degrees as its real magnitude), while being acute from some points of view and obtuse from others. Reid thinks that it is ultimately through touch that real or absolute geometrical values are ascertained, but I need not take a stand on that. The proposal I am making is that visibles are none other than the familiar objects around us, and that the geometry of visibles is the geometry that investigates the geometrical properties possessed by these objects from a point of view. Any triangle has an angle sum of 180 degrees absolutely, but a sum greater than that relative to any chosen point of view. The sum will vary depending on the point of view, but will always be more than 180 degrees.

This proposal may sound like the suggestion of our direct realist in section I, who resisted the introduction of visibles as a special class of entities and insisted that visible objects merely *appear* to have non-Euclidean properties (or properties that would yield a non-Euclidean object if all combined in the same whole). The four angles in Lucas's ceiling *look* obtuse to the viewer in the center of the room, but they are really right angles. In fact, however, I am going just part of the way with that direct realist. I am identifying visibles with ordinary objects, as he does, but in the relativized approach to visible figure I am suggesting, I am not saying that quadrilaterals merely *appear* to have angles that sum to more than 360 degrees. (That would sound too much like an error theory.) The corner of the ceiling does not merely *look* obtuse from here—it *is* obtuse, *from here*. Compare: the mouth of a soccer goal does not merely *look* narrow from the sidelines; it *is* narrow from there, as shown by the greater difficulty of putting the ball in the net from there.[36]

---

[36] The relativized approach to visible figure is similar to the Multiple Inherence theory discussed in Broad 1925:160ff. and the Multiple Location theory discussed in Price 1932:55–58. It has more recent incarnations in Harman's "larger from here" (1990), Hill's appearance properties (2009:ch. 5), and Noë's perspectival properties (2004:83–84).

How far should we go with such relativized predication? If one post obscures another from a certain point of view, should we say there is only one post from there?

The present way of construing visibles leaves the way clear for a direct realism of vision. What we see are not special visible intermediaries that inherently possess non-Euclidean properties, but ordinary objects that possess non-Euclidean properties relative to our point of view. In the same way, the present approach gives us a way of avoiding the inconsistent triad about the objects of sight and touch that was brought to light in section K. What we see are indeed the very things we touch. Things we touch (and so of course also things we see) have Euclidean properties absolutely. Things we see (and so of course also things we touch) have non-Euclidean properties relative to our point of view. There is no inconsistency in that. In fact, this way out of the triad is reminiscent of Reid's own way with Hume's table argument: what I see is nothing other than the table, which varies in its apparent or perspectival magnitude while remaining constant in its real or intrinsic magnitude.[37]

Two questions remain to be asked about the conception of visibles as ordinary objects and visible figure as a relativized property of them. Did Reid think of things in this way? And does doing so give rise to a non-Euclidean geometry?

Did Reid think of things in this way? Probably not. He says that visible objects are two-dimensional (IHM 6.23:188, among many other places), whereas visibles on the conception I am now proposing are three-dimensional. Throughout IHM 6.9 he talks of "visible right lines," implying that visible right lines are a species of right (i.e., straight) lines, whereas the more apt phrase on the present conception would be "visibly right line," a phrase that may apply to a line that is absolutely curved.[38] Finally, his language tends to suggest two domains of objects—visible objects seen

---

[37] There is this difference: in chapter 3, section C, I construed apparent magnitude and visible figure as dyadic relations; I am now construing visible figure not as a dyadic relation but as a relativized property (in the sense indicated in n. 35). But either construal could be used to block the conclusion of the table argument.

[38] Note also that the present construal of visibles has trouble accommodating Reid's Proposition 1: "Every right line being produced, will at last return into itself." On the present construal, that proposition should be understood as follows: every line that is straight to the eye, when continued so as to make a longer line that is also straight to the eye, at last returns into itself. (A line is straight to an eye at p iff it lies in a plane containing p but does not pass through p.) That is true of *some* lines and methods of continuation: a segment of the equator is straight to the eye at the center of the globe and may be continued round the globe as a line that is straight to the eye and rejoins itself. But it is false of others: a *really* straight line may be continued indefinitely in a really straight line that is straight to the eye all the way but never rejoins itself. It will end at the limits of one's field of view if the eye remains stationary; it will end at the midpoint of one's field of view if the eye rotates until its axis is parallel with the line; it will end at points short of the midpoint as the eye continues to rotate. So visibles under the present construal of them do not satisfy Reid's Proposition 1. But that may well be a problem with Proposition 1 itself rather than the construal: although Proposition 1 is true if "right line" is interpreted as "great circle or segment thereof," I have been unable to find any good construal of "visible right line" that makes Proposition 1 true, as it is supposed to be, of all such lines.

immediately and the tangible objects they suggest to the mind. But no deep doctrine of his philosophy would have prevented Reid from adopting the present conception of visibles, and he would perhaps have welcomed alternative suggestions about where visibles might have their lodging in the categories.

Does the present conception give us a non-Euclidean geometry? If to propound a non-Euclidean geometry it suffices to point out that there are objects that have non-Euclidean properties from any point of view—even though these same objects are Euclidean in themselves—the answer would be yes. But there is reason to question the antecedent of that conditional. What does it mean to say that objects have non-Euclidean properties from a point of view? Here we may note that there is generally an equivalence between facts about the properties an object has in relation to a point p and facts about the nonrelational properties of larger configurations including the object and p. Here is one example:

> Triangle ABC has an angle sum of more than 180 degrees from p *iff* the pyramid with ABC as base and p as apex has more than 180 degrees as the sum of the three dihedral angles made by its three walls.[39]

The right-hand side of that biconditional is a purely Euclidean fact. So how can the left-hand side report a non-Euclidean fact?

If we are to obtain genuinely non-Euclidean results, I think we must make an assumption like the following—as I suspect Reid implicitly does:

> If object O has property F in relation to point p, then if your eye were placed at p and directed at O, an object with F would be presented to you.[40]

This principle implies that if O is F in relation to p, then there is something that is F *simpliciter*. For example, if a circle is elliptical from p, an observer with eye at p would be presented with an object that is elliptical, period. If an ordinary triangle has an angle sum of more than 180 degrees from p, then there is a special visible

---

[39] Recall that a dihedral angle is the angle between two planes, such as the walls pBA and pBC. Except in special cases, this will be broader or narrower than the angle ABC.

[40] Two questions may occur to the reader about this principle. (i) Does the F object exist regardless of whether there is an eye at p? I suspect Reid would say yes. To make this explicit, we could change the right-hand side to "there is an F object that would be presented to any observer with eye at p and directed at O." (ii) Would the F object be presented even in a fog or to an astigmatic eye? Here Reid is obviously making the idealizing assumption that what figures are presented to the eye is determined solely by geometrical considerations—the real figure of O and the location of p.

triangle—whatever exactly its ontological status may be—that has more than 180 degrees, period.

We have now arrived at genuinely non-Euclidean facts, but only by introducing special visible objects for them to be facts about. If no more is said, that leaves unallayed the worry I have had from the beginning—that Reid can secure a non-Euclidean geometry of visibles only at the cost of abandoning a direct realism of vision.

## M. MEDIATED BUT DIRECT?

I now make one last attempt to reconcile the geometry of visibles with direct realism. The reconciliation I propose can be effected even if the original objects of vision are special visible objects, differing from tables and chairs in possessing two dimensions and obeying non-Euclidean laws.

At the end of chapter 3, I suggest that what matters in securing direct perception is not downgrading our cognitive relation to any intermediaries, but upgrading our cognitive relation to the thing perceived. If we perceive or otherwise apprehend some intermediary along the way to perceiving a certain external object, no problem—just so long as we *do* in the end achieve perception of the object (that is to say, acquaintance with it). Reid himself allows for this possibility in the following passage:

> There is a sense in which a thing may be said to be perceived by a medium. Thus any kind of sign may be said to be the medium by which I perceive or understand the thing signified. The sign, by custom, or compact, or perhaps by nature, introduces the thought of the thing signified. But here the thing signified, when it is introduced to the thought, is an object of thought no less immediate than the sign was before: And there are here two objects of thought, one succeeding another, which we have shown is not the case with respect to an idea, and the object it represents. (EIP 2.9:134)

Perception might involve a sign as a perceived medium, yet still be immediate (or direct, in the sense I have been using). I refer to this possibility henceforth as the possibility that perception is (in Copenhaver's apt phrase) *mediated, but direct*.[41] How can we exploit this possibility to reconcile the geometry of visibles with direct realism?

In Reid's view as I am now taking it, the original objects of vision are two-dimensional visible figures; these are the intermediaries in the acquired visual

[41] I take the phrase from Copenhaver's "A Realism for Reid: Mediated, but Direct" (2004), but adapt its meaning to some extent for my own purposes. The direct realisms Copenhaver and I attribute to Reid differ in the following way: for her, the key to directness is whether the relation between sign and thing signified is an external relation; for me, it is whether we have acquaintance with the thing signified and not merely with the sign.

perception of three-dimensional figures, which are given originally only to touch. Our question is whether the acquired and mediated perception of three-dimensional figures can qualify as direct. The answer will be *yes* if we achieve acquaintance with three-dimensional figures through vision. So what *is* our cognitive relation to three-dimensional figures? What state of mind are we put into as a result of being aware of the two-dimensional cues?

To help answer this question, let us consider first Berkeley's view about the suggestion of tangible figure by visual cues, which was Reid's main model for acquired perception. According to Berkeley, we go through a period of learning during which we come to associate visual cues with tactile data entirely heterogeneous from them. Once the associations are formed, tactile imagery comes flooding in whenever we see a two-dimensional array, and therein lies our "seeing" of three-dimensional objects. To me, it seems quite doubtful that such "seeing" should count as direct visual perception, for it is doubtful that it counts as visual perception at all. For Berkeley, we see three-dimensional objects only in the sense in which we see the heat of a glowing red poker, the coldness of a white-capped peak, or the shame in another's soul.

If Reid followed Berkeley all the way, it would therefore be doubtful that acquired perception of three-dimensional objects is direct visual perception. But Reid does *not* follow Berkeley all the way. Remember the *experimentum crucis*: the conception of extended three-dimensional objects we get from our tactile sensations is *nothing like* those sensations. In coming to associate visual cues with conceptions previously acquired by touch, we are not associating the cues with anything inherently tactile. It is an open possibility for Reid that the conception of three-dimensional figure a blind person obtains by touch is very much the same as the conception of three-dimensional figures the sighted get from vision—and this not because the visual conception is "touchy," but because the tactile conception is "looky."[42]

To get a sense of what mediated but direct perception of three-dimensional figures might be like for Reid, think of what happens when you have a change of aspect while viewing a wireframe box. At first, you see the edges of the box as forming

---

The combination I defend in this section under the "mediated, but direct" label was adumbrated in Van Cleve 2004a; a similar position is developed in Quilty-Dunn 2013.

The term "immediate" (and its neighbor "not mediated") have now been used in this book to describe four different statuses. To say that the perception of x is immediate may mean (i) that the belief about x involved in the perception of x is psychologically noninferential, (ii) that the belief in question is epistemically basic, (iii) that the perception of x is not mediated by the perception or awareness of anything else, or (iv) that x is perceived *in propria persona* and not merely by proxy. The "mediated but direct" combination of this section is (iv) without (iii).

[42] If some "touchy" conception of figure were delivered to touch and then subsequently associated with visual cues, then of course the same conception would be delivered to both senses, but that is not the possibility I have in mind. Take instead the putatively purely visual conception of

a flat network of polygons. A moment later, you see the edges as forming a three-dimensional cube, with one square face frontmost and another lying in a deeper plane. You see the three-dimensional cube as directly as you see the flat array, the perception of the flat array coming first and prompting the perception of the cube. I am suggesting that Reidian acquired and mediated visual perceptions of three-dimensional objects might be like *that*.[43]

For my part, I think I do have direct visual perceptions of three-dimensional objects, even if my perception of them is occasionally mediated by two-dimensional cues. But unlike Reid, I do not think that my original perceptions through sight are of two-dimensional objects only. I know, as Reid did not, that having two eyes makes it possible to have original perceptions of objects in depth. See the story of Stereo Sue in appendix K.

---

three-dimensional figure that the man on the street, uninstructed in Berkeley's theory of vision, takes himself to get from vision alone. (I think the man on the street is right, thanks to stereopsis; see appendix K.) I am suggesting that *that* conception of three-dimensional figure could be a hardwired response to tactile sensations and a learned response to visual perceptions of two-dimensional figures.

In saying that the conception of figure delivered by touch might be "looky" for Reid, I do not mean that tangible and visible figures could ever be congruent, but that they could resemble each other as closely as the difference between Euclidean and non-Euclidean figures permits.

[43] In allowing that the acquired perception of real figure may be direct, I must retract one of the premises in the first argument in section B of chapter 5 for the conclusion that no acquired perception is genuine perception. The second, third, and fourth arguments of that section may stand, however, as their conclusion is only that *not all* acquired perception is perception.

The possibility that the perception of three-dimensional figure is direct despite being acquired and mediated is further developed in Quilty-Dunn 2013. According to Quilty-Dunn, our perception of visible figure is direct, unmediated, and original, while our perception of real figure is direct, mediated, and acquired. The direct/indirect distinction thus cuts across the unmediated/mediated and original/acquired distinctions.

While we are investigating possible cross-cuttings, we should also ask whether the unmediated/mediated distinction could cut across the original/acquired distinction. I believe the answer is yes. In an unpublished manuscript I learned about from Grandi 2003 (MS 2131/8/II/21 in the Aberdeen University Library), Reid raises the possibility that the connection between visible cues and outward distance—and hence in principle the connection between visible figures and the tangible figures signified by them—might have been hardwired into us, even though with our present constitution we learn the connection by experience. Had the connection been hardwired, our perception of three-dimensional figure would have been original but mediated. The other cross-cutting combination, perception that is acquired but unmediated, seems also to be possible. It would be realized if the medium in the acquired visual perception of real figure, namely, visible figure, ever did become truly effaced, dropping out of awareness altogether and leaving unconscious retinal impressions as the only cues.

# 7

## ERECT AND INVERTED VISION

In this explication of vision, there occurs one mighty difficulty. The objects are painted in an inverted order on the bottom of the eye, the upper part of any object being painted on the lower part of the eye, and the lower part of the object on the upper part of the eye; and so also as to right and left. Since therefore the pictures are thus inverted, it is demanded how it comes to pass that we see the objects erect and in their natural posture? (George Berkeley, *An Essay Towards a New Theory of Vision*, section 88).

## A. THE NAÏVE PUZZLE AND ROCK'S QUESTION

It was "the sagacious Kepler," Reid tells us, who first discovered that images on the retina are inverted with respect to their objects (IHM 6.11:114).[1] Kepler's discovery, already common knowledge in Berkeley's day, gives rise to the "mighty difficulty" Berkeley formulates above: if our images are inverted, why don't we see the world upside down? The puzzle comes naturally to children,[2] and it has exercised many philosophers as well, including Descartes, Malebranche, Berkeley, and Reid.

It is easy to dismiss the problem as a pseudo-problem, resting on one or the other of two false presuppositions. One false presupposition is that images on the retina are the proper objects of vision, seen perhaps by a homunculus, in which case it may

---

[1] Kepler's discovery dates from 1604 (Wade 1998:9).

[2] Mathews 1980:8–9. The naturalness of the assumption that an inverted image should produce inverted vision is shown also by the following facts: (1) Believing that the eye might receive an inverted image because it works like a camera obscura, Leonardo da Vinci posited a second inversion within the eye to account for upright vision (Wade:322–23). (2) The eighteenth-century naturalist Comte de Buffon thought that until touch teaches them the truth, very young children actually *do* see things upside down (Morgan 1977:97–99).

seem natural to ask: if what we see is an image and the image is upside down, why don't we see things upside down? If such homuncular thinking is really what the puzzle turns upon, however, one could venture the solution that the homunculus dangles from his heels, so all looks fine to him. A weaker presupposition would be that if I see something by having an image of it (not by *seeing* the image this time, just by *having* it) and the image has feature F, then what I see has feature F. But when stated generally in this way, even the weaker presupposition is ridiculous. It implies that if the image on my retina is slimy or three millimeters across, so is what I see.

Even if we dismiss the original problem as a naïve pseudo-problem, though, there remains an important question about vision that we need to answer. Granted that having an inverted image does not imply that we should see the world upside down, is that because the orientation of the image *does not matter*? Or is it because an inverted image is actually the *means* of upright vision, positions lower in the retina somehow signifying to the perceiver positions higher in ambient space? This point has been well made by the psychologist Irwin Rock (Rock 1975:460).[3]

The second alternative—that the inverted image is the mechanism of upright vision, by virtue of lower image points signifying higher object points—actually divides into three subalternatives. If lower image points signify higher object points, is that something we figure out by geometrical reasoning? Is it something we come to learn by empirical association? Or is the signification relation programmed into us innately? We thus have four alternatives to consider in all:

I. It doesn't matter what the orientation of the image is; we would see the world as we do however the image were oriented.

II. The inverted image is the means of upright vision; a lower point in the retinal image signifies a higher point in ambient space—

A. As we know by geometrical reasoning.

B. As we know by empirical learning.

C. As we know (or are programmed to take into account) by an innate law of our constitution.

All four answers to Rock's question have advocates among seventeenth- and eighteenth-century philosophers. IIA is the classical view, advanced by Kepler,

---

[3] Rock notes that even after the original puzzle is diagnosed as a pseudo-puzzle, we still have to choose between two alternatives: "Because the image is inverted and vision is upright, either the lower retina innately signifies an 'up' egocentric direction (and vice versa) ... or it does not matter at all what the orientation of the image is" (460). However, as I explain in the text, Rock's innatist alternative is in fact only one of three subalternatives that should be considered under the general alternative that an inverted image is the means of upright vision.

Descartes, and Malebranche; I and IIB are solutions that have a strong basis in Berkeley's *New Theory of Vision*; finally, IIC is the view advocated by Reid in the *Inquiry*.

In this chapter I examine the answers of Berkeley and Reid to the original naïve puzzle and to Rock's follow-up question. In section B, I sketch the classical solution along with Berkeley and Reid's reasons for rejecting it. In section C, I expound Berkeley's response to the naïve puzzle, arguing that he actually has two responses that he and his commentators do not always distinguish. In section D, I present Reid's critique of Berkeley and his own positive solution. In section E, I turn to Rock's question, spelling out the differences among Reid's answer and Berkeley's two answers, one corresponding to each of his two answers to the naïve puzzle. Finally, in sections F and G, I turn to comparative assessment of Berkeley's and Reid's answers, especially in light of the famous experiments with inverting lenses first conducted by Stratton in the 1890s. Although the inverting lens experiments are often regarded as a confirmation of Berkeley, I shall argue that they can be accommodated as well or better by Reid.

## B. THE CLASSICAL SOLUTION

The received solution to the problem of the inverted image in Berkeley's day was that of Kepler, Descartes, and Malebranche. Given the manner in which the lens of the eye focuses all the rays coming from a given point of the object in one point on the retina, we know that a ray of light reaching a point low in the retina proceeds from a point high in the object, and that rays striking points high in retina proceed from points low in the object. Being thus aware of the geometry of the situation, we make correct judgments about the orientation of external objects—for example, that a man whose head is "painted" low on the retina and whose feet are painted high is actually standing upright. This is the solution Descartes illustrates with the figure of a blind man holding two crossed sticks: knowing that the sticks are crossed, he correctly judges that the part of the object he feels with the stick held in his upper hand is lower than the part of the object he feels with the stick held in his lower hand.[4]

The classical account answers Rock's question by saying the inverted image is a means of erect vision, being an essential part of the information from which we draw inferences to correct judgments. It answers the naïve question by saying that the judgments thus arrived at constitute perceptions in their own right, superseding any previous perceptions (if there ever were any) of objects as inverted.

---

[4] Descartes's drawing of the blind man with sticks accompanies the Sixth Discourse of his *Optics* and was reproduced by Berkeley in the Appendix to the second edition of the *New Theory of Vision*.

Berkeley objects to the classical account for the same reason he objects to the standard account of how we perceive distance (by the angle of convergence our eyes must make to bring an object into focus)—namely, that we are in fact not aware of the geometry of the situation. "To me it seems evident that crossing and tracing of the rays is never thought on by children, idiots, or, in truth, by any other, save only those who have applied themselves to the study of optics" (NTV 90).

Reid agrees entirely with Berkeley in rejecting the classical solution. He breaks his objection in two:

> First, because it supposes our seeing things erect, to be a deduction of reason, drawn from certain premises; whereas it seems to be an immediate perception. And, secondly, Because the premises from which all mankind are supposed to draw this conclusion, never entered into the minds of the far greater part, but are absolutely unknown to them. (IHM 6.11:115)

In the second of these points, Reid is repeating Berkeley's objection. In the first, he is adding a trenchant objection of his own: even if we were aware of the geometry of optical processes, it is not true that we *reason* our way to correct judgments about orientation—we simply *see* things as erect or inverted. He might well have added that even if we *do* reason our way to correct judgments, a judgment is not the same as a perception.

## C. BERKELEY'S SOLUTION(S) TO THE NAÏVE PUZZLE

The original naïve puzzle of the inverted image may be generated from two assumptions:

1. What we see are images on the retina.
2. In the images, things are upside down: for example, the head of a standing man is lower than his feet.

From these assumptions it apparently follows that we should see an erect man as upside down, his head lower than his feet. So why don't we? As Berkeley puts it in his *Theory of Vision Vindicated*:

> How comes it to pass that the objects whereof the pictures are thus inverted do yet seem erect and in their natural situation? For the objects not being perceived otherwise than by their pictures, it should follow that as these are inverted, those should seem so too. (TVV, section 49)

Did Berkeley really believe that we see our own retinal images? In the NTV he seems to say so (see NTV 114–15), but commentators are divided on whether he really meant it.[5] In the TVV, published twenty-five years later, he says not. Images on the retina, he there says, "are so far from being the proper objects of sight that they are not at all perceived thereby, being by their nature altogether of the tangible kind. . . . I deny that they are, or can be, the proper immediate objects of sight. This indeed is vulgarly supposed by the writers on optics; but it is a vulgar error which, being removed, the foregoing difficulty is removed with it." (TVV, section 50)

I need not take a stand on the question of whether Berkeley ever believed we see our own retinal images. However that question is answered, Berkeley has a good overall response to the naïve puzzle, taking the form of a dilemma. If the things we see are *not* retinal images (as he says in TVV), the first assumption generating the naïve puzzle is false. If the things we see *are* images on the retina (as NTV assumes, if only for the sake of argument), then assumption 2 of the naïve puzzle is false, for there is no good sense in which the retinal image is upside down. Either way, the naïve puzzle evaporates.

Why does Berkeley hold in the NTV that the retinal image is not, after all, upside down? To answer this question, we must consider two different senses in which he says we call items in a visual field high, low, above, below, erect, inverted, and the like.[6] They are the derivative or touch-based sense of NTV 91–98 and the purely visual sense of NTV 111. I shall show that in neither of these senses is the retinal image inverted.[7]

*The derivative senses of "high" and "low."* In NTV 91–98, Berkeley develops the thesis that the terms "higher" and "lower" have no proper meaning as applied to visible objects. They apply originally only to tangible objects or ideas. In application to visible objects, they can have only a derivative meaning—a meaning derived from the senses these terms have when applied to tangible objects. He illustrates this thesis by inviting us to consider the frame of mind of a man born blind and made to see. Such a one, he tells us, "would not at first think that anything he saw was high

---

[5] According to Turbayne 1955, Berkeley assumed in NTV that retinal images are the proper objects of vision only for the sake of argument. According to Armstrong 1960:9–10 and 51–52 and Thrane 1977, Berkeley was committed to this assumption himself.

[6] Berkeley sometimes focuses on some of these terms, sometimes on others. To some extent, they are interdefinable; for example, a man is erect iff his head is higher than his feet.

[7] I actually believe that Berkeley distinguishes *four* senses of directional terms such as "erect" and "inverted." The two not discussed here are the mixed modality sense of NTV 115 and the interpersonal comparative sense of NTV 116. I discuss the bearing of these two further senses on the naïve puzzle in Van Cleve 2003b.

or low, erect or inverted" (NTV 95).[8] These terms would have only a tangible meaning for him. For example, that part of an object "on which he felt himself supported, or toward which he perceived his body to gravitate, he would term 'lower,' and the contrary to this 'upper'" (NTV 93).[9] But there would be nothing in the visual field to support the application of such terms to it. In time, however, the newly sighted man would come to correlate visible objects with tangible objects, and even to call correlated objects (e.g., a visible apple and a tangible apple) by the same names. Once he had established such correlations, he could apply terms such as "higher" and "lower" to visible objects in a derivative or analogical sense.

What is the derivative sense? I shall discuss two proposals, one that Berkeley actually gives and another that he might have given. Berkeley's actual proposal is that visible objects are denominated high or low according as the eyes must be turned up or down in order for them to be distinctly seen:

> And this seems to me the true reason why he should call those objects uppermost that are painted on the lower part of his eye. For, by turning the eye up they shall be distinctly seen; as likewise those that are painted on the highest part of the eye shall be distinctly seen by turning the eye down, and are for that reason esteemed lowest. (NTV 98)

The relevant piece of background information here is that as I turn my eye up toward an apple hanging on a branch above me, its image comes to occupy a position nearer the centrally located fovea of my retina, where vision is sharpest; that is why by turning the eye up, I see the apple more distinctly. We may call this the "look up" or eye-movement theory; it is one way of defining visual "upness" in terms of upness as ascertained by another sense.

If there really are correlations of the sort Berkeley supposes between visible and tangible objects, then there is a natural alternative account he could have given of the derivative sense of "high" and "low." I will call it the "reach up" theory. He does not actually give this account, but it is Berkeleian in spirit, and I believe some such account is what Reid and other students of Berkeley have actually taken to be his doctrine. In any case, the reach-up theory will serve below as a useful foil to the

---

[8] If the visual field is extended in two dimensions (as Berkeley believes), must some items in it not be above or below others, that is, higher or lower than others? *Pace* Atherton 1990:150 and 159, I believe it is possible to say *no*: two dimensions give relations of adjacency, but not necessarily of above and below or left and right. For more on this point, see Van Cleve 2003b:49, note 12.

[9] Gravity had better not be essential to Berkeley's explanation, however, for he holds that the terms "right" and "left" also have a meaning as applied to tangible objects, and in this case there is nothing analogous to gravity.

look-up theory. In the reach-up theory, a visible object x is high (or higher than visible object y) iff the tangible correlate of x is high (or higher in the proper sense than the tangible correlate of y). For example, to say that the apple I see on the branch before me is high would mean that I have to reach upward to grasp the tangible apple correlated with it.[10] Once again we would be defining visual upness in terms of nonvisual upness—this time in terms of straightforwardly tangible or kinesthetic upness.[11]

Berkeley has two possible explications, then, of directional terms as applied to visible objects: to say that a visible object is high can mean either that my eye must be turned up to see it distinctly (the look-up or eye-movement theory) or that my hand must reach up in order to grasp its tangible correlate (the reach-up or hand-movement theory). How do these senses apply to the puzzle of the inverted image?

Assumption 2 in the pair of assumptions generating the naïve puzzle was that the retinal image is upside down—for example, that in the image of a man who stands erect before me, the head is lower than the feet. Given the identification of what I see with the image (which is operative in this stretch of the argument), this means that the visible head is lower than the visible feet. But in either of the two derivative senses we have just explained, this assumption is false. To say that the visible head is lower on the eye-movement theory means that I must turn my eyes down to bring it into clear view, and to say that it is lower on the hand-movement theory means that I must reach down to touch its tangible correlate. Precisely the opposite is the case: when a man stands erect before me, I must turn my eyes up to see his head distinctly, and I must reach up to feel it. So assumption 2 is false.

---

[10] In fact, I think it is very doubtful that Berkeley can make sense of the correlations that the reach-up theory requires. He can have correlations between existential statements about visibles and existential statements about tangibles—for instance, when there is a certain sort of red, round patch in my visual field, a certain sort of tangible object will be available to my grasp. But I do not see what in his system would ground the correlation of one particular visible apple with one particular tangible apple. Which of the hundreds of tangible apples on the tree is the correlate of the visible apple I see *there*, at that location in my visual field? The obvious answer—that it is the tangible apple that occupies the same location as the visible apple—is not open to Berkeley and would indeed be repudiated by him, since he believes the spaces of sight and touch to be totally disparate (NTV 112).

[11] Some readers may wonder if there is really anything inherently "uppish" or "downish" about the sensations I have when I turn my eyeballs. Perhaps an "uppish" sensation can only mean a sensation of the sort I have when I turn my eyes in the way required to bring (the visual correlate of) a high tangible object into clear view. In that case, the look-up theory would presuppose the resources of the reach-up theory.

*The purely visual senses of "high" and "low."* Sections 91–98 seem to imply that there is *no* purely visual sense in which visible items can be high or low. But when we get to section 111, Berkeley allows that there is such a sense after all:

> We say any object of touch is "high" or "low," according as it is more or less distant from the tangible earth; and in like manner we denominate any object of sight "high" or "low," in proportion as it is more or less distant from the visible earth. (NTV 111)

Here, then, is a nonderivative sense in which one visible item may be higher or lower than another, without any reference to tangible objects or kinesthetic sensations.

Using directional terms in the purely visual sense, we may again deny the assumption that what we see in viewing an erect man is upside down. To say that the retinal image (still assumed for the sake of argument to be the proper object of sight) is upside down in the purely visual sense would be to say that the head is nearest the visible earth and the feet are nearest the visible sky. But that is simply not true, as anyone can tell simply by consulting what he sees. Berkeley makes this point in the following passage:

> If we confine our thoughts to the proper objects of sight, the whole is plain and easy. The head is painted farthest from, and the feet nearest to, the visible earth; and so they appear to be. What is there strange or unaccountable in this? Let us suppose the pictures in the fund of the eye to be the immediate objects of the sight. The consequence is that things should appear in the same posture they are painted in; and is it not so? The head which is seen seems farthest from the earth which is seen; and the feet which are seen seem nearest to the earth which is seen. And just so they are painted. (NTV 114)

Thus again no puzzle arises.

## D. REID'S ALTERNATIVE TO BERKELEY'S SOLUTION

Reid devotes two sections of the *Inquiry* to the question of why we see objects erect with inverted images, the first (6.11) containing his criticisms of the solutions of Descartes and Berkeley and the second (6.12) containing his own positive solution. In his critique of Descartes, he repeats one of Berkeley's points and adds one of his own, as we saw in section 2. In his critique of Berkeley, he makes three separate criticisms, two explicit and one implicit.

Reid begins his exposition of Berkeley's solution by noting that for Berkeley, outward distance and tangible figure are ideas given properly only to touch. Nothing similar to them is given to vision, but we can learn that certain visible ideas are signs of certain tangible ideas, for example, that a certain visual array is a sign of something that will be felt to be square. The same goes for erect or inverted position. We do not originally see a man to be erect, but we learn that a certain visible appearance of a man is a sign of a tangibly erect man (one whose face will be felt by reaching up):

> In the same way, finding from experience, that an object in an erect position, affects the eye in one manner, and the same object in an inverted position, affects it in another, we learn to judge, by the manner in which the eye is affected, whether the object is erect or inverted. In a word, visible ideas, according to this author, are signs of the tangible; and the mind passeth from the sign to the thing signified, not by means of any similitude between the one and the other, nor by any natural principle; but by having found them constantly conjoined in experience, as the sounds of a language are with the things they signify. (IHM 6.11:116)

Reid applauds Berkeley for his groundbreaking work in distinguishing between the immediate objects of sight and what they signify. However, he notes that it is "almost unavoidable, for one who has made an important discovery in philosophy, to carry it a little beyond its sphere" (IHM 6.11:117).

*Reid's critique of Berkeley.* The first of Reid's criticisms, developed over IHM 6.11:117–19, is that Berkeley is wrong to think that spatial attributes are not given to sight in the same manner as to touch. It culminates in the following remark: "Bishop Berkeley proceeds upon a capital mistake, in supposing that there is no resemblance betwixt the extension, figure, and position which we see, and that which we perceive by touch" (IHM 6.11:119). On Reid's own view, the figures we perceive by sight and those we perceive by touch "are to all sense the same" (118).[12] The same goes for situation or orientation: when I say that the head of my walking cane extends above the horizon, I mean the same thing whether I am reporting the verdict of feeling or seeing, cane and horizon being common objects of sight and touch (119). So a key presupposition of Berkeley's theory of upright vision is false.

The second of Reid's criticisms is ad hominem, directed not against Berkeley's solution to the inverted image problem per se, but against the idealist framework in which it is embedded. Reid, like many of Berkeley's readers, takes the *New Theory* to be a halfway house on the road to Berkeley's full idealism:

> In his theory of vision, he seems indeed to allow, that there is an external material world: but he believed that this external world is tangible only, and not visible; and

---

[12] As discussed in chapter 6, this claim requires qualification. Since any visible triangle that we can take in at one view has slightly more than 180 degrees in it, no visible triangle *exactly* resembles any tangible triangle. Nonetheless, visible triangles and tangible triangles are nearly indistinguishable, not completely heterogeneous as on Berkeley's view.

that the visible world, the proper object of sight, is not external, but in the mind. (IHM 6.11:119)

Though the tangible world exists outside the mind, the visible world does not. Reid continues:

> If this be supposed, he that affirms that he sees things erect and not inverted, affirms that there is a top and a bottom, a right and a left in the mind. Now, I confess I am not so well acquainted with the topography of the mind, as to be able to affix a meaning to these words when applied to it. (IHM 6.11:119)

I take Reid's point to be that if Berkeley's idealism about the visible world is taken seriously, we cannot even *state* the problem of the inverted image: "When we propose the question, Why objects are seen erect and not inverted? we take it for granted, that we are not in Bishop Berkeley's ideal world, but in that world in which men, who yield to the dictates of common sense, believe themselves to inhabit" (119).[13]

I come now to the third criticism, which I take to be the most important one even though Reid never states it explicitly. It is this: in taking the perception of situation or orientation by sight to be a matter of learned association rather than original constitution, Berkeley's theory *makes the wrong predictions* about what would happen in certain hypothetical cases. This point is implicit in a corollary Reid draws from Berkeley's view by way of distinguishing it from his own: that an erect image might have signified an erect object for us as readily as an inverted image does now (116). To appreciate this difference between the philosophers, we must now set forth Reid's own positive view.

*Reid's own solution.* Reid begins by pointing out that one of the presuppositions of the naïve problem, namely, that we perceive our own retinal images, is false. Pictures on the retina are a means of vision, but not themselves things seen (IHM 6.12:120).

> [There is not] any probability that the mind perceives the pictures upon the retina. These pictures are no more objects of our perception, than the brain is, or the optic nerve. (121)

---

[13] Falkenstein advances an alternative interpretation in which Reid is not criticizing Berkeley but merely reporting an inference that Berkeley would accept himself—from the ideality of the objects of sight to their being devoid of any directional characteristics (2000b:36–37). I think to the contrary that Reid is charging Berkeley with an inconsistency—believing that the visual field is extended in two dimensions while embracing an idealism that rules this out. See Van Cleve 2003b:436.

He goes on to make an eloquent exposé of homunculus fallacy associated with the assumption that we perceive our retinal images:

> If any man will shew how the mind may perceive images in the brain [or on the retina], I will undertake to shew how it may perceive the most distant objects: for if we give eyes to the mind, to perceive, what is transacted at home in its dark chamber, why may we not make these eyes a little longer-sighted? (121)

But Reid does not rest there. To scotch the assumption that retinal images are objects of sight is not to be done with the puzzle of the inverted image. As noted in section 1, the question remains whether the inverted image is irrelevant to erect vision or instrumental to it, and if instrumental, whether it signifies an erect object by virtue of geometrical reasoning, empirical learning, or an innate law of our constitution. Reid's answer is the last.

Reid asks, "By what law of nature is a picture upon the retina, the mean or occasion of my seeing an external object of the same figure ... in a contrary position, and in a certain direction from the eye?" (122) He answers by citing the following as a law of nature:

> Every point of the object is seen in the direction of a right line passing from the picture of that point on the retina through the centre of the eye. (122–23)

Reid notes that for a hemispherical retina, this law is equivalent to a law formulated by Porterfield: "That a visible object appears in the direction of a right line perpendicular to the retina at that point where its image is painted" (123).[14] It is a consequence of the law in either Reid's or Porterfield's formulation that a point whose image is projected high on the retina will be seen as low in ambient space, and a point whose image is projected low will be seen as high. I shall refer to this law henceforth as the "receive low, perceive high" law. It is easy to see that this law explains why we see objects erect by means of our inverted images: if a man's feet are "painted" (or etched) high on our retinas and his head low (as they are when a man stands erect before us), we shall see his head as high and his feet as low.

Reid notes that the law he invokes may or may not be deduced someday from a higher law, but in any case, he takes it to be an inductively confirmed generalization about human vision. He devotes the remainder of *Inquiry* 6.12 to describing various experiments that he takes to confirm it. I present one striking additional

---

[14] Hamilton claims that Porterfield was only one among many to have formulated this law, which he calls "the law of *the line of visible direction*" (Hamilton 158b and 177a).

confirmation of the law in appendix P. Unfortunately, I must also point out an apparent inconsistency between the law and another Reidian principle in appendix R.

I have encountered the complaint that Reid has really done nothing to *explain* erect vision—he has merely restated the phenomenon that needs explaining, namely, that we see objects as erect despite the fact that our images of them are inverted. But this complaint underestimates the force of what Reid is saying. His explanation has enough content to conflict with rival explanations of the phenomenon, including Berkeley's, as shown below.[15] If Reid's explanation were a mere restatement of the phenomenon, there could be no such conflict—unless the rival explanations were actually inconsistent with the phenomenon, which they are not.

*How Reid's theory differs from Berkeley's.* Reid draws the following corollary from what he takes to be Berkeley's solution to the problem of the inverted retinal image:

> So that if the images upon the retina had been always erect, they would have shown the objects erect, in the manner as they do now that they are inverted: nay, if the visible idea which we now have from an inverted object, had been associated from the beginning with the erect position of that object, it would have signified an erect position, as readily as it now signifies an inverted one. (IHM 6.12:116).

The images upon the retina would have been always erect in the case of someone who had worn inverting lenses from birth. Berkeley actually hypothesizes such an individual in his Philosophical Notebooks—let us call him Invertus—and queries what he would think of up and down.[16] According to Reid's theory, Invertus would see objects upside down with his erect images, because the "receive low, perceive high" law is a law of human nature. We are innately so constituted that we would see objects upside down if our images were made erect. Reid claims that Berkeley's theory has the opposite implication, however: Invertus would see objects erect with his erect images just as easily as we do with our inverted images. Is Reid correct in drawing this corollary from Berkeley's theory?

The answer depends in part on whether Berkeley holds the look-up theory or the reach-up theory. Consider first the reach-up theory. This theory agrees with Reid's own in what it implies about what we shall see in our actual situation. Both theories predict that an inverted image (as we have in our normal situation) will signify an erect object, though for different reasons. In Reid's theory, the reason is that when

---

[15] To anticipate, the Berkeleyan theories I and IIB and the Reidian theory IIC all differ in their implications about what would happen in experiments with inverting lenses.

[16] "Suppose inverting perspectives bound to the eyes of a child, & continu'd to the years of Manhood, When he looks up or turns up his head he shall behold what we call under. Qu: what would he think of up & down?" (*Philosophical Notebooks*, entry 278).

the head of an erect man is imaged low on our retina, we are innately disposed to see it is as high. For the reach-up theory, the reason is that when the head is imaged low, we must reach up to feel it (or rather, its tangible correlate). As applied to the hypothetical situation involving Invertus, however, the two theories diverge in their predictions. For Invertus on Reid's theory, an erect image would show the object inverted: the head of an erect man would be imaged high on his retina, so he would see it as low. For Invertus on the reach-up theory, by contrast, *an erect image would show the object erect* (as soon as it showed any orientation at all). This is because with the head imaged high, he would have to reach high to feel it, and a high retinal position would therefore come to signify an erect man. As soon as the retinal image signified *anything* to him about the orientation of the object, it would signify an erect orientation. So far, then, Reid's corollary is correctly drawn.

Suppose on the other hand that Berkeley holds the look-up theory. Would the corollary Reid draws still be correctly drawn? That turns out to depend on further questions about the precise arrangement of the inverting lens.[17] Suppose the lens places before the eye an optical array that is inverted with respect to its object, and that the eye is free to pan over this array. Since the array is placed before the eye's own lens, it will project onto the retina an erect image of the object, as required. With this arrangement, the look-up theory makes the same predictions about Invertus as Reid's own theory. Invertus's erect image will show the object inverted, because with the head imaged high on his retina, he will have to turn his eyes *down* to bring it into clear view. Somewhat surprisingly, then, the look-up theory diverges in this case from the reach-up theory, making the same predictions as Reid's own. Reid's corollary would not be correctly drawn.

But what if instead of presenting the eye with an array over which it may pan, the inverting lens is fastened to the eye itself, so that the inverted array moves with the eye? This would be the case with an inverting *contact* lens (an idea I owe to Lorne Falkenstein in correspondence and conversation). As before, the image projected on the retina will be erect. But in this case, the eye must turn *up* to see the head of an upright man—if it turns down, it will receive rays from the man's feet. With an inverting contact lens, then, the look-up theory makes the same predictions as the reach-up theory about what Invertus will see. When a man's head is imaged high on his retina, he must look up to see it, and he will therefore (according to the look-up theory) perceive the man as upright.[18] Reid's corollary would once again be correctly drawn.

---

[17] I am indebted here to conversations with Gideon Yaffe and Lorne Falkenstein.

[18] This prediction is false, however. Looking through an inverting contact lens is analogous to looking at the peak of a gabled house through an astronomical telescope. As Falkenstein notes (2000b:40), even though one has to turn the scope up to bring the peak into clear view, one will see it as inverted.

To summarize, Reid is correct in drawing his corollary—that for Berkeley an erect image could yield erect vision—under two of the three suppositions we have considered. He is right if Berkeley holds the reach-up theory or if he holds the look-up theory and the inverting lens produces an array that moves with the eye. He is wrong if Berkeley holds the look-up theory and the inverting lens produces an array over which the eye may rove. But in any of the three cases, he is right to note that his theory differs significantly from Berkeley's. For Berkeley, we see objects as oriented only *after* we have made associations with appropriate movements of the arm or the eye. For Reid, we see objects as oriented as soon as we see at all.[19]

## E. ANSWERS TO ROCK'S QUESTION

I return now to Rock's question. I distinguished four answers at the outset, three of which (I, IIB, and IIC) are to be found in Berkeley and Reid. The relations among the various positions may be further clarified by noting the stands they would take in regard to the following four propositions, arranged in a classical square of opposition (Figure 7.1):

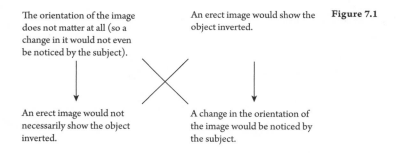

The orientation of the image does not matter at all (so a change in it would not even be noticed by the subject).

An erect image would show the object inverted.

**Figure 7.1**

An erect image would not necessarily show the object inverted.

A change in the orientation of the image would be noticed by the subject.

The two strongest propositions are the two at the top, which are contraries of each other. Each of them entails the proposition below it, but not conversely. The propositions at opposite ends of diagonals are contradictories of each other. Finally, the two propositions at the bottom are subcontraries; they might both be true, but cannot both be false.

[19] Turbayne observes that although Berkeley never directly answered his own query about the man with inverting lenses, the whole tenor of his theory implies that Invertus would see things as we do (1955:353). He thus, in effect, endorses Reid's corollary. But he also notes that the eye-movement theory, which Berkeley embraced in the *New Theory*, implies that Invertus would see things upside down. He surmises (in note 72) that Berkeley came to notice this (by his own lights) incorrect implication, and therefore dropped the eye-movement theory in the *Theory Vindicated*. He replaced it with a *head*-movement theory, which (adding to the confusion in an already confusing set of issues) agrees with the reach-up theory rather than the eye-movement theory in its implications.

Answer I affirms the top left proposition, that image orientation does not matter to what we see. I attribute this answer to the philosopher I shall call Berkeley₁. This is the Berkeley who operates with the purely visual sense of "up" and "down," proclaiming that nothing matters but relations internal to the visual field, such as the relative distances of visible head and feet to visible earth and sky. Such relations are preserved even if the retinal image is flipped: so long as the visible feet of the man you see are nearest the visible earth, all's right with your world.

Reid affirms the proposition at top right—he definitely thinks that the orientation of the retinal image matters. Thanks to the "receive low, perceive high" law, it is *because* we have an inverted image that we see objects erect, and if lenses brought the image to an upright position, we should then see objects inverted. Moreover, the "receive low, perceive high" law is an innate law of our constitution. Thus Reid affirms answer IIC.

The eye-movement theory, though distinct from Reid's theory, may agree with it in affirming the top right proposition (depending on the questions about the mechanism of inversion raised in the previous section).[20] The geometrical theory of Kepler and Descartes, IIA, may also agree with Reid's theory in affirming the upper right proposition, provided that the subject's beliefs about the geometry of visual processes stay constant through image inversion.

The remaining position is IIB, according to which an inverted image signifies an erect object in virtue of nomologically contingent and experientially learned correlations. This is the position of the philosopher I shall call Berkeley₂, who gives pride of place to the derivative senses of "up" and "down." Berkeley₂ affirms the two propositions at the bottom of the square. He affirms the lower left proposition because, as Reid points out, he is committed to saying that an erect image might have indicated an erect object as easily as an inverted image does now: with inverting lenses from birth, we would have learned a different set of visuo-tactile correlations, whereby an erect image signifies an erect object. He also affirms the lower right proposition, or else he would be Berkeley₁ rather than Berkeley₂.

Note that although there are four propositions in our square, they determine only three general philosophical positions. That is because any position that denies both of the contraries at the top must embrace each of the subcontraries at the bottom. In effect, the three positions are these: embrace the two left propositions (Berkeley₁), embrace the two right propositions (Reid, the eye-movement theory), and embrace the two bottom propositions (Berkeley₂). No other pairs in the square are consistent.

[20] Even if the eye-movement theory and Reid's theory agree in affirming the top right position, they differ in this; in the eye-movement theory, learning is required to see objects as high or low, whereas in Reid's theory it is not. In Reid's theory, we would see objects as high or low even if our eyes had always been totally immobilized.

# F. EXPERIMENTS WITH INVERTING LENSES

A variant of the experiment Berkeley envisioned in his notebooks was actually carried out by the American psychologist G. M. Stratton in the 1890s. Stratton wore a blindfold over one eye and a set of lenses over the other that reinverted his retinal image, thus becoming (according to R. L. Gregory) the first man in the history of the universe to see with an upright retinal image (1997:139). He recorded the results over a period of three days and then in a subsequent experiment over a period of eight days (Stratton 1896 and 1897). The highlights of the three-day experiment, which were substantially the same as in the eight-day experiment, are summed up in Stratton's own words as follows. I distinguish three phases.

Phase 1: When he first looked through the lenses, everything looked upside down. "All images at first appeared to be inverted; the room and all in it seemed upside down" (1896:613).
Phase 2: As time wore on, he learned to adjust to the new scene, and things sometimes seemed normal again. "When . . . full attention was given to the outer objects, these frequently seemed to be in normal position" (1896:616).
Phase 3: "On removing the glasses on the third day, there was no peculiar experience. Normal vision was restored instantaneously and without any disturbance in the natural appearance or position of objects" (1896:616).

I pause to note a difference between the Stratton experiment as actually reported by Stratton and the Stratton experiment of academic folklore. Time and again I have been told by students or colleagues that in the inverting lens experiment, things at first looked upside down to the subject, subsequently came to look normal, and then looked upside down again (that is, inverted from their just previous state) when the subject removed the lenses.[21] That is not what Stratton says. He does indeed report that things initially looked upside down and that they came to seem, if only briefly and in a fragmentary way, rightside up again, but he does not say that the world flipped yet again upon removal of the lenses. On the contrary, "there was no peculiar experience."

Of course, it is natural to expect that if Stratton really achieved perceptual adaptation to the erect image during Phase 2, then his world should have seemed upside

---

[21] According to Nöe 2004, "Once full adaptation has been achieved, the result of *removing* the lenses is comparable to the initial effects of putting them on" (9; see also 91–92). The only post-removal effect he mentions, however, is experiential blindness, the confused state he takes to be the first effect of putting the lenses on. He is not explicit on whether he takes there to be an inversion of perceptual content upon removal of the lenses.

down again during Phase 3, when the image was restored to its normal inverted position. This has led Rock, a critic of Stratton's account, to doubt whether Stratton really did achieve perceptual adaptation (as opposed simply to motor adaptation) during Phase 2. If he had, there should have been a negative after-effect in Phase 3, but there was none (Rock 1975:470–71). Stratton's own account of Phase 3, then, both contradicts the account of academic folklore and throws doubt on his account of Phase 2.

Further doubts about Stratton's account of Phase 2 are raised in a recent experiment by Linden et al., which deserves to be more widely known. Four subjects wore inverting goggles for several days, learning to ride bicycles and negotiate shopping malls adeptly, but by their own testimony and independent tests, they perceived things upside down all the while. I describe the experiment in greater detail in appendix Q.[22]

Nonetheless, it is of great interest to inquire what the implications of perceptual adaptation would be for the various positions in our square if it were accepted as a genuine phenomenon. In what follows, therefore, I shall take Stratton's word for it that perceptual adaptation did occur during Phase 2.

What are the lessons of the Stratton experiment if we take it at face value? Stratton himself took the experiment to refute those theories according to which "the inversion of the retinal image is necessary for the perception of things as upright" (1896:611). These are the theories that imply the proposition in the upper right corner of our square—that an erect image would perforce give us inverted vision.[23]

---

[22] A more recent authority sometimes cited in support of the claim that upright vision returns in wearers of inverting lenses is Ivo Kohler, who does report that his subjects experienced a negative aftereffect during the first few minutes after the goggles were removed ([1951] 1964). But Kohler's results in particular are challenged by Linden et al.

A twelve-minute video purporting to be a record of one of Kohler's experiments is available at http://www.youtube.com/watch?v=jKUVpBJalNQ as of June 2014. It is hard to believe that the video is not an exaggerated dramatization. It is especially hard to believe that the scenes of what the subject supposedly saw—for instance, a man seen first upside down and then (as he is felt with a stick) right side up—are anything but film images of the external scene run first inverted and then in normal orientation. Even if miniature cameras had been available in 1950, where would they have been placed—in the subject's sensorium?

[23] Our square is useful here in warding off a possible confusion. Stratton's class of theories that hold the inversion of the image to be necessary for upright vision and Rock's class of theories that declare the orientation of the image to be irrelevant might seem to be opposites. And so they are—but they are contrary opposites, not contradictory opposites. We must not let the terminology of "necessary" versus "irrelevant" or "does not matter" blind us to the possibility of associationist theories like Stratton's own, which affirm the bottom two propositions in the square. For these theories, image orientation matters (we would notice a change in it), but an inverted image is not necessary for perceiving objects in any particular orientation (insofar as we could learn to perceive objects as erect via erect images of them).

Stratton places two theories in this category, the eye-movement theory and the projection theory. The eye-movement theory is the same as the look-up theory we have discussed above, and the projection theory is the same in intention as Reid's "receive low, perceive high" theory.[24] Stratton claims that the eye-movement and projection theories both predict that a human subject who donned inverting lenses would see the world upside down and, moreover, would do so for as long as he wore the lenses. Whether he is right about this in the case of the eye-movement theory depends on the questions about the mechanism of re-inversion discussed in section D.[25] In the case of Reid's version of the projection theory, however, I believe he is right without qualification. This is because the "receive low, perceive high" law is a law of our constitution, not to be undone by any relearning of habits. In any case, Stratton is right to claim that Phase 2 of his experiment, in which the subject *does* come to see the world aright with an erect image, refutes theories in the upper right corner of our square.

By the same token, the Stratton experiment confirms theories in the lower left corner of our square, where we have placed Berkeley$_2$. As psychologist Michael Morgan says, "[Stratton] reasoned that if Berkeley were right, his subjects should eventually come to see the world the right way up, since the inverted optic array would come to suggest, or be the 'mark' for (as Berkeley would have said) normally oriented actions and tactile experiences" (1977:171). Stratton never actually mentions Berkeley by name, but Morgan is correct to claim that his experiment confirms a Berkeleyan view. Schematically, the situation is as follows: A

---

[24] I say "the same in intention" because the projection theory as actually formulated by Stratton is not equivalent to Reid's. Stratton puts it thus: "objects are projected back into space in the directions in which the rays of light fall upon the retina" (1896:611). But as Reid points out at IHM 6.12:126, the rays coming to any one point of the retina from any one point of the object are actually a cone of rays, having *many* directions (some having been refracted by the upper portion of the lens, some by lower portions, etc.); "yet the object is seen in only one of these directions, to wit, in the direction of the rays that come from the centre of the eye." Reid therefore insists on formulating the law in the manner in which we have stated it above. I suspect that proponents of the projection theory really had a theory equivalent to Reid's in mind, but were careless in stating it.
[25] Here is Stratton's explanation of why the eye-movement theory makes an inverted image necessary for upright vision: "Upper and lower, according to this theory, mean positions which require an upward or downward movement of the eye to bring them into clear vision. But an upward movement of the eye brings into clear vision only what lies below the fovea of the retina. So that here too the perception of objects as upright requires that their retinal images be inverted" (1896:611). With either no inverting lenses or Stratton's own device in place—"a short adjustable tube, and at either end of the tube a pair of good lenses of equal focal length" (612)—the second premise would be true. But with the inverting contact lens we discussed above, the second premise would be false. As Will Bernstein has pointed out to me, it would also be false if the inverting device were a second lens placed *between* the eye's existing lens and the retina.

subject who has formed the appropriate associations with touch sees an object as erect or inverted according as his image of it signifies a tangible object that is inverted or erect. In Phase 1, the image (now erect) has the character that formerly signified an inverted tangible object, so the subject sees things as upside down. But after enough experience with the lenses, he gets used to the new correlations. The same erect character of the image that signified an inverted tangible object in Phase 1 now signifies an erect tangible object in Phase 2, and in consequence the subject now sees the object as erect.[26] In this way, the experiment confirms a Berkeleyan view.

It confirms *a* Berkeleyan view, but not *every* Berkeleyan view. Those who cite Stratton in defense of Berkeley often overlook the fact that the Stratton experiment *refutes* another Berkeleyan view, namely, the position of Berkeley$_1$ at the upper left corner of our square (as pointed out by Rock on pp. 463–64 and 495). For Berkeley$_1$, all that matters to upright vision is relations internal to the visual field—that the visual head be placed against the visual sky and so on. These relations are preserved by inversion of the image. We should therefore see things the same way no matter how the image were turned—donning the lenses should make no difference in what we immediately see. But that runs afoul of Phase 1, for Stratton tells us that things *did* look upside down as soon as he put on the lenses.

To sum up, then, it seems on first reflection that the bearing of the Stratton experiment on the theories in our square is as follows: Phase 2 refutes Reid along with others at the upper right; Phase 1 refutes Berkeley$_1$ at the upper left; and the experiment as a whole confirms Berkeley$_2$ at the bottom.[27] It also confirms the position of the neo-Berkeleyan Noë, who holds that perceptual content is determined by practical knowledge of sensorimotor contingencies (2004).

---

[26] The account of the last four sentences is independent of whether the image is the proper object of vision.

[27] Actually, the experiment as a whole may *not* confirm Berkeley$_2$, since it seems on further thought that Phase 1 of the experiment makes trouble for Berkeley$_2$ as much as for Berkeley$_1$. Berkeley$_2$ holds that the meaning of "there is an apple high in my visual field" is exhausted by conditionals such as "if I reach or look up, I shall feel or distinctly see an apple." But in that case, why should the subject in Phase 1 have an impression that something has changed *even before he stretches out his arm or turns up his eyes*? The problem here is symptomatic of a deeper potential incoherence in Berkeley. If there is really nothing about a visual field that would let a Stratton subject know prior to reaching that anything has changed, then how could the subject have learned to begin with the associations with touch that supposedly constitute the difference between a field with apple visually high and a field with apple visually low? No subject can attach different associations to cues between which he cannot discriminate! I discuss possible ways of averting this incoherence in Van Cleve 2003b, section 13.

## G. PERCEPTUAL ADAPTATION

If we take Stratton's account as given, is Berkeley$_2$ the only contestant left standing in the field? Not necessarily, for Reid's views can be understood in such a way that they accommodate all facets of the experiment.

The problem for Reid is that he holds that the "receive low, perceive high" law is a *law of our constitution*, or a consequence of such a law. The subject in a Stratton experiment should therefore see upside down not only immediately after donning the lenses, but for as long as he wears them, even if for the rest of his life.[28] Perceptual adaptation, if it means the world's coming to be seen right-side up again as Stratton said it sometimes did in Phase 2, should not occur.

What sort of view *would* accommodate Phase 2? Before we get to Reid's view, let us canvass three other possibilities.

1. A pure behavioral theory of perception: to see an object as high means that you reach up if you want to feel it. Obviously, you will "see upside down" when you first put on the lenses, for you will reach in the wrong places. Equally obviously, the motor adaptation you eventually achieve will amount to perceptual adaptation.

2. A pure belief theory of perception: to see the object as high is to believe that it is high, for example, that you have to reach up to feel it. (A behavioral theory of belief would collapse this option with the preceding one.) This theory accommodates Phases 1 and 2 as readily as the behavioral theory. The lenses will make you believe during Phase 1 that the crown of the tree is low and its trunk high, but as you get used to the lenses you will replace this false belief by a true one, thereby seeing the world aright again in Phase 2.

3. Nöe's "enactive" theory of perception: what you see (as well as perceptual content generally) is determined by knowledge of how sensation would change as a result of movement (Nöe 2004:8 and *passim*). Depending on whether knowledge is construed as knowledge-how or knowledge-that, this view may be assimilated to 1, 2, or a blend of the two.

---

[28] In this respect, the law of visible direction contrasts with what Reid calls "the principle of credulity" (IHM 6.24:194–95). Children have a beneficial tendency to believe what they are told—a tendency that is weakened somewhat as they grow older and wiser. But the "receive low, perceive high" law is not modifiable in this way. It is more like the laws by which Reid seeks to explain single and double vision, stated in IHM 6.13 and discussed in Van Cleve 2008. Reid takes it to be a consequence of these laws that squinters (people who cannot direct both eyes to the same object) should see double for their entire lives, and he devotes several sections of the *Inquiry* (6.13–19) to squaring this consequence with apparent exceptions to it.

Although the foregoing theories deal neatly with the possibility of adaptation, I believe all of them can be faulted precisely for leaving the *perception* out of perception. Perception is not merely behavior, nor merely belief, nor a blend of the two; it is at least partly a matter of having things *look* to you a certain way. To his credit, Reid allows in his theory of perception for this essential phenomenal element.[29] To see a man as erect is to have a certain appearance before the mind—an appearance in which the man's head is high, seen up there, and his feet are low, seen down there.[30] Reid does not merely say that our original inverted image *signifies* an erect object— he says it *shows* an erect object (IHM 6.11:116, line 30).

But does not just this feature of Reid's theory, together with the "receive low, perceive high" law, make him vulnerable to refutation by Stratton's Phase 2? So long as I am wearing the lenses, I will be determined to have an appearance before my mind in which my upright friend's head is low and his feet high.

In reply, I concede that Reid is indeed committed to saying that so long as I wear inverting lenses, I will have an appearance before my mind in which objects are shown inverted with respect to their real positions. But although the appearance is there, it is one that I can come to disregard. Reid gives us many examples of appearances that are regularly before the mind, but seldom noticed. When I hold a finger before my eyes while focusing on a more distant object, I actually have an appearance of two fingers, as I can tell by attending to the finger without shifting focus. But one normally pays no attention to the appearance of doubling, and "you may find a man that can say with a good conscience, that he never saw things double all his life" (6.13:134). Yet

> The same double appearance of an object hath been a thousand times presented to his eye before now; but he did not attend to it; and so it is as little an object of his reflection and memory, as if it had never happened. (IHM 6.3:134)

Here is more in the same vein, from the section of the *Inquiry* (5.3) entitled "Of the visible appearances of objects":

> Every one who is acquainted with the rules of perspective, knows that the appearance of the figure of the book must vary in every different position: yet if you ask a man

---

[29] On the score of phenomenality, the theory of Berkeley$_2$ is intermediate between a pure belief theory and Reid's theory. Up or down orientation is not a proper object of sight for Berkeley as it is for Reid, but neither is it merely an object of belief, if belief is just a propositional attitude. For Berkeley, the relevant belief is at least partly a matter of associated tactile imagery, which may become "blended" with the visual cues. See NTV 51.

[30] Of course, this talk of appearances should not be taken to implicate Reid in a theory of reified inner objects or ideas. It is physical arrays that present themselves to our minds.

that has no notion of perspective, whether the figure of it does not appear to his eye to be the same in all its different positions? he can with a good conscience affirm, that it does. He hath learned to make allowance for the variety of visible figure arising from the difference of position, and to draw the proper conclusions from it. But he draws these conclusions so readily and habitually, as to lose sight of the premises: and therefore, where he hath made the same conclusion, he conceives the visible appearance must have been the same. (IHM 6.3:83–84)

Reid makes similar observations concerning color and size: we see the book as constant in these respects, even though the appearances of it are constantly changing. The variegated appearances are present to the mind, but none but painters have reason to attend to them, and it is almost as though they are not present to consciousness at all.

My suggestion is that if we can become oblivious to the color, size, figure, and even the number of the appearances that are present to the mind, we can do so just as well in regard to their up or down orientation. The inversion of the appearances consequent upon donning Stratton's lenses comes as a shock when first noticed and never goes away—but we can learn to ignore it.[31] In this fashion, Reid can accommodate the results of Stratton's experiment at least as plausibly as Berkeley$_2$ and neo-Berkeleyans such as Noë.

---

[31] It is an empirical commitment of my suggestion that a wearer of Stratton lenses could become aware at any time that his scene was inverted simply by paying attention. Stratton concedes that in his case this was indeed so: "If the attention was directed mainly inward, and things were viewed only in indirect attention, they seemed clearly to be inverted" (1896:616).

# 8

## MOLYNEUX'S QUESTION

Suppose a man born blind [and taught to distinguish globes and cubes by touch]. . . . Suppose . . . the blind man to be made to see: *quaere*, whether by his sight, before he touched them, he could now distinguish and tell which is the globe, which the cube? (William Molyneux)

Although Reid never addresses Molyneux's famous question by name, he has much to say that bears upon it, particularly in his discussions of the capacities of the blind and the relations of visible to tangible figure.[1] My goal in this chapter is to ascertain and evaluate Reid's answer. It can seem that Reid gives two inconsistent answers, but I argue that the inconsistency goes away once we distinguish different versions of what is being asked. I also argue that Reid's answer of *yes* to one important Molyneux question is more plausible than Berkeley's answer of *no*.

## A. MOLYNEUX'S QUESTION

Molyneux posed his question in a letter to Locke, which Locke quoted along with an endorsement of Molyneux's answer in the second edition of the *Essay Concerning*

---

[1] Molyneux's name does not occur in the index to the Brookes edition of the *Inquiry*. It occurs in the index to the Brookes edition of the *Intellectual Powers* only in connection with moral topics.

*Human Understanding* (1694).² Berkeley in turn quoted Locke in his *Essay Towards a New Theory of Vision*. Here is the question as it appears in Berkeley's text, differing only in capitalization and inessential punctuation from Locke's:

> *Suppose a man born blind, and now adult, and taught by his touch to distinguish between a cube and a sphere of the same metal, and nighly of the same bigness, so as to tell when he felt one and the other, which is the cube, which the sphere. Suppose then the cube and sphere placed on a table, and the blind man to be made to see: quaere, whether by his sight, before he touched them, he could now distinguish and tell which is the globe, which the cube?*

> To which the acute and judicious proposer [Molyneux] answers: *Not. For though he has obtained the experience of how a globe, how a cube affects his touch; yet he has not yet attained the experience, that what affects his touch so or so must affect his sight so or so; or that a protuberant angle in the cube, that pressed his hand unequally, shall appear to his eye as it does in the cube.* I [Locke] agree with this thinking gentleman, whom I am proud to call my friend, in his answer to this his problem; and am of opinion, that the blind man, at first sight, would not be able with certainty to say which was the globe, which the cube, while he only saw them. (NTV 132)

There are several clarifications or possible amendments to Molyneux's question that we should consider. The first, proposed by Diderot in his *Letter on the Blind*, is that we change the question from *globe versus cube* to *circle versus square*.³ His reason is that a subject gaining sight for the first time might not be able to perceive depth (as Berkeley maintained), in which case he would not yet be able to see *anything* as a three-dimensional globe or cube,⁴ but he could nonetheless still presumably distinguish from one another two-dimensional figures like circles and squares. I agree with Gareth Evans that Diderot's substitution leaves us with a question that still

---

² Locke quoted from the second of two letters on this topic from Molyneux, dated March 2, 1693. An earlier letter from 1688, to which Locke never responded, had raised as well the question of whether a newly sighted man could see things as being at a distance from him.

³ Substantial portions of Diderot's *Letter on the Blind* of 1749 are translated and discussed in Morgan 1977. According to Marjolein Degenaar, the first thinker to propose the circle/square substitution was actually the Dutch philosopher Bouillier in 1737 (Degenaar 1996:46).

⁴ This is arguably Locke's reason for answering Molyneux's question *no*: the newly sighted man would be unable to recognize three-dimensional shapes in his two-dimensional visual ideas. If this is his reason, it would explain his placement of Molyneux's question in the *Essay* at the end of section 2.9.8, whose main point is that past associations with tangible ideas make us confuse our two-dimensional visual ideas with ideas of three-dimensional solids.

poses the key issues about the recognition of shapes presented in different sensory modalities (Evans 1985).

The next two twists are due to Leibniz, who discussed Molyneux's question in the section of the *New Essay Concerning Human Understandings* dealing with Locke's treatment of it. Here is Leibniz's spokesman Theophilus:

> I believe that if the blind man knows that the two shapes which he sees are those of a cube and a sphere, he will be able to identify them and to say without touching them that this one is the sphere and this the cube. . . . I have included in [my answer] a condition which can be taken to be implicit in the question: namely that it is merely a problem of telling which is which, and that the blind man knows that the two shaped bodies which he has to discern are before him and thus that each of the appearances which he sees is either that of a cube or that of a sphere. Given this condition, it seems to me past question that the blind man whose sight is restored could discern them by applying rational principles to the sensory knowledge which he has already acquired by touch. ([1765] 1981:136–37)

There are two amendments here that we should distinguish. One is that the subject be told that one of the objects before him is what he formerly knew by touch as a cube and the other what he knew as a globe. Molyneux's own formulation is silent on whether the subject is to be given this hint. The other is that the subject be given the opportunity to work things out "by applying rational principles to the sensory knowledge which he has already acquired by touch" (for example, that a cube but not a sphere has eight distinguished points). In his discussion of Leibniz's version of the question, Evans gives prominence to the "let him work it out" aspect, but Leibniz's own emphasis is on the "give him a hint" aspect—that the subject be told "that, of the two appearances or perceptions he has of them, one belongs to the sphere and the other to the cube" (138). It seems to me that the hint is the more significant factor of the two (or at any rate, that the hint together with the time to work things out is more significant than the time alone).

A fourth clarification is due to Evans. The important question according to Evans is not whether a newly sighted subject will be able to *distinguish* circles and squares, but whether a subject who *can see* circles and squares will *recognize* them as shapes he formerly knew by touch.[5] Perhaps his visual field at first will be a chaos in which

---

[5] The difference between *distinguishing* and *recognizing* is already explicit in Molyneux's original statement of the question as quoted by Locke: could the newly sighted man *distinguish, and tell, which is the globe, which the cube?* The second question, which presupposes that an affirmative answer to the first has already been given, is unfortunately lost sight of by the many writers who misreport the Molyneux question using only the verb "distinguish."

no distinct figures stand forth.[6] But once the subject *is* able to see figures, will he be able to recognize them as the very figures he previously knew by touch? That is what we really want to know, and when the question is so understood, some apparently negative results involving subjects whose sight was restored are seen to be irrelevant.

To these four qualifications or amendments, I add a fifth: let the question concern the subject's ability to recognize the shapes that now *visually appear* to him for the first time, regardless of whether these shapes are *actually possessed* by the objects before him. If we do not make this stipulation, the answer to Molyneux's question threatens to be negative for an irrelevant reason. Suppose that because of some systematically distorting property in the conditions of observation or in the subject's sensory transducers, tangible globes appear to his vision with corners poking out and tangible cubes appear with their corners smoothed away.[7] If the subject in a Molyneux experiment could not rule out such a hypothesis about how tangible globes and cubes affect his sight, he would not be in a position to say which of the objects before him is a globe and which a cube. But this is an utterly boring reason for answering *no*. It would also be a reason for answering *no* to the following question: would a man who had become acquainted with red and white things in London be able to recognize them again when he saw them in Amsterdam? For all he knows, there are strange lights in the new city that make white things look red and red things look white, leaving him unsure or mistaken in his judgments about the colors of objects. Let it be so; it is still a question of interest whether he could recognize the *visual presentations* of red and white things. A parallel question about presentations is what interests us in the Molyneux problem: could the subject recognize visually presented shapes as the shapes he previously knew by touch?[8]

Diderot was aware of the complication I have just raised, but he does not reformulate the instructions to the subject so as to remove it. In consequence, he says he

---

[6] Oliver Sacks's patient Virgil reported that "he had no idea what he was seeing. There was light, there was movement, there was color, all mixed up, all meaningless, all a blur" (Sacks 1995).

[7] Could there be a situation in which what feels like a globe (i.e., feels how globes normally feel in our world) looks like a cube (i.e., looks how cubes normally look in our world) and vice versa? Judith Thomson apparently takes this sort of possibility to be at the root of Molyneux's and Locke's negative answers to Molyneux's problem (Thomson 1974). She questions whether the possibility is a genuine one by noting various anomalies that would result if it obtained—for example, that one could not stick one's finger in the visible gap between two contiguous visible circles if they were produced by contiguous tangible squares. As I am proposing to understand Molyneux's question, possibilities of the sort Thomson discusses would not support a negative answer to it.

[8] By a "visually presented shape" I do not mean a shape *sensation*. Recall from chapter 2 that for Reid, there is no such thing as a sensation of shape.

would expect the following response in a Molyneux experiment if the subject were philosophically minded: "This seems to me to be the object that I call square, that to be the object I call circle; however, I have been asked not what seems, but what is: and I am not in a position to answer that question" (Morgan 1977:50). I would take such a response as warranting an answer of *yes* to the Molyneux question as I conceive of it.[9] Diderot's philosophical subject would show by his words that he connects one visual presentation with tangible squares and the other with tangible circles.

We have, then, five possible variations or specifications of Molyneux's question: (1) replace globe/cube in the problem posed to the subject by circle/square; (2) tell the subject one of the objects now before him is what he formerly knew by touch as a globe (circle) and the other is a cube (square); (3) let him work out his answer by reasoning rather than insisting on immediate recognition; (4) assign the recognitional task only after the subject is able to see circles and squares as distinct figures; (5) let the question concern the shapes presented to the subject's vision rather than the shapes actually possessed by the objects before him.[10]

In what follows, I take stipulations (2), (4), and (5) for granted. I give separate consideration to how Molyneux's question should be answered depending on whether stipulations (1) and (3) are in place.

## B. EMPIRICAL EVIDENCE

Though merely a thought experiment when first propounded, Molyneux's question is apparently a straightforwardly empirical question. One might think that it ought to have been decided by now by actual cases of persons born blind and made to see. Nonetheless, three centuries after the question was first asked, the evidence drawn from cases of restored vision does not conclusively settle it. Such, at any rate, is the conclusion of three writers who surveyed the evidence available as of the late twentieth century: Morgan (1977), Evans (1985), and Degenaar (1996).

There have been just a few scores of reported cases of persons blind from birth or a very early age whose sight was restored surgically, most often by the couching or

---

[9] Here is another reason for insisting on the qualification I am proposing: even *after* attaining the experience that what affects his touch in a certain way normally affects his sight in a certain way—in other words, even after learning what it takes according to Berkeley to perform Molyneux tasks—the subject could not authoritatively say which object is actually a globe/circle and which is a cube/square. For how could he be sure that the conditions of observation are normal and not such as to distort the visual appearances he has come through past experience to expect?

[10] Does the Leibniz hint in condition (2) obviate the need for my condition (5)? I think not, because cross-wiring could make the appearance normally produced by a cube or a square come from a globe or a circle in the test situation.

removal of cataracts.[11] Some of these patients were explicitly given Molyneux tasks and others not (though their relevant reactions were recorded). Some of them could perform Molyneux tasks (for example, name figures or answer which-is-which questions) and others not.[12] The evidence thus points in divergent directions and is often simply ambiguous. Many questions have been raised about the reported cases. Could the postoperative patients really see? How blind were they initially, and for how long? Had they really been denied any opportunity to learn by association? Were they asked any leading questions? Evans notes that many of the "can't tells" may have been "can't sees" and that many of the "can tells" may already have had relevant experience (1985:380–82).

One of the best-known cases of a cataract patient restored to sight is that reported in 1728 by the surgeon William Cheselden, whose patient was a thirteen-year-old boy who had lost sight so early that he had no memory of it. Berkeley, Reid, Voltaire, and many others commented on Cheselden's published report of the boy's experiences.[13] Some, including the optical writer Robert Smith, cited the Cheselden case as supporting their own negative answer to Molyneux's question (Degenaar:61), but others questioned its relevance, noting that the Cheselden lad apparently could not at first distinguish figures at all. It seems clear to me that the questioners are right. Cheselden says that when the boy first saw, "he knew not the shape of anything, nor any one thing from another, however different in shape" (Morgan 1977:19). He thus belongs in the class of "can't sees" rightly deemed irrelevant by Evans.

Degenaar concludes her review of three centuries of empirical evidence bearing on the Molyneux question with the following sentence: "We have not answered Molyneux's question—and, indeed, we think that it cannot be answered because congenitally blind people cannot be made to see once their critical period is passed" (132). She is referring to a period early in life during which if there is no

---

[11] Couching, the earliest treatment for cataracts, consists in moving them aside rather than extracting them.

[12] Degenaar reports that the first researcher explicitly to pose a Molyneux task with sphere and cube was J. C. A. Franz in 1841. Franz's patient could not recognize the sphere and cube as such, but identified them instead as circle and square. Some sixty years later, A. M. Ramsay conducted a Molyneux test with a ball and a brick, telling his newly sighted patient which two objects he would be shown. The patient was able to identify each correctly. These cases highlight for me the significance of Diderot's variation and Leibniz's hint. See Degenaar 87–97 for further details.

[13] See Degenaar 60–65 for details. Berkeley cites the Cheselden case at TVV 71 as confirming by experience points to which he had been led by reasoning, but he does not say which points he has in mind. Probably one of them is that depth is not given to sight prior to associations with touch, since he quotes the boy's remark that at first all objects he saw seemed to touch his eye. That is inconclusive, however, as it may take time for nonassociative mechanisms of depth perception to develop; see appendix K.

appropriate retinal stimulation, there is no formation of the feature analyzer cells that are needed for subsequent discrimination of shapes—or so it has been believed until fairly recently. If there really is a critical period, though, how can there have been *any* positive results to date in Molyneux experiments? And how can the subjects described in appendix S have demonstrated an ability to discriminate visible shapes after being cured of congenital blindness?[14]

Although tests on adults or adolescents restored to sight would be the only direct tests of Molyneux's original question, there have been experiments on infants that potentially bear on the underlying issue. I have in mind the various experiments over the last three decades on "Molyneux babies"—infants too young to have learned any associations between sight and touch who are given Molyneux-like tasks. In one such experiment, days-old infants were allowed to grasp either a cylinder or a triangular prism out of sight in their right hands (Streri and Gentaz 2003). They were then shown a cylinder and a prism side by side, whereupon they gazed longer and more often at the shape they had not previously grasped. Since independent experiments have shown that novel objects rather than familiar objects tend to capture an infant's attention, Streri and Gentaz took their results to indicate that the infants recognized one of the seen shapes as what they had already felt and regarded the other as new.[15] As the authors put it, "This is experimental evidence that newborns can extract shape information in a tactual format and transform it in a visual format before they have had the opportunity to learn from the pairings of visual and tactual experience" (11).

Such was the state of things until 2011, when the prospects for answering Molyneux's question empirically became dramatically better thanks to Project Prakash—a humanitarian and scientific project under whose auspices congenitally blind children in India are operated on to cure their blindness and then given vision-to-touch matching tests (see Held et al. 2011 and appendix S for details). The answer to Molyneux's question emerging from the Prakash researchers is negative, but as I note in the appendix, their results to date bear only on the globe-cube version of the question, not the circle-square version.

Those who addressed the Molyneux question early in its history, including Berkeley and Reid, could only offer theoretical grounds for their answers to it. To these grounds I now turn.

---

[14] Until recently it has also been believed that there is a critical period for the development of the binocular neurons that enable one to perceive depth. That *this* critical period is a myth is one of the main lessons of Barry 2009, discussed in appendix K.

[15] Brian Glenney has pointed out to me that it does not matter for purposes of the experiment whether novelty or familiarity draws an infant's attention. Just so long as the experimental group exhibits preferential looking and the control group (which was not habituated to shapes by touch) does not, that indicates that some sort of cross-modal transfer is taking place.

## C. BERKELEY'S ANSWER

The fourth main thesis of Berkeley's *New Theory of Vision* is that there is no idea or kind of idea common to sight and touch—the objects of these senses are entirely heterogeneous (NTV 121 and 127). He says that the extension and figure perceived by sight are "specifically distinct" from those perceived by touch, by which he means that they are different in species or kind. He agrees with Molyneux and Locke in their answer to Molyneux's question, and he takes the supposed correctness of their answer as an important confirmation of his heterogeneity thesis. As he puts the point in his table of contents entry summarizing NTV 133, the Molyneux problem "is falsely solved, if the common supposition [of ideas common to sight and touch] be true."

Berkeley, in other words, offers us the following *modus tollens*:

1. If visible squares resemble tangible squares, the answer to Molyneux's question is *yes*.
2. But in fact the answer is *no*.
3. Therefore, visible squares do not resemble tangible squares.

He explains as follows why he takes the first premise to be true:

> Now, if a square surface perceived by touch be the same sort with a square surface perceived by sight, it is certain the blind man here mentioned might know a square surface as soon as he saw it. It is no more but introducing into his mind, by a new inlet, an idea he has been already well acquainted with. (NTV 133)

He goes on to say that since the blind man is supposed to have known by his touch that a cube is terminated by square surfaces and a globe is not, he could know (on the supposition of similarity between visible and tangible squares) "which was the cube, and which not, while he only saw them." Berkeley thus returns negative answers to both the globe-cube and circle-square versions of the question, basing his negative answer to the first on a negative answer to the second.

In Berkeley's view, a seen square and a felt square have nothing more in common with each other than do a square of either variety and the *word* "square." (See NTV 140.) The connection between them is a brute correlation of the sort that can be learned only through repeated experience. One could no more expect a newly sighted man to know that the square figure he sees belongs to a tangibly square object than one could expect a neophyte in English to know that the word "square" denotes squares.

## D. REID'S ANSWER(S)

We find material relevant to Molyneux's question in four sections of the *Inquiry*: 5.6, 6.3, 6.7, and 6.11.

I begin with *Inquiry* 5.6, in which Reid discusses how we obtain the conception of extension through touch. By touching things we obtain both tactile sensations and a conception of hard, extended, and figured objects. But the conception does not in any way resemble the sensations; nor could it have been derived from them by any process of abstraction or ratiocination. We obtain the conception only because it is a law of our constitution that such-and-such sensations are the occasion for the formation of such-and-such conceptions. This is the moral of the *experimentum crucis*.

I remind the reader of this aspect of Reid's philosophy because it shows that he would repudiate a reason some thinkers have for answering Molyneux's question in the negative. Lotze and von Senden hold that the blind do not have spatial concepts at all, because (a) spatial concepts must be concepts of things existing side by side simultaneously, and (b) the blind do not have any such concepts of the simultaneously side by side, but only concepts of what *sequences* of tactile sensations they would obtain if they ran their fingers around the edges of an object (Evans: 366–68). If the blind do not have spatial concepts at all, then they presumably would not recognize a square as such upon seeing it for the first time. Reid might agree with point (a), but he would certainly dispute point (b). The touch-derived conception of extension that the sighted and the blind alike possess is not the conception of any sequence of sensations, because it is not the conception of anything sequential, nor of anything sensational. It is the conception of points arrayed thus and so in space. It is an open possibility (so far as what Reid says in 5.6 goes) that the conception of extension given to the blind as a hardwired response to cutaneous stimulation is the same conception as that given to the sighted as a hardwired response to retinal stimulation.[16]

I turn next to *Inquiry* 6.3, where Reid discusses the perspectival variation in the figures given to sight. A round coin seen at an angle will look elliptical; a rectangular table seen from one end will appear trapezoidal. These facts are well known to painters, who must reproduce the appearances of things on canvas, but they are easily overlooked by common folk, who may swear (if they do not give the matter

---

[16] Well, not *quite* the same, since there are these differences as discussed in chapter 6: touch can give a conception of both two- and three-dimensional objects, whereas sight originally gives the conception of two-dimensional objects only, and touch gives a conception of objects governed by Euclidean geometry, whereas sight gives a conception of objects that deviate at least slightly from Euclid.

sufficient attention) that the seen shape of a table is constant as they walk around it. The important point for our purposes comes in the final paragraph of the section:

> To a man newly made to see, the visible appearance of objects would be the same as to us; but he would see nothing at all of their real dimensions, as we do. He could form no conjecture, by means of his sight only, how many inches or feet they were in length, breadth, or thickness. He could perceive little or nothing of their real [three-dimensional] figure; nor could he discern, that this was a cube, that a sphere. (84–85)

*Nor could he discern that this was a cube, that a sphere*: that sounds like a definite *no* to Molyneux's question. Before we jump to conclusions, however, let us read on.

In *Inquiry* 6.11 Reid has us imagine what amounts to a Molyneux scenario involving Dr. Nicholas Saunderson, a blind mathematician whose acquaintance Reid made on a visit to Cambridge in 1736:

> Let us suppose such a blind man as Dr Saunderson, having all the knowledge and abilities which a blind man may have, suddenly made to see perfectly. Let us suppose him kept from all opportunities of associating his ideas of sight with those of touch, until the former become a little familiar; and the first surprise, occasioned by objects so new, being abated, he has time to canvass them, and to compare them, in his mind, with the notions which he formerly had by touch; and in particular to compare, in his mind, that visible extension which his eyes present, with the extension in length and breadth with which he was before acquainted....
>
> ... If Dr Saunderson had been made to see, and had attentively viewed the figures of the first book of Euclid, he might, by thought and consideration, without touching them, have found out that they were the very figures he was before so well acquainted with by touch. (IHM 6.11:117–18)

That sounds like a definite *yes*! What gives? Has Reid given us two conflicting answers to Molyneux's question?

If we keep in mind the various versions of Molyneux's question I distinguished at the outset, we see that there is no conflict; Reid is not returning answers of *yes* and *no* to one and the same question. There are three relevant differences between the 6.3 and 6.11 passages that make this clear.

The first difference is that 6.3 is dealing with globes and cubes, whereas 6.11 is dealing with circles and squares. Here is 6.3 again, with a bit of Reid's explanation:

> [A man newly made to see] could perceive little or nothing of their real figure; nor could he discern, that this was a cube, that a sphere; that this was a cone, that a

cylinder. His eye could not inform him, that this object was near, and that more remote. (85)

Reid agrees with Berkeley that depth is not an original object of sight. We come to be able to perceive by sight the outward distances of things only after we have learned associations between visual cues and information gained by touch and locomotion. For that reason, a newly sighted person could apprehend only two-dimensional shapes, not the three-dimensional shapes Reid refers to as "real figure." Upon seeing a cube for the first time, he would not recognize it as the cube he formerly knew by touch because he would not see it as a cube at all. That, of course, was precisely Diderot's reason for recommending that we replace the globe-cube version of Molyneux's question by the circle-square version. He wanted us to be able to raise questions about cross-modal shape recognition independently of questions about depth perception.

In 6.11, Reid is addressing the circle-square version of the question. This is clear for two reasons. First, he speaks of Dr. Saunderson's viewing the figures of "the first book of Euclid." Book I of the *Elements* is concerned with two-dimensional figures only, solids not making their appearance until Book XI. Second, in the paragraph explaining why he thinks Dr. Saunderson could recognize such figures (elided in my quotation from IHM 6.11:118 above) Reid discusses plane figures explicitly, emphasizing how great he takes the similarity between visible and tangible plane figures to be.

The second salient difference between the passages is that the subject of Reid's thought experiment in 6.11 is not just any blind person (as it was in 6.3), but Dr. Saunderson (1682–1739), the Lucasian professor of mathematics at Cambridge and successor but one to Newton. Saunderson had been blinded by smallpox at the age of one, but that did not keep him from teaching a remarkable range of subjects, including not only algebra and geometry, but optics, the nature of light and colors, the theory of vision, and the effects of lenses.[17]

The third salient difference between the two passages is that in 6.11 the subject is allowed to use "thought and consideration," whereas in 6.3 there is no such stipulation.[18]

---

[17] For more on Saunderson, see Degenaar 49–50, and Morgan ch. 3, especially 42ff. It was his attribution (in the *Letter on the Blind*) of a blasphemous deathbed remark to Saunderson that got Diderot thrown into jail for a month in 1749.

[18] Robert Hopkins identifies the same three differences between the passages in 6.3 and 6.11 (2005). We agree that there is no contradiction between Reid's answers in 6.3 and 6.11, but we disagree on what his main point in 6.11 is; see n. 25.

From now on, I am going to lump the second and third differences together, since it seems to me that they work only in concert. "Thought and consideration" probably would not enable a newly sighted plain man to recognize a cube by sight if he lacked Dr. Saunderson's sophistication, and sophistication might not suffice for Saunderson if he were not given time to exercise it. That gives us the following two-by-two matrix (Table 8.1), in which we can enter Reid's answers to two versions of Molyneux's question—one with both of stipulations (1) and (3) in place and the other with neither:

**Table 8.1**

|  | *Plain man on first view* | *Dr. Saunderson after thought and consideration* |
|---|---|---|
| Globe-cube | 6.3: No |  |
| Circle-square |  | 6.11: Yes |

When I say "on first view," I do not mean that quite literally. The subject is to be given time to get over any dazzlement and confusion. But once things have settled down enough that he can differentiate figures before him, we are to ask what strikes him rather than what he can work out.

The blank spots prompt the question of what Reid would say about the remaining two cases. Although he does not address either case explicitly, he provides us with the basis for answers of *yes* in each of the two unfilled slots.

To take the upper right slot first, could Dr. Saunderson, upon gaining sight, tell which is the globe and which the cube? Reid provides us with a clear case for *yes* in his discussion in *Inquiry* 6.7 of the relation of visible figure (which is always two-dimensional) to real figure (which may be either two- or three-dimensional). Reid distinguishes the two types of figure as follows: "as the real figure of a body consists in the situation of its several parts with regard to one another, so its visible figure consists in the position of its several parts with regard to the eye" (96). Position with regard to the eye is direction out from the eye, regardless of distance: points that lie on the same straight line drawn from the center of the eye have the same position with regard to the eye. If lines are drawn from the eye (considered as a single point) to all points on an object, the intersections of all these lines with a sphere centered on the eye (or any other intercepting surface) will mark out the object's visible figure. The visible figure of a tilted coin will be an ellipse, while that of a cube will be a network of polygons. These matters are familiar to us from chapter 6.

The visible figure of an object is mathematically deducible from its real figure plus its distance and orientation, as Reid explains in the following passage from *Inquiry* 6.7:

> The visible figure, magnitude, and position, may, by mathematical reasoning, be deduced from the real. . . . Nay, we may venture to affirm, that a man born blind, if he were instructed in mathematics, would be able to determine the visible figure of a body, when its real figure, distance, and position are given. Dr. Saunderson understood the projection of the sphere, and perspective. Now, I require no more knowledge in a blind man, in order to his being able to determine the visible figure of bodies, than that he can project the outline of a given body, upon the surface of a hollow sphere, whose centre is in the eye. This projection is [determines] the visible figure he wants. (95)[19]

> From these principles, having given [to him] the real figure and magnitude of a body, and its position and distance with regard to the eye, he [our blind mathematician] can find out its visible figure and magnitude. He can demonstrate in general, from these principles, that the visible figure of all bodies will be the same with that of their projection upon the surface of a hollow sphere, when the eye is placed in the centre. (96)

Reid is telling us that Dr. Saunderson could have worked out, in advance of ever seeing them, what visible figures are normally presented by globes and cubes when seen from various perspectives.[20] This knowledge is not fully tantamount to knowing how they would look, if only because it omits any information about color. But it ought to be enough to enable him to know by reflection after he sees them that the object that looks this way is a cube and the object that looks that way is a globe. At any rate, Dr. Saunderson could surely know this if he had been given the Leibniz

---

[19] Reid should have said that the projection determines, specifies, or represents the visible figure, not that it *is* the visible figure. The projection is curved and at a certain distance from the eye; the visible figure has neither of these properties.

[20] In a paragraph at IHM 6.7:97, Reid distinguishes two routes to the conception of a figure such as a parabola or a cycloid: by means of a mathematical definition and by means of seeing or feeling a specimen of it drawn on paper or cut out in wood. He says the blind mathematician forms his conceptions of visible figure in the first way, the mathematically naïve sighted person in the second. He does not say the resulting conceptions are different. I think Reid would be suspicious, as I am, of C. D. Broad's distinction between geometrical properties and sensible forms as set forth in 1925:171–72.

At any rate, I think Reid would acknowledge the possibility of a blind mathematician whose conceptions of visible figure are the same in all ways as those of the sighted, except that they are not got through the channels of sight. I have in mind someone whose cortical structures are the same as in the sighted (and who can therefore visualize a square) but whose blindness is due to a problem somewhere in the visual pathways to the cortex and not in the cortex itself. Such a person could visualize squares as readily as the sighted, but could have only tactile or other nonvisual cues for doing so.

hint (which I am taking for granted) that globe and cube are the only choices.[21] Without the hint, he could suppose that the round figure he is now seeing for the first time is the visible figure of any number of objects—a cylinder or an egg viewed endwise, perhaps, or even just a two-dimensional circle. Visible figure by itself does not uniquely determine the real figure of the object that projects it.

Let us turn now to the plain man. Lacking the sophistication of Dr. Saunderson, he may be unable to answer the question about globes and cubes, but there is a good Reidian basis for thinking that he could answer Diderot's question about circles and squares. The reason for *yes* this time comes out in Reid's discussion (in *Inquiry* 6.9 and 6.11) of the *similarity* between visible and tangible figures. Reid is very much opposed to Berkeley's doctrine of the radical heterogeneity of the objects of sight and touch. According to Berkeley, a visible square and a tangible square are no more alike than a tangible square and the *name* "square" (NTV 140). But according to Reid, a visible square and a tangible square, though not "strictly and mathematically" alike as regards shape (6.9:106), may be "to all sense the same" (6.11:118).

Why not strictly and mathematically alike? That is because (as discussed in chapter 6) visible squares and tangible squares are governed by different geometries. Tangible squares always have angle sums of 360 degrees; visible squares have angle sums larger than that. But in the case of any visible square small enough to be taken in at one view, the departure from Euclidean values will be negligible. That is why a visible square and a tangible square are "to all sense the same." As Reid explains:

> It is true, that of every visible triangle, the three angles are greater than two right angles; whereas in a plain [plane] triangle, the three angles are equal to two right angles: but when the visible triangle is small, its three angles will be so nearly equal to two right angles, that the sense cannot discern the difference....
>
> Hence it appears, that small visible figures (and such only can be seen distinctly at one view) have not only a resemblance to the plain tangible figures which have the same name, but are to all sense the same. (IHM 6.11:118; see also 6.9:106, lines 3–23)

This, then, is the reason Reid gives for saying that Dr. Saunderson could recognize the figures of Euclid when first seen in a book as the figures he formerly knew by touch: they are "to all sense the same."[22] It is true that the visible figures are colored

---

[21] Saunderson is reported to have had an opinion on the Molyneux question himself—that the subject could indeed know, if given the Leibniz hint (Degenaar:49). I daresay that if Saunderson was capable of having this opinion, it must have been right!

[22] In saying that a visible triangle and a tangible triangle are "to all sense the same," is Reid saying outright that they are the same no matter what sense modality they are presented in? No, his immediate point is simply that they are sensibly indiscriminable despite not being exactly congruent. But that paves the way for the view that they are nearly enough the same *for all senses*.

and the tangible not, but "they may, notwithstanding, have the same figure; as two objects of touch may have the same figure, although one is hot and the other cold" (6.11:118).

But if this is the reason in Dr. Saunderson's case, it seems an equally good reason in the plain man's case.[23] Visible squares and tangible squares are as much alike in point of figure as hot squares and cold squares. What better reason to think that a subject acquainted with them in one modality or medium would be well placed to recognize them in the other?

To sum up, then, I think the rest of our table should be filled in like this (Table 8.2):

**Table 8.2**

|  | Plain man on first view | Dr. Saunderson after thought and consideration |
| --- | --- | --- |
| Globe-cube | 6.3: No | 6.7: Yes (implicitly) |
| Circle-square | 6.11 Yes (implicitly) | 6.11: Yes |

If I am right about this, Reid's answer of *yes* in the lower right cell is doubly determined. The considerations that yield *yes* at the upper right and those that yield *yes* at the lower left are each sufficient on their own to yield *yes* at the lower right.[24]

## E. IS BERKELEY'S *MODUS TOLLENS* REID'S *MODUS PONENS?*

The reasons I have attributed to Reid for answering *yes* to the circle-square question apparently involve attributing to him an argument like the following:

1. If visible squares resemble tangible squares, the answer to Molyneux's question is *yes*.
2. Visible squares *do* resemble tangible squares.
3. Therefore, the answer to Molyneux's question is *yes*.

---

[23] I am assuming that the circle and the square are presented head-on rather than obliquely to the plain man's sight. If they were presented obliquely (so as to present an ellipse and a trapezoid), the subject might need something of Dr. Saunderson's sophistication (along with the Leibniz hint) in order to know which is the circle and which the square.

[24] One reason that Reid's case for *yes* is of interest is that it does not rely on the neo-behaviorist assumptions of Evans 1985: that to know you are confronted with a square array, whether visible or tangible, is to be disposed to reach in the right directions to find the corners.

That would be replacing Berkeley's *modus tollens* with his own *modus ponens*. Would Reid approve of that argument? The question breaks in two: Does Reid affirm the antecedent of Berkeley's conditional? And does he affirm the conditional itself?

I think it is clear that Reid does affirm the antecedent—that visible squares resemble tangible squares. As noted in the previous section, visible squares and tangible squares have angles that are not "strictly and mathematically equal" (IHM 6.9:106), but if the visible figures are small enough to be seen at one view, they have "not only a resemblance to the plain tangible figures, which have the same name, but are to all sense the same" (IHM 6.11:118). His discussion of the Molyneux question in 6.11, which is embedded in a critical discussion of Berkeley's heterogeneity thesis, closes with the words, "Berkeley therefore proceeds upon a capital mistake, in supposing that there is no resemblance betwixt the extension, figure, and position which we see, and that which we perceive by touch" (IHM 6.11:119).[25]

So Reid affirms the antecedent of Berkeley's conditional, but would he affirm the conditional itself? And is that a reasonable thing for a philosopher to do? There are doubts, not unconnected, on each score. One may think that the Molyneux question is a thoroughly empirical question, even if not settled by the evidence available to date, and that it is bad strategy for a philosopher to have a stake in the eventual outcome. If Reid affirms Berkeley's conditional along with its antecedent, he unwisely gives hostage to future empirical enquiry. This concern has led some friends of Reid to question whether he is or ought to be committed to the conditional.[26]

"If visible squares are like tangible squares," runs Berkeley's conditional, "the answer to Molyneux's question is *yes*." But *yes* to exactly what question? As with Reid's *experimentum crucis*, we may ask whether it is it a question about *woulds, coulds,* or *shoulds*. This is a new dimension of variation in the Molyneux question, cutting across the five dimensions distinguished above.

Is the Molyneux question a question about what the subject *would* say or do in the envisaged setup? If so, it is an empirical question, and philosophers should make no bets. However similar visible circles and squares may be to their tangible counterparts, there can be no a priori assurance about what a Molyneux subject would actually say. Cognitive dysfunction or an idiosyncratic quality space might prevent someone from recognizing even a *perfect replica* of what he has been presented with

---

[25] Hopkins (2005) denies that Reid means to affirm in IHM 6.11 that visible figures and tangible figures are "common sensibles"; he takes Reid's main point to be that there are concepts (namely, of visible figure) that are not constitutively tied to sensations. I do not see why Reid's discussion cannot be taken as supporting both points.

[26] This point has been urged forcefully on me by Ben Jarvis.

many times before—he might not judge a red square seen now to be the same as a red square seen earlier.

Is the Molyneux question a question about what the subject *could* do? No, for then the answer is too easily *yes*. There is nothing impossible about a subject's correctly identifying the shape he used to know by touch as square, if only by luck.

In asking the Molyneux question, we do not mean to ask merely whether there is a possibility of a subject's being set a Molyneux task and getting the answer right. We mean to ask whether he would be in a position to give an answer *knowingly*— with adequate warrant or a good rational basis or something of that sort. But this is to shift to the third alternative, in which "could" gives way to "should" or some kindred notion. Under the third construal, to say that the answer to Molyneux's question is *yes* is to say that in the envisaged setup, something along the following lines would be true of the subject:

—he *should* be able to tell which seen figure is a circle and which a square;
—he would have *sufficient evidence* for judging that this figure is a circle, that a square;
—he would be in a position to *know* which seen figure is a circle and which a square (unless he were suffering from some cognitive dysfunction), etc.

These formulations all make the consequent of Berkeley's conditional a *normative* assertion.[27] As such, it hazards no predictions about what any subject would actually do in the envisaged setup. So it is safer now to affirm Berkeley's conditional, and Reid's commitment to the consequent of it is more defensible than it would be on an empirical construal.

Unfortunately, if we insulate Reid's answer to Molyneux's question from experimental disproof by the strategy above, we also renounce the right to claim experimental confirmation for it. Consider again the experiments with Molyneux babies described in section 2. The infants apparently recognize the seen cylinder as something they have touched, but who can be sure that the mechanisms subserving this recognition are such as to make it a rational phenomenon? Perhaps the infants' behavior is explained not by any similarities of visual and tactile shape experience that would rationalize it, but by innate or hardwired connections between disparate

---

[27] Locke states his opinion thus: "that the Blind Man, at first sight, would not be able *with certainty* to say, which was the Globe, which the Cube" (emphasis mine). If this certainty has to do with strength of evidence rather than strength of conviction, it may be that Locke, too, understood the question in a normative way. For further discussion of what "certainty" might involve, see Levin 2008.

concepts of shape properties accessible through the two sensory modalities—a possibility pointed out by Evans (1985:377–78 and 381).[28]

## F. THE ONE-TWO MOLYNEUX QUESTION

Aristotle ranked figure, magnitude, motion, and number as "common sensibles," that is, features that can be perceived by more than one sense. In developing his thesis of the radical heterogeneity of the objects of sight and touch, Berkeley explicitly denies that the first three characteristics are common sensibles. What would he say about number?

This question is connected with another: how would Berkeley answer the one-two Molyneux question, a question we might frame in Molyneux's style as follows?

> Suppose a man born blind and taught to distinguish by his touch a single raised dot from a pair of raised dots (as Braille readers can do). Suppose the blind man made to see, and presented with a single visible dot on the left and a pair on the right. Quaere: whether by his sight and before he touched them, he could now distinguish and tell, which is the single and which the pair?

In the case of figure, we have seen that Berkeley offers the following argument:

1. If visible squares resemble tangible squares, the answer to Molyneux's question is *yes*.
2. But in fact the answer is *no*.
3. Therefore, visible squares do not resemble tangible squares.

Would he give the following parallel argument about number?

1. If visible pairs resemble tangible pairs, the answer to the one-two question is *yes*.
2. But in fact the answer is *no*.
3. Therefore, visible pairs do not resemble tangible pairs.

To me, it seems that there would be something bizarre and incredible about a subject who was stymied by the cross-modal number recognition task. But the

---

[28] In view of the hardwiring possibility, Evans contends that although a negative answer to Molyneux's question would refute the hypothesis of a shape concept common to vision and touch, a positive answer would not necessarily prove it.

number task seems to me in principle on a par with the shape task, so I am tempted to regard the parallel argument as a reductio ad absurdum of Berkeley's original.

But is it legitimate to extend Berkeley's views in the way I am suggesting? Is he really committed to saying that the Molyneux man would not know by sight which is the single and which the pair?

There are more and less radical ways of interpreting Berkeley's philosophy as it bears on this point, but either way, I think the answer is *yes*. Among the attributes discussed in the *New Theory* are outward distance, size, orientation, figure, and number. The radical line about any of these attributes says that it is a proper object of touch alone, not really manifested in vision at all. The moderate line about one of the attributes says that vision displays an analog or counterpart of the tactile attribute, but that the counterpart is heterogeneous from the tactile attribute and only contingently connected with it.

With regard to distance or depth, Berkeley takes the radical line. There is no such thing as visual depth; there are only visual cues from which we may infer degrees of distance once we have correlated the cues with distance as gauged by locomotion and touch. I believe he also takes the radical line about up or down orientation.

With regard to size, Berkeley takes the moderate line. There is such a thing as visible magnitude, as a being endowed with sight alone could tell that one visible line was longer than another. However, visible magnitude has no resemblance to tangible magnitude, and it is only after learning correlations between the two that anyone can predict one from the other.

What line does Berkeley take about number?

Reid interpreted Berkeley as taking the radical line about number (as well as figure and orientation). Under Reid's understanding, it is Berkeley's view "that we do not originally, and previous to acquired habits, see things either erect or inverted, of one figure or another, single or double, but learn from experience to judge of their tangible position, figure, and number, by certain visible signs" (IHM 6.11:117). As an instance of this general position, "if the visible appearance of two shillings had been found connected from the beginning with the tangible idea of one shilling, that appearance would as naturally and readily have signified the unity of the object, as now it signifies its duplicity" (116). On this reading of Berkeley, his views clearly imply that the Molyneux man would be unable to recognize a pair of visible dots as a pair. Number would have no meaning as applied to visible things except by courtesy of association with variously numbered tangible things, and the Molyneux man has had no opportunity to learn the required associations.

I myself think that Berkeley took the moderate line about number, assimilating it to size rather than depth. We find evidence of this in his reply to an objection to his view that a newly sighted man, upon first seeing heads and feet, would not connect these visible objects in any way with the tangible objects he calls head and feet. The objection is that the subject could infer that because there are two visible feet, they correspond to the man's tangible feet rather than to his head. Berkeley's reply is as follows:

> In order to get clear of this seeming difficulty we need only observe that diversity of visible objects does not necessarily infer [imply] diversity of tangible objects corresponding to them. . . . I should not therefore at first opening my eyes conclude that because I see two I shall feel two. How, therefore, can I, before experience teaches me, know that the visible legs, because two, are connected with the tangible legs? (NTV 108)

Here Berkeley is granting that I do see the visible feet as two; I just cannot draw any inferences regarding the number of tangible feet.

For present purposes, it does not matter which interpretation of Berkeley is correct, since the moderate line has the same implications as the radical line. On the moderate line, there is such a thing as visible number, but it is wholly disparate from tangible number and only contingently connected with it. In short, visible number is related to tangible number as visible figure to tangible figure. But the supposed disparity in the case of visible and tangible figure is enough to make Berkeley confident that the answer to the circle-square Molyneux question is *no*. He therefore ought to insist that the answer to the one-two Molyneux question is *no* and give the parallel argument I attributed to him above. That strikes me as a reductio ad absurdum of his original *modus tollens* and an indirect recommendation of Reid's *modus ponens*.

## G. CONCLUDING CONFESSION

I have taken for granted in this chapter that whether a property apprehended previously is being presented again is a matter of objective fact, capable of rationalizing a subject's opinion about it rather than being constituted by it. Some philosophers take the opposite tack. According to Quine, whether the same predicate applies to each of two things is as much a function of the subject's innate quality space as it of any features of the things (1960). According to Wittgenstein in the *Brown Book* (1958), whether two things are the same in some respect is a matter of whether they strike the speaker as the same.[29] According to some contemporary theorists

---

[29] "Striking the subject as the same" is ambiguous between (i) "S's response to x is the same as S's response to y" and (ii) "S judges that x is the same as y." These are not equivalent. If (i) is made a necessary condition of sameness, it gives rise to a vicious regress, since "same" occurs in the statement of the condition itself. Taking (ii) as the condition does not necessarily give rise to a regress, since "same" occurs in the statement of the condition only inside a propositional attitude context. It nonetheless makes urgent the question: what is the content of the subject's judgment of sameness?

of radical response-dependence, whether a given concept is instantiated always depends on what a subject is disposed to say or do when confronted with a putative instance of it (Smith and Stoljar 1998).

If we review the questions asked in this chapter, persuaded of these principles, what havoc must we make? Obviously, I am not myself persuaded of the principles, but I must leave the examination of them for another occasion.

# 9

## MEMORY AND PERSONAL IDENTITY

Once, I smelled a tuberose in a certain room where it grew in a pot, and gave a very grateful perfume. . . . The very thing I saw yesterday, and the fragrance I smelled, are now the immediate objects of my mind when I remember it. (Thomas Reid, *IHM 2.3:28*)

## A. THINGS OBVIOUS AND CERTAIN WITH REGARD TO MEMORY

Reid begins Essay 3 of the EIP with a list of things "obvious and certain" with regard to memory, enumerated below.

(1) "It is by memory that we have immediate knowledge of things past" (EIP 3.1:253).

That formula can be taken as the expression of either of two theses. The first is that the operations of memory yield *basic knowledge* about things past—knowledge of truths about the past not reached by inference, nor dependent for their justification on any other justified beliefs. The second is that the operations of memory give us *direct awareness* of things past—an awareness of past events in no way mediated by awareness of present intermediaries, but putting us directly in cognitive contact with pieces of the past. These two theses are the analogs of two theses about perception distinguished in chapter 3, epistemic direct realism and presentational direct realism.[1] It is clear that Reid affirms the first of the theses in regard to memory, but controversial whether he affirms the second. I argue that he affirms them both.

(2) "Memory must have an object" (253).

As Reid goes on to explain, every man who remembers must remember *something*. In this way, he says, "memory agrees with perception, but differs from sensation."[2]

(3) "Every man can distinguish the thing remembered from the remembrance of it" (253).

With memory as with all other mental operations (with the possible exception of sensations), there is a distinction between act and object.

(4) "The object of memory, or thing remembered, must be something that is past" (254).

In this way memory is distinguished from perception and consciousness, which must have present objects, and from imagination, whose object need not exist at all.

Is memory distinguished from perception *solely* by the fact that its object lies in the past rather than the present? If so (as Marina Folescu has pointed out to me), that would invite the question how we know on a given occasion whether we are perceiving or remembering. Reid has an answer: "I am conscious of a difference *in kind* between sensation and memory, and between both and imagination" (IHM 2.3:29, emphasis mine).

What is this difference in kind? Russell makes some apposite remarks. He lays down the principle that if experiences with the same object differ intrinsically, they must involve different relations to the object ([1913] 1992:54), and he goes on to say that in sensation (what Reid normally calls perception) the object is given as present, in memory it is given as past, and in imagination it is given without any temporal relation to the present (58). These differences in how the same object may be "given" are differences in relation, reminiscent of Reid's remark that in sensation, memory, and imagination, the same smell is "presented to the mind three different ways" (IHM 2.3:27).[3]

---

[1] I discuss an analog of perceptual direct realism in the final paragraph of section C.

[2] If the sentence ended here, it would support the no-object theory of sensations, but it continues with "which has no object but the feeling itself," inviting once again the surmise that he holds the reflexive theory.

[3] Russell's writings on memory from 1912 and 1913 strongly support the contention in Beanblossom 1978 that Russell must have been influenced by Reid, though he never cites him. Among the Reidian points in Russell are these: the object of memory is a past event, not an image; memory, perception, and imagination may have the same object, but differ in kind or relation; it is contingent that we have cognition of the past but not of the future; finally, there is no necessary

(5) "Memory is always accompanied with the belief of that which we remember" (254).

In this way, memory is like perception, but unlike imagination.

In connection with point (5), an issue arises parallel to one discussed in chapter 1 regarding perception: does memory have a belief in the past existence of its object as an *ingredient* or merely as a *concomitant*? Hamilton (2003) and Copenhaver (2006:179, 182–84) say the former, van Woudenberg (2004) the latter.

In favor of the ingredient reading, one may cite the following two passages:

> I find in my mind a distinct conception and a firm belief of a series of past events; but how this is produced I know not. I call it memory. (EIP 3.2:255)

> I remember distinctly to have dined yesterday with such company. What is the meaning of this? It is, that I have a distinct conception and firm belief of this past event; not by reasoning, not by testimony, but immediately from my constitution. (EIP 2.20:232)

If a firm belief in a past event is *called* memory and is part of the *meaning* of it, it seems to follow that the belief is a constituent or ingredient of the memory. Moreover, Copenhaver cites the following passage as explicitly saying that belief is an ingredient of memory (2006):

> There are many operations of mind in which, when we analyse them as far as we are able, we find belief to be an essential ingredient. A man cannot be conscious of his own thoughts, without believing that he thinks. He cannot perceive an object of sense, without believing that it exists. He cannot distinctly remember a past event without believing that it did exist. Belief therefore is an ingredient in consciousness, in perception, and in remembrance. (EIP 2.20:228)

In my opinion, however, this passage is not decisive. In the first place, the reason Reid gives for saying belief is an ingredient of the three operations—that the operations never occur without the appropriate belief—is not a reason for saying that belief is an ingredient rather than a concomitant. In the second place, by his own confession he sometimes uses the term "ingredient" when "concomitant" would be equally acceptable (EIP 6.1:409 and COR 108).

---

connection between a memory and the existence of its object. (Compare Russell's famous remark that there is no logical impossibility in the supposition that the entire world came into existence five minutes ago together with a population that "remembered" a wholly unreal past.) By the time Russell wrote the *Analysis of Mind* in 1921, however, he had gone over from a Reidian to a Humean account of memory. See the excerpts in Huemer 2002:88–90.

In favor of the concomitant reading, one may cite passages such as the following:

> Why sensation should compel our belief of the present existence of the thing, memory a belief of its past existence, and imagination no belief at all, I believe no philosopher can give a shadow of reason. (IHM 2.4:28)

> Every man feels that he must believe what he distinctly remembers, though he can give no other reason of his belief, but that he remembers the thing distinctly. (EIP 3.2:254)

If memory is either a cause of belief or a reason for it as these passages say it is, it must be distinct from the belief to which it bears these relations (van Woudenberg 2004:207-208). I agree with van Woudenberg. Like perception, memory elicits and justifies belief in its object rather than being partly constituted by such a belief.

> (6) "This belief, which we have from distinct memory, we account real knowledge, no less certain than if it was grounded on demonstration" (EIP 3.2:254).

Memory is a source not merely of belief, but also of knowledge and therefore of evidence. This claim supports the interpretation of Reid's "first principles" I advance in chapter 11—that they are principles of evidence and not merely principles of belief.

> (7) "Things remembered must be things formerly perceived or known" (EIP 3.2:254).

In contemporary theorizing about memory, this requirement is known as the Previous Awareness Condition. Reid gives the following example of its application: "I remember the transit of Venus over the sun in the year 1769. I must therefore have perceived it" (EIP 3.2:255).[4] Presumably, another application would be that if I remember hearing a whistle (a mental event), I must previously have been conscious of hearing a whistle.

The Previous Awareness Condition provides good occasion for discussing a distinction drawn by contemporary theorists of memory: "personal memory" versus "factual memory" (Malcolm 1963) or "episodic memory" versus "semantic memory"

---

[4] Reid further elucidates the claim that we can remember only what we have formerly perceived by saying, "Memory can only produce a continuance or renewal of former acquaintance with the thing remembered" (EIP 3.2:255). This implies (at least verbally) that perception for Reid is a form of acquaintance, as I argue in chapter 1, section D.

(Tulving, cited in Copenhaver 2006). Two marks distinguish personal or episodic memory from factual memory (Copenhaver 2006:176, following Martin).[5] First, factual memory is reported using that-clauses, as in "I remember that Cheyenne is the capital of Wyoming" or "I remember that I was born in Minnesota," whereas personal or episodic memory is reported using names or phrases designating past objects or events, as in "I remember the transit of Venus across the sun in 1769" or "I remember my eighth birthday party." Second, episodic memory is subject to the Previous Awareness Condition, whereas factual memory is not. I can remember my eighth birthday party only if I experienced it when it happened, but there is no parallel requirement of past experience governing my remembrance that Cheyenne is the capital of Wyoming.[6] Theorists are divided about which of the two forms of memory (if either) is more fundamental.[7]

Most of Reid's examples of memory are cases of personal or episodic memory. How much room does he make for factual memory? The answer is either none at all or none for factual memory not based on personal memory. According to van Woudenberg, Reid holds that all memory (as opposed to beliefs based on memory) is personal memory (van Woudenberg 2004:207–8). According to Copenhaver, Reid allows for both types of memory, but holds that we have factual memory *that* I did such-and-such only if the memory is based on personal memory *of* my doing such-and-such. On this issue, I side with Copenhaver. Here is a passage in which Reid uses a factual memory locution: "I believe that I washed my hands and face this morning . . . [because] I remember it distinctly" (EIP 3.1:255–56). The antecedent of "it" in "I remember it" is "that I washed my hands and face this morning." But I do not think Reid would say he remembers that he washed his hands and face this morning unless he also remembered washing them (as opposed, say, to having been told he did so by his wife). Otherwise, one's supposed memory that p would be comparable to other things one has learned about one's past but does not strictly remember. As Reid observes, "I know who bare me, and suckled me, but I do not remember these events" (EIP 3.4:264).

---

[5] I prefer "factual" to "semantic" so as not to build into one's terminology the substantive assumption that memory that p is tied to language.

[6] Copenhaver (n. 22) credits Sydney Shoemaker with pointing out that factual memory has a Previous Awareness Condition of its own: one remembers that p only if one previously knew that p. Factual memory is nonetheless distinguishable from personal memory by this, that there is no requirement on factual memory of previous relevant *perception* or *experience*. Reid may be formulating a broad Previous Awareness Condition that applies to both forms of memory when he says, "Things remembered must be things formerly perceived *or known*" (EIP 3.2:254, emphasis added).

[7] Russell holds that factual memory depends on personal memory, but not conversely; Malcolm argues for the opposite direction of one-way dependency.

Malcolm observes that when one remembers that p, the verb in the subordinate sentence of the that-clause may be in any tense. For instance, one can remember that there will be an eclipse of the moon tomorrow or that dinner will be served at six o'clock. Van Woudenberg tries to square Malcolm's observation with Reid's insistence that the object of memory be past by reconstruing Reid thus: "the objects of memory are past, present, or future things about which we have learned in the past" (205–6, citing EIP 3.2:254). I doubt, however, that Reid would really let us say that if I have learned that there will be an eclipse tomorrow, the object of my memory is tomorrow's eclipse. Given that all memory for Reid is either personal or based on the personal, I believe we should deal with Malcolm's examples by excluding them rather than trying to accommodate them. One does not really remember that there will be an eclipse tomorrow; one knows that there will be one because one remembers reading about it.[8]

(8) "The remembrance of a past event is necessarily accompanied with the conviction of our own existence at the time the event happened" (EIP 3.2:255).

Moreover, as Reid makes clear later, memory is a source not just of conviction, but of *knowledge* of our own "personal identity and continued existence, as far back as we remember anything distinctly" (EIP 6.5:476).

## B. CRITIQUE OF THE IMPRESSION AND IDEA THEORIES OF MEMORY

In EIP 3.7, Reid expounds and criticizes theories of memory that are rivals to his own—the impression theory of the ancients and the idea theories of Locke and Hume.

*Impression theories.* Recall that in Reid's parlance, an impression is always a physical event or state leading up to perception or some other mental operation, such as the falling of light on the retina. He sketches an ancient theory according to which the impressions caused by external objects persist after the objects are removed, not at our sensory surfaces, but more inwardly in our brains. By their survival, these impressions (or traces, as we might call them) enable memory. Reid faults the trace

---

[8] Reid makes one remark that is inconsistent with the views I attribute to him in the previous two paragraphs: "After all, many things are remembered which were never perceived by the senses, being no object of sense" (EIP 3.7:282). That either contradicts the Previous Awareness Condition or else acknowledges that there is a kind of factual memory not derived from personal memory.

theory for running afoul of the two Newtonian requirements he likes to cite as conditions for an adequate explanation: the proposed cause must be sufficient to produce the effect, and there must be evidence that the cause actually exists (see EIP 1.3:51 for the general rule and 3.7:280 for its application to the case at hand). As for the first requirement, Reid says no one knows how the impression would give rise to a memory. That may be true but is irrelevant. On Reid's own view of "what it is to account for a phenomenon in nature" (EIP 2.6), one need only show that the explanatory factor is lawfully followed by the explanandum. Science is never in the business of finding true causes, so Reid should not fault the trace theory for not doing so. As for the second requirement, Reid stands here on firmer ground. In his own century and well into the twentieth, no one had identified any localized structures in the brain that could play the theoretical role of traces (Lashley 1950). It should be said, though, that one of Reid's objections to traces is easily answerable. He claims that so long as they persist, so should the memory, if not the original perception. Anyone who posited traces would say that they are not functional equivalents of impressions on organs and that they must be activated to produce their effects. In other words, there is a difference on the side of the cause to account for the difference in effect.

*Idea theories.* Locke's theory, when stated without his metaphor of a repository, says that for the mind to remember something is for it to "revive Perceptions [or ideas], which it once had, with this additional Perception annexed to them, that it has had them before" (ECHU 2.10.2:150). Noting that ideas or perceptions are interrupted in their existence and therefore have no true identity over time, Reid emends Locke's theory thus: to remember a previous idea is to generate a distinct and present idea resembling it, along with the "perception" that one has had an idea resembling this one before. He then makes three criticisms. First, "perceiving" a present idea to be like one we had before presupposes memory, which is the very thing Locke is trying to explain. Locke could easily have sidestepped this objection by rewriting his theory thus: S remembers e (a past idea) iff S has a present idea e* that resembles e & S believes that e* resembles some idea he had in the past. This existential belief on S's part would not presuppose memory of e because it is not directed at e in particular. Second, on Locke's theory, the only things we can remember are ideas, not external objects and events. Well, yes, because the only things we can perceive in the first place for Locke are ideas. This objection is not an objection to Locke's theory of memory as such; if we could perceive trees, his theory of memory would give a sense in which we may also remember them, namely, this: we believe truly of a present image that it resembles some tree we have perceived in the past. Such was Russell's theory in 1921 (Huemer 2002:89). Third, Locke's definition would classify as remembering a case in which one "revives" one's idea of a tree simply by looking at the tree again and believing that one has had a similar idea before—but this would be perceiving, not remembering. To get around this objection, Locke would need to say when an idea is perceptual and when it is memorial, but this he has not done.

Now for Hume. Reid quotes the essentials of Hume's theory of memory as follows:

> We find by experience, that when any impression [in Hume's sense, not Reid's] has been present with the mind, it again makes its appearance there as an idea; and this it may do after two different ways, either when in its new appearance it retains a considerable degree of its first vivacity, and is somewhat intermediate betwixt an impression and an idea, or when it entirely loses that vivacity, and is a perfect idea. The faculty by which we repeat our impressions in the first manner, is called the memory, and the other the imagination. (EIP 3.7:287, quoting THN 1.3.3:8)

In brief, to remember a previous impression is to have an appropriately faded idea of it, to which we should probably add that the idea was caused by the impression.

Reid makes three objections. He introduces the first by asking what Hume can mean by the "experience" through which we find that impressions are often superseded in the mind by ideas that resemble them (but have less vivacity). Reid answers that he can only mean *memory* in the common sense of immediate knowledge of the past. But "Our author does not admit that there is any such knowledge in the human mind. He maintains that memory is nothing but a present idea" (EIP 3.7:287). That sets the stage for Reid's trenchant objection:

> So that it appears from Mr. Hume's account of this matter, that he found himself to have that kind of memory, which he acknowledges and defines, by exercising that kind which he rejects. (EIP 3.7:288)

The objection here is not an objection of circularity, but of self-confessed incompleteness. Reid is not accusing Hume of presupposing the notion he is trying to define; he is accusing him of presupposing a notion that his theory has no place for and in fact rejects.[9]

---

[9] Compare Russell (1912) 1999:83: "We are certainly able to some extent to compare our image with the object remembered, so that we often know, within somewhat wide limits, how far our image is accurate; but this would be impossible unless the object, as opposed to the image, were in some way before the mind." And Price 1940:5: "If [Hume] is to know what he professes to know about the derivation of ideas from impressions . . . he requires an immediate apprehension of past impressions themselves."

A similar objection may be raised against Hume in another context. One of his arguments for his copy principle—that there is no (simple) idea that has not been copied from some prior impression—is to invite the reader to make a survey of his ideas and try to find an exception. For any of your ideas, Hume says, if you consult your memory, you will find that you once had a resembling impression. But if there is no more to memory than having present ideas, the only principle in the neighborhood of the copy principle that can be confirmed by Hume's procedure is this: for every idea, there is a resembling *idea*. We may take the idea to be "of" a previous impression, but that would be exercising that kind of memory for which Hume's theory has no place.

Reid's second objection begins life as a repeat of one of his objections to Locke—that as there is no literal "reviving" of past impressions, so there is no "reappearing" of an impression as an idea. What there is is the appearing of an idea similar in content but differing in vivacity from an earlier numerically distinct impression. What Reid's objection then turns into is an incisive criticism of Hume's "force and vivacity" criterion for distinguishing impressions from ideas, which I paraphrase as follows:

> Suppose a man strikes his head smartly against a wall; the result is an impression. Let him now strike his head again, but somewhat less forcefully. The result, being somewhat less vivacious, will be what Hume's theory classifies as memory. Finally, let him just barely touch the wall with his head; the result, having a very low degree of vivacity, will be what Hume's theory classifies as imagination. Yet in fact—and as Hume himself would agree—all three touchings of head to wall will result in impressions (or what Reid would call sensations or perceptions). (cf. EIP 3.7:289)

Touché.

Reid's third objection is that although Hume says *we* reproduce our impressions, his official view is that *impressions* cause the subsequent appearance of ideas resembling them (THN 1.1.1:5). Reid observes,

> The impression, after it is gone, and has no existence, produces the idea. Such are the mysteries of Mr. HUME's philosophy. (EIP 3.7:289)

If Reid finds Hume's view mysterious, it must be because he takes for granted that items that no longer exist cannot be causes. But what on Reid's own view is the cause of my memories? Must it not be either a no-longer existent event or a presently existing trace, in either case putting him in company with a theory he disparages?

Reid concludes his criticism of the idea theory of memory with an objection that echoes one of his criticisms of the idea theory of perception—that just as the idea theory of perception engenders skepticism about the external world, so the idea theory of memory engenders skepticism about the past. If the object of memory is only a present idea, how can we possibly infer the existence of anything at any other time? In my view, Reid should not press this objection, because it applies to Reid himself as much as to the philosophers he is criticizing. By his own admission, there is no necessary connection between remembrance as a present act of the mind and the past event that is its object (EIP 2.2:256).

## C. MEMORY AS DIRECT AWARENESS OF THINGS PAST

As noted above, the phrase "immediate knowledge of things past" can refer both to basic knowledge of past-tense propositions and to direct awareness or acquaintance with past objects or events. Reid believes in both. The strongest intimation of the latter view comes out in the following passage from the *Inquiry*:

> Suppose that once, and only once, I smelled a tuberose in a certain room where it grew in a pot, and gave a very grateful perfume. Next day I relate what I saw and smelled. When I attend as carefully as I can to what passes in my mind in this case, it appears evident, that the very thing I saw yesterday, and the fragrance I smelled, are now the immediate objects of my mind when I remember it. Further, I can imagine this pot and flower transported to the room where I now sit, and yielding the same perfume. Here likewise it appears, that the individual thing which I saw and smelled, is the object of my imagination. . . . Philosophers indeed tell me, that the immediate object of my memory and imagination in this case, is not the past sensation, but an idea of it. . . . Upon the strictest attention, memory appears to me to have things that are past, and not present ideas, for its object. . . . I beg leave to think with the vulgar, that when I remember the smell of the tuberose, that very sensation which I had yesterday, and which has no more any existence, is the immediate object of my memory. (IHM 2.3:28)

By calling the past sensation the *immediate* object of his memory, Reid means there is no intervening image or present idea such as the philosophical theory calls for. It is the past sensation itself that comes before one's mind in memory (and also in imagination).

The thesis that memory is in this sense direct awareness of things past has scandalized some of Reid's readers. After quoting the tuberose passage above, Malcolm observes that Reid is right in his negative remarks—one does not remember a present idea. But he then goes on to say, "But one wonders whether Reid was struggling to say something more—namely, that yesterday's odor, or the sensation of it, is there, in my mind, *now*" (1976:3). Malcolm thinks this something more would be out of the question. He says that there is one good sense in which memory can be direct knowledge of the past—it can be "immediate knowledge of things past" in the first sense distinguished above, namely, knowledge not based on inference. But when he tries to understand the second sense introduced above, all he can say by way of explicating it is this: if B's memory M of X is direct awareness of X, then M and X *coexist* (5).[10] No wonder he has trouble with the notion of direct awareness of the past!

Another writer who disparages direct awareness of the past is Andy Hamilton, who claims that "immediate knowledge" of the past in Reid cannot possibly mean direct awareness of the past. The latter, he claims, would involve a "telescope into the past" view of memory, implying the absurdity that memory and the thing remembered are contemporaneous. He also claims that "immediate awareness of the past" (as opposed to immediate knowledge of the past) is a contradiction (2003:231–32). I cannot see why he makes either of these claims unless he shares Malcolm's assumption about what direct awareness of the past would have to mean.

Joining in the conclusion of Malcolm and Hamilton (though not necessarily in their arguments) is Copenhaver: "It is impossible to currently apprehend any events in the past" (Copenhaver 2009:181).

What is the problem about direct awareness of things past? I surmise that the basic argument in the back of the minds of its opponents is something like this:

1. If S has a (direct) remembrance of event e, S stands in some relation to e.
2. A relation holds at t only if its relata all exist at t.
3. If e is past, it no longer exists.
4. Therefore, S does not now have (direct) remembrance of any past event.

Premises 1 and 2 would yield the assumption of Malcolm and Hamilton that direct remembrance of an event would require its being contemporaneous with the remembrance of it.[11]

---

[10] What he actually says is that if B is directly aware of X, then B and X coexist. But since B is a continuant who may indeed have coexisted with X in the past, that formulation does not bring out what Malcolm regards as problematic with direct awareness of the past.

[11] We could equally well arrive at the argument's conclusion by using the following premise in place of 2, deleting both occurrences of "at t": A relation holds only if its relata all exist. I use 2 as stated to rationalize what Malcolm and Hamilton say. An instance of 2 is identified by Reid as one of the fundamental prejudices giving rise to the theory of ideas—"in all the operations of understanding there must be an object of thought, which really exists *while* we think of it" (EIP 4.2:312, emphasis mine).

Before we evaluate this argument, let us note that if it is sound, it threatens to prove much more than intended. It threatens to prove that there is never *any* remembrance of a past event, whether the remembrance is construed as direct awareness or not. That is because the first premise seems equally true if we drop the parenthetical word "direct."

Consider what the rival theory of ideas would have us put in the place of direct remembrance. When I remember e, the only immediate object of my awareness is a present image. This image stands in certain relations to the remembered event—perhaps it was caused by the original event; perhaps it resembles or copies that event. My remembrance of e is thus indirect in the sense that it decomposes into two other relations: my awareness of the image and the image's causal relation or resemblance relation to e. But, of course, if the other premises of the argument are true, there cannot really be any resemblance of the image to e, nor any causal relation between the two, since e no longer exists. Neither, therefore, can there be any indirect remembrance of e. This is no doubt a more sweeping consequence than the arguers intended.[12]

What could a defender of memory as direct awareness of the past say against the 1-2-3-4 argument? There are two main possible responses: deny 3 or deny 2.

Premise 3 is the bone of contention between presentists on the one hand and four-dimensionalists or eternalists on the other. Presentists do indeed say that what is no longer present (or not yet present) does not exist; that is why Augustine laments his lost boyhood and wonders how there can be anything with a duration of nonzero extent. Eternalists say that things past and things future exist just as much as things present; the smoke that rose from the Battle of Gettysburg and the Martian outposts of 2115 are fully there, but they are located in different parts of the four-dimensional manifold from that in which we find ourselves. If the eternalists are right, premise 3 is simply false and the entire puzzle about relations to things past is much ado about nothing.[13]

What side does Reid take in the presentism-eternalism debate?[14] As far as I can tell, his texts leave that undetermined. He simply does not have much to say about

---

[12] Janet Levin has suggested to me that an idea theorist could avoid being hoist on her own petard if she modified the first two premises of the argument thus: (1') If S has a direct remembrance of event e, S stands in some *direct* relation to e, and (2') a *direct* relation holds at t only if its relata all exist at t. A direct relation is a relation that is not the logical product of two or more further relations. What the idea theorist would have to do now is construe the relation of causation (say) between present image and past event as an indirect relation strung together from other relations that hold only between contemporaneously existing relata.

[13] See Quine 1987:196–99 on the four-dimensional scheme of things as a way of accommodating relations between things existing at different times.

[14] According to Bigelow 1996, every human being who lived before the twentieth century was a presentist. Ergo, Reid was a presentist—unless Bigelow exaggerates.

the metaphysics of time. We do learn this much from him: time (or duration) is one-dimensional; it is continuous; it is infinite; and it is absolute or substantival, as Newton taught (EIP 3.3:259–60). As for presentism versus eternalism, there are a few suggestive hints, but nothing conclusive. On the side of presentism, he says that yesterday's sensation of the tuberose "has no more any existence" (IHM 2.3:28; cf. EIP 3.7:289, lines 24–25). He says that what is "past and gone" may be an object of memory, but not of perception (EIP 3.1:254). "Past and gone" is an apt phrase for a presentist, but not for an eternalist, who should say "past and remote." He says that he cannot conceive of time standing still (EIP 3.3:261)—perhaps an endorsement of the idea that time passes, which some eternalists deny. On the eternalist side, there are passages brought to my attention by Brian Glenney in which Reid says he believes in prescience, or knowledge of the future—God has it (EAP 4.10:253) and he could have given it to human beings (EIP 3.2:255). Prescience is sometimes thought best accounted for in a four-dimensional scheme. But surely it does not *require* four-dimensionalism, or else the fact of memory by itself would by parity of reasoning already require it.

The other option for avoiding the 1-2-3-4 argument is to deny premise 2, the principle that relations require existing relata. This is a deeply entrenched assumption in much metaphysical thinking (Bigelow 1996), but there are philosophers who deny it, Meinong being the best known. According to Meinong, I can think of a golden mountain and thereby stand in a cognitive relation to it, even if no golden mountain exists. And Reid is arguably in the same company:

> But we may conceive or imagine what has no existence, and what we firmly believe to have no existence.... Every man knows, that it is as easy to conceive a winged horse or a centaur, as it is to conceive a horse or a man. (EIP 1.1, 24)

The Meinongian side of Reid's views is the topic of chapter 10. Suffice it to say for now that Reid holds that the relations of perceiving, imagining, and remembering differ in this: the object of perceiving is something that exists at present, the object of imagination something that perhaps never did and never will exist, and the object of memory something that once existed, but no longer does. That it no longer exists is no barrier to our standing in a cognitive relation to it.[15]

---

[15] In the course of defending a view of memory as direct awareness of the past, William Earle propounds a view intermediate between eternalism and Meinongism: "As past, [the remembered item] is the subject of true propositions, and precisely what would such propositions be *about* if their subject matter had fallen back into pure nothingness.... The past therefore has its own distinctive and determinate mode of being" (Earle 1956:23). Earle thus believes in a half-way mode of being similar to that of the pseudo-Meinongians I discuss in chapter 10.

Our findings to date on the 1-2-3-4 argument may be summarized as follows: If the four-dimensionalist view is correct, there is no problem with direct awareness of things past or any other relation to them. If the presentist view is correct, (i) any problem with direct awareness of the past is on the face of things also a problem for indirect awareness of the past, but (ii) there may be no problem to start with for those who cast their lot with Reid and Meinong.

We should canvass one more view before we leave the 1-2-3-4 argument behind. Some there may be who say that the objects of memory are exclusively propositional; we do not remember things or events. A soldier remembers that he was flogged at school for robbing an orchard. The object of his memory (or perhaps better, the content of it) is a past-tense proposition that exists at the time of his remembrance, so we abide by premise 2. One who takes this line may accept everything in the 1-2-3-4 argument against direct awareness of the past without going over to a present-image theory of memory in its place. The resulting theory may be compared with a propositional theory of perception such as that of Armstrong, but with one significant difference. A propositionalist about perception may define a derivative sense in which one perceives objects: S perceives O iff S perceives to be true some proposition about O. But we cannot say S remembers e iff S remembers to be true some proposition about e, for if there are no relations to nonexistent relata, nothing can be about what no longer exists. There is only factual memory; there is no episodic memory or any other relation to past events.

## D. THE SPECIOUS PRESENT

As an aside to his discussion of Locke's account of how we get the ideas of succession and duration, Reid says this:

> It may here be observed, that if we speak strictly and philosophically, no kind of succession can be an object either of the sense, or of consciousness; because the operations of both are confined to the present point of time, and there can be no succession in a point of time; and on that account the motion of a body, which is a successive change of place, could not be observed by the sense alone without the aid of memory. (EIP 3.5:270).

He concedes that the vulgar sometimes use the term "present" to cover extended periods of time (as in "the present hour"), but insists that in philosophically correct usage, "the present" can only denote an indivisible point of time. He is thus led to reiterate:

> When as philosophers we distinguish accurately the province of sense from that of memory, we can no more see what is past, though but a moment ago, than we can

remember what is present; so that speaking philosophically, it is only by the aid of memory that we discern motion, or any succession whatsoever: We see the present place of the body; we remember the successive advance it made to that place: The first can then only give us a conception of motion, when joined to the last. (3.5:271)

On Reid's view, then, we do not perceive motion. We only infer it from a perception of the present position of an object together with a memory of its previous position.

Reid's view is squarely at odds with a famous doctrine defended by William James and later by Russell and Broad: the doctrine of the specious present. James asks us to contrast the way in which we know that the hour hand of a clock is moving with the way in which we know that the second hand is moving. Reid's account is tolerably accurate as an account of how we know the hour hand is moving: we see that it is now pointing straight up at the numeral "12" while remembering that it previously pointed at "11," and we conclude that it has moved. But the way in which we know the second hand is moving is not at all like that—we simply *see* it move.

To accommodate this phenomenon, proponents of the specious present hold that we can literally peer into the past, apprehending in a perceptual way rather than a memorial way the recent phases of an object. The portion of the past to which we still have perceptual access is called the specious present—specious because it is not really present, but is perceived as though it were. James memorably describes the phenomenon as follows:

> We are constantly aware of a certain duration—the specious present—varying from a few seconds to probably not more than a minute, and this duration (with its content perceived as having one part earlier and another part later) is the original intuition of time. ([1890] 1950, vol. 1:642)

> The practically cognized present is no knife-edge, but a saddle-back, with a certain breadth of its own on which we sit perched, and from which we look in two directions into time. The unit of composition of our perception of time is a *duration*. ([1890] 1950, vol. 1:609)[16]

As Russell further explains the theory, we can be aware of succession even within the arena of what seems present to us ([1913] 1992:65 and 73). The specious present extends as far back into the past as an object may lie and still be sensed, even though it has ceased to exist (68).

---

[16] James holds that the specious present extends a bit into the future as well as the past, as does Husserl.

Sean Kelly has presented a number of objections to the specious present doctrine (Kelly 2005). One of them is expressed in a supposedly rhetorical question—"How can I be directly aware of something that is no longer taking place?"—to which his answer is that I cannot. Why is he so confident about that? I conjecture that it is for the same reason that Malcolm and Hamilton are scornful of memory as direct awareness of the past—that awareness is a relation, and that relations can only hold among coexisting relata.

Kelly considers the following reply to his contention that we cannot be aware of events that are no longer taking place: owing to the finite speed of light, we are *always* seeing events that are no longer taking place.[17] This is what some philosophers (e.g., Huemer 2001) say in response to the puzzle of how we can see a distant star that for all we know has burned out by the time light from it has reached us.[18] Kelly claims that this reply does not save the specious present theory, but instead contradicts it, since the theory says we perceive the events in a window that includes the present. I offer two points by way of rejoinder. First, we could modify the specious present theory so that it says we perceive the events in a window that includes (not the present but) the slightly past and the slightly more past. Second, Kelly does not acknowledge what is undeniably true—that Huemer's point contradicts Kelly's own contention that we cannot be aware of events that are no longer taking place.

There are other arguments that can be given against the contentions of Reid and Kelly that we cannot perceive anything but what happens in the instantaneous present. One proceeds from the intransitivity of apparent simultaneity. There may be an appearance of simultaneity (or at any rate no appearance of succession) between events A and B and again between events B and C, yet discernible succession between A and C. If A, B, and C are external events that we perceive, it must be that A actually preceded B or B actually preceded C (or both), even though we saw A and B as co-present and B and C as co-present. Therefore, some events that we perceive as present are really in the past.[19] A proponent of ideas or sense data might jump in at this point and say that my conclusion depends on the false assumption that

---

[17] As a lecturer on physics and astronomy as part of his regent's duties at Aberdeen, Reid would have known of the finite velocity of light, first demonstrated by Roemer in 1676. See Wood 2004:60.

[18] It does not follow from the finite speed of light alone that we are always seeing events that lie in the past. There must be unstated assumptions in the argument, perhaps including these: we see only what belongs to some causal chain leading to our perception, and the links in such chains are dated events rather than enduring things.

[19] Perhaps the point can be proved by Locke's simpler example of a cannonball that carries off a man's arm and slams into the wall behind him (ECHU 2.14.10). One of these events preceded the other even if the victim cannot discern their successiveness.

external events are what we see. She might reconstrue the situation as follows: A and B appeared simultaneous, that is, they presented us with sense data A' and B' that really were simultaneous and both of which existed in the present. Likewise, B and C presented us with sense data B' and C' that both existed in the present. In this way, the sense-datum theorist could uphold the thesis that things sensed always lie in the present. In point of fact, however, the intransitivity of apparent simultaneity may be used to *refute* the sense datum theory (Armstrong 1988:136–37). The relation of *real* simultaneity between sense data must clearly be transitive, so A' must be simultaneous with C'—contradicting the fact that A and C do not seem simultaneous. The sense datum theorist's claim, after all, is that A and C seem simultaneous if and only if they present the subject with sense data A' and C' that *are* simultaneous.

A more formidable objection to the specious present doctrine than Kelly's was raised by Paton ([1929] 1951:105–7). If we are somehow still seeing the previous positions of the clock hand when we see it pointing straight up, then our experience should really be as of a *fan*—a wedge-shaped black expanse with vertices at the center of the clock, "12" at the top, and a point a little to the left of "12." This objection may at first seem to rest on a misunderstanding of what proponents of the specious present are saying. After all, they do maintain that we see the hand's pointing just to the left of "12" as *preceding* its pointing to "12." On second thought, it is not obvious how the objection is to be resisted. LePoidevin (2011) puts the objection this way:

1. What we perceive, we perceive as present.
2. We perceive motion.
3. Motion occurs over an interval.
4. Therefore, there are some things we perceive as present that occur over an interval.

As LePoidevin points out, two events each seen as present are seen as simultaneous, in which case it does seem to follow that we should see a wedge-shaped expanse on the face of the clock. How is a proponent of the specious present to avoid this consequence?

One possibility would be to endorse 2 and 3 without endorsing 1. Perhaps successiveness is a relation we can perceive without perceiving any intrinsic properties on which it supervenes. (The relation of comparative size may be like this.) Or perhaps the intrinsic properties we perceive are presentness and just-pastness.

Another possibility would be to adopt a propositional theory of perception, despite the misgivings about such theories I raise elsewhere in this book. The idea would be that when closely successive positions of a clock hand register on us, we are induced to form a perceptual representation or belief with the content *x has moved*. We do not see motion in any further sense, such as what Russell tries to account for. Nor do we merely *infer* the content *x has moved*, as Reid would have it. Rather, it is a genuinely *perceptual* content. But spelling out the force of the adjective "perceptual" as applied to propositional contents seems to me to be a formidable problem for propositional theories.

Before leaving the topic of the specious present, I wish to call attention to a contradiction in Reid's views first noticed by Marina Folescu (2013). Reid affirms each of the propositions in the following inconsistent triad:

1. I remember the transit of Venus across the sun.
2. What I remember, I formerly perceived (the Previous Awareness Condition).
3. Motion is never perceived.

One way out would be to replace 2 by a liberalized Previous Awareness Condition: what I remember, I formerly *experienced*, where experiencing may be either simple perceiving or a compound of perceiving, remembering, comparing, and inferring, such as Reid thinks is involved in our "seeing" of motion. But I think a better way out would be to deny 3, even if that involves embracing the doctrine of the specious present. Surely a follower of common sense should think that we perceive motion as immediately as we perceive color or shape!

What happens when I remember hearing the bird call *Bob WHITE*? If Reid's account of the original hearing were accurate, I would remember the complex act of hearing *WHITE* while remembering *Bob* and quickly concluding that *Bob* preceded *WHITE*. Yet that is not what I remember; I simply remember the sound sequence *Bob WHITE*. This shows, I think, that the elements in a temporal sequence can be grasped in a single mental act occurring later than the first element. If that can happen in memory, why not also in perception, as in the doctrine of the specious present?

## E. PERSONAL IDENTITY

No book on Reid would be complete without some discussion of his views on personal identity, including his famous criticisms of Locke.

The problem of personal identity is posed in questions like these: What makes me the same person as the first infant my mother bore? If there are such phenomena as reincarnation and time travel, what would make me the same person as someone who walked the earth centuries ago? If someone wakes up in the body formerly possessed by a certain cobbler, but with memories just like those formerly possessed by a certain prince, is he the prince or the cobbler or neither? To solve the problem, we must fill in the blank in the following formula, where A is a person who exists now and B is a person who existed at some time t in the past:

A = B if and only if _____.

Locke's answer is given at ECHU 2.27.9: "As far as this consciousness can be extended backwards to any past action or thought, so far reaches the identity of that person."

There are two ways to interpret Locke's answer. The first is

1. A = B iff the consciousness with which A now does something = the consciousness with which B did something at t.

Here the identity of persons is explicated in terms of the identity of acts of consciousness. This answer is suggested by his restating his view thus: "as far as any intelligent being can repeat the idea of any past action with the same consciousness it had of it at first ... so far it is the same personal self" (2.27.10).

The second and more commonly discussed interpretation is the memory theory of personal identity:

2. A = B iff A now remembers doing things B did at t.

This answer is suggested by his talking of "recollection" in 2.27.24 and of "finding himself conscious of any of the actions of Nestor" in 2.27.14. It is also suggested by the example of the prince and the cobbler in 2.27.15: the person who wakes up in the cobbler's body is identical with the prince and not the cobbler because he has memories of the prince's life.

Locke maintains that under his account, it is possible to have the same person where you have two intelligent beings or substances (if consciousness is transferred from one substance to another) and two persons where you have the same intelligent being (if the intelligent being has lost its consciousness of earlier actions). But Locke also says that a person *is* an intelligent being. Reid complains that this combination is inconsistent (EIP 3.6:275)—and so it is, except under the problematic doctrine of relative identity. I criticize the doctrine of relative identity and its attribution to Locke in appendix T.

Some of Reid's objections to Locke's theory of personal identity presuppose interpretation 1 while others presuppose interpretation 2. Reid passes from one objection to another as though he is unaware of this fact.

Two of Reid's objections are directed against Locke's theory under interpretation 1. The first is that personal identity cannot consist in sameness of consciousness, for states of consciousness perish every moment (EIP 3.6:278). Reid is here contrasting states or modes, which are transitory, from substances, which alone endure and maintain identity across time. The second is that the same consciousness cannot be "continued through a succession of different substances" as Locke envisions, because it is impossible that the same individual operation should be in different substances (EIP 3.6:279). You can have a headache tomorrow perfectly similar to the one I have now, but I cannot transfer my headache (or any other mental "operation") to you. Modes cannot migrate from one substance to substance.

Reid's more famous objections are directed against Locke's theory under interpretation 2, the memory theory. The first of these is terminological: Locke misuses the word "consciousness." Reid thinks this word should be confined to the awareness we have of our current states of mind; Locke should therefore have spoken instead of *remembrance* (EIP 3.6:277). Here, obviously, Reid is presupposing interpretation 2.

The second objection is that Locke confounds identity with the evidence we have for it. Remembering doing an act is not what *makes* me the person who did it; it is what gives me *evidence* that I did it (EIP 3.6:277, reprising 265). To say that remembrance constitutes identity is like saying that similitude, which is the owner's evidence for the identity of a found horse with one that was stolen from him, constitutes the identity through time of horses. With Butler, Reid makes it a general rule that evidence or knowledge does not constitute truth (Stewart 2004).

The third and most famous objection is the Brave Officer counterexample. I reproduce it in Reid's words:

> Suppose a brave officer to have been flogged when a boy at school, for robbing an orchard, to have taken a standard from the enemy in his first campaign, and to have been made a general in advanced life: Suppose also, which must be admitted to be possible, that when he took the standard, he was conscious of his having been flogged at school, and that when made a general he was conscious of his taking the standard, but had absolutely lost the consciousness of his flogging.
>
> These things being supposed, it follows, from Mr Locke's doctrine, that he who was flogged at school is the same person who took the standard, and that he who took the standard is the same person who was made a general. Whence it follows, if there be any truth in logic, that the general is the same person with him who was flogged at school. But the general's consciousness does not reach so far back as his flogging, therefore, according to Mr Locke's doctrine, he is not the person who was flogged. Therefore the general is, and at the same time is not the same person with him who was flogged at school. (EIP 3.6:276).

Reid falls in here with Locke's use of the terms "was conscious of" and "consciousness," which he suggests in his next paragraph be replaced with "remembers" and "memory."

The counterexample is utterly destructive of Locke's theory as stated above.[20] However, there are modifications of the theory that might be proposed to save its general idea. The most obvious modification is to allow indirect as well as direct memory links: A now has an indirect memory link to something B did at t if A remembers doing something C did at intervening time t,' and at t' C remembered doing something B did at t. Obviously, we could allow as many intervening links as we like. This would enable the general to be the boy despite not having a direct memory link to anything the boy did.

A neo-Lockean theory along these lines (with a few other tweaks) was proposed by H. P. Grice ([1941] 1975). Grice was working within a bundle theory of persons (à la Hume), but his proposal could be adapted by substance theorists as well. He supposes that a person is composed of a series of time slices or total temporary states, a total temporary state being a collection of all the experiences, memories, and so forth that a given person is having at a given time. Let us give Grice the relation of synchronic unity among elements making up a total temporary state or person slice so that we may consider his account of diachronic unity for such states. The task is to say under what conditions a collection of total temporary states constitutes a person series—that is, adds up to the history of one continuing person.

Grice sums up his answer compactly as follows:

A person series is an interlocking series of memorative and memorable total temporary states. (88)

A state or stage is "memorative" if it remembers another state, that is, if some element of it is a memory of an experience in the other state. A state is "memorable" if some other state in the same sense remembers it. A series is "interlocking" if you can pass from any member of the series to any other by a chain of relations of remembering or being remembered by.

---

[20] I was disappointed to learn from Stewart 2004 (crediting Stewart-Robinson 1989:397) that the Brave Officer counterexample is not original with Reid. In an unpublished manuscript from 1758 (MS 2131/6/III/5, 2), he attributes it to his friend George Campbell. Berkeley gives a structurally similar counterexample in *Alciphron*: A's being the same person as B cannot be analyzed in terms of A's being conscious of some of the same ideas B was conscious of, since the former relation is transitive and the latter is not ([1732] 1950, vol. 3:299).

What Grice has done is in effect to disjoin Locke's relation of remembering with its converse and then employ the ancestral of the disjunctive relation.[21] We can see this by restating his analysis in the following equivalent form: a person series is a series of states any two members of which are related by the ancestral of the relation *remembers or is remembered by*. The analysis easily accommodates the general and the boy, for we may pass from the general's total temporary state at the time he remembers taking the flag to the boy's state at the time of the flogging in two hops. It also allows past states that are not remembered at all to belong to a person series, provided they remember states that are themselves remembered by yet other members of the series.

Grice's theory can be given one more equivalent formulation:

A series of person stages constitutes a persisting person iff (i) every stage in the series remembers or is remembered by some other stage in the series, and (ii) there is no isolated subseries.

A subseries is isolated if it is not possible to pass from any member of it to a stage outside the subseries by the designated relations.

We can see how the theory works by considering Figure 9.1, in which boxes represent person stages and arrows passing from one box to another mean that (some element of) the one stage remembers (some element of) the other.

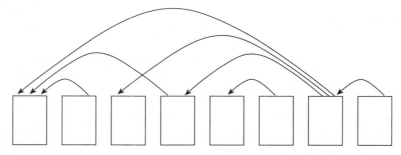

**Figure 9.1**

The entire sequence does not constitute a person, because it contains an isolated subseries (the fifth and sixth boxes from the left). But the rest of the sequence does constitute a person, because it no longer contains an isolated subsequence, and you

---

[21] The ancestral of a relation R is the relation x has to y iff either xRy or there is an item z such that xRz and zRy or there are items u and v such that xRu, uRv, and vRy, etc. Grice makes one other liberalization I have not mentioned: where I have "remembers," he has "remembers or would remember given certain conditions," thus allowing for dispositional as well as occurrent memories.

can pass from any box to some other (indeed, to any other) by tracing arrows from tail to head or head to tail.[22]

We are now in a position to assess some of the consequences of the neo-Lockean theory. For this purpose I describe an example once used by Chisholm for a somewhat different purpose (1976:110). You are about to undergo a painful operation, and you may choose either of two procedures. One involves standard anesthesia; it eliminates all pain, but is terribly expensive. The other is cheap. It does not block the pain, which will be excruciating, but instead involves two drugs (or two sessions with a brain erasing and reprogramming device) that manage your memories. One is given before the operation, obliterating all your memories; the other is given after the operation, obliterating any memories of the operation itself, but restoring all your previous memories. (I have added the second feature of the second drug, as Chisholm may have intended.) Assume your values are such that (i) you will avoid needless expense, but (ii) you will avoid pain at any cost, provided it is *your* pain. (You are not concerned about the pain of others.) The question is now this: would you choose the cheap operation?

The example is a good diagnostic of whether you believe the neo-Lockean theory.[23] If you said no to the cheap operation, you presumably do not believe the theory, since the theory makes the cheap operation totally reasonable. The situation may be diagrammed in Figure 9.2:

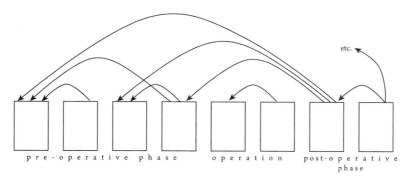

**Figure 9.2**

[22] How could we incorporate Grice's approach without adopting his bundle theory of persons? Taking a cue from Yaffe (2010:179), perhaps we could say that A = B iff A is the subject of a total temporary state that is part of the same person series as a total temporary state of which B is the subject. But would it not be possible for distinct subjects to be subjects of such total temporary states, opening up Locke's divorce between "same person" and "same substance"? If so, it would follow, *pace* Locke, that persons are not substances, but at best some sort of construction—if not out of experiences as in the bundle theory, then out of substances as in Chisholm's theory of *entia successiva* (1976:97–104).

[23] Chisholm deploys the example in the course of arguing that the question "Will I be he?" always has a definite answer, knowable or not, independent of any conventions. He does not note how perfectly suited the example is to test Grice's theory of personal identity, which has nothing conventional about it.

Whoever that wretch on the operating table is, it is not you. It is an isolated sub-series, and as such it is no part of the series that constitutes *you*.[24]

If Reid does not accept Locke's way of filling the blank in our identity formula above, how does he fill it? His view is that the identity of persons is primitive, not to be analyzed in terms of anything else. Moreover, he thinks persons endure through time in a strict sense, whereas ordinary physical objects like trees and houses do not, since they gain and lose parts. For more on these matters, see van Woudenberg 2004.

---

[24] I have included memory arrows connecting phases within the operation, but what if the pain is so intense that it crowds out all memories during the operation? Then there will be a separate person for every moment of the operation.

# 10

## CONCEPTION AND ITS OBJECTS

All these writers [Meinong, Findlay, Anscombe, et al.] are walking on a tightrope; though Reid in particular contrives to suggest that it's quite a low and thick one, and that you don't have to be much of an acrobat to toddle along it quite easily. (Arthur Prior, *Objects of Thought*)

Essay 4 of the *Essays on the Intellectual Powers of Man* is devoted to *conception*. As Reid explains at the outset, what he means by conception is what the logicians of his day called *simple apprehension*—a way of having a thing before the mind without having any judgment or belief about it (EIP 4.1:295). One of the cardinal truths about conception is that it always has an object—"he that conceives, must conceive something" (EIP 4.1:311). Another is that conception is the most fundamental and pervasive of all mental operations—none of the other operations can take place without it, but it can take place without them. "There is no operation of the mind without conception, yet it may be found naked, detached from all others" (EIP 4.1:296). For example, you cannot will without having some conception of what you will, or believe without having some conception of what you believe, but you can conceive something without making it the object of any other mental operation. Putting the two cardinal truths together, we arrive at something close to Brentano's thesis that reference to an object is the distinctive feature of the mental.[1]

---

[1] If Reidian sensations are objectless as I take them to be in chapter 1, they are the sole exception to Brentano's thesis.

After explaining many of the other features of conception, Reid comes round to this important one: [2]

> Ninthly, the last property I shall mention of this faculty, is that which essentially distinguishes it from every other power of the mind; and it is, that it is not employed solely about things which have existence. I can conceive a winged horse or a centaur, as easily and as distinctly as I can conceive a man whom I have seen. (EIP 4.1:310; cf. also 321)

> Conception is often employed about objects that neither do, nor did, nor will exist. This is the very nature of this faculty, that its object, though distinctly conceived, may have no existence. (EIP 4.1:311)

Passages such as these have put many of Reid's readers in mind of Alexius Meinong, who developed an elaborate theory of nonexistent objects about a century and a quarter after Reid. According to Meinong,

> The totality of what exists, including what has existed and will exist, is infinitely small in comparison with the totality of the Objects of knowledge. (Meinong [1904] 1960:79)

Could it be that Reid was a Meinongian before Meinong?[3] That is the first question of this chapter, and I argue that the answer is *yes*.

Reid explicitly develops his Meinongism only for the objects of conception, but given that conception is a core constituent of perception, it has occurred to some of his readers to wonder whether his Meinongism can be extended to the objects of perception—or more accurately, to the objects of erroneous perception such as hallucination. Can Meinongism be used to help secure Reid's direct realism against objections based on hallucination, such as Malebranche's Master Argument? That is the second question of this chapter, and I explore it in sections D, E, and F.

---

[2] The other features in his list of nine in EIP 4.1 are these: (i) "Conception enters as an ingredient in every operation of the mind" (295–96). (ii) "In bare conception there can be neither truth nor falsehood, because it neither affirms nor denies" (296). (iii) Conceiving, unlike painting, does not produce an image distinct from itself. (iv) Our conceptions [i.e., the objects of which we conceive] may be divided into three kinds: existing individuals (such as the Westminster bridge), universals (such as triangularity), and creatures of the conceiver's own imagination (such as Don Quixote). (v) Conceptions may differ in their degree of liveliness. (vi) They may also differ in their degree of clarity and distinctness. (vii) We can conceive of simple things only if we have previously been acquainted with them by some other power of the mind, such as perception. (viii) We may form compound conceptions as we please.

[3] The phrase is Wolterstorff's (2001). His own answer to the question is *no*, as discussed below in section B.

## A. WAS REID A MEINONGIAN BEFORE MEINONG?

We must begin by distinguishing the real from the mythical Meinong. Meinong's name is often associated with a doctrine he did not in fact hold—that there are two modes of being, one of them solid and substantial and the other shadowy and ethereal. There is ordinary existence, which is possessed by the planet Mars and the keyboard on which I am typing, and there is a less substantial and more inclusive mode of being, which is possessed by the golden mountain I am thinking of and by fictional objects such as Sherlock Holmes.

The thesis that there are two modes of being is well expressed in the following passage:

> *Being* is that which belongs to every conceivable term, to every possible object of thought—in short to everything that can possibly occur in any proposition, true or false, and to all such propositions themselves. . . . *Existence*, on the contrary, is the pre-rogative of some only amongst beings. . . . This distinction is essential, if we are ever to deny the existence of anything. For what does not exist must be something, or it would be meaningless to deny its existence; and hence we need the concept of being, as that which belongs even to the non-existent. (Russell 1903:449)

That is not Meinong speaking, however. It is Bertrand Russell, who held the suppos-edly Meinongian view himself when he wrote those words in 1903. Russell was the perfect incarnation of the mythical Meinong up until 1905, when his newly minted theory of descriptions gave him the resources for avoiding it.

What Meinong really held is that (i) some objects do not exist *in any manner whatever*, but (ii) we can nonetheless think about them and make them topics of discourse.

If the real Meinong did not invest his objects with a special mode of being, why is the impression to the contrary so widespread? There are terminological reasons that may have played a minor role,[4] but I believe the main explanation is as follows. The presumption that things must exist in some way if there are to be truths about them

---

[4] Here are two. First, those who distinguish (as Russell did) between being and existence some-times use the term "subsistence" for the more inclusive notion, and Meinong, too, draws a dis-tinction between subsistence and existence. But for Meinong, the subsistent is a subset and not a superset of what Russell would call the existent. His subsistence (*Bestand*) is simply *Sein* as re-stricted to abstract objects. Second, Meinong attributes to his Objects a status he calls *Aussersein*, which may sound like a distinctive mode of being. But his explanation makes clear that it is not. To say that an object has Aussersein or "indifference to being" is simply to say that its own nature leaves open the question whether it has being.

(or if they are to have any properties) runs deep. It runs so deep in most of us that we tend automatically to ascribe it to others in trying to make sense of what they say. So when Meinong tells us that the golden mountain is golden, even though it does not exist, we naturally take him to mean that although the golden mountain does not exist in the ordinary way, it must nonetheless exist in some extraordinary way. Again, when Meinong enunciates his famous paradoxical sentence—"There are objects of which it is true that there are no such objects"—we naturally suppose that he intends "there are" at the beginning of the sentence to express a mode of being different from that which is expressed by "there are" at the end of the sentence. We take him to be saying that there are (in the distinctively Meinongian way) objects that lack the Russellian prerogative of existence. It does not occur to us that his initial quantifier may range over things that do not exist in any sense at all.

The situation may be illustrated by a trenchant passage from Hume. In the *Treatise*, Hume challenges the necessity of the principle that every event has a cause. In the course of so doing, he dismisses a number of bad arguments for the principle, including the argument that an event with no cause would have itself for its cause, which is absurd (because a thing would then exist before it existed), or nothing for its cause, which is also absurd (since *nothing* cannot be a cause). He aptly remarks:

> 'Tis sufficient only to observe, that when we exclude all causes we really do exclude them, and neither suppose nothing nor the object itself to be the causes of the existence. (THN 1.4.3:81)

Meinong could well have issued a similar protest: "When we exclude all varieties of being, we really do exclude them."

The principal views of the real Meinong may be summed up in four theses. First, there can be cognitive relations to utterly nonexistent objects:

> (M1) There is thus not the slightest doubt that what is supposed to be the Object of knowledge need not exist at all. (Meinong [1904] 1960:81)

Second, an object can have properties regardless of whether it exists:

> (M2) The *Sosein* [being thus] of an Object is not affected by its *Nichtsein* [nonbeing]. The fact is sufficiently important to be explicitly formulated as the principle of the independence of *Sosein* from *Sein*.... The principle applies, not only to Objects which do not exist in fact, but also to Objects which could not exist because they are impossible. Not only is the much heralded gold mountain made of gold, but the round square is as surely round as it is square. (Meinong [1904] 1960:82)

This is the exact opposite of the view Plantinga calls "serious actualism" (1983).

Third, there is Meinong's notorious paradoxical sentence:

> (M3) Those who like paradoxical modes of expression could very well say: "There are objects of which it is true that there are no such objects." (Meinong [1904] 1960:83)

That would be not just paradoxical but downright contradictory if we were using at both ends of the sentence the existential quantifier now employed in standard logic. The moral, though, is that at the beginning of the sentence Meinong is using his own distinctive quantifier, which lacks existential import. It might rather be called the *particular* quantifier, as it allows us to say things like "Some things do not exist." For more on the properties of this quantifier, see Routley 1966.

I regard M3 as a simple corollary of M2. If you think the golden mountain is golden without existing, then you ought to be willing to generalize and say that some things have properties without existing, which implies that some things do not exist.[5]

The final tenet is not explicitly formulated by Meinong, but is implicit in much of what he says:

> (M4) Many objects are incomplete—they need not possess one property from every pair consisting of a property and its complement.

For instance, the golden mountain is neither less than 10,000 meters high, nor greater than or equal to that in height.

Turning now to Reid, I find ample evidence that he accepts each of M1 through M4. As for M1, he tells us again and again that "conception is often employed about objects that neither do, nor did, nor will exist" (EIP 4.1:311). Here are some passages in point:

> But we may conceive or imagine what has no existence, and what we firmly believe to have no existence.... Every man knows, that it is as easy to conceive a winged horse or a centaur, as it is to conceive a horse or a man. (EIP 1.1:24)

> When we conceive any thing, there is a real act or operation of the mind; of this we are conscious, and can have no doubt of its existence: But every such act must have an object; for he that conceives, must conceive something. Suppose he conceives a centaur, he may have a distinct conception of this object, though no centaur ever existed. (EIP 4.1:311)

---

[5] The folly of accepting M2 without M3 is illustrated by the absurdity of the following dialogue:
 A: Santa Claus has properties—for example, he is fat and jolly—but he does not exist.
 B: What? Did you just say that something has properties but does not exist?
 A: No, I didn't say that anything has properties but does not exist. I said that *Santa* has properties but does not exist.

I know no truth more evident to the common sense and to the experience of mankind [as that men may barely conceive things that never existed] (EIP 4.1:311; I have inverted Reid's order of clauses.)

The unlearned . . . know that they can conceive a thousand things that never existed. (EIP 4.2:314)

As for M2, Reid does not hesitate to say that centaurs are animals, even though they do not exist. He also tells us that universals have all the attributes Plato said they did (being without place, being immutable, being entire in every individual without multiplication or division, being merely determinable, and so forth) *except* for existence:

It may further be observed, that all that is mysterious and unintelligible in the Platonic ideas, arises from attributing existence to them. Take away this one attribute, and all the rest, however pompously expressed, are easily admitted and understood. (EIP 4.2:318; for the list of attributes, see EIP 4.2:318 and 5.5:386)

As for M3, it is a natural corollary of M2, as noted above. Moreover, Reid implicitly commits himself to M3 when he tells us that *there are* attributes on the same page on which he tells us that attributes *do not exist*:

If any man can doubt whether there be attributes that are really common to many individuals, let him consider whether there be not many men that are above six feet high, and many below it; whether there be not many men that are rich, and many more that are poor. . . . It is certain therefore, that there are innumerable attributes that are really common to many individuals. (EIP 5.3:367; see also 356, lines 9 and 10)

Presumably "there are" in these sentences must be the particular quantifier, not the existential quantifier. (See Lehrer 1985/86, especially 582–83, for more on the need for an existence-neutral quantifier in Reid.)

Marian David (1985) gives us further reason for attributing M2 and M3 to Reid. He says that Reid denies the right-to-left half of the principle *x exists iff* $\exists FFx$, which is to affirm M2. And he says that M3 is needed in order to resolve the apparent tension between the following two theses (which Arthur Prior calls "Reid's first master thesis" and "Reid's second master thesis"):[6]

---

[6] Prior formulates the first master thesis as "all operations of the mind have objects" and the second as "the objects of conception need not exist" (116–17). He strongly hints that the two theses are incompatible. Grave (1960:168) explicitly accuses Reid of holding two incompatible theses.

(A) To conceive is to conceive of something.

(B) We sometimes conceive of what does not exist.

(B) can be heard as taking back precisely what (A) says.[7] If we do not want this to happen, we must construe (B) as

(B') (∃x)(S conceives of x & x does not exist).

which implies by simplification that some things do not exist, just as M3 says.

Finally, Reid subscribes to M4, though for reasons foreign to Meinong's. In a number of passages, he says that objects of conception are nothing more nor less than what they are conceived as being:

> And to suppose that there can be any thing in a conception [i.e., object conceived] that is not conceived, is a contradiction. (EIP 5.3:371, restated on 372)

> [Things merely conceived] are nothing more than they are conceived to be. (EIP 6.3:440)[8]

This feature of objects of conception will make many of them incomplete. If I do not conceive of a triangle as being either isosceles or scalene, it will not possess either of these attributes. If Cervantes does not conceive of Don Quixote as being either more or less than six feet tall, he will be indeterminate in height.[9]

I say that Reid's reason for incompleteness is different from Meinong's because I do not detect in Meinong any suggestion that Objects are dependent for their nature on how they are conceived.[10] Incompleteness for Meinong may simply be a consequence of some sort of comprehension principle or principle of plenitude regarding objects: for any set of properties, there is an object having just those properties and

---

[7] (B) would renege on (A) if we interpreted (A) as "If S conceives, then ∃x(S conceives x)" and (B) as "S conceives, but ~∃x(S conceives x)."

[8] If we leave it at this, it will be a corollary that property possession for objects of mere conception is not closed under entailment, for an object conceived of as F need not be conceived of as G, even if F entails G. At EAP 4.11:261, however, Reid adds an amendment: "Things merely conceived have no relations or connections but such as are implied in the conception, *or are consequent from it*" (italics added).

[9] Such indeterminacy, as well as the reason for it, is characteristic of intentional objects as expounded by McGinn: they have only those properties that mental acts confer upon them (2004:498 and 499).

[10] Meinong tells us, "It is no more necessary to an object that it be presented in order not to exist than it is in order for it to exist" ([1904] 1960:83). Assuming that *Sein* depends on *Sosein*—that a thing cannot be without being some way—it follows that an object would depend on being presented for its *Sosein* only if it depended on being presented for its *Sein*. But in the sentence I have quoted, Meinong denies that objects depend on being presented for their *Sein*. Hence they do not depend on how they are presented for their *Sosein*, either. This point sets Meinong apart from Reid.

no others.[11] That principle will give us an object whose only properties are being golden and being a mountain. For Reid, by contrast, if a golden mountain has no definite size or shape, that is because the act by which it is conceived has given it none.

Reid does not believe that *all* objects of conception are incomplete, for we may conceive of things that exist as well as things that do not exist, and whatever exists is necessarily complete:

> I can likewise conceive an individual object that really exists, such as St. Paul's church in London. . . . The immediate object of this conception is four hundred miles distant. (EIP 4.2:324)

He is not saying that being 400 miles distant is part of what I conceive in regard to St. Paul's, but only that its location is a sidebar fact about it. Any existing object of conception will have thousands of features that I do not conceive it to have, thanks simply to the completeness and determinacy of the existent together with the limitations on human powers of conception. God alone knows the whole nature of any existing thing (4.1:302). It may seem strange that a unitary faculty of conception should take two such very different types of objects, existent complete ones and inexistent incomplete ones, but such is arguably Reid's view.[12]

The thesis that there are objects that do not exist can sound exotic and perhaps even contradictory, but Reid makes it sound like just one more piece of common sense. Here is a simple-minded argument for it (cf. EIP 4.1:310 and 4.2:321)

1. We can and do think of centaurs.
2. Centaurs do not exist.
3. So we can and do think of what does not exist.

Assuming that what we think of has the property of being thought of by us, it follows from 3 that some things that do not exist have properties. It also follows that some things do not exist.

Many thinkers will balk at this argument. They might combine Reid's initial conclusion, 3, with two other theses to form an inconsistent triad:

P. We can and do think of things that do not exist.
Q. Thinking-of is a relation.
R. There can be no relations to the nonexistent.

---

[11] Parsons attributes such a principle to Meinong as a generalization of his practice (1980:19).

[12] Finding the disparity between conceptions of the existent (as in perception) and conceptions of the nonexistent (as in imagination) so wide, Marina Folescu argues that Reid should have acknowledged that two different faculties are in play (2013).

Reid himself would readily accept the first two propositions and would have no compunctions about denying the third. But his opponents, who include Prior, would try to enjoin acceptance of the third. Prior says that for every genuine relation, there is a converse relational property. If I stand in the thinking-of relation to Pegasus, then Pegasus has the converse relational property of being thought of by me. He also employs the principle

$$x \text{ exists iff } \exists FFx$$

as a virtual definition of existence, or at any rate a necessary truth about it—a thing exists iff it has some property, or if something is true of it.[13] It follows that there can be no relations to the nonexistent.

A true Meinongian would not be cowed by this argument. As noted, a cardinal Meinongian tenet is M2, the independence of *Sosein* from *Sein*, which is precisely the denial of the principle $\exists FFx \rightarrow x$ *exists*. It is part of the Meinongian package that a thing can have relational properties, including the property of standing at one end of a cognitive relation to a thinker, even if it does not exist.

Nonetheless, let us explore the options for those who hold fast to the thought that there can be no relations to the nonexistent. They will have to deny either the first proposition in the P-Q-R triad, maintaining that what is called "thinking of the nonexistent" really reduces to thinking of something existent, or the second, maintaining that thinking-of is not a relation at all. I discuss each option in turn.

## B. ALTERNATIVES TO MEINONGISM: IDEAS AND UNIVERSALS

*Thinking by way of existents: ideas.* The most popular candidates in Reid's day for the existent items mediating thought of the nonexistent were *ideas*. Their use in this role gives rise to his observation that one of the two chief prejudices underlying the theory of ideas is "That in all the operations of understanding there must be an object of thought, which really exists while we think of it" (EIP 4.2 312).

The idea theorist says that when I think of a centaur, the *immediate* object of my thought is a centaur *idea*, which *does* exist as a piece of mental furniture. Insofar as

---

[13] Ryle says the same thing: "A thing's being real or being an entity or being an object just consists in the fact that it has attributes" (quoted in Smith 2002:256).

my idea represents a centaur, my thought can be said to have a centaur as its mediate or remote object.

To this version of the theory, Reid raises two objections. The first is

> I am certain there are not two objects of this conception, but one only; and that one is as immediate an object of my conception as any can be. (EIP 4.2:321)

This is the "double object" objection, which we have encountered before as an objection to the idea theory's account of perception.

Perhaps the idea theorist could sidestep the double-object objection by saying that only one of the two objects is presented to the mind. What we call "thinking of a centaur" is really the logical product of two other relations, the relation of our act of thinking to an idea and the relation of the idea to a centaur. Only the idea is present to the mind, for the centaur does not exist. But the problem with this version of the theory is obvious. Relations to the nonexistent are precisely what the theory is trying to explain away, yet here they are taken for granted. If an idea can be related to the nonexistent, our thoughts may as well be related to the nonexistent directly, without the mediation of ideas. Rather than saying that our idea is *of* a nonexistent object, then, the idea theorist would do better to say that it has *no* answering object.

Another way to avoid the double-object objection would be to say that when you think of a centaur idea, you *thereby* think of a centaur; that is what thinking of a centaur *is*. But this suggestion is not very plausible. You no more think of a centaur by thinking of a centaur idea than you hang a man by hanging him in effigy.

Regardless of how issues about double objects are resolved, Reid has a second objection to the idea theory—that it gets the objects of our conceiving wrong:

> *Secondly*, This one object which I conceive, is not the image of an animal, it is an animal. I know what it is to conceive an image of an animal, and what it is to conceive an animal; and I can distinguish the one of these from the other without any danger of mistake. (EIP 4.2:321)

Commenting favorably on this objection, Prior says, "The theory that Reid is attacking here is now a dead one, and it has been killed precisely by this argument, either in Reid's hands or in those of others" (Prior 1971:118–19).[14]

A third objection to the idea theory's account of conceiving the nonexistent, not made by Reid, is worth mentioning. If ideas are my proper objects when I think of

---

[14] Prior cites Mill and Russell as having made the same point. For further discussion of the argument, see Nichols 2003, in which prominence is given to Reid's assumption that we have inerrant access to the contents of our own thinking.

the nonexistent, they must also be my proper objects when I think of the existent; thus even when the object I am trying to think of *does* exist, I am not really thinking of *it*. The point is well made by Anscombe as follows:

> If the idea is to be brought in when the object doesn't exist, then equally it should be brought in when the object does exist. Yet one is thinking, surely of Winston Churchill, not of the idea of him, and just that fact started us off. (Anscombe [1965] 1981:5)

As Prior notes, Anscombe is taking for granted the "same analysis" principle: thinking is the same sort of thing wherever it occurs, so if its proximal object is an idea when no distal object exists, its proximal object must also be an idea when the distal object does exist. Thinking must be given the same analysis in both cases. This principle is denied by disjunctivists, a sect not known when Anscombe wrote; I criticize their view below in section D.

*Thinking by way of existents: universals.* Another way to analyze thought of the nonexistent in terms of thought of the existent has recourse to universals. Universals, unlike ideas, do have a place in Reid's philosophy, and Gallie and Wolterstorff have both suggested that Reid himself uses them at just this juncture (Gallie 1989: chapter 5; Wolterstorff 2001:73). On Wolterstorff's interpretation, Reid is *not* a Meinongian:

> Reid was not a Meinongian; I see no evidence that he even so much as entertained the thought that the substances that exist might constitute a subset of those that have being. Fictional characters, fictitious beasts, plans for unbuilt buildings—all are, on his view, not nonexistent particulars but complex universals. (Wolterstorff 2001:73)

Notice, by the way, that Wolterstorff subscribes to the Meinong stereotype, attributing to him the view that existing things are a subset of those that have being.[15]

When Reid says that we can think of Don Quixote even though he does not exist, his meaning according to Wolterstorff is as follows: Don Quixote is not a nonexistent particular, but a cluster of existent universals (courage, knightliness, and so forth). In thinking of Quixote, we do therefore think of something that exists. When we say that Quixote is merely a creature of fiction, we mean that the universals in the cluster are not instantiated by anything, not that they do not exist.[16]

---

[15] "The president of my university not only has being but also existence, whereas Don Quixote has being without existence" (Wolterstorff 2001:73).

[16] This is Wolterstorff's own view in his 1980. I conjecture that he attributes it to Reid in imagined solidarity with that philosopher—an interpreter's prejudice to which I confess I may myself at times succumb.

Universals admittedly have advantages over ideas as proxy existents. Since in the Platonic account of them they are necessary beings, they are better suited than ideas for answering the ancient riddle of nonbeing. How do you say that unicorns do not exist if they are not there in some sense to have nonexistence predicated of them? The idea theorist says that the *idea* of a unicorn, which exists in our minds, has no answering objects. But surely there are possible worlds in which there are neither unicorns nor any minds with ideas. What can the nonexistence of unicorns amount to in such worlds? Universals, on the other hand, are generally accorded the dignity of existing in every possible world, including worlds in which they are not instantiated, so they are there in mindless worlds to ground the nonexistence of unicorns.

If we adhere to the "same analysis" principle advocated by Anscombe and Prior, the Wolterstorff view would have us say that even when I think of someone existent like my wife, I am really thinking of a bundle of universals. It might be argued that this consequence is less objectionable than the corresponding consequence of the theory of ideas, since my wife is more intimately related to the universals she instantiates than to whatever ideas I have of her; indeed, it would be said by some (though not by Reid or by me) that my wife simply *is* a bundle of co-instantiated universals. But in the absence of such a bundle theory, the Wolterstorff view is open to the objection that it does not let me think of my wife *in propria persona*.

Aside from that consequence, there is one major rub with Wolterstorff's suggestion as an interpretation of Reid: though Reid has a place in his philosophy for universals, he explicitly says they are among those objects of conception that *do not exist*. Take note of this striking pair of passages:

> It may further be observed, that all that is mysterious and unintelligible in the Platonic ideas [a.k.a. universals according to 319], arises from attributing existence to them. Take away this one attribute, and all the rest, however pompously expressed, are easily admitted and understood. (EIP 4.2:318)

> Take away the attribute of existence, and suppose them not to be things that exist, but things that are barely conceived, and all the mystery is removed; all that remains is level to the human understanding. (EIP 5.5:386)

If universals themselves are things that are conceived but do not exist, they can hardly be employed in an alternative to a Meinongian theory!

Wolterstorff is aware of this objection to his interpretation. He seeks to defuse it by giving a deflationary account of what Reid means by saying universals do not exist. On this account, when Reid says universals do not exist, he merely means they are *outside the causal order* (73). In support of this claim, Wolterstorff cites the following sentence:

> If we can conceive objects which have no existence, it follows that there may be objects of thought which neither act upon the mind, nor are acted upon by it; because *that which has no existence can neither act nor be acted upon.* (EIP 4.2:313, italics added)

I disagree with Wolterstorff's reading of the sentence. The context for the sentence is Reid's observation that the theory of ideas is underwritten by two prejudices:

> There are two prejudices which seem to me to have given rise to the theory of ideas in all the various forms in which it has appeared in the course of above two thousand years. . . . The *first* is, That in all the operations of the understanding there must be some immediate intercourse between the mind and its object . . . [whereby the one acts] upon the other. The *second*, That in all the operations of understanding there must be an object of thought, which really exists while we think of it. (EIP 4.2:312) [17]

Reid goes on to say that the first prejudice implies the second, though not conversely. The sentence Wolterstorff quotes is Reid's explanation of why the first implies the second: things that do not exist cannot enter into causal relations.

My objection to Wolterstorff's reading of the sentence is that if "has no existence" *just means* "neither acts nor is acted upon," the sentence he quotes in his support would be a tautology. It would amount to "that which neither acts nor is acted upon can neither act nor be acted upon." Moreover, the second of the "two fundamental prejudices" would be a trivial corollary of the first, hardly worth stating separately or being billed as fundamental. I cannot believe that Reid meant things this way.[18]

---

[17] I have substituted "whereby one acts upon the other" for Reid's "so that the one may act upon the other" to make his meaning clearer.

[18] I am tempted to raise this further objection to Wolterstorff: if "has no existence" is synonymous with "does not enter into causal relations," then the second of the two prejudices would entail the first, which Reid says it does not do. Contrary to this tempting objection, the second prejudice would not quite entail the first, since to say that the object of any act must stand in *some* causal relations is not to say that it must stand in causal relations *to the act.* On the other hand, why would Reid state the prejudice as "the object must exist (= stand in causal relations) while we think of it" unless the causal relations he had in mind were causal relations to the act of thinking?

## C. ALTERNATIVES TO MEINONGISM: THE ADVERBIAL THEORY OF THINKING

I turn now to the other way out of the P-Q-R triad for those not willing to countenance relations to nonexistent relata—that thinking, rather than being a relation to the existent, is not a relation at all. The likeliest form of this option would be an *adverbial theory of thinking*, analogous to the adverbial theory of sensing I discussed and attributed to Reid in chapter 1. The idea would be that when we think of a horse or of a centaur, we do not stand in the thinking-of relation to some *object*, but instead simply think in a certain *way*. Such a theory is intimated by Brentano, and it has been advocated in recent times by Sellars (1969).[19]

I am not attributing an adverbial theory of thinking to Reid. As I understand him, Reid, like Kant, makes a fundamental distinction between sensing and other forms of thinking. Thinking is intentional or object-directed; sensing is not. Sensing alone among acts of the mind has no object, and this fact is most naturally accommodated by construing Reid as holding an adverbial theory of sensing. If he had an adverbial theory of thinking as well, the fundamental difference between sensing and thinking would evaporate. Nonetheless, it behooves us to consider the credentials of an adverbial theory of thinking, since if it were viable, Reid's commonsense argument for our ability to think of the nonexistent would not go through. Moreover, as discussed below in section F, there are reasons for thinking that a direct realist theory of perception is best served by an adverbial theory of perception, which in Reid's case would have to incorporate an adverbial theory of thinking, even if he himself contemplated no such thing.

Recall that Reid argues as follows:

1. We sometimes think of centaurs.
2. Centaurs do not exist.
3. Therefore, we sometimes think of things that do not exist.

The proposal of the adverbial theory is that premise 1, though doubtless true in some sense, does not express a relation between us and centaurs, but is to be construed instead as

---

[19] After an initial period in which he believed in "intentional inexistence" as a mode of being (or nonbeing) possessed by objects of thought, Brentano came round to something more like an adverbial theory, as suggested by the following pair of quotations: "'There is something which is the object of thought' may be equated with 'There is something which thinks'"; "its being an object, however, is only the linguistic correlate of the person experiencing it *having* it as object" (1966:68 and 78).

1.' We sometimes think centaurly.

The logical form of 1' is not *aRb*, but simply *Fa*, involving a monadic property of the thinker. Presumably, the conclusion is also to be understood in some adverbial fashion, so that it no longer implies that we stand in cognitive relations to nonexistent relata.

Is the adverbial theory viable? A problem for it arises immediately. Did the reader not recognize the original 1–2–3 argument as valid, whatever his opinion of its soundness? And yet it would *not* be valid on the adverbial reconstruction of it. Upon that reconstruction, the argument amounts to this:

1.' We sometimes think centaurly.
2. There are no centaurs (= centaurs do not exist).
3. Therefore, we sometimes think of things that do not exist.

The problem is that if 1 just affirms a monadic property of us and does not relate us to centaurs, it makes no logical contact with premise 2. Therefore, no conclusion can be drawn.

The problem I have just raised is essentially the same as a problem Chisholm raised for adverbial alternatives to Meinong ([1973] 1982). Chisholm observed that the argument

1. Jones thinks of a unicorn.
2. Jones thinks only of things that exist.
3. Therefore, there are unicorns (i.e., a unicorn is a thing that exists).

is valid, but becomes invalid if the first premise is replaced by

1.' Jones thinks unicornly.

The similarity to the problem raised just above should be obvious.[20]

To highlight the fact that the recast first premise no longer engages with the second, Chisholm puckishly points out that the recast premise has nothing more to do with unicorns than the following sentence does:

---

[20] If we swap unicorns for centaurs and Jones for us, the 1–2–3 argument considered by Chisholm is the antilogism of the argument I attributed to Reid. That is, if we number the premises and conclusion in either of the arguments as 1, 2, therefore 3, the other argument is equivalent to 1, ~3, therefore ~2.

The emperor decorated his tunic ornately.

"Neither sentence has to do with unicorns," he observes, "despite the fact that the word 'unicorn' may be found in each" ([1973] 1982:41).

William Rapaport (1979) has offered a defense of the adverbial theory against Chisholm's objection.[21] He claims that we *do* preserve the validity of the argument if we also construe the *second* premise adverbially. He offers the example

1. Jones thinks unicornly.
2. Jones thinks only existentially.
3.' Therefore, Jones's unicornly thinking is existentially thinking.
   and claims that 3' implies the further conclusion
3. Therefore, unicorns exist.

He also offers a parallel example in which Jones has a singular thought:

1. Jones thinks Quinely (i.e., thinks of Quine).
2. Jones thinks only existentially.
3.' Therefore, Jones's Quinely thinking is existentially thinking.
3. Therefore, Quine exists.

I see two objections to Rapaport, both answerable, but of value in showing how the new second premise must be understood. The first objection invites us to consider the argument

1. Jones thinks Quinely.
2. Jones thinks only quickly.
3.' Therefore, Jones's Quinely thinking is quickly thinking.

If the first Quine argument implies that Quine exists, should this one not imply that Quine is quick?

The objection goes wrong because "quickly" is not the sort of adverb that is meant to figure in Rapaport's adverbial theory (except when it is meant to indicate that Jones is thinking of quickness). "Quickly" is not a content-specifying adverb like "Quinely."

---

[21] I leave aside the question whether Rapaport's theory should be thought of as a form of Meinongism or a rival to it.

This brings us to the second objection. Rapaport says that in the complete paraphrase of the arguments whose validity we are trying to secure, both premises must be construed adverbially, which suggests that the adverb in the second premise should be understood in a manner parallel to the adverb in the first. Well, if the occurrence of "existentially" in the second premise functions as "Quinely" or "unicornly" does in the first, it serves only to specify the *content* of Jones's act of thinking. The two premises together would imply only that Jones has a thought with the content *existent unicorn* or *existent Quine*, a fact that leaves it open whether Quine or any unicorns exist. If Hume is right, whenever we think of *any* F, we are thinking of an existent F,[22] but we should not conclude from this that whatever we think of exists. There is a difference between "Jones is thinking of unicorns-that-exist" and "Jones is thinking of unicorns, which exist."

Using Scholastic and Cartesian terminology, we may say that the problem alleged in my first objection (that the argument proves too much) arises if the second premise concerns only the "formal reality" of Jones's act of thinking, whereas the problem alleged in the second objection (that the argument proves too little) arises if the second premise concerns only the "objective reality" of Jones's act of thinking. Is there a way between the horns of this dilemma?

What we need is a premise linking the "objective reality" of our acts with the "formal reality" of things in the world—a bridge principle similar to one that Descartes employs in his Third Meditation proof of the existence of God.[23]

Rapaport supplies us with just such a premise in a formalization of the Quine argument given in a footnote. Using "R" for the relation of representing and "S" for the relation of exemplifying, we have

1. Jones thinks mly & (mly)RQ. (That is, Jones thinks in a manner that represents Quine's properties.)
2. (mly)(Jones thinks mly → $\exists x(F)((mly)RF \rightarrow xSF)$). (That is, in whatever manner Jones thinks, some actual object x exemplifies all of the properties represented by his manner of thinking.)
3. Therefore, $\exists x(xSQ)$. (That is, something exemplifies Quine's properties.)

But if we appeal thus to the representation of properties by manners of thinking, are we not moving out of the adverbial camp and into the Wolterstorff camp? I noted

---

[22] "To reflect on anything simply, and to reflect on it as existent, are nothing different from each other" (THN 1.2.6:66–67).

[23] Viz., the cause of an idea must have at least as much formal reality as the idea has objective reality. This is to be found in paragraph 14 of Meditation 3.

that there are two alternatives to admitting Reidian cognitive relations to the nonexistent: treating conceiving as not a relation at all and treating it as a relation to the existent (for example, to properties, which exist even if they are not instantiated). The adverbial theory was supposed to be an instance of the first alternative, but in Rapaport's hands, it is turning out to be an instance of the second.

Let's cut to the chase and see if we can come up with a second premise that combines with the adverbially formulated first premise to yield the desired conclusion without using any resources going beyond those of the adverbial theory. The following premise appears to do the trick (with the stipulation, of course, that the premise holds only for content-specifying adverbs):

(F)(If Jones thinks Fly, there are Fs).

An instance of this premise would be "If Jones thinks unicornly, there are unicorns," which combines with the first premise to yield the desired conclusion.

The question to raise now is this: is it legitimate to quantify into the interiors of content-specifying adverbs? Chisholm would presumably have said *no*. In raising his original objection, he regarded "unicornly" as an unstructured predicate with nothing to quantify into; "unicorn" does not occur relevantly in "unicornly" any more than it does in "decorated his tunic ornately." From his point of view, inferring from "Jones thinks unicornly" to "$\exists F($Jones thinks Fly$)$" would be comparable to inferring from "The emperor decorated his tunic ornately" to "$\exists x($the emperor decorated his t-x-ately$)$." On this note, I leave the adverbial alternative to Meinong for the time being, shrouded in doubts that need to be resolved.[24]

Before we give the palm to Reid's Meinongian theory, however, we need to ask how the Meinongian theory itself can meet Chisholm's challenge. Presumably, it is because the theory has objects over which we can quantify that it allows us to represent the validity of the 1–2–3 argument. But what is the representation? A first pass might be

---

[24] I do not mean to suggest that there is no hope of resolution. Investigation of the adverbial theory of sensing has taught us that the theory must have recourse to semantically structured predicates. Frank Jackson (1977, chapter 3) challenges the adverbial theorist to show how to understand in adverbial fashion what a sense-datum theorist would analyze as "S senses a round, red sense datum." "S senses redly & S senses roundly" is plainly not sufficient, as it would be true if S senses redly in regard to one object and roundly in regard to another spatially separated object. What the adverbialist needs to say is that S is sensing (red&round)ly, where the adverbial predicate is compounded (in a way that needs further elucidation) out of two adverb stems. Tye 1984 provides some of the needed elucidation. In any case, there is structure here and thus room for quantification. If the adverbialist about sensing can solve Jackson's problem, the adverbialist about thinking can solve Chisholm's problem.

1. ∃x(Ux & Tjx).
2. (x)(Tjx → x exists).
3. ∃x(Ux & x exists).

But in this representation, we cannot take "∃x" as the standard existential quantifier, or the existence of unicorns would be implied already by the first premise without any help from the second. Moreover, the conclusion of the antilogism, "Jones sometimes thinks of things that do not exist," would come out as the contradictory "∃x(Tjx & x does not exist)." So the quantifiers must be the Meinongian particular quantifier and its companion universal quantifier, which are silent on questions of existence. The argument must be regimented as follows, using Routley's symbols for Meinongian quantifiers (1966):

1. Σx(Ux & Tjx)
2. Πx(Tjx → Ex)
3. Σx(Ux & Ex)

But this representation has at least two problems of its own.

The first problem (which was already a problem for the regimentation using the standard quantifier) is that the first premise may impute too much particularity to the content of Jones's thinking. Is there really a particular unicorn Jones is thinking of when he thinks of a unicorn? Recall Quine's example of the man who wants a sloop—not any particular one, but merely relief from slooplessness (1956:177).

The second problem is that the conclusion may now be too weak. It says that some unicorns exist—but as the quantifier is nonexistential, how does that imply that there *exists* a unicorn that exists? No problem, some may say, since ∃xUx may be defined as Σx(Ux & Ex) (Routley 1966:254). But recall that in Meinongian systems, predication is supposed to be neutral on questions of existence: "Ux" does not imply that x exists, and in that case, why should "Ex" imply that x exists, even though existence itself is the predicate? Moreover, if neither "Ux" nor "Ex" nor their conjunction entails the existence of unicorns, how can "Σx(Ux & Ex)" entail the existence of unicorns, being no stronger than that conjunction?[25]

Both the adverbial and the Meinongian reconstructions of the unicorn argument have their problems. In the hope of circumventing them, I now turn to two theses of Arthur Prior. Recall that Prior is opposed to the relations to the nonexistent espoused by Reid, but some of his other views may afford a compromise with Reid.

---

[25] For further elucidation, see Van Cleve 1999:198–200, where I raise a similar point in criticism of a Meinongian version of the ontological argument.

The first thesis is that all thinking-*of* is a case of thinking-*that* (1971:131; [1968] 1976: 200). To think of Churchill is to think something *about* Churchill, for example, that he was Britain's prime minister during the Second World War. More generally, to think of x is to think Fx, where "F" is some verb (in the broad sense of any expression that combines with a subject term to make a sentence). To think of Fs is similarly to think a thought such as all Fs are Gs, Tom is an F, etc.

The second thesis is that it is legitimate to quantify into predicate position, and that such quantification carries no ontological commitment (Prior 1971, chapter 3). From "Tom is bald" it is legitimate to infer "∃F(Tom is F)"—in English, if Tom is bald, then Tom is *something*—without being committed to anything besides Tom. Prior's views are thus at odds with the more widely received views of Quine on ontological commitment and quantification into predicate position. Quine would claim that "∃F(Tom is F)" commits one to the existence of a property or attribute possessed by Tom. But Quine's views are anomalous, insofar as he does not think the original "Tom is bald" commits one to an attribute of baldness. How can a generalization of something noncommittal suddenly be committal? Prior thinks that the only linguistic practice that is in the first instance ontologically committing is the use of names. "∃x(x is bald)" is ontologically committing not simply because it contains a quantifier, but because it quantifies into a position occupied by a name.[26] "∃F(Tom is F)" is *not* ontologically committing, because it quantifies into the position occupied by a predicate.

Now let's put the two theses together to formalize Chisholm's unicorn argument. (So far as I know, Prior never envisioned this application of his views.) If Jones is thinking of unicorns, he must in accordance with the first thesis be thinking something about them:

1. ∃φJones thinks unicorns φ.

For example, he might be thinking that unicorns have horns, or that some of them are white. Availing ourselves of the other notion, quantification into predicate position, we may render the premise that Jones thinks only of things that exist as

2. (F)(∃φJones thinks Fs φ → ∃xFx).

That is, if Jones thinks something about Fs, then there are Fs. The two premises together yield

3. ∃x(x is a unicorn)

---

[26] For more in criticism of Quine and in defense of Prior (though composed before I knew of Prior's views), see Van Cleve 1994, especially p. 587. For Prior's defense of quantification into predicate position and its ontological innocence, see his 1971, chapter 3.

This reconstruction unquestionably reaches the intended conclusion, unlike the Meinongian reconstruction, which we suspected of reaching a conclusion that was too weak. It also avoids the adverbialist's questionable quantification into the "F" of "Fly." It quantifies into the positions of stand-alone predicates, but not into predicates inside the context "Fly."

While avoiding the difficulties of the adverbial and Meinongian approaches, the Prior-inspired approach nonetheless borrows features from each of them. Prior holds that *Jones thinks that p* does not assert a relation between Jones and a proposition, but simply states a monadic fact about Jones.[27] He thus has a theory of thinking that is in a broad sense adverbial. At the same time, what we predicate of Jones in saying what he thinks has further structure into which we can quantify. If Jones thinks that pigs fly, then for some φ, Jones thinks pigs φ. Prior thus has something like the quantificational resources of a Meinongian theory.

How stands the Priorian reconstruction in relation to the views of Reid—is it a way of implementing them or a way of avoiding them? The answer, I think, is some of each. In holding that all thinking-of is thinking-that, Prior goes against the position I have attributed to Reid in chapter 1: that there are forms of conceiving and perceiving that are objectual rather than propositional.[28] Moreover, in going on to say that thinking-that is nonrelational, he parts with Reid's relational account of conceiving.

In another way, though, Prior's views are reminiscent of Reid's. Reid holds that there are universals, but they do not exist—an assertion that plainly requires a particular quantifier with no existential force. There is at least something of the flavor of that in Prior's view that "$\exists F(\text{Tom is } F)$" and "$\exists\varphi$Jones thinks unicorns φ" (and for that matter, "$\exists\psi\exists\varphi$Jones thinks ψs φ") can all be true even though there are no entities referred to by the predicate variables.

## D. A MEINONGIAN DEFENSE OF DIRECT REALISM

Reid's Meinongism can be put to work in other places in his philosophy. One is his treatment of abstract general ideas, as discussed in appendix U. Another is the

---

[27] He parses "Jones thinks that p" not as "Jones thinks / that p," which sounds like the assertion of a relation between Jones and something named by a that-clause, but as "Jones thinks that / p," in which an operator has been prefixed to a sentence. He holds further that prefixing operators to sentences is not predicating anything of propositions. See 1971, chapter 2.

[28] On the other hand, Reid may need to suppose that our thinking about *nonexistent* objects is always propositional. He says that nonexistent objects have only those properties they are conceived to have, and conceiving x to be F is propositional. As he notes at EIP 1.1:25, the use of an infinitive construction rather than a noun to denote the object of a conceiving generally indicates that the object is propositional.

defense of his direct realist theory of perception, as discussed in the remainder of this chapter.

The classic account of Reid's direct realism as crucially incorporating Meinongism was put forth by Phillip Cummins (1974). Cummins does not compare Reid to Meinong by name, but the similarities between Meinong and Reid as interpreted by Cummins are patent. He advances the following theses, all further elaborated below: for Reid, conception and perception are not E-relations (= existence-entailing relations); Reid is an intentional direct realist, not an E-relation direct realist; E-relation direct realism is refuted by standard cases of hallucination and illusion; Reid's intentional direct realism is not refuted by such cases.

Cummins defines an E-relation as a relation that can hold among two or more relata only if all the relata exist. Familiar examples of E-relations are kicking and giving: you can kick a football only if you and the football both exist, and Tom can give Mary a ring only if Tom, Mary, and the ring all exist. But there are many psychological relations that are arguably not E-relations: the Greeks worshipped Zeus, even though no such deity exists, and Ponce de León searched for the Fountain of Youth, even though no such fountain exists.[29] Psychological relations are *intentional* relations—they are directed at something—but what they are directed at need not exist.

It is beyond question that *conceiving* is not an E-relation for Reid: it is one of the hallmarks of this operation "that it is not employed solely about things which have existence" (EIP 4.1:310). It is less obvious, but nonetheless true according to Cummins, that *perceiving* is not an E-relation for Reid. He gives two reasons for thinking so. First, there are passages in which Reid says outright that there are cases of perception in which the object perceived does not exist. (Notice that I do not say that in these cases "perception has no object.") Here is one of them:

> Thus, a man may feel pain in his toes after the leg is cut off. He may feel a little ball double by crossing his fingers. He may see an object double, by not directing both eyes properly to it. By pressing the ball of his eye, he may see colours that are not real. (EIP 2.22:251; cf. 2.18:214)[30]

Second, Reid says that conceiving is an ingredient in perception. As Cummins takes it, conceiving is the *intentional core* of perception. That is, perception has an object

---

[29] For critical discussion of the thesis that psychological relations are not existence entailing, see Bigelow 1996.

[30] These are the only genuine errors of the senses Reid admits after dismissing many other alleged errors of the senses as really errors of judgment or inference.

only because the act of conceiving within perception provides the object.[31] If conception can have a nonexisting object, it might then seem to follow that perception can have a nonexisting object. More on this presently.

Cummins characterizes direct realism as the view that external physical objects are what is perceived—they are the objects presented in perception. Indirect realists may wish to appropriate the same language, saying we "perceive" the moon, but I have already had occasion to excoriate that usage. For an indirect realist, external objects are not *presented* to us; they are inferred from (or otherwise believed in on the basis of) other things that are presented to us—ideas. Cummins distinguishes two varieties of direct realism: *E-relation direct realism* is the view that perception itself, or some intentional relation within it, is an E-relation; *intentional direct realism* is the view that the object of perception is an *intentional object*, that is, an object of an intentional relation that need not exist in order to stand in that relation.[32] Cummins goes on to maintain that E-relation direct realism is refuted by familiar arguments against direct realism invoking illusions and hallucinations, while intentional direct realism is spared.

The basic problem for E-relation direct realism is this: if perceiving is an E-relation, you must be presented with some existent in every case of perception, but in some cases (hallucination) there is no external existent, and in other cases (illusion and perspectival distortion) the only relevant external existent has properties incompatible with those of the existent you are presented with. In these cases, what

---

[31] The other intentional component within perception is believing. Since Cummins takes belief for Reid to be "assent to what one conceives" (323), he regards the intentionality of belief as parasitic on the intentionality of conception.

Buras generalizes what Cummins says about belief to all other mental operations, maintaining that "Conception is Reid's term for the simple acts of apprehension by which the mind secures objects for its operations" (2005:223). For example, remembering is conceiving of an object or event and believing oneself to have experienced that object in the past.

I distinguish four progressively weaker theses that Reid might have in mind when he says there is no operation of the mind without conception: (i) *every* act of mind has the conception of some object as an ingredient, and it has that object because the conception does; (ii) every act of mind *that has an object at all* has that object because the conception ingredient within the act has that object; (iii) whenever any act of mind has an object, there is an act of conception that *also* has that object—here it is allowed that the conception may not be an ingredient of the original act, but something made possible by it, as in what Reid says about perception preceding simple apprehension; (iv) whenever there is any act of mind, there is also a conception that takes as its object either the object of the original act *or the act itself*. The last is the thesis I attribute to Reid in chapter 1, section G.

[32] A terminological caveat: as Cummins uses the phrase, a presented object must exist, so he does not characterize Reid's direct realism by saying material objects are presented objects. I nonetheless put things as I do in this paragraph to harmonize with what I say about "presentational direct realism" in chapter 3.

you are presented with must therefore be an existent internal to the mind. Once such mental existents have been acknowledged to be the presented objects in some cases, they must be acknowledged to be the presented objects in all cases, thus refuting direct realism.

To see in more detail how the dialectic goes, let us consider the argument from hallucination, as formidable an argument against direct realism as any. Here I follow Smith 2002:230 fairly closely:

1. When Macbeth hallucinated his dagger, he was presented with a daggery *something*.
2. But not with a *physical* dagger, as no physical dagger was existent anywhere in his chamber.
3. Therefore, Macbeth was presented with a daggery *mental* object—a dagger-shaped image or sense datum.
4. If mental images are the presented objects in cases of hallucination, they are also the presented objects in cases of veridical perception.
5. Therefore, the presented object in *all* cases of perception is a mental object, contrary to direct realism.

It is overstating things to say as Cummins does that this argument refutes every would-be direct realist except the intentional direct realist, since there is more than one step at which defenders of E-relation direct realism may try to block it. Nonetheless, the intentional direct realist is in a position to block the argument at an unexpected place, and his strategy might turn out to be the best. To judge of this, let us review the various options, previously canvassed in chapter 3, sections D and E.

Disjunctivists may allow the argument to proceed as far as step 3, but they deny step 4 and the attendant inference to 5. Step 4 rests on the auxiliary premises that hallucinatory experience and veridical experience can be phenomenologically just alike, and that if so, they must be given similar ontological assays—the "ontology recapitulates phenomenology" principle. That principle is exactly what disjunctivists deny; they typically allow the qualitative similarity of hallucinatory and veridical experiences, but they deny that the two types of experience have any factor in common.

To my mind, disjunctivism is exceedingly implausible. Consider what it would have us say in response to the burned-out star scenario. While the star still exists, I am seeing *it*—the star. When the star ceases to exist, I continue to have a qualitatively similar experience as of a star, since light from the star continues to reach my retina, but the star itself is no longer there for me to see. Therefore, what I am seeing is a starlike sense datum in my mind. WHAM—in the twinkling of an eye, out goes the star and in goes the star datum.[33] That is too much for me to believe.

Another objection to disjunctivism rests on considerations about causation. Hallucinations and veridical perceptions can theoretically be caused by exactly the same brain states—indeed, that is the best explanation of their indistinguishability. By the principle "same proximate cause, same immediate effect," it is therefore reasonable to conclude that if the hallucination involves an internal image, so must the veridical perception. "If the mechanism or brain state is a sufficient causal condition for the production of an image, or otherwise characterized subjective sense-content, when the table and wall are not there, why is it not so sufficient when they are present? Does the brain state mysteriously know how it is being produced . . . or does the table, when present, inhibit the production of an image by some sort of action at a distance?" (Robinson 1994:153–54). Such are the mysteries of disjunctivism.

Two of the authors discussed in section C above, Anscombe and Prior, wrote before the advent of the disjunctivist theory, and they in effect dismiss it without acknowledging the existence of this corner of logical space. I think this is testament not to any logical blindness on their part, but rather to the fundamental implausibility of the theory.

Adverbialists and propositionalists refuse to let the argument get as far as step 1. Adverbialists would say that Macbeth was not presented with some *thing*, but was only presented-to in some *way*. Propositionalists would say that Macbeth underwent an experience with a certain propositional content, but not an experience with any object, since there was no object (not even a sense datum) satisfying that content.[34]

Finally, the novel strategy of intentional direct realists is to deny the inference to step 3. That step follows from its predecessors only with the help of an unstated premise: that one can be presented with things only if they exist, or in other words, that presentation is an E-relation. Meinongians can say that Macbeth was indeed aware of something, but this something was only an intentional object, which in

---

[33] A disjunctivist need not analyze hallucinations in terms of sense data. He could analyze them in terms of adverbially modified states, for instance, or he could resurrect an Aristotelian account and say that during hallucinations the mind is stamped with the form of the object even though the object is not there. He might even refuse to give any positive account of hallucination at all. But there is presumably *something* that goes on during hallucinations, and whatever it is, there must for the disjunctivist be a sudden onset of it when the star ceases to exist. There is still a WHAM.

[34] As noted in chapter 1, section E, propositionalism is usually called intentionalism, but in the present context that would beget intolerable confusion, as Cummins and Smith both use the term "intentionalism" for their own quite distinct view.

his situation did not exist. Freed from the prejudice that there must be an existing object for every presentation, the intentionalist is not forced to posit inner images or ideas when no suitable external object exists.

It is instructive to compare the views of Reid-Cummins (as I henceforth call Reid as Cummins interprets him) with those of A. D. Smith, who has independently advanced what he bills as a Meinongian solution to the problem of hallucination.[35] Smith begins by correctly defending Meinong against two of the common misunderstandings—that he overpopulates the universe and that he gives to nonexistents the special ontological status of subsistence (239–40). He then applies Meinongian views to the argument from hallucination, blocking the argument at step 3: Macbeth's dagger is not an existing mental object, but an intentional object that does not exist. So far, the affinities with Reid-Cummins are strong.

In the end, however, I believe Smith is an ersatz Meinongian rather than an *echt* Meinongian. Citing Brentano, he says that having an intentional object is not standing in a relation, and citing Husserl, he says that having an intentional object supervenes on phenomenological states (242–44). If these things are true, how does Smith's brand of Meinongism differ from an adverbial theory, broadly construed? He makes the having of an object a monadic state of the subject rather than a relation to something nonexistent—something with the logical form $Fa$ rather than the form $aRb$.

To bring out why I think it is important for a genuinely Meinongian solution to the argument from hallucination to allow the intending of an object to be relational, recall Chisholm's objection to adverbial theories of thinking: that unless we allow thinking to be relational in a sense permitting us to quantify over its objects, we cannot represent certain intuitively valid arguments as valid. Indeed, without so allowing, we cannot even exhibit the 1–3 portion of the argument from hallucination as valid. Premise 1 says that the hallucinating Macbeth is aware of something daggery; premise 2 says that he is not aware of anything daggery, physical, and existent; the unstated premise says that all awareness is of existents; and step 3 concludes that Macbeth is aware of a *non*physical daggery existent. If we represent the premises as $\Sigma x(Amx \ \& \ Dx)$, $\sim\exists x(Amx \ \& \ Dx \ \& \ Px)$, $\Sigma x(Amx \ \& \ Dx) \rightarrow \exists x(Amx \ \& \ Dx)$, therefore $\exists x(Amx \ \& \ Dx \ \& \sim Px)$, the argument is valid, but only because it construes awareness or intending as a relation to an object and allows objects introduced in one

---

[35] Smith is evidently unaware that he has been preceded in his approach by Reid-Cummins. On p. 238, he says the only previous philosopher who has used intentionalism to counter the argument from hallucination is Routley (1980). His only reference to Cummins (n. 42 on p. 279) misidentifies him as Robert Cummins.

premise to be reached by the quantifiers of another. How would Smith represent the argument as valid if he thinks intentional states are really nonrelational?

Even Cummins seems to me to stop short of pure Meinongism. In a footnote he observes, "One who rejects the E-relation view of intentionality can either hold that intentional states are relational, but not E-relational, or else that they are not relational at all" (n. 10). I take the Meinongian alternative to be the first rather than the second, but Cummins professes neutrality.[36]

One more thing Cummins says makes me wonder whether Reid-Cummins is a pure Meinongian. He notes that for a would-be direct realist who is an E-relation theorist, "presented objects and their features are the sole determinants of what is perceived" (i.e., of the phenomenal character of a perceptual state) (331). Thus, if a tilted coin looks elliptical, some presented object must *be* elliptical. If the coin itself is round, the presented object must something other than the coin—an image or sense datum, undoing direct realism. For Reid, on the other hand, Cummins says, "Conceptions [i.e., acts of conceiving], not actual objects, determine the objects intended in perception and the objects intended need not exist" (332). Since the appearance of ellipticality is contributed by the act, not by any elliptical object, there is no rival to the coin as the perceived object. So far, so good, as far as upholding direct realism goes. But if Reid-Cummins were a genuine Meinongian with intentional objects available as the relata of perceptual relations, it would be more natural for him to say that the presented intentional object is the determinant of the phenomenal character of the perceptual state. Objects should determine what acts are like rather than vice versa. If the order of determination is reversed, Reid-Cummins is more like an adverbialist than a Meinongian.[37]

---

[36] In another footnote (n. 53), he explains that by intentionalism he means (a) that the intentional character of acts of perceiving is not different in kind from the intentionality of thought and belief, and (b) that the object of an act is not specified in terms of an existent to which the act is related. This still leaves the answer to my question open: (a) suggests that the intentional object of perception is a proposition, but even so, propositional views can either be relational à la Russell or nonrelational à la Prior. I note with regret that (a) seems to imply that perceiving is not an A-relation, making Reid-Cummins not a presentational direct realist.

[37] Under prompting from his student Twardowski, Meinong introduced *content* as an intrinsic feature of acts determining which objects they are directed to. (For more on content in this sense, see Hopp, chapter 1.) After bringing content into his account, not even Meinong was a pure Meinongian by my standards, since he no longer made relation to an object with certain features the sole determinant of phenomenal character. A pure Meinongian should uphold a doctrine of perceptual transparency such as that espoused in Moore 2003 and explained in Van Cleve 2015, though without holding as Moore did that intended objects are existent.

# E. ASSESSMENT OF THE DEFENSE

We must now address two questions, one exegetical and the other philosophical. First, how plausible is intentional direct realism as an interpretation of Reid? Second, how plausible is intentional direct realism in its own right?

The first question divides into two more. Did Reid think that perception is not an E-relation? And if so, did he exploit this fact in defense of direct realism?

The first reason Cummins gives for saying perception is not an E-relation for Reid is the passage quoted above about doubled objects and pains in phantom limbs, in which Reid does indeed speak of perceiving things that do not exist. But in other passages, much more numerous, he says that perception always has an object that exists. Here are two:

> I acknowledge that a man cannot perceive an object that does not exist. (EIP 4.2:321)

> It seems to be admitted as a first principle by the learned and the unlearned, that what is really perceived must exist, and that to perceive what does not exist is impossible. (EIP 2.8:126)

Moreover, Reid says this about conception: "that which essentially distinguishes it from *every other* power of the mind [emphasis mine] . . . is, that it is not employed solely about things which have existence" (EIP 4.1:310). This implies that perception *is* employed solely about things that have existence.[38]

The other reason Cummins gives for saying that Reidian perception is not an E-relation is that its core ingredient is conception, and conception is not an E-relation. Against this, two things must be said. First, it may be Reid's view that only *one species* of conception sometimes has nonexistent objects—for example, the type of conception that is involved in imagining a centaur—and not that conception wherever it occurs may have nonexistent objects. Second, from the fact that perception has a constituent that is not an E-relation, it would not follow that perception itself is not an E-relation. Compare: knowledge has belief as a constituent and belief is not factive (i.e., truth-entailing), but knowledge is factive for all that.

The last point would not much matter if Reid's only reason for saying that perception always has an existing object were "grammatical"—that we would not *call* any operation perception that did not have an existing object, though there could *be* an

---

[38] Cummins notes this point, but seeks to disarm it by reading the passage, implausibly, as saying that what is distinctive about conception is that it need not induce *belief* in the existence of its object (326).

operation just like perception that did not have an existing object.[39] Call such operations ostensible perceptions. We could then say a hallucination is an ostensible perception whose object does not exist, whereas a veridical perception (now a redundant term) is an ostensible perception of an object that does exist. We could still block the argument from hallucination in the Meinongian way—denying its third step, in which hallucination is said to have an existing mental object.

I think we must agree with Cummins that Reid had the resources for blocking arguments against direct realism in the Meinongian way, but the question remains whether he actually envisioned employing his resources in that way. My impression is no.[40] There are two contexts in which Reid could have invoked intentionalism in defense of direct realism, but did not take the opportunity do so.

Here is a passage (not cited by Cummins) that at first sight seems strongly suggestive of intentional direct realism:

> [The second of two prejudices giving rise to the theory of ideas is] that in all the operations of understanding there must be an object of thought, which really exists while we think of it. (4.2:312)

If Reid thinks the prejudice in favor of the existent underlies the theory of ideas as incarnated in the theory of *perception*, we would have strong reason for thinking that he is an intentional direct realist. In the lines that follow, however, Reid does not implicate this prejudice in indirect theories of perception, but only in indirect theories of conception and memory (EIP 4.2:313, lines 3–30). What he lays at the basis of indirect theories of perception is the *first* of the two prejudices he identifies, which is the assumption that the object of perception must be causally related to the act of perception and therefore not spatially distant from it (EIP 4.2:312, lines 21–28). He rejects this prejudice in replying to the "no action at a distance" argument against direct realism.

The other argument against direct realism about perception that Reid singles out for critical attention is Hume's table argument. Recall the argument: as I retreat from the table, what I see gets smaller, but the table does not get smaller, so what I see is not the table. Reid does not invoke Meinongian views in replying to this argument; for example, he does not say that some nonexistent object is getting smaller.[41]

---

[39] I am not sure that Reid's reasons are grammatical. If they were, he would not need to say as he does at EIP 2.8:126 that it is a first principle that what is perceived exists. Tautologies need not be listed as first principles.

[40] Cummins does not hold otherwise. His claim is that intentional direct realism was available to Reid and that it is the more defensible form of realism.

[41] It is actually not so clear what the application of Meinongism is to arguments from perspectival variation; it is more straightforwardly applied to cases of hallucination and double vision.

He says that the existent table is getting smaller in apparent size while remaining the same in real size.

My answer to the exegetical question, then, is this: Cummins has woven genuinely Reidian motifs into a promising pattern, but Reid himself provided us only with the threads.

I turn now to the philosophical question: how viable is intentionalism as a way of securing direct realism?

To start toward an answer, let me call attention to a feature that intentional direct realism arguably must have if it is to have a leg up on the competition: it must hold that intentional objects, though nonexistent in cases of hallucination, can exist and be identical with real objects in cases of veridical perception. Suppose the hallucinating Macbeth is aware of an intentional object that does not exist. By an analog of the principle that if sense data are the objects of hallucination, they must also be the objects of veridical perception, one could argue that intentional objects must be present in all cases of perception. The worry then arises that intentional objects usurp the place of material objects as the objects of perception, in which case direct realism would be lost. It would be lost, at any rate, unless intentional objects in veridical cases could *be* existing material objects. This, then, is the wanted feature of intentional direct realism: in some cases intentional objects fail to exist, as in hallucination, but in other cases they exist, as when one sees a dagger that is really there, and in the latter cases one's intentional object is *identical* with an existent physical dagger. "Your intentional object—that which your perception is *of*—is on favorable occasions identical with a real object in the external world." That sounds almost like the definition of direct realism.

Smith agrees:

> This, after all, is the whole point of our examining the intentionalist position as a way of sustaining Direct Realism. . . . A perceptual state does not forfeit its intentional object in virtue of being veridical. Rather, because of its veridicality, its intentional object is a *real* denizen of our actual environment. Its intentional object *exists*. If we deny this by suggesting that in non-hallucinatory perception the subject is aware of an intentional object *in addition to* a real object, we shall simply forsake Direct Realism. (257, italics added)

A simple and economical view satisfying Smith's desideratum would have it that the same object can be in one situation a nonexisting object of hallucination and in another situation (or at a later time) an existing real object. Suppose, for example, that I am seeing a real dagger, which is suddenly vaporized or whisked away, while at the same instant a backup brain stimulator kicks in to sustain in me an experience qualitatively just like the one I was having before. On the simple view, I see the same dagger-like object all along; first it existed and then it did not. Or one could have it the other way around, a hallucination giving way to a veridical experience of the same persisting object when a real dagger supplants the brain stimulator as cause of my experience.[42]

The simple view is untenable, however, for reasons adumbrated above in connection with the incompleteness of mere objects of conception. The real dagger I am seeing was made in China and was once wrapped in silk. The hallucinatory dagger I saw a few minutes ago did not have those properties or their complements, for it was incomplete. On some accounts, this is because it had only those properties that my perception conferred upon it.[43] Therefore, there can be no identity between the object formerly hallucinated and the object now perceived.[44] It will not do to suggest that the hallucinatory dagger *acquired* the richer set of properties when my experience became veridical, for nothing can acquire historical properties.[45]

Perhaps in recognition of considerations like these, Smith denies that there can be identity of intentional objects across hallucinatory and veridical experiences. Nonetheless, he maintains that it is crucial for direct realism that in veridical cases, one's intentional object be identical with some real object in the environment. Are there any obstacles to this more limited claim of identity?

There are. Smith cites the following inconsistent triad as a problem for the view to which he aspires (257–58):

1. Facts about intentional objects supervene on phenomenological facts.
2. Facts about real objects do not thus supervene.
3. When an experience is non-hallucinatory, its intentional object *is* a real object.

Statement 1 is the Husserlian thesis noted in the previous section, statement 2 is an obvious fact, and statement 3 is Smith's intended view. When we put them together,

---

[42] There is a hint of this possibility in the following remark by Reid: "An intelligent artificer must conceive his work before it is made; he makes it according to that conception; and *the thing conceived, before it exists*, can only be an idea [in the Platonic sense, but stripped of existence]" (EIP 6.3:441, italics added).

[43] "When an object is merely intentional there is nothing to confer properties on it *but* the mental acts of its entertainers" (McGinn 2004:499).

[44] Kenny Pearce has suggested to me that the identification problem is worse when the hallucinated object comes first, as in the present example. When the perceived object comes first—as in the case of hallucinating a dead relative—we do sometimes speak as though the object now being hallucinated is the same as someone previously encountered in the flesh.

[45] In the case where the dagger is whisked away rather than vaporized, there is a further argument against identifying the presently hallucinated dagger with the formerly seen dagger: the seen dagger still exists and the hallucinated one does not (cf. McGinn 2004: 502 on Fido and Rex).

we generate a contradiction: there are objects whose properties both do and do not supervene on phenomenological facts.[46]

Smith responds by qualifying statement 1: it is only facts about *nonexistent* objects, not facts about intentional objects in general, that supervene on phenomenological facts. The existing intentional objects of veridical perception have their properties in their own right.

The qualification removes the inconsistency, but at a cost. We have now introduced a bifurcation into the theory of intentional objects—there are incomplete nonexistent intentional objects and complete real intentional objects, just as in Reid's theory of the objects of conception.[47] Moreover, in the scenarios in which we pass from a veridical experience to a qualitatively identical hallucinatory experience, we must say that we lose one intentional object and gain another of which we were not previously aware. Even though the newly acquired intentional object is not an existent object, something like the WHAM objection to disjunctivism still applies.

Smith is not the only contemporary philosopher who has brought Meinongian intentional objects into the theory of perception; two others are Routley (1980) and McGinn (2004). While Smith holds that it is only objects of hallucination that have all their properties conferred upon them by perception, Routley and McGinn hold that even intentional objects in veridical perception have all their properties conferred upon them by perception. How, then, can intentional objects ever be identical with real objects, like St. Paul's cathedral in London? And if they cannot be, how can intentional objects be anything but obstacles to direct realism?

Routley (if I understand him correctly) holds that intentional objects can be identical with real objects despite the fact that the properties of the real far outstrip

---

[46] We reach the contradiction noted in the text if we symbolize the statements as follows: for any experience e and object o, if e has o as its intentional object, then for any property φ of o, o has φ because Fe; for any e and o, if e has o as its real object, then it is *not* the case that for any property φ of o, o has φ because Fe; for some e and o, e has o as its intentional object and e has o as its real object.

[47] The qualification Smith proposes is more nuanced than what I have described. Using the terms "formal" and "objective" in Descartes's way (roughly, an item has a property P formally if it really has P, and it has P objectively if it is presented as having P), he says that the properties possessed *objectively* by an intentional object supervene on the subject's phenomenological state, while the properties possessed *formally* by an intentional object do not. This enables him to say that when a red tomato looks black to me, the same tomato is both a real and an intentional object; it is formally red for reasons of its own and objectively black in virtue of my phenomenological state. However, the *only* properties of a hallucinated object are those it possesses objectively, so it remains true that all of the properties of a hallucinated object supervene on the subject's phenomenological state. There is still a bifurcation between merely intentional objects and intentional objects that are also real objects, as I claim in the text.

those of the intentional. How is this possible? Routley's answer is that intentional objects are objects of a kind for which Leibniz's Law does not hold (1980:662–65). At this point, I can follow him no further.

McGinn holds that whenever we have any perceptual experience, whether hallucinatory, illusory, or veridical, we are aware of some intentional object with only those properties perception confers upon it.[48] Unlike Smith and Routley, he holds that this intentional object cannot be identical with any real object in the environment. In veridical perception, there are actually *two* objects before us—an intentional object that would be there even if we were hallucinating and a real object that is there precisely because we are not hallucinating. There are two objects because in the transition from a veridical situation s1 to a qualitatively matching hallucinatory situation s2, (i) there is a real object, say the dog Fido, as an intentional object for us in s1, (ii) there is a nonexistent doggish intentional object, call him Rex, in s2, (iii) Rex is not identical with Fido, and (iv) Rex was already there as an intentional object in s1—otherwise we pick up a new intentional object in s2 despite the continuity of our experience.[49] The "situations" may be possible worlds as well as times, so there are two intentional objects in every case of veridical perception (502–3).

At this point, I fear direct realism is lost. Recall what Reid says in answer to his question whether according to idea theorists, we perceive ideas only or both external objects and their ideas in the mind:

> If the last be their meaning, it would follow, that, in every instance of perception, there is a double object perceived: That I perceive, for instance, one sun in the heavens, and another in my own mind. But I do not find that they affirm this; and as it contradicts the experience of all mankind, I will not impute it to them. (EIP 2.7:106)

Instead, he takes them to hold that we perceive ideas only. McGinn's intentional objects are not ideas, but is he not confronted with the same alternatives—renounce direct realism or accept a preposterous doubling of objects perceived?

---

[48] McGinn holds that intentional objects are given by the "b" in "aRb," where "R" is a psychological verb, "a" is the name of a person, and "b" is a singular term. Intentional objects need not exist, and some of them do not. We must introduce them in the theory of perception because it sometimes appears as if something is F when no existing thing is F, and intentional objects are needed as the bearers of the presented properties.

[49] Though I object as McGinn does to saying that I acquire a new intentional object when hallucination sets in, I do not share his reason: that the new object would violate the continuity of my experience. I take him to hold something analogous to the sense datum principle: if there is an appearance of identity between what I see in s1 and what I see in s2, then there must be something that really is identical across the two situations. I question whether there is such a thing as the appearance of numerical (as opposed to qualitative) identity.

If McGinn's two objects were presented side by side, as in a case of double vision, his view would be absurd. However, nothing prevents him from saying that the two objects coincide in their visible location. After all, if nonexistent objects can have any property but existence (498), they can have location.[50] Moreover, McGinn can dispel further worries about double intentionality by holding that we see the real object *by* seeing the merely intentional object. Direct realists do not mind saying that we see a table by seeing its surface, so why should they object to saying that we see an external object by seeing a nonexistent intentional object? (McGinn:506).

At this point, we could enter into a discussion of when seeing x by seeing a distinct thing y is a genuine case of seeing x. Seeing a table by seeing its surface seems legitimate; seeing a table by seeing a sense datum sounds like a sham. To which of these paradigms should seeing an external object by seeing a nonexistent intentional object be assimilated? The Pappas definition of direct perception considered above in chapter 3, section F, allows that one may directly perceive something by way of perceiving one of its own parts. The surface of a table is part of it, but I daresay no nonexistent intentional object is a part of any real table.[51] Is it nonetheless intimately enough related to the table that one may perceive the table by perceiving it?

I do not try to settle this issue, and to explain why, I must make a confession. I have tried to give Reid and Meinong a run for their money above, but when all is said and done, I do not believe that there are any nonexistent intentional objects—even in the sense of "there are" expressed by the Meinongian particular quantifier. Only existing things have properties. I suspect that some self-proclaimed Meinongians implicitly agree, as when Smith says that all the features of nonexistent intentional objects logically or metaphysically supervene on intrinsic features of the subject's mental state. What Smith says strongly suggests to me that intentional objects are objects only in a manner of speaking, like the "virtual objects" I discuss in connection with Kant (Van Cleve 1999:8–12).

---

[50] Reid balks at saying nonexistent objects can have place or time (EIP 6.3:440), and McGinn says that a simple causal theory of reference cannot govern reference to nonexistent objects because the latter cannot be causes (499). But why cannot nonexisting objects have spatiotemporal properties and causal properties as easily as they have other properties? Are Reid and McGinn failing to abide by their own principles, or is there a distinction between two modes of property possession that I am missing here?

[51] Thanks here to Jasper Heaton.

## F. DIRECT REALISM REDUX

As I have been expounding Reid in this book, he is a presentational direct realist; he holds that perception (or the conception that lies at its core) is a matter of our being directly acquainted with external objects.

A formidable challenge to presentational direct realism is provided by the phenomena of doubled fingers, burned-out stars, and hallucinated daggers, all of which are epitomized in Malebranche's Master Argument. Perceptual experience sometimes does occur in the absence of any relevant physical object, and it always can. What, then, gives perception its phenomenal character? Must it not be some entity of a special type that is always there, getting in the way of direct realism?

*Yes*, says the sense-datum or way-of-ideas theorist. Erroneous experiences require special mental objects, guaranteed to be there even if a corresponding physical object is not, and it is such objects that we are aware of even in normal veridical perceptual experience. This doctrine is Reid's bête noire, and exorcising it is one the chief aims of his philosophy.

If we are not to give in to the way of ideas, what are the alternatives?

One alternative is to go disjunctivist. Ideas may indeed be the objects of hallucination, but they need not on that account be the objects of veridical experiences. Hallucinations and veridical experiences have no mental factor in common, however similar qualitatively they may be. This alternative I dismiss in section D as fundamentally implausible.

Another alternative is to go propositional. When I have an experience as of seeing an apple, I apprehend that there is an item that is red and round and shiny; such propositional contents characterize my experience regardless of whether there is an apple present, and the phenomenal character of the experience is exhausted by its having such contents. I have recorded my misgivings about propositional theories in appendices C, D, and E.

Yet another alternative is to go Meinongian, in the way explored in this chapter. The phenomenal character of my experience is conferred on it by a relation to an object that may or may not exist—it exists in normal cases, but not if I am hallucinating. There is some danger that the intentional object introduced to account for hallucination will remain on the scene in veridical cases as an object distinct from any environmental object, thus complicating direct realism. But my main reason for rejecting Meinongism, as lately confessed, is that it is as hard for me as it is for nearly everyone else to understand how there can be relations to the nonexistent.

That leaves us with the adverbial theory. When I have an experience as of a red apple, I am not thereby experiencing any object; I am experiencing in a certain way or exemplifying a certain intrinsic property. It should not be objected to this theory that it does away with the seeming intentionality or object-directedness of perceptual states, for intrinsic states can be states in which you seem to be presented with an object. That is why some theorists, such as Smith and Rapaport, try to *implement* Meinongism with what amounts to an adverbial theory. I have favorable regard for their suggestions in their own right, but if I am correct in my understanding of Meinong, they abandon his view rather than incorporating it.

I believe there is pressure toward an adverbial view in the following consideration. Suppose the phenomenal character of an experience is determined by a relation of the experience or the experiencer to some object—be it a sense datum, an existing object in the perceiver's environment, or a potentially nonexisting Meinongian object. On that supposition, any change in the quality of your experience is a relational change in you. If you stop having one kind of experience and start having another (as when you pass from seeing red to seeing green), all that changes is *which objects you are related to*. You yourself do not change in any intrinsic way, any more than you change when the red car next to you in a line of traffic is replaced by a green car. This is a consequence I find strange and counterintuitive. It seems to me that a change in what I perceive is ipso facto a change in *me*—that I am different in some *intrinsic* way when I stop seeing red and start seeing green.

What, then, is the status of the property I have when I am seeing red, but no longer have when I am seeing green? To use old-fashioned terminology, it is a modification of my mind—some manner in which I am sensing or perceiving. If there are such modifications, they account for (indeed, they constitute) the phenomenal character of my experience regardless of what objects are or are not there. We have been brought around to an adverbial theory, not just of sensing, but of perceiving.

It is no part of the adverbial theory that *what* you are aware of in perception is an experience. The experience is the vehicle of awareness, not its object. More accurately, the experience by itself has no object, but in veridical cases it is part of a larger complex that does have an object.

I claimed in chapter 1 that Reidian perception (or the conception involved therein) is a form of acquaintance. This claim now needs to be qualified. Insofar as acquaintance theories are contrasted with theories that make perception belief- or judgment-like, the claim may stand. But insofar as acquaintance, whenever it occurs, is a relation to an object, it can no longer stand. When there is no object, acquaintance cannot be a relation.

Although I regard the adverbial theory as the most promising way of securing direct realism, it faces stiff challenges, both as a view for Reid to adopt and as a theory of perception in its own right.

As for adoptability by Reid, it is fairly clear that he holds an adverbial theory of *sensation*, as I argue in chapter 1. But we are now envisioning an adverbial theory of *perception*. What becomes of the distinction between sensation and perception, on which Reid lays so much stress, if perception itself is adverbial?

One possible answer is that Reid is a dual or multi-component theorist of perception in the sense set forth by Smith (2002, chapter 2). Sensation is one component of perception, constituting part of "what it is like" to be in a perceptual state. Conception and belief are two further components, giving perception its intentionality—conception providing an object and belief providing a proposition affirmed of the object. In developing this view further, however, we encounter the problem of the nonexistent object. How can conception provide the object in cases of hallucination? We need to take one of the alternatives canvassed above (disjunctivism, propositionalism, Meinongism, or adverbialism) in regard to conception itself, and I am now advocating the last. So the question persists: what is the difference between sensation and perception? I see two possible things to say. One is that although conception, like sensation, is adverbial, it has an "object-presenting" phenomenological character that sensation lacks. The other is that perception is distinguished from mere sensation by its belief component, as in the views of Chisholm. According to Chisholm, when you perceive x to be F, you do not merely sense in a certain way, but you correctly believe that x's being F is the cause of your sensing in that way (1957:3, 77, 148, and 149).

As for the prospects of the adverbial theory in its own right, the outstanding problem is to spell out the sense in which perceptions have objects when they are veridical. Under the adverbial theory, a perceptual experience as such has no object, but it can be embedded in a veridical perception that does have an object. One can perceive of-a-green-tree-ly when there is no tree, but one can also perceive in that manner under further conditions that make it true to say you see a tree, or that you have a green tree as the object of your veridical perception. What makes a perceptual experience veridical—what gives it an object when it has one?

For one thing, there must be a green tree. For another thing, the tree must cause your experience in the right way. But now comes the hard part: the tree must suitably *match* your experience. What is this matching? The other theorists are ready with answers. For the sense datum theorist, matching is literal resemblance between idea and object. For the propositionalist, it is the object's satisfying the propositional content of the experience (or that proposition's being true of the object). For the Meinongian, it is the object's existing—that is, the very object on which the experience is directed (and on which it would be directed even if the object did not exist) does exist. But what is matching for the adverbialist?[52]

I doubt that this question can be satisfactorily answered unless the adverbial experience has some internal structure into which we can quantify. We do not want to quantify over any *object* constituents of the experience, however, lest we be led back to the way of ideas. It would be better to quantify only into predicate place. For this purpose, it may be necessary to impute some propositional content to the experience, as discussed in connection with Prior in section C. If we do this, we can say that an experience to the effect that something is F is veridical only if it is caused by an object that really is F, matching the experience in that regard. Arguably, saying this would not be reverting to a *purely* propositional account of perception, for we would not be saying that *every* aspect of an experience supervenes on its propositional content.[53]

Much more needs to be said, of course, about how adverbially characterized experiences—or perhaps experiences under *any* construal of them—can match or fail to match objects in the external world. That is the *Weltknoten*.

---

[52] Suppose ersatz Meinongians like Smith have an answer to the question, "On what phenomenological features of S's experience does S's having an intentional object with properties F, G, and H supervene?" Adverbialists can then simply take over this answer in giving their account of veridicality conditions. For example, if features F*, G*, and H* of the experience are held to give it an intentional object with properties F, G, and H, adverbialists can say that the experience has no immanent object, but is veridical iff it caused by a material object with F, G, and H.

[53] Instructive in this connection are two papers by Michael Pendlebury (1990, 1998), one defending a propositional account of experience and the other an adverbial account compatible with it. In his view, (i) every experience with content has some propositional content, (ii) an experience is veridical iff its propositional content is true, and (iii) phenomenal character is not exhaustively determined by propositional content. I worry whether a view like his (and like the one I am floating in the text) implies that the only aspects of an experience that can be veridical or not are those that are propositionally encoded.

# 11

## EPISTEMOLOGY 1

## FIRST PRINCIPLES

I know what I distinctly perceive by my Senses; I know what I distinctly remember; I know when I am pained; I know that two & three make five. In all these cases the knowledge is immediate. There is no *medium* of proof. But there is belief upon good Evidence. (*Letter from Reid to Kames, December 1, 1778, COR 107*)

In Essay 6, Chapter 5, of the *Intellectual Powers*, Reid presents us with a list of "the first principles of contingent truths." Some of the principles in the list are purely or primarily metaphysical; for example, Principle 2 tells us that thoughts require a thinker, and Principle 6 tells us that we have some degree of power over our actions. But others are plainly intended to have epistemological significance, proclaiming the trustworthiness of consciousness (Principle 1), memory (Principle 3), perception (Principle 5), our faculties in general (Principle 7), our beliefs concerning the minds of others (Principles 8 and 9), testimony (Principle 10), and induction (Principle 12). (See appendix V for the complete list.) My concern in this chapter is with the epistemological principles, and my main question is this: are they principles of *truth* or principles of *evidence*?

There is a third possibility: that they are principles neither of truth nor of evidence, but merely of *belief*. It is clear that they are *at least* principles of belief; this is something Reid tells us again and again. For example, he says, "All reasoning must be from first principles; and for first principles no other reason can be given but this, that, by the constitution of our nature, we are under a necessity of assenting to them" (IHM 5.7:71). A "naturalist" interpretation of Reid might maintain that

that is *all* they are—that his principles begin and end as principles of belief—and go on to make the most of it. I discuss such interpretations in the next chapter; here I simply take for granted that Reid's principles are not merely principles of belief but are meant in addition to be principles of truth or evidence. The question is which.

According to Lehrer and Alston, Reid's principles are in the first instance principles of truth, not evidence. Lehrer writes, "When one considers the first principles Reid articulates, one finds beliefs telling us about truth instead of evidence" (1989:197). And Alston notes,

> The only [first principles] that are distinctively epistemological are those that have to do with the reliability of our faculties. There are no principles that tell us the conditions under which one or another sort of belief is justified, rational, evident, or the like. (Alston 1985:437).

Lehrer and Alston both hold that in the end Reid's principles do add up to a theory of evidence—in Alston's case, because he takes Reid to hold a reliability theory of justification, and in Lehrer's case, because "evidence for Reid just is information about what is true or false" (1989:198).

As Lehrer elaborates,

> The first principles state that the convictions of our faculties are true rather than evident, but the information that our convictions are true is the evidence that grounds them. These first principles are, therefore, principles of evidence as well as principles of truth. (1989:157)

But it remains the case according to both commentators that Reid's principles are *in the first instance* principles of truth.[1] In this chapter I propose an alternative interpretation according to which Reid's principles are principles of evidence right from the start.

The direct textual grounds for my interpretation are somewhat equivocal, but there are philosophical grounds that recommend it. Only on the evidentialist interpretation of his principles, I argue, are certain central Reidian claims plausible.

On the interpretation of Reid's principles I advance, they make possible a way of establishing the reliability of our cognitive faculties by using those very faculties—a procedure sometimes known as bootstrapping. In this chapter I show how bootstrapping is possible; in the next I discuss whether it is an embarrassing bug or a desirable feature.

---

[1] In a later publication (1990), Lehrer maintains that Reid does advance principles that are directly about evidence. I say more about this in section J.

## A. FIRST PRINCIPLES AND EPISTEMIC PRINCIPLES

What is a first principle? As the name implies, it is a principle that comes first in all reasoning or inquiry; that is to say, it is a principle on which we base other beliefs, but which is based on nothing in turn. In company with tradition going back to Aristotle, Reid thinks that a principle is fit to play this role only if it is self-evident:[2]

> It is demonstrable, and was long ago demonstrated by Aristotle, that every proposition to which we give a rational assent, must either have its evidence in itself, or derive it from some antecedent proposition. And the same thing may be said of the antecedent proposition. As, therefore, we cannot go back to antecedent propositions without end, the evidence must at last rest upon propositions, one or more, which have their evidence in themselves, that is, upon first principles. (EIP 6.7:522; see also 6.2:426 and 6.4:454–55)

Reid affirms the self-evidence of first principles in many other passages as well, including the following:

> There are other propositions which are no sooner understood than they are believed. The judgment follows the apprehension of them necessarily.... There is no searching for evidence; no weighing of arguments; the proposition is not deduced or inferred from another; it has the light of truth in itself, and has no occasion to borrow it from another.
>
> Propositions of the last kind, when they are used in matters of science, have commonly been called *axioms*; and on whatever occasion they are used, are called *first principles, principles of common sense, common notions, self-evident truths*. (EIP 6.4:452)

> [That] we perceive it so plainly, and so certainly, that it neither needs, nor is capable of any proof... [is] the very definition of a first principle. (EIP 6.7:522)

When Reid says first principles are "incapable" of proof, I take him to mean that they are not derivable from any premises more evident than they already are themselves—not that there can be no sound arguments having them as conclusions (see EAP 5.1:276, lines 29–33, for corroboration). The principle that identity

---

[2] Some philosophers acknowledge the need for principles to play this role without granting the need for them to have any special epistemic privilege, such as self-evidence. They say that the status of first principle accrues to a proposition simply in virtue of its being compulsorily believed (as in the naturalist views I discuss in the next chapter) or simply in virtue of its being a recognized argument-stopper in our language game (as in the view of Wittgenstein). But I hope it will become abundantly clear as this chapter progresses that Reidian first principles must be self-evident.

is transitive may be derived from Leibniz's Law, but it is a first principle for all that, being as evident to start with as Leibniz's Law.

I shall take it, then, that the defining mark of a first principle is its self-evidence.[3] But here a note of terminological caution is in order. Following Alston, let us distinguish the self-evident proper (that which is evident on merely understanding the proposition) from the *immediately* evident (that which is evident, but not on the basis of support from other propositions believed or known) (1985:440). Immediate evidence is the genus of which self-evidence proper is one species. Reid does often attribute self-evidence in the narrow sense to first principles, as in the next to the last passage quoted above.[4] But not everything he regards as a first principle may plausibly be thought of as self-evident in that sense. In general, it would seem that self-evidence in the narrow sense belongs only to those first principles that are necessary truths; with only a few exceptions (for instance, Descartes's propositions *cogito* and *sum*) first principles that are contingent seem to possess self-evidence only in the broad sense of immediate evidence. To save a few syllables in what follows, I shall generally follow Reid's own loose practice, using "self-evident" in the broad sense in which it is equivalent to "immediately evident."[5]

First principles should be distinguished from *epistemic* principles (or principles of evidence). An epistemic principle is a general principle specifying the conditions under which beliefs of various types are justified, rational, evident, or the like. There are clearly first principles that are not epistemic principles (for instance, axioms of mathematics or metaphysics), and a case can be made that there are also epistemic principles that are not first principles.[6] Whether there are any epistemic principles that *do* qualify as first principles is an interesting question, addressed below in section J.

## B. A CRUCIAL AMBIGUITY

I turn now to the main question of this chapter: are the epistemological-sounding principles in Reid's list principles of truth or principles of evidence? I think the

---

[3] Reid lists other traits of first principles as well (e.g., universal consent among mankind), but none seems to me have as good a claim to be the defining mark. For enumeration and discussion of the traits, see EIP 5.4:459–67, as well as Alston 1985:441–42 and Lehrer 1989:156.

[4] Another example: "[Certain propositions] are first principles, because their truth is immediately discerned as soon as they are understood" (EIP 6.7:519).

[5] For further clarification of the status of being immediately evident or immediately justified, including a list of seven things that it is *not*, see Pryor 2000:532–36.

[6] Such is implicitly Alston's position in 1985. Alston takes Reid's epistemic principles to be reliability principles and argues that reliability principles are not self-evident.

answer depends on a crucial but little noted ambiguity in the wording of Principle 1 and several others of the principles. Here is how Reid formulates Principle 1:

> First, then, I hold, as a first principle, the existence of every thing of which I am conscious. (EIP 6.5:470)

I propose that we systematically transmute Reid's talk of existence into talk of truth. Thus, when he says "if I am conscious of a certain thought, it exists," I rewrite it as "if I am conscious that I am thinking thus and so, then I *am* thinking thus and so." That will facilitate symbolization without distorting Reid's views.[7]

The ambiguity to which I wish to call attention may now be brought out by the following two ways of symbolizing Principle 1 (where "Cp" is short for "I am conscious that p"):

1.1. It is a first principle that $(p)(Cp \rightarrow p)$.
1.2. $(p)(Cp \rightarrow$ it is a first principle that p).

What 1.1 specifies as a first principle is a principle of truth—a single principle laying down that all the deliverances of consciousness are true. (On reliabilist assumptions this would amount to a principle of evidence, but on other assumptions it would not.) By contrast, 1.2 is a principle laying down that each of the deliverances of consciousness is itself a first principle. Unlike 1.1, which gives us *one general* first principle, 1.2 gives us *many particular* first principles.[8]

The next of the epistemological sounding principles, Principle 3, concerns memory: "Another first principle I take to be, that those things did really happen which I distinctly remember" (EIP 6.5:474). The wording here does not share the ambiguity of Principle 1, and it seems that our symbolization should run parallel to 1.1:

3.1 It is a first principle that $(p)(Rp \rightarrow p)$.

---

[7] Indeed, the rewrite is quite in line with Reid's views on the ontological status of mental entities: they are acts or states of a substance rather than existents in their own right. The logical form of "I have a thought" is not "Rab" or "∃xRax" but "Fa."

[8] It is potentially misleading that under the heading "First Principles" Reid gives a list of sentences that themselves contain such phrases as "it is a first principle that . . ." This does not necessarily mean that his first principles themselves employ the concept of a first principle. It is rather as though someone headed up a list with "What I Believe" and then made entries such as "I believe that all men are created equal." What he is listing as his belief is the proposition that all men are created equal, not the proposition that he believes this. Similarly, I take what is a first principle according to 1.1 to be the general proposition $(p)(Cp \rightarrow p)$ and what are first principles according to 1.2 to be a host of particular propositions. One should not assume automatically that 1.1 or 1.2 themselves are meant to be first principles.

However, in his gloss on the principle in the ensuing paragraph, Reid tells us "the testimony of memory, like that of consciousness, is immediate; it claims our assent upon its own authority." That suggests a symbolization parallel to 1.2:

3.2 $(p)(Rp \rightarrow$ it is a first principle that p).

We can also raise the question whether Principle 5, concerning things perceived by our external senses, ought to be understood in the first manner as

5.1 It is a first principle that $(p)(Pp \rightarrow p)$.

or in the second manner as

5.2 $(p)(Pp \rightarrow$ it is a first principle that p).

It is true that Reid's formulation in EIP 6.5 more strongly suggests 5.1: "Another first principle is, That those things do really exist which we distinctly perceive by our senses, and are what we perceive them to be" (EIP 6.5:476). However, his formulation of the principle in other places has the same ambiguity we have found in Principle 1. At IHM 7:210, he says the way to avoid skepticism is "to admit the existence of what we see and feel as a first principle, as well as the existence of things whereof we are conscious." At EIP 2.5:100, he says, "The constitution of our power of perception determines us to hold the existence of what we distinctly perceive as a first principle, from which other truths may be deduced." And at EIP 6.7:516, he says that the existence of what we perceive by our senses is self-evident (see appendix W on paragraph 33).

The relevance of this ambiguity to the main question of the chapter may now be stated. If the first style of formulation of each principle is correct, then Reid's principles are in the first instance principles of truth.[9] They would amount to principles of evidence only in the company of further assumptions connecting evidence with truth, such as Alston's assumption that Reid is a reliabilist or Lehrer's assumption that evidence is information concerning what is true and false. But if the second style of formulation is correct, Reid is laying down principles that are principles of evidence in their own right, despite not overtly containing the *term* "evidence."

---

[9] If Reid's principles *are* principles of truth, they are not meant to hold simply because "perceive" and "remember" are factive verbs. If those verbs were meant to be factive, there would be no need for Reid to add the qualification "distinctly" in Principles 3 and 5. Nor would there even be much point in citing those principles as first principles, for they would be trivially true.

They are epistemic principles attributing first-principle status to the propositions in various classes (those attested by consciousness, memory, and so on), and such status is to be explicated in terms of immediate evidence.

## C. CLUES FROM REID'S DISCUSSION OF DESCARTES

How did Reid understand the principles on his list—in the generalist and truth-oriented style of 1.1, or in the particularist and evidence-oriented style of 1.2? The textual evidence bearing on this question is mixed: there are many passages that suggest or imply the generalist reading and many others that imply the particularist reading. In this section, I provide a sampling of the ways in which the textual evidence is equivocal. In sections E and F, I build a philosophical case for favoring 1.2, and in section G, I return to the textual evidence.

In "Opinions Ancient and Modern about First Principles" (EIP 6.7), Reid discusses the systems of Aristotle and Descartes. He tells us that Aristotle operated with too many first principles and Descartes with too few—indeed, that Descartes tried to get by with just one first principle, regarding consciousness. Since Reid takes the principle he attributes to Descartes to be the same as one of his own first principles, we may try to see whether we can learn anything about his own by paying attention to what he says about Descartes's.

Some of the things Reid says about Descartes simply reproduce the syntactical ambiguities in the formulation of his own principles. For example, he says that Descartes was justified "in assuming, as a first principle, the existence of thought, of which he was conscious" (EIP 6.7:515). That could be taken either as 1.1 or as 1.2.

Other things Reid says point definitely toward 1.1. He says repeatedly that Descartes operated with just one master principle, about consciousness, and that he believed that "upon this one first principle, he could support the whole fabric of human knowledge" (515). If there is indeed only *one* first principle, the formulation of it must be as in 1.1, giving us a single general principle rather than a battery of particular principles.

But still other things Reid says point toward 1.2. He often formulates the principle he attributes to Descartes by using epistemic terms—"certain" or "self-evident"—in the consequent. For example:

> This, therefore, may be considered as the spirit of modern philosophy, to allow of no first principles of contingent truths but this one, that the thoughts and operations of our own minds, of which we are conscious, are self-evidently real and true; but that every thing else that is contingent is to be proved by argument. (EIP 6.7:516)

Here the "one principle" is that for any p, if we are conscious that p, then it is true *and self-evident* that p. Since self-evidence is the prime mark of a first principle, what we are really getting here is a single epistemic principle that specifies a multitude of first principles, in the style of 1.2.

I examine Reid's various remarks about Descartes at greater length in appendix W, exhibiting several more that support 1.1 and several more that support 1.2. From his discussion of Descartes one can easily get the impression that Reid was either not clear in his own mind about the difference or not aware of the importance of it.

## D. PARTICULARS VERSUS GENERALS

Although Reid often seems oblivious or indifferent to the distinction between 1.1 and 1.2, there are two passages in which he draws a similar distinction himself. One occurs in EIP 6.7, where Reid endorses Locke's observation that "the particular propositions contained under a general axiom are no less self-evident than the general axiom, and that they are sooner known and understood" (521). As an example, he notes that "it is as evident, that my hand is less than my body, as that a part is less than the whole" (521.). Symbolizing "a part is less than the whole" as "$(x)(y)(xPy \rightarrow xLy)$," we might at first take what is "contained under" the formula to be its instances, such as "$hPb \rightarrow hLb$." However, what Reid cites as "contained under" the general maxim is not that conditional, but its *consequent*, "$hLb$." In parallel fashion, what is "contained under" the general principle $(p)(Cp \rightarrow p)$ would be consequents of its instances, that is, particular propositions I am conscious of, such as "I am now wondering whether God exists." This distinction between the evidence of general principles and the evidence of particular propositions contained under them is exactly what is involved in the distinction between 1.1 and 1.2.

The other passage occurs in EIP 6.5: "It is another property of this and of many first principles that they force their assent in particular instances, more powerfully than when they are turned into a general proposition" (482). As an example, he points out that skeptics who maintain that their senses are fallacious nonetheless trust them in particular instances. As another example, we may cite the Descartes of the early stages of the Third Meditation, before he has proved the veracity of God. He is then capable of doubting the general proposition that whatever he perceives clearly and distinctly is true, but he is not capable of doubting particular propositions when he clearly and distinctly perceives them. (See Van Cleve 1979:66–67.) What is involved here is a scope distinction formally analogous to that between 1.1 and 1.2:

It is indubitable that $(p)(CDp \rightarrow p)$ (false of Descartes)
$(p)(CDp \rightarrow$ it is indubitable that p) (true of Descartes)

Indeed, to the extent that Reid takes indubitability as a mark of first principles, we have here exactly the distinction that is involved in 1.1 and 1.2.

This distinction may explain one apparent inconsistency in Reid. He tells us repeatedly that a key feature of first principles is that we cannot help believing them, but he also tells us that there can be disputes about first principles and says that modern philosophers are to be faulted for not acknowledging certain principles to be first principles that really are such. (See, for example, EIP 1.2:41, and EIP 6.7, *passim*.) If what some philosophers dispute are the generals and what everyone believes are the particulars, the inconsistency vanishes.

Even if Reid does at times distinguish 1.1 and 1.2, we are left with the question of which model to follow in understanding the principles on his list. Which are the first principles properly so called, the particulars or the generals? In the next three sections, I argue that the particularist answer fits better with Reid's philosophical commitments and occasionally with his explicit pronouncements.

## E. THREE REASONS FOR PARTICULARISM

First principles are supposed to be self-evident. They are supposed to be things we cannot help believing. And they are supposed to be ultimate premises, lying behind all other beliefs. The general principles about truth that are first principles according to 1.1 and its analogs do not have a strong claim to possess any of these features. The particular propositions about the contents of consciousness, memory, and perception that are first principles according to 1.2, 3.2, and 5.2 have a much better claim. These are excellent reasons for adopting the particularist construal, and I now say more about each.

1. Reid says that first principles are self-evident. I think it will be conceded that particular deliverances of consciousness have a better claim to this status than the general proposition that all such deliverances are true. I think it will be even more readily conceded that particular deliverances of perception and memory have a better claim to self-evidence than the general proposition that all deliverances of *these* faculties are true.[10]

2. Reid tells us repeatedly that a key feature of first principles is that we cannot help believing them. It is possible to doubt (as Descartes did) whether all deliverances of consciousness, perception, and memory are true, but it is not so easy to doubt

---

[10] I do not oppose calling "all deliverances of memory are true" immediately evident simply on the ground that it is false, for that would also be a reason for refusing to attribute self-evidence to the particular deliverances of memory—some of them are false, too.

a particular deliverance of one of these faculties at the moment of delivery. As I pointed out in the previous section, Reid makes this point himself, and it is one more reason for favoring 1.2 and company over 1.1 and company.

3. If $(p)(Cp \to p)$ is a first principle as claimed by 1.1, how would we use it in coming to know particular propositions about the operations and contents of our mind (*cogito*-propositions, as I shall call them)? Presumably, we would enlist it as a major premise alongside some instance of its antecedent, $Cq$, as minor premise; from the two premises together we would then deduce the conclusion $q$ (*I am now in pain*, or whatever it might be). But that procedure gives rise to two absurdities. First, how would we know $Cq$, the minor premise? By deducing it from $CCq$ and another application of the major premise? That would launch an absurd infinite regress.[11] Second, Reid would think it absurd that we have to deduce *cogito*-propositions from anything else. Such propositions are self-evident if anything is.

We avoid these difficulties if what underlies our knowledge of *cogito*-propositions is 1.2 rather than 1.1. Principle 1.2 tells us that if we are conscious of any *cogito*-proposition, then *that proposition* is (for the time being) a first principle for us. It does not need to be deduced from anything else, because it is immediately evident. It is immediately evident because we are conscious of it, but that is not to say that some proposition about our state of consciousness is a mediating premise. In order to know that p by means of consciousness, we do not have to know that we are conscious that p; nor do we have to know that whatever we are conscious of is true; we simply have to be *in* the state of consciousness that p. Similarly, we do not have to know that 1.2 is true in order to acquire knowledge by its means; we need only fall under that principle.

An important difference between principles of truth and principles of evidence emerges from the considerations of the last two paragraphs. Principles of truth contribute to our knowledge only in so far as they (and instances of their antecedents) are themselves evident or known; that is why the 1.1 construal of Reid's principles gives rise to the regress we have noted above. But principles of evidence contribute to our knowledge simply by being *true*. We do not have to *know* that they are true;

---

[11] Richard Feldman has pointed out to me that this regress argument may only show the need for *one* of Reid's principles to be of the 1.2 form—namely, 1.2 itself. If I can know by consciousness that I am in a state of perceiving or remembering (a supposition that seems all right as long as verbs like "perceive" and "remember" are not taken to be factive), I can then combine that knowledge with $(p)(Pp \to p)$ or $(p)(Rp \to p)$ to deduce truths about what lies beyond the sphere of present consciousness (for instance, that I walked beside the ocean yesterday). However, the first two arguments I employ in this section for the 1.2 style apply equally well to the principles governing memory and perception.

we simply have to fall under them. Since this point is of crucial importance below, I repeat it in a slogan: principles of truth contribute to our knowledge by being evident; principles of evidence contribute to our knowledge by being true.

## F. OTHER MINDS AND NATURAL SIGNS

Another reason for favoring the particularist over the generalist interpretation of Reid's principles comes to light when we consider Principle 9, one of the principles underlying our knowledge of other minds:

> Another first principle I take to be, that certain features of the countenance, sounds of the voice, and gestures of the body, indicate certain thoughts and dispositions of mind. (EIP 6.5:484)

This principle echoes Reid's teaching in the *Inquiry* (sections 4.2 and 5.3) that certain features, sounds, and gestures are natural signs of inward thoughts and sentiments. How exactly are we to understand the principle? One possibility is

> It is a first principle that there are bodily features $B_1$-$B_n$ and mental features $M_1$-$M_n$ such that $B_1$ is a sign of $M_1$, $B_2$ is a sign of $M_2$, and so on.

On this reading, what Principle 9 would lay down as a first principle is simply that *there are* correlations between inner states and their outward manifestations. We would have a license to look for such correlations, but no hint in advance of what they are. It seems to me, however, that Reid's position in the *Inquiry* involves more than this. He argues that artificial language presupposes natural language—that there could not be signs whose meaning is fixed by convention unless there previously existed signs (e.g., facial expressions) whose meaning "every man understands by the principles of his own nature" (IHM 4.2:51). What would have to function as first principles according to this argument are not just beliefs that *there are* psychophysical correlations to be discovered, but beliefs in particular psychophysical correlations, such as that between smiling and approval or affirmation. In other words, the correct reading of Principle 9 must be

> There are bodily features $B_1$-$B_n$ and mental features $M_1$-$M_n$ such that it is a first principle that $B_1$ is a sign of $M_1$, a first principle that $B_2$ is a sign of $M_2$, and so on.

This understanding of Principle 9 is confirmed in Reid's subsequent discussion of it. He notes that infants know how to interpret a threatening tone of voice almost as soon as they are born (EIP 6.5:484), and he says that by the constitution of our nature, the figure and color in an expressive face make us conceive of and believe in a certain passion in the mind of another, just as certain tactile sensations make us conceive of and believe in a round hard body (EIP 6.5:486). There is no need to learn correlations between facial or vocal signs and the sentiments they signify. Indeed, there is not even any *possibility* of learning such correlations by experience, since we have access to inner thoughts and passions in another only *via* their outward signs (EIP 6.5:485–86, beginning on line 31).

In Principle 9, then, Reid is positing a plurality of particular first principles rather than a single general first principle. I take this as further evidence for a particularist interpretation of Reid's principles.[12]

## G. MUST PRINCIPLES BE GENERAL?

It may ring odd in some ears to hear the particular deliverances of consciousness or perception called *principles*. Is not a principle something inherently general? How, then, can it be a first principle that I am now seeing a tree or feeling a twinge of pain? Self-evident these things may be, but it is an abuse of language to call them principles—or so I have been told.

Since the "firstness" of the propositions I am classifying as first principles matters to me more than their principlehood, I could simply take this objection in stride, perhaps using instead Leibniz's phrase "first truths." But it also seems to me that I am entitled to brush the objection aside, since it is clear that Reid himself has no scruple about calling particular propositions principles. When he introduces the topic of first principles, he tells us that "first principle" and "self-evident truth" are interchangeable terms (EIP 6.4:452), and I think my discussion to date has made it amply clear that particular propositions may be self-evident. Moreover, there are plenty of passages in which Reid unequivocally either cites particular propositions as first principles or implies that particular propositions may be first principles. Here is one from the *Inquiry*, immediately following a sentence in which he has offered "my perception of the tree" as an example of a perception:

> All reasoning is from principles. The first principles of mathematical reasoning are mathematical axioms and definitions; and the first principles of all our reasoning about existences, are our perceptions. (IHM 6.20:172)

[12] Perhaps it will be objected that it is not very plausible to classify propositions about particular psychophysical correlations as self-evident—no matter how instinctive our belief in them may be. I concede this objection and acknowledge that it is grist for the naturalist interpretations of Reid discussed in chapter 12.

Here is one from the *Active Powers*:

> The truths immediately testified by the external senses are the first principles from which we reason, with regard to the material world, and from which all our knowledge of it is deduced. (EAP 3.3.6:176)

And here are two from the *Intellectual Powers*:

> The operations of our minds are attended with *consciousness*; and this consciousness is the evidence, the only evidence, which we have or can have of their existence.... Every man finds himself under a necessity of believing what consciousness testifies, and every thing that hath this testimony is to be taken as a first principle. (EIP 1.2:41–42)

> The greatest Sceptics admit the testimony of consciousness, and allow, that what it testifies is to be held as a first principle. (EIP 6.4:463)

Among the things having the testimony of consciousness is the pain I am feeling right now. There could hardly be a stronger endorsement of particular propositions as first principles.[13]

## H. ESTABLISHING RELIABILITY WITHOUT CIRCULARITY

I come now to the noteworthy feature advertised above of the particularist reading (or as it may equally well be called, the evidentialist reading) of Reid's principles: it would enable us to establish the reliability of various of our cognitive faculties through the use of those very faculties. Such a procedure is often condemned as circular, but I argue that if there are correct epistemic principles in

---

[13] Wolterstorff (2004) raises a legitimate difficulty for my particularist interpretation of Reid's principles. It is this: Reid holds that first principles are principles of *common sense*, which implies that they are believed by all sane adults; but the first principles specified by 1.2, such as *I have a headache*, are *not* believed by every sane adult; they are only believed by those who are conscious of having a headache. The objection is fair enough, and it remains after we reformulate 1.2 as "(p)(S)(if S is conscious that p, then it is a first principle for S that p)." But I think the objection is trumped by other considerations, and that Reid should have relaxed or reformulated the requirement of commonality. He certainly does consider as first principles singular propositions that are believed only by their subjects. Moreover, it would be disastrous if he accepted the conclusion to which Wolterstorff's objection leads—that only general principles are first principles. He would then be confronted with the regress noted as point 3 of section E and be left with no way of accounting for the evidence of *cogito*-propositions.

the style of 1.2 governing consciousness, memory, perception, and other cognitive faculties, there is no vicious circle in using those faculties in support of
themselves.

A noncircular argument for the reliability of our faculties is often thought to be
inherently impossible. Indeed, Reid himself is often credited with making precisely
this point. After enunciating his Principle 7—"the natural faculties, by which we
distinguish truth from error, are not fallacious"—he goes on to disparage any attempt to *prove* the reliability of these faculties:

> If a man's honesty were called in question, it would be ridiculous to refer it to the man's
> own word, whether he be honest or not. The same absurdity there is in attempting to
> prove, by any kind of reasoning, probable or demonstrative, that our reason is not fal-
> lacious, since the very point in question is, whether reasoning may be trusted. (EIP
> 6.5:480)

A few paragraphs later he criticizes Descartes for failing to see this point. In effect,
he is calling attention to the problem of the Cartesian Circle:

> Descartes certainly made a false step in this matter; for having suggested this doubt
> among others, that whatever evidence he might have from his consciousness, his
> senses, his memory, or his reason; yet possibly some malignant being had given him
> those faculties on purpose to impose upon him; and therefore, that they are not to be
> trusted without a proper voucher: to remove this doubt, he endeavours to prove the
> being of a Deity who is no deceiver; whence he concludes, that the faculties he had
> given him are true and worthy to be trusted.
>
> It is strange that so acute a reasoner did not perceive, that in this reasoning there is
> evidently a begging of the question.
>
> For if our faculties be fallacious, why may they not deceive us in this reasoning as
> well as in others? And if they are to be trusted in this instance without a voucher, why
> not in others?
>
> Every kind of reasoning for the veracity of our faculties, amounts to no more than
> taking their own testimony for their veracity; and this we must do implicitly, until
> God give us new faculties to sit in judgment upon the old. (EIP 6.5:480–81; see also
> EIP 6.7:516–17)

Despite the seeming probity of this point, I maintain that a noncircular argument for the reliability of our faculties is possible after all. Moreover, Reid's own
principles—construed in the evidentialist and particularist manner I have been
advocating—are what make it possible.

How might such an argument go? Descartes took an indirect route. Using his clear and distinct perceptions, he fashioned a proof of the existence of a God who is no deceiver; from this in turn, he deduced the reliability of his clear and distinct perceptions. But let us consider instead a more direct route, in which we compare the deliverances of a given faculty directly with the facts to which they testify. In the case of sense perception, such an argument might take the following form, which Alston (1986:9) has dubbed a "track-record argument":

1. At $t_1$, I formed the perceptual belief that p, and p.
2. At $t_2$, I formed the perceptual belief that q, and q.
      (and so on)
C. Therefore, sense perception is a reliable source of belief.

In such an argument we consider a wide sample of perceptual beliefs, note that the vast majority of them have been true, and conclude by induction that perception is reliable.[14]

Note that the conclusion of the argument does not appear anywhere among the premises. Why, then, are such arguments typically thought circular? The answer is obvious as soon as we focus on the second conjunct in a typical premise. How do I know that the perceptual belief I formed at $t_1$ is true, that is, how do I know that p? Presumably, I know this only on the basis of perception itself—for example, subsequent perceptions corroborating those that initially prompted my belief that p. Even if my corroborative knowledge is reached by some other means, such as the testimony of a witness, I must presumably rely on perception to know what the witness says—and the witness herself must rely on perception to ascertain the facts to which she testifies. So it appears that ultimately, if not in the first instance, I must rely on perception in order to know that the premises of a track-record argument on behalf of perception are true. Assuming that perception yields knowledge only if it is reliable, it follows that the truth of the conclusion of the track-record argument is a necessary condition of our gaining knowledge of its premises. That is why track-record arguments are generally thought circular.

And yet they are *not* circular in any sense that prevents us from acquiring knowledge by means of them. Let us suppose that Reid's Principle 5 takes the particularist form I have suggested—that it lays down that any deliverance of sense perception may function as a first principle, implying that if we perceive or seem to

---

[14] Insofar as the reliability need only be of the "for the most part" variety, it is allowable that some of the premises tell of occasions on which I formed perceptual beliefs that I subsequently learned to be false.

perceive that p, it is thereby immediately evident for us that p.[15] Let us suppose further that Principle 5, so construed, is true. We may then come to know a great many things *through* sense perception without having to know anything *about* the epistemic powers (especially, the reliability) of sense perception. That we need not know anything about the epistemic powers of sense perception is implicit in what we have just supposed: that the deliverances of that faculty are *immediately* evident. So by its means we can acquire evident beliefs about our environment, and if the beliefs in question are true, they will constitute knowledge. In this fashion we may arrive at knowledge of the various *p*s and *q*s in the track record argument above, and in so doing we need no antecedent knowledge of the reliability of sense perception itself. That is why I maintain that track-record arguments for the reliability of a faculty are not circular in any debilitating sense.[16]

There is, to be sure, *a* sense in which such arguments are circular: on the assumption that sense perception (or any other faculty) yields knowledge only if it is reliable, it would not be possible to gain knowledge of the premises of a track-record argument unless the argument's conclusion were true. Alston has proposed that arguments with this feature be labeled as "epistemically circular," and in his article on Reid's epistemology he maintains that circularity in this sense vitiates an argument just as much as ordinary logical circularity (1985:443 and 447). But I suggest that if the label of circularity is to be a stamp of worthlessness, we should not apply it to an argument simply because the truth of the argument's conclusion is a precondition of obtaining knowledge of the premises.[17] We should apply it instead only to arguments in which *knowledge* of the conclusion is a precondition for knowledge of the premises. Such arguments *are* circular in a way that makes them useless for acquiring knowledge, but track-record arguments are not like that.[18]

---

[15] I add "or seem to" for those who insist that "perceive" is factive, implying the truth of what is perceived. The point is that perceptual experiences, even when unveridical, confer evidence on their propositional contents.

[16] I concede that track-record arguments are not dialectically effective against a skeptic. As Reid observes in discussing Hume's skepticism regarding reason, "what can be more absurd than to attempt to convince a man by reasoning [or any other faculty] who disowns the authority of reason [or whatever faculty it is]" (EIP 7.4:739). I maintain nonetheless that such arguments can be means of acquiring knowledge of their conclusions, as argued at greater length in Van Cleve 1979 and 1984.

[17] I say "precondition" and not just "necessary condition" because in *any* valid argument, the truth of the conclusion is a necessary condition of anyone's having knowledge of the premises.

[18] A year later in his 1986, Alston is more sanguine about the prospects for "justifying, or being justified in accepting, claims that one or another source of belief is reliable" on the basis of track-record arguments. He concludes that even when an argument for a reliability claim is epistemically circular in his stipulated sense, "one may still justify, and *be justified* in, the reliability claim by virtue of basing it on the reasons embodied in the epistemically circular argument." See

Crucial to the possibility of establishing the reliability of our faculties without vicious circularity is a point made above at the end of section E. I note there that principles of truth (such as those given by 1.1 and its analogs) contribute to our knowledge *only insofar as they are themselves known*. But principles of evidence (such as 1.2 and its analogs) contribute to our knowledge *simply by being true*—or more accurately, by their being true and our falling under them. There is no need of our knowing that they are true (or that the faculties they concern are reliable). The Reid I am showcasing is therefore an *epistemological externalist*—someone who thinks there are important knowledge-making factors that do their work regardless of whether they are themselves known.[19]

There are many places in Reid where the externalist strain in his thinking is prominent. For example, he says that when light from an object strikes the lower portion of one's retina, that gives one *knowledge* that the object lies in an upward direction from the eye (IHM 6.12:124–25). More generally, he says that signs produce "knowledge and belief" of the things they signify (IHM 6.24: 190–92). For example, by a law of our constitution, certain tactile sensations produce in us the belief in a hard, extended object; this belief can be knowledge even for one who has no knowledge that such sensations are reliably connected with such objects.

Why is it that on externalist principles there is nothing objectionably circular about using a faculty to obtain knowledge of its own reliability? This is so for two reasons taken together. First, an argument is vitiatingly circular—that is, circular in a way that makes it inept as a means for acquiring knowledge of its conclusion—*only if knowledge of the conclusion is a precondition of acquiring knowledge of its premises*.[20] Second, if the variety of externalism I attribute to Reid is correct, knowledge of the reliability of sense perception is *not* a precondition of using sense perception to gain knowledge. In particular, *knowledge of a track-record argument's conclusion is not a*

---

especially pp. 12–13, where some of the points I have noted above are acknowledged. What epistemic circularity stands in the way of is only "full reflective justification," something that Alston argues to be impossible in any case.

[19] On this point (Reid as externalist) I am in agreement with what Plantinga says about Reid in 1993a (v) and 1993b (viii). I also agree with Plantinga that Reid is a nonclassical foundationalist—someone who holds that the range of properly basic or immediately evident propositions extends beyond the Cartesian basis to include propositions about the external world, the past, and the minds of others (1993a:86, and 1993b:95–96 and 183–84). I add that it is only the construal of Reid's principles in the particularist style I recommend—1.2., 3.2, and so on—that accommodates the interpretation of him as an externalist foundationalist.

[20] Or of the argument's validity or inductive strength—a consideration that arises in inductive arguments for induction, but not in the track-record arguments currently under consideration.

*precondition of acquiring knowledge of its premises.* The senses need merely *be* reliable or justification-producing in order to be means of acquiring knowledge, whether a subject knows them to be or not. On externalist principles, then, track-record arguments are not subject to any reproach.

## I. REID ON CONFIRMING THE TESTIMONY OF OUR FACULTIES

Although he seems to come down hard on attempts to prove the reliability of our faculties, I suggest that Reid may not be altogether hostile to what I am proposing here. Several of his remarks suggest that he may, after all, countenance the possibility of confirming the reliability of our cognitive faculties, even though those very faculties would have to be used in the undertaking.

After enunciating the last of his principles, concerning induction—"in the phenomena of nature, what is to be, will probably be like to what has been in similar circumstances" (EIP 6.5:489)—he makes the following observation: "This is one of those principles, which, when we grow up and observe the course of nature, we can confirm by reasoning" (EIP 6.5:489). What he seems to oppose is not the idea that we *can* confirm the reliability of induction, but rather the idea that we *must* do so before we are entitled to use inductive inferences or before we can acquire any knowledge by their means.

He makes a similar point about sense perception:

> The credit we give to both [the testimony of nature given by our senses and the testimony of men given by language] is at first the effect of instinct only. When we grow up, and begin to reason about them, the credit given to human testimony is restrained, and weakened, by the experience we have of deceit. But the credit given to the testimony of our senses, is established and confirmed by the uniformity and constancy of the laws of Nature. (IHM 6.20:171; see also 170)

And also about memory:

> Perhaps it may be said, that the experience we have had of the fidelity of memory is a good reason for relying upon its testimony. I deny not that this may be a reason to those who have had this experience, and who reflect upon it. But I believe there are few who ever thought of this reason, or who found any need of it. It must be some very rare occasion that leads a man to have recourse to it; and in those who have done so, the testimony of memory was believed before the experience of its fidelity; and that belief could not be caused by the experience which came after it. (EIP 3.2:256)

Strikingly absent from the last remark is any suggestion that experience of the fidelity of memory—by which Reid can only mean *memorial* experience of its fidelity—would be worthless for purposes of ascertaining or demonstrating its fidelity. The point is rather that it is essential to our cognitive functioning that we believe the deliverances of memory before we have any such demonstration.

In retrospect, it seems that some of Reid's readers may have misappropriated the passage in which he castigates Descartes for trying to prove the reliability of our faculties when we have nothing to use in the enterprise but those very faculties. Here is a crucial part of that passage:

> For if our faculties be fallacious, why may they not deceive us in this reasoning as well as in others? And if they are to be trusted in this instance without a voucher, why not in others? (EIP 6.5:481)

The main moral is "Do not insist on a proof of the reliability of your faculties *before* you trust them"—otherwise you will get nowhere. This injunction allows us to *begin* by trusting our faculties, which "we must do implicitly, until God give us new faculties to sit in judgment on the old" (EIP 6.5:481). It allows us to come to know various things through the use of our faculties (without prior proof or knowledge of their reliability), and on the basis of the things thus known, to confirm the reliability of those faculties.

What Reid castigates is *not* the very idea of arguing for the reliability of our faculties, but doing so under the requirement that our faculties do not yield knowledge unless their reliability is already known. Under that requirement, arguments for reliability cannot get off the ground. But when the requirement is rejected as Reid recommends, there is no longer anything wrong with such arguments.

## J. CAN EPISTEMIC PRINCIPLES BE FIRST PRINCIPLES?

What I have been advocating under the name "particularism" is the view that Reid's first principles are, or at least include, particular deliverances of consciousness, memory, and perception. I raise now the question of whether they might also include general principles of evidence—in other words, whether epistemic principles might themselves be first principles.[21]

---

[21] This possibility—that Reid's first principles include *both* particular beliefs and general principles of evidence—is advocated by Lehrer in 1990. He expresses it by saying, "Our knowledge of both the first principles [which he here takes to be general principles of evidence] and the particular beliefs to which they give rise [e.g., particular perceptual beliefs] are both immediate" (40).

The question whether epistemic principles might themselves be first principles for Reid hinges on two other questions: (1) Does Reid hold a reliability theory of justification? (2) Does Reid hold that first principles (or self-evident principles) must by their very nature be true?

I have called Reid an epistemological externalist, meaning by this someone who thinks that knowledge-making factors do their work regardless of whether they are themselves known. The most clear-cut variety of externalism on the contemporary scene is reliabilism—the view that a necessary and sufficient condition for a belief's being justified is its having issued from a reliable faculty, that is, a faculty all or most of whose deliverances are true. (See Goldman 1979 for a paradigm exposition.) Is Reid a reliabilist in this sense? To this question, Alston (1985) and de Bary (2002) say yes; Lehrer (1989) says no. Without trying to settle the issue in this chapter, I note its bearings on other issues I discuss.

I note first that if Reid is a reliabilist, the distinction between 1.1 and 1.2, on which I have made so much hang, threatens to collapse. According to 1.1, it is a first principle that all deliverances of consciousness are true. If first principles must be true, it follows from 1.1 that consciousness is a reliable faculty, and if reliabilism is correct, it follows that all deliverances of consciousness are justified (or evident). Given that our beliefs in the deliverances of consciousness are not inferred from other beliefs, it follows further that the deliverances of consciousness are *immediately* evident.[22] That is exactly what 1.2 says, so we have shown that if reliabilism is correct, the first principle specified by 1.1 implies 1.2.[23]

---

He concludes from this that Reid is neither a particularist nor a methodist in Chisholm's senses of these terms (Chisholm 1973). Particularists hold that we derive general principles of evidence from propositions saying that this or that particular belief is evident; methodists hold that we derive the latter propositions from the former. According to Lehrer, Reid holds that there is no derivation in either direction, since both types of proposition are immediately evident.

Particularism in my sense does not automatically imply particularism in Chisholm's sense. The particularism I attribute to Reid holds that some particular propositions are self-evident, but it does not necessarily imply what particularism in Chisholm's sense implies: that some propositions *ascribing the property of being evident* to particular propositions are self-evident.

[22] The reason it follows that the deliverances of consciousness are *immediately* justified or evident is that (to use Goldman's terms) they are the outputs of a reliable *belief-independent* process, that is, a belief-forming process whose inputs are not other beliefs, but simply the conscious states themselves. See 1979:13.

[23] In discussion, Hud Hudson has raised the question whether there may not also be a collapse in the other direction. Suppose I were conscious of the general truth $(p)(Cp \to p)$; it would then by 1.2 be a first principle that $(p)(Cp \to p)$, just as 1.1 says. However, I believe that Reid would deny that $(p)(Cp \to p)$ can be a proper object of consciousness. He defines consciousness as "that immediate knowledge which we have of our present thoughts and purposes, and in general, of all the present operations of our minds" (EIP 1.1:24). General facts about consciousness are not themselves present operations of our minds.

However, this collapse would not undermine the main results for which I have argued above. It would remain true that Reidian first principles include particular propositions, and it would also remain true that track-record arguments for the reliability of a faculty are not viciously circular. Indeed, with the reliability theory in the background, such arguments are all the more obviously legitimate: if the reliability of a faculty is all it takes to make its deliverances justified, it is perfectly clear that one may come to know that the premises of a track-record argument are true without already having to know that its conclusion is true.[24]

I turn now to the bearing of reliabilism on the question of this section, whether epistemic principles can be first principles. If reliabilism is correct, epistemic principles are simply reliability principles, that is, principles affirming the reliability of one or another faculty or belief-forming process. Our question would therefore reduce to this: are reliability principles ever self-evident? For example, is it immediately evident that everything distinctly perceived is true, or that everything distinctly remembered is true? Is it even immediately evident that perception and memory yield truth most of the time? I am reluctant to say yes, at least if self-evidence connotes any sort of obviousness or inescapability.[25] The main ground for my reluctance is that no proposition that is both *general* and *contingent* seems to be a good candidate for being self-evident. There are, of course, general propositions that are self-evident (e.g., all triangles have three angles), and there are also contingent propositions that are self-evident (e.g., I am now conscious), but are there any self-evident propositions that are *both* general and contingent in the way that reliability principles are?[26] It is hard for me to see how there could be.[27]

Having said this, I must confess that Reid may think otherwise. He states his Principle 7 thus: "Another first principle is, that the natural faculties, by which we distinguish truth from error, are not fallacious" (EIP 6.5:480). He also speaks of the truth and fidelity of our faculties as well as their nonfallaciousness. So he does seem to be claiming self-evidence for the contingent and general proposition that

---

[24] It is incongruous, then, for Alston to attribute reliabilism to Reid in his 1985 and then go on to commend him for exposing the circularity of arguments for the reliability of our faculties.

[25] Alston (1985) expresses similar reluctance. It leads him to downplay Reid's attributions of self-evidence to epistemic principles; it leads me to wonder whether Alston is right in construing Reid's epistemic principles as reliability principles.

[26] Reliability principles are not only contingent, but *deeply* contingent in the sense marked out by Evans (1985a): a mere understanding of sentences expressing them does not suffice for knowing that those sentences are true, as in Kripkean examples of the so-called contingent a priori.

[27] On the other hand, it may be that in saying this I am not adhering consistently to the hypothesis of reliabilism. If I came to believe immediately in the reliability of some faculty through a faculty that was itself reliable, would it not follow on reliabilist assumptions that my belief was immediately justified?

our faculties are reliable, or at least not unreliable in a wholesale way. That Reid holds the reliability of our faculties to be self-evident is a cardinal point of Lehrer's interpretation of Reid, discussed in chapter 13, but I do not see how Reid can get away with it.

The other issue bearing on the question of this section is whether first principles carry a guarantee of truth. If the answer were yes, then every epistemic principle in the style of 1.2 would imply a reliability principle. For example, if deliverances of sense perception are first principles (as 5.2 says) and if being a first principle implies being true, it would follow that all deliverances of sense perception are true. Consequently, if it is implausible to regard reliability principles as self-evident (as I have suggested), it would also be implausible to regard epistemic principles as self-evident.

So we need to know whether Reid holds that anything having the evidence of a first principle is true. In other words, is the evidence of first principles for Reid infallible or merely presumptive and prima facie?[28] Here I think Reid's answer varies depending on which of our faculties is at issue.[29] He clearly thinks that the evidence conferred by consciousness is a guarantee of truth:

> The testimony of consciousness can never deceive. . . . The testimony of consciousness is always unerring, nor was it ever called in question by the greatest skeptics, ancient or modern. (EAP 1.1:9; see also EIP 6.7:522)

On the other hand, he equally clearly thinks that beliefs about other minds and beliefs based on testimony may be mistaken, even though (as I interpret him) such beliefs may be immediately evident (EIP 6.4:483–84; IHM 6.20:171). Despite some ambivalence on his part, I believe he also allows that immediately evident beliefs of perception, memory, and reason can be mistaken. In the chapter entitled "Of the Fallacy of the Senses," he argues that many alleged errors of the senses are really errors in reasoning, but he seems prepared to concede in the end that some so-called deceptions of the senses (e.g., pains felt in an amputated limb) are properly so called (EIP 2.22:251 and 2.18:214; see also EAP 3.3.6:179). At EIP 1.2:42, he says that the evidence of memory is "next to" that of consciousness. If memory were infallible,

---

[28] For the term "presumptive evidence" (*Vermutungsevidenz*), see Meinong (1886) 1973. For discussion of the similar idea of prima facie evidence, see Pollock 1974.

[29] Reid nearly states the view I want to attribute to him at EIP 6.4:455: "Some first principles yield conclusions that are certain, others such as are probable." Had he been operating with my distinction between first principles and epistemic principles, he would have put the point by saying, "Some epistemic principles yield first principles that are certain, others first principles that are probable."

why would its evidence not be on a *level* with that of consciousness? Finally, he suggests that even the evidence of a proposition in Euclid is comparable to that of a credible witness, subject to either confirmation or weakening by further scrutiny (EIP 7.4:568; see also EIP 6.4:465–66). I take these points to corroborate the classification of Reid as a fallibilist in epistemology, even as regards first principles.

If Reid were either a reliabilist or an infallibilist about evidence, it would be implausible for him to regard epistemic principles as first principles, as argued five paragraphs back. But suppose instead that he is a *normativist*—someone for whom evidence (that is, the quality of being evident) is a normative category not logically tied to reliability, as in the epistemological writings of R. M. Chisholm. And suppose further (as suggested in the previous paragraph) that he has a fallibilist conception of evidence, allowing that a proposition can be evident (and even self-evident) without being true. Then epistemic principles would not entail reliability principles, and it would be easier to classify them as self-evident. The epistemic principle governing memory, for example, would not say that all or even most memory beliefs are true; it would say that remembered propositions are presumptively evident or prima facie justified simply in virtue of being remembered.

Epistemic principles would still be general, so if nothing both contingent and general can be self-evident, the classification of epistemic principles as self-evident would require that epistemic principles be necessary truths. That is not out of the question. Reid believes that there are necessary general truths in taste and morals, so why not also in epistemology, if the epistemic is another species of the normative?

Alston raises the possibility that Reid is a normativist, but proceeds to downplay it. He says, "Reid distances himself from Chisholm by giving a psychological characterization of evidence" (1985:438), citing the following passages:

> We give the name of evidence to whatever is a ground of belief. (EIP 2.20:228)

> [The different kinds of evidence] seem to me to agree only in this, that they are fitted by nature to produce belief in the human mind. (EIP 2.20:229)

Alston's verdict is premature. Within a page of the remarks he cites, we find this as well:

> I shall take it for granted, that the evidence of sense, when the proper circumstances concur, is *good* evidence, and a *just* ground of belief.... All good evidence is commonly called *reasonable* evidence, and very justly, because it *ought* to govern our belief as reasonable creatures. (EIP 2.20:229–30, emphases added)

Moreover, here is a passage that indicates that Reid does not want to reduce the evident to a purely psychological matter of what we must believe:

> This, however, is certain, that such is the constitution of the human mind, that evidence discerned by us, forces a corresponding degree of assent. And a man who perfectly understood a just syllogism, without believing that the conclusion follows from the premises, would be a greater monster than a man born without hands or feet. (EIP 6.5:481)

Since monsters are not logical impossibilities (chimeras are not round squares), Reid is implying that it is contingent that our assent follows upon evidence. It would *not* be contingent if the evident were *defined* as what compels assent.[30]

I end this section by commenting on the striking passage in which Reid compares evidence to light:

> How then come we to be assured of this fundamental truth on which all others rest? [Reid is speaking of his Principle 7, that our faculties are not fallacious.] Perhaps evidence, as in many other respects it resembles light, so in this also, that as light, which is the discoverer of all visible objects, discovers itself at the same time; so evidence, which is the voucher for all truth, vouches for itself at the same time. (EIP 6.5:481)

Is Reid not saying here that general principles about evidence may be self-evident themselves, and thus that epistemic principles may be first principles?[31] The matter is not entirely clear, for there are at least two readings of the passage. On the first, Reid is saying that whatever makes something evident also makes it evident that it is evident—a principle we might symbolize as $(p)(Ep \rightarrow EEp)$. This reading is supported by the formulation "evidence, which is the voucher for all truth, vouches for itself at the same time." On the second, Reid is saying that whenever it is evident through a faculty F that p, it is also evident that it is evident through F that p, or that F is a source of evidence. In symbols, $(p)[(Ep \text{ because } Fp) \rightarrow E(p)(Fp \rightarrow Ep)]$. Perhaps this is the reading that is required if the analogy with light is to answer Reid's question: how we come to be assured that our faculties are not fallacious. On both readings, propositions ascribing evidence are themselves evident, but there is an important difference: on the first reading, the second-level propositions that are evident are propositions ascribing evidence to *single* propositions, whereas on the second reading, they are propositions ascribing evidence to *all* propositions

---

[30] For more on Reidian evidence as not merely a psychological notion, see Rysiew 2005.

[31] This has been proposed to me by Dale Tuggy. See also Lehrer 1990:41.

vouched for by a given source. Only in the latter case would a *general* principle about evidence be evident; hence, only in the latter case would Reid be implying that epistemic principles are themselves first principles.

## K. THE EPISTEMIC STATUS OF RELIABILITY PRINCIPLES

What is the epistemic status of principles affirming the reliability of one or more of our cognitive faculties? There seem to be just three possible answers: either they are immediately justified (justified despite not being inferred from anything else), or they are mediately justified (justified because they are inferred from something else), or they are not justified at all.

Alston opposes assigning either of the first two statuses to reliability principles. He says it is implausible (as I agree) to take any proposition about the reliability of a faculty, such as sense perception, to be immediately justified or self-evident.[32] And he dismisses the possibility that they are mediately justified on the ground that they could have that status only through an argument that is epistemically circular.

If reliability principles are neither mediately nor immediately justified, where does that leave us? Here is what Alston has to say:

> What the circularity thesis [i.e., "epistemic circularity infects all attempts to demonstrate the reliability of a basic ground of belief"] shows is that there is no possibility of establishing either the reliability or the unreliability of our basic cognitive faculties. This means that there is, as we might say, no *theoretical* problem as to their reliability; i.e., there is no such theoretical problem *for us*, none to which we can address ourselves. The most we have is a practical problem. (1985:447)

He goes on to suggest that the solution to the practical problem is that we should "acquiesce gladly" in our native tendencies of belief.

I have two questions to raise about Alston's suggestion. First, does Alston believe that a supposed theoretical problem ceases to be a problem (or at any rate, ceases to be a theoretical problem) once it is determined that no solution is possible? Would that all theoretical problems were so easily dissolvable! Second, is Alston insinuating that there is a *fourth* position on the status of reliability principles, distinct from the three we have mentioned? But how *can* there be—our threefold division was

---

[32] "Any tendency to suppose [a principle affirming the reliability of sense perception] to be self-evident can be put down to a confusion between self-evidence and being strongly inclined to accept the proposition without question" (1986:4).

logically exhaustive! A principle is either justified or not, and if justified, justified either mediately or immediately.

Reid agrees:

> With regard to this point, we must hold one of these three things, either that it is an opinion, for which we have no evidence, and which men have foolishly taken up without ground; or, *secondly*, that it is capable of direct proof by argument; or, *thirdly*, that it is self-evident, and needs no proof, but ought to be received as an axiom, which cannot, by reasonable men, be called in question. (EIP 6.6:497; see also EAP 5.1:369, lines 7–8)

I believe some of the attractiveness of any "practical" solution is bound to dissipate as soon as we squarely recognize that it places reliability principles in the first of the categories Reid mentions here—namely, opinions for which we have no evidence and have taken up without ground.

If we *do* wish to assign to reliability principles some positive epistemic status, but cannot see our way to calling them immediately evident, I do not think we have any other option but to embrace the allegedly circular justification of them I outline in section H.

## L. CONCLUSION

In the interpretation I have proposed here, the epistemological principles Reid formulates in EIP 6.5 are principles of evidence rather than principles of truth. They are epistemic principles telling us that the particular deliverances of consciousness, memory, and perception (among other faculties) are first principles, that is, self-evident propositions from which we may derive further knowledge. The epistemic principles may or may not be first principles themselves—that is a point on which I reached no definite answer. Principles of truth corresponding to the epistemic principles—that is, principles affirming the reliability of consciousness, memory, and perception—may be justified in noncircular fashion by appeal to the first principles Reid's epistemic principles lay down.

# 12

## EPISTEMOLOGY 2

## REID'S RESPONSE TO THE SKEPTIC

Reason, says the sceptic, is the only judge of truth, and you ought to throw off every opinion and every belief that is not grounded on reason. Why, Sir, should I believe the faculty of reason more than that of perception; they came both out of the same shop, and were made by the same artist; and if he puts one piece of false ware into my hands, what should hinder him from putting another? (Thomas Reid, *IHM 6.20:169*)

Reid is renowned for his response to the skeptic. But does he really have one? If ridicule is a response, the answer is yes.[1] But does he have a *refutation* of skepticism, or anything to offer by way of undercutting it? To answer that question, I discuss the potential bearing against skepticism of three Reidian motifs—direct realism, naturalism, and externalism. (A fourth motif, nativism, was discussed in chapter 2 and found to have no bearing against epistemological skepticism.) I argue that Reid's externalism is the most potent anti-skeptical element in his epistemology. But externalism has been disparaged of late precisely *because* it affords an easy reply to the skeptic. I therefore consider criticisms of externalism and examine a prominent contemporary alternative to it.

[1] For example, Reid says the upshot of believing the skeptic's injunction not to believe my senses would be this: "I break my nose against a post that comes in my way; I step into a dirty kennel; and, after twenty such wise and rational actions, I am taken up and clapt into a mad-house" (IHM 6.20:170). Reid even endorses ridicule as "the proper method of refuting an absurdity" (EIP 6.6:507). He notes that "to discountenance absurdity, Nature hath given us a particular emotion, to wit, that of ridicule, which seems intended for this very purpose of putting out of countenance what is absurd, either in opinion or practice" (EIP 6.4:462). For more on the epistemic force of ridicule in Reid's thought, see Grandi 2008.

Epistemological skepticisms may be distinguished by asking two questions. First, what epistemic commodity does the skeptic deny us: certainty, knowledge, justification adequate for knowledge, or any degree of justification whatever? Second, in what sphere of belief is the commodity denied us: beliefs about the external world, the past, the future, the minds of others, the truths of reason, or all beliefs whatsoever? I shall focus here mainly on skepticism that denies that we have knowledge or adequately justified belief concerning objects in the external world. Such was Reid's main focus, though he also discusses skepticism in other domains or says things about one that carry over to others.

## A. DIRECT REALISM

In Reid's view, the main source of skepticism about the external world is the theory of ideas, which is why he spends so much effort in exorcising it. If I do not see the tree in my back yard, but only an idea of it, how can I know that the tree is anything like my idea? More radically still, how can I know that the tree (or any external object) is there at all? It would evidently have to be by some kind of inference, but the inference is notoriously problematic. As Hume argues, the inference would presumably go from the idea as effect to the object as cause. But if Hume's philosophy is correct, we have reason to believe in a causal connection between Xs and Ys only if we have experienced Xs conjoined with Ys in the past. And if the theory of ideas is correct, we have *never* experienced any of the Ys—any objects beyond our ideas. It follows that we are trapped behind the veil of ideas and are in no position to make any causal inferences to external objects (ECHU, section 12).[2]

Having discussed Reid's critique of the theory of ideas and his direct realist alternative in previous chapters, we have only two questions to address here: Does the theory of ideas inevitably lead to skepticism? Conversely, may we avoid skepticism by rejecting ideas and embracing direct realism?

Reid thought the answer to both questions is *yes*—that the theory of ideas and skepticism stand or fall together. Here are three passages in which he affirms that the theory of ideas is sufficient to engender skepticism:

> The theory of ideas has skepticism "inlaid in it, and reared along with it." (IHM 1.7:23)

> The natural issue of [the ideal system] is scepticism with regard to every thing except the existence of our ideas, and of their necessary relations which appear upon comparing them. (IHM 7:212)

---

[2] For a similar argument, see the Fourth Paralogism in Kant's *Critique of Pure Reason*, A366–67.

But that which chiefly led Descartes to think that he ought not to trust to his senses without proof of their veracity, was, that he took it for granted, as all Philosophers had done before him, that he did not perceive external objects themselves, but certain images of them in his own mind, called ideas. He was certain by consciousness, that he had the ideas of sun and moon, earth and sea; but how could he be assured that there really existed external objects like to these ideas? (EIP 2.8:116; see also IHM 2.3:28, IHM 7: 10, EIP 2.14:186, EIP 3.7:289, EIP 6.3:446 and 450)

And here are two passages in which he implies that the theory of ideas is necessary for engendering skepticism:

The sceptical system "leans with its whole weight" upon the theory of ideas. (IHM Dedication:4)

All the arguments urged by Berkeley and Hume against the existence of a material world are grounded upon this principle, That we do not perceive external objects themselves, but certain images or ideas in our own minds. (EIP 6.5:478)

If the theory of ideas is necessary for engendering skepticism, denying that theory and affirming direct realism instead should be sufficient for avoiding skepticism. But is affirming direct realism really sufficient for avoiding skepticism? Here is one reason for thinking not: directly seeing (or otherwise perceiving) something that is in fact a K is not sufficient for knowing that there is a K there to be seen. This is immediately clear if we let "K" stand for a kind of thing that is the least bit esoteric. I may see a carburetor without knowing that it is a carburetor I am seeing.

Even if we restrict the permissible values of "K" to some narrowly demarcated range of easily recognizable things, it is not clear that directly seeing a K is sufficient for knowing that a K is there. Direct realism by itself does not give us sufficient resources for answering skeptical arguments along the following lines:

1. I know that there is a hand in front of me only if know that I am not in an elaborate dream or Matrix set-up making me believe erroneously that there is a hand in front of me.[3]
2. I do not know that I am not in any such elaborate dream or Matrix set-up.
3. Therefore, I do not know that there is a hand in front of me.

---

[3] This premise can be derived from the principle that knowledge is closed under known implication together with the assumption that I do know such obvious implications as that from "there is a hand in front of me" to "I do not erroneously believe that there is a hand in front of me."

The premises of this argument are compatible with direct realism. Let me perceive a hand as directly as you please; I still do not thereby know that I am not dreaming or caught up in the Matrix.

So direct realism is not sufficient for avoiding skepticism. Is it necessary? This, too, can be questioned. There are three types of thinkers who aspire to be anti-skeptical without embracing direct realism: phenomenalists, advocates of inference to the best explanation, and proponents of sui generis epistemic principles.

Phenomenalists renounce realism but keep directness. For an ontological phenomenalist like Berkeley, a table or a cherry is a congeries of ideas, so in perceiving an idea I am ipso facto aware of something that is (or may be) part of a physical thing. For a linguistic phenomenalist like A. J. Ayer or C. I. Lewis, any statement about a table is logically equivalent to a complicated statement about what sense data are being sensed or would be sensed under various conditions, so in sensing a sense datum, one can know that part of the logical content of the table statement is true. I set aside the question whether phenomenalism is true. Suffice it to say that as an epistemological strategy, phenomenalism still has significant gaps to deal with. How do I know, on a given occasion of perceiving a table-shaped expanse of brown, that all the other sense data are there or in the offing that would have to be there if I really am perceiving a table? These sense data include appropriately shaped expanses visible from other viewpoints, rapping sounds heard if I strike with my knuckles, and so on into the thousands.

Partisans of the second strategy, inference to the best explanation, retain realism while abandoning directness, claiming that we can secure knowledge of the external world even if ideas are all we perceive. They maintain that Hume's strictures on causal inference, which permit us to infer the existence only of kinds of things that we have previously observed directly, are too narrow. We can postulate a world of objects that is in some way isomorphic to our ideas, and if this postulate is the best explanation of our ideas (best because simplest, perhaps), we are adequately justified in believing it even if we cannot know for certain that it is true. Skepticism of all but the first degree (which denies us *certainty* concerning the external world) is avoided. This sort of anti-skeptical strategy has been defended in recent epistemology by Jonathan Vogel (1990) and Laurence BonJour (2002, chapter 7).[4]

Inference to the best explanation is not a strategy that would have appealed to Reid. In his discussion of proper philosophical method, Reid inveighs against the acceptance of hypotheses. By a hypothesis he means a proposition whose only recommendation to our belief is that it would, if true, explain other things that we know

---

[4] BonJour is explicitly an indirect realist. I am not sure about Vogel, but direct realism forms no part of his anti-skeptical strategy.

to be true, but whose truth is not open to verification by any more direct method. An example is the Indian philosopher's hypothesis of a great elephant supporting the earth on its back, offered to explain why the earth does not hurtle downward. "His elephant was a hypothesis, and our hypotheses are elephants" (IHM 6.19:163). By what Reid takes to be proper Newtonian method, a hypothesis is legitimately invoked to explain phenomena only when it is supported by induction from the phenomena themselves—either the phenomena to be explained or other related phenomena. Hypotheses that transcend the phenomena altogether—and if any nonphenomenalist version of the theory of ideas is true, that includes even humdrum hypotheses about tables and chairs—are to be abjured (EIP 1.3:47–52).

The third way of circumventing skepticism without essential reliance on direct realism ironically has precedent in Reid's own philosophy. I have in mind epistemologies such as Chisholm's, which lay down epistemic principles whereby beliefs in certain sorts of propositions are justified by certain sorts of experiences or in certain sorts of conditions. For example, one of Chisholm's principles is the following:

> For any subject S, if S believes, without ground for doubt, that he is perceiving something to be F, then it is beyond reasonable doubt for S that he perceives something to be F [and thus that there is something F]. (1977:76)[5]

Reid lays down similar sounding principles, as discussed in the preceding chapter. It is a question of some moment what justifies such principles themselves; promulgating them may simply invite the charge that one is begging the question against the skeptic. Be that as it may, my point for now is just that the legitimacy of such principles governing some domain need not be tied (or so it may be argued) to direct realism about that domain.

To illustrate, here again is Reid's principle pertaining to our justification for believing in other minds:

> Another first principle I take to be, That certain features of the countenance, sounds of the voice, and gestures of the body, indicate certain thoughts and dispositions of mind. (EIP 6.5:484)

Reid does not believe that anything like direct realism is true about the minds of other people. He does not believe that we have any access to the mental states of

---

[5] By "believing that one perceives," Chisholm is not referring to a second-order act of believing directed at a first-order act of perceiving, but to *ostensible* perceiving—a state just like perceiving, but not necessarily veridical.

others not mediated by their faces, words, and gestures. If it is nonetheless permissible to lay down the principle above, why should it not also be permissible for an indirect realist, who believes our access to the physical world is mediated by our own ideas, to lay down a parallel principle such as the following?

> Another first principle I take to be, that certain ideas and images presented to the senses, indicate certain objects and happenings external to the mind.

I do not say there is no good answer to this question, but until we have one, we may not assume that indirect realism inevitably engenders skepticism.[6]

I myself think that the fight for direct realism is a fight well worth fighting, and I am grateful to Reid for his contributions to the campaign. However, I do not see the avoidance of skepticism as the main thing at stake. When I look at the sky at sunset, I like to believe that the colors and forms I see are there on the horizon, not simply splashed across some screen inside my mind. This is not merely because I desire to *know* what my environment is like. Even if God were to assure me that there is a systematic correspondence between what I see and what is there, my pleasure in the experience would be diminished by the thought that the beauties I see are only in me.[7]

## B. NATURALISM

Reid tells us again and again that we cannot help believing in the existence of external bodies when we have perceptual experiences of them. Here are two representative passages:

> Even those philosophers who have disowned the authority of our notions of an external material world, confess, that they find themselves under a necessity of submitting to their power.
>
> Methinks, therefore, it were better to make a virtue of necessity; and since we cannot get rid of the vulgar notion and belief of an external world, to reconcile our reason to it as well as we can. (IHM 5.7:68)

---

[6] As John Greco points out (2004:151), Reid notes that the ancient Greek philosophers believed in a materialized version of the theory of ideas, but were not skeptics (IHM 7:210). This is either a tacit admission on Reid's part that the theory of ideas alone does not entail skepticism or a tacit charge that the ancients were inconsistent. Greco also suggests that one who adheres to the theory of ideas could still hold a theory of evidence that provides for noninferential knowledge of external things (1995).

[7] Contrast the attitude of Whitehead: "The poets are entirely mistaken. They should address their lyrics to themselves, and should turn them into odes of self-congratulation on the excellency of the human mind. Nature is a dull affair, soundless, scentless, colourless; merely the hurrying of material, endlessly, meaninglessly" (1925:80).

My belief is carried along by perception, as irresistibly as my body by the earth. And the greatest sceptic will find himself to be in the same condition. (IHM 6.20:169)

Is there any leverage to be gotten here against the external world skeptic? Yes, say those philosophers who promote what they call *naturalism*. A recent book devoted to this topic begins thus:

Historically, one of the ways in which people have attempted to counter scepticism has been by appeal to . . . "the natural"—to how we are constituted, to what we, as human beings, are and do in the arena of believing. (Ferreira 1986:vii)

In a similar vein, Derek R. Brookes says in his introduction to Reid's *Inquiry* that skepticism is untenable because "the operation of mind by which we form beliefs is largely involuntary and irresistible, much like breathing or swallowing" (IHM:xiii).

P. F. Strawson has championed the naturalist attitude in his book *Skepticism and Naturalism* (1985, especially chapter 1). Strawson says that according to the naturalist position, "whatever arguments may be produced on one side or the other of the question, we simply *cannot help* believing in the existence of body" (10). Skeptical arguments are therefore to be *neglected*: "neglected because they are *idle*; powerless against the force of nature, of our naturally implanted disposition to belief" (13).

Ironically, Strawson finds that a leading exponent of the naturalist attitude is the great skeptic Hume himself.[8] Here are some relevant quotations from Hume:

Nature, by an absolute and uncontrollable necessity has determin'd us to judge as well as to breathe and feel. (THN 1.4.1:183)

Nature has not left this [whether to believe in body] to [our] choice, and has doubtless esteem'd it an affair of too great importance to be trusted to our uncertain reasonings and speculations. (THN 1.4.2:187)

Other observers have also pointed out that Hume is no less aware than Reid of the fact that we cannot help believing as we do (Loeb 2007). In a famous remark in 1812, Thomas Brown declared that the difference between Reid and Hume on this score is only one of emphasis:

Reid bawled out, We must believe an outward world; but added in a whisper, We can give no reason for our belief. Hume cries out, We can give no reason for such a notion; and whispers, I own we cannot get rid of it. (Quoted in Galen Strawson 1990)

---

[8] Strawson's other main model of the naturalist attitude is the Wittgenstein of *On Certainty* (1969). For an interpretation of Reid highlighting similarities with Wittgenstein, see Wolterstorff 2000 and 2001:231–44.

What exactly is the anti-skeptical significance of the fact that we cannot help believing certain things? If skepticism is the position that we have no knowledge or adequately justified belief in the existence of bodies, I cannot see that it has any. I think it likely that Hume would agree. In the following passage Hume is speaking of induction, but his point is equally applicable to our beliefs about the material world:

> My practice, you say, refutes my doubts. But you mistake the purport of my question. As an agent, I am quite satisfied in the point; but as a philosopher, who has some share of curiosity, I will not say skepticism, I want to learn the foundation of this inference. (EHU 4.2:38)

A philosopher who believes in material things as irresistibly as the next person may nonetheless be curious about whether and how such beliefs have justification (or amount to knowledge), and he may conclude that they do not.

We have not yet found in either Reid the naturalist or Hume the naturalist anything to counter Hume the skeptic. Naturalism as so far delineated is an antidote to skepticism only in the sense that it saves us from unbelief. It does nothing to show that our beliefs are justified or that they constitute knowledge.[9]

Naturalism may not yet be dismissed, however, for there are two proposals we should consider about how the fact that we cannot help believing certain things may be exploited against the skeptic. The first appeals to the principle that *ought* implies *can*; the second contends that the evident or justified in the way of belief must be defined in terms of what we cannot help believing.

*Ought implies can.* Reid takes it to be a first principle of morals that you cannot be blamed for doing something if it was not in your power not to do it (or blamed for not doing something if it was not in your power to do it). In effect, he holds with Kant that *ought* implies *can*. A corollary of *ought* implies *can* is that *must* implies *may*: if you must do a certain thing (cannot but do it), then it is not the case that you ought not to do it, which is to say that you are permitted to do it. If these ideas carry over into epistemology, anything you must believe is something that you may permissibly believe, and are in that sense justified in believing.

---

[9] Compare Lemos 2004:21: "If the only thing to be said in favor of our common sense beliefs is that they are irresistible, why should we not view them the way we view bad habits, such as smoking or overeating, that we continue to engage in even when reason convinces us that they should be given up?" And here is Russell, putting a speech in the mouth of a skeptic: "Let us recognize undoubtingness, therefore, as, like rage and hate and lust, one of the unfortunate passions to which our animal ancestry exposes us" ([1913] 1992:163).

Such considerations underlie Wolterstorrf's account of "Reid's way with the skeptic." Wolterstorrf characterizes Reid's skeptical opponent as saying we have an obligation to suspend our beliefs in the deliverances of perception and memory until such time as we have demonstrated that those faculties are reliable—without using perception and memory in the process. No one has ever done this (and arguably no one could). Reid's "way with the skeptic" according to Wolterstorff is this:

> There is a decisive reason for concluding that at no time . . . did they [the skeptics themselves, but the rest of us, too] have an obligation to throw off those purported believings. That reason is that they could not have done so if they had tried. (194)

Very well; we have no obligation to stop believing as we do; we are permitted to keep on believing those things we cannot help believing. But even if this permission is of a distinctively epistemic sort, not a moral sort, it seems to me to fall short of what epistemologists typically mean by warrant or justification. Knowledge is more than permitted true belief.

*The evident as the forced.* There is another way in which the fact that we cannot help believing certain things might be exploited against the skeptic. If in circumstances C we cannot help believing proposition P, then in C we have evidence for P, it might be urged, *because that is what having evidence is.* Evidence is simply whatever forces our assent, so if our sensory experiences make us believe in bodies, we thereby have evidence for that belief.

We can find a hint or two of such a position in Reid. He writes:

> We give the name of evidence to whatever is a ground of belief. . . . I confess that, although I have, as I think, a distinct notion of the different kinds of evidence above mentioned [of sense, memory, consciousness, testimony, axioms, and reasoning] . . . yet I am not able to find any common nature to which they may all be reduced. They seem to me to agree only in this, that they are all fitted by Nature to produce belief in the human mind. (EIP 2.20:228–29)

Alston cites this passage as raising the possibility that Reid meant to offer a purely psychologistic characterization of evidence (1985:438). He might also have cited IHM 5.7:71: "For first principles no other reason can be given but this, that, by the constitution of our nature, we are under a necessity of assenting to them."

A conception of evidence as what forces belief may be motivated by the following question: If God wanted to make something maximally evident to you, what would he do? Would he surround the proposition with a special kind of glow? Or would he simply make you believe it willy-nilly? It might seem that he could scarcely do better than the latter, suggesting that irresistibility is all that evidence ever is or could be.[10]

When all is said and done, however, I do not believe that Reid would define evidence as what forces belief. Perhaps there is normally an alignment between what is evident and what we must believe, but it is not a matter of definition, as may be brought out by asking a Euthyphro question: are things evident because we are forced to believe them, or are we forced to believe them because they are evident? I think Reid would endorse the latter alternative, thereby implying the falsity of the former.[11]

One reason to think that Reid would not define evidence as what forces assent is afforded by the following passage, already cited in the previous chapter:

> This, however, is certain, that such is the constitution of the human mind, that evidence discerned by us, forces a corresponding degree of assent. And a man who perfectly understood a just syllogism, without believing that the conclusion follows from the premises, would be a greater monster than a man born without hands or feet. (EIP 6.5:481)

Here it is the natural constitution of our minds that is responsible for evidence forcing our assent, not the definition of evidence. Moreover, if evidence were *defined* as what compels assent, a man who refused to accept an evident syllogism would not be a "monster," as Reid says, but an impossibility.

Another reason not to define evident beliefs as forced beliefs emerges when we consider the analog of an argument Reid gives about moral principles. In his discussion of morals, Reid considers the view that right and wrong are simply matters of agreeing or disagreeing with our moral sense—of eliciting approbation or condemnation from us. He argues against the view as follows (EIP 6.6:494–95; see also EIP 7.2):

---

[10] A notion of evidence along these lines is discussed by Plantinga under the name "impulsional evidence"—a strong inclination to believe something, along with a perception of the attractiveness or inevitability of believing it in the circumstances. He does not, however, regard impulsional evidence as sufficient for warrant or justification. See Plantinga 1993b:192–93.

[11] As in Socrates' original question—is the action pious because the gods love it, or do the gods love it because it is pious?—"because" is not univocal in the two alternatives. In the first Reidian alternative (things are evident because we are forced to believe them), the "because" is constitutional; in the second (we are forced to believe them because they are evident—or more accurately, because we perceive their evidence), the "because" is causal. The equivocation does not harm the argument, though, because nothing can cause what it is constituted by.

1. If right and wrong were correctly definable as agreeing or not with our moral sense, then moral principles—principles specifying which types of action are right and which wrong—would be contingent. (It is contingent that actions of a given type elicit approval rather than disgust from our moral sense.)
2. But in fact moral principles are necessary truths.
3. Therefore, right and wrong are not correctly definable as agreeing or not with our moral sense.

The analogous argument in epistemology would run thus:

1. If being evident were just a matter of forcing our assent, then epistemic principles—principles specifying which types of belief are evident—would be contingent.
2. But in fact epistemic principles are necessary truths.
3. Therefore, being evident is not just a matter of forcing our assent.

Whether Reid would give this argument depends on whether he agrees with the premise that epistemic principles are necessary. I return to this question in section C of this chapter and in section D of chapter 16.

I end this section with one more comparison of Reid to Hume. Hume, like Reid, occasionally says things that imply an equation of the evident with that which we cannot help believing. He defines belief in terms of the force and vivacity of ideas, but then goes on to define evidence in the same way (THN 1.3.13:154). He also treats it as an objection to his philosophy that "the evidence of ancient history will decay on my system, yet posterity will believe in Caesar"—as though there must be evidence where there is belief. But again like Reid, Hume also says things that imply that the evident *cannot* be equated with what must be believed. In the essay on miracles, he says "A wise man, therefore, proportions his belief to the evidence" (EHU 10.1:110). If strength of evidence were simply defined as strength of belief, wisdom would be the lot of every man, and there would have been no need for Hume to compose his "everlasting check to all kinds of superstitious delusion."

## C. EXTERNALISM

The third anti-skeptical motif is *externalism*. The name is not to be found in Reid, but the doctrine almost certainly is, as argued in the previous chapter. Externalism is so called because it holds that there are important knowledge-making factors that lie (or may lie) outside the subject's knowledge—they do their work of conferring or enabling knowledge regardless of whether the subject knows they obtain. In this section I bring out the externalist side of Reid's epistemology further and show how it undercuts one of the most powerful arguments in the skeptic's arsenal.

The argument I have in mind is sometimes called "the Problem of the Criterion." It may be expressed in a pair of supposedly rhetorical questions: How can I know that any of my methods of obtaining knowledge are reliable (or that some criterion for knowing is correct) unless I know some other propositions from which to derive these facts? But how can I know those other propositions are true unless I already know, concerning some method of obtaining knowledge, that it is reliable? (See Chisholm 1973, Van Cleve 1979, and Huemer 2001:11–13.)

To sharpen the argument, let's convert the rhetorical questions into premises. One premise endorses a requirement on knowledge accepted by many thinkers and articulated by Stewart Cohen as follows:

(KR) A potential knowledge source K can yield knowledge for a subject S only if S knows K is reliable. (Cohen 2002)

"KR" is short for "knowledge of reliability." What the principle says is that no alleged source of knowledge, such as perception, memory, or reason, yields knowledge for a person unless the person knows that the source is reliable, in the sense of producing true beliefs all or most of the time. In short, knowledge of the reliability of K is a necessary condition for having any knowledge by means of K. Moreover, in the version of the premise I use here, the necessary condition is an *antecedent* condition of knowledge—one cannot know anything through K unless one *first* knows K is reliable.

The other premise affirms that knowledge of the reliability of a source can come about in one way only, namely, by inference from premises obtained through that very source. For example, to know that perception is reliable, I would have to tote up a wide range of instances in which I believed things on the strength of perception (that here is a hand, there is a goat, and so forth), note that the vast majority of things I believed in these various instances were true, and conclude by induction that perception is reliable. In other words, I would have to give a track-record argument of the sort described in the previous chapter. Now a key feature of a track-record argument for the reliability of a supposed source of knowledge is apparently this: to establish that its premises are true, one must rely on the very source on behalf of which the argument is given. How could I verify that most of my perceptual beliefs have been true—that there really were hands or goats and so forth on the occasions when I thought I saw or felt them? Presumably, only by further exercises of perception.[12]

---

[12] It might be thought that I could rely in some cases on means of knowing other than perception, such as the testimony of witnesses or the information provided by surveillance cameras. But I would still be relying on perception to know what the witnesses are saying or what the cameras are showing, and I would also need to rely on my own previous perceptions to know that witnesses and cameras generally do not lie. There is no escaping reliance on perception to ascertain the veracity of perception.

So it appears that the reliability of a source (at least if it is a fundamental source, that is, a way of knowing about its domain on which all other ways of knowing about that domain depend) can be vouchsafed only by using deliverances of that very source.[13]

If we put these two points together, we are confronted with the following skeptical dyad:

(1) We can know that a deliverance of K is true only if we first know that K is reliable.

(2) We can know that K is reliable only if we first know, concerning certain of its deliverances, that they are true.

If (1) and (2) are both true, skepticism is the inescapable consequence. Clearly, if we cannot know either of two things without knowing the other *first*, we cannot know either of them at all. It thus follows from (1) and (2) that we cannot know that any source is reliable *or that any single deliverance of any source is true*. And if we cannot know that any deliverance of any source is true, we cannot know anything at all.

How are we to avoid this sweeping skeptical result? Plainly, we must deny either (1) or (2). In this section, I consider two interpretations of Reid as an externalist who would have us deny (1). In section E and chapter 13, I consider epistemologies and interpretations of Reid that would have us deny (2) instead.

The first interpretation of Reid as an externalist takes him to be a Goldman-style reliabilist. According to reliabilism, a necessary and sufficient condition for a belief's being justified (and so potentially a piece of knowledge) is its having been produced by a reliable process or, in language closer to Reid's, its having issued from a reliable source or faculty (Goldman 1979). For a belief to be justified according to reliabilism, it is not necessary that the subject *know* that the process that produced the belief is reliable; it suffices that the process *be* reliable. The KR requirement is explicitly rejected.

The most fully developed interpretation of Reid as a reliabilist is that put forth by Philip de Bary (2002).[14] According to de Bary, when Reid draws up his list of first principles, he is in the first instance simply formulating psychological laws about human belief formation—laws specifying what sorts of things people instinctively and inevitably believe in various circumstances. When I have a perception of a tree or a star, I automatically believe that one is there; when I remember walking on the beach yesterday, I believe that I did so; and so on. On a naturalist interpretation of

---

[13] Huemer (2001) adds that if we *did* use another source to vouch for the reliability of the original source, the same skeptical problem could be raised concerning the further source, setting in motion a regress that ends only if we eventually use some source on its own behalf.

[14] Alston attributes a reliability theory to Reid in Alston 1985. Plantinga attributes to Reid something like his own "proper function" theory, which is a cousin of reliabilism (1993b:50).

Reid, that would be the end of the matter. But according to de Bary, if Reid went no further than this, his list of first principles would "lack any epistemological bite" (65). Reid does go further, says de Bary, by embedding his principles in a framework of reliabilism. Reid believes that "the instinctive beliefs of healthy people . . . tend towards the truth" and that such a tendency is sufficient for their being justified and amounting to knowledge when they are true (83). So the various classes of belief marked out in Reid's list of first principles are not only psychologically immediate and irresistible, but epistemically justified. When true, they qualify as knowledge, and this is so regardless of whether the believer knows anything about the reliability of his own cognitive mechanisms. As advertised, the KR requirement and its attendant skepticism are rejected.

In the second externalist interpretation of Reid, which is the one I favor, he is an externalist, but *not* a reliabilist. This is a combination whose possibility is often overlooked. To satisfy ourselves that it is possible, we may note that there are non-reliabilist views, including views often considered to be paradigms of internalism, that are externalist in the sense I have defined above. A case in point is Chisholm:

> The concept of epistemic justification is . . . *internal* . . . in that one can find out directly, by *reflection*, what one is justified in believing at any time. (Chisholm 1989:7)[15]

That sentence makes Chisholm an internalist in at least one sense of the term—he holds that the epistemic status of a belief must be reflectively accessible to the subject.[16] At the same time, however, it makes him an externalist in the sense that is important here. "What one is justified in believing" is a function of two things, certain justifying states and the relations whereby they confer justification on what they justify. To know by reflection that one is justified in believing $p$, one must therefore know by reflection, with respect to some factor $f$, (i) that $f$ obtains and (ii) that $f$ confers justification on belief in $p$. Knowing (ii) by reflection arguably implies that justifying factors do their work even if they are not reliably connected with the truth of what they justify, since reliability relations do not seem to be the sort of thing that can be known to obtain simply by reflection. So for Chisholm, justifying factors need not be reliably connected with what they justify.[17] *A fortiori*, justifying factors

---

[15] Compare page 76 of the same work (Chisholm 1989): "The internalist assumes that, merely by reflecting upon his own conscious state, he can . . . find out, with respect to any possible belief he has, whether he is *justified* in having that belief."

[16] This position is a species of what is sometimes called access internalism. For a taxonomy of internalisms and externalisms, see Van Cleve 2003a:45–46. In the scheme offered there, Chisholm is an internalist of the 1bi and 2bi varieties.

[17] We find confirmation at Chisholm 1989:76: "According to the traditional conception of 'internal' epistemic justification, there is no *logical* connection between epistemic justification and truth."

need not be *known* to be reliably connected with what they justify. And that means that Chisholm is an externalist in the sense that matters here: there are sources of justification or knowledge that deliver their goods even if the subject does not know they are reliable.

In the interpretation of Reid I favor, he is an externalist in just this sense.[18] What makes this interpretation possible is the construal of his epistemic principles in the particularist style I advocate in the preceding chapter. When Reid says that he holds as a first principle the existence of everything of which he is conscious, he does not mean that the general principle "every mental operation of which I am conscious exists" is a first principle; he means that if he is consciousness of this or that mental state, it is a first principle that the state in question exists. A similar point holds for the objects of perception and memory. In other words, the various particular deliverances of consciousness, perception, and memory are all self-evident.

Two things follow. First, Reid is a broad or nonclassical foundationalist. He thinks the range of self-evident or basic propositions extends considerably beyond the classical Cartesian basis, including not just deliverances of consciousness and rational intuition, but also propositions about the physical world and the past. Second, and more important for present purposes, he is an externalist in the sense I am highlighting. He holds that the mere fact that a proposition is a deliverance of perception, memory, or consciousness suffices to make that proposition evident. In order for someone to be justified in believing that there is a tree over there, she need only have a perception as of a tree being over there. Nothing else is necessary. In particular, it is not necessary that the subject know anything about the reliability of sense perception. She need take no thought of that. For Reid as I understand him, consciousness, memory, and perception are knowledge- or evidence-conferring factors that do their job regardless of whether the subject knows anything about their reliability. So once again, the KR requirement that forms one half of the skeptical predicament is rejected.

I must acknowledge as an obstacle to my interpretation one or two passages in which Reid seems to endorse the KR requirement after all. Here is the starkest one:

> If any truth can be said to be prior to all others in the order of nature, this [our natural faculties are not fallacious] seems to have the best claim; because in every instance of

---

[18] Externalism in this sense is compatible with internalism in another contemporary sense, sometimes called mental-state internalism: subjects alike in all their mental states must also be alike in what they are justified in believing. I do not try to settle here whether Reid is a mental-state internalist. Nor do I say that Reid arrives at his externalism via the Chisholm route through the doctrines labeled 1bi and 2bi in note 16.

assent, whether upon intuitive, demonstrative, or probable evidence, the truth of our faculties is taken for granted, and is, as it were, one of the premises on which our assent is grounded. (EIP 6.5:481)

But Reid should not have said that. If he is really saying here that the reliability of our faculties is a premise needed to support anything else we claim to know, he is contradicting his frequent insistence that perceptual beliefs, memorial beliefs, and many of our other beliefs are first principles. For this reason, Lemos regards this passage as constituting "Reid's wrong turn" (Lemos, ch. 4).[19] (On the other hand, the passage is the centerpiece of the interpretation of Reid's epistemology offered by Lehrer, which I discuss in chapter 13.)

The anti-skeptical strategy I am attributing to Reid is very much of a piece with the position in recent epistemology called *dogmatism* (with no pejorative intent) by Pryor (2000). Those who prefer a more neutral term may call it *liberalism* (Silins 2008). As Pryor characterizes it, dogmatism or liberalism is the position that there are certain things you can know without any proof, such as G. E. Moore's proposition *here is a hand*. You can know such things without proof because "whenever you have an experience as of *p*'s being the case, you thereby have immediate *prima facie* justification for believing *p*" (532). Such justification can be defeated, but in normal circumstances it gives you knowledge. Liberalism has anti-skeptical import according to Pryor because it implies the falsity of a premise that figures in many skeptical arguments: that you cannot know *p* on the strength of your experience unless you have antecedent knowledge that things are not going bad somehow—for example, that your experience is being manipulated by a Cartesian demon. Liberalism has additional anti-skeptical import according to me because it implies the falsity of KR: if perceptual experience by itself can give you knowledge of *p*, then, contrary to KR, you do not need to know first that perceptual experience is a reliable source.[20]

The particularist reading of Reid's principles is compatible with reliabilism, but does not imply it. It is compatible with reliabilism because a reliabilist may well hold

[19] Reid may be aware of the tension between the quoted remark and his other views, for he says the reliability of our faculties is "as it were" a premise on which our assent to anything else is grounded.

[20] This may be a good place to reprise the definitions of the multiple labels I am applying to Reid's epistemology. As I understand him, he holds that having an ostensible perception of a tree over there suffices to make it immediately evident that there is a tree over there. This position is particularist because what is immediately evident is a *particular* proposition, not a general proposition (for instance, one to the effect that all perceptions are true). It is dogmatic or liberal because the perception *is sufficient by itself* to confer evidence—no further knowledge is required. And it is externalist because (as was just implied) *no knowledge about the reliability of perception* is required for this evidence to be conferred.

that there are self-evident or immediately justified particular beliefs. If the belief *there is a tree over there* is both psychologically immediate (not inferred from other beliefs) and reliably formed, it will count as immediately justified for a reliabilist. But the particularist reading does not imply reliabilism, since it need not be held in conjunction with the view that being reliably formed is either necessary or sufficient for being justified. It could be joined instead with the view that being justified is a sui generis normative status not logically tied to reliability, as in the view of Chisholm discussed above.[21] There is a hint of this position in Reid's remark that he can find no common denominator to evident beliefs except that they are "fitted" to produce belief. If "fitted" is a normative term, Reid's epistemology would be more like Chisholm's normativist externalism than Goldman's reliabilist externalism.

The question of whether Reid's externalism is of the reliabilist or the normativist variety connects with the question raised in the previous section about the modal status of epistemic principles. Is it plausible to regard such principles as necessary? For a reliabilist, the answer would be no. Epistemic principles would imply reliability principles, principles affirming that beliefs formed in specified ways are always or usually true, and such principles are contingent. On the other hand, if Reid is a normativist, the answer could well be yes. Epistemic principles could have the same necessity Reid attributes to principles saying this or that type of action is right.[22] The normativist Reid is the one I find more attractive, but regardless of whether his externalism is of the normativist or reliabilist variety, it gives him an answer to the skeptical dyad.[23]

## D. PROBLEMS FOR EXTERNALISM

Liberal externalism like that I attribute to Reid has come in for censure in recent epistemology. Here I present criticisms of it advanced in Wright 2004 and Cohen 2002.

---

[21] And in the view of Pryor as well: "Perceptual justification would be in place no matter how reliable our experiences were" (536).

[22] It does not count against this possibility that Reid presents his epistemic principles under the heading "First Principles of Contingent Truths." As noted in appendix V, they are so called because they are principles that make knowledge of contingent truths possible, regardless of whether they are themselves contingent.

[23] There are two ways of circumventing the skeptical dyad I do not discuss here because they are not found in Reid. One involves a form of coherentism advocated by Cohen. Cohen accepts that knowledge of the reliability of a source and knowledge of the truth of its particular deliverances *require* each other, but denies that either must be *prior* to the other. Rather, they develop together—light dawns simultaneously over the whole. The other involves Sosa's distinction between animal knowledge (which is not subject to a KR requirement) and reflective knowledge (which is). For further discussion of these strategies, see Van Cleve 2003a.

Wright's target is the "proof of the external world" offered by G. E. Moore ([1939] 1962). Moore argued in effect as follows:

I. I have an experience as of a hand at the end of my arm—an ostensible perception of a hand.
II. There is a hand at the end of my arm.
III. Therefore, there is an external world.

In a variation of the argument, the conclusion could instead be

III.' Therefore, I am not falsely dreaming that there is a hand at the end of my arm.

Though I refer to the I-II-III sequence as an argument, the transition from I to II need not be thought of as a piece of reasoning. It could be thought of simply as a transition from having the experience described in statement I to being justified in believing the proposition expressed in statement II.[24] The point is simply that the Moorean subject comes to be justified in believing there is a hand on the strength of the experience described in I. The same thing happens countless times every day according to Reid's epistemology as I am interpreting it. In normal circumstances (if there really is a hand and the subject is not in a Gettier situation), the subject will also come to *know* there is a hand in front of him.[25]

Moore took it to be a conceptual truth that hands are external objects, so the existence of hands would entail the existence of an external world. In addition, it is a simple matter of logic that if there is hand at the end of my arm, I am not falsely dreaming that there is a hand at the end of my arm. Thus, II entails both III and III.' Moreover, it does so in an obvious enough way that an alert subject will be justified in believing that these entailments hold. Let us suppose (and add as a step in the sequence if you like) that our subject is such a subject. It will then follow, in accordance with the principle that justification is closed under justifiably believed entailment (= if S is justified in believing that p entails q and also justified in believing p, he is justified in believing q) that the subject is justified in believing III. If he has arrived at *knowledge* that II is true, then by the analogous principle that knowledge is closed under known entailment, he will also arrive at knowledge that III is true.[26]

---

[24] See the discussion of point 3 in chapter 11, section E.

[25] An example of a Gettier situation would be this: what the subject is seeing is actually a mirror reflection of a hand behind him, but by a lucky accident his own hand is in the place where he seems to see a hand. See Gettier 1963.

[26] These closure principles are disputed by some epistemologists, but accepted by most. For discussion of the issue, see Dretske 2005 and Hawthorne 2005.

Such is the Moorean route to knowing there is an external world. Moore offered his proof to end what Kant called the "scandal" that philosophy had not proven the existence of an external world, but some of Moore's readers have thought the real scandal is that Moore should offer such a "proof."

According to Wright, the I-II-III procedure described above could never be the means whereby one comes to know that there is a material world (or that one is not merely dreaming that one's environment is as it appears to be). Having warrant for the III-type propositions is a *precondition* for acquiring justification for II-type propositions on the strength of I-type propositions or experiences. If so, that explains why Moore's procedure strikes many of his readers as question-begging.

In giving this assessment, Wright is implying that liberalism is false. Having an experience as of hands is *not* enough to make you justified, even defeasibly, in believing that you have hands. In addition, you must have antecedent and independent justification for believing that there is an external world and that your ostensible experience of a hand is not merely a dream. You must already have justification for the III-type propositions before you can acquire justification for the II-type propositions.

At this point, Wright's objection to Moore threatens to turn into an argument for the inescapability of skepticism about the external world. He lays down the requirement that knowing anything about external matters of fact through perceptual experience presupposes having antecedent justification for the belief in an external world. But how could one acquire justification for that belief if not through perceptual experiences ostensibly revealing facts about the material world? It appears that there is a circle of mutual priority into which we could never gain entry, analogous to the (1)-(2) dyad, preventing us from knowing the most mundane of facts.

Formally parallel skeptical predicaments could be set up in other departments of human knowledge or would-be knowledge, such as knowledge of the past through memory or of the future through induction. For example, we could let our three propositions be

I. I seem to remember eating eggs for breakfast yesterday.
II. I did eat eggs for breakfast yesterday.
III. It is not the case (contrary to what Russell once entertained) that the entire world came into existence complete with phony records and memories five minutes ago.

As before, Wright claims that only a subject who is already justified in believing III can acquire justification for believing II on the strength of I. He would deny Reid's liberal assumption that certain experiences of perceiving or remembering are *all it takes* to give one justified beliefs about the external world or the past.

I turn now to Cohen's criticisms. His targets are epistemological views according to which its seeming to you as if p is enough by itself to make you prima facie justified believing that p—in other words, liberal epistemologies, like those of Reid (as I am interpreting him), Moore, and Chisholm.[27] According to such epistemologies, I can know that a table is red merely on the basis of its looking red to me. I do not need to know that its looking red is a reliable indicator of its being red; I need only be in a state in which the table does look red to me.[28] Cohen raises two problems of "easy knowledge" for such epistemologies: knowledge by closure and knowledge by bootstrapping.

Easy knowledge by closure would come about as follows: In accordance with a liberal epistemology, one comes to know that a table is red simply on the strength of its looking red to one. From one's knowledge that the table is red, one deduces that it is not white and, *a fortiori*, that is not white with red lights shining on it. By closure, one thereby comes to know that the table is not white with red lights shining on it, despite not having any independent reason to believe anything about the lighting conditions. To many, that seems too easy. The subject's procedure is analogous to the I-II-III procedure discussed in connection with Moore and Wright.

Easy knowledge by bootstrapping (the stigmatizing term introduced in Vogel 2000) would arise as follows: On occasions when one takes a wall or a table to be red merely on the strength of its look, one also notes introspectively how it looks, thus eventually amassing a body of evidence of the form "On occasion 1, an object looked red to me, and it was red; on occasion 2, an object looked red to me, and it was red; . . .; on occasion n an object looked red to me, and it was red; moreover, there were no occasions on which an object looked red to me and was not red." From this body of evidence one infers by induction that one's color vision is reliable. To many, the resultant knowledge looks too easy, since one's endorsement of the accuracy of one's vision is arrived at using nothing other than vision. The procedure here is precisely a track-record argument of the sort discussed in chapter 11, section H, but now regarded as a bug rather than a feature.

---

[27] He calls them "basic knowledge epistemologies" in the following stipulated sense: they are epistemologies that allow you to have knowledge from a source without knowing that the source is reliable. Such knowledge need not be basic knowledge in the more usual sense of being knowledge not depending on any other knowledge whatever.

[28] I gloss over the difference between "it appears to me that the table is red" (explicitly propositional) and "the table looks red to me" (arguably nonpropositional), as the same epistemological issues arise regardless of which is taken to be the prima facie justifier.

Cohen's recommended way of blocking easy knowledge of either variety is to insist on the KR requirement across the board. Knowing that a source is reliable is, if not a prerequisite, at least a corequisite of knowing anything through that source.[29]

The objections we have canvassed have a common theme: liberalism makes knowledge too easy because it holds certain experiences to be *sufficient by themselves* to make a subject prima facie justified in believing certain things, whereas in fact something more is required. In Wright's case, the something more is having antecedent and independent justification for type-III propositions (which he calls "cornerstone" propositions). In Cohen's case, the something more is having knowledge of the reliability of the relevant knowledge source.[30] The question to be addressed next is how the something more could ever be achieved.

## E. RATIONALIST ALTERNATIVES

How are we ever to know the crucial extra propositions that, according to Wright and Cohen, we must know as conditions of knowing anything whatever on the basis of perception? The answer favored by Wright, Cohen, and a number of other contemporary philosophers is that the special propositions can be known a priori, without appeal to any perceptual evidence. This position may aptly be called *rationalism*.[31]

A traditional view is that the things we know a priori are either intuitively or demonstratively evident—we either see that they are true by a kind of intellectual vision, or we demonstrate that they are true, which is a matter of intuiting that they follow from other things known a priori (and thus, at bottom, things known intuitively). For the sake of the discussion that follows, I assume that our rationalist holds that the special propositions are known by intuition, but my remarks apply equally to the supposition that they are known by demonstration.

Descartes challenged our perceptual knowledge by raising the possibility that all of our perceptual experience is occurring in a dream. Rationalists hope to exclude this possibility a priori. But Descartes also challenged our a priori knowledge by raising the possibility that an evil demon with God-like powers is making

---

[29] It is clear how KR blocks bootstrapping—one could not acquire knowledge of the reliability of a source by a track-record argument, since one would already need this knowledge to get knowledge of the premises. It is not clear to me how KR blocks knowledge by closure, unless reliability is reconstrued as a propensity to get things right under the circumstances prevailing in a particular instance.

[30] According to Roger White, another critic of liberalism, the something more is having justification for the simple conditional linking evidence with conclusion—as it might be, if something looks red, then it is red (White 2006).

[31] I take the name of the position and some of the strategy I use in criticizing it from Stang (forthcoming).

us wrong even about the deliverances of intuition. How, then, is our rationalist to maintain that we have a priori knowledge of the special propositions—or of *any* propositions—in the face of the following skeptical argument? Here T can be $2 + 3 = 5$ or any proposition that is intuitively evident to the subject, including the special propositions if they are evident:

1. S does not know that no demon is bringing it about that he intuits T while everything he intuits is false.
2. If S does not know that no demon is bringing it about that he intuits T while everything he intuits is false, then S does not know that T is true.
3. Therefore, S does not know that T is true.

If we assume that the entailment from *T is true* to *no demon is bringing it about that S intuits T while everything S intuits is false* is obvious enough that S knows it, premise 2 will be a consequence of one of the closure principles mentioned above.

How can the knowledge posited by the rationalist withstand the foregoing skeptical argument? One possibility is that the argument should simply be turned on its head:

~3. S *does* know that T is true.
  2. As before, if S does not know that no demon is bringing it about that he intuits T while everything he intuits is false, then S does not know that T is true.
~1. Therefore, S knows that no demon is bringing it about that he intuits T while everything he intuits is false.

This argument is as valid as the original. It is exactly the argument H. A. Prichard suggested Descartes should have used in the first person in his grapplings with the demon. To secure our knowledge of simple truths of geometry against the supposed possibility of a demon deceiving us about such things, Prichard said, "We can answer that we know that there can be no such fact, for in knowing that a triangle must have such angles we also know that nothing can exist which is incompatible with this fact" (Prichard 1950:90).

How would a subject acquire the knowledge attributed to him in premises~3 and~1? A traditional rationalist would say that she does it by going through the following steps (which need not be an argument, as explained above):

  I. I have an intuition that T is true.
 II. T is true.
III. Therefore, no demon is bringing it about that I have an intuition that T is true while everything I intuit is false.

The rub, of course, is that this procedure has the same pattern as the Moorean argument criticized by Wright. If having warrant for *no dream is giving me false appearances of hands* is a precondition for getting knowledge of hands through perception, then presumably having warrant for *no demon is giving me false intuitions of T* is a precondition of knowing any proposition T through intuition. As a precondition of acquiring a priori knowledge, it cannot itself be known a priori. Formally, at least, rationalism appears to be subject to the same criticisms as Mooreanism.

If the rationalist is not to be done in by the criticism Wright levels against Moore, he must evidently claim some special privilege for rational modes of knowing. He must say you can know things a priori without having first to clear away worries about reason-deceiving demons, or that rational intuition is so powerful that it sweeps such worries aside every time it is used. Reid is aware that there are such rationalists, and here is what he has to say about them:

> I am aware, that this belief which I have in perception, stands exposed to the strongest batteries of skepticism. But they make no great impression upon it. The sceptic asks me, Why do you believe the existence of the external object which you perceive? . . . Reason, says the sceptic, is the only judge of truth, and you ought to throw off every opinion and every belief that is not grounded on reason. Why, Sir, should I believe the faculty of reason more than that of perception; they came both out of the same shop, and were made by the same artist; and if he puts one piece of false ware into my hands, what should hinder him from putting another? (IHM 6.20:168–69).

Traditional rationalism cannot be a way of avoiding problems with Mooreanism. If reason and perception come from the same shop, then the rationalist and the Moorean are in the same boat.[32]

Wright's own brand of rationalism is not the traditional kind portrayed above. He says the kind of warrant we need for the cornerstone propositions is a kind of warrant, called "entitlement," that does not consist in having evidence. Now if "having evidence" means having reasons or premises and drawing conclusions from them, the traditionalist as I portray him above does not see intuitive knowledge as resting on evidence, either. What justifies someone in believing an elementary truth of mathematics is simply the person's being in an intuitional state, not drawing any inferences. But Wright's "warrant without evidence" is not akin to the warrant conferred by being in an intuitional state, since it is not a status that is *acquired* at all. It is a status that cornerstone propositions have all along. What exactly is this entitlement, then? Wright sketches several varieties of it, all of which have in common

---

[32] The "same boat" thesis is well argued for by Stang.

that they are a sort of pragmatic justification for proceeding on certain assumptions. For example, the cornerstone proposition underlying of our use of induction is the thesis of the Uniformity of Nature, and our entitlement with respect to it consists in the fact (pointed out by Reichenbach in his "pragmatic vindication of induction") that if the thesis is true, induction will enable us to learn regularities, while if it is not, no other method will work any better. Induction works if anything does.

My objection to Wright is that if entitlement is merely a pragmatic status, it is not what it takes to give us knowledge of type II propositions. The original skeptical challenge was that some favorable epistemic status for type III propositions is required before perception gives us any knowledge of hands or memory gives us any knowledge of yesterday's breakfast. Assuming the closure principle, if the type II propositions are to possess justification, the status required of the type III propositions would also have to be justification or something equally robust. If the status possessed by type III propositions is only entitlement, then on the assumption that a chain is no stronger than its weakest link, nothing stronger than entitlement is conferred by experience on propositions about hands.[33] But entitlement is not what you need to add to true belief to get knowledge.[34]

I turn now to Cohen's rationalist attempt to navigate between liberalism on the left and skepticism on the right. For him, the special proposition that anyone must know in order to know anything on the basis of perception is that perception is reliable. How are we to know this without using any deliverances of perception? Cohen's answer is that we may use the liberal's own principles to construct an a priori proof

---

[33] Wright discusses this problem under the name "leaching" in the final section of his paper, but as far as I can see, he has no good answer to it.

[34] Wright offers entitlement as an alternative to the dogmatism of Moore, who was following in Reid's footsteps in his defense of common sense. I therefore find it ironic that some see Reid himself as advancing an entitlement approach (Wolterstorff 2000, White 2006). Interpretations of Reid along these lines have three features in common. First, when Reid gives us his list of the first principles of contingent truths, he is identifying the cornerstone propositions in various areas of knowledge. For example, Principle 5—"those things do really exist which we distinctly perceive by our senses"—is the cornerstone proposition for knowledge of the external world. Second, our attitude toward these propositions is not properly characterized as *believing* them. Instead, it would more aptly be called what Reid himself sometimes calls it, *taking them for granted*—a notion that Wright and Wolterstorff both explicate by reference to Wittgenstein 1969. Third, the special status possessed by the things we take for granted is to be understood in practical terms rather than epistemic terms. "If there are certain principles . . . which we are under a necessity to take for granted in the common concerns of life, without being able to give a reason for them; these are what we call the principles of common sense" (IHM 2.6:33). These themes do undeniably resonate with some things Reid says, but I nonetheless resist an entitlement interpretation of his epistemology. As indicated in the previous chapter, it seems to me that when Reid calls something a first principle, he is attributing to it not a merely pragmatic status but a high epistemic status—a status as high or nearly as high as anything ever gets.

of the reliability of perception. He reconstrues epistemic principles as rules of reasoning, rules that authorize defeasible inferences or transitions such as that from "That object looks red" or "I seem to see a tree over there" to "That object *is* red" or "There *is* a tree over there." He then notes that such rules can be used in reasoning analogous to what logicians call *conditional proof*—establishing a conditional proposition by assuming its antecedent and deriving its consequent. We suppose that an object looks red to us; we infer from that assumption (as allegedly licensed by the rule) that the object is red; we then "discharge the assumption" by concluding that if the object looks red to us, it is red. Since the rule applies to any object and to a wide range of sensory predicates, we may generalize the conclusion: when we have an ostensible perception as of something's being F, there really is something F there. In other words, perception is reliable. We thus establish by a priori reasoning (though defeasibly, since the inference rule was defeasible) that perception is reliable.

Cohen's strategy concedes that the liberal's principles or rules of justification are correct—indeed, it uses these rules. His strategy also concedes that the bootstrapping reasoning sketched above contains no mistake. It is just that it does not give you any *additional* reason to believe in the reliability of perception, that is, any reason that was not already available to you just by virtue of your competence in the defeasible rules—bootstrapping does not let you learn anything new. The main point for our purposes is that Cohen's strategy involves affirming (1) and denying (2) in the skeptical dyad—to know anything through perception, you must know that perception is reliable, but you can know this a priori and without any reliance on perception itself.

I have two criticisms of Cohen's approach. The first, developed at greater length in Van Cleve (no date), is that it is questionable whether epistemic principles should be construed as rules of reasoning in the way Cohen requires. Having an ostensible perception of a tree makes it immediately evident that there is a tree, yes; but that does not mean that the *assumption* that you are having such a perception authorizes you (even defeasibly) to conclude that there is tree over there. Reid's "rule" gives knowledge to subjects if and only if they *fall under it* (that is, satisfy its antecedent). One who does not fall under the rule, but merely assumes he does, may not infer or justifiably believe its consequent unless he knows the rule is correct. Where is that knowledge supposed to come from? Without it, there can be no knowledge via a priori reasoning of the reliability of perception.

My second criticism, already noted above, applies to *any* rationalist approach. By using reasoning to vouch for the reliability of perception, Cohen is letting one faculty be the guarantor of another. But how does he know that reasoning is reliable? In particular, how does he know that if assuming P lets you derive Q , you thereby know that *if* P, *then* Q? Perhaps that is only a delusion of demon-addled brains.

In short, Cohen incurs Reid's "same shop" challenge: if perception is not on its own a source of knowledge, why should reason be?

Reid's rationalist critics accuse him of making perceptual knowledge too easy, but in their own turn they make rational knowledge easy. If knowledge is to be possible at all, some knowledge must be easy.

## F. CONCLUSION

I have canvassed four anti-skeptical strategies in this chapter and chapter 2. *Direct realism* is touted by many of its proponents, including Reid, as a way of undercutting skepticism about the external world, but it is not by itself sufficient. What is really needed is for beliefs about the external world to be epistemically basic, which requires epistemological doctrine going beyond direct realism. *Nativism* can be used to dispel one kind of skepticism, namely, semantic skepticism or skepticism about understanding, but it leaves epistemological skepticism standing. *Naturalism* also leaves epistemological skepticism standing, however much it bowls over skeptics themselves by making them believe the things they profess not to know. Of the four strategies, only *externalism* has genuine anti-skeptical force, since it undercuts the powerful argument for skepticism based on the KR requirement.

But can the skeptic's position itself, as distinct from the arguments for it, be refuted? Let us heed some of Reid's remarks on this topic.

> But are we to admit nothing but what can be proved by reasoning? Then we must be skeptics indeed, and believe nothing at all. The author of the *Treatise of human nature* appears to me to be but a half-sceptic . . . and yields himself a captive to the most common of all vulgar prejudices, I mean the belief of the existence of his own impressions and ideas. . . . I affirm, that the belief of the existence of impressions and ideas, is as little supported by reason, as that of the existence of minds and bodies. . . . A thorough and consistent sceptic will never, therefore, yield this point [that not even the existence of ideas and impressions merits credence]; and while he holds it, you can never oblige him to yield any thing else.
>
> To such a sceptic, I have nothing to say; but of the semi-sceptics, I should beg to know, why they believe the existence of their impressions and ideas. (IHM 5.7: 71)

> Reason, says the sceptic, is the only judge of truth, and you ought to throw off every opinion and every belief that is not grounded on reason. Why, Sir, should I believe the faculty of reason more than that of perception; they came both out of the same shop, and were made by the same artist; and if he puts one piece of false ware into my hands, what should hinder him from putting another? (IHM 6.20:169)

Thus the faculties of consciousness, of memory, of external sense, and of reason, are all equally the gifts of Nature. No good reason can be assigned for receiving the testimony of one of them, which is not of equal force with regard to the others. The greatest Sceptics admit the testimony of consciousness, and allow, that what it testifies is to be held as a first principle. If therefore they reject the immediate testimony of sense, or of memory, they are guilty of an inconsistency. (EIP 6.4:463)

If a Sceptic should build his skepticism upon this foundation, that all our reasoning and judging powers are fallacious in their nature, or should resolve at least to withhold assent until it be proved that they are not; it would be impossible by argument to beat him out of this strong-hold, and he must even be left to enjoy his skepticism. (EIP 6.5:480)[35]

In these passages, Reid distinguishes two kinds of skeptics. *Semi-skeptics*, such as Reid took Descartes and Hume to be, trust the deliverances of one or two of our faculties, reason and perhaps also consciousness, but refuse to admit anything that is not provable by reason from the deliverances of consciousness. *Total skeptics* refuse to trust even the deliverances of consciousness and reason. Reid concedes that total skeptics cannot be refuted; before them we must be silent. But semi-skeptics can be charged with inconsistency, or at least arbitrariness. They trust some faculties but not others, with no real reason for doing so.[36]

To what Reid has said, I add just one observation. He says we cannot refute the thoroughgoing skeptic, that is, prove that he is wrong using premises that he would accept. We cannot *show* that he is wrong. But can we nonetheless *know* that he is wrong? After all, we can sometimes know things that we cannot prove to the satisfaction of another.[37] If Reid's externalist epistemology is correct, we can know many of the things the skeptic says we cannot know—we can know things our knowing of which implies that the skeptic is wrong.[38]

---

[35] This remark is echoed in Russell (1913) 1992:159: "The position of the sceptic who questions without denying is impregnable."

[36] See Greco 2004:151–55, for more on this point. In one of his few criticisms of Reid, Brentano says there *is* a difference between inner consciousness and reason on one side and all other faculties on the other: the former are infallible, the rest not ([1916] 1975). Brentano owes us an explanation of why only infallible faculties can be justification sources.

[37] For more on this point—that arguments or procedures that are dialectically ineffective against an opponent may nonetheless be epistemically successful for the agent himself—see Van Cleve 1979, Alston 1986a, Pryor 2000, Bergmann 2004, and Lemos 2004.

[38] Which is not yet to say that we know the skeptic is wrong; for that, we would have to know that we know the things that we do. We would need second-order knowledge, which I have not discussed in this chapter.

# 13

## EPISTEMOLOGY 3

## LEHRER'S REID

Perhaps evidence, as in many other respects it resembles light, so in this also, that as light, which is the discoverer of all visible objects, discovers itself at the same time: so evidence, which is the voucher for all truth, vouches for itself at the same time. (Thomas Reid, *EIP 6.5:481*)

In the person of Keith Lehrer, a distinguished epistemologist and a distinguished Reid scholar come together. In this chapter, I discuss the principal features of Reid's epistemology as interpreted by Lehrer, noting points where he and I disagree. I concentrate on three of Lehrer's distinctive theses: that a Reidian knower must know that his faculties are reliable, that one among Reid's principles of common sense stands above the others as an indispensably important metaprinciple, and that some faculties vouch for themselves.

### A. MUST A KNOWER KNOW THAT HIS FACULTIES ARE RELIABLE?

One issue on which Lehrer and I differ is discussed in chapter 11: does Reid give us principles of truth or principles of evidence? Lehrer says truth, I say evidence. With this difference goes another, to be discussed in greater depth now: must a knower know that Reid's principles are true? I say no, Lehrer says yes.

As I understand Reid's principles, they say that the mere fact that a proposition is a deliverance of perception, memory, or consciousness suffices to make that proposition evident. In order to know that there is a tree in front of one, for example, one need only perceive that there is. Nothing else is necessary. In particular, it is not necessary that the subject know anything about the reliability of sense perception. This is the respect in which I claim that Reid is an epistemological externalist.

Lehrer is opposed to externalist views in epistemology, however, and he finds Reid to be no less opposed:

> Reid is not a reliabilist of the sort Goldman describes. It would be possible for a belief to be a product of a reliable belief-forming process without our having any idea that this was so, without, that is, our having any information about the trustworthiness of the belief. (1989:198)

> The theory of evidence is based on the innate first principles of the mind. It is, however, not sufficient for a belief to be evident that it be a product of an innate principle, even a trustworthy and reliable one. A belief could be the product of such a principle and not be evident for the person because the person had no idea whether the belief originated in a way that is trustworthy or deceptive. In fact, the first principles of our nature not only yield beliefs but also information about those beliefs, to wit, that they are trustworthy and not fallacious in origin. (1989:187)

Lehrer's remarks also imply that Reid is not an externalist of the normativist variety I have described. He is saying that in order to be justified in believing that there is a tree over there, it is *not* enough to perceive that there is a tree there, even if we do so in accordance with a reliable innate tendency of our constitution. We must in addition have the *idea* (or the *information*) that perception is a reliable source of belief.

What is it to have such information? Is it merely to *believe* that perception is reliable? Or is it something stronger—to believe with evidence and truth, and thus to *know*, that perception is reliable? Let us consider what Reid says or might say about each of these requirements.

In order to have knowledge from a given source, must we *believe* that the source is reliable? If so, then the generality of mankind does not know very much, for people are seldom as reflective as that. A child or an unreflective adult may take little thought about the faculties whose deliverances she accepts. This is Reid's own position in the following passage:

> We may here take notice of a property of the principle under consideration [that our faculties are not fallacious] that seems to be common to it with many other first principles . . . and that is, that in most men it produces its effect without ever being attended to, or made an object of thought. No man ever thinks of this principle, unless when

he considers the grounds of skepticism; yet it invariably governs his opinions. When a man in the common course of life gives credit to the testimony of his senses, his memory, or his reason, he does not put the question to himself, whether these faculties may deceive him; yet the trust he reposes in them supposes an inward conviction, that in this instance at least, they do not deceive him. (EIP 6.5:632)

It is another property of this and of many first principles that they force assent in particular instances more powerfully than when they are turned into a general proposition. (EIP 6.5:632.)

In light of passages such as these, Lehrer qualifies the requirement that subjects must believe in the reliability of their own faculties. He says that principles such as "What I perceive to be the case is generally so" must be "operative" in us even if we do not explicitly believe them,[1] and that general principles must be "in us" in the sense that they *cause* us to believe their particular instances (1990:40).

In what sense do we have general beliefs that cause us to have beliefs in their particular instances? Two observations will help answer this question. First, what Reid and Lehrer mean by an "instance" of a general belief is really an instance of its consequent, obtainable by subsumption (universal instantiation and modus ponens). If the general proposition is *all deliverances of perception are true*, symbolizable as $(p)(Pp \rightarrow p)$, then an instance of it would be *there is a tree over there* (if a tree is what I am now perceiving).[2] Second, there is a sense in which one believes implicitly that all Fs are Gs simply by having the disposition to believe, concerning anything one believes to be F, that it is G. In symbols, we could say that one has an implicit belief in $(x)(Fx \rightarrow Gx)$ if one has the disposition expressed by "BFx $\rightarrow$ BGx" (where "B" stands for believing).[3] If one has such an implicit belief, one will be caused to believe instances of the consequent of "$(x)(Fx \rightarrow Gx)$" whenever one believes instances of its antecedent. Even a person who never entertained the proposition that perceptual beliefs are generally true might still be so constituted that whenever she believes she perceives that p, she also believes that p. (Alternatively, if we wish to accommodate the possibility that sometimes we perceive things without believing that we

---

[1] This was Lehrer's way of putting it in a lecture at the NEH Seminar on Thomas Reid, Brown University, August 2000.

[2] A substitution instance of the generalization "$(x)(Fx \rightarrow Gx)$" would be the conditional "Fa $\rightarrow$ Ga"; a confirmation instance of it would be the conjunction "Fa & Ga" (or perhaps an object that is both F and G). What Reid and Lehrer mean by an instance is neither of these things, but simply "Ga."

[3] Sosa offers an analysis of "implicit commitments" along these lines in Sosa and Van Cleve 2001, beginning on page 190. For the more radical view that general belief is never anything over and above such $BFx \rightarrow BGx$ dispositions, see Armstrong 1972, chapter 6.

perceive them,[4] we could say that a general belief in the reliability of perception is operative in S if S is so constituted that whenever he is conscious of perceiving that p, he believes that p.)

We have now identified one plausible sense in which ordinary subjects believe in the reliability of their faculties. Even if they do not have general propositions such as "When I perceive something to be the case, it is the case" explicitly before their minds, their opinions are governed by them, in the sense that whenever they are aware of falling under the antecedent, they will believe the consequent.

Let us turn now to the second and stronger requirement envisioned above—that to know something through a faculty, you must *know* that the faculty is reliable. Lehrer accepts this requirement, and he takes Reid to accept it as well. Of course, if the sense in which we believe in reliability is only the implicit sense just identified, the sense in which we have knowledge of reliability would presumably be implicit in a corresponding sense, but I ignore this complication here.

What we have just affirmed is that Lehrer and Lehrer's Reid both accept the KR requirement discussed in chapter 12:

(KR) A potential knowledge source K can yield knowledge for a subject S only if S knows K is reliable.

That means we are threatened once again by the skeptical dyad:

(1) We can know that a deliverance of K is true only if we first know that K is reliable.
(2) We can know that K is reliable only if we first know, concerning certain of its deliverances, that they are true.

To avoid the skeptical result, Lehrer's Reid must deny (2). How is such a denial possible—how can we know that a faculty is reliable if not through its own deliverances? I return to that question after we have discussed the special role Lehrer assigns to Reid's Principle 7.

---

[4] Reid may be committed to rejecting this possibility. In his account of the system of Leibniz, he explicitly disapproves of Leibniz's distinction between perception and apperception. "As far as we can discover, every operation of our mind is attended with consciousness, and particularly that which we call the perception of external objects. . . . No man can perceive an object, without being conscious that he perceives it" (EIP 2.15:190–91). In another place (EIP 3.1:254), he says that consciousness is always attended with belief of that whereof we are conscious. Putting these two points together, it follows that we never perceive without believing that we perceive.

## B. A SPECIAL ROLE FOR PRINCIPLE 7?

Here is the seventh in Reid's list of the principles of contingent truths:

> Another first principle is, that the natural faculties, by which we distinguish truth
> from error, are not fallacious. (EIP 6.5:480)

Shortly after enunciating it, Reid says

> If any truth can be said to be prior to all others in the order of nature, this seems to
> have the best claim; because in every instance of assent, whether upon intuitive, de-
> monstrative, or probable evidence, the truth of our faculties is taken for granted, and
> is, as it were, one of the premises on which our assent is grounded. (EIP 6.5:481)

Reid seems here to be assigning to Principle 7 a special role. According to Lehrer, Principle 7 is the most important principle of all (1989:162), special in two ways. First, it
is a *meta*-principle, affirming the truth of all the others (1989:144, 157, 162, and 187).
Second, it is a *looping* principle. "The principle vouches for itself. It loops around and supports itself" (1990:43). For these reasons, Lehrer calls this principle "the keystone principle of the first principles" (1990:42). He also calls it "the *first* first principle" (1998:15).

If Principle 7 is really the first in importance, why does it occur seventh in a list of
twelve? And does its place in the middle of the list not suggest that it really concerns
just some faculties, not all?

There are ways of understanding Principle 7 as co-ordinate with the other principles, treating of just certain faculties rather than all of them, and thus deserving
its place in the middle. De Bary (2000) has noted that the clause "by which we distinguish truth from error" may have been intended by Reid as a restrictive clause,
singling out a subset of the faculties, rather than as a parenthetical gloss on what all
faculties do.[5] And yet do not *all* cognitive faculties enable us to distinguish truth
from error, informing us that some things are true and others false? What possible
restriction on cognitive faculties could Principle 7 be incorporating?[6]

---

[5] De Bary reports that in Reid's manuscript of the *Intellectual Powers* at Aberdeen University Library, there are no commas surrounding "by which we distinguish truth from error" (2000:380,
n. 22). As far as I have been able to glean, however, Reid's writing does not consistently adhere to
any convention that nonrestrictive clauses are surrounded by commas and restrictive clauses not.
For instance, at IHM 6.11:119, lines 24–25, EIP 5.3:366, lines 33–36, and EAP 5.1:270, line 25,
he puts commas before clauses that are clearly restrictive. I ask readers who find an instance of the
converse combination, a nonrestrictive clause with no commas, to let me know.

[6] If the restriction is just to cognitive faculties themselves (as opposed to practical faculties such
as willing), Lehrer is vindicated—Principle 7 pertains to all cognitive faculties.

One suggestion for a restricted Principle 7 would take the faculties "by which we distinguish truth from error" to be *second-order* faculties, that is, faculties whereby we judge of other faculties.[7] If we do this, Principle 7 would be a principle about metafaculties, but it would not necessarily be a metaprinciple. Nor would it be a principle of supreme generality, for it would concern some faculties among others, even if those faculties are of special importance. In any case, it counts against this suggestion that Reid twice uses the phrase "until God give us new faculties to sit in judgment upon the old" (6.5:481 and 6.7:517), implying that we have nothing to judge of our faculties but those faculties themselves.

Another suggestion for a restricted Principle 7 would take it to be concerned with *reasoning*, which is not mentioned elsewhere in Reid's list of principles.[8] Reasoning, Reid tells us, is "the process by which we pass from one judgment to another" (EIP 7.1:542). There is some support for this suggestion in the fact that many of Reid's illustrations of Principle 7 are cases of reasoning. For example, immediately follow-ing his enunciation of Principle 7, he says, "If any man should demand a proof of this it is impossible to satisfy him . . . because *to judge of a demonstration*, a man must trust his faculties" (EIP 6.5:480, emphasis mine). He follows this up by observing that the very point in question in Principle 7 is *whether reasoning may be trusted*.

These remarks are not decisive, however. If Principle 7 concerned *all* our faculties, as Lehrer holds, it would concern reasoning, too, so Reid could still make his point that it would beg the question to offer reasoning in support of Principle 7. Moreover, as we read further in Reid's commentary on Principle 7, we find him saying that it is concerned with "all our reasoning and judging powers" (480 and 481), which suggests a considerably broader scope for Principle 7.

But how much broader? De Bary suggests a broader but still restricted scope for Principle 7. Noting that Reid devotes separate essays in the *Intellectual Powers* to perception, memory, judging, and reasoning, he proposes that the scope of Prin-ciple 7 is *just* judging and reasoning, not our faculties in general. Against this sug-gestion, however, is the fact that Reid views perception and memory as *special cases* of judgment. He says, for example, "There is no more reason to account our senses fallacious, than our reason, our memory, or *any other faculty of judging* which nature has given us" (EIP 2.22:251–52, emphasis mine). Confirming this point, Essay 6, "Of Judgment," makes points applicable to all our faculties; indeed, it is in that Essay that we find the list of principles that is our current topic. Moreover, as we read Reid's thirteen paragraphs of commentary on Principle 7, I think it becomes fairly clear that Principle 7 is meant to cover all our faculties. The trust we repose in our

---

[7] I thank Gideon Yaffe and Sue Cox for this suggestion.
[8] I thank Alan Hazlett, Nick Treanor, and Ali Eslami for this suggestion.

senses, our memory, our consciousness, and our reason are all said to be instances of the general trust that is affirmed in Principle 7 (EIP 6.5:481–82).

I agree with Lehrer, then, that Principle 7 concerns *all* of our cognitive faculties—not just some specially delineated faculty or faculties. But a question potentially dividing us remains: In what way does Principle 7 go beyond the other principles on Reid's list? Why is it not merely redundant—perhaps simply a device enabling Reid to make points concerning all the principles by discussing just one of them?

To this question, Lehrer's answer, as noted above, is that Principle 7 is a meta-principle, affirming the truth of the other principles, and a looping principle, affirming the truth of itself as well. In this last way it goes beyond the other principles.

If we take Reid's formulations at face value, however, there does not appear to be anything particularly "meta" about Principle 7. The sequence

Consciousness is reliable;
Memory is reliable;
Perception is reliable; . . .;
All our faculties are reliable.

is comparable to the sequence

My dogs are friendly;
My cats are friendly;
My birds are friendly; . . .
All my pets are friendly.

The last item on each list does not seem to be much more than a summary of what has gone before. If Principle 7 goes beyond the other principles, it is only by virtue of implying either that I have no faculties not already mentioned or, if I do, that they are reliable, too.[9]

Nonetheless, the "meta" and "looping" character of Principle 7 may be brought out clearly if we rewrite Principle 7 in a way Lehrer has proposed. Principle 7 may be recast, he suggests, as a principle affirming that *all first principles are true*.[10] So

[9] In order that Principle 7 not convey *less* information than the preceding principles, I am assuming that a reference to the faculties already mentioned is implicit—"the above-mentioned faculties, as well as any others that I possess, are reliable."

[10] Lecture at the NEH Seminar on Thomas Reid, Brown University, August 2000. Lehrer's actual formulation was "all first principles are trustworthy," where being trustworthy implies both being evident and being true. The fact that trustworthiness implies truth generates the worry about ungroundedness that I raise in the text.

construed, Principle 7 does indeed convey what the other principles convey—that consciousness is reliable (since Principle 1 is true), memory is reliable (since Principle 3 is true), and so on. But Principle 7 also conveys more, because it is itself a first principle. It therefore implies its own truth by way of self-subsumption:

All first principles are true (= Principle 7).
Principle 7 is a first principle (i.e., it is a first principle that all first principles are true).
Therefore, Principle 7 is true.

The self-subsuming character of Principle 7 may not have been obvious in Reid's formulation, because "all our faculties are reliable" talks of faculties rather than principles.[11] But Lehrer's rewrite makes the self-subsuming feature manifest, and it is precisely this feature, he thinks, that enables Principle 7 to play its keystone role.

I have two questions about Lehrer's rewrite. First, is it a legitimate transcription of Reid's original? "All first principles are true" would be equivalent to "All our faculties are reliable" provided the following biconditional were true: P is a first principle iff P is a principle affirming the reliability of some faculty or faculties of ours. The right-to-left half of this biconditional depends on whether it can be self-evident that a faculty is reliable—a debatable question, but one to which Lehrer clearly thinks Reid would answer yes, as we see further below. The left-to-right half of the biconditional is problematic. There are first principles that do not affirm reliability (for example, particular propositions such as *there is a tree in front of me* and metaphysical principles such as *thoughts must belong to a thinker*). But I shall assume that we may qualify Lehrer's rewrite of Principle 7 so as to get around this problem.

Second, what do we gain by the rewrite? Lehrer's answer is that we obtain a principle that explains its own truth. He is worried by the prospect of *epistemic surds*—that is, epistemological principles for which there is no explanation. Given a choice between a surd and a loop—an unexplained principle and a principle that explains itself—he would prefer the loop (1997:22–23).

By making Principle 7 self-subsuming, do we really enable it to play this special explanatory role? A qualm about this may be engendered by considering the following list:

$2 + 2 = 4$.
Aberdeen is northeast of Glasgow.
Water boils at 212 degrees Fahrenheit.
All the sentences in this list are true.

[11] If we render "all our faculties are reliable" as "all deliverances of our faculties are true," however, we would obtain a principle that is self-subsuming provided it is itself a deliverance of our faculties.

The concern is that the final sentence is semantically ungrounded, just like the truth-teller sentence, "this sentence is true." If one of the sentences preceding it were false, that would make the final sentence false. But if all others on the list are true, whether the last is true comes down to—whether it is true! Yet there seems nothing to determine that. There is nothing to *make* it true or false, so arguably it is neither. The situation seems similar with Principle 7. If the other first principles are all true, then Principle 7 goes beyond them just to the extent that it ventures out over the void, with nothing to sustain a truth value for it. So the worry is that in trying to come up with a keystone principle that explains the others and itself in the bargain, we obtain a principle that explains nothing at all because it lacks truth value.

I do not wish to suggest that there is anything automatically defective about general principles that subsume themselves. *All necessary propositions are true* is itself a necessary proposition, and therefore may be subsumed under itself. But there is no question about its truth value; it is an accepted axiom of modal logic. Similarly, *everything that God believes is true* would be both self-subsuming and true (indeed, necessarily true) if there were an essentially omniscient and infallible God who believed it. But it is significant that these examples of self-subsuming propositions that are unproblematically true are *necessary* truths. There is a necessary connection between the properties that figure in antecedent and consequent, and that is what makes them true. Lehrer, however, does not think that Principle 7 is a necessary truth. He thinks that Reid's first principles of contingent truths are themselves contingent.[12] So he does not have this way of alleviating the worry that under his construal of it, Principle 7 is semantically ungrounded.

I return to this worry below. We must first learn how two important aspects of Lehrer's interpretation of Reid—the KR requirement and the endorsement of looping principles—are connected.

## C. FACULTIES THAT VOUCH FOR THEMSELVES?

The problem we left unresolved in section 1 is this: if we cannot know anything through a faculty without knowing that the faculty is reliable (the first proposition in the skeptical dyad), how can we know anything at all? Plainly, we must deny the other proposition in the dyad—that knowledge of the reliability of a source can be collected only from particular deliverances of that source. But if not derived from

---

[12] As I note in appendix V, the "first principles of contingent truths" are so called because they make knowledge of contingent truths possible; this leaves it open whether they are themselves necessary or contingent. It is clear from 1989:157, however, that Lehrer takes them to be contingent.

knowledge of its own particular deliverances, from what other knowledge *could* knowledge of K's reliability be derived? One answer (possibly agreeing with the rationalism discussed in the previous chapter) is that it is derived from *no* other knowledge. Knowledge of the reliability of our faculties is epistemically basic.[13]

That is the answer given by Lehrer's Reid. We know that our faculties are reliable not by deriving this knowledge from any other knowledge, but simply because the reliability of our faculties is self-evident (1990:40 and 1998:22–23). It is a self-evident first principle that consciousness is reliable; it is likewise a self-evident first principle that perception is reliable; and so on for all our other faculties. In this way, we have a way of breaking the skeptical impasse set up by propositions (1) and (2). We can accept the condition that KR lays down for all knowledge, but affirm that that condition is thankfully met, owing to the first principles of human knowledge.

Let us look more closely at the implications of this proposal. For Lehrer's Reid, we are enabled to know that particular deliverances of sense perception are true because it is a piece of basic knowledge, inferred from no other, that sense perception is reliable. We are still entitled to ask: what is the source of this basic knowledge?[14] Presumably, it is not perception itself, which does not yield truths of such generality.[15] If only to give the source a name, let us call it *intuition*. (A good Reidian name for it would be *common sense*, since Reid tells us that "the sole province of common sense" is "to judge of things self-evident" (EIP 6.2:433).) By KR, intuition yields knowledge only if we know that intuition is reliable. What is the source of *that* knowledge? This time we may answer that it is intuition itself—intuition intuits its own reliability. Indeed, it seems plausible that we *must* give an answer of that form sooner or later—KR can accommodate basic knowledge of the reliability of a source only if there is at least one source that gives basic knowledge of its own reliability.

But now we must go back to the principle that perception is reliable. How can that be a first principle if knowledge of it depends on the knowledge that some other faculty, namely, intuition, is reliable? Perhaps the answer is something like this: although it would not be evident (or known) that perception is reliable unless it were evident (or known) that intuition is reliable, that is not because the former proposition derives its evidence from the latter. Rather, intuition confers evidence

---

[13] This answer may, but need not, intersect with rationalism. Rational knowledge need not be basic (it could be demonstrative) and basic knowledge need not be rational (it could be empirical), but some knowledge is both rational and basic. Lehrer and the rationalist would agree if they both held knowledge of the reliability of our faculties to be rational and basic.

[14] It is not contradictory to say that basic knowledge has a source. On this point, consult the distinction between *sources* and *grounds* in Van Cleve 1979:69.

[15] Lehrer may disagree; he says at 1998:22 that the first principle about perception comes from the faculty of perception itself.

simultaneously on its primary object (in this case, that perception is reliable) and also on its own reliability.[16]

The Reidian view that is emerging evidently requires that there be certain faculties or sources that deliver knowledge not only of their primary objects, but also of their own reliability. This may be what Reid himself is getting at in the passage comparing evidence to light, which follows immediately upon his suggestion that if any truth be prior to all others, it is Principle 7:

> How then come we to be assured of this fundamental truth on which all others rest? Perhaps evidence, as in many other respects it resembles light, so in this also, that as light, which is the discoverer of all visible objects, discovers itself at the same time: so evidence, which is the voucher for all truth, vouches for itself at the same time. (EIP 6.5:481)[17]

The idea would be that as light discloses features both of visible objects and itself, so at least some among our cognitive faculties disclose features both of their primary objects and of themselves—in particular, their own reliability.

With this answer, we have drawn close to Lehrer's interpretation of Principle 7. Recall that for Lehrer, Principle 7 undergirds all the others and itself at the same time. It is a principle that affirms its own truth along with the truth of the other principles. We are now suggesting that there are faculties that apprehend their own reliability along with the reliability of other faculties. We have thus arrived at a view structurally similar to Lehrer's, incorporating the looping strategy he favors. And we have been led to do so in the attempt to show that knowledge is possible even under the stringent demands of KR. It is no accident, then, that a philosopher

---

[16] We see here, by the way, that the Reid who gets around the skeptical impasse by denying (2) must also deny (1). Though he accepts KR, he denies that to have knowledge through K you must have knowledge of K's reliability *first*. Otherwise, there could be no such thing as basic knowledge of the reliability of a source. Rather, there are cases in which knowledge through K and knowledge of K's reliability arise simultaneously.

[17] Lehrer draws on this passage for a somewhat different purpose. He poses a question about Reid from Chisholm: "How can we tell that a belief is evident if not by appeal to a general principle?" He cites the paragraph about light as Reid's answer, glossing it as "The evidence of some beliefs is itself evident. . . . If there are some beliefs whose evidence is evident to us, we have no need for a criterion to pick them out as evident" (1990:41). This is the first of the two readings of the light passage distinguished in chapter 11, section J, symbolized as $(p)(Ep \rightarrow EEp)$ or, more weakly, as $\exists p(Ep \& EEp)$. The second reading mentioned there, symbolizable as $(p)[(Ep$ because $Fp) \rightarrow E(p)(Fp \rightarrow Ep)]$, is closer to what I am envisioning now. It implies what I am envisioning now if, with Lehrer, we take the reliability of a source to be a necessary condition of its being a source of evidence.

who, like Lehrer's Reid, holds that there is no knowledge through a faculty without knowledge of its reliability, also holds that there are faculties that vouch for their own reliability.

I now return to a worry left unresolved above—that self-subsuming principles of the sort Lehrer favors would be semantically ungrounded. Is there an analogous worry about self-authenticating faculties? Suppose that intuition intuits its own reliability—that is, that I have an intuition whose content is that all intuitions are true. If all other intuitions are true, what would make that one true? As before, I think it would have to be some sort of necessary connection between the properties of being an intuition (that is, an act of intuiting) and being true. If it were simply a matter of the individual truth values of all intuitions, ungroundedness would threaten. Is there plausibly a necessary connection between being an intuition and being true, and if so, could Lehrer accept it? As noted above, he does not believe that Reid's principles are metaphysically necessary truths, so he would deny that there is any metaphysically necessary connection between being an intuiting and being true. But I expect he might allow that there is a *nomologically* necessary connection between being an intuition and being true, and perhaps such a connection would suffice as a truth-maker for the intuition that all intuitions are true. I leave further exploration of this suggestion for another occasion.[18]

It is time to take stock of what I accept in the package of views held by Lehrer's Reid. *To have knowledge through a faculty, a subject must know that the faculty is reliable.* This I have resisted all along, since it is a requirement that threatens to make knowledge impossible. *The reliability of perception is intuitively and immediately evident.* This I find difficult to accept for the reason noted in chapter 11, section J: I do not see how a deeply contingent general truth can be self-evident. *The reliability of intuition is intuitively and immediately evident—intuition vouches for itself.* This also I find difficult to accept, but less so, the difference being that the reliability of intuition, unlike that of perception, could be claimed to be a necessary truth. I am again reminded of H. A. Prichard, whom I can imagine declaiming as follows: "When I reflect on my current condition (of clearly and distinctly perceiving p), I see that I

---

[18] Would the suggestion work in conjunction with Reid's view of laws? A law is a true generalization that is true because God arranges the world in accordance with it (see chapter 14, section C). To make it true that all intuitions are true, God would see to it that p is true when I intuit p (perhaps better, that I intuit p only if it is true), q is true when I intuit q, and—what?—is true when I intuit that all intuitions including this one are true. The question enclosed in dashes raises the grounding problem again—there does not seem to be anything that even God could do to make such a self-referential intuiting true. Perhaps matters would be otherwise if God could insert a relation of nomic necessitation between the properties of being an intuiting and being true, but that would be adopting an un-Reidian account of laws.

could not be related to any proposition as I am related now to p unless that proposition were true."

What I *do* find it plausible to accept as a necessary and intuitively knowable truth about intuition (alongside some of our other cognitive faculties) is not their reliability, but their *justificatory power.* I would not balk at a claim to find it intuitively evident that epistemic principles affirming that things intuited, perceived, remembered, or inductively inferred from premises already justified are thereby prima facie justified. But if *that* is what our epistemic principles proclaim, we are back to be being liberals, dogmatists, and externalists. We are back to saying that states of intuiting, perceiving, or remembering, unsupplemented by any knowledge of the reliability of those operations, can give us justified beliefs about their objects, amounting in favorable cases to knowledge. We are making bootstrapping possible. If knowledge of the reliability of our faculties is not required in our first cognitive endeavors, it may be obtained eventually through the use of those very faculties.[19]

The point of solidarity that remains between Lehrer and me (or between his Reid and mine) is that we both hold that it is possible to know that a faculty is reliable through the use of that very faculty. We differ on whether such knowledge is immediate, as it is for Lehrer, or mediated by the faculty's own deliverances, as it is for me. Our critics will say that the difference scarcely matters—we are both trying to pull ourselves up by our own bootstraps, Lehrer tugging directly with his fingers while I use a pulley.

In a passage sometimes quoted to illustrate the alleged absurdity in using our faculties to demonstrate their own reliability, Reid says, "If a man's honesty were called in question, it would be ridiculous to refer it to the man's own word, whether he be honest or not" (EIP 6.5:480). Yes; but it would be equally ridiculous to believe a man's testimony about various matters before the court (the time of the crime and so forth), but to balk for the first time when he said, "Moreover, I am a truthful witness." If we are not justified in believing what a faculty tells us about itself, we are not justified in believing anything it tells us about anything else, either—in which case, none of our sources can be trusted, and we know nothing.

---

[19] The earliest anticipation I have found of the possibility of bootstrapping comes in a single sentence from Chisholm: "I think we can inductively confirm the hypothesis that those 'sensible takings' we have called marks of evidence are also marks of *truth*" (1957:89).

# 14

## THEORY OF ACTION 1

## CAUSATION, ACTION, AND VOLITION

The name of a cause and of an agent, is properly given to that being only, which, by its active power produces some change in itself, or in some other being. (Thomas Reid, *EAP 4.2:203*)

This chapter and the next are devoted to Reid's theory of action, which is presented in the third of his three works, the *Essays on the Active Powers of Man* (1788). I have made no effort to provide a comprehensive treatment of Reid's philosophy of action, which would require a book of its own. Two excellent books on this subject already exist, Rowe 1991 and Yaffe 2004, as well as an excellent book on Reid and his predecessors in the British tradition, Harris 2005. On some topics, I simply refer the reader to them.

## A. THE NOTION OF ACTIVE POWER

Active power is that by exerting which an agent brings about some effect, such as moving his limbs or directing the course of his thoughts. The opposite of "active power" is not "passive power," a Lockean term that Reid regards as an oxymoron, but "speculative power," of which seeing and remembering would be instances (EAP 1.3:21 and 1.1:12).[1] Reid begins his discussion of active power by remarking

---

[1] So he tells us, but would he not regard perception as passive? If so, the speculative powers would include some passive powers.

that it is something perfectly well understood, but incapable of being defined (EAP 1.1:7). He nonetheless offers several observations about it, of which I focus on two here: that the concept of power is not an empirical concept, and that our notion of it is distinct despite being relative.[2] I also examine his contention that power is exercised only by beings with will and understanding.

*Power as an exception to empiricism.* Reid's first observation is that active power is "not an object of any of our external senses, nor even an object of consciousness" (EAP 1.1:8). This makes power a suspect notion for any concept empiricist. According to Locke and Hume as Reid portrays them, we have no conceptions not derived from either our external or our internal senses (or compounded from others so derived); in Locke's language, all our simple ideas are derived from sensation or reflection (EAP 1.3:22). Reid points out that Locke never noticed that his empiricist principles prohibit our having any conception of power. Hume did notice this, and he does not hesitate to conclude that we have no idea of power:

> *Efficacy, agency, power, force, energy*—these terms all mean the same thing, which is to say, nothing. (THN 1.3.1:157)

> As we can have no idea of any thing which never appeared to our outward sense or inward sentiment, the necessary conclusion *seems* to be that we have no idea of connexion or power at all, and that these words are absolutely without any meaning, when employed either in philosophical reasonings or common life. (EHU 7.2:74)[3]

Reid agrees that Hume's empiricist principles are "repugnant" to our having any conception of active power (EAP 4.2:204–05).

Reid observes that Locke's empiricist principles are in practice less strict than Hume's (EAP 1.4:22–23). Locke holds that all ideas are "derived" from ideas of sensation and reflection, but he is lax in what he allows to count as a derivation. He begins his chapter "Of Power" with a section entitled "This idea, how got" (2.21.1), which comes down (after we eliminate some prolixity) to this: the mind, noting that one type of change is often followed by another type of change, concludes that changes of the first type will continue to be followed by changes of the second type, "and so comes by the idea of power" (ECHU 2.21.1) All Locke is doing here is

---

[2] Reid's remaining observations in EAP 1.1 are that power must belong to a subject, that it may be present even when not exerted, and that it has no contrary (11–12).

[3] Hume is actually of two minds on this issue, sometimes forthrightly declaring that we have no idea of power or necessary connection and other times saying that we do, deriving it from the alleged "feeling" we have of one idea giving way to another with which it has become firmly associated. He italicizes "seems" in the passage just quoted to leave room for the second option, but in my view, that option is inconsistent with his core principles.

pointing out the experiential occasions on which we acquire the concept of power. He does not require that power be *on display* in our experience or that instances of it actually be set before our minds—or if he has such a requirement, he does not enforce it. Hume, by contrast, does operate with a requirement of displayability; he holds that all our simple ideas are *copies* of prior impressions, and by this standard, he concludes that we have no idea of power.

Reid claims that Locke has "imposed upon himself" if he thinks our having the notion of power is reconcilable with the letter of his empiricist principles (EAP 1.3:21–22). He points out that in order to get the idea of power in the way Locke sketches, we must have not only the Lockean sources of sensation (= Reidian perception) and reflection (= Reidian consciousness), but memory and reason as well. We may add that not even these sources are sufficient if by "reason" one means the drawing out of necessary consequences. Or does Reid think power is necessarily implied in change in a way in which hardness is not implied in the tactile sensations that suggest it to us? I return to this question below.

One of Reid's overarching principles is that when philosophical theory is at odds with commonsense fact, the theory must yield. So much the worse, then, for concept empiricism. He had already argued in the Inquiry's *experimentum crucis* that there is one family of conceptions that every one agrees we possess, yet are not displayed in sensory experience: extension and its kin, such as figure and motion. He now adds power to the list of exceptions to empiricism.

What are the arguments for concept empiricism? Hume says there are two: that when you exclude any sense, such as vision to the blind, you cut off a range of ideas, and that if anyone will make an inventory of his ideas, he will see that there are none not copied from prior impressions (THN 1.1.1:4–5; EHU 2:19–20; letter to Reid, IHM 256–57). The second of these arguments is an inductive argument. Yet Hume subsequently employs the principle polemically to banish exceptions, as though it were a necessary truth. Reid notes how Hume changes the game:

> For it is a conclusion that admits no proof, but by induction; and it is upon this ground that he himself founds it. . . . [Therefore, there can be no assurance] that this conclusion holds without any exception. . . . [Yet throughout Hume's *Treatise*] this general rule is considered as of sufficient authority, in itself, to exclude . . . every thing that appears to be an exception. This is contrary to the fundamental principles of the experimental method of reasoning. (EAP 1.4:23)

Reid takes Hume to be almost alone among philosophers in denying that we have any idea of power. He offers five points against the Humean stance, summarized at EAP 1.2: 19–20. The most powerful of the five is this: there are many things we can affirm or deny concerning power with understanding—for example, power re-quires a subject and it need not be exerted—but how could we understand what these things mean if we had no notion of power? Later on he encapsulates the point by saying, "A false opinion about power, no less than a true, implies an idea of power; for how can men have any opinion, true or false, about a thing of which they have no idea?" (EAP 1.4:25–26).[4]

Wright (1987) claims that Hume would deny Reid's premise that we can have beliefs only about things concerning which we also have ideas. For my part, I do not see how Hume could possibly deny Reid's premise, given his account of belief as consisting of lively ideas. A hard-core Humean should say that we do not even have the *beliefs* Reid says we do—we only bandy about words like "power" without expressing any beliefs thereby.

A good part of Reid's efforts against Hume are therefore devoted to showing that we do indeed have the beliefs in question. He argues that human beings engage in various activities that presuppose a belief on the agent's part that he has this or that power. For example, deliberation and promising presuppose a belief on the agent's part that he has the power to do the promised or deliberated-upon thing (EAP 1.2:18; see Yaffe 2007 for a reconstruction of the argument concerning promising). If we have the belief, we must have the constituent notion. Such is Reid's brief for our having the notion of power.

*Relative, yet distinct.* Reid's second observation concerning power is that our con-ception of it is relative rather than direct. Recall that this distinction is the key to Reid's account of what he thinks right in the distinction between primary and sec-ondary qualities (chapter 4). He explains the terms again:

> Of some things we know what they are in themselves; our conception of such things I call *direct*. Of other things, we know not what they are in themselves, but only that they have . . . certain relations to other things; of these our conception is only *relative*. (EAP 1.1:9)[5]

Reid mentions two categories of things of which we have direct conceptions: the primary qualities of bodies and the operations of our own minds (EAP 1.1:10). Of other things we have only relative conceptions; for example, when we conceive an

---

[4] Reid is using "idea" here broadly to cover what he himself usually calls conceptions or notions. He does not mean to imply that having beliefs requires having ideas in Locke's or Hume's sense.
[5] Reid fills the ellipsis with "certain properties or attributes, or." I have elided this phrase to high-light what is relational about relative conceptions; "having certain properties" is simply a special case of having relations, as is clear in Reid's discussion of the notion of substance.

object to be red, all we conceive about it is that it has some property that produces a certain sort of sensation in us.

What is our relative conception of power relative *to*? Its exertions or effects, Reid says, as when we speak of the power *to walk*. "It is relative to the effect, and to the will of producing it" (EAP 1.5:32). In section D below, I discuss how exertion, will, and effect are related.

In the *Active Powers* Reid claims that a relative conception need not be indistinct; it may even be more distinct than a direct conception of the same thing. This is a departure from the *Intellectual Powers*, in which he says that relative notions are ipso facto obscure, not distinct.[6] I suspect that he changed his tune between the two books simply because he did not want to have to confess that our conception of active power is obscure.

To illustrate his contention that a relative conception may be distinct, Reid cites Descartes's example of the chiliagon, or thousand-sided polygon. Our direct conception of such a figure through sight or visual imagination is not distinct, not being distinguishable from the conception we would form of a polygon with 999 sides. "But when I form a relative conception of it, by attending to the relation it bears to polygons of a greater or less number of sides, my notion of it becomes distinct and scientific" (EAP 1.1:11).

I must register a complaint against Reid's use of the chiliagon example. *A figure having 997 more sides than a triangle* is a relative conception involving an *internal* relation—a relation supervening on intrinsic characteristics of the relata and enabling us to deduce some of the intrinsic characteristics of one relatum if we know those of the other. *The power exerted in walking* is, for all we have been told, a relative conception involving an *external* relation, leaving us in the dark about the intrinsic nature of the power or quality that stands in the relation. If Reid wants us to believe that our notion of power is one of those relative notions that manages not be obscure, he has not yet made out his case.[7]

---

[6] Locke operates with two oppositions, clear versus obscure and distinct versus confused. Reid has only a single opposition, distinct versus obscure. He sometimes uses "clear" instead of "distinct."

[7] Here is another way to make my point: If we know that x has the property of having one more side than a chiliagon, we do thereby know something about how x is in itself, just as much as we do in knowing something to be square. Although we have used a relational expression in describing the property, the property itself is (or at least implies) an intrinsic property. So the example of the chili-plus-one-agon is not an example of a notion that is *merely* relative, yet distinct—it is an example of a notion that is (or at least yields) a direct notion. By contrast, "the power that gives rise to walking" involves a relation that is arguably external, and therefore it is a *merely* relative notion, about which no claim of clearness or distinctness can be made.

*Power and Will.* Section 1.5 of the *Active Powers* is entitled "Whether Beings that have no Will nor Understanding may have Active Power?" The answer Reid announces in the final paragraph of the section is negative: "It seems, therefore, to me most probable, that such beings only as have some degree of understanding and will, can possess active power" (EAP 1.5:33). If Reid is right, active power cannot be ascribed to inanimate objects—fire does not have the power to consume wood, nor water the power to dissolve sugar.

Reid cites Locke as holding (in Reid's paraphrase) that "the only clear notion or idea we have of active power, is taken from the power which we find in ourselves to give certain motions to our bodies, or a certain direction to our thoughts; and this power in ourselves can be brought into action only by willing or volition" (EAP 1.5:29). From this it follows, Reid says, "that the active power, of which [alone] we can have any distinct conception, can be only in beings that have understanding and will." He goes on to endorse Locke's opinion himself: "From the consciousness of our own activity, seems to be derived, not only the clearest, but the only conception we can form of activity, or the exertion of active power" (EAP 1.5:30).[8]

I wish to discuss two questions. First, why does Reid think our clearest notion of active power (if not our only notion of it) is gotten from our own voluntary activity? Second, is Reid warranted in concluding that only beings with will and intelligence can have any power?

The notion of active power is an innate concept in the sense introduced in chapter 2: it is not copied from any external item of perception, nor from any internal item of consciousness. Nonetheless, the notion is *suggested* to us (in Reid's sense) by our consciousness of certain internal items—our own volitions. We may be reminded at this point of Reid's examples of innate concepts in the *Inquiry*—the notions of hardness and extension, which he thinks are not copied from our sensations or extracted from them in any rational way, but which arise in us on certain sensory occasions by a law of our constitution. Is the notion of active power related to our volitions as the notion of hardness is related to the sensations that suggest it? In other words, is the notion of power related to the occasions on which we form it not by virtue of any internal relation to those occasions, but simply because it is a law of our constitution that we form the notion on those occasions?

In two of my remarks above, I assumed that the answer is yes—that power stands to our volitions as hardness stands to our tactile sensations. I noted that in his discussion of Locke's account of how we get the idea of power, Reid should not have allowed that all we need add to the sources acknowledged by Locke is reasoning, by

---

[8] Is this claim compatible with Reid's earlier claim that we have no consciousness of active power? Yes, for he is claiming here only that we are conscious of our own *exertions* of active power.

which we trace internal connections. I also complained that Reid should not have insinuated that active power may be one of those notions that is clear despite being relative, like *figure having one more side than a chiliagon*, since the relation of active power to its exertions or effects is not an internal relation like *having one more side than*. But perhaps I was wrong on both counts; perhaps Reid does think that active power is internally related to its effects, in such a way that we can deduce its existence and something of its character from its manifestations.

Reid holds that we get a clearer conception of active power from observing our own voluntary activity than we would get from seeing the wind topple a tree in a storm. It is not really a matter of degrees of clarity, but of all or none: we *do* get the conception of active power from observing our own activity, whereas we would never get it just from observing events in nature. Why is that? On the hardness model, the answer would be that it is a simply a brute fact about our constitution—it is part of our nature that voluntary actions make us think of power and falling trees do not. The matter is as unaccountable as would be a scenario in which red sensations somehow gave us the notion of color in objects while blue sensations did not. It is hard to believe that Reid thinks of things in this way. He seems rather to think that there is something about voluntary activity that bears an inherently intelligible relation to the power that it manifests—that it somehow *smacks* of power, making "manifest" the appropriate word.[9] This throws some light, I think, on why he thinks our voluntary activity is our best and perhaps our only source of the notion of power.[10]

I turn now to the second question: whether Reid is warranted in concluding that there is active power only in beings with will and understanding. For Reid, all willing has an object (EAP 2.1:47–48), so is it is easy to see why understanding (or the ability to form conceptions of things) is a requisite of will. But why must will be a requisite of power?

Here is the conclusion of EAP 1.5 again:

> It seems, therefore, to me most probable, that such beings only as have some degree of understanding and will, can possess active power. (EAP 1.5:33)

In a letter, Reid states the point with no qualification in terms of mere probability:

> I am not able to form a conception how power, in the strict sense, can be exerted without will; nor can there be will without some degree of understanding. Therefore,

---

[9] Whence, I surmise, the title of Yaffe's *Manifest Activity* (2004); see pp. 21–22 of that book.
[10] There is perhaps a hint of this idea in his remark that we do have "consciousness of the manner in which our own active power is exerted" (EAP 1.5:30).

nothing can be an efficient cause, in the proper sense, but an intelligent being. (Letter to James Gregory, June 14, 1785, COR 174–75; cf. EAP 4.2:204)[11]

How does Reid reach this remarkable conclusion?

I begin by warning against a non sequitur. What Reid has contended for earlier in the section is that it is exclusively from our experience of our own voluntary activity—our willings and the actions they effect—that we get our notion of active power. There is no other source for the notion. Granting this much, I claim that it does not follow that we cannot conceive of active power in a being that lacks will, nor that there cannot be active power in such a being. An analogy should make the point clear. Some philosophers (including Pollock 1974) hold that we get our concept of the past from one source only: our experiences of remembering (or ostensibly remembering), in which items seem to be presented to us as past.[12] (Perhaps Reid would agree with these philosophers, but it does not matter whether he would.) Does it follow that we can form no conception of a past event lying beyond the scope of our own memories? Or that there could not *be* a past event antedating our own memories? Not in the slightest. Having gotten the concept of the past from its circumscribed source, we can extrapolate it and apply it to items that transcend the source. Reid needs to show us why something similar may not also be the case with active power.[13]

I do not say that Reid commits this non sequitur. He may simply claim outright that we can form no conception of power in beings without will, rather than invalidly inferring it from the premise that our original source of the notion of power is our own volitions. But the question remains how he arrives at the further conclusion that there can *be* no power in beings without will.

Yaffe proposes that Reid is using the principle that what we cannot conceive of is impossible. Reid is well known for criticizing Hume's principle that whatever is conceivable is possible (EIP 4.3:327–33), but Yaffe maintains that Reid has no

---

[11] "It is certain that we can conceive no kind of active power but what is similar or analogous to that which we attribute to ourselves; that is, a power which is exerted by will and with understanding" (EAP 4.2:204).

[12] Others (including Furlong 1951:104) hold that we get our concept of the past from experiences of items within the specious present. That being so, we may still go on to think of a past that stretches beyond the advent of life on earth.

[13] Berkeley says we get our concept of existence for sensible things only by perceiving them (PHK section 5)—a plausible enough premise. He goes on to conclude that we can form no "abstracted" concept of sensible things existing unperceived. Any interpretation of Reid's argument linking power to will must show why a similar argument would not lead to Berkeleyan idealism.

One may cite Wittgenstein 1953:302 as another instance in which Reid's method of arguing would lead to a conclusion of which he himself would disapprove: "If one has to imagine someone else's pain on the model of one's own, this is none too easy a thing to do: for I have to imagine pain which I do not feel on the model of the pain which I do feel."

qualms about the converse principle, that whatever is *in*conceivable is *im*possible (Yaffe 2004:25).

I myself have defended the principle that finding something inconceivable gives one a prima facie reason for regarding it as impossible (Van Cleve 1983). However, I have defended it only under the following meaning of "finding it inconceivable that p": intuiting (or "seeing" in a nonfactive sense) that it is impossible that p. I do not find it inconceivable in this sense that there are beings that possess active power but lack will. Would Reid? I am not sure. He claims only that he can *form no conception* of beings who have power but not will (or who exert power otherwise than by willing). Being unable to form a conception of something is *not* a prima facie reason for regarding it as nonexistent or impossible. That is true, at any rate, under either of two meanings of "being unable to form a conception of X." (i) It could mean drawing a blank when you try to think of anything answering to the description "X." If that is your condition, you are in no position to regard X as impossible. The blind man who can form no conception of scarlet things is in no position to regard scarlet things as impossible.[14] Moreover, that is presumably not Reid's condition, since he takes sides in the debate whether there can be beings with power but not will.[15] (ii) It could mean being able to form a conception of Xs, but not being able to see that Xs are possible. That, I would wager, is Reid's true condition with respect to beings that have power but not will. But being in that condition does not warrant one in believing Xs to be impossible. I am unable to see how there can be more than three mutually perpendicular lines meeting in a single point, but I am hesitant to conclude from that fact alone that four-dimensional spaces are impossible. Reid himself gives a similar example: "Though we can have no conception how the future free actions of men may be known by the Deity, this is not a sufficient reason to conclude that they cannot be known" (EAP 4.10:258).[16] The claim that power cannot be exercised by beings who lack will is unproven by any considerations canvassed here.[17]

---

[14] Reid notes at EAP 1.5:30 that "if all men had been blind, we should have no conception of the power of seeing." He should also have noted that we would have been in no position to affirm that there is no such power.

[15] In a remark directed against Hume, Reid says "The very dispute, whether we have the conception of an efficient cause, shows that we have. [Men] cannot dispute about things of which they have no conception" (EAP 4.2:205). This point may be re-directed against Reid himself: since he participates in a dispute over whether unintelligent beings can be causes, he must have the conception of an unintelligent cause. (Is there any inconsistency here with EAP 1.5:33, lines 5–7?)

[16] He adds that we cannot conceive how God created the world *ex nihilo*, or even how we manage to remember past events or be conscious of our own thoughts. But we do manage somehow to be conscious of our thoughts!

[17] Anyone who would render a final verdict on this question, however, must assess the resourceful reconstructions of two Reidian arguments from power to will in Chapters 1 and 2 of Yaffe 2004.

## B. TWO TYPES OF CAUSATION

In Reid's philosophy there are two types of causation, agent causation and event causation or, as he usually calls them, efficient causation and physical causation. He prefers to
say that there are two senses of the word "cause," as he thinks the two types are so different that they are not even species of a common genus (letter to James Gregory, July 30,
1789, COR 206). The two types of causation are distinguished both by their relata and
by the nature of the relation itself. In event causation, both of the relata are events, such
as the striking of ball 2 by ball 1 and the careening off of ball 2. In agent causation, the
relatum on the cause side is a substance or an agent, not an event. The relation in event
causation is *following in accordance with a law*: e is followed by f, and e and f are of types
E and F such that all E-type events are followed by F-type events. The relation in agent
causation is sui generis and indefinable, but Reid thinks we get our clearest notion of it
when we are aware of what we ourselves do in initiating a voluntary action, as discussed
in the previous section. He goes so far as to say (in company with Berkeley) that the
only true efficient causes are conscious beings endowed with will.[18]

The standard view about causation nowadays is that the relata of the causal relation
are *always* events. Those who embrace the standard view may allow that we use locutions in which the cause is specified only as a substance, as in "the stone caused the
window to break," but they maintain that such locutions are elliptical; they are short
for something along the lines of "the stone's coming into contact with the window
at velocity v caused it to break." More generally, statements of the form "S causes e"
(where "S" is the name of a substance rather than an event) can be true only if there
is some event c of which S is the subject such that c causes e. I once heard Wilfrid Sellars say that Mrs. O'Leary's cow caused the Chicago fire, but she did it *by* kicking over
the lantern. I take his point to have been that apparent cases of agent causation are
always reducible to event causation: "*the cow* caused the fire" is true only in the sense
that the cow was the subject of an *event* that caused the fire.[19] A true believer in agent
causation, on the other hand, believes that there are cases of causation by agents that
are *not* thus reducible to event causation; the cause of e is not S's V-ing, but simply S.

---

[18] The distinction between efficient causation, exercised only by conscious agents, and physical
causation, understood merely as regular sequence, is one of most prominent Berkeleyan elements
surviving in Reid's philosophy. For Berkeley's view, see Works, vol. II, 280.

[19] I do not know whether the Sellars remark occurs in print. An alternative interpretation of it
would be that he was allowing Mrs. O'Leary's cow as an irreducible agent cause, but saying that
her causing the Chicago fire was not a *basic* action of hers, but an action she accomplished by
doing something else, kicking over the lantern—which she presumably also did by doing something else, moving her foot. An agent-causation theorist would say that wherever this series of
actions bottoms out, we have an action or event not caused by any event, but simply by the agent
herself. I doubt that this is what Sellars had in mind.

When spelled out that way, agent causation can seem mysterious and even unintelligible. How can the cause simply be the agent, period? C. D. Broad once complained that the cause of an event must be something whose existence or occurrence explains why the event happened when it did, but that no enduring agent provides any such explanation:

> How could an event possibly be determined to happen at certain date if its total cause contained no factor to which the notion of date has any application? And how can the notion of date have any application to anything that is not an event? (1952:215)

Similar puzzlement is expressed by Brody in the introduction to his edition of the *Active Powers*:

> The agent presumably existed for a long time before that particular act of willing, so it is not the mere existence of the agent that produces the act of willing. What then causes the act of willing to take place when it does? The answer to this question is the missing link in Reid's theory of human liberty. (Brody 1969:xix)

It is understandable, then, that irreducible agent causation has few contemporary proponents.[20]

The situation in this regard has changed 180 degrees since Reid's day (Donagan 1979:218). Today event causation is the norm and agent causation the mystery. In Reid's day, agent causation was taken for granted and event causation regarded as a Humean innovation of doubtful intelligibility. Reid observes that the definition of *cause* by his adversary Priestley, a follower of Hume on this point, "[puts] a *cause* under the category of *circumstances*, which I take to be new" (EAP 4.9:249).

The turnabout is well described in Taylor 1966 (9–17). Taylor identifies four theses bound up in what he calls "the original idea of a cause" and which he could have taken straight from the pages of Reid: that efficient causation has nothing to do with constant conjunction, that causes are substances (typically persons), that causes make things happen by exercising their power to do so, and that exercises of power necessitate their effects. He notes that there has been a significant shift in the meaning of "cause" from ancient days to the present, causes once being thought of as objects and now being thought of as events.

---

[20] A survey of contemporary opinion on the relata of the causal relation (Schaffer 2008) mentions events and other event-like entities (such as facts and states of affairs) as candidate relata, but not substances or agents. I classify facts and states of affairs as event-like (despite their not being individuated in the same manner as events) because they involve predicates as well as subjects, not just subjects themselves.

Reid's views about agent causation and event causation are well expressed in a series of letters to his physician and friend James Gregory, written not long after he had treated of these topics in drafts of the *Active Powers*. I reproduce passages from four of these letters here:

> The word *cause*, is very ambiguous in all languages. . . .
>
> In the strict and proper sense, I take an efficient cause to be a being who had power to produce the effect, and exerted that power for that purpose.
>
> Active power is a quality which can only be in a substance that really exists, and is endowed with that power. Power to produce an effect, supposes power not to produce it; otherwise it is not power but necessity, which is incompatible with power taken in a strict sense.
>
> In physics, the word *cause* has another meaning. . . . When a phenomenon is produced according to a certain law of nature, we call the law of nature the cause of that phenomenon. (June 14, 1785, COR 174–76)

> I think we agree in this, that a cause, in the proper and strict sense . . . signifies a being or mind that has power and will to produce the effect. But there is another meaning of the word cause, which is so well authorized by custom, that we cannot always avoid using it, and I think we may call it the physical sense; as when we say that heat is the cause that turns water into vapour, and cold the cause that freezes it into ice. A cause, in this sense, means only something which, by the laws of nature, the effect always follows. I think natural philosophers, when they pretend to shew the *causes* of natural phenomena, always use the word in this last sense; and the vulgar in common discourse very often do the same. (September 23, 1785, COR 178)

> What D. Hume says of causes, in general, is very just when applied to physical causes, that a constant conjunction with the effect is essential to such causes, and implied in the very conception of them. (March 1786, COR 180; see also the letter of October 1793, COR 234)

> I think [the word cause] has one strict and philosophical meaning which is a single relation, and it has a lax and popular meaning which includes many relations. The popular meaning I think I can express by a definition. *Causa est id, quo posito ponitur Effectus, quo sublato tollitur.*[21] (Spring 1786, COR 181)

We have what Reid calls physical causation when one event follows another according to a law. What is the cause—the earlier event or the law? In the first letter

---

[21] A cause is that which, being affirmed, the effect is affirmed; and being denied, the effect is denied.

above (and frequently in his published writings), he says that *the law* is the cause. (See, for example, EIP 2.6:103; EAP 4.3:211, lines 16–21, and 4.9:251, lines 3–4.) In the second letter, he says *the earlier event* is the cause. As it sounds more natural to me to call the earlier event the cause, I shall generally follow that terminological practice, but nothing important turns on the choice.

Despite believing that agent or efficient causation is the only causation in the "strict and philosophical" sense of the term, Reid himself uses the word "cause" in its "lax and popular" sense over and over again in his published writings.[22] To cite just one example, I remind the reader of Reid's account of secondary qualities, as discussed in chapter 4. What we mean in calling an object red, Reid says, is that there is something in the object that causes sensations of red in us. He certainly does not mean that the object itself is (or contains) a causal agent, endowed with will and intelligence, or that some other agent is really playing the relevant causal role. What plays that role is a physical property in the object, even if God or some other intelligent agent was required to endow it with that role. Redness is in the rose, not in God or some other agent.

We can say what is involved in physical causation: it is simply what Hume calls constant conjunction. (See the next to the last remark in the excerpts above from his letters to Gregory.) What can we say about what is involved in agent causation? Rowe has helpfully summed up Reid's view in three conditions, individually necessary and jointly sufficient for *X caused event e* (Rowe 1991:49):

1. X is a *substance* that had *power* to bring about e;
2. X *exerted* its power to bring about e;
3. X had the *power* to refrain from bringing about e.

Rowe notes that these conditions are not meant to be a definition, as they themselves use causal language ("bringing about") (69). He also notes that the third condition is redundant in Reid's view, being already implied by the first as well as the second (as we shall see later). All three conditions may be found in the first of the letters to Gregory quoted from above, as well as in multiple passages in the *Active Powers*.[23]

Agent causation is thus characterized in terms of active power. Recall from the previous section that on Reid's view, the only beings possessed of active power are

---

[22] In a letter to Gregory of July 30, 1789, he says we must bear with the imperfections of language in this regard (COR 207).

[23] Condition (1): "That power may exist without any being or subject to which that power may be attributed, is an absurdity" (EAP 1.1:11). Condition (2): "That which produces a change by the exertion of its power, we call the *cause* of that change" (EAP 1.1:13). Condition (3): "Power to produce any effect implies power not to produce it" (EAP 1.5:29); "a power to walk implies a power not to walk" ("Of Power," 11).

beings with intelligence and will. Combining these points, we see that the only agents—the only exercisers of causality in the strict and philosophical sense of the term—are intelligent beings. All other "causes" are causes only in the lax and popular sense; they are events regularly followed by other events. On this point Reid's views are strikingly reminiscent of Berkeley, with whom he so strenuously disagrees on other matters.

It is necessary in this connection to correct a remark made by von Wright: that for Reid we understand causation in the realm of nature by means of the analogy cause:effect = agent:action (1971:n.40). The analogy holds for efficient causation, but not for physical causation. In the inanimate world, there is nothing like the agent:action relation between physical causes and their effects; there is only regular succession.[24]

## C. UNIVERSAL AGENT CAUSATION

Reid affirms that it is a first principle that everything that happens has an efficient cause (EAP 1.5:26, 4.2:202–03; COR 174).[25] He also maintains, as we have just noted, that efficient causation is only exercised by intelligent agents. To these contentions of his, let us now add another: that natural science never discovers anything but physical causes:

> We deceive ourselves, if we conceive, that we can point out the real efficient cause of any one of [the phenomena of nature]. (EAP 1.6:37)

> Supposing natural philosophy brought to its utmost perfection, it does not discover the efficient cause of any one phenomenon in nature. (EAP 1.6:38)

A sailor and a Newtonian natural philosopher will both say that a magnet causes a compass needle to swerve, but neither of them knows the real cause, and the Newtonian knows he does not know. Both of them use the word "cause" simply because the motion of the needle regularly follows the approach of the magnet.

Reid is thus committed to two remarkable theses, one negative and one positive. Negatively, when we say that a magnet causes a needle to move or a storm causes a

---

[24] It is true, as discussed in the next section, that Reid believes that the laws of succession are the rules by which God, the supreme agent, acts. But that point pertains to the explanation of physical causal relations, not the analysis of them, and in any case does not make the physical cause itself anything like an agent.

[25] There is also EIP 6.6:497, but there he does not make it explicit that everything that comes to be has an *efficient* cause.

tree to fall, the cause strictly speaking is not the magnet or the storm or any other natural event. Positively, the real cause is an intelligent agent.

As regards the negative thesis, Madden maintains that in denying that there are any real causes in nature, Reid is flying in the face of the common sense he is normally concerned to defend (1982, discussed in Rowe 51–54). Do not people the world around say that water has the power to dissolve sugar and that bricks sometimes cause windows to break? And does not Reid himself say that forms of speech embodied in all languages are hallmarks of common sense?

This is one of the few places where Reid does not heed the dictates of common language. He explains our saying such things as "the ocean wore away the dune" as relics of a bygone age in which human beings believed that all objects in nature were animate. (See EAP 1.2:13–18 and 3.3:206–9.) We say that the sun warms the stone because our ancestors believed that the sun was a being with intelligence and will, quite capable of being an efficient cause in Reid's sense. We have shed the animism, but its effects on our language remain. We still say the sun warms the stone, just as we still say that the sun rises even though we now believe it is the earth that moves. Thus does Reid explain away linguistic evidence of a sort that he normally cites as authoritative.[26] Apparently, the evidence provided by what is common to all languages is defeasible.

Let us turn to the positive thesis—that every event in nature is caused by some intelligent agent. Reid's view is reminiscent of Malebranche's, for whom God is the only real cause and everything else we call a cause is merely an occasion on which God acts. Reid's view is not as extreme as Malebranche's, though, for he allows that human beings are the causes of some of their own bodily motions and acts of mind, and that conscious agents other than God (angels, perhaps?) may for all we know be the causes of events in nature.

How radical is Reid's positive view? We may distinguish a stronger and a weaker form of it. According to the stronger, every event in nature is *directly* caused by some intelligent agent, whether that agent be God or some finite intelligence. According to the weaker, every event in nature is *directly or indirectly* caused by some intelligent agent. The weaker thesis allows that the proximate cause of the fall of a tree might be a physical cause, such as a windstorm, whose own proximate cause was also a physical cause, such as the collision of two air masses, and so on back until we reach

---

[26] For example, at EIP 1.2:44 Reid defends the principle that attributes require subjects by noting that in all languages adjectives require substantives. At EIP 6.4:466, he notes that features common to all languages, such as the dependence of adjectives on substantives, are marks of first principles.

an agent cause that initiated the chain of physical causes. The choice is between two pictures. The stronger view may be portrayed as in Figure 14.1:

```
A    A    A    Figure 14.1
↓    ↓    ↓
e  –  f  –  g
```

It would not have to be the same agent in each column. The weaker may be portrayed as in Figure 14.2:

```
A              Figure 14.2
↓
e  –  f  –  g
```

Tuggy (2000) and Yaffe (2004:70) take it that Reid's view is the stronger, but I wish to investigate the possibility that it is the weaker.[27]

Here are several passages that seem to leave the weaker thesis open:

> But whether he [God] acts immediately in the production of [events in the natural world], or by subordinate intelligent agents, *or by instruments that are unintelligent* . . . I apprehend to be mysteries placed beyond the limits of human knowledge. (EAP 1.5:28, emphasis mine)

> Thus, that a body put in motion continues to move till it be stopped, is an effect which, for what I know, may be owing to an inherent property in matter; if this be so, this property of matter is the physical cause of the continuance of the motion; but the ultimate efficient cause is the Being who gave this property to matter. (Letter to James Gregory, July 30, 1789, COR 206; cf. COR 175, lines 10–15)

> A law of nature requires a Being who has not only enacted the law, but provided the means of its being executed, *either by some physical cause,* or by some agent acting by his order. (Letter to James Gregory, July 30, 1789, COR 206; cf. COR 175, lines 10–15, emphasis mine)

> Nature appears as one great machine, where one wheel is turned by another, that by a third; and how far this necessary succession may reach, the Philosopher does not know. (EAP 4.3:207)

---

[27] How, it might be asked, can the agent in the second picture be said to be the cause of g? I do not see a problem here; A is the indirect agent cause of g insofar as A is the direct agent cause of an event that (by transitivity of event causation) is an event-cause of g.

The notion of indirect agent causation is required if Reid wants to say (as he does in passages to be discussed below) that we are the agent causes of our own bodily motions while conceding the possibility (as he also does) that we only directly agent-cause certain antecedents of those motions.

These remarks seem to allow that chains of physical causation, once set in motion by an agent, can proceed on their own.

On the other side, we must consider Reid's view that physical causes are only such in virtue of God's acting in accordance with certain laws.

Reid believes that the laws of nature are established by God. But how does God establish them? In what way are they the products of his will? I see two possibilities. First, he might establish them once for all by a single stroke of will (or at least by only one act of will per law). If laws take the form $(x)(Ax \rightarrow Bx)$, this alternative may be symbolized as $W(x)(Ax \rightarrow Bx)$. Second, he could establish them by making $Bx$ happen on every occasion on which $Ax$ happens, which would require a separate act of will for every happening of $Ax$. This alternative may be symbolized as $(x)(Ax \rightarrow WBx)$. It should be clear that on the second alternative, God is the immediate cause of every event in nature,[28] whereas on the first he may only be the ultimate cause of it, standing at the head of every chain $Ax \rightarrow Bx \rightarrow Cx \rightarrow$ (etc.) that spools out according to the laws he has ordained in the first way.

How would God will a law once for all in the $W(x)(Ax \rightarrow Bx)$ way without doing it piecemeal the $(x)(Ax \rightarrow WBx)$ way? The main possibility that occurs to me is that he might institute some sort of nomically necessary connection between the properties A and B, such as envisioned by D. M. Armstrong in his theory of laws (1985), whereby any occurrence of $Ax$ must be followed by an occurrence of $Bx$.[29]

The distinction I have just drawn between $W(x)(Ax \rightarrow Bx)$ and $(x)(Ax \rightarrow WBx)$ may call to mind Malebranche's distinction between general and particular volitions of the Deity. On closer scrutiny, however, I believe Malebranche's distinction is not the same as mine. Here is how Malebranche characterizes general volitions:

> I say that God acts by general volitions when He acts in consequence of the general laws which He has established. For example, I say that God acts in me by general volitions when He gives me a sensation of pain when I am pricked, since in consequence of the general and efficacious laws of the union of my soul and body which He has established, he makes me suffer pain when my body is ill-disposed. (1992:263)

---

[28] Or it could be that one of his agents is the immediate cause—but that would still give us the stronger form of the thesis that every event has an agent cause.

[29] Another possibility that comes to mind is this: God might arrange the total Humean mosaic in spacetime so that the supervenience base for the law $(x)(Ax \rightarrow Bx)$ under David Lewis's theory of laws (Lewis [1994] 1999) obtains. But that seems to me no different from the $(x)(Ax \rightarrow WBx)$ account. Perhaps the procedure would not have to involve a separate act for each tile; God might envision the entire mosaic and say "Let it be like that." But the procedure would still be one under which the placement of every tile is directly willed by God, even if only as part of a single cosmic act.

That is at least compatible with, and I believe strongly suggestive of, what I am calling the piecemeal approach. I take it the final clause should be punctuated as "he makes me suffer pain (when my body is ill-disposed)" rather than "he makes me (suffer pain when my body is ill-disposed)."

Here is Malebranche's contrasting characterization of particular volitions:

> I say, on the contrary, that God acts by particular volitions when the efficacy of His will is not determined by some general law to produce some effect. Thus, supposing that God should make me feel the pain of pricking without there occurring any change in my body or in any creature whatsoever, which determines Him to act in me by some general law, I say that then God acts by particular volitions. (264)

The contrast is between God's making me feel pain on an occasion of a type lawfully connected with feeling pain (general volition) and his making me feel pain when there is no such occasion for it (particular volition). Either way, the pain is caused by something God does there and then. Both types of volition are particular in the sense that their objects are particular states of affairs; they differ just in whether they happen in consequence of God's resolution to act in accord with some general law.[30]

Would Malebranche allow that God might implement a law by inserting a necessitation relation between universals, à la Armstrong? I think not. He says God could not delegate causal powers to his creatures, since they are incapable of having them, and the point seems no less applicable if the "creatures" are universals or event-types (1992:96–97).[31]

Let us now return to Reid. How does he think of God's enacting a law? Here are several relevant pronouncements:

> The laws of nature are the rules according to which the effects are produced; but there must be a cause which operates according to these rules. (EAP 1.6:38)

> But a law of nature . . . is only the rule, according to which the efficient cause acts. (EAP 4.9:251; see also EAP 4.3:211)

> The physical laws of nature are the rules according to which the Deity commonly acts in his natural government of the world; and, whatever is done according to them, is

---

[30] As I understand Malebranche, a particular volition may or may not constitute a miracle, depending on whether the willed particular state of affairs happens in the presence of a circumstance that normally contraindicates it (miracle) or in the absence of any circumstance that normally positively indicates it (no miracle).

[31] On the other hand, Malebranche does speak of "efficacious laws" on pp. 263–64. (Thanks to Kenny Pearce for pointing this out.)

not done by man, but by God, either immediately or by instruments under his direction. (EAP 4.9:251)

A law of nature is a purpose or resolution of the author of nature, to act according to a certain rule—either immediately by himself or by instruments that are under his direction. There must be a real agent to produce the phenomenon according to the law. (COR 176)

In each case, Reid says God (or the deputized efficient cause) acts *according to* the law he has envisioned and resolved to follow. He does not say God acts *by means of* the law or that he lets *the world* unfold in accordance with the law. This strongly suggests to me the $(x)(Ax \rightarrow WBx)$ answer to our question. I suspect also that Reid may have something like Malebranche's reason for not wanting properties or events themselves to be invested with any sort of efficacy: they are not agents, and power can reside only in an agent.

In the end, then, I side with Tuggy and Yaffe: Reid holds that every event in nature is produced *directly* by an agent cause.

Assuming that this is so, I wish to consider two objections to Reid's view.

First, how can Reid hold it to be a first principle—a self-evident truth—that every event has an efficient cause, if that implies that every event in nature is produced by an intelligent cause? Surely there is nothing self-evident about the latter proposition! In reply (thanks here to Tuggy), I think Reid could say that what is self-evident is simply that every event has an *efficient* cause. That every event has an *intelligent* cause follows only when we add the further premise that only beings with intelligence can be efficient causes. Reid certainly believes the further premise, but he may not regard it as self-evident. (See EAP 1.5:28, lines 1–3.)[32] What follows from something self-evident together with something not self-evident need not be self-evident.

Second, if God is the immediate cause of every event in nature, does that imply that every event in nature is really God's action? And would that in turn imply a sort of Spinozism, in which God is the subject of all events in nature?

Reid is not committed to Spinozism, for two reasons. First, he does not hold that God is the cause of *every* event in nature—human beings cause some events in nature, such as their own bodily motions. Second, even if God *were* the cause of all events in nature, it would not follow that all events in nature are God's actions.

---

[32] See also the letter to Gregory of June 14, 1985, in which he spells out what an efficient cause is without mentioning will or intelligence, then says, "That every event must have a cause in this proper sense, I take to be self-evident." On the other side of the issue, however, is the following passage from EAP 4.9:250: "Why may not an efficient cause be defined to be a being that had power and will to produce the effect? . . . This, I think, is the proper meaning of the word cause, when it is used in metaphysics; and particularly when we affirm, that every thing that begins to exist must have a cause."

If God causes a tree to fall, then making it fall is one of his actions, but the tree's falling is not. The tree's falling is a *component* of one of God's actions, but it is not itself one of God's actions, since it has the tree and not God as its subject.[33] We could reach Spinoza's conclusion if we added the Spinozistic premise that no substance can cause an event in any other substance, but Reid's God is not under that prohibition.

## D. ACTION AND VOLITION

"We digest our food, our blood circulates, our heart and arteries beat . . . all these things must be done by the power of some agent; but they are not done by our power" (EAP 1:5:31). They are not our *doings*, Reid says. What distinguishes our actions, the things that we *do*, from events that we merely undergo, of which we are merely the subject?

This is the issue posed by Wittgenstein in his pregnant question:

> When 'I raise my arm,' my arm goes up. And the problem arises: what is left over if I subtract the fact that my arm goes up from the fact that I raise my arm? (1953, paragraph 621)

The mere fact that my arm went up does not entail that I raised it, since someone else may have pushed it up, or it may have jerked up in a spasm. So what must be added to make it true that I raised my arm?[34]

There are two main answers to this question. According to the first, what must be added is the fact that a *volition* or *act of will* on my part caused my arm to go up. According to second, the needed fact is that *I*, an agent, caused my arm to go up. These are not the only answers, but they are the leading contenders.[35] Reid's theory of action combines the two: he thinks volition and agent causation are *both* essential ingredients in actions.

[33] I presuppose here that an action of S's must be an event of which S is a subject; hence I deny what some causal theorists of action affirm, that if S (or one of S's intentions, etc.) causes x's Ving, then x's Ving is an action of S's. I say instead that x's Ving is a *component* of an action of S's. See paragraph 5 of section D below.

[34] It would be safer to put the question thus: how is one to analyze statements such as "I raise my arm" so as to reveal how they entail (without being entailed by) statements such as "my arm goes up"? One should not presuppose (as the subtraction formulation encourages us to do) that there is a statement R such that (i) R is logically independent of "my arm goes up" and (ii) the conjunction of R and "my arm goes up" is logically equivalent to "I raise my arm." See Jaeger 1973.

[35] A third answer is that my action resides in some interior physical event, perhaps a neural event, that causes my arm to go up. This view is attributed to Hornsby by Alvarez and Hyman (1998).

"Voluntary action" is the phrase Reid often uses to distinguish actions in the sense we are now concerned with from events I merely undergo, such as the jostlings and jerks of two paragraphs back. Some would find the phrase "voluntary action" redundant, but it is nonetheless useful as a reminder. In this use, "voluntary action" does not have the meaning it has in some moral contexts. If I yield to the order to raise my arms at gunpoint, my action is not voluntary in a moral sense, but is nonetheless voluntary by contrast with my arms' going up as the result of someone else's hoisting them.[36, 37]

For the sake of brevity in what follows, I sometimes use two ways of speaking that I regard as inaccurate. I speak of raising one's arm as an action caused by the agent, whereas strictly speaking, what is caused by the agent is his arm's going up. Raising one's arm is not the action caused; instead, it is an action that consists in causing something else, the event of one's arm going up. I also speak of an arm's going up as an action when it is appropriately caused, but it would be more correct to say that it is a *component* of an action, the action being the larger state of affairs of the agent's appropriately causing the arm to go up. For further elucidation and defense of these points, see Alvarez and Hyman.

*Volitions and agency.* One of the ingredients Reid thinks essential to action— volition—was a commonplace in late seventeenth- and eighteenth-century philosophy. Here is Locke:

> We find in our selves a *Power* to begin or forbear, continue or end several actions of our minds, and motions of our Bodies, barely by a thought or preference of the mind, ordering, or, as it were commanding the doing or not doing such a particular action. This *Power* . . . is that which we call *the Will*. The actual exercise of that power, by directing any particular action, or its forbearance is that which we call *Volition* or *Willing*. (ECHU:2.21.5)

And Hume:

> I desire it may be observ'd that by the *will*, I mean nothing but *the internal impression we feel and are conscious of, when we knowingly give rise to any new motion of our body, or new perception of our mind.* (THN 2.3.1:399)

---

[36] Two further refinements: (i) Reid also distinguishes things done voluntarily from things done by instinct or habit (EAP 2.1:48 and 2.2:52). (ii) He thinks if there are things done under *irresistible* coercion, such as torture, they are not even voluntary in the metaphysical sense (EAP 2.2:56–58).

[37] Gideon Yaffe tells me that from the standpoint of the law (as distinct, perhaps, from morals), acts done under coercion are voluntary, though excusable.

Such impressions Hume elsewhere calls volitions:

> An act of volition produces motion in our limbs, or raises a new idea in our imagination.... Volition is surely an act of the mind, with which we are sufficiently acquainted. (EHU 8:64 and 69)[38]

Many thinkers of the period accepted what we may call the volitional theory of action: a bodily motion (or a "movement" of thought) by A is an action (or, more accurately, is part of an action) if and only if it is caused by a volition on A's part. The main controversies concerned not whether this analysis of action is correct, but what it takes for an action so analyzed to be a *free* action, or one possessed of moral liberty. (See Rowe 1995 for a good account of these matters.)

Some twentieth-century philosophers, of whom Richard Taylor (1966) is an outstanding example, have regarded volitions with suspicion and contempt. According to Taylor, volitions are philosophers' fictions. They have been given a name, "volition," that makes it look as though they are just the items needed to convert mere movements into voluntary actions. But when we look for these items, we do not find them:

> No one has ever arrived at a belief in volitions by observing them. They find no place in the data of empirical psychology, nor does it appear that anyone has ever found volitions occurring within himself ... by any introspective scrutiny of his mental life. It is doubtful, in fact, whether any such thing as a volition, as construed by this theory, has ever occurred under the sun. (66)

He also makes the following charge, meant to be damning:

> They are always referred to and described in terms of their effects, never in terms of themselves, leading one to suspect that perhaps they have no inherent characteristics. ... It is quite impossible to describe any volition or act of will except in terms of its alleged effects. (68)

For example, all that can be said about the supposed volition that one's arm should move is that its content is that one's arm should move.[39]

---

[38] Had Hume entered more intimately into himself, he might have realized that he never catches any volition, but always stumbles on some particular action, such as wiggling a finger or conjuring up an idea. But I am getting ahead of myself; this matter will shortly be discussed in connection with Taylor.

[39] As Gideon Yaffe has pointed out to me, this is a description of a volition in terms of its intended effect, which may not be its actual effect. Taylor's claim is therefore not strictly correct.

This second feature of volitions is alleged to be problematic for two reasons. First, it undermines the claim that volitions are causes of movements. The connection between a cause and its effect is supposed to be contingent, says Taylor, but it cannot be if the cause can be described only in terms of its effect. Second, it undermines the claim that volitions exist at all. Anything that exists must presumably have some intrinsic character, but volitions, if describable only in terms of their actual or intended effects, are intrinsically characterless.

The objections of the preceding paragraph are inconclusive, as we may see by considering their analogs regarding perceptual states. It is a fairly common doctrine in contemporary philosophy of mind that perceptual states are *transparent* in the following sense: the only features of them we can detect are their intentional or relational features. One knows that one's perception of a tree is *of* a tree, but knows nothing about its intrinsic character (Harman 1990). From this transparency doctrine it by no means follows that perceptions of trees cannot be caused by trees. Still less does it follow that perceptions of trees are too characterless to exist. Perceptions may have intrinsic features to which we have no access, or (as in the radical transparency doctrine of Moore) they may have no intrinsic character at all (see Van Cleve 2015).

But what of Taylor's initial point—that no one has ever found a volition? This has been contested by Carl Ginet, a contemporary proponent of the volitional theory of action (1990).[40] Ginet maintains that we do experience volitions, though we seldom attend to them—the very thing Reid so often says about sensations (24). He says volitions have an "actish phenomenal quality" that is easily recognized (15, 20). He argues that if we did not experience volitions, there would be no difference between the experience of voluntary activity and the experience of involuntary activity, as there plainly is (23–29).[41] And he says that volition is none other than *trying*, which seems to be an everyday phenomenon rather than an elusive one (10–11, 15, 30).

Taylor is as disdainful of *trying* (conceived of as a special interior act) as he is of willing. He says trying to do one thing is always doing something else, a manifest bodily act, with the goal of doing the first thing—for instance, trying to open a door is pushing on it with the goal of making it open. To this suggestion it may be objected that one may try to move one's limb when (perhaps unbeknownst to

---

[40] More accurately, Ginet's view is that actions are either basic actions or events generated by basic actions. The basic actions are "simple mental acts," which include volitions but are not limited to them. See his first chapter for a more accurate statement yet.

[41] This argument seems to me inconclusive. There is a difference between the experience of pleasurable activity and the experience of unpleasurable activity, but it does not follow that there is a distinctive experience of pleasure.

one) it is paralyzed. (This sort of consideration goes back to Reid; see EAP 2.1:50.) One tries and nothing bodily happens—so the trying must be purely mental. Taylor replies that there must be *something* bodily you are doing—straining your muscles, perhaps—and that if you are so paralyzed that you cannot even do that, then you cannot even try (1966:chapter 6).

As luck would have it, Taylor's book was fresh in mind while I recuperated from surgery to repair a torn rotator cuff. I was given a nerve block that numbed my right arm and paralyzed my fingers, effects which lasted for several hours after the operation, thus giving me the perfect opportunity to test Taylor's claims. I tried lifting now this knuckle, now that. With my left hand, success; with my right hand, failure. What did I feel? In the left hand, kinesthetic sensations; in the right hand, nothing. Of course, I said to myself, "Now I'll try moving the right middle finger," but that was the announcement of a plan rather than the execution of it. I think there was also a heightening of attention on the finger I was trying to move—but that was probably the looking for the trying rather than the trying itself. If there is a distinctive phenomenology of trying, it eluded me. So far, Taylor is vindicated. Yet Taylor also maintains that all trying is doing one bodily thing with the purpose of doing another, implying that in my postoperative condition, I could not even *try* to move my finger. I was confident to the contrary that I *did* try—I tried on the left with success and on the right with failure—and that there was something common to the two efforts, even though I cannot say anything about what the common element was *like*. I was also certain which finger on the right hand I was trying to lift, even though all the fingers on that hand felt the same, which is to say, no way at all.[42] As far as I am concerned, tryings remain in contention as plausible candidates for volitions.[43]

---

[42] My conviction that I tried to move my fingers while they were paralyzed is reinforced by McCann 1975.

[43] I have been asked, "Why not let things like this be settled by MRI tests?" An MRI investigation of the physiology of volition in subjects under nerve block has indeed been proposed (US National Institutes of Health 2011). The investigators expect to find correlates of the sense of agency in the inferior parietal lobule, but as of December of 2011, no results had been announced. However, thanks to Gideon Yaffe, I know of one actually performed study that indicates the possibility of volition without overt action (Desmurget 2009). The investigators administered direct electrical stimulation to areas within the inferior parietal cortex of patients undergoing awake brain surgery. A low level of stimulation produced the consciousness of an intention to move a hand or a foot, though without any actual muscle activity; a higher level produced an illusory sense of actually having performed the movement. This shows, perhaps, that there are tryings in the absence of any muscle activity. It does nothing, though, to demonstrate two other tenets of the classical volitional theory of action—that volitions are purely mental and that they are initiators of action.

In sum, nothing in the considerations adduced by Taylor shows that volitions do not exist or that they cannot stand in causal relations to bodily motions.

Nonetheless, Taylor does raise one good objection to the volitional theory of action. He notes that an event's being (part of) an action cannot consist simply in its being caused by an event internal to the agent, be that event a volition or something else. The point is easy to see if the internal event is something purely physiological with which the agent has nothing to do. Heartbeats are not made actions of mine just because they are caused by electrical impulses from within my sinoatrial node. Now let the inner event be a volition instead of an electrical impulse, but suppose that the volition is caused by a physician's giving me a drug or a jolt of electricity. The volition-caused event seems now just to be something I undergo, not anything I do. Inner event causes do not bestow action status unless they are themselves actions of mine—but now infinite regress and circular analysis both threaten. The moral Taylor draws is that action cannot be analyzed in terms of a special kind of inner event as cause. Actions can only be understood as those events of which the agent himself is the cause. In other words, we cannot understand the concept of action unless we bring in the concept of agent causation.

We have now circled back to Reid. Reid, unlike Taylor, has room for volitions in his theory of action, but they do their job only if they are caused by the agent himself.[44] On this point—agent causation as central to the concept of action—Reid was doubtless Taylor's principal inspiration.[45]

*Exerting, willing, and acting.* In one way of thinking about what is involved for Reid when I wiggle my finger, there are three distinct ingredients: the exertion of my power, a resultant volition, and the ensuing movement of my finger (Rowe 1991). Three things—exerting, willing, and acting! That seems too many. Is there any way to reduce the number by identifying some two out of the three with each other?[46]

In some passages, Reid seems to equate exertion with volition. He quotes the following passage from Locke with approval:

We find in ourselves a power to begin or forbear, continue or end several actions of our minds or motions of our bodies, barely by a thought or preference of the mind,

[44] Or, alternatively, if they are causings by the agent. I return to this difference presently.

[45] The index to Taylor's book contains only two proper names, those of his teachers Chisholm and Ducasse, but they were themselves distinguished Reidians.

[46] This is one place where I am using "action" in the imprecise way I warned of in paragraph 5 of section D. "Action" properly denotes the entire complex rather than the behavioral element of it.

ordering, or, as it were, commanding the doing or not doing such a particular action. This power . . . is that which we call *the will*. The actual exercise of that power, by directing any particular action, or its forbearance, is that which we call *volition* or *willing*. (EAP 1.5: 29, quoting ECHU 2.21.5; see also ECHU 2.21.15 ("Volition") and 2.21.28 ("Volition, what"))

Here willing and exerting our active power seem to be the same thing. Another passage with this implication is the following:

The only clear notion or idea we have of active power, is taken from the power which we find in ourselves to give certain motions to our bodies, or a certain direction to our thoughts; and *this power in ourselves can be brought into action only by willing or volition*. (EAP 1.5: 29, emphasis added; see also 1.5: 31, line 14)

There is this passage as well:

We perceive not any necessary connection between the volition and exertion on our part, and the motion of our body that follows them. (EAP 1.7:40)

From this passage we may draw one and perhaps two inferences. First, the moving of a bodily part is not to be identified with the volition or exertion that led to it (contrary to a proposed identification to be considered presently). Second, it is at least left open, and is perhaps even implied, that the volition and the exertion are the same thing. The conjunctive phrase "volition and exertion" may be a redundancy used for the sake of emphasis, as in "aiding and abetting."

That volition and exertion are coextensive for Reid is an interpretive principle adopted by Yaffe (2004:24) and also by Hoffman (2004).[47]

Matters are muddied, however, by the fact there is also textual evidence *against* the equation of exertion with volition. In an essay entitled "Of Power," bearing a date four years later than the publication of the *Active Powers*, Reid explicitly says that exertion and willing are not to be identified, since either can occur without the other.[48] This remark is not decisive for settling Reid's EAP views, as it may simply indicate a change of mind, or it may be that he is not here using "exertion" in the EAP sense (as suggested in Yaffe:26–28). But there is also evidence against the

---

[47] More accurately, Yaffe takes it to be a Reidian premise that all human exertion is volition and a Reidian conclusion that all exertion whatever is volition. See note 56 below for further articulation of Hoffman's position.

[48] He cites resolving to do something in the future as a case of willing without exertion and walking with your mind lost in other matters as a case of exertion without willing.

exertion-volition equation in the EAP itself. For example, he says, "I consider the determination of the will as an effect" (EAP 4.1:201). "Determination of the will" is a synonym of "volition."[49] If volitions are effects, they are not effectings (or exertions of power), but things effected by them.

It is hard to reach a settled verdict on the question whether exertions and volitions are identical, as Reid is not careful and systematic in his use of these terms.[50] In the next subsection, however, I cite a philosophical problem that Reid can avoid if he distinguishes them.

The next identification to be considered is that of willing with acting, at least when the acting is voluntary. It is only under such an identification that Taylor admits that there are such things as "acts of will" at all:

> Such expressions as "an act of will." . . . have perfectly good and familiar referents. . . . To perform an act of will is only to act willfully, that is to say, intentionally and deliberately. . . . To act willfully is not . . . to perform or to undergo some inner, unobservable twitch or convulsion of the soul in the hope or expectation that this will somehow produce a desired twitch or jerk of the body, like the motion of a limb or the tongue. (1966:75–77).

I know of no reason, however, to think, that Reid himself would take any such line.[51]

On the contrary, he lays down as an important characteristic of volitions that they have objects and that their objects are always our own actions (EAP 2.1: 47–48). This feature stands in the way of any general identification of willing with acting. Willing to walk (even when successful) cannot be the same as walking, since walking has no object.[52]

The last identification to be considered is that of exertion with action.[53] A number of passages in Reid seem to support this identification. He says, "Every operation of the mind is the exertion of some power of the mind" (EAP 1.1:8). Since some

---

[49] For confirmation, see EAP 2.1:47: "The determination of the mind is only another term for volition." In context, it is clear that Reid could have substituted "the will" for "the mind."

[50] For example, at EAP 4.2:204, Reid says our conception of active power "is derived from our voluntary exertions in producing effects." If "voluntary" means produced by volition, he is saying here that volition produces exertion, yet elsewhere he says that exertion produces volition.

[51] In chapter 15, section E, I discuss views of Yaffe's that imply that willing and acting are sometimes identical for Reid, though I do not think Yaffe intended this consequence.

[52] Interestingly, Ginet holds that every volition is self-referential: it is the volition to accomplish something by means of this very volition (35). The thing to be accomplished, however, cannot be identical with the volition to accomplish it.

[53] Here "action" refers not to action proper, but to the bodily or mental movement that is the result-constituent of it.

operations of the mind are actions no less than any bodily action,[54] this remark could be taken to suggest that exerting one's power to attend to something (for instance) is nothing distinct from the attending. Again, he says, "Our conception of power is relative to its exertions or effects" and then goes on to give as examples "the power to speak" and "the power to walk" (EAP 1.1:11). This suggests that speaking and walking might count as exertions of power.

In evaluating passages such as these, we must be mindful of the fact that nouns ending in the suffix *–ion* can be ambiguous between an activity and the result or product of it, as with "construction." So it is with "exertion": it could denote either an exerting or what is brought about by an exerting.[55] Our current question is whether *exertings* might be identical with actions. The passages above do not give us unequivocal reason for saying yes. They might simply tell us that walking, speaking, and operations of the mind are all exertions in the product sense.[56]

Here is another group of passages that might seem to support an equation of exertion with action:

> The exertion of active power we call *action*. (EAP 1.1:13)

> From the consciousness of our own activity, seems to be derived, not only the clearest, but the only conception we can form of activity, or the exertion of active power. (EAP 1.5:30)

> And the exertion of that active power in producing the effect, is called *action, agency, efficiency*. (EAP 4.2:203)

In these passages, it is plausible that "exertion" means "exerting" rather than its products. However, now a possible ambiguity in the terms "action" and "activity"

---

[54] Reid should not have said that *every* operation of the mind is the exertion of some power. Some operations of the mind, such as sensing, are things we are made to undergo willy-nilly, and are therefore not exertions of our power. They are only manifestations of "passive power," which Reid regards as an oxymoron.

[55] We cannot characterize this as "ing"/"ed" ambiguity as we may with "construction," since the thing exerted by an exertion is not the thing brought about, but a certain power.

[56] The distinction I have just drawn is similar to Hoffman's distinction between exertions$_A$ and exertions$_E$. Exertions$_A$ are activations of one's power, whereas exertions$_E$ are the things effected by such activations. Hoffman thinks Reid's term "exertion" is ambiguous, sometimes having the first of these senses and sometimes the second. He also thinks the same distinction can be drawn within the will itself, so that we have exertions$_A$ of the power of willing as well as exertions$_E$ of that power, the volitions produced. This opens up the possibility of there being *four* ingredients in the action of walking: (1) an exertion$_A$ of will, (2a), an exertion$_E$ of will, (2b) an exertion$_A$ of the power of walking, and (3) an exertion$_E$ of the power of walking. But Hoffman favors identifying the middle two elements in the series; it is in this sense that he advocates identifying exertions with volitions.

comes into play. Exertings and willings count as actions for Reid; as we shall see, they may even be the actions par excellence. But "action" may be also be used more broadly to include such things as speaking and walking, which are brought about by actions in the narrower sense, and when "action" is used in the broader way, it is no longer clear that the passages above support an equation of actions with exertings.[57]

As textual evidence *against* the equation of exertion with action, we may cite the various places where Reid says we bring about various changes (in the position of our legs, for instance) *by* the exertion of our active power (EAP 1.1:13). If I V *by* U-ing, V-ing and U-ing are arguably not the same thing.[58]

To summarize, we have reached no definite verdicts on the identification of exerting with willing or of exerting with acting, but we did reject the identification of willing with acting. If we go on to accept the identity of exerting with willing, then (having rejected the identity of willing with acting), we should also reject the identity of exerting with acting. (If E = W and W ≠ A, then E ≠ A.)

*How far do my actions extend?* Let us suppose (adapting a well-known example from Davidson [1963] 1980:4) that I will to move my finger, thereby causing my finger to move, which in turn causes a switch to flip, which then causes a light to come on, which next causes a prowler to be alerted. It is clear that in suitable surrounding circumstances, an initial action or volition may thus generate a series of ever-expanding actions or putative actions: moving my finger, flipping the switch, turning on the light, and so on. Reid is well aware of such possibilities:

> The command of a mighty prince, what is it, but the sound of his breath, modified by his organs of speech? But it may have great consequences; it may raise armies, equip fleets, and spread war and desolation over a great part of the earth. (EIP 1.7:42)

The question is this: how many of these putative actions are genuine actions of the agent, as opposed to mere consequences of them? How many of them are his doings?

---

[57] If we reject the identification of exerting with acting, we could nonetheless allow that the following is a true principle for Reid: if S has the power to V, then S exerts his power to V iff S Vs. This says two things. First, if S has the power to V and exerts this power, S Vs. Reid affirms this as a necessary truth at several places, including EAP 4.2:203. Second, if S has the power to V and Vs, S exerts the power to V. At first there may appear to be counterexamples to this second conditional. Suppose I have the power to collapse into a chair and I *do* collapse into a chair; have I thereby exerted my power to do so? No, I simply collapsed! But here it could be said that what was truly in my power was not collapsing, but allowing myself to collapse, and if I did *that*, I *did* exert my power to do so. So Ving and exerting one's power to V are arguably equivalent (given that one has the power to V), but that does not imply that they are identical.

[58] This principle is controversial, however. Anscombe (1957) repudiates it; Alvarez and Hyman defend it.

An austere answer is that nothing beyond the original volition is the agent's action, all else being consequences of the action, but not action itself. This is the position taken by the old-line Oxford philosopher H. A. Prichard (1949:190 and 193).

A liberal answer is that *all* of the items in the series (mushrooming out, perhaps, to the destruction of the globe) are genuine actions. The captain expelled air through his vocal chords and mouth, thereby giving a command, thereby firing a cannon, thereby sinking an enemy ship, thereby starting a war—all of these being actions of his. Theorists who give this answer typically distinguish between derivative or nonbasic actions, which one does *by* doing other things (for instance, sinking a ship by firing a cannon) and basic actions, which one does *not* by doing other things (for instance—but contestably, as we shall see—expelling air through one's lips or contracting one's finger). Once the liberal answer is given, there is the further question, much pursued in the literature, whether all the actions are distinct or whether some of them are really the same action under different descriptions. (See Ginet 1990, chapter 3 for further discussion of this issue and 15–20 for discussion of action-generating relations in addition to causation that can underlie the *by*-relation.)

In EAP 1.7, "Of the extent of human power," Reid at first appears to give an answer intermediate between the preceding two, letting our actions encompass more than just our volitions, but not the movements of anything outside our own bodies and minds:

> The effects of human power are either immediate, or they are more remote.
>
> The immediate effects, I think, are reducible to two heads. We can give certain motions to our own bodies; and we can give a certain direction to our own thoughts.
>
> Whatever we can do beyond this, must be done by one of these means, or both.
> (EAP 1.7:39)

It is tempting to see Reid as claiming here that the basic actions are giving motions to our bodies and giving direction to our thoughts; everything beyond these two is not a basic action and perhaps not an action at all.[59]

---

[59] Alvarez and Hyman (1998) understand Reid as circumscribing basic actions in just this way. Following von Wright 1963, they distinguish the *result* of an action from its *consequences*. The result is the event the causing of which constitutes the action; thus, the rising of my arm is the result of my raising it. The consequences are the effects of the result. By the "immediate effects" of my power, they take Reid to mean the results of my actions. Under this construal, my basic actions would include giving motion to my body and direction to my thoughts, but nothing more. My nonbasic actions (if any) would be actions whose results are the consequences of other actions of mine and ultimately of basic actions.

Before long, however, Reid registers second thoughts about whether our bodily movements are really within our immediate power. He notes that between our volitions and our bodily movements there are various intervening events, such as nerve impulses and muscle contractions, of which most of us know little or nothing:

> Anatomists inform us, that every voluntary motion of the body is performed by the contraction of certain muscles, and that the muscles are contracted by some influence derived from the nerves. But, without thinking in the least, either of muscles or nerves, we will only the external effect, and the internal machinery, without our call, immediately produces that effect. . . .
>
> It is possible therefore, for any thing we know, that what we call the immediate effects of our power, may not be so in the strictest sense. (EAP 1.7:40–41)[60]

He says that a similar point applies just as much to our mental actions.

---

[60] The full passage from which I have taken this quotation raises several questions of Reid exegesis that I find puzzling. Here is a fuller version of the passage:

> Anatomists inform us, that every voluntary motion of the body is performed by the contraction of certain muscles, and that the muscles are contracted by some influence derived from the nerves. But, without thinking in the least, either of muscles or nerves, we will only the external effect, and the internal machinery, without our call, immediately produces that effect. . . .
>
> That there is an established harmony between our willing certain motions of our bodies, and the operation of the nerves and muscles which produces those motions, is a fact known by experience. This volition is an act of the mind. But whether this act of the mind have any physical effect upon the nerves and muscles; or whether it be only an occasion of their being acted upon by some other efficient, according to the established laws of nature, is hid from us. . . .
>
> It is possible therefore, for any thing we know, that what we call the immediate effects of our power, may not be so in the strictest sense. Between the will to produce the effect, and the production of it, there may be agents or instruments of which we are ignorant.
>
> This may leave some doubt, whether we be in the strictest sense, the efficient cause of the voluntary motions of our own body. (EAP 1.7:40–41)

My questions are these. (i) Why does Reid say only that "for any thing we know," what we call immediate effects of our power may not really be such? Has he not said that there definitely are mediating causes, even if the average person knows nothing of them? Perhaps he thinks the question of immediacy turns on whether the intervening causes are *physical causes* or mere *occasions* on which another agent acts. But that raises two further questions. (ii) How can Reid distinguish between physical causes and occasions? According to the position I ascribe to him in section C, *all* physical causes are merely occasions on which an intelligent agent acts. Is he now wavering from that doctrine? (iii) In any case, why would the distinction matter? Whether my volitions have their effects by the mediation of physical causes or occasions for the actions of another agent, do I not fail in either case to be the immediate cause of them?

Reid's observation suggests three potential difficulties for us to consider. The first is that our bodily motions (and mental actions), not being immediate effects of our power, are not basic actions, despite being attractive candidates for that status. A second and more unsettling problem is that bodily motions may not be actions of ours at all.[61] If their proximate causes are muscle contractions and neuron firings, how can we be said to cause the motions unless we also cause the neuron firings? Yet most of us know nothing of such things, and Reid insists that we can exert our power only with respect to things of which we have some conception.[62] The presumed upshot of these two problems would be the Prichard position or something close to it—our only basic actions and perhaps our only actions, period, are volitions.

A third problem comes from Hume. Hume, too, calls attention to the fact that we do not know what the immediate effects of our volitions are, and he uses this fact to discredit the idea that we get our idea of power from observing what goes on when we will things (EHU 7.1:66–67). It is not surprising, then, that Hoffman says Reid is making a "deep confession" when he says we are in the dark about what our volitions immediately produce.

One issue left unsettled above may be relevant to the second and third difficulties. I stayed noncommittal on whether volitions are to be identified with exertings of our power or whether they are the "first effects" of such exertings. It would be more economical and perhaps less mysterious to identify them with exertings. However, Hume's problem then arises with a vengeance: when we exert our power in willing, we have no idea what we directly bring about, so how can such exercises be the source of our idea of power? The second problem also threatens: if we have no idea what the "first effects" of our volitions are, we cannot on Reid's view be said to cause those effects, and if we cause nothing in the causal chain leading up to our bodily movements, how can they be actions of ours?

Suppose, on the other hand, that volitions are distinct from exertions of power and are the "first effects" of them. We then have the triad of exerting, willing, and acting regarded with suspicion above, but we do solve two of the problems now under discussion. We solve Hume's problem because when we exert our power, we are aware of the effect immediately produced, namely, a volition. We are not hopelessly adrift in the search for relata of the causal relation. We also solve the second problem. In order to be causes of our own bodily movements, we do not have to conceive of everything in the causal chain leading up to them; we only have to conceive

---

[61] Compare Malebranche: "There is no man who knows what must be done to move one of his fingers by means of animal spirits. How, then, could men move their arms?" (96).

[62] Reid's view is not merely that will presupposes intelligence in general, but that willing $X$ presupposes a conception of $X$. See EAP 2.1:48, lines 3–5.

of one such item. We agent-cause a volition, of which we do have a conception, and that volition is the first link in a chain of event causes leading up to our action. In that way, we are remote causes of our own bodily actions, even though we are ignorant of many of the intervening links.

We are still left with the first difficulty, that bodily motions and mental operations are not basic actions of ours, not being "immediate effects of our power." That consequence is probably one Reid can take in stride, but let's look at some attempts to avoid it. Other action theorists have wrestled with the problem of how supposedly basic actions like bodily movements can really be basic (or how they can be actions at all) if they are caused by neural events of which we know nothing. Chisholm (1964:29–30) draws a distinction between what I *do* and what I *make happen*, suggesting that I can perform an action such as moving my finger by making happen some unknown neural event that event-causes the finger motion. My finger movements are thus actions of mine even though I know nothing of their intervening event causes, and they are basic in so far as I accomplish them not by *doing* anything else. This is a departure from Reid insofar as that of which I am agent cause—the neural event—is something of which I may have no conception. (For further discussion of Chisholm's views, see appendix Y.) Von Wright (1971: 76–77) resorts to the mind-boggling expedient of retroactive causation: "By performing basic actions we bring about earlier events in our neural system." We do not perform basic actions by bringing about the neural events, but do the converse instead. Alvarez and Hyman (1998) say that the cause of the neural events that are the event causes of an agent's bodily movements is not the agent himself, but some impersonal part of him. My raising my arm can still therefore be a basic action, because it is not *I* who cause the neural events leading up to it.[63] By this expedient they preserve the basic status of my raising my arm if it is an action at all, but they leave unexplained how it can be an action in the first place.

We are now embroiled in some of the hardest problems in the metaphysics of action. As one may be initially tempted to read Reid at this juncture, he simply shrugs them off, admitting that perhaps our volitions are our only actions metaphysically speaking and turning to a moral issue he regards as both more tractable and more important.

> [The foregoing consideration about intervening causes] may leave some doubt, whether we be in the strictest sense, the efficient cause of the voluntary motions of

---

[63] If *I* caused the neural events, they would be the result-components of actions of mine, and I would be raising my arm by doing something else at the neural level. My raising my arm would no longer be basic.

our own body. But it can produce no doubt with regard to the moral estimation of our actions.

The man who knows that such an event depends upon his will, and who deliberately wills to produce it, is, in the strictest moral sense, the cause of the event; and it is justly imputed to him, whatever physical causes may have concurred in its production.

Thus, he who maliciously intends to shoot his neighbour dead, and voluntarily does it, is undoubtedly the cause of his death, though he did no more to occasion it than draw the trigger of the gun. He neither gave to the ball its velocity, nor to the powder its expansive force, nor to the flint and steel the power to strike fire; but he knew that what he did must be followed by the man's death, and did it with that intention; and therefore he is justly chargeable with the murder. (EAP 1.7:41)

Perhaps the man did not in the strict sense even do so much as pull the trigger—he merely willed his finger to move in a certain direction. But knowing and intending as he did, he was the moral cause of everything that ensued. We can make declarations about the morals even if we wash our hands of the metaphysics.

On further reflection, that cannot be the right way to understand Reid. Moral accountability depends on and is determined by metaphysical fact. It is a first principle, Reid tells us, that we are morally accountable only for conduct that is within our power—this is a principle as evident as anything in Euclid (EAP 1.7:39; see also 4.1:198, 4.7:237, and EIP 6.6:494). Elsewhere he expands upon the point thus:

It is self-evident that no man can be the object either of approbation or of blame for what he did not. But how shall we know whether it is his doing or not? If the action depended upon his will, and if he intended and willed it, it is his action in the judgment of all mankind. (EAP 1.5:31)

My actions, I therefore want to say on Reid's behalf, are my agent-caused volitions along with all the actions that consist in my causing some other foreseen and intended event indirectly (that is, by causing a volition that initiates a chain of physical causes leading to that event). Starting a war can thus be an action of mine, though of course not a basic action; perhaps nothing but causing my volitions counts as basic action. Moral accountability for any happening implies that it was my action, but not conversely: some things that are my actions (because event-caused by things agent-caused by me) are not things for which I am accountable because I did not foresee that they would result from my basic actions.

# 15

## THEORY OF ACTION 2

## DETERMINISM, FREEDOM, AND AGENCY

Either the man was the cause of the action, and then it was a free action, and is justly imputed to him; or it must have had another cause, and cannot justly be imputed to the man. (Thomas Reid, *EAP 4.9:246*)

### A. TWO FORMS OF DETERMINISM

The shortest formulation of determinism is five words long: every event has a cause. A somewhat longer formulation appeals to the idea that the world is governed by laws that, together with a complete description of the world at any one instant, let you deduce the state of the world at any subsequent instant. An implication of determinism in the second formulation is that if the same total state of the world should recur, it would be followed by the same total state that followed upon it previously—for short, same total circumstances, same total sequel. It is sometimes assumed that these two formulations of determinism, which I shall call determinism$_1$ and determinism$_2$, are equivalent. It is therefore surprising to find that Reid vigorously affirms determinism$_1$ while just as vigorously denying determinism$_2$. How is this possible? The key, as we shall see, is his belief in agent causation.

Reid's combination of views is well brought out in his critical discussion of Leibniz's Principle of Sufficient Reason, which he puts as follows: "For every existence, for every event, for every truth, there must be a sufficient reason" (EAP 4.9:244). When this principle is applied to actions or determinations of the will, Reid tells us, there are three ways to understand it, depending on which of three meanings we give to "sufficient reason" (EAP 4.9:246).

1. If "sufficient reason" means "a motive for the action justifying it as wise and good," the principle is false. People sometimes act foolishly.
2. If "sufficient reason" means "a cause of the action," the principle is true. *Either the man was the cause of the action*, and then it was a free action, and is justly imputed to him; *or it must have had another cause*, and cannot justly be imputed to the man" (EAP 4.9:246, emphasis mine).
3. If "sufficient reason" means "something previous to the action upon which the action followed necessarily," the principle is false. At any rate, it is false if there are any free actions. (In such contexts Reid uses the word "necessarily" without any modal force; it could be replaced by "in accordance with an exceptionless law.")

In delivering a verdict of "true" in case 2, Reid is affirming determinism$_1$ as regards human actions. In delivering a verdict of "false" in case 3, he is denying determinism$_2$.

Reid affirms the principle that every event has a cause in many passages, often adding that it is a first principle. Here is one of them:

> Every thing that begins to exist, must have a cause of its existence, which had power to give it existence. And every thing that undergoes any change, must have some cause of that change.
>
> That neither existence, nor any mode of existence, can begin without an efficient cause, is a principle that appears very early in the mind of man; and it is so universal, and so firmly rooted in human nature, that the most determined scepticism cannot eradicate it. (EAP 4.2:202)

The references to power and efficiency show that Reid is thinking of agent causes. The references to universality and ineradicability show that he regards this causal principle as a first principle.[1]

---

[1] A small sample of other passages in which Reid affirms the principle of universal causation would include EAP 1.1:13, 1.4:25–26, 4.3:212, and 4.9:248. In the *Intellectual Powers*, the principle that every event has a cause is listed among the first principles of necessary truths (EIP 6.6:497–503), though with nothing said there about whether the principle calls for agent causes, event causes, or their disjunction.

It may seem that some of Reid's formulations of the causal principle—e.g., "every thing that begins to exist, must have a cause of its existence"—imply only that beginnings of existence must have causes, not changes generally. In fact his principle has no such restriction, given his ontology of tropes. (See EIP 5.3:367 on the whiteness of this sheet of paper.) If anything that was formerly not F comes to be F, there is something (the Fness of x) that comes to be *simpliciter*, and its so doing requires a cause.

Reid's denial of the second form of determinism comes to the fore in his discussion of the views of Joseph Priestley (he of phlogiston fame).[2] Priestley defends a doctrine he calls "the doctrine of necessity," which he formulates as follows: "throughout all nature, the same consequences should invariably result from the same circumstances."[3] This, of course, is none other than determinism$_2$.

Reid says Priestley's principle is questionable even when restricted to inanimate nature. There might be miracles, which are events contrary to the normal laws of nature, or there might be events that are simply not covered by any law of nature (EAP 4.9:247 and 251). In either case, it would not be true that the same circumstances always have the same consequences.[4] But whether Priestley's principle holds in inanimate nature or not, Reid is convinced that it does not hold in the realm of human actions.

Priestley defines causation in a Hume-like way: "such previous circumstances as are constantly followed by a certain effect" (EAP 4.9:249). He then attempts to prove his principle by arguing that denying it would involve "an effect without a cause," which is absurd.

Is Priestley right about this? Reid says no, for two reasons. In the first place, what follows from the denial of determinism$_2$ would not be an *effect* without a cause (which is contradictory), but at most an *event* without a cause.[5] Second, it would not even follow that there would be an event without a cause unless we insist that causes in Priestley's sense (necessitating prior circumstances) are the only admissible causes. If there are such things as agent causes, an event with no prior necessitating circumstance would not thereby be an event without a cause.[6] There is thus no absurdity in denying determinism$_2$.

---

[2] Priestley is credited with the discovery of oxygen (though as a defender of the phlogiston theory, he called it "dephlogisticated air"). He was also a leading figure in the development of Unitarianism. In the present connection, his most important work is *The Doctrine of Philosophical Necessity Illustrated*, published in 1777.

[3] Priestley, like Hume (EHU, section 8) refers to determinism$_2$ as the "doctrine of necessity," even though neither of them believes that determination involves any kind of necessity going beyond constant conjunction.

[4] On the other side, it should be noted that in his discussion of secondary qualities, Reid betrays belief in pervasive if not universal physical causation. He says we all believe by our nature that our sensations (of red, for instance) must have an external cause, and we give the name of redness to this cause (or the property of containing such a cause). What we believe to be in the external object is plainly a physical cause, not an efficient or agent cause.

[5] Compare the argument, lampooned by Hume at THN 1.3.3:82, that every man must be married, because otherwise some husband would lack a wife.

[6] Reid could have made this point in either of two ways: first, deny that an event without a Priestley cause would have to be an event without a cause, since there are also agent causes; second, admit that there are events without causes (that is, Priestley causes), but deny that such events are impossible.

Reid's response to Priestley brings into the limelight one of the puzzling features of agent causation: when an event has an agent cause, "another event might have arisen from the same cause, in the same circumstances" (EAP 4.10:256). If an agent causes e in total circumstances C, it does not follow that if the same agent were placed again in C—with the stars in the same pattern overhead, the same motives present, and every other detail the same—he would again cause e. An agent might will to move his hand (in a gesture of clemency, perhaps) the first time around but not the second, despite the sameness of all circumstances and motives. He was nonetheless the cause of his hand's moving the first time around. I revisit this feature of agent causation in section G.

I end this section by spelling out just how the two varieties of determinism are logically related. First, I show that determinism$_1$ implies determinism$_2$, but only if we make two assumptions: (i) that the cause of an event is always itself an event, and (ii) that an event cause is followed regularly by its effect, as Hume and Priestley both hold. Let A and B denote total momentary states of the universe, and let A' and B' denote states perfectly similar to them. Suppose A was immediately followed the first time around by B, and that we now get an occurrence of total state A' just like A. We must show that what happens next is B', and for this purpose it will suffice if we can show that an event is part of what happens next if and only if a perfectly similar event was part of B. (For ease of exposition, I am assuming that time is discrete.) Let e be any event that was part of B. By determinism$_1$ and assumption (i), e had an event cause in A, which cause recurs by hypothesis in A', and which upon its recurrence must (by assumption (ii)) be followed by the same effect as before. Thus, every event in B that occurred before will occur again in the moment just after A'. Moreover, everything that occurs in this moment must have occurred previously as part of B. For suppose f is some event occurring just after A'; by determinism$_1$ and (i), it will need an event cause in A', which by hypothesis was also part of A, so by (ii) its regular effect must also have been in B. So the total state that occurs after A' is B', a replication of B. Q.E.D.[7]

Thus, determinism$_1$ may be shown to imply determinism$_2$, but only if we use an assumption Reid would reject: that the cause of an event is always itself an event. We must also use the assumption that if e causes f, events of e's type are always followed by events of f's type, but that is an assumption Reid accepts for event causation.

---

[7] If time is not discrete, we need at least one more assumption to complete the proof: that if every event is caused by an earlier event, then every event has a chain of event causes stretching arbitrarily far back in time. Its causal chain cannot converge to a particular moment finitely far back. Without this assumption, we could not trace the causes of events in B back to A. The need for this assumption (in a slightly different context) is explained in van Inwagen 1983:4–5 and 225n7.

(See COR 180.) The main point to take away is that Reid's view that some events are caused by agents rather than by events enables him to uphold determinism$_1$ while rejecting determinism$_2$.

What of the converse implication, from determinism$_2$ to determinism$_1$? It looks as though we can prove this if we make three assumptions: (i) that every state of the universe is preceded by some other state, (ii) that total states of the universe count as very large events, and (iii) that regular succession is sufficient for causation.[8] Let e be any event, and call the total state of which e is a part B. The total state A that by (i) precedes B is by (ii) an event, which by determinism$_2$ is always followed by B, and B includes e. So A is always followed by e and thus by (iii) counts as a cause of it. Q.E.D.

From now on, let us understand determinism$_2$ as having built into it the assumption that every state of the universe is preceded by some other state.[9] It thus implies that every event e is preceded by some state such that whenever you get that state again, you get an event of e's type again. If we add assumptions (ii) and (iii), that is tantamount to the thesis that every event is caused by an earlier event.

Paul Studtmann has asked me whether Reid's theory of agent causation is at odds with Newtonian physics. Given Reid's general admiration for Newton, it would be surprising if the answer were yes; nonetheless, it does seem to be yes.[10] Consider the first physical event in a chain of events inaugurated by an agent. Either there is no physical antecedent from which events of that sort regularly follow, which would be contrary to Newtonian physics, or there is an implausible pre-established harmony whereby agents cause only those physical events that also have Newtonian physical causes. Moreover, it would have to be a harmony built around agents. God would have to arrange for the course of the physical world to evolve deterministically in synchronization with our decisions (which he foresees) rather than fitting our decisions to the course of the world (which would infringe on our liberty).

Reid's suggestion that determinism$_2$ might fail even in the inanimate world constitutes a further clash with Newton, a clash not avertable like the first one by invoking pre-established harmony between what agents cause and what physical events cause.

---

[8] The need for the first of these assumptions was overlooked in Van Cleve 1999:230–31.

[9] Without this assumption, determinism$_2$ could be true even if there were a first moment of time containing a state determined by nothing.

[10] The threat to Newtonian physics I describe in this paragraph is posed not by agent causation as such, but by any view that allows physical events to have causes outside the physical realm, as also happens in Cartesian dualism with mental events as causes.

# B. WHAT FREEDOM IS *NOT*: THE WILLIWIG ACCOUNT

What is it for an action to be free, or to be possessed of what eighteenth-century philosophers called moral liberty? In this section I discuss the nearly identical answers given by Locke and Hume, which Reid thinks inadequate. He rejects them in large part because they allow an action to be free even though it is determined by prior causes. I consider Reid's alternative answer in the next section.

I begin with some definitions that capture the essence of Locke's view in *Essay* 2.21, the long chapter on power, along with supporting quotations:

> (D1) S performed A voluntarily = df A was caused by a volition of S's.[11]

> The forbearance or performance of [an] action, consequent to such order or command of the mind [i.e., volition] is called voluntary. (2.21.5)

> (D2) S is free with respect to A = df (i) if S were to will A, A would occur, and (ii) if S were to will ~A, A would not occur. In other words, whether A happens depends on what S wills.

> So far as a Man has a power to think, or not to think; to move, or not to move, according to the preference or direction of his own mind, so far is a Man *Free*. Where-ever any performance or forbearance are not equally in a Man's power; where-ever doing or not doing, will not equally follow upon the preference of his mind directing it, there he is not *Free*, though perhaps the Action may be voluntary. (2.21.8)

The preference or direction of the mind of which Locke here speaks is none other than what he elsewhere calls volition. Having a power to move or not to move according to your preference (as Locke calls it in the first sentence) is a matter of its being true (as his second sentence says) that moving would follow upon your preference to move and not moving on your preference not to move. Hence I have rendered the definiens above as a pair of subjunctive conditionals.[12]

The definition just given can be adapted to actions already performed rather than prospective actions as follows:

> (D3) S performed A freely = df (i) S performed A, and (ii) A happened because S willed it, and (iii) if S had willed otherwise, A would not have happened.

---

[11] Perhaps it would be truer to Locke to define voluntary actions as simply being *in accordance* with one's volitions rather than being caused by them, since he notes in 2.21.11 that a paralytic voluntarily remains in one place if that is what he prefers to do. I cannot help thinking, though, that my definition is better. Is there any place where Locke implicitly uses it?

[12] See Rowe 1991:13–14 for reasons for rendering Locke's clauses as conditionals about what I *would* do if I willed, not what I "could" do if I willed.

I say "A happened because S willed it" in clause (ii) instead of "if S were to will A, A would occur" in light of the close connection between causation and subjunctive conditionals.[13]

The definitions I have given imply that whatever is done freely is done voluntarily, but not conversely, which agrees with Locke's explicit pronouncement. Had I stopped with clause (ii) in D3, that would have been a good definition of a voluntary action, but not yet of a free action.

The need for adding clause (iii) in the definition of free action is the moral of the famous example of the locked room in 2.21.10 of the *Essay*. Locke asks us to imagine a man's waking up in a room into which he had been carried while asleep. He finds himself in pleasant company and chooses to stay—not knowing that he is securely locked in. Does he remain freely? Locke says no. He remains voluntarily, but not freely, since he could not leave if he chose to. He does not satisfy clause (iii) of the definition of acting freely.[14]

Locke's definition of freedom is meant to be a compatibilist definition, that is, a definition of freedom under which an action might be free even if determinism$_1$ or determinism$_2$ is true. Suppose I acted as I did because I willed to, and that my

---

[13] There may be some question whether the antecedent of (iii) should be rendered as "W~A" or "~WA." In Locke's own view, the question does not arise, since he thinks (perhaps mistakenly) that they are equivalent: see 2.21.23–24. Suppose for the moment, though, that we render the antecedent as "~WA." Then the immediate adaptation of D2 to actions already performed would be

> (D2a) S performed A freely = df (i) S performed A, and (ii) if S had willed A, A would have occurred, and (iii) if S had not willed A, A would not have occurred.

On the analysis of causation offered in Lewis 1973, if A and S's willing of it are events that actually occurred, then A was caused by S's willing A iff (a) if S had willed A, A would have occurred, and (b) if S had not willed A, A would not have occurred. (Lewis would not bother to state (a), since on his view it is automatically true if A actually occurred.) Thus, clauses (ii) and (iii) in D2a may be replaced by "A occurred because S willed A," giving us

> (D2b) S performed A freely = df (i) S performed A, and (ii) A occurred because S willed A.

In the text, I retain clause (iii) as a reminder, giving us

> D3) S performed A freely = df (i) S performed A, and (ii) A occurred because S willed A, and (iii) if S had willed otherwise, A would not have occurred.

[14] In his section title, Locke misleadingly states the moral of his example as "liberty belongs not to volition." If that simply means an act is not free simply in virtue of being voluntary, fine. But it would more naturally be taken to mean that willing itself cannot be considered free or not free—a conclusion he argues for in subsequent sections (principally 2.21.25), but which is not at all shown by the example of the locked room.

willing as I did was itself caused or determined to happen by prior circumstances—as Locke supposes will always be the case. Locke says the action is nonetheless free, just so long as clause (iii) is satisfied—that had I willed otherwise, I would have done otherwise.

> But though the preference of the Mind always be determined . . . ; yet the Person who has the power . . . to act, or not to act, according to such preference, is nevertheless free. . . . He that has his Chains knocked off, and the Prison doors set open to him, is perfectly at liberty, because he may either go or stay as he best likes; though his preference be determined to stay by the darkness of the Night, or illness of the Weather, or want of other Lodging. He ceases not to be free; though that which at that time appears to him the greater Good absolutely determines his preference, and makes him stay in his Prison. (2.21.33)

Hume gives an account of freedom that is in all essentials equivalent to Locke's. Here is his definition of liberty in section 8 of the *Enquiry*:

> By liberty, then, we can only mean *a power of acting or not acting, according to the determinations of the will*; that is, if we choose to remain at rest, we may; if we choose to move, we also may. (EHU 8.1:95)

I am not sure why he merely says "may"; the point is clearly that if we chose to remain at rest, our remaining at rest *would* be the result, and similarly for choosing to move. His definition thus incorporates the same two subjunctive conditional clauses we used above in explicating Locke, and like Locke's definition, Hume's is offered in the project of reconciling freedom with determinism.

Before Locke and Hume, Hobbes had given a definition of liberty very similar in form to theirs:

> He is free to do a thing, that may do it if he have the will to do it and may forbear, if he have the will to forbear. ([1654] 1962:240; cf. 1651:164)

Hobbes, too, believes that liberty so defined is perfectly compatible with determinism.[15]

---

[15] On the same page with his definition and affirmation of liberty in the *Leviathan*, Hobbes says, "Every act of man's will . . . proceedeth from some cause, and that from another cause, in a continual chain, whose first link is in the hand of God" (1651:164).

I like to sum up the views of Hobbes, Locke, and Hume in an acronym. In the early days of word processing, there was an acronym, WYSIWYG, meaning "what you see is what you get"—that is, whatever is displayed on the screen is what you will get if you print it out. Nowadays all word processing programs have that feature, so there is little need for the acronym. Locke and Hume's accounts of freedom may be summed up in a similar acronym, WYWIWYG, meaning "what you will is what you get." If you choose to move, you move; if you choose not to move, you remain at rest.[16] (Or for an act already accomplished, it was free if it was what you willed, and had you not willed it, it would not have happened.) Not wishing to sound like Elmer Fudd, I henceforth spell and pronounce the acronym as *williwig*.

What is the williwig account meant to be an account *of*—freedom or power? I take it to be an account of freedom, but Yaffe takes it to be an account of power (2004:15 and 2007:268–69). He calls it the analysis of "necessitarian power," that is, power of a sort that a determinist or necessitarian can believe in. In support of my way of taking the account, I note two things.

First, when Locke and Hume state the definitions quoted above, their definiendum is freedom or liberty. To be sure, they both use the word "power" in their definientia. But the "power" that occurs there refers to a power of acting or not acting *if we will*. That is, it is a conditional power—a power (indeed, a reliable propensity) to act this way if we will and not this way if we do not so will. Their definientia do not imply that it is in our power to do A, period, and in my opinion they were not even meant to do so.[17]

Second, as a definition of power, the williwig account is seriously deficient, or so it seems to me. There are, to be sure, some williwiggers, notably including G. E. Moore, who do explicitly offer the analysis as an analysis of power ([1912] 1965: 84–95). According to Moore, the proposition

---

[16] I am not saying that *whatever* you will is what you get, which is the prerogative of omnipotence alone.

[17] Yaffe sometimes takes the *single* conditional "If S were to will A, A would occur" as an analysis of necessitarian power (2004:15, and 2007:268–69). I do not think necessitarians themselves thought of that conditional as an analysis of power. I would argue the point at least in the case of Locke's follower Anthony Collins as follows: According to Collins, freedom is compatible with determinism, but the conjunction of the power to do A with the power not to do A is *not* compatible with determinism. (See Weinstock 1976:97, and Rowe 1991:104.) Freedom (for a good Lockean) equals the conjunction of the conditionals (WA → A) and (W~A → ~A). Therefore, (WA → A) and (W~A → ~A) are not respectively sufficient for the power to do A and the power to do ~A. If they were, we would have a contradiction in the necessitarian view—freedom would be the conjunction of the power to do A with the power not to do A, and would thus not be compatible with determinism after all.

(a) *He could have done otherwise*

is equivalent to

(b) *If he had chosen to do otherwise, then he would have done otherwise.*

In opposition to Moore, Chisholm (1964, section 3) objected that (b) by itself does not imply (a), and that in order to pass from (b) to (a), we would need the further premise

(c) *He could have chosen to do otherwise.*

To see that Chisholm is right, we may note two things: that the conjunction of (b) & ~(c) clearly does not imply (a), and that if the conjunction of two things does not imply a third thing, then neither does either of the two things alone. Therefore, (b) does not imply (a).[18]

Perhaps Yaffe is operating with the assumption that freedom worthy of the name must include the power to do otherwise. When Locke and Hume set forth conditions for freedom, he therefore takes them to be setting forth conditions for power as part of the bargain. As I read Locke and Hume, however, they do not share the assumption that freedom requires the power to do otherwise, but only the power to do otherwise *if we will*. As Locke puts it, "We can scarce tell how to imagine any *Being* freer, than to be able to do what he *wills*" (2.21.21).[19]

---

[18] If you are not yet convinced, consider the formally parallel purported analysis of (a') *He could have opened an escape route from the cave* as (b') *If he had pushed aside the 1000-pound boulder, he would have opened an escape route from the cave*. Clearly, (b') does not imply (a'), as may be seen by noting that the conjunction of (b') with (c') *He could not have pushed aside the 1000-pound boulder* does not imply (a'). What difference does it make if we now change the antecedent of (b') to *If he had willed to open an escape route from the cave*? None, so far as securing the implication to (a') is concerned. Perhaps some will think that the *freedom* of the agent to open an escape route is now implied, but his power to do so is not.

[19] My point may be put another way. There are two ways to be a compatibilist: hold that determinism does not take away our power to have done otherwise, or concede that determinism does do this, but hold that no such power is required by freedom (not, at any rate, by that freedom which is essential to moral responsibility—as Jonathan Edwards puts it in his title, "that Freedom of the Will, which is supposed to be essential to Moral Agency, Virtue and Vice, Reward and Punishment, Praise and Blame."). There are compatibilists of the former sort (e.g., Lehrer in 1980, Lewis in 1981, Vihvelin in 2013), but I take Locke, Hume, and Edwards all to be compatibilists of the latter sort. In effect, I take them to be "semi-compatibilists" in the sense of the term introduced by Fischer (2002).

Having set aside the williwig account as an account of power, we may now ask, How plausible is the williwig account as an account of freedom? May we really conceive no greater freedom than it articulates? I shall mention two objections to it, both discussed by Rowe ([1987] 1995:154–56) and both Reidian in spirit.[20]

The first objection is that the conditions of the definition could easily be satisfied in a world in which every event was caused by a prior event. I might do something because I willed to do it, and I might be such that had I willed otherwise, I would not have done it; yet at the same time, it might be true that my willing as I did was caused by prior factors, which were themselves caused by prior factors, and so on until we reach causes lying outside my skin and before I was born. If my willing and doing as I did were caused by factors already in place in dinosaur days, surely I did not do what I did freely, despite satisfying all of the conditions in the williwig account.

I find this objection convincing myself (for reasons given at the end of section C below), but it cannot be counted upon to sway williwiggers. Their definition is *designed* to establish conditions for freedom that are compatible with determinism, so they will not be impressed when it is pointed out that they have succeeded.

The second objection has more bite. Suppose there is someone who did A because he willed to do so and whose will was efficacious, in the sense that had he willed to do something else instead, he would not have done A. Suppose further that there is some manipulator who by the use of hypnotism or electrodes planted in the brain caused the subject to will as he did. Surely the subject did not do what he did freely—he was caused to do it (with the mediation of his own volitions) by the manipulator. He was no more free than a marionette—the only difference is that the manipulator's strings were attached inwardly to his volitions rather than outwardly to his limbs. And yet our subject satisfies all the conditions in the williwig account.

There is an obvious way to remedy the williwig account to get around this objection: we simply add a clause in the definiens stipulating that the subject not only willed A, but willed A *freely*. But this is a suggestion that williwiggers are unanimous in rejecting. They insist that freedom may be ascribed to our actions when

---

[20] I refer the reader to Yaffe 2004:15–24 for a reconstruction of a third argument against the williwig account, based on Reid's principle "To say that what depends upon the will [some action] is in a man's power, but the will [the willing of that action] is not in his power, is to say that the end is in his power, but the means necessary to that end are not in his power, which is a contradiction" (EAP 4.1:201). Yaffe states the conclusion of the argument inconspicuously as "S has a power only if S has the power to exert it," but given his equation of exertion with volition, this amounts to "S has the power to do something only if S has the power to *will* to do that thing," which runs counter to the williwig account taken as an account of power.

they flow from our willing, but not to willing itself. Locke suggests at one point that the remedy advocated by the objector would beget an infinite regress:

> The next thing demanded is, *whether a man be at liberty to will which of the two he pleases, motion or rest.* This question carries the absurdity of it so manifestly in itself, that one might thereby sufficiently be convinced that liberty concerns not the will. For to ask, whether a man be at liberty to will ... which he pleases, is to ask, whether a man can *will,* what he *wills*; or be pleased with what he is pleased with. A question, which, I think, needs no answer: and they, who can make a question if it, must suppose one will to determine the acts of another, and another to determine that; and so on *in infinitum.* (2.21.25, suppressing one confusing clause)

The regress Locke alleges can be illustrated thus:

S did A freely only if he did A because $W_f A$ (he *freely* willed to do A)

i.e., WA because $W_f WA$

i.e., WWA because $W_f WWA$

i.e., (etc.)

where each "i.e." clause unpacks the italicized clause just above it.[21] This regress does indeed arise if we understand the free willing insisted upon by the objector as a special case of free acting as defined by Locke.[22]

And therein lies the duply to Locke's reply. ("Duply" is the term in Scots law for the reply to a reply.) Locke has not shown that a regress is generated by the objector's remedy itself; it is generated only by the remedy *as it would have to be understood within Locke's own theory.* The objector would say that Locke's theory is at fault, and that the freedom of willing he insists upon, rather than being understood as a special case of Lockean free action, must be understood in some other way. This is

---

[21] The regress still arises if we replace everything of the form "because $W_f A$" by "because WA and $W_f A$", putting "$W_f A$" outside the scope of "because."

[22] Hobbes raises a similar regress objection, but he may think the regress is already absurd at the second step: "to say I can will if I will, I take to be an absurd speech." See IV:69 though: "a man can no more say he will will, than he will will will and so make an infinite repetition of the word [will]." Jonathan Edwards also raises the regress of willing objection; see Edwards (1754) 2012:2.1:30–32, 2.5:49 and Harris 2005:113–17.

Sometimes the objection to willing as you will is not that it launches a regress, but that it is tautological. There is a hint of this in the passage quoted from Locke at 2.21.25, and it is explicit in Berkeley's presentation of the objection at *Alciphron* 7.19–20. To make the charge of tautology, however, is to misread "willing what you will" as "willing A if you will A" rather than the higher-order "willing to will A."

essentially Reid's response to the regress objection (which he ascribes to Hobbes): "It is grounded upon a definition of liberty totally different from that which I have given, and therefore does not apply to moral liberty, as above defined" (EAP 4.1:200).[23]

So how does Reid define moral liberty?

## C. WHAT FREEDOM *IS*: THE AGENT-CAUSATION ACCOUNT

Here is Reid's positive characterization of moral liberty or freedom:

> *By the liberty of a moral agent, I understand, a power over the determinations of his own will.*
> *If, in any action, he had power to will what he did, or not to will it, in that action he is*
> *free.* But if, in every voluntary action, the determination of his will be the necessary consequence of something involuntary in the state of his mind, or of something in his external circumstances, he is not free; he has not what I call the liberty of a moral agent, but is subject to necessity. (EAP 4.1:196, italics added)

There are three important things to notice about this definition. The first is that Reid's definition brings to the fore what was crucially lacking in the williwig account: power over willing itself.[24] But it does not thereby incur the objection of

---

[23] Lehrer offers a conditional analysis of "I could have done otherwise" that may be instructively compared with Locke's williwig account of freedom. Locke says you did something freely if it was what you willed and you wouldn't have done it if you had willed otherwise. He declines to say that you must have been free to will otherwise, for fear of generating an infinite regress. Lehrer may be seen as taking the bait Locke shuns and running off with it. What does it mean to say that although A is what I did, I could have done otherwise? It is not enough, Lehrer says, that I would have done otherwise had I preferred otherwise, for perhaps I could not have preferred otherwise. But we do get a sufficient condition for "I could have done otherwise" if we add "if I had preferred to prefer ~A, I would have preferred ~A," *and so on up.* At each level, we say that if I had preferred to have the preference one level below, I would have had it. In this way, we get an infinite hierarchy of subjunctive conditionals, but not of actual acts of willing (Lehrer 1980).

Though Lehrer is not committed to an infinite series of acts, there are views in the neighborhood that would be so committed. For example, suppose we say that I did A freely only if I could have done otherwise (in the sense Lehrer articulates—I would have done otherwise if I had preferred otherwise, would have preferred otherwise if I had preferred to prefer otherwise, and so on) AND that A was what I preferred, and that had I not preferred to prefer A, I would not have preferred A. It follows that I preferred to prefer A, which is but the second step in an infinite regress of preferences.

[24] What are "determinations of the will"—willings or the actions effected by them? I take it that Reid means the former. In the second sentence of his definition he unpacks "power over the determinations of his own will" as "power to will what he did . . . ", not "power to do what he did. . . . " For confirmation, see EAP 2.1:47: "the determination of the mind [will] is only another term for volition."

Hobbes and Locke—that insisting on power over the will would beget an infinity of willings. The basic idea of their argument is that since power is being able to do what you will, there cannot be power over the will itself, for that would imply being able to will what you will. The same basic idea is present in a number of structurally similar arguments, such as *moving is changing your relation to space; therefore, space cannot move* and *being justified is being sanctioned by your first principles; therefore, your first principles cannot be justified.* These arguments are not mere sophisms, but they may be resisted. In the case at hand, the proper course of resistance is to take power as a primitive notion, not definable as being able to do what you will.

The second thing to notice is that the power Reid insists upon is a two-pronged power. It is the power both to will a certain way *and* the power not to will that way. This fact may be obscured by Reid's use of the word *or* in the phrase "power to will what he did, or not to will it." Having the power to will A or not to will A does not mean either having the one power or having the other; it means having them *both*.[25] Reid probably avoided the conjunctive phrase "power to will A and not to will A" because it sounds contradictory—the power to (will A and not will A). But if the conjunctive phrase is taken as an ellipsis of "power to will A and *power* not to will A," it is not contradictory and is exactly what is intended.

To see the rationale for insisting on a two-pronged power, suppose I had the power to will A, but did *not* have the power *not* to will A. Then I would *have* to will A; no other course would be open to me. And in that case, I could hardly be free in willing A or in whatever is consequent upon it.

In Reid's philosophy, the two-pronged power requirement is actually overdetermined. As we saw in chapter 14, section B, Reid holds that whenever anything has the power to produce any effect, it also has the complementary power not to produce that effect (EAP 1.5:29). Hence, the power to will a certain way requires the power not to will that way. But even a philosopher who did not hold this view about the two-pronged nature of power might hold, for the reason just given, that *freedom* requires having each of two complementary powers. In a way, that is the view of Locke and Hume: they require a free agent to have the power to move (if he chooses) as well as the power not to move (if he chooses)—although they do not say there is power over choosing itself.

Yaffe points out that Locke's example of the locked room may be used (though in my opinion this was not its original intent) as a counterexample to Reid's thesis that

---

[25] Compare: "She likes oatmeal or bran flakes for breakfast" does not mean "She likes oatmeal for breakfast OR she likes bran flakes for breakfast," which would be true if she only liked oatmeal. It means "she likes oatmeal for breakfast AND she likes bran flakes for breakfast" (though not necessarily on the same morning).

the power to do anything implies having the power not to do that thing. The man in the room allegedly has the power to stay, but not the power not to stay (39–40). Yaffe offers one response on Reid's behalf to the counterexample, Rowe another.[26] But even if Reid turns out to be wrong in holding that a power requires having the complementary power, he may be quite correct in holding that *freedom* requires having each of the two complementary powers.

The third thing to notice about Reid's account of freedom is that it has both negative and positive implications (as noted in Rowe [1987] 1995:157–58). The negative implication is that in a free action, one's willing of that action cannot have been caused by prior events, whether internal or external. The positive implication is that the willing must have been caused by the agent whose willing it is. Reid's official definition (italicized in the quotation at the head of this section) does not mention either of these things—it simply defines freedom in terms of the power both to will and not to will in a certain way. But I agree with Rowe that the negative and positive theses about causation are necessarily bound up with freedom in Reid's scheme of things.

The negative thesis comes out immediately after the official definition of liberty in the sentence characterizing the opposed notion of necessity. If your willing is the necessary (i.e., invariable) consequence of something outside your will—an involuntary state of mind or of something in your external circumstances—it is not free. This follows from the official definition together with Reid's belief that if your willing was causally necessitated by some other event, it was not in your power *not* to will as you did. Here Reid's incompatibilism (to be discussed further below) is on full display.

The positive thesis comes out when we remember Reid's conditions for *substance X caused event e* from chapter 14, section B above: X had the power to bring about e, exerted this power, and had the power to refrain from bringing about e. Acting freely and being the agent cause of something both involve two-pronged powers for Reid, and it is not surprising that they turn out to be coextensive, as he affirms in the following passages:

> [The determination of the will] must have a cause which had power to produce it; and the cause must be either the person himself, whose will it is, or some other being. . . .

---

[26] Yaffe argues, invoking the principle of Efficient-Causal Exclusivity, that Reid is correct in holding that having the power to V requires having also the power not to V, and that in Locke's example, the man really does not have the power to stay in the room (39–47, summarized on 47). By way of mitigating the counterintuitiveness of the latter claim (or is it really exacerbating it?), I note that the man may be credited with the power to remain within a ten-foot radius of his chair, even if not with the power to remain within the room. Rowe maintains that Reid holds something weaker than the *power to V → power not to V* principle, namely, that if an agent has the power to will in a certain way, he also has the power not to cause his willing in that way. See note 30 below for the reasons for Rowe's view.

*If the person was the cause of that determination of his own will, he was free in that action,* and it is justly imputed to him, whether it be good or bad. But, if another being was the cause of the determination, either by producing it immediately, or by means and instruments under his direction, then the determination is the act and deed of that being, and is solely imputable to him. (EAP 4.1:201, emphasis mine)

To say that a man is a free agent, is no more than to say, that in some instances he is truly an agent, and a cause. (EAP 4.3:212)

There are free actions only where there are agent-caused willings.

There are two further questions to be taken up regarding how Reid's definition is to be understood. First, is the definition meant to apply just to willings or to actions more broadly, including those we effect by willing? Here is the key sentence again:

If, in any action, he had power to will what he did, or not to will it, in that action he is free. (EAP 4.1:196)

The exegetical question about this sentence is whether "that action" is just the willing itself or whether it is a further action accomplished by the willing, such as raising one's arm. I expect Reid wants to cover both cases, but they need slightly different treatment. For willing itself, we can perhaps just say that the agent exerted his power to will a certain way and had the power not to will that way.[27] For further actions, we cannot say simply what is said in the displayed sentence above, for that could be true even if one's willing had no further issue. But Reid is no doubt assuming that the actions we are talking about were event-caused by one's willing. Thus to extend the definition beyond willings themselves, we may say what Rowe does:

An action is free just in case the agent willed to perform it, performed it as a result of willing to perform it, and the agent was the cause [in the sense above, implying the freedom of the willing] of the act of will to perform the action. (Rowe 1991:80)

The second question is whether Reid's conditions for liberty are meant as a *supplement* to the williwig conditions or a *replacement* for them. In other words, should we retain the williwig conditions alongside Reid's conditions or discard them?[28] One reason for retaining them is that if we do not, we must in some cases ascribe

[27] We should not say that the agent had the power to will to will as he did and also the power not to will to will as he did. That would be taking the first step in the regress alleged by opponents of liberty as predicated of willing.

[28] Rowe calls supplementation the "standard" account (78). Hamilton (599), Duggan (1976:106) and Weinstock (1976:95) all attribute it to Reid without discussion.

freedom regarding prospective actions to someone whose willings are totally inefficacious. I have the power to will to walk as well as the power not to will to walk, but since I am paralyzed, nothing will happen however I will. Am I free to walk? Or consider the following example: A malicious driver swerves to kill a turtle on the road, his hands and steering wheel obeying the commands of his will, which could easily have been directed otherwise. Did he swerve freely? According to Reid's conditions, yes. But suppose that unbeknownst to the driver, his wheels had just entered a rut, and he would have swerved and killed the turtle even if he had not willed to. This, of course, is Locke's room all over again, and Lockean intuitions may lead some to say that the driver did not swerve freely. This is an argument for retaining the williwig conditions alongside Reid's conditions for freedom.

On the other side, Rowe has pointed out a reason why Reid should *not* accept the williwig conditions as necessary for freedom. One of Reid's cardinal principles is that we are accountable or morally responsible for actions only if we performed them freely (EIP 6.6:494, EAP 1.7:39, 4.1:198, 4.7:237).[29] Was the driver responsible for swerving and killing the turtle? Rowe thinks Reid would say yes ([1987] 1995:164). If so, Reid cannot hold that swerving freely requires that the driver would not have swerved if he had not willed to swerve, for that is false in the example. We might put the point this way: Reid thinks responsibility requires freedom in his sense; he does not think it requires freedom in Locke's sense; therefore, Reidian freedom does not imply Lockean freedom. Reidian freedom differs from Lockean freedom not only in requiring that I could have *willed* otherwise, but also in *not* requiring that I would have *done* otherwise had I so willed ([1987] 1995:164).[30]

In this book I do not discuss Reid's reasons for believing that human beings possess moral liberty in the sense we have just articulated. Reid says that the arguments that have the greatest weight with him are the following three: "*First,* Because [any person] has a natural conviction or belief, that, in many cases, he acts freely;

---

[29] Sometimes Reid puts the principle in terms of power, sometimes in terms of liberty. Since the principle is the cornerstone of one of his arguments for moral liberty (EAP 4.7), it is clear that for him the two formulations come to the same thing.

[30] Actually, Rowe thinks it is not quite right to say that Reidian freedom requires that the agent could have willed otherwise or refrained from willing as he did. He calls our attention to a scenario (like those in Frankfurt 1969) in which an evil scientist monitoring my brain stands ready to make me will a certain act if he sees that I am not going to will it myself. As it happens, I do will it. Rowe thinks Reid would say I am responsible for the ensuing act, and therefore I must have performed it freely. Yet it was not within my power to refrain from willing as I did, given that the scientist would have ensured that I will that way no matter what. Rowe proposes that Reid be understood as laying down as a requirement for freedom not (1) *that it was in my power not to will that way* but rather (2) *that I caused the volition and had it within my power not to cause it.* In Frankfurt scenarios, 1 is false, but 2 is true. See Rowe 1991:83–85.

*secondly,* Because he is accountable; and, *thirdly,* Because he is able to prosecute an end by a long series of means adapted to it" (4.5:228). For reconstruction and appraisal of these arguments, I refer the reader to Lehrer 1989, Rowe 1991, McDermid 1999, Yaffe 2004, and Harris 2005.

I end this section by discussing the rationale for Reid's incompatibilism. Incompatibilists hold that freedom and determinism are incompatible because (a) my doing or willing something freely requires my having been able to do or will otherwise and (b) if determinism is true, I could not have done or willed otherwise than I did on any occasion.[31] I present below an argument for incompatibilism that takes point (a) for granted and marshals considerations in support of point (b). The considerations in support of (b) are known in contemporary philosophy as the Consequence Argument (after van Inwagen, one of its staunchest defenders, in 1975, 1983:16 and chapter 3, and 2008). Letting A be some action I performed as the result of willing it, we may set forth one version of the argument as follows:

1. My doing A was free only if I could have willed something other than A.
2. If determinism$_2$ is true, my willing A was implied by some past state of the world together with the laws of nature.
3. If my willing A was implied by some past state of the world together with the laws of nature, I could have willed something other than A only by doing something that either "undid" the past or "undid" the laws of nature.
4. I cannot do anything that undoes the past or the laws of nature.
5. Therefore, if determinism$_2$ is true, I cannot have willed anything other than A (from 2, 3, and 4).
6. Therefore, if determinism$_2$ is true, my doing A was not free (from 1 and 5).

Though its merits are debated in contemporary philosophy, I find this argument compelling.[32]

In Reid's day, the 2 through 5 part of the argument, or at least the subconclusion 5 itself, would have been relatively uncontroversial. The controversy was almost

---

[31] Denying (a) and (b) are the two ways of being a compatibilist noted in n. 19 above.

[32] Premise 3 seems quite intuitive to me, but it rests on two assumptions that some contemporary critics of the Consequence Argument have seen fit to challenge. To expose the assumptions, let us symbolize premise 3 using the following abbreviations: "A" for "the agent wills to do A," "P" for a complete description of the world at some past instant, "L" for the laws of nature, and "Cp" for "the agent can bring it about that p" (or "the agent could have brought it about that p"). "~C~p" is an approximation to what van Inwagen expresses by saying the proposition that p is *untouchable* (2008:45–52). Premise 3 may now be symbolized as follows:

(3) If (P & L) entails A, then C~A only if C~P or C~L.

entirely about 1, Clarke and Reid affirming it and williwiggers denying it. We have already discussed Reid's reasons for 1. What are his reasons for 5?

In particular, what would Reid's attitude have been toward the 2–5 argument? He certainly agrees with the subconclusion, 5. His own reasons for accepting this conclusion appeal to his view, discussed in chapter 14, section C, that the laws of nature are the rules followed by God or his subordinate agents in producing phenomena. If I do something as a consequence of past states and laws, it follows for Reid that *someone else made me do it*. (See EAP 4.9: 246, lines 13–18, bearing in mind that a cause that exerts its power must for Reid be an agent). *That* is why "the system of necessity" (determinism) is at odds with freedom. If Reid had held a purely secular or naturalist conception of the laws of nature—for example, if he had conceived of them as brute regularities à la Hume or governing principles à la Armstrong—would he still have been moved to incompatibilism by considerations like those in 2–5? I like to think so, but I cannot be sure.[33]

---

Here is a proof of (3) that proceeds by assuming its antecedent, denying its consequent, and deriving a contradiction:

a. (P & L) entails A (antecedent of 3)
b. C~A & ~(C~P or C~L) (denial of consequent of 3)
c. ~C~P & ~C~L (DeMorgan applied to right conjunct of b)
d. ~C~(P & L) (c and the assumption that untouchability is conjunctive or agglomerative)
e. ~A entails ~(P & L) (contrapositive of a)
f. If C~A, then C~(P & L) (e and the assumption that "can-do-ability" is transferred by entailment)
g. C~(P & L) (from b and f, but contradicting d).

The assumptions sometimes challenged are agglomeration at step d and transfer at step f. For a discussion of the role of these assumptions, see Šuster 2012.

Since some of my readers have professed not to recognize anything like van Inwagen's Consequence Argument in my version of it, let me comment on several differences or apparent differences. (i) His version concerns *doing* otherwise, mine *willing* otherwise, but if either of these is shown incompatible with determinism, so is the other by a formally parallel argument. (ii) Where I speak of "undoing" the past or the laws, he speaks in 1975 of rendering them false. (iii) I say explicitly that you cannot undo the past; he does not in 1975. But he does say that you can render the conjunction of the laws and some past state P false only if you can render the laws false. Why say that unless you are presupposing that you cannot render P false? Moreover, in 2008, he explicitly states the argument using the premise that the past is "untouchable." (iv) Although he does not appeal explicitly to the transfer and agglomeration principles, he uses two other principles that together do the same work, the necessitation rule and the conditional rule (1983:94–95 and 2008).

In another article, van Inwagen acknowledges counterexamples that have been raised to the agglomeration principle, but offers a reformulation of the Consequence Argument designed to get around them (2002).

[33] Yaffe tells me that he is fairly sure Reid would *not* have been an incompatibilist in that case.

# D. THE FUNDAMENTAL DILEMMA
# FOR LIBERTARIANISM

Let us call the view that some actions are free (or that they have moral liberty in Reid's sense) *libertarianism*.[34] If an action is free in that sense, it was produced by the agent's willing it, and he had the power not to will it. Reid takes it that his having that power entails that there were no event causes sufficient for his having willed as he did. In other words, he takes it that the existence of free actions is incompatible with determinism, as we saw in the previous section.

But now we need to ask whether *in*determinism is any more hospitable to free actions than determinism. There is reason to think the answer is *no*. If my action had no cause at all (as indeterminism allows), would it not simply have been an accident—a random occurrence? And in that case, it would not have been a free action of mine; indeed, it would not have been an action of mine at all, but simply something that happened out of the blue.[35]

The horns are now in place for the fundamental dilemma for libertarianism. If determinism is true, every action of mine has a cause, which has a prior cause, and so on until we get back to dinosaur days.[36] An action cannot be free if it was deter-mined to happen by events that occurred before I was born. If determinism is *not* true—if my action was simply uncaused—it was not an action of mine at all. In either case, there are no such things as free actions. This is a harsh dilemma, and it led C. D. Broad to conclude that human freedom is a delusion, being impossible under each of two assumptions he took to be exhaustive (Broad [1934] 1952).

Actually, the second horn of the dilemma has not yet been correctly stated. The mere falsity of determinism owing to the occurrence of an uncaused event some-where in the universe would neither help nor hurt the libertarian thesis. What the indeterminist libertarian seeks to exploit in his defense of freedom—and what his opponent claims is in fact his undoing—is not any old uncaused event, but an un-caused event *in the causal chain culminating in a given action*. The horns are more properly formulated as follows: either an action A is caused by an earlier event, which is caused by a still earlier event, and so on ad infinitum, or else the causal chain culminating in A contains an uncaused event, either A itself or one of the events in the chain leading up to it. The horns still have the appearance of being

---

[34] Reid credits his minor adversary Alexander Crombie with coining the term "Libertarian" in 1793, but the OED reports an earlier use in 1789 (COR:233 and 318).

[35] Jonathan Edwards states this horn of the dilemma as follows: if free acts of the soul have no cause, then the soul is "subjected to what accident brings to pass . . . as much as the earth that is inactive, is necessarily subjected to what falls upon it" ([1754] 2002 2.13:114).

[36] Taking the chain back to dinosaur days requires the assumption identified in n7.

exhaustive, and they yield the same dismal results as before: on the first horn, A is not free, and on the second, A is not an action at all, but only a random occurrence.[37]

Agent causation to the rescue! The horns may appear to be exhaustive, but in fact they are so only if we assume that *all causation is event causation*. Under that assumption, the causal ancestry of an action must be a chain of events either stretching infinitely into the past or containing an uncaused event. But if an action can be caused not by any other event, but by an agent, *we can go right between the horns of the fundamental dilemma for libertarianism.*

We may make the present point by restoring the subscripts from our discussion of determinism in section A. The determinism that is affirmed in the first horn is determinism$_2$, the thesis that every event is caused by previous events or states (in the sense of following lawfully upon them). The determinism that is denied in the second horn is determinism$_1$. If we avoid the first horn by saying of an action or volition of mine that it was not caused by a prior event, we are not thereby thrown on the second horn (uncaused events), for the action may have been caused by *me*, the agent.

This is exactly what Reid says:

> In certain motions of my body and directions of my thoughts, I know, not only that there must be a cause that has power to produce these effects, but that *I am that cause.* (EAP 1.5:30, emphasis added)

> Was there a cause of the action? Undoubtedly there was: Of every event there must be a cause. [If the action was free] *the man was the cause of the action.* . . . (EAP 4.9:246, emphasis added)

> The question that remains is whether a volition, undetermined by motives, is an event uncaused. This I deny. *The cause of the volition is the man that willed it.* (COR 234, emphasis added)

The notion of agent causation is exactly what is needed, it now appears, to go between the horns of the fundamental dilemma. Chisholm, following Reid, invokes agent causation for exactly this purpose:

> We must not say that every event involved in the act is caused by some other event; and we must not say that the act is something that is not caused at all. The possibility

---

[37] What if we grasp Horn 2, but say the uncaused event in A's causal ancestry lies two centuries in the past? Is it then so obvious that A is a random event? Perhaps not, but we are now granting that A is caused by events so far back in the agent's past that he cannot be said to have performed A freely. We get the same result as from Horn 1.

that remains, therefore, is this: We should say that at least one of the events that are involved in the act is caused, not by any other events, but by something else instead. And this something else can only be the agent—the man. (1964:28)

The theory of agent causation thus provides a tantalizing glimmer of hope for escaping a harsh dilemma for human liberty. Yet it faces potentially debilitating problems of its own, to which I now turn.

## E. THE REGRESS OF EXERTION

Perhaps the most formidable objection to Reid's agent-causation account of freedom is that it generates an absurd infinite regress of acts by the agent. I am not referring to the alleged infinite regress of ever higher-order acts of willing, advanced as an objection by Hobbes and Locke to the view that nothing can be free unless the will itself is free. In section B I dismissed that objection as not applicable to Reid's view, but only to the amalgam of his view with theirs. I am referring instead to an infinite regress of acts of exertion, which may be advanced against Reid's view in particular, or an infinite regress of agent causings, which may be advanced against theories of agent causation in general. I discuss the exertion regress in this section and the more general regress in the next.

The regress of exertion has been well articulated by Rowe as follows:

On Reid's theory, when an agent wills some action, the act of will is itself an event and, as such, requires a cause. If the act of will is free, its cause is not some event, it is the agent whose act of will it is. Being the cause of the act of will, the agent must satisfy Reid's three conditions of agent-causation. Thus the agent must have had the power to bring about the act of will as well as the power to refrain from bringing about the act of will, and she must have *exerted* her power to bring about the act of will. It is the last of these conditions that generates an infinite regress of events that an agent must cause if she is to cause her act of will. For what it tells us is that to produce the act of will the agent must *exert* her power to bring about the act of will. Now an exertion of power is itself an event. As such, it too must have a cause. On Reid's view that cause must again be the agent herself. But to have caused this exertion the agent must have had the power to bring it about and must have *exerted* that power. Each exertion of power is itself an event which the agent can cause only by having the power to cause it and by *exerting* that power. As Reid reminds us, "In order to the production of any effect, there must be in the cause, not only power, but the exertion of that power: for power that is not exerted produces no effect." The result of this principle, however, is that in order to produce any act of will whatever, the agent must cause an infinite number of exertions. (Rowe 1991:147–48 or [1987] 1995:161–62; for a more formal presentation of the argument, see appendix X.)

Another passage that Rowe might have cited as grist for his regress is this: "The exertion of active power we call *action*; and as every action produces some change, so every change must be caused by some exertion, or by the cessation of some exertion of power" (EAP 1.1:13). As exertions and cessations of them are both changes, the regress appears to be well under way.

Rowe identifies four possible responses to this argument: (1) accept the infinite regress; (2) abandon the principle that all events have causes; (3) hold that acts of will are not events (or, in a variant of this response, that the exertions producing acts of will are not events); and (4) deny that agents cause their effects by means of their exertions ([1987] 1995). I now comment on (2) through (4), as well discussing an additional "outside the box" solution proposed by Yaffe.

In (1987) 1995, Rowe favors response (4). He writes as though the idea that some acts are caused by the agent but not by exerting her power simply goes with the territory of basic action theories:

> Perhaps we should think of the act of will as in some way a special sort of action, a *basic act*. A basic act of an agent is one that she causes but not by any exertion of power or any other act. ([1987] 1995:162)

Or with the territory of agent causation theories:

> The whole idea of agent-causation is that . . . in addition to event-causes there are causes of a wholly different kind—agents. . . . In short, once we fully grasp the idea of agent-causation we can see, I believe, that it implies that when an agent causes his action there is some event (an act of will, perhaps) that the agent causes without bringing about any other event as a means to producing it. (163)

Hoffman advocates a similar solution, except he proposes that the acts not achieved by means of any prior exertion are exertions themselves, rather than volitions (443–45).[38]

It is not clear to me that the Rowe-Hoffman tactic manages to avoid the regress of exertion. It may be true that acts of will (or the exertions producing them) are not produced *by means of* any other exertion. It does not follow, however, that no further

---

[38] He also says that he differs from Rowe in holding that this solution *is* Reid's theory, not a modification of it (445).

exertion *occurs* when an agent causes an act of will or an exertion. Perhaps the exertion is a by-product of the causing, rather than anything by means of which the agent performed the causing. If any further exertion occurs, the regress is under way.[39]

In his 1991, Rowe no longer favors this tactic. He seems to think that in order to obviate one of the fundamental mysteries about agent causation—why did the agent's effect occur when it did rather than earlier or later in her lifetime?—we must appeal to her exerting her power at a certain time (156–57). So Rowe explores a different response, number (2), which involves giving up the principle of universal causation (though he initially presents it under the "exertions are not events" rubric). He says that what requires a cause according to Reid's causal principle is any change that a substance undergoes. He goes on to say that exertions of power are not *changes subjects undergo*, but *activities*. As such, they need not have causes. It seems to me that this tactic is more aptly classified as one that gives up the universality of the causal principle (as I think Rowe agrees in the end: see 154). It shrinks the sphere of events that are required to have causes to changes passively undergone by substances, affirming that changes not passively undergone need not have causes. Rowe tries to make this departure from determinism₁ more palatable by arguing that exertions, as episodes of causing by agents, are not the sorts of things that *could* have causes (154–55).

A version of strategy (3) more clearly deserving the name "exertions are not events" is attributed to Reid by O'Connor:

> The proper solution . . . is to see that an exertion of active power, according to Reid, is not any kind of event at all. Rather, it is the instantiation of a causal relation between agent and volition, and Reid does not consider this to be an event. (2000:47).

Reid does say that exertion is a relation between an agent and the event effected by it, but why should that imply that exertions are not events? Lighting a fire is a relation between an agent and an event, but is it not also a paradigm event? O'Connor himself does not think this solution is philosophically defensible (48).

Yaffe has proposed an ingenious solution different from any of the foregoing. As noted in chapter 14, section D, Yaffe takes exertions to be the same thing as willings or volitions. When he addresses the exertion regress, he proposes that exertions may also be identified with what in ordinary parlance we call *tryings*. The gist

---

[39] An analogy may help explain the possibility I am indicating here. When I believe that I am thinking, my belief is not justified *by* any other justified proposition, but at the same time it would not be justified unless certain other propositions were justified in the bargain, such as the proposition that I exist. Similarly, even though I perform an act of will not *by* exerting my power to do so, it may be that an exertion of my power to will necessarily occurs when I will.

of his solution is this: When you try to V and fail, there is a trying. But what happens when you try and succeed? Are there then two things, V-ing and trying to V? Yaffe says no. "We do not . . . prosecute the successful murderer for both murder and attempted murder" (154), and this, he says, is for reasons of metaphysics and not merely jurisprudence. Where, then, does the trying go in the case of success? It gets absorbed into the accomplished act: "If it is anything at all, it is just the action that the agent succeeds in performing, the murder say, or the bodily movement" (156). So the regress of exertion does not arise. If I try to V and succeed, there is only my V-ing and not in addition the exertion of my power to V. If I try to V and fail, then I succeed in something, namely, the trying or exerting itself. By similar reasoning, there is no trying to try or exerting of the power to exert. The regress stops with the "inmost" thing I succeed at. In the case of a failed attempt to move some part of my body, the inmost item will be the exertion that failed, but since I did accomplish the exertion, there was no trying to exert or exertion of the power to exert distinct from the exertion itself.

I do not dispute this solution on its merits, but I worry that it is inconsistent with Reid's larger scheme of things, at least as set forth by Yaffe. In his first chapter (21ff), Yaffe attributes to Reid the view that all actions inherit their status as actions from basic actions. Basic actions are actions I perform without doing anything else as a means thereto, and every action is either a basic action or something I bring about ultimately by means of basic actions. The basic actions are my exertions or volitions, which Yaffe takes to be coextensive. The resulting constellation of views gives rise to the following potentially inconsistent triad:

1. Some actions (namely, successful ones) involve no exertions [distinct from themselves].
2. All actions involve basic actions.
3. All basic actions are exertions (= volitions).

If we erased the bracketed phrase in statement 1, we would have outright inconsistency: all actions involve exertions (by 2 and 3), yet some do not (by 1). We could avoid the inconsistency by including the bracketed phrase and saying that some actions involve exertions that are identical with the actions. But since for Yaffe exertions are coextensive with volitions, we would have to go on and say that some actions involve volitions that are identical with the actions—that there are instances in which walking and willing to walk are the same thing.[40] And that is

---

[40] Not every willing to walk would be a walking, but every (voluntary) walking would be a willing to walk.

something Reid would surely *not* want to say. Willing to walk is an intentional state with an object; walking is a physical state without an object.

## F. THE REGRESS OF AGENT CAUSATION

I turn now to the more general regress objection to agent-causation theories of freedom. This objection does not turn on any exegetical issues about what Reid meant by "exertion" or about how exertions fits into the rest of his scheme (for example, whether they are productive of or identical with volitions). It can be developed without using the word "exertion" at all. It is a problem that flows, I believe, from the very notion of agent causation, or at any rate, from any notion of it fit to play its intended role of avoiding the fundamental dilemma for libertarian theories.

Consider an action that is free because it is caused by a volition that is free. (Or if, like Taylor, you think volitions are fictions, consider the action itself.) We do not want to say that the volition is caused by another event (and that event by another, and so on), or we land on the determinist$_2$ horn of the fundamental dilemma. Nor do we want to say that the volition is uncaused, or we land on the indeterminist$_1$ horn. So we say that the volition is caused by the agent, A, and in so saying we uphold determinism$_1$. Since agents are not events, neither variety of determinism requires us to posit a further cause, and our regress stops with the agent as prime mover.

The question that is now unavoidable is this: Why did A cause his volition, or whatever the inmost event is in the series of events culminating in the action? Call the inmost event e. Why did the agent cause e? To ask what may seem to be the same question in other words, what caused the agent to cause e? We cannot say that some other event (or some other agent) caused the agent to cause e, or we forfeit freedom. We cannot say that nothing caused the agent to cause e, or we embrace randomness. We must say that what caused A's causing of e is simply A, the agent: A caused A to cause e.[41] And now we may ask what caused A to cause his causing of e, setting us off on our regress.

To present the regress a bit more formally, let me use the following notational conventions: "Ace" means "agent A causes event e," and when a formula of the form "Ace" is enclosed in parentheses, it becomes a term, denoting the event that is A's

---

[41] Rowe argues that it is a conceptual impossibility in Reid's framework for something to cause an agent to cause an event, even if the "something" is the agent himself (1991:151–53). I see how the argument works in the case where the cause of the causing is *another* agent or event: Reid holds that an agent causes something (exerts his power to produce it) only if he has the power *not* to produce it, and he would not have this power if some other agent or event caused him to produce it. I cannot see, however, why an agent cannot cause *himself* to cause something. I cannot see why I cannot make myself make a cake, at least if the makings are simultaneous.

causing of e. Thus "Ac(Ace)" is to be read as "A causes A's causing of e." Letting e be an exertion, a volition, or some free action of A's, we may argue as follows:[42]

1. Assume Ace and A was free in so doing (it was in A's power not to cause e).
2. If Ace, then there is an event (Ace) of A's causing of e.
3. Every event has a cause.
4. So something caused (Ace). What was it?
5. Not nothing, as we have already said in step 3.
6. Not another event, or we are back on the determinist$_2$ horn.[43]
7. Not another agent, or A was not free in causing e.
8. So A himself caused (Ace): Ac(Ace). What caused (Ac(Ace))?

Now the pattern of reasoning repeats itself, generating a regress of the following form:

Ace; Ac(Ace); Ac(Ac(Ace)); Ac(Ac(Ac(Ace))); and so on.

We can keep on adding parentheses and "Ac" operators in front of them ad infinitum.

Something seems absurd or impossible about such a regress. What are the ways out this time? I find three worth discussing, two of which are partial echoes of responses to the exertion regress: (1) we could *accept* the regress, but deny that it is vicious; (2) we could say that when A causes e, there is no *event* of his so doing, and

---

[42] If volitions are effectings, they would be represented in "Ace" by the verb "c"; if they are first effects, they would be represented by the noun "e."

[43] More needs to be said by way of justifying step 6, for we are not really back on the determinist horn unless we say (Ace) was caused by another event and that by another event ad infinitum. What if instead we say that (Ace) was caused by an event f, f by A, (Acf) by g, g by A, and so on, in a sequence oscillating between agent and event causes?

Reid would say that as soon as *any* event causes (Ace), A was not free in causing e and was not truly the cause of it. Not all incompatibilist arguers reach their verdict of unfreedom so quickly; some would rest their case only when we reach an event in the causal ancestry of (Ace) that was clearly beyond A's control, such as one lying before his birth. But sooner or later, it seems, we must reach such an event.

What if we say, as in some Hindu cosmologies, that selves are beginningless, so however far back an event may lie in the causal ancestry of one of my current actions, I was there to cause that event? That, it seems to me, would at most show that I am *responsible* for my current action. It would not show that I am *free* in performing it, since what I did in the irrefrangible past leaves me no alternative now. And Reid would not even agree that I am responsible for my current action, for he holds that I am accountable for an action only if doing it and forbearing from it are both within my power at the time of the action. The sailor who cuts off his fingers to avoid having to climb aloft is guilty of a crime, Reid says, but his crime lies in the mutilation and not in the subsequent failure to climb, for climbing is no longer in his power (EAP 4.7:238; see also 5.4:292–93).

therefore nothing that requires a cause; or (3) we could seek to collapse the regress by denying that successive members of it are *distinct* events.

(1) In a number of his writings in defense of agent causation, Chisholm explicitly accepts an infinite regress of agent-causings. For example, in *Person and Object* he embraces the principle that if a person contributes causally to event p, then he also contributes causally to his contributing causally to p (1976:71). He acknowledges in response to an objection from Donagan that his views imply an infinite series of ever more complicated events of causal contribution (Donagan 1979, Chisholm 1979). But he denies that the regress is vicious, as it would be if every instance of causing required a *prior* instance of causing. He suggests that the infinitely many causings could be accomplished in one fell swoop:

> It is not as though a and e were dominoes with all these other events falling between them, each such that it must be preceded by another. If we use the domino figure, then we should think of the other events, not as standing between a and e, but as attached to the right and left of e, so that, when [one] falls, it brings down the whole group at once (1979:372). [In Chisholm's notation, a is an event.]

Nonetheless, even if there is no problem of the agent's never being able to do anything because he must always do something else first, one may balk at the idea there are infinitely many events of ever-increasing complexity each time I wiggle a finger.

In addition to any other objection to the infinite regress, there is a special objection to it in the Reidian setting. Causing for Reid is willing, and willing requires having some conception of what one wills. Hence one could not cause all of the successively more complicated events in the series without having a conception of each of them, a feat no finite mind could manage.

(2) The next strategy sounds initially more promising: we deny that A's causing of event e is itself an event, in which case we need not inquire about its cause. But why is (Ace) not an event, or as we may better phrase the question, why is there no such event as (Ace) when by hypothesis Ace? One prominent theory of events holds that there is an event whenever an object has a property or two or more objects stand in a relation (Kim 1993:35).[44] On a liberal theory such as this, when Ace, *of course* there is the event (Ace). To avoid countenancing this event, we would have to take either of two options. First, we could refuse

---

[44] Kim's "Existence Condition" says that event (x, P, t) exists just in case substance x has property P at time t, with similar principles holding for dyadic and higher-place events.

to countenance such entities as events altogether, as in the no-event ontology of A. N. Prior. According to Prior, when we say such things as "the marriage of Tom and Estella occurred at noon," that is really just an inflated way of saying that Tom married Estella at noon—there are no entities involved in addition to Tom and Estella (Prior 2003:7–19). Second, we could hold a sparse theory of events—a theory holding that when certain objects have certain properties or stand in certain relations, there is in some cases a corresponding event, but not in all. Now I would be willing to embrace a liberal ontology of events à la Kim or a no-event ontology à la Prior, but it is hard for me to see any rationale for a sparse theory. Don't mess with Mr. In-Between. It seems to me that one who wishes to discountenance the event of A's causing of e should do away with events altogether.

Suppose, then, we adopt a no-event theory like Prior's. Do we then avoid the questions about causation that generate a regress? Not at all. A world without events is not a world without causation, any more than it is a world without moving or shoving or loving. There are still causal truths, but we must state them using sentences and sentential connectives rather than terms and relational expressions—"Jack broke his crown because he fell down" or "Jack fell down and thereby caused it to be the case that his crown broke" rather than "Jack's fall caused the breaking of Jack's crown." A no-event ontologist can still believe in universal causation, but it must be expressed by saying that it is never the case that p unless for some q, it is the case that p because it is the case that q.[45]

This brings me to the important point for present purposes: because universal causation may be stated in Prior's framework, neither a no-event ontologist nor a sparse event ontologist can duck the question "What causes A's causing of e?"[46] Let it be granted that there is no such event as A's causing of e; still, A *does* cause e, and one can inquire about the cause of that.[47] Either *nothing* causes it to be the case that A causes e (the indeterminist answer), or A causes e because (for some x and F) *x is F* (the determinist answer), or *A* causes it to be the case that A causes e (the agent-causalist answer). We are confronted with the same alternatives as before, and the

[45] On Prior's view, the quantifier "for some q" carries no commitment to events or fact-like entities; see his 1971, chapter 3.

[46] Let me make it clear, then, that my dismissal of the "not an event" strategy does not rest on repudiating sparse or in-between theories in favor of extreme theories, though I do repudiate them. Consideration of Prior's theory, whether one embraces it or not, reveals the resources for raising the regress problem even in the setting of a sparse theory.

[47] If a professed determinist said that although A causes e, there is no cause for this because A's causing of e is not an event, we would not take his profession of determinism seriously.

agent-causation theorist can afford to give no answer but the last. We get essentially the same regress as before, now written without parentheses (and with "Ac..." read as "A causes it to be the case that..." and "e" functioning as a formula rather than a term):

Ace, AcAce, AcAcAce, AcAcAce, and so on.

The strategy of saying there is no such event as A's causing of e therefore fails of its purpose. Having made this point, I will go back to event notation for purposes of discussion.

(3) The third strategy has no exact analog among the responses we discussed to the exertion regress,[48] but it does have an analog among responses to the infinite regress of conscious states, discussed in chapter 1, section G, and appendix F. Recall that we contemplated the possibility that the apparently infinite regress involved in A's being aware of O, A's being aware of his awareness of O, his being aware of his awareness of his awareness of O, and so on could be collapsed down to its bottom element if each apparently more complicated higher-level state could be *identified* with the state below it. Could any such identification strategy be made to work here? The idea would be that in the supposed regress

Ace; Ac(Ace); Ac(Ac(Ace)); (Ac(Ac(Ace))); and so on.

any two adjacent formulas really report the same event. Thus (Ace) = (Ac(Ace)) = (Ac(Ac(Ace))) and so on. The entire series collapses down to its simplest element.

There is an objection that might appear to trip the identification strategy right out of the starting blocks. If (Ace) is identical with (Ac(Ace)), the effect-constituent of (Ace), namely e, must be identical with the effect-constituent of (Ac(Ace)), namely (Ace). But recall what e is: it is the rising of A's arm, or his willing this or that: it is something without any causal structure.[49] (Ace), on the other

---

[48] The Yaffe strategy comes closest to being an analog; he can be seen as identifying exertion and action in cases in which the exertion is successful.

[49] I am trying to stay noncommittal on the question whether volitions are effectings (exertings of power) or the first effects of such effectings, even though I suggest in chapter 14, section D that the latter view has advantages for Reid. If volitions are first effects, they are links in a causal chain, but they lack causal structure themselves, and what I say in the text about them is true. If they are effectings, they do have causal structure—they are causings—but then they are denoted by "(Ace)" rather than "e" in my notation. The role of e will now be played by the rising of an arm or the firing of a neuron, but in any case, something without causal structure. Whatever e is, it is not the causing of anything.

hand, does have causal structure. So (Ace) cannot be identical with e,[50] and there-fore (Ac(Ace)) cannot be identical with (Ace).

Though the foregoing argument is seductive, there is a subtle mistake in it. It is wrong to say that (Ace) is identical with (Ac(Ace)) only if *the* effect-constituent of the former is identical with *the* effect-constituent of the latter, since that presupposes that an event has at most one effect-constituent.[51] What we should really say is the following, which is an instance of Leibniz's Law: if (Ace) = (Ac(Ace)), then every effect-constituent of either is an effect-constituent of the other. (That is, every effect-constituent of the event denoted by either side of the identity is an effect-constituent of the event denoted by the other side of the identity.) That could be true if (Ace) and (Ac(Ace)) each had the same *pair* of effect-constituents, namely, e and (Ace). In other words, (Ace) has as effect-constituents both e and itself; and (Ac(Ace)) has those same two effect-constituents. Neither has any other effect-constituent, any-thing apparently more complicated reducing down to (Ac(Ace)).

The resulting view is reminiscent of Brentano's view about self-reflexive aware-ness, discussed in chapter 1. According to Brentano, the act of seeing a tree has the tree for its primary object and the act itself for its secondary object, as portrayed in Figure 15.1:

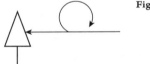

**Figure 15.1**

According to the present suggestion, the act or event of causing a ground-level effect (such as a volition or a bodily movement) has the ground-level item as its pri-mary effect-constituent and itself as a secondary effect-constituent. The situation may be portrayed in a diagram of exactly the same structure, the arrow now stand-ing for causation rather than awareness (Figure 15.2):

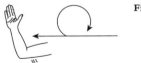

**Figure 15.2**

When I cause my arm to go up, I cause in the bargain my causing of my arm's going up. It is also true to say that I cause my causing of my causing my arm to go up,

---

[50] As Alvarez and Hyman put the point, "my causing an event is not identical with the event caused, any more than my making or breaking a pot is identical with the pot I make or break" (1998:229). As will soon emerge, I accept this as an argument against ground-level identities.

[51] I am using the term "effect-constituent" rather than "effect" because (Ace) does not *cause* e; it is a complex event that *includes* e.

but this added complexity of description is matched by no corresponding complexity in the fact described—or so it may now safely be maintained.[52]

I close by discussing three apparent consequences of the identity strategy that some may find paradoxical. The first apparent consequence is not really a consequence, the second is not really paradoxical, and the third (which arises independent of the identity strategy) may be avoided by a moderate revision of Reid's philosophy.

(a) Buras, who espouses an identity theory of sensations and the awareness of them, points out that such theories are at odds with causal theories of intentionality (2009). In brief, his argument is that because there are cases of *x is aware of x*, but no cases of *x causes x*, *x is aware of y* cannot be analyzed so as to imply *y is a cause of x*. In floating an identity strategy, am I flouting Buras's premise that there can be no cases of an item causing itself? No: I am suggesting that in causing e, A causes her own causing of e; but I am not saying that (Ace) is an event that causes itself. What causes (Ace) is not (Ace) but A.

(b) In saying that (Ac(Ace)) may be identical with (Ace) even though (Ace) is not identical with e, I am implying that there are exceptions to the rule that if A's V-ing of x is identical with A's V-ing of y, then x is identical with y.[53] Is there any precedent for denying this rule? Well, on a Davidsonian theory of events, if Tom tips his hat to Mary and Sally as they approach him on the sidewalk, Tom's greeting of Mary *is* his greeting of Sally, even though Mary and Sally are not identical (Davidson [1969] 1980). I am not sure whether a Davidsonian theory best serves Reid all things considered, but it serves him well in dealing with the present objection.[54]

Suppose we say that A causes (Ace) *by* causing e, rather than saying that A's causing e *is* his causing of (Ace). That would be returning to Chisholm's course, which *does* involve an infinite series of distinct and ever more complicated effects, all brought about by A's causing of e: (Ace), (Ac(Ace)), (Ac(Ac(Ace))), and so on, as with the dominoes that go down all at once. Apart from any other objection to the regress, there is a special objection to it in the Reidian setting, as we saw above. Causing for Reid is willing, and willing requires having some conception of what one wills. An

---

[52] Thorp (1980) proposes an identity strategy to forestall the regress of agent causation, but in my opinion he applies it one level too soon: he says (in my notation) that Ace = e, for example, that the agent's decision is his causing his decision, and that his arm's going up is his causing his arm to go up (102–3).

[53] Thanks to David Robb for pressing me on this point.

[54] On Kim's rival theory of events, an event represented as <A, V, x> is identical with an event represented as <A, V, y> only if x = y, which looks like trouble for the identification strategy proposed in the text. See Bennett 2002, however, for criticisms of this aspect of Kim's theory.

infinite regress of causing would therefore involve a series of ever more complicated objects of conception, eventually exhausting the capacities of a finite conceiver.[55]

(c) With or without the identity strategy, Reid's view that causing an event requires conceiving of it has a consequence some would regard as implausible. Whether causing e is the same as causing (Ace) or not, in doing the former one does the latter according to the dialectic of agent causation. Therefore, any agent A who causes any event e must have a conception of (Ace). It follows that infants are not the causes of any of their bodily motions until they have acquired the conception of causation, as well as the conception of themselves as agents. It was perhaps with this consequence in mind that Reid wrote "Of Power," his last piece of philosophical writing ([1792] 2001), which qualifies his former views. He suggests there that infants may exert their power (that is, cause things) involuntarily before they have the conception of power, and that such exertions eventually give them the notion of power they need to exert their power voluntarily. See Walsh for an exposition of Reid's revised views. For another approach to this third objection, in which the notions of causing and having an intentional object are allowed to come apart even in mature subjects, see appendix Y.

In sum, I think the best way out of the regress of agent causings for an agent-causation theorist is the identity strategy, in which an agent's causing of e is the same as his causing of his causing of e, collapsing the regress. If we take this approach, agents are not analogous to "the prime mover unmoved" (as Chisholm says), but to "the prime mover that moves itself."

## G. ANOMIC EXPLANATION

One more serious challenge to the idea of agent causation remains to be discussed. When an agent acts in some way—that is to say, when A causes some event to take place in her body or in her mind, thereby perhaps also causing further events to take place in the wider world—*why* did she act in that way? What is the explanation of her causing the initial event, e? Event causes of A's causing e are excluded, as are other agent causes. We may correctly say that A caused her causing of e, but if we take the line suggested in the previous section for avoiding an infinite regress, we may not correctly say that (Ace) is *explained* by A's having caused it (= (Ac(Ace))). Since (Ac(Ace)) = (Ace), that would

---

[55] A second thought: if volitions are the first effects of an agent's exertions, there may be a sense in which not all causing is willing; rather, it is productive of willing. The present objection would nonetheless still be in play if Reid held that all exertion requires the conception of what it produces.

be tantamount to saying that (Ace) is explained by the fact of its own occurrence. It looks as though A's causing e is simply a surd, an event with no explanation.[56]

At this juncture, patrons of agent causation are wont to protest that there are commonly recognized and entirely satisfactory explanations of why A caused e. Perhaps A caused his hands to move as he did because he wanted to open the window and let smoke out of the kitchen. Perhaps B moved her legs as she did in order to climb the ladder and retrieve her hat from the roof. Perhaps C concentrated his attention on the left side of the diagram in the hope of noticing the figure that was camouflaged there. In short, the familiar idiom of reasons, motives, intentions, and purposes is fully available to explain why agents cause what they do. Explanations in terms of purposes are paradigms of explanation in everyday life—this is one of the guiding themes in the work of Taylor (1966) and many other action theorists.

And yet it may be questioned whether explanations of action in terms of motives and purposes are really possible within an agent-causal framework like Reid's. Recall that Reid denies determinism$_2$ as applied to human action: he denies that when an agent acts, there are antecedent circumstances that, if repeated, would necessarily or invariably be followed by her acting again in the same way.[57] If we say that

---

[56] This problem should be distinguished from another, a solution to which it presupposes: what is the difference between A's causing e and e's happening without A's causing it or, in other words, in what does the truth of "A causes e" consist?

[57] Reid can admit that there are some agents who always act the same way under repetitions of certain circumstances—for example, agents who adhere to their resolution always to keep promises they have made. What he denies is that for *any* agent S, *any* action A, and *any* total antecedent circumstance C, if S does A in C, then S will again do A in any recurrence of C.

The question arises whether we should change "S will again do A in any recurrence of C" to "S *must* again do A in any recurrence of C." I have assumed until now that when Reid and Priestley speak of circumstances as "necessitating" an action, they just mean that those circumstances are invariably followed by an action of that type. That assumption seems right to me on the whole; it is hard to see what physical necessity can amount to for Reid beyond God's acting in accordance with the rule that whenever C obtains, A follows. However, there is a problem with the assumption in the present connection. If the world is so complex that the same total set of antecedent circumstances is never in fact repeated, then Priestley's determinism$_2$ is vacuously true, and Reid would be wrong to deny it.

One way around the vacuity problem would be to bring an element of necessity into necessitarianism after all, formulating it thus: for any agent S, any action A, and any total antecedent circumstance C, if S does A in C, then, *necessarily*, S will again do A in any recurrence of C. Reid could deny this merely by affirming the *possibility* of C's recurring without S's doing A.

Another way around the vacuity problem would be bring in an element of necessity, but only at the head of the thesis, formulating it thus: *necessarily*, for any agent S, any action A, and any total antecedent circumstance C, if S does A in C, then, S will again do A in any recurrence of C. Reid could deny this merely by affirming the possibility of worlds in which recurrences of the same antecedent circumstances are not followed by recurrences of the same actions. (Thanks to Gideon Yaffe for helping me get clearer on these matters.)

A's resigning her position is explained by the motive of protesting the policies of her employer, we must at the same time confess that in identical circumstances with the same motives, she might *not* resign. What kind of explanation is that?

In a word, it is an *anomic* explanation (Ginet 1990:124). It is an explanation in which the factors cited in the explanans need not be followed in accordance with a law by the thing to be explained. The question before us now is whether anomic explanations can ever be adequate explanations. Some philosophers say *no*. They say an explanation can only consist in citing factors (perhaps very complicated and far flung ones) that as a matter of law are always followed by the thing to be explained.[58] If determinism$_2$ is true, everything that happens has such an explanation; if not, not; and proponents of the nomic requirement would say that if there are any exceptions to determinism$_2$, they can have no explanation at all.

It should be emphasized that under the nomic requirement, not only are undetermined actions not explained by motives or purposes as Reid or Taylor would have it;[59] they are not explained by *anything*. No matter how much we cite in our explanation, it will not be enough, since all of that could happen again without the explanandum event's occurring.

One thinker committed to the nomic requirement on explanations is J. S. Mill, as revealed in the following passage:

> When we think of ourselves hypothetically as having acted otherwise than we did, we always suppose a difference in the antecedents: we picture ourselves as having known something that we did not know ... or as having desired something, or disliked something, more or less than we did. (Quoted in Ginet:132)

Also revealed here is Mill's commitment to determinism$_2$.

Defenders of anomic explanation, such as Taylor and Ginet, maintain that the nomic requirement is simply untenable. According to them, explanations in terms

---

[58] In a more liberal version of the nomic requirement, there must *be* factors that in combination with the laws and our cited explanatory factors necessitate the thing to be explained, even if we have not identified them in our explanation.

[59] Explanations in terms of reasons are not as such anomic. Proponents of the nomic requirement may say explanations in terms of reasons are legitimate, provided there are circumstances that combine with the agent's having the reasons he has to yield a nomically sufficient condition.

Nor does Reid hold that explanations in terms of motives or purposes are automatically anomic. As mentioned in n. 54, Reid allows that a resolutely honorable person will keep his promises in all circumstances, making his acts of promise-keeping explainable by subsuming them under a law. Nonetheless, *some* good explanations in terms of motives and purposes will be anomic, setting Reid at odds with proponents of the nomic requirement.

of purposes and the like are deeply entrenched in our ordinary explanatory practice and are perfectly proper despite not satisfying the requirement.

This is an issue on which I feel pulled both ways. Without attempting to resolve it here, I cite three features of anomic explanations I find puzzling.

The first feature pertains to "why this rather than that?" questions. Some anomic explanations allegedly explain why an agent did a certain thing without explaining why he did that thing rather than some other thing. "Why did you put that bill in the slot?" I may be asked. According to Ginet, I may answer satisfactorily by saying I intended to obtain a Coke, even though I do not thereby answer the question "Why did you put *that* bill in the slot rather than an identical bill that was next to it in your wallet?" (134–35)

I do not know whether Reid would agree with Ginet on this point. He does say that a person may hand over a shilling to a merchant without having any reason for paying with one shilling rather than another (EAP 4.4:215–16). I am not sure, though, whether he would say (as Ginet would) that the person's handing over *that* shilling (not simply his handing over *a* shilling) is explained by his intention to complete the purchase.[60]

The second puzzling feature has to do with probability. Reid notes that in many cases we reason from men's motives to their actions with great probability, though never with certainty (EAP 4.4:220). A true believer in the nomic requirement would insist that we cannot explain something by an explanans that merely makes the explanandum probable; we must have the inevitability that goes with exceptionless covering laws. My present point is that an even weaker requirement proposed by some philosophers of science as an alternative to the nomic requirement is not always satisfied by anomic explanations. Hempel relaxes the nomic requirement by holding that an explanation need not show that the explanandum event was inevitable, but only that it was to be expected—that it was highly probable, or at least more probable than not, given the factors cited in the explanans (1965:381–86). A Reidian explanation need not do even this much. Reid allows possibilities of the following sort: An agent is confronted with a pair of motives, M1 favoring A1 and M2 favoring A2, and he is such that in 90 cases out of 100, he (or agents of a similar character) would do A1; yet on the occasion in question, he does A2. His acting as he did is explained by

---

[60] Alexander Pruss denies that anomic explanations in terms of reasons have the feature accepted by Ginet. He says that in explaining X, you *thereby* explain why X rather than Y (Pruss 2006:148–55).

citing M2 as his motive;[61] yet given that motive, it was actually *unlikely* that he would do A2.[62]

The third puzzling feature of anomic explanations has to do with the possibility of explaining either of two incompatible actions using the same explanatory resources. Before I say more about this, it will be useful to have before us Reid's criticism of the view, common among the necessitarians of his day, that agents always act from their strongest motive.

Reid paraphrases the view he wishes to criticize as follows:[63]

> 'Every deliberate action,' they say, 'must have a motive. When there is no motive on the other side, this motive must determine the agent; When there are contrary motives, the strongest must prevail.' (EAP 4.4:213)

He goes on to say that according to adherents of the doctrine, we reason from motive to action as certainly as we do from any physical cause to its effect. Reid holds to the contrary that motives function not like causes (or weights in a balance), but like advice, which an agent may or may not follow (EAP 4.4:214 and 217).

Reid confronts the "strongest motive" doctrine with a devastating dilemma (EAP 4.4:216–20). How, he asks, shall we measure the strength of motives so as to know which is the strongest? If we define the strongest motive as the one that actually prevails (that is, the one in accordance with which the agent acts), we make it a tautology that agents always act from their strongest motive. We convert "He did A because the motive favoring A was the strongest" into the worthless "He did A because A was the thing he did." If we do *not* define the strongest motive as the one that prevails, but in some independent way—for instance, as the one that requires

---

[61] What exactly is the explanans in an explanation by appeal to motives? Is it my having a certain motive (the one on which I acted)? Is it my having a certain *array* of motives, including the one on which I acted? Or is it my "going with" a certain motive, that is, acting on it? The last seems to entail the explanandum, in which case we do not have the anomic feature anymore. A similar puzzle arises for me in regard to Ginet's account. He says that a statement of the form "S V-ed with the intention of thereby U-ing" could be a true explanation. The explanandum is S's V-ing; what is the explanans? I do not see how to state it otherwise than "S V-ed with the intention of thereby U-ing." It is not merely having the intention of U-ing, for the intention refers to the very act of V-ing that is being explained. So it looks to me as though the explanans entails the explanandum, in which case the explanation is no longer anomic.

[62] Explanations of this sort might nonetheless satisfy a weaker requirement than Hempel's, proposed in Salmon 1984: that the explanans raise the probability of the explanandum beyond its antecedent level, that is, that the probability of A2 given M2, though less than 0.5, be greater than the prior probability of A2.

[63] Adherents of the view include Hume, Kames, Edwards, and Priestley, all discussed in Harris. For an especially forceful presentation of it, see d'Holbach (1770) 2008.

the greatest felt effort to resist—then we do not know that agents always act from their strongest motive, and indeed we have evidence against it. Under one construal, then, the "strongest motive" doctrine is trivial, and under any of several others, it is not known to be true. For more detailed discussion of this argument, see Yaffe 2004, chapter 6.

I return now to the third puzzling feature. Suppose an agent has an array of conflicting motives, some giving him reason to do X and others giving him reason to do Y instead. He deliberates and finally does X. It is a feature of Reid's indeterminism$_2$ that the agent might be placed again in the same situation with the same array of motives and end up doing Y rather than X, and it is a feature of anomic explanation that those same circumstances and motives will explain what he does each time.[64] Ginet forthrightly embraces this feature:

> But the same antecedent state can explain in the anomic, reasons way any of several alternative possible subsequent actions. If the antecedent situation contains the agent's having a desire for each of two or more incompatible ends or her being indifferent between alternative means to an intended end, then it has the potential to explain in the reasons way whichever of the alternative actions occurs. (Ginet 1990:147).

Edwards, d'Holbach, and Mill would insist that the motive acted upon the second time must have been relatively stronger than it was the first time, but that is precisely the claim Reid claims to be unknowable unless rendered tautological by defining the strongest motive as the one that prevails.

What troubles me about the feature highlighted by Ginet is that if Reid embraces it, he becomes in one way a partner in sin with the "strongest motive" necessitarians he criticizes. Both parties are in a position to explain the agent's action no matter what it turns out to be. If the agent acts from motive M, the necessitarian will say that she did so because M was the strongest—but of course had she acted from another motive, that one would have been the strongest. Reid will say that the agent acted as she did because her motive, strongest or not, was M—but of course had she acted from one of the other motives, that one would have explained her action. No matter what the agent does, each party has an explanation. Moreover,

---

[64] Some may object to my saying that *the same* motives explain what happens each time—it is rather that different subsets of the motives in play explain the contrary outcomes. It is nonetheless true that the same cluster of explanatory factors contains a potential explanation of each of two contraries in such a way that whatever happens will have an explanation drawn from the cluster.

each party knew in advance that it would have an explanation, though neither knew what it would be.[65]

For an illustration, consider the scenario depicted in the classic short story by Frank Stockton, "The Lady or the Tiger?" Reid and his necessitarian opponent can each know everything about the motives in play (love, jealousy, and whatever else). Neither can say in advance which door the princess will point to. But each can be sure in advance that he will be able to explain her action, whatever it turns out to be, and each will give an explanation he considers adequate after the fact. If the tiger comes bounding out, each will say, "She indicated the room containing the tiger because she was jealous." If the lady lies in waiting, each will say, "She indicated the room containing the lady because she loved him." The necessitarian will tack on "and jealousy (love) was her strongest motive" while Reid demurs, saying merely that jealousy (love) was the motive on which the princess chose to act, but each will be satisfied with the explanation he gives. It seems to me that there is something profoundly unsatisfying about an explanation constructed ex post facto from resources that could have been drawn upon equally well to explain the agent's action no matter what it turned out to be.

The three features I have cited—not explaining why this rather than that, running against the probabilities, and being available no matter what the agent does—make me wonder whether anomic explanations really explain. I close, however, by pointing out a potential advantage of anomic explanations that may for some minds go some way toward offsetting their puzzling features.

Suppose one is enough of a rationalist to believe or hope true some version of the Principle of Sufficient Reason, according to which nothing is true unless there is some reason or explanation of why it is true. One very big thing that needs explaining is why there is something rather than nothing or, more precisely, why there are any contingent beings (= beings whose nonexistence would have been possible). According to the classical cosmological argument (as set forth, for instance, by Samuel Clarke), the explanation can only lie in the existence of a necessary being: if we are trying to explain why there are contingent beings in general (as opposed to certain specific ones), our explanation cannot have recourse to contingent beings. Suppose the necessary being is God. The explanans cannot be the sheer existence of God, for that is a necessary fact, the necessity of which would get transferred by entailment

---

[65] Here is a slightly different way of phrasing my point. For the necessitarians, which motive was strongest (and thus which one was acted upon) depends on which action took place. For Reid, which motive was acted on (whether strongest or not) depends on which action took place. For either party, which motive was explanatory depends on which action took place—if Y had taken place rather than X, the motive favoring Y would have been the one acted on.

to the explanandum, making the existence of contingent beings not contingent after all. The explanans must therefore be some contingent fact about God, presumably his willing or doing one thing rather than another. As a contingent fact, this fact requires an explanation, but what could it be? If we require the explanation to be some circumstance that necessitates the primal act, this circumstance will either be contingent, in which case we have yet another unexplained fact, or necessary, in which case everything that flows from it is necessary. So how are we to avoid the alternatives of brute unexplained facts on the one hand and Spinozistic necessity throughout the universe on the other?[66]

I see only one way. Let the primal act be an act necessitated by no further circumstance, but not on that account shunted into the box of unexplained surds: let it be an act performed for some reason or purpose. If anomic explanations by reference to purposes really do explain—if they satisfy the demands of the Principle of Sufficient Reason, or at any rate, those of the Principle of Pretty Good Reason—we have a way between the horns of brute facts and universal necessity.[67]

---

[66] For further discussion of this problem, see Bennett 1984:114–19 or Van Cleve 1999:204–11.

[67] The suggestion briefly floated in this paragraph is pursued in detail by Pruss (2006, chapters 6 and 7). Drawing on van Inwagen 1983, Pruss sets out the argument from the Principle of Sufficient Reason to the loss of all contingency as follows: If the totality of contingent fact is explained by something outside the totality, it is explained by something necessary and is therefore itself necessary, since (i) p explains q only if p entails q and (ii) necessity is transmitted by entailment. If the totality of contingent fact is explained by something within the totality, we have a case of something's explaining itself, since (iii) what explains a conjunction explains every conjunct. But (iv) no contingent fact can explain itself; nothing contingent can be self-explanatory. Therefore, there can be no explanation for the totality of contingent fact.

Pruss considers two ways around the argument, one denying (i) and the other denying (iv). Both ways invoke the idea of an agent cause who acts freely. In the strategy that denies (i), we say that *God appreciated the reasons for actualizing world w and chose what to create* is a necessary fact that explains the existence of w without entailing it. It does not entail the existence of w, since God also appreciated the reasons for actualizing other worlds without creating them. In the strategy that denies (iv), we say that facts of the form *the agent chose A* (e.g., *to create w) for reason R*, though contingent, are self-explanatory—"We can read off the explanation right from the fact" (Pruss:147). Pruss also entertains a Jamesian variant of this strategy according to which even reasonless choices can be self-explanatory. Thanks to Kenny Pearce for bringing Pruss's work to my attention.

# 16

## REID VERSUS HUME ON MORALS

The sum of what has been said in this chapter is, That by an original power of the mind, which we call *conscience*, or *the moral faculty*, we have the conceptions of right and wrong in human conduct, of merit and demerit, of duty and moral obligation, and our other moral conceptions; and that, by the same faculty, we perceive some things in human conduct to be right and others to be wrong; that the first principles of morals are the dictates of this faculty; and that we have the same reason to rely upon those dictates, as upon the determinations of our senses, or of our other natural faculties. (Thomas Reid, *EAP 3.3.6:180*)

In moral philosophy as in many other matters, Reid's principal adversary is Hume. In this chapter I discuss some of the competing arguments offered by Reid and Hume on the nature of morals.[1] I close with comparisons of positions and arguments in meta-ethics with analogous positions and arguments in epistemology.

## A. HUME AND REID IN THE BROAD SCHEME OF THINGS

A good entrée to our topic is the taxonomy of meta-ethical theories offered by C. D. Broad in the course of giving an exposition and defense of so-called moral sense theories of ethics (1945). The items in Broad's scheme of classification are theories about what is meant by calling things right or wrong—analyses of deontic sentences, as Broad calls them—but his scheme applies as well to theories about what is meant by calling things good or bad.

---

[1] There is much that I do not discuss, including Reid's criticisms of Hume on the obligation of promises, on justice as an artificial virtue, and on reason as the slave of the passions.

Broad first divides theories into those that hold that deontic sentences express *judgments*—items that are true or false—and those that hold they do not express judgments, but simply evince one's *attitude*, like exclamations of "Boo!" or "Hurrah!" The former are what we now call cognitivist and the latter what we now call expressivist theories; Broad aptly calls the latter "interjectional theories."

Cognitivist theories are further divided into objective and subjective theories, depending on whether moral sentences ascribe objective properties to acts or are simply about human feelings.

Subjective cognitivist theories are subdivided by their answers to three questions: (i) Are the "feelings" with which moral judgments are concerned *sensations* or *emotions*? (ii) Do deontic sentences make assertions only about one's *own* feelings or about *everyone's* feelings? (iii) Do they say a feeling is *actually occurring* or only that humans are *disposed* to have a certain feeling upon contemplating actions of a certain sort? In the latter case, the disposition could equally well be ascribed to the action as a disposition to elicit a certain sort of feeling in those who contemplate it. An example of a subjective theory of the emotional, trans-subjective, and dispositional variety would be one that analyzed "It is right to keep promises" as "Any person contemplating what he believed to be an act of promise-keeping would tend to have a moral pro-feeling [emotion] in so far as he confined his attention to that aspect of the act" (136). The same example serves as a paradigm of the type of "moral sense" theory Broad regards as most plausible.

Objective cognitivist theories are subdivided by their answers to two questions: (i) Are moral properties *definable* or are they *simple* and therefore indefinable? (ii) If they are definable, are they definable only by means of other ethical terms, or are they definable without using ethical terms? Broad classifies as "naturalistic" all subjective theories and all objective theories that hold ethical terms to be definable by means of nonethical terms. He classifies as "nonnaturalistic" all theories according to which ethical terms are either indefinable or definable only by means of other ethical terms. Mill is a prototypical objective naturalist (to be right is to promote the greatest happiness for the greatest number),[2] Moore a prototypical objective nonnaturalist (goodness is a simple nonnatural property). Objective nonnaturalism is typically accompanied by a moral epistemology in which ethical concepts are a priori concepts and ethical principles are synthetic necessary truths known by intuition; hence it is also known as intuitionism.

---

[2] In taking Mill to be a cognitivist, I assume that his utilitarianism is a theory of the meaning of "right" and not merely a normative theory paired with an expressivist meta-ethic. (Thanks here to Kenny Pearce.) In taking him to be an objectivist, I assume that producing the greatest happiness is an objective property, even though it makes reference to a mental state.

Let us now situate Hume and Reid in Broad's scheme of things. "There has been a controversy started of late," says Hume, "concerning the general foundation of Morals";

> whether they be derived from Reason, or from Sentiment; whether we attain the knowledge of them by a chain of argument and induction, or by an immediate feeling and finer internal sense; whether, like all sound judgements of truth and falsehood, they should be the same to every rational intelligent being, or whether, like the perception of beauty and deformity, they be founded entirely on the particular fabric and constitution of the human species. (EPM 170)

Hume comes down on the second side of each of the three alternatives: moral determinations are derived from sentiment, they are known by feeling, and they depend on the fabric of the human species.

Here are several more passages expressing his view:

> The hypothesis which we embrace is plain. It maintains that morality is determined by sentiment. It defines virtue to be *whatever mental action or quality gives to a spectator the pleasing sentiment of approbation*; and vice the contrary. (EPM 289)

> So that when you pronounce any action or character to be vicious, you mean nothing, but that from the constitution of your nature you have a feeling or sentiment of blame from the contemplation of it. Vice and virtue, therefore, may be compar'd to sounds, colours, heat and cold, which, according to modern philosophy, are not qualities in objects, but perceptions in the mind. (THN 3.1.1:469)

> An action, or sentiment, or character is virtuous or vicious; why? Because its view causes a pleasure or uneasiness of a particular kind. (THN 3.1.2:471)

On the whole, these passages seem to give voice to a moral sense theory in Broad's sense of the term—in particular, a subjective theory of the emotional, transsubjective, and dispositional type. (The title of THN 3.1.2 is "Moral distinctions deriv'd from a moral sense.") There are two complications, however.

First, recall from chapter 4 that there is an ambiguity in the early modern use of the term "secondary quality": secondary qualities were sometimes said to be dispositions of objects to produce sensations or experiences in us (thus residing in objects), but were also sometimes said to be the sensations themselves (thus residing in us). The same ambiguity infects Hume's comparison of virtue and vice to secondary qualities in the middle quotation above: virtue and vice may be properties of actions that elicit feelings of approval or disapproval in us, or they may be the feelings themselves.

Second, alongside the passages above, which seem to put forth a cognitivist account of moral qualities, there is a strong noncognitivist or expressivist strain in Hume's theory. Witness, for instance, the following:

> To have the sense of virtue, is nothing but to *feel* a satisfaction of a particular kind from the contemplation of a character. The very *feeling* constitutes our praise or admiration. (THN 3.1.2:471)

Feeling is not judging. If feeling *constitutes* finding something virtuous or vicious, then moral findings are not judgments. As Hume says a page earlier, "Morality, therefore, is more properly felt than judg'd of" (THN 3.1.2:470).

The noncognitivist side of Hume's theory comes out more strongly yet in Hume's arguments that "moral distinctions [are] not derived from reason" (the title of *Treatise* 3.1.1). Hume sometimes uses "reason" narrowly to refer to that faculty by which we have knowledge of "relations of ideas" or a priori matters; he also sometimes uses it broadly to cover as well all our knowledge of "matters of fact" or contingent a posteriori truths. (See EHU 4.1 for the divide between relations of ideas and matters of fact.) When Hume argues that moral determinations are not exercises of reason, he means reason in the broad sense (THN 3.1.1:463–69). Since truth and falsehood are for Hume the province of reason alone, it follows that moral determinations are not susceptible of truth or falsehood (THN 3.1.1:458).

Through not applying his "sifting humour" sufficiently to his own views, then, Hume propounds at least two incompatible positions in Broad's scheme of things. He comes across sometimes as a subjective cognitivist (of either of two varieties, depending on whether secondary qualities are construed as dispositions in objects or experiences in subjects), but other times as a noncognitivist.[3]

Reid is fortunately easier to classify: he is a cognitivist of the objective nonnaturalist variety.

Hutcheson, Hume, Smith, and Reid have all been called moral sense theorists, but they are not all moral sense theorists in Broad's sense of the term, nor in any other univocal sense of the term. Reid calls himself a moral sense theorist, but only with an important proviso: that a sense be understood as a faculty that delivers *judgments* as well as feelings (EAP 3.3.6:175–76). He is thus opposed to the noncognitivist strain in Hume. It is also clear what variety of cognitivist Reid is: he is an

---

[3] Some see yet a fourth position in Hume: *projectivism*, a variant of expressivism in which sentiments are not only expressed in our moralizing but somehow "spread on the world." See Stroud 1993 and Blackburn 1993 for attributions of projectivism to Hume along with opposing appraisals of the merits of the position.

objective nonnaturalist. Much of what Reid says about *right* anticipates what Moore was later to say about *good*: that it is indefinable, that we understand what it is by an original power of the mind, and that our moral faculty provides us with first principles about which types of acts are right and which wrong. Witness:

> I take [the notion of duty or rightness in conduct] to be too simple to admit of a logical definition. We can define it only by synonymous words or phrases . . . as when we say it is what we ought to do. (EAP 3.3.5:169)

> Some Philosophers, with whom I agree, ascribe [our ability to determine that this is right and that is wrong] to an original power or faculty in man, which they call the *moral sense*, the *moral faculty, conscience.* . . . As by [our external senses] we have not only the original conceptions of the various qualities of bodies, but the original judgments that this body has such a quality, that such another; so by our moral faculty, we have both the original conceptions of right and wrong in conduct, of merit and demerit, and the original judgments that this conduct is right, that is wrong; that this character has worth, that demerit. . . . The truths immediately testified by our moral faculty, are the first principles of all moral reasoning, from which all our knowledge of our duty must be deduced. (EAP 3.3.6: 175–77; see also EAP 3.3.6 180, 5.5:300, and the letter to Kames of December 3, 1772, COR 66)

Let us delve deeper into the analogies between the operations of our external senses and the operations of the moral sense. Recall that a perception of the external senses typically involves these three things: (i) a sensation or feeling, (ii) a conception of some quality of an external thing, and (iii) a belief that some external thing has the quality. We find three corresponding items involved in operations of the moral sense: (i) a feeling of approval or disapproval, (ii) a conception of some moral quality, and (iii) a belief that some action or character has the moral quality.[4] There is one key difference, however: in the operations of external perception, the sensation is the cause of the conception and the belief; in the operations of the moral sense, the belief ascribing some moral quality is the cause of the feeling of approval or disapproval (EAP 5.7:348–49 and 350). The importance of this reversal in the direction of causation is well brought out in Broadie 1998.

---

[4] I find Reid often inexplicit and perhaps sometimes inconsistent on whether the moral judgments delivered by our moral sense are general or particular. Insofar as moral judgments are first principles, I would expect them to be general, for instance, that lying as such is wrong. Insofar as moral judgments correspond to the beliefs involved in sense perception, I would expect them to be particular, for instance, that this act (of lying) is wrong, mediated by a general principle and further beliefs about the empirical character of the act. For further discussion of this issue, see Cuneo 2004.

I just said that moral judgments *cause* feelings of approval and disapproval, but is the relation really a causal relation, or is it some stronger form of necessitation? I return to this question in section C.

## B. REID AGAINST HUME

EAP 5.7 is entitled "Moral approbation implies a real judgment." By this slogan, Reid means that moral approbation and disapprobation are not merely feelings with no truth value, but also include a judgment, true or false, that some action is right or wrong. In urging this view, Reid takes his chief adversary to be Hume. He characterizes Hume's view thus: "Moral approbation and disapprobation are not judgments, which must be true or false, but barely, agreeable and uneasy feelings or sensations" (EAP 5.7:345). Moreover, feelings cannot be true or false (346).[5] Alarmed by the noncognivist strain in Hume, Reid undertakes to refute it.

Reid asks us to consider two speeches, both made in regard to the same piece of conduct: *That man did well and worthily* and *That man's conduct gave me a very agreeable feeling*. If Hume's theory is true, says Reid, the two speeches must have exactly the same meaning. But they cannot have the same meaning, for two reasons. First, the former speech "expresses plainly an opinion or judgment of the conduct of the man, but says nothing of the speaker," whereas the second "only testifies a fact concerning the speaker, to wit, that he had such a feeling" (EAP 5.7:350). One is about the agent, the other about the speaker. Second, the former speech

> may be contradicted without any ground of offence, such contradiction being only a difference of opinion, which, to a reasonable man, gives no offence. But the second speech cannot be contradicted without an affront; for, as every man must know his own feelings, to deny that a man had a feeling which he affirms he had, is to charge him with falsehood. (EAP 5.7:350)

To dispute the second speech would be to accuse the speaker of lying, but there is no such accusation in disputing the first.

These are excellent objections to *one* of the views Hume held, but they do not apply to the view Reid actually imputes to Hume. What the objections show to be in error

[5] It should not be thought that Reid's framing of the issue leaves available to Hume the option that while moral approbations are mere feelings, there exist alongside them true-or-false judgments in morals. On the contrary, Reid uses "moral approbation and disapprobation" broadly to cover the *entire sphere* of "operations of our moral faculty" (as he calls them at EAP 5.7:353). If there is nothing in this sphere but feelings, then there is no truth or falsity in morals.

is not noncognitivism, but a subjective form of cognitivism—the form Broad would classify as the occurrent intra-personal form, in which "that action was right" means "that action gave me an agreeable feeling." The objections do not apply to Hume the expressivist, for if moral speeches merely *express* feelings (as distinct from *reporting* them), they are not *about* anything and cannot be contradicted as a proposition can.[6]

How could Reid have failed to notice that the target he sets up is not the one he proceeds to knock down?[7] His lapse may be explained to some extent by the fact that Hume himself makes the same conflation in presenting his views. I also offer the following conjecture as a potential explanation of Reid's switch. One way to state Hume's expressivism would be to say

> Finding M's action right = having an agreeable feeling as the result of contemplating M's action.

I intend the word "finding" to leave open the question whether moral determinations involve judgment. When we state Hume's equation, we close the question, saying that moral findings do *not* involve judgment. But from the equation as stated, it is all too easy to slide illicitly to

> Finding it to be the case that M's action is right = finding it to be the case that M's action gives me an agreeable feeling.

If we then suppose (as is natural, though perhaps not mandatory) that the equation *finding it to be the case that p = finding it to be the case that q* holds only if p and q are logically equivalent propositions, we arrive at the cognitivist position Reid criticizes.[8]

Reid does make one critical point that applies to expressivism proper:

> That moral approbation is merely a feeling without judgment, necessarily carries along with it this consequence, that a form of speech, upon one of the most common

---

[6] The latter fact may give rise to an objection that does apply to expressivism: that moral speeches *can* be contradicted, with or without affront.

[7] The question is all the more perplexing because (as noted in Cuneo 2004) Reid shows awareness that although feelings lack truth values, an affirmation that one has a feeling does have a truth value (EAP 5.7:346).

[8] Kenny Pearce has pointed out to me that there may be counterexamples to "finding that p = finding that q only if p and q are logically equivalent" if the identity holds between token findings (e.g., finding that the fingerprints match and finding that Jones is the criminal). It is not obvious that there are counterexamples, though, if the identity is an identity of types, as intended in the Humean equation.

topics of discourse, which either has no meaning, or a meaning irreconcilable to all rules of grammar or rhetoric, is found to be common and familiar in all languages and in all ages of the world, which every man knows how to express the meaning, if it have any, in plain and proper language.

Such a consequence I think sufficient to sink any philosophical opinion on which it hangs. (EAP 5.7:351)

A form of speech used in all languages as though it were the expression of judgment is actually no such thing: this consequence, offered by Reid as a *reductio*, is precisely the consequence that one contemporary defender of expressivism embraces and seeks to ameliorate. I have in mind Simon Blackburn in the project he calls "quasi-realism" (1993).[9] His project, in brief, is to show that although moral claims are merely expressions of feelings, they may be appropriately cast as assertoric forms of speech.

In addition to opposing expressivist theories, Reid opposes moral sense theories of the subjectivist variety current in his day and espoused in our own by Broad (1945) and McDowell (1985) among others. According to these theories, for an action to be right is for it to arouse favorable moral emotion in those who contemplate it. Reid offers one argument squarely directed against such theories, and he provides the key premise in a second argument against them.

The first argument is the argument from the necessity of moral principles, most clearly stated at EIP 6.6:494–95 (but see also EIP 7.2:549, EIP 7.3:584, and EAP 5.7:361–62).

The argument may be presented as follows, letting A be helping the needy or keeping one's promises or some kindred type of right action:

1. It is *necessary* that any action of type A is right.
2. It is *not* necessary that any action of type A is approved (that is, is such that the contemplation of it elicits agreeable feelings from human beings).
3. Therefore, rightness is not necessarily equivalent to (and cannot be defined as) a disposition to elicit approval. By the same token, wrongness cannot be defined as a disposition to elicit condemnation.

---

[9] Blackburn extends his expressivism to many matters beyond the moral sphere, including causal relations, and he interprets Hume as having done likewise (1993). In a similar vein, there are places where Reid takes Hume to have been an expressivist about *everything* (EAP 5.7:344–45 and EIP 8.3:583–84). He presents a series of steps he says modern philosophers have taken, attributing the status of being "nothing but sensations in the mind" successively to secondary qualities, primary qualities, aesthetic qualities, (the ascription of?) moral qualities, and beliefs in general. "Mr. Hume made the last step in this progress, and crowned the system by what he calls

This argument is valid in any modal logic. Reid gives a parallel argument about aesthetic properties, and I conjecture that he would do likewise about epistemic properties.

Broad defends moral sense theories against this argument (which he attributes to Reid's contemporary Richard Price) by claiming that the moral sense theorist's definition of rightness should carry a qualification: right actions are those that elicit approval from *normal* human beings. He then contends, in opposition to premise 2, that it is necessary after all that acts of promise keeping and the rest are approved by normal human beings, since approving them is part of what it means to be normal. It is *analytic* that acts of type A are approved by normal human beings. But by the same token, it now becomes analytic according to Broad's definition that acts of type A are *right*. A Reid or a Price could rejoin that it is a *synthetic* necessary truth that acts of a given type are right. Against an argument with this new starting point, Broad would have no recourse but to challenge the very notion of synthetic necessary truths.[10]

The second argument against moral sense theories (stated by Broad at 149 and 160–66) is trickier. It is not advanced by Reid, but it uses a very Reidian premise: that moral feeling is mediated by moral judgment. As discussed above, Reid holds that in operations of the moral sense, feelings do not give rise to judgments (as happens in the case of external perception), but conversely: judgments of rightness or wrongness give rise to moral feeling. This fact can be made the basis of a charge of vicious circularity against the account of right and wrong given by moral sense theorists.

Moral sense theories are sometimes characterized as theories that draw an analogy between moral qualities and secondary qualities in the dispositional sense. It will therefore provide useful background to the Reid-Broad argument if we first consider difficulties for a dispositional account of secondary qualities advanced by a contemporary philosopher. John McDowell defines redness roughly as follows (1985):

x is red = Df in normal viewing conditions, x looks red to human beings.

---

his *hypothesis*, to wit, That belief is more properly an act of the sensitive, than of the cogitative part of our nature." The sentence from Hume occurs in THN 1.4.1 at p. 183, where Hume is talking about beliefs in cause and effect in particular. In context, his point seems to be that the beliefs in question are thrust upon as ineluctably as the perceptions of our senses; there is no suggestion that the beliefs are merely feelings. Reid is therefore out of line in quoting Hume as though he takes the last step in the five-step progression.

[10] Though he does not have the Kantian terminology of synthetic a priori judgments, Reid clearly has the notion of them. He says that the proposition that some event has occurred without a cause is *impossible* and *absurd*, but not *contradictory* (EAP 4.9:249 and COR 234). That makes its negation, the proposition that every event has a cause, necessary and a priori, but not analytic.

As discussed in chapter 4, Reid offers a similar account. But there is one signifi-cant difference: whereas Reid takes "looking red" to be a matter of causing a certain type of sensations in us, McDowell understands looking red to be an *intentional* rather than a *merely sensory* state—a matter of its *seeming to be the case that x is red*, where seeming to be the case is a propositional attitude. Two distinct problems now threaten to arise. One is circular analysis—the analysandum, *x is red*, shows up in the analysans. The other is infinite involution—if we substitute in the analysans in accordance with the analysis, we get "x looks to human beings to be such that it looks to human beings to be red," and we can repeat this indefinitely. Symbolizing the definition as $Rx = Df L(Rx)$, we have $Rx$ iff $L(Rx)$ iff $L(L(Rx))$ iff $L(L(L(Rx)))$, and so on.

To generate the latter difficulty, we need to make an assumption that some would challenge: that items that are definitionally equivalent may be interchanged within intentional contexts. Intentional contexts, such as "S believes that ___" and "it appears to be the case that ___" are often held to be hyperintensional, meaning that interchange of necessarily equivalent formulas within them does not always preserve truth value. (You can believe that $1 = 1$ without believing that $\sin^2 x - \cos^2 x = 1$.) But what about formulas that are not only necessarily equiva-lent, but equivalent by *definition* or *analysis*—are they interchangeable *salva veri-tate*? Here opinions differ. Broad holds that you can believe a proposition without believing a proposition that correctly analyzes it (163–64). On the other hand, Moore and Sellars hold that there is an epistemic criterion for the adequacy of analyses, whereby if B is the analysis of A, then you cannot know or believe A without knowing or believing B (Moore 1942:663; Sellars 1963:141).[11] Whether the infinite involution objection succeeds thus depends on who is right about the criterion for a correct philosophical analysis.

What of the circularity objection—does it remain even if the involution objection is blocked? In support of the negative answer, someone might say that if we make "Rx" inaccessible to substitution in "L(Rx)," we also make it occur so opaquely in the analysans that there is no longer any circle. But I think the case is stronger for the positive answer. "L(Rx)" is conceptually parasitic on "Rx" in a way that makes "L(Rx)" not permissible as an ingredient in the analysis of "Rx." You would already have to understand the analysandum in order to understand the analysans.

---

[11] Prior lays down a law of propositional identity that seems at first sight to be at odds with Broad: if the proposition that p is the same as the proposition that q, then the proposition that δp is the same as the proposition that δq, where δ is any operator, including belief (1971:153–56). How-ever, Prior's law is not really at odds with Broad unless we make the further debatable assumption that the correct analysis of a proposition must yield a proposition identical with the original.

With this background, let us return to the Reid-Broad objection. As noted, its central premise is that moral feeling is mediated by moral judgment—as Broad puts it, we feel moral pro- or anti-emotion toward an action only in respect of its rightness or wrongness (149). Broad calls the objection based on this premise a "circularity" objection (163). To make it such, we must somehow bring belief in rightness or wrongness into the analysis itself, as for example in

An act of type A is wrong = Df people who contemplate an act of type A in the belief that it is wrong will feel moral anti-feeling toward it.

If that is how the analysans must be filled out, we have an almost classic case of the analysandum occurring within the analysans.

In developing the objection further, however, Broad changes tack. He substitutes for "wrong" in the analysans the longer expression that supposedly analyzes it: "in the belief that it is wrong" becomes "in the belief that people who contemplate it in the belief that it is wrong will have moral anti-feeling toward it" (163). To go this route is to press the infinite involution objection rather than the circularity objection.

Broad's reply to the objection in our latest statement of it is to make the point I attributed to him above: it is possible to believe a proposition without believing its correct analysans (even if you accept the analysis, since you might not be thinking of it at the time) (163–64). Granting him that, the infinite involution objection is blocked. The original circularity objection is arguably still with us, though; it arises as soon as we need to use "in the belief that it is wrong" on the right-hand side of the analysis.

I have two observations to make about the Reid-Broad objection. First, I have doubts about the truth of the premise it takes from Reid—that moral emotion is always mediated by moral belief. Moral emotion is not evoked by naked actions, to be sure, but only by actions conceptualized or apprehended in certain ways. However, why must the characteristics under which the actions are apprehended be *moral* characteristics? Why may they not instead be the natural characteristics upon which the moral characteristics supervene—being an act of ingratitude, for instance, or of self-sacrifice?[12, 13]

---

[12] Broad makes a similar point on p. 166.

[13] In an interesting counterpoint to Reid, Roeser (2009) claims that feelings sometimes guide moral judgments and do not merely follow in their wake. She may be right, but I do not think her example about the victim of sexual abuse on p. 187 illlustrates her claim. It seems to me to be a case in which one's emotional sensibilities help one determine what the naturalistic profile of an action is, rather than what moral evaluation should attach to the profile.

Second, Reid himself is in grave danger of incurring an objection very like the one we are discussing. He holds that an action is not truly praiseworthy—which he often equates with being right—unless it is done in the belief that it is right. Conversely, he holds that an agent is praiseworthy for doing an action that is wrong considered in itself so long as he did it in the belief that it is right. (See EAP 5.4:291–93.) He verges on holding, even if he does not hold explicitly, that an act is right if and only if the agent believes it to be right. That raises with real urgency the question of what the content can possibly be of the belief in rightness that confers rightness on an act.[14]

## C. HUME AGAINST REID

One of Hume's arguments for his noncognitivist account of moral determinations is the argument from the influence of moral determinations on action, still a leading argument today. One version of the argument runs as follows (THN 3.1.1:457–62):

1. Morality has an influence on action.
2. Reason has no influence on action (by the arguments of THN 2.3.3).
3. Therefore, morality is not discovered by reason.

A more refined version of this argument, occurring a few pages later (465–66), is this:

1. Moral evaluations are necessarily motivating.
2. No judgment of reason (such as the supposed judgment that one ought to do A) is necessarily motivating.
3. Therefore, moral evaluations are not judgments of reason.

A *locus classicus* of this argument in contemporary philosophy is Mackie 1977.

Using the term "finding" in the neutral way I proposed above, we could state the idea of the argument as follows: finding something right necessarily inclines you to do it; no judgment of reason (even in the broad sense including all judgments about

[14] We have here the springboard for Hume's argument that justice is not a natural virtue (THN 3.2.1)—an argument that strikes me as deeply penetrating and probably correct despite the considerable difficulty of reconstructing it. I believe Reid mistakes the force of Hume's argument, taking it to be an argument that believing something cannot magically make it so (EAP 5.4:295) rather than an argument that belief in rightness would be without content unless rightness had some delineation antecedent to an agent's beliefs about it.

"matters of fact") necessarily inclines you to do anything; therefore, finding something right is not a judgment of reason.

I note one difficulty with the argument right off the bat. To have any chance of being true, the second premise must be understood as saying that no judgment of reason *by itself* gives you any inducement to do anything. What then follows by way of conclusion is that moral evaluations are not *merely* judgments of reason. And that is something Reid could accept: operations of the moral sense are, according to him, complex operations consisting of both judgment and feeling. His central claim against Hume—"moral approbation implies a real judgment"—is left standing by Hume's argument. But I set this difficulty aside to consider more direct challenges to Hume.

Price responds to Hume's argument by accepting the first premise but rejecting the second (Cuneo 2004). How would Reid respond? I shall approach this question by taking a closer look at a point broached above—the nature of the link between moral judgment and feeling. Moral judgments, says Reid, do carry feelings along with them:

> Our moral judgments are not like those we form in speculative matters, dry and unaffecting, but, from their nature, are necessarily accompanied with affections and feelings. (EAP 3.3.7:180)

Moral judgments are in some sense necessarily connected with feelings, and feelings are just the sorts of things that Hume allows *do* have a necessary connection with action. By transitivity, then, there would be a necessary connection between moral judgments and action, contrary to Hume's second premise—provided the necessity of the first link were of the same sort as the second. Humeans take the necessity of the second link to be logico-metaphysical necessity. So our question is this: is the necessity with which Reid says moral judgments are "necessarily accompanied" by feelings logico-metaphysical necessity or physico-nomological necessity?

Evidence can be adduced on either side of this question. Here is one quotation suggesting that the necessity is logical:

> I am very apt to think, with Dr Price, that, in intelligent beings, the desire of what is good, and aversion to what is ill, is necessarily connected with the intelligent nature; and that it is a contradiction to suppose such a being to have the notion of good without the desire of it, or the notion of ill without aversion to it. (EAP 3.3.2:156)[15]

---

[15] For Price's own statements of his view, see (1758) 1991:143 and 150. But see also pp. 150–51 for apparent backsliding.

If having the notion that something is good can logically necessitate desiring it, why cannot believing that an action is right logically necessitate having pro-feelings toward it?

Reid again recommends the views of Price in connection with the analogous question in aesthetics:

> Whether the pleasure we feel in contemplating beautiful objects may have any necessary connection with the belief of their excellence, or whether that pleasure be conjoined with this belief, by the good pleasure only of our Maker, I will not determine. The reader may see Dr Price's sentiments upon this subject, which merit consideration. (EIP 7.4:592)

He says, however, that he will not himself try to determine the answer.

There are other passages—greater in number by my count—in which Reid suggests that the necessary connection between moral belief and moral feeling is only nomological. Here is one:

> Nor can we conceive a greater depravity in the heart of man, than it would be to see and acknowledge worth without feeling any respect to it; or to see and acknowledge the highest worthlessness without any degree of dislike and indignation. (EAP 3.3.7:181)

Assuming that no one would denounce as depraved what he regards as logically impossible,[16] this passage implies that moral estimation does not logically require moral feeling.

> Esteem and benevolent regard, not only accompany real worth by the constitution of our nature, but are perceived to be really and properly due to it. (EAP 3.3.7:181)

If esteem and regard were logically necessitated by our judging an action worthy, the constitution of our nature would not enter into it.

> In [sense perception], the belief or judgment is the consequence of the sensation, as the sensation is the consequence of the impression made on the organ sense. . . . [In other complex operations, including exercises of the moral sense], the feeling is the consequence of the judgment. (EAP 5.7:348–49)

---

[16] Lewis Powell has proposed to me the following counterexample: someone might say, "There is no greater depravity than stealing from those who have nothing." However, Reid himself says, "In judging of men's conduct, we do not suppose things which cannot happen, nor do the laws of God give decisions upon impossible cases" (EAP 5.4:294).

The "consequence" relation that runs from organic impressions to sensations is not logical, but nomological, so the same must go for the consequence relation that runs from moral judgment to moral feeling.

> I know, that what a man judges to be a very worthy action, he contemplates with plea-sure. . . . But the judgment and the feeling are different acts of his mind, though con-nected as cause and effect. (EAP 5.7:350)

This last passage is as explicit as one could like: moral judgments *cause* moral feel-ings rather than logically necessitating them.

I conclude, then, that Reid would respond to the Humean argument from moti-vation in the opposite way from Price: he would concede the second premise, but reject the first. There is no logically necessary connection between moral evalua-tions and being motivated to act.[17]

Ironically, this is a point on which Hume himself should agree. Insofar as moral determinations have a necessary influence on action in Hume's philosophy, it is because moral determinations are items of a conative rather than a cognitive sort. Moral findings are feelings rather than judgings; they are emotions with a certain phenomenal character. But how then can they be necessarily connected with ac-tions or tendencies to action? It is a cardinal principle of Hume's philosophy that there can be no necessary connection between distinct existences (THN 1.1.7:18, 1.3.3:79–80, and 1.3.6:86 among many other passages), and feelings and actions are distinct. If Hume should reply that there can nonetheless be a *causally* neces-sary connection between feelings and actions, that is to say, a constant or regular conjunction between them, the rejoinder is that there can be *that* sort of necessary connection between moral judgments and actions, just as Reid allows. It is, after all, another tenet of Hume's philosophy that in principle, anything might be the cause of anything (THN 1.3.15:173).

## D. ETHICS AND EPISTEMOLOGY

Having examined some of the arguments by which Reid and Hume seek to estab-lish their own meta-ethical positions and refute those of their opponents, I now ask

---

[17] On this point, I am in total agreement with Cuneo (2004)—when necessity is construed in the logical sense Hume requires, Reid would accept Hume's second premise, but deny the first. Un-fortunately, a typo on p. 255 has Cuneo saying that Reid rejects the second premise.

I am also in agreement with Broadie (1998), who suggests that on Reid's view, moral judgments are attended with feelings because it is part of God or nature's plan to help us act morally. That implies that the linkage is contingent.

whether any of these arguments carry over to epistemology—as would be expected if epistemic properties, like ethical properties, are normative. I consider two arguments in particular: the epistemic analog of Reid's modal argument that rightness cannot be defined as eliciting approval from human beings and the epistemic analog of Hume's motivational argument that moral evaluations are expressions of feelings rather than being judgments with truth values.

Moral sense theories in ethics have as epistemic counterparts theories that define being evident as soliciting or forcing our belief. A self-evident proposition in the narrow sense of "self-evident" associated with the a priori might be defined as a proposition such that human beings ineluctably believe it upon the bare contemplation or understanding of it. A self-evident proposition in the broader sense associated with the immediately evident might be characterized as a proposition such that human beings cannot help believing it when they are in certain states of consciousness, perceiving, or remembering. I consider a view along these lines in chapter 12, section B, finding hints of it in Reid himself—as when he says, "For first principles no other reason can be given but this, that, by the constitution of our nature, we are under a necessity of assenting to them" (IHM 5.7:71).[18] I suggest there that a reduction of the evident to the forced cannot be Reid's final view, but the matter deserves a further hearing.

An across-the-board reduction of the evident to the forced would need to say something not just about immediately evident propositions (as in the preceding paragraph), but about mediately or inferentially evident propositions as well. For this purpose, we could bring in the notion of one belief's forcing another belief upon us, or of p and q's being such that anyone who believed q would be irresistibly driven to believe p as well—for short, q's forcing p. We could then give a recursive definition of the evident as follows: p is evident for S iff either (i) S is in some nondoxastic state (for instance, of contemplating, perceiving, or remembering) that forces S to believe p,[19] or (ii) for some q, q is evident and q forces p. It is to be understood that being forced to believe something means being under a necessity of assenting to it

---

[18] Compare Reid's discussion of memory at EIP 3.2:255–56. "I believe most firmly what I distinctly remember," he tells us, "but I can give no reason of this belief." Read one way, this statement contradicts an analysis of reasons for believing in terms of forced assent. But read another way, with "no reason" as elliptical for "no other reason," it could perhaps be taken as supporting such an analysis.

A few lines earlier he says, "The knowledge which I have of things past by my memory, seems to me as unaccountable as an immediate knowledge would be of things to come; and I can give no reason why I should have the one and not the other, but that such is the will of my Maker." He notes that there is no necessary or intelligible connection between the fact of remembrance and the fact remembered, as there is between the subject and the predicate in a mathematical axiom.

[19] I am assuming here that perceiving and remembering have beliefs as consequences rather than constituents.

by the *constitution of our nature* and not because (for instance) we have been temporarily hypnotized to believe it whenever the hypnotist snaps his fingers.

A forced-assent theory of the evident would have the following implication: if human beings were so constituted that perceiving the sun made them believe it was raining and perceiving rain made them think it was sunny, then rain beliefs would be justified by experiences of the sun and sun beliefs by experiences of rain.

Despite the hints he occasionally drops in their favor, I think Reid would reject forced-assent theories. One of his arguments against moral sense theories in ethics, the modal argument, works just as well against forced assent theories in epistemology. We cannot equate *it is right to keep your promises* with *human beings who contemplate acts of promise-keeping have an agreeable feeling* because the first is necessary while the second is contingent. In just the same way, it can be argued that *a person is justified in believing that a tree exists when he has the experience as of seeing a tree* cannot be held equivalent to *human beings cannot help believing a tree exists when they have the experience as of seeing a tree* because the first is necessary and the second contingent.

How can it be necessary that tree-experiences make tree-beliefs justified? Instructive in this connection are Reid's views on the nature of beauty and of judgments of taste. An exercise of our sense of beauty, Reid tells us, consists in "an agreeable feeling or emotion, accompanied with an opinion or judgment of some excellence in the object, which is fitted by Nature to produce that feeling" (EIP 8.4:594). Beauty is the excellence in the object that is "fitted" to produce the feeling, and Reid's remarks elsewhere strongly suggest that being "fitted" is a normative notion. He tells us that there are qualities in beautiful objects that *ought* to give us pleasure (EIP 6.6:494), and that grandeur is a degree of excellence that *merits* our admiration (EIP 8.3:582). These normative terms, I suggest, are the key to Reid's own escape from the modal objection he levels against moral sense theories and their aesthetic counterparts—that they run afoul of the fact "that what is true or false in morals, or in matters of taste, is necessarily so" (EIP 6.6:495).[20]

To see how Reid himself can accommodate this fact, consider the following three propositions, in which Q is some structural property of an object that makes it beautiful:

(1) Objects with Q are *beautiful*.
(2) Objects with Q *produce* a pleasurable response in human beings.
(3) Objects with Q *merit* a pleasurable response from human beings.

---

[20] In fairness to McDowell, cited in section B as a moral sense theorist, I should note that his view of moral qualities is actually like Reid's of aesthetic qualities: to be right is to have a property that *merits* a certain response. He thus avoids the modal argument to moral sense theories. However, insofar as he treats the response as including a belief in the act's rightness, he incurs the circularity objection discussed in section B.

(1) cannot be equated with (2), Reid says, because (1) is necessary and (2) contingent. But (1) *can* be equated with (3), since (3) is a proposition of a sort that is necessarily true if true at all. I suggest that matters stand likewise for Reid in epistemology. The evident cannot be defined as that to which assent is compelled, but it may be defined as that to which assent is merited. Since meriting is a relation that holds necessarily if at all, correct principles about what is evident under what circumstances are necessary truths. That enables Reid to accommodate the modal fact that is denied by forced-assent theories.[21]

I turn now to analogs in epistemology of meta-ethical expressivism and Hume's motivational argument for it. The idea that epistemic evaluations are merely expressive is considered (though not endorsed) in Chisholm 1957, and it is discussed at length in Cuneo 2007, where it is attributed to Gibbard. As Chisholm develops the idea, saying that some proposition is evident, justified, or the like is not saying anything true or false, but is a way of evincing one's approval of believing it (1957, chapter 7). An argument for this position parallel to the Humean argument considered in section C would run as follows:

1. Ascribing evidence to *p* necessarily inclines you to believe *p*.
2. If ascribing evidence to *p* were a judgment of reason—a belief in a true or false proposition to the effect that *p* is evident—it would *not* necessarily incline you to believe *p*.
3. Therefore, ascribing evidence is not a judgment of reason—it is not anything that is true or false.

In criticism of the Humean original, I said that the first premise is false if the necessity spoken of is logical and the second premise false if the necessity is nomological. Does the same criticism apply here?

It is not unheard of for people to say, "I acknowledge that the evidence is all against there being a God, but I believe in God nonetheless." (Think Kierkegaard!) I take such declarations at face value, and I therefore take premise 1 to be false regardless of whether the necessity spoken of is logical or nomological. There can be, and there actually are, cases in which people are not inclined to believe things they regard as evident; by a miracle in their own person, they may even believe the opposite. In

---

[21] I acknowledge that Reid's views on memory at EIP 3.2:255–56 are troubling for my interpretation. Reid asserts there that it is not necessary that if one has a remembrance of e, then e actually happened. So far, no problem, because it could still be necessary that one who remembers e is prima facie justified in believing that e happened. Nonetheless, what he says about the "unaccountability" of our belief in the truth of what we remember seems at odds with there being a necessary relation of meriting between acts of remembrance and beliefs in facts remembered.

short, belief, like action, may be akratic—one may fail to believe (or even positively disbelieve) things one takes to be well supported by the evidence.[22] If this is so, premise 1 is false in *either* sense of necessity, and it does not matter whether there is any sense in which premise 2 is true.

An interesting problem for epistemological expressivism arises when we consider the ascribing of evidence to evidential ascriptions themselves. (See Cuneo 2007, chapter 5, for a good development of the problem.) Recall Reid's comparison of evidence to light at EIP 6.5:481: "as light, which is the discoverer of all visible objects, discovers itself at the same time; so evidence, which is the voucher for all truth, vouches for itself at the same time." On one interpretation of this remark, Reid saying that whenever a proposition *p* is evident, so is the proposition that *p* is evident: in symbols, Ep → EEp. Whether this claim is true in full generality or not, it seems undeniable that there are *some* cases in which we ascribe evidence to statements ascribing evidence. As Russell once remarked, "The degree of credibility to be attached to a proposition is itself sometimes a datum" (1948:381). What can the expressivist make of this? On the plausible assumption that only performances evaluable for truth or falsity are subject to epistemic evaluation, she cannot make anything of it all. Favorably evaluating Ep, or approving the believing of it, would presuppose that the ground-level Ep is itself a truth-evaluable proposition, not something merely expressive. Putting it the other way around, if saying Ep merely expresses one's approval of believing p, then it would be confused at best and impossible at worst to voice your approval of believing this approval. Believings can be approved, but approvals cannot be believed. Nothing happens at the first level the believing of which can be approved at the second level.[23]

What if epistemic appraisals are held to express not states of approval or disapproval, but one's own impulse to believe or not believe various things? I am not referring to the forced-assent theory discussed above, but to an expressivist appropriation of it.[24] It might be thought that by adopting this version of the expressive theory, we both rehabilitate the Humean argument for expressivism and get around the problem of higher-order appraisals. But in fact we do neither.

---

[22] For a defense of this position, see Chislenko, forthcoming. One of his examples is the anorexic who cannot shake the belief that he needs to lose weight despite believing the evidence is all against this belief.

[23] Disregarding a few subtleties, the main point of Cuneo's chapter 5 can be distilled down to the following syllogism: any epistemic evaluation can itself be epistemically evaluated; only truth-apt states can be epistemically evaluated; therefore, epistemic evaluations are truth-apt and not merely expressive.

[24] Under the expressivist appropriation, one who ascribes evidence to p is not *reporting* that he finds himself under an impulse to believe it; he is *evincing* this impulse, which is not an act with a true-or-false content.

As for the Humean argument, is not a sincere evincing of one's impulsion to believe p necessarily accompanied by one's believing p, in line with the first premise of that argument? Let that much be granted.[25] All that follows is that ascribing evidence is not *merely* believing some true-or-false proposition. It could still be a complex act containing such a belief alongside a noncognitive component.[26] This is a problem that undercuts the epistemological version of Hume's argument as much as it does the moral version.

As for the problem of higher-order appraisals, it is still with us. You can no more believe an evincing than you can believe an approving or a whistling. There is therefore no such thing as evincing a belief in an evincing, for there are no such beliefs to be evinced. If higher-order epistemic appraisals are to be possible, first-order epistemic appraisals must be items that are truth-evaluable. In contest with Hume in matters meta-epistemological, Reid rules.

---

[25] The evincing is not what does the inclining; nonetheless, one who sincerely evinces the belief necessarily possesses it.

[26] Compare what was said in section A about the complex character of approbation according to Reid. Compare also what Chisholm says about "the performative fallacy" in 1966:16–17.

# APPENDICES

## APPENDIX A

# Is There Knowledge by Acquaintance?

"Is There Knowledge by Acquaintance?" was the title of an Aristotelian Society symposium in 1919 among C. D. Broad, G. E. Moore, and two other symposiasts. Complaining that the title of the symposium committed "the fallacy of many questions," Broad distinguished the following three for consideration:

Q1: Is there such a thing as acquaintance?

Q2: Is acquaintance itself knowledge?

Q3: If acquaintance is not itself knowledge, is there nonetheless such a thing as knowledge *by* acquaintance?[1]

His answers, with which I agree, were Yes, No, and Yes.

Prior to all three questions, of course, is the question *what is acquaintance*? Russell's answer in the *locus classicus* on this topic is given as follows:

> I say that I am *acquainted* with an object when I have a direct cognitive relation to that object, i.e. when I am directly aware of the object itself. When I speak of a cognitive relation here, I do not mean the sort of relation which constitutes judgment, but the sort which constitutes presentation. In fact, I think the relation of subject and object which I call acquaintance is simply the converse of the relation of object and subject which constitutes presentation. (1910:108)

The crucial feature of acquaintance is that it is a relation between a person and an *object*, not between a person and a proposition.[2] Its logical form is S-A-O, not S-Verb-that-p; nor does it analyze into or depend on anything of the latter form. In the overarching divide between knowledge of *things* and knowledge of *truths*, acquaintance falls on the *thing* side, and it does not depend on any knowledge of truths.[3]

---

[1] Broad also distinguished two more questions, which arise on the supposition that acquaintance *is* knowledge: is there such a thing as knowledge *by* acquaintance, and how is it related to the knowledge that *is* acquaintance?

[2] Compare (1913) 1992:156, where Russell says acquaintance is cognition of single objects and knowledge is cognition of propositions.

[3] Russell's phrase "knowledge by description" is sometimes erroneously equated with knowledge of truths. Knowledge by acquaintance and knowledge by description are *both* species of knowledge of *things*. The former is knowledge of things that does *not* depend on knowledge of truths, while the latter is knowledge of things that *does* depend on knowledge of truths. I have knowledge by description concerning x when I know some proposition of the form "The F is G," and x uniquely satisfies the description "the F."

Many philosophers nowadays doubt that there is such a thing as a primitive relation of acquaintance. If they allow the objectual form of locution S-A-O at all, it is only to the extent that it is short for ∃F(S knows that O is F). All knowledge and (more broadly) all cognitions are propositional or judgmental. Any cognitive relation to a thing simply consists in knowing some truth about it.

I hold, with Russell and Broad, that there is such a thing as acquaintance. Broad notes that you have acquaintance with a panoply of things when a scene is suddenly illuminated by lightning and you have not had a chance to make any judgments. Even if you do make judgments, they would not take the acquaintance away; as H. H. Price once noted, judgment may be a companion of acquaintance without being its executioner (1932).

One argument for the existence of acquaintance may be based on a famous Russellian principle, the Principle of Acquaintance:

> The fundamental epistemological principle in the analysis of propositions containing descriptions is this: *Every proposition which we can understand must be composed wholly of constituents with which we are acquainted.* ([1912] 1999:40; 1910:219)

This principle does not say that understanding a proposition requires *temporally* prior acquaintance with its constituents. But just so long as it implies that understanding a proposition presupposes acquaintance with its constituents in a sense of "presupposing" that has two of the logical features of temporal priority—irreflexivity and transitivity—we can give the argument that follows. Somewhat reminiscent of Reid's paradox about conception and judgment (appendix B), it is a *reductio* of two assumptions:

(1) Every judgment presupposes acquaintance with the constituents (individuals or properties) of the proposition judged (Principle of Acquaintance).
(2) Every act of awareness (and thus every supposed act of acquaintance) itself consists in a judgment (or something with propositional content).

(1) and (2) generate an endless regress of judgments. A judgment J1 would presuppose acquaintance A1 with the constituents of J1, which would consist in J2 about those constituents (together perhaps with other constituents), which would presuppose A2 with the constituents of J2, which would consist in J3 about them, and so on. The properties of the presupposing relation guarantee that no judgment that has already occurred in the sequence may occur again, so the sequence goes on forever. To complete the argument, we claim that the regress is absurd and that it is best avoided by denying assumption (2). In other words, we admit cognitive acts that are not judgments—acquaintance in precisely Russell's sense of the term.

Broad argues in another way from the Principle of Acquaintance to the nonjudgmental character of acquaintance. He says that if acquaintance with O were *defined* as knowing some proposition about O, then the claim of the Principle of Acquaintance that to know anything about O, you must be acquainted with O would be *analytic*, whereas in fact it is synthetic. The rub with this argument is that the theorist Broad is attacking could define acquaintance not just as having *any* old knowledge about O, but as having some especially intimate kind of knowledge about it, and it would not be analytic that all knowledge about O requires knowledge of the intimate kind.

I pass now to the remaining two questions. (Q2) Is acquaintance knowledge? Russell assumed *yes*, and when he used the phrase "knowledge by acquaintance" he often meant "that knowledge which *is* acquaintance." Broad said *no*, insisting that knowledge is always a form of belief or judgment. I side with Broad, while also admitting with him that the issue may be verbal.

(Q3) Even if acquaintance is not itself knowledge, is there a special kind of knowledge made possible by acquaintance? With Broad, I say *yes*. You have such knowledge when you are acquainted with some object and the acquaintance lets you "read off" some of its manifest properties, such as its color or its shape.

# APPENDIX B

# Conception and Judgment: The Chicken or the Egg?

At EIP 6.1:413–19, Reid presents a paradox about conception and judgment that is resolved, it seems to me, only if there are acts of conception that do not involve or presuppose any judgment. This gives us one more reason for supposing that Reidian conception is an A-relation.

Reid leads us into the paradox with the observation that "some exercise of judgment is necessary in the formation of all abstract and general conceptions, whether more simple or more complex; in dividing, in defining, and in general, in forming all clear and distinct conceptions of things" (EIP 6.1:413). The paradox then consists in the following pair of propositions:

(1) There can be no conception without some previous judgment.
(2) There can be no judgment without some previous conception (of the proposition judged or the various constituents of it).

If (1) and (2) are both true, Reid notes, it follows that there is a "labyrinth of absurdity"—a downward spiral into a bottomless abyss. But something must have gotten things started: "if we go back to the origin of things, there must have been some bird that did not come from any egg, or some egg that did not come from any bird" (EIP 6.1:415–16).

A solution is afforded if we insert the qualifier "distinct" before "conception" in (1). "The reader may please to observe, that I have limited what I have said to distinct conception, and some degree of judgment; and it is by this means I hope to avoid this labyrinth of absurdity" (6.1:415). What lets things get started, then, is the fact that there are indistinct conceptions that require no previous judgment. As he notes in concluding his discussion of the issue, "there are therefore notions of the objects of sense which are gross and indistinct" (EIP 6.1:419; see also EIP 3.5:269).

Why, then, does Reid say that he does not know which came first, the bird or the egg? (EIP 6.1:415, lines 34–36). I conjecture that it is because he thought another of his qualifications, "some degree of judgment," might afford another solution. Perhaps there are primal judgments of such a low degree that they require no prior conception. Against this solution, however, there are two objections. First, what even can be *meant* by a degree of judgment—something that is an affirmation or a denial only to some degree? (Degrees of *conviction* are not at issue here.) Second, are not the reasons for thinking that judgment requires some conception of the things judged about also reasons for thinking that *any* degree of judgment, however low, requires such conception? Indeed, Reid says as much elsewhere: "although conception may be without any degree of belief, even the smallest belief cannot be without conception" (EIP 4.1:295) It can easily seem, then, that Reid should have proclaimed that the egg of conception preceded the bird of judgment (just as in the biological case: see Sorensen 1992).

Trouble for this suggestion comes from a remark at EIP 4.3:327: "Simple apprehension, therefore, though it be the simplest, is not the first operation of the understanding." The first operations, he says, are probably sensation and perception.

If the first operation of the understanding is perception, and if perception involves both conception and judgment, then it cannot be true that conception precedes any act of judgment. Conception and judgment would be coeval, though it would still be true that judgment logically presupposes conception and not conversely. After there were a few cases of conception accompanied by judgment, there could be subsequent cases of bare conception without any judgment.

\* \* \* \* \*

There is a potential inconsistency in Reid that I propose to forestall with some terminological legislation.

Reid claims that conception is an ingredient of all other mental operations (EIP 4.1:295), but he arguably means that conception is either an ingredient *or a concomitant* of all other mental operations. Either way, you cannot love something without having some conception of what you love, believe something without having some conception of what you believe, and so on. And either way, Reid's claim implies

1. Where there is belief about x, there is conception of x.

Reid defines conception as simple apprehension, and he says that by "simple apprehension" logicians mean apprehension without belief. "Without belief" might mean "not having belief as an ingredient" or "not having belief as a concomitant." Suppose it means the latter. We then get the following consequence:

2. Where there is conception of x, there is no belief about x.

The problem is that 1 and 2 together imply

3. Where there is belief about x, there is no belief about x.

That gives rise to a contradiction as soon as there are such things as beliefs at all. Surely Reid meant to imply no such contradiction.

The moral I draw is that Reid should have defined "simple apprehension" in the first way— as apprehension having no belief as an *ingredient*. That would free him from commitment to 2, allowing him to say that a conception having no belief as an ingredient could nonetheless have a belief as a companion.

Alternatively, Reid could have said that "apprehension having no belief as a concomitant" is not the definition of conception as such, but of *bare* conception. That would also free him from commitment to 2, which would now be true only of bare conception.

The two strategies are complementary, and my recommendation is that we adopt them both by employing the following definitions:

Conception of x = Df apprehension of x with no belief as ingredient.
Bare conception of x = Df apprehension of x with no belief about x as concomitant.

Reid could then go on to espouse all the following doctrines without any inconsistency: (i) where there is belief about x (or any other operation about x), there is conception of x (the *caput mortuum* doctrine of EIP 4.1:296); (ii) where there is bare conception of x, there is no accompanying belief (by definition); (iii) conception comes at least as early as the earliest judgment (a partial answer to the chicken-or-egg riddle); (iv) operations that combine conception and judgment (e.g., perception) come before bare conception (asserted at IHM 2.4:29 and EIP 4.3:327).

# APPENDIX C

# Experience as a Source of Concepts

Reid is not a concept empiricist. In his view, there are many important concepts that we either possess innately or come to have without abstracting them from experience, such as the concepts of power, self, and body. But there are *some* concepts, such as that of the color red or of a piny smell, that we *do* get from experience. That is enough for purposes of the present argument, the thrust of which is that in order to be a source of concepts, experience cannot be exclusively propositional.[4]

My argument consists in setting forth an inconsistent tetrad of statements and then contending that the best way to remove the inconsistency is to reject the propositionality of experience. Here is the tetrad:

1. All experience, including perceptual experience, has propositional content; it is experience that p.
2. No one can have any propositional attitude (or any other experiential relation) toward a propositional content who does not already grasp whatever concepts are involved in the articulation of that content. (You cannot entertain or be experientially related to the proposition that *a is F* unless you grasp the concept of an F thing.)
3. As Locke taught (and as Reid would agree), there are many concepts that are first acquired through perceptual experience; it is experience that makes it possible for you subsequently to entertain contents involving the concept.
4. If concept F is acquired through experience E and E has propositional content, then F is a constituent of that content.

To see that these four statements are indeed inconsistent, assume (as 3 says we may) that concept F is acquired through experience E. According to 1, E has a propositional content. According to 4, F is a constituent of that content. According to 2, no one can have E who does not already possess or grasp F. But that contradicts our initial assumption that F is first acquired through E.

---

[4] Others who have argued along these lines are Heck (2000) and Roskies (2008).

There are four possible responses to the tetrad.

Reject 1: This is what I recommend. There is such a thing as seeing an expanse of red or a shiny apple or a vista of the Grand Canyon without thereby being cognitively related to any proposition. You may, of course, entertain or believe various propositions in response to your experience, but your experience is not constituted by any cognitive relation to those propositions. In holding this, I am rejecting the position known elsewhere as intentionalism (Byrne 2001) and in this book as propositionalism.

Reject 2: This seems to be the position of many of those who espouse what is called (misleadingly, in my view) "nonconceptual content." In particular, it is the position of those who espouse what is sometimes called "state nonconceptualism," the view that there are contents that can be grasped by individuals who do not possess the concepts involved in those contents (Byrne 2005). But if the contents are indeed propositional, this view seems to me highly dubious. See Van Cleve 2012.

Reject 3: This is what Sellars (1963) and McDowell (1994) do; they reject empiricist-abstractionist theories of concept formation along with their rejection of the so-called Myth of the Given. I think the Myth is no myth, for reasons I have given elsewhere.[5]

Reject 4: This alternative may seem strange at first, but I shall mention two reasons that might be given for questioning 4.

First, it might be suggested that a complex concept can be acquired from a sequence of experiences no one of which has that concept as a constituent, as when one constructs the concept Unicorn from the concepts Horse and Horn, each acquired separately from experience. That, of course, was explicitly allowed for in Hume's version of concept empiricism. However, this consideration only shows that it would be false to say that if concept F is acquired from experiences $E_1$ through $E_n$, then F is a constituent of one of $E_1$-$E_n$. It does not show that 4 is false as stated. Moreover, we could avoid this objection altogether simply by stipulating in 3 that some *simple* concepts are acquired through experience, which is what concept empiricists typically assert.

Second, it might be suggested that besides having propositional content, an experience has a surrounding phenomenal halo or aura from which a concept could be abstracted even if the content did not contain that concept. However, it is clear that this suggestion runs contrary to the spirit of propositionalism and could hardly be used in defense of it. A properly formulated propositionalism goes beyond 1 to 1': all perceptual experience has its phenomenal character *exhaustively determined* by its propositional content. Under this assumption, it is plausible that a phenomenal feature of an experience could permit the acquisition of concept F from the experience only if F were a constituent of the propositional content of that experience.[6]

---

[5] See Van Cleve 1985 for a limited defense of the Myth of the Given; see Roskies 2008 for an argument that those who deny that concepts are learned from experience must endorse either an implausible nativism about all concepts or an implausible theory of concept acquisition through brute-causal processes occurring at some sub-personal level.

[6] In effect, I am suggesting that if the second challenge to 4 is taken seriously, one should rewrite 4 as 4': If concept F is acquired through experience E and E has a propositional content that determines its phenomenal character, then F is a constituent of that content.

Of course, if 1 is strengthened to 1' in this way, the conclusion I obtain by denying the first proposition in the tetrad will have to be correspondingly weakened. The conclusion will now be that not all experience has a propositional content that exhaustively determines its phenomenal character. I am content with the weaker conclusion.

# APPENDIX D

# Perception as Analog Representation

An argument that perception cannot be exhausted by belief or any other attitudes with propositional content may be based on ideas from Dretske 1981 about analog versus digital forms of representation.

Here is how Dretske draws the analog-digital distinction:

> I will say that a signal (structure, event, state) carries the information that s is F in digital form if and only if the signal carries no additional information about s, no information that is not already nested in S's being F. If the signal *does* carry additional information about s, information that is *not* nested in s's being F then I shall say that the signal carries this information in analog form. When a signal carries the information that s is F in analog form, the signal always carries more specific, more determinate, information about s than that it is F. (1981:137).

For example, a digital odometer tells you how far you have gone to the nearest tenth of a mile. An old-fashioned analog odometer with revolving numeral plates tells you more; it tells you that you have gone at least 10.8 miles, but it also tells you roughly what fraction of a tenth of a mile you have gone beyond 10.8 miles.

Dretske offers a further illustration. The verbal signal "The cup has coffee in it" tells you just that and no more. A photograph tells you more—how full the cup is, how dark the coffee is, the color of the tablecloth, and perhaps further facts about the cup's environment. The sentence carries information in digital form, the photograph in analog form.[7]

Dretske goes on to suggest that conceptualization is by its very nature a process of digitalization that involves loss of information (1981:142). When we go from raw awareness of a scene to some judgment or proposition about it—that we have gone at least ten miles or that the tablecloth is red—we inevitably leave out information that was encoded in analog form. We do this for good reasons, of course; we want to highlight some respect of similarity or note whether some important threshold has been reached. But we do so at the cost of losing information.

I maintain that in a given perceptual experience, I am aware of more *things*, more *properties* of those things, and *more determinate levels* of those properties than I deploy any concepts of. I am not saying that I lack concepts of all the things that I see, though I believe that is

---

[7] We are not supposed to conclude from the example that all analog representation is pictorial and all digital representation linguistic.

generally the case; I am saying that even if I have the concepts, I do not deploy them all. Moreover, the conceptualizations or "propositionalizations" that I do bring forth will fall short of describing all aspects of what I perceptually experience; my perceptual state will carry more information than any conceptual encoding of it in a belief or judgment.

I am quite prepared to concede that *for any level of detail in the scene before me, there is a possible digital encoding that would adequately capture it.* At the same time, I believe that my opponents must concede that *for any actual digital encoding, there are details in the scene not yet captured by it.* The latter proposition suffices for my point: perception is not exhausted by judgments. There must be more to perception than judgment, and acquaintance with objects or scenes is a good candidate for what that "more" is.

# APPENDIX E

## Byrne versus Reid

Alex Byrne argues for intentionalism, the view that phenomenal character supervenes on propositional content, and criticizes Reid for holding otherwise. I defend Reid.

*Intentionalism, what.* Philosophers who speak of the "intentional" character of mental states may have any of four characteristics in mind: (i) being *of* something, that is, being directed upon some object; (ii) being of something that *does not exist* (or at any rate, that need not exist just in virtue of some mental state's being *of* it); (iii) having a *propositional* object or content; and (iv) having a propositional content concerning things in one's *environment.* (i) is the etymological meaning; the Latin verb "intendo" means to *aim* at something, as with a bow and arrow. (ii) is the meaning connected with the doctrine of intentionalism discussed in chapter 10 and associated with Brentano and Meinong. (iii) is the meaning connected with the contemporary doctrine that people most often have in mind when they speak of intentionalism. (iv) is the meaning connected with one variety of intentionalism in the previous sense.

An exemplary exposition and defense of intentionalism in the main contemporary sense (which I sometimes call propositionalism to distinguish it from intentionalism in the sense associated with Meinong) is Byrne 2001. As Byrne formulates it, intentionalism is the thesis that phenomenal character supervenes on intentional ( = propositional) content: for any phenomenal character P of a mental state M, there is an intentional content C such that M has C, and any state with C would also have P. This has two implications: (I) there is no phenomenal character in states without intentional content, and (II) there is no difference in phenomenal character between two states without difference in intentional content.

*How Reid is at odds with intentionalism.* For Reid, the phenomenal character of a perceptual episode is contributed by some combination of sensation (which is objectless or non-intentional) and conception (which is intentional but not always propositional). When we perceive secondary qualities, sensation predominates as the determinant of phenomenal character; when we perceive primary qualities, conception predominates. The propositional content of perception is carried by belief. When Reid says that perception proper (conception and belief) might vary independently of sensation, some of the possibilities he has in mind are at odds with intentionalism. He allows each of the following four possibilities:

(a) We might perceive quality Q by means of *different* sensations from those that are signs of Q now; for example, we might perceive hardness by the sensations we now get through smell (IHM 5.2:57 and 6.21:176). This is holding content the same and varying character, contrary to (II).

(b) We might perceive quality Q by means of *no* sensations (IHM 6.21:176; EIP 2:20:227), and in fact Reid thinks this is what actually happens in our perception of visible figure (IHM 6.8:99–101 and IHM 6.21:176). This does not mean there is no phenomenal character in the perception of visible figure, but rather that the phenomenal character must be carried by conception. Since the conception has no propositional content, this is contrary to (I).

(c) We might have sensations with *no* perceptions or other intentional states (EIP 2.20:227). Since bare sensations still have phenomenal character, this is also contrary to (I).

(d) We might have the same sensations with *different* perceptions (IHM 5.2:57 and 6.8:100).[8] This does not contradict the letter of the intentionalist's supervenience thesis, which allows for the "multiple realization" of phenomenal character in intentional states, but I think some intentionalists would find it strange. Those strong intentionalists who *identify* phenomenal character with representational content (discussed in Siegel 2010) would find it impossible.

*Byrne's argument for intentionalism.* Pared down to its essentials, Byrne's argument for intentionalism runs as follows:

Premise A: If S has consecutive experiences e and e* that differ in phenomenal character, S will notice the difference.

Premise B: If S notices a difference between e and e*, the way things seem to S when she undergoes e differs from the way things seem when she undergoes e*. That is (?!), the intentional contents of e and e* differ.

Conclusion C: If S has consecutive experiences e and e* that that differ in phenomenal character, e and e* differ in intentional content.

My main criticism of this argument is that in his rewrite of the consequent of B, Byrne has simply assumed that something's seeming some way to a person is an intentional state. He has ignored the substantial tradition (represented by Chisholm 1957 and Alston 1999) in which seeming is irreducibly phenomenal, not intentional.

*Byrne's "localization" objection against Reid.* Reid holds that pains, which for him are the paradigms of sensations, are lacking in intentional content. Byrne argues against Reid as follows:

1. This pain seems to come from my toe.
2. A state whereby things seem a certain way has intentional content.
3. Therefore, pains have intentional content.

---

[8] (i) Smell sensations now trigger the perception of smell and (ii) certain tactile sensations trigger the perception of hardness. Reid says (iii) smell sensations might have triggered the perception of hardness (IHM 5.2:57). (ii) and (iii) yield possibility (a) in the text; (i) and (iii) yield (d).

I would reply on Reid's behalf that premise 2 is false. As just noted, Byrne does not argue for this premise.

One way to account for the pain's seeming to come from my toe is to say it is a matter of the pain's eliciting in me the belief that the cause of the pain lies in the toe. It is a matter of the intentional content of an accompanying belief, not of the content of the pain itself. This seems to be Reid's own way at IHM 6.12:125: pain has no relation "from its own nature" to any part of the body, but we know where the cause of a pain lies by a constitutionally associated belief. (Presumably, the nerve impulses that signal the pain "know" where its cause lies and "tell" us what to believe in this regard.)

To this suggestion, Byrne has a good rejoinder. As Reid himself acknowledges, a man who knows his foot has been cut off may still feel pains that seem to come from his toe (EIP 2.18:214 and 2.22:251).[9] Presumably, he does not believe the pain really does come from his toe. So localization is not always a matter of concomitant belief about location.

A second response on Reid's behalf would be to put the seeming into the pain itself without making it intentional, holding that some intrinsic feature of the pain suggests one place rather than another as its cause. The trouble with this suggestion is that it would undermine the *experimentum crucis* of *Inquiry* 5.6. If sensations inherently suggest places, could we not get the notion of extension (which at bottom is just the idea of spatial separation) from two separated pricks of a pin?

A third response on Reid's behalf, consistent with the *experimentum crucis*, would be to analyze a pain's seeming to have a certain location in terms of an associated experience with *representational* content. As Peacocke notes, an experience can represent x as being F without the subject's believing this representational content (1981, chapter 1). So we could say that the amputee seems to feel pain in his toe because his sensation has annexed to it an experience that represents the pain as coming from his toe. It would be important to add, however, that the experience is not *part* of the sensation, but only something contingently conjoined with it by our constitution.

## APPENDIX F

## Infinity and Reflexivity

It is well to distinguish between *perception*, which is the inner state of the monad representing external things, and *apperception*, which is *consciousness*, or the reflective knowledge of this inner state. (Leibniz, *Principles of Nature and Grace*, paragraph 4)

[9] At EIP 2.18:214, Reid offers the then-standard explanation of pains in phantom limbs, which had been given by Descartes: severed nerve pathways that formerly came from the toe still occasionally get activated, culminating in a brain state sufficient for the perception of pain in the toe. In a fascinating discussion of this topic, Ramachandran (1999, chapter 2) offers an alternative explanation: brain areas that used to respond to the foot get invaded and enervated by adjacent brain areas responding to the face, so that stimulation of receptors in the face can bring about an experience as though of pain in the toe. This hypothesis might also explain a phenomenon once reported to me by Jaegwon Kim: that he used to feel an itch in his elbow that could be relieved only by scratching his shoulder.

In an article defending the Aristotle-Brentano (A-B) doctrine of self-reflexive mental states (2003), Uriah Kriegel notes that many people are under the impression that the A-B view, which is expressly designed to avoid an infinite regress of mental *acts*, itself generates a problematic infinite regress of ever more complicated *contents* of mental acts. One may be put in mind here of Royce's example of the complete map of England inscribed within the soil of England: it would have to contain a replica of itself, a replica of the replica, and so on ad infinitum.

Whether the A-B theory generates a regress of contents may depend in part on whether the contents of mental acts are taken to be objects or propositions. Let's assume first that the content of an apperceptive act is an object. The A-B theory then says that an act of perceiving a primary object O is also an act of apperceiving itself as secondary object: $A(O) = A(A(O))$. We can repeatedly substitute in the right side of the identity as permitted by the identity itself to get $A(A(O)) = A(A(A(O))) = A(A(A(A(O))))$ and so on. But this string of ever more complicated terms is harmless, as the same identity that gives rise to it also collapses it down to its initial member, $A(A(O))$. No act A has for its scope anything more complicated than $A(O)$ (alongside O).

But content regresses threaten to be more problematic when we consider the contents of apperception to be propositional, as Kriegel does. Consider the following identity claim, entertained by Kriegel as one possible statement of the A-B theory:

(*) The act whereby one thinks that p = the act whereby one thinks that one thinks that p.

By expanding the right side of (*) in accordance with an instance of (*) itself, we get the third term in the following chain of identities, which may be prolonged indefinitely:

The act whereby one thinks that p = the act whereby one thinks that one thinks that p = the act whereby one thinks that one thinks that one thinks that p = etc.

Here the contents of the act do appear to get successively more complicated.

There are two promising strategies for dealing with this regress: collapsing it (as with the object regress above) and denying that it arises in the first place (which is what Kriegel does).

In the collapse strategy, we claim that *one thinks that one thinks that p* is logically equivalent to *one thinks that p* and is therefore not really more complicated than it. But this strategy fails, for there is no such equivalence. Perhaps the act by which one thinks the sky is blue is of necessity an act whereby one thinks that one thinks that the sky is blue, but from this it would not follow that the two *contents* of the act are equivalent. If they were, the sky could not be blue in a world without thinkers.

In the Kriegel strategy, we claim that the regress does not advance beyond the second content. To generate a regress above, we had to use principle (*), understood thus: *for any proposition p, if we think that p, we thereby think that we think that p*. But according to Kriegel, the A-B view is not committed to (*), but only to this: *for any proposition p at the ground level* (e.g., the sky is blue), if we think that p, we thereby think that we think that p. From this principle alone, no infinite regress arises.

It seems to me, however, that if we bring in one more assumption, we do get a regress. Let us assume that a mental state M2 directed at a mental state M1 represents (i) that M1 represents its primary object, O, and also represents (ii) any *intrinsic mental* facts about M1.

(We need not suppose, of course, that M2 represents *extrinsic* facts about M1, such as its having occurred when the clock struck one, or *physical* facts about M1, such as its having been implemented in part by neuron #344's firing.) Among the intrinsic mental facts about M1 will be the following:

M1 occurs; M1 represents itself; M1 represents M1 as representing O.

Now by applying (ii) to the last item on this list, we get

M2 ( = M1) represents M1 as representing M1 as representing O

which is one more intrinsic fact to be added to the list. Applying (ii) to this fact, we get

M1 represents M1 as representing M1 as representing M1 as representing O.

And now it is clear that we are off on our regress of ever more intricate contents.

A defender of the A-B position could reply that I have made a gratuitous assumption to which he is not committed—namely (ii), which is an assumption of omniscience by mental states with respect to their own intrinsic features or, putting it conversely, of the transparency of mental states to themselves as apperceptive. A mental state can apprehend its own existence and its own directedness upon O without apprehending absolutely *every* intrinsic feature of itself, or so the defender might say.

There we might leave things, except for one last twist: Reid sometimes says things that seem to imply that sensations are transparent, in the sense of disclosing all their intrinsic features to attentive consciousness.[10] If we combine this transparency doctrine with a view of sensations as apperceiving themselves (such as Buras wants to attribute to Reid), we do get an infinite regress like the one sketched here. So Reid had better not accept both transparency (à la Ganson) and self-reflexivity (à la Buras).

# APPENDIX G

# Programming the Obvious

A common Reidian mode of argument runs along the following lines: We inevitably conceive of and believe in Y when we experience X. For example, we conceive of and believe in hard bodies when we have certain sorts of tactile sensations, and we conceive of and believe

---

[10] Beware the many (and indeed sometimes incompatible) meanings of "transparent." Some who call sensory experiences transparent (e.g., Ganson) mean we are aware of all their intrinsic features. Other who call sensory experiences transparent (e.g., Harman) mean we are aware of *none* of their intrinsic features. I conjecture that the difference in usage may come about as follows: those in the former group take any supposed obstruction between us and the features of our experience to be transparent, whereas those in the latter group take the experiences themselves to be transparent—we look right through them to their objects.

in the occurrence of a certain event in the past when we have a memory experience of it. But there is no intrinsic or necessary connection between X and Y, no relation between them that reason can discern. Therefore, it must be a brute law of our constitution that being aware of X makes us conceive of and believe in Y.

Hume employs a similar modus operandi. Finding no rational or intelligible connection between the fact that A and B have gone together in the past and the fact that they will continue to go together in the future, Hume supposes it must simply be a principle of human nature that when we have been exposed to many cases of A being accompanied by B, we expect the next A to be accompanied by B (*Enquiry*, sections 4 and 5).

Arguments of this sort prompt the following thought: What if there *were* a necessary connection, discernible by reason, between X and Y? Would there then be no need to posit an innate mechanism whereby we believe in Y when presented with X? Of course, the inference "not necessary, therefore part of our constitution" does not imply its converse, "necessary, therefore not part of our constitution." Yet I believe Reid does endorse the converse inference along with the original, as intimated below:

> Is it possible that this act [of remembrance] should be, if the event had not happened? I confess I do not see any necessary connection between the one and the other. If any man can shew such a necessary connection, then I think that belief which we have of what we remember will be fairly accounted for; but if this cannot be done, that belief is unaccountable, and we can say no more but that it is the result of our constitution. (EIP 3.1:255–56)

Many other thinkers also endorse the converse inference in various contexts. Locke rejects the argument that a hypothesis of innate principles is needed to explain why we believe certain principles as soon as we think of them. He says no such hypothesis is necessary because the principles are simply self-evident (ECHU 1.2.18). Quine and Davidson hold that certain principles are so obvious that they are built into translation or interpretation. They are so obvious that anyone we seek to understand *must* believe them; there is no need for any hardwiring hypothesis to explain why people hold them. (See Van Cleve 1992.) Wittgenstein holds that if a principle is a necessary truth, then it is also a necessary truth that people believe it, in which case no account in terms of the human constitution of why people believe it is called for. That assumption underlies the Wittgensteinian methodology of seeking to show that this or that principle is not a necessary truth by imagining a tribe of people who do not believe it or act in accordance with it.

In disagreement with Reid and the other thinkers listed above, I cannot see why our native constitution does not have to collaborate in *whatever* we believe. Let a principle be ever so obvious or necessary: must we still not be programmed to believe it or operate in accordance with it?

In a somewhat similar vein, it seems to me that no matter how inherently valuable something is, it is a further question whether anyone actually values it. A child's song of thanksgiving gives thanks for various things, including the moonlit night and the stars above, then concludes by giving thanks for the wonder in me. The last verse is not redundant; the intrinsic wonderfulness of the nighttime sky provides no guarantee that I will in fact take wonder in it.

## APPENDIX H

# The Sun in the Sky and the Sun in My Mind
## OR Why Arnauld Is Not Steadfastly a Direct Realist

Reid's claim to be unique among philosophers of the early modern period in rejecting the way of ideas and endorsing direct realism is sometimes challenged by those who put forth another philosopher as having the same distinction: Antoine Arnauld. Reid himself realized that Arnauld may have a claim in this regard, but he hesitated to endorse it, remarking in his chapter on Arnauld in the EIP that "it seems difficult to determine whether he adopted the common theory of ideas, or whether he is singular in rejecting it altogether as a fiction of Philosophers" (EIP 2.13:165). Disparaging Reid's reluctance, Nadler has argued (i) that Arnauld was indeed a direct realist, and (ii) that Reid's failure to recognize this fact puts his credibility as a historian of philosophy in doubt (1986, 1989). In this appendix, I argue that Reid's reluctance is not without reason.

Arnauld's views are best characterized by contrast with those of Malebranche, with whom he had a famous running debate. (See Nadler 1989 for a fuller account.) Malebranche espoused a tripartite theory of perception, according to which there are three items involved in any perceptual situation in addition to the perceiving subject: a mental act or modification of the mind, an idea, and an external object. What the subject perceives directly is not the external object, but only the idea, which represents the object. In his *Of True and False Ideas* (1683), Arnauld propounded a bipartite theory, according to which the only items in addition to the subject are the act and the external object. There is no need for ideas as special representative entities, since an act (or modification of the mind) can represent or intend an external object directly. Arnauld did, to be sure, say that there are such things as ideas, but he used the term "idea" to refer to the act, not to any *tertium quid*. (He also thought that in using the term "idea" in this way, he was simply following the lead of Descartes.)[11] The difference between a bipartite act theory of ideas like Arnauld's and a tripartite object theory like Malebranche's is taken with some plausibility to line up with the difference between a direct and an indirect realist theory of perception.

It must be acknowledged that Arnauld's official view is bipartite, and that he made some of the key moves that are needed to secure direct realism. If Reid was not prepared to embrace Arnauld as a forerunner, why not?

It is not because Reid was misled by Arnauld's admission of items to which he gave the name "idea." Reid knew that Arnauld defined the idea of a thing to be the perception of it in the act sense (EIP 2.13). He was also clear on the fact that ordinary speakers often use the word "idea" to refer to operations of the mind, and that in this sense "idea"-talk is quite harmless:

---

[11] Some contemporary commentators, including Yolton and Nadler, follow Arnauld in his interpretation of Descartes, thus disputing Reid's contention that Descartes was a paradigm proponent of ideas as third things.

If by ideas are meant only the acts or operations of our minds in perceiving, remembering, or imagining objects, I am far from calling in question the existence of these acts; we are conscious of them every day, and every hour of life. (EIP 2.14:171).

Indeed, Reid often uses the word "idea" in this sense himself in stating his own views.

The main thing that seems to have made Reid unsure whether Arnauld was a direct realist is that Arnauld devoted chapter 6 of his 1683 book to showing that the following words are not to be rejected, but express something true when rightly understood:

that we perceive not things immediately; that it is their ideas that are the immediate objects of our thoughts. (EIP 2.13)[12]

Nadler refers to this formula as P. Why did Arnauld affirm P, and how could he do so while remaining a direct realist?

Evidently, Arnauld thought he had to accept P under some construal of it in order to be faithful to Descartes (Nadler 118). At the same time, he did not want P to implicate him in a tripartite theory. He proposed that P is true because it expresses the thesis that perception is self-reflexive in the Brentano sense explored in chapter 1, section G: a perception never has any material thing as its object without having *itself* as its object as well. Since perceptive acts are what Arnauld calls ideas, it follows that we never perceive any material thing without being aware of an idea. There need be nothing in this at odds with direct realism.[13]

Under Arnauld's gloss of it, then, formula P is compatible with direct realism. It should be noted, however, that the gloss leaves unexplained one troublesome aspect of P in its original wording: that ideas are "the" (implying *the only*) immediate objects of our thoughts. It is understandable that Reid should have had his doubts.

Moreover, there is another feature of Arnauld's thought that is even more antithetical to direct realism: he aligns himself with what Descartes has to say about the "objective reality" of ideas.[14] I now argue that the relevant remarks of Descartes's can only be understood if ideas are "third things" in addition to acts and external objects.

Descartes uses the scholastic terminology of "objective reality" and "formal reality" in presenting his Third Meditation proof of the existence of God. There is an aspect of our ideas, their objective reality, that requires a cause, and the cause of an idea must have at least as much formal reality as the idea has objective reality. Since our idea of God has an infinite

---

[12] I am giving Reid's words, which are an accurate translation of Arnaulds's French as quoted by Nadler on p. 120. Reid adds one more clause: "that it is in the idea of every thing that we perceive its properties."

[13] It does seem right to me that holding a self-reflexive theory of perception should not stand in the way of being a direct realist (as discussed in chapter 3, section G). To accommodate this result, however, one must take some care in defining direct realism. The definition from Cornman quoted in n. 27 of Nadler's chapter 1 would *not* allow a self-reflexive theory to count as direct realist.

[14] "Objective reality" is a term that is apt to confuse a contemporary reader. For an account of the way in which the term "objective" has undergone a 180-degree turn of meaning between Descartes's day and our own, see Anscombe (1965) 1981:3–4.

amount of objective reality, its cause must have an infinite amount of formal reality, which means that it must be God himself.

What is the "objective reality" that Descartes ascribes to ideas, and why does it require a cause? Caterus pressed these questions in the first set of objections to the Meditations.[15] Here is Descartes's summary of Caterus's objection, along with his reply:

> "Objective being in the intellect," he [Caterus] says, "is simply the determination of an act of the intellect by means of an object, and this is merely an extraneous label which adds nothing to the thing itself." Notice here that he is referring to the thing itself as if it were located outside the intellect, and in this sense "objective being in the intellect" is certainly an extraneous label; but I was speaking of the idea, which is never outside the intellect, and in this sense "objective being" simply means being in the intellect in the way in which objects are normally there. For example, if anyone asks what happens to the sun through its being objectively in my intellect, the best answer is that nothing happens to it beyond the application of an extraneous label which does indeed "determine an act of the intellect by means of an object." But if the question is about what the idea of the sun is, and we answer that it is the thing which is thought of, in so far as it has objective being in the intellect no one will take this to be the sun itself with this extraneous label applied to it. "Objective being in the intellect" will not here mean "the determination of an act of the intellect by means of an object," but will signify the object's being in the intellect in the way in which its objects are normally there. By this I mean that the idea of the sun is the sun itself existing in the intellect—not of course formally existing, as it does in the heavens, but objectively existing, i.e. in the way in which objects normally are in the intellect. Now this mode of being is of course much less perfect than that possessed by things which exist outside the intellect; but as I did explain, it is not therefore simply nothing. (Descartes 1984:74–75)

Especially telling is the penultimate sentence, which I offer again in the more evocative translation of Haldane and Ross:

> Hence the idea of the sun will be the sun itself existing in the mind, not indeed formally, as it exists in the sky, but objectively, i.e., in the way in which objects are wont to exist in the mind. (Descartes 1911, Vol. II:10)

[15] I have always found Descartes's use of "objective reality" ambiguous between a relational property and its converse: sometimes it means an object's property of being referred to by a mental act, other times it means an act's property of referring to an object, and sometimes it is not clear which. I was therefore given hope of greater understanding by Nadler's suggestion that Descartes systematically marks this distinction himself, using "objective reality" for the property of acts and "objective being" for the property of objects (Nadler 159). However, on rereading the relevant passages (Meditation 3, the First Replies, and the *more geometrico* section of the Second Replies) I could not see that Nadler's claim is consistently borne out. In Meditation III, Descartes generally uses "objective reality" for the feature of ideas that requires a cause; in the First Replies, he generally uses "objective being." Also, in Definition III of the *more geometrico* section, "objective reality" is defined in a way that can only make it a property of objects represented.

What can it mean to identify the idea of the sun with the sun itself existing in the mind?

"The sun itself existing in the mind" is not an act, for it is a represent*ed*, not a represent*er*. After all, it is represented items that are "in the mind in the way in which objects are wont to be there." In addition, if the ideas he is speaking of were acts, it would not have been necessary for Descartes to point out that the mode of being he attributes to them is more than "mere nothing," for acts have formal reality as modifications of the mind.

Nor can the idea of the sun be identified with the sun in sky. There are three reasons for this in the long passage quoted above. First, if the sun in the mind were identical with the sun in the sky qua being represented, its having "objective being in the intellect" would then be an extrinsic denomination of it, just as Caterus alleges. But that is precisely what Descartes denies. Second, Descartes says that the sun he is speaking of "at no time exists outside the mind" (1911:10). Therefore, it cannot be the astronomical sun. Third, Descartes says the objective mode of being possessed by the sun in the mind is more than mere nothing, but also less perfect than the formal being possessed by things outside the mind. Therefore, once again, the idea of the sun, or the sun in the mind, cannot be the astronomical sun.

So why does Descartes say that the idea of the sun is *the sun itself existing in the mind*? It is time to point out an ambiguity in that phrase, corresponding to two possible ways of punctuating it. It can be read as *the sun itself, existing in the mind*, or it can be read without the comma as *that (second) sun which exists in the mind in that special way in which objects are wont to exist there*. I have been arguing, in effect, that the second reading is the one needed to make sense of Descartes's reply to Caterus. John Monfasani tells me that this point is even clearer in the Latin.[16]

There is admittedly one feature of the Cottingham and Haldane and Ross translations that favors the first reading: the pronoun "it" in "the sun itself existing in the mind, not indeed formally, as it exists in the sky" suggests that *the same sun* exists both in the mind and in the sky. But the Latin is just "ut in coelo"—there is no pronoun. "Ut in coelo" requires the addition of a noun or pronoun upon being translated into English, but if no issues are to be prejudged, what is added should be "the sun"—"as the sun exists in the sky."

In the First Replies, then, what Descartes means by "ideas" can neither be acts nor external objects. They must be third things.

Let us return to Arnauld. In chapter 5 of his 1683 book, Arnauld defines the idea of an object as the perception of it (definition 3) and says that a thing is objectively in my mind when I conceive of it (definition 5). Had he stopped there, one could attribute a bipartite theory to him. But he goes on to say, "*The idea of an object* must not be confused with *the object conceived*, unless one adds, *insofar as it is objectively in the mind*. . . . *the idea of the sun is the sun itself, insofar as it is objectively in my mind*" (definition 10). He explicates "being objectively in the mind" exactly as Descartes does in reply to Caterus—as a property of representeds rather than representers, and as a property not possessed by the astronomical sun. A represented item other than the sun in the sky can only be a second sun in my mind. It appears,

---

[16] The relevant stretch of Latin is "adeo ut idea solis sit sol ipse in intellectu existens, non quidem formaliter, ut in coelo, sed objective, hoc est eo modo quo objecta in intellectu esse solent."

then, that by falling in with Descartes on these matters, Arnauld falls into a tripartite theory, if only implicitly and in spite of his best intentions.[17]

We may give the final words to Reid:

> But what they [philosophers who say external objects are not immediate objects of perception, but are nonetheless objects of perception] mean by a mediate object of perception I do not find clearly explained; whether they suit their language to popular opinion, and mean that we perceive external objects in that figurative sense, in which we say that we perceive an absent friend when we look on his picture; or whether they mean, that really, and without a figure, we perceive both the external object and its idea in the mind. If the last be their meaning, it would follow, that, in every instance of perception, there is a double object perceived: That I perceive, for instance, one sun in the heavens, and another in my own mind. But I do not find that they affirm this; and as it contradicts the experience of all mankind, I will not impute it to them. (EIP 2.7: 105–6)

We do not perceive two suns. If Descartes and Arnauld think there is a sun represented in our minds that is other than the sun in the sky, it follows that we do not perceive the sun in the sky. It is no wonder that Reid does not regard them as direct realists.

## APPENDIX I

## Secondary Qualities: Can We Have It Both Ways?

By the "capital part" thesis, I mean Reid's thesis that sensations play a capital part in the notions we form of secondary qualities, the qualities being conceivable only in terms of the sensations. As Lehrer puts it, sensations are "semantic constituents" of our secondary quality concepts (1989:27). This thesis would be true on standard dispositional understandings of secondary qualities.

By the "physical supervenience" thesis, I mean the thesis that the color of an object supervenes on its intrinsic physical character in the following sense: anything just like a given red object in all intrinsic physical respects would itself be red (Wright 1992:113). This thesis would be espoused by any physicalist worth his salt; it would presumably also be attributed to Reid by anyone who thought he identified colors with the causal bases of dispositions rather than the dispositions themselves.

Is it possible to define secondary qualities in a way that makes *both* theses true?

---

[17] Kenny Pearce has pointed out that the ambiguity I note above in 'the sun itself existing in the mind' is not present in Arnauld's French rendition, which is *le soleil même, en tant qu'il est objectivement dans mon esprit.* In the same paragraph, however, Arnauld falls in with Descartes on one of the points that makes it impossible to identify the sun in my mind with the sun in the sky: he says the sun existing objectively in my mind has "a way of being much more imperfect than that by which the sun actually exists" ([1683], 1990:67).

Three ways of defining or specifying secondary qualities are discussed in chapter 4. The first is the simple conditional definition of red as a disposition:

D1. x is red = df if x were placed in view of a normal human observer in normal circumstances, the observer would be caused to experience red* sensations.

The second is the second-order property definition of red as a disposition:

D2. x is red = df there is some property P such that x has P & P causes red* sensations in normal human observers in normal circumstances.

From now on, let's abbreviate "causes red* sensations in normal human observers in normal circumstances" to "causes red* sensations in humans." The third definition identifies red with the causal base of the disposition defined by D1 or D2, using sensations only to fix the reference of "red":

D3. There is a property P such that P causes red* sensations in humans; x is red = df x has that property P.

How do our two theses fare under these definitions?

D1 makes the capital part thesis true, since sensations figure in its definiens. (I am relying on the old-fashioned idea that the definiendum in an apt definition must, in Spinoza's language, be "conceived through" the definiens.) But it makes the physical supervenience thesis false, since a thing in another world just like a red thing in our world might *not* be such that humans who looked at it would get red* sensations. Perhaps the neural structure of humans is different in that world, or perhaps the laws of nature are different there.

D2 also makes the capital part thesis true, since it again defines color in terms of sensations. And like D1, it makes the physical supervenience thesis false, because humans or the laws might be different in some world containing a physical duplicate of a red object. In such a world, the duplicate need not have any property making things that have it look red (= cause red* sensations).

D3 reverses the verdicts yielded by D1 and D2. It makes the capital part thesis false, since it mentions sensations only outside the definition proper, using them merely to fix the reference of "red." Redness under this definition is a certain microphysical property, and you can grasp that property without conceiving of red* sensations. By the same token, it makes the physical supervenience thesis true, because if redness just is a certain physical property, then anything physically just like a red thing would be red, regardless of whether it causes red* sensations in humans.

None of our definitions, then, makes both theses true. Is there any way of understanding secondary qualities that *does* make both theses true? The answer is *yes*, although it involves a tricky device of contemporary philosophical logic that was unknown to Reid.

Definitions imply the necessary truth of their corresponding biconditionals, which must hold in all possible worlds. The most natural way to understand D2 in terms of possible worlds would be this:

D2a. For all worlds w: x is red in w = df for some property P, x has P in w & in w P causes red* sensations in humans.

But we can also understand D2 in another way—and here comes the trick—by indexing the second conjunct in the definiens to the actual world, @:

> D2b.  For all worlds w: x is red in w = df for some property P, x has P in w & in @ P causes red* sensations in humans.

D2a and D2b both imply the same verdict on the capital part thesis, since as with D1 and D2, they define redness in terms of sensations. But they part ways on the supervenience thesis, D2a making it false (as D2 did) and D2b making it true. D2b makes it true because if an object x in @ has a property P making it look red, any physical duplicate of x in another world w will also have that property P; and since P makes things *in* @ look red, possession of P by the duplicate in w makes it red even if it does not *look* red in w.

Our results so far may be summed up in Table I.1.

**Table I.1**

|  | *D1* | *D2a* | *D2b* | *D3* |
|---|---|---|---|---|
| Is the capital part thesis true? | yes | yes | yes | no |
| Is the physical supervenience thesis true? | no | no | yes | yes |

Yet there are a number of problems or puzzles that arise if we try to explicate Reid's views using definitions in the style of D2b. Ryan Nichols has suggested that a definition parallel to D2b would be equally true in the case of a primary quality like hardness (2007:179):

> D2b.'  For all worlds w: x is hard in w = df for some property P, x has P in w & in @ P causes hard* sensations in humans.[18]

This might be thought problematic for two reasons. Does it not imply that hardness counts as a secondary quality? And does it not also imply that sensations of a certain sort are a capital part of our notion of hardness? Both implications would be un-Reidian.

In reply to these supposed difficulties, I note two things. First, what makes something a primary quality is not that it cannot be defined in the D2b way, but that it *can* be defined in some other way. Reid defines hardness thus: a thing is hard when its parts "adhere so firmly, that it cannot easily be made to change its figure" (IHM 5.2:55), which is a definition that tells us how a hard thing is in itself, as befits the definition of a primary quality. Second, though the biconditional corresponding to D2b' is a necessary truth, that does not mean that D2b' is correct as a definition. The symbol " = df" is a hyperintensional connective, which is to say that a statement of the form "P = df Q" is not automatically true simply because the

---

[18] Nichols is addressing an earlier version of my proposal that was couched in terms of laws of nature rather than causation; I have adapted his point to apply to my proposal in its current wording.

corresponding biconditional "P iff Q" is a necessary truth. So D2b' may not be true in the definitional way needed to sustain the capital part thesis in the case of hardness.

But other drawbacks of using D2b to explicate Reid's thought remain. I have wanted to keep alive the interpretive possibility that Reidian secondary qualities are dispositions rather than their bases. Is the property defined by D2b a disposition? It is a second-order property like the property defined by D2a, which we agreed was a disposition; yet it is necessarily co-extensive with the property defined by D3, which I said was a base. By including the reference to @ in D2b, we may have constructed a definition that no longer defines a disposition.

The suspicion that D2b does not define a disposition is reinforced if we use a diagnostic scheme offered by Wolterstorff (2001:112). Suppose that camellias in some world w have the same intrinsic physical characteristics as our camellias, but look green rather than red to inhabitants of w. Are camellias in that world red or green? If you say green, you are thinking of colors as dispositions; if you say red, you are thinking of them as bases. The property defined by D2b does not satisfy this test for being a disposition.

The bottom line is that we cannot have things all *three* of the following ways: colors are conceived in terms of the sensations they produce, they supervene on the intrinsic physical characteristics of things, and they are dispositions.[19]


# APPENDIX J

## The One-Point Argument

By what arguments are we supposed to be convinced that depth is not perceived? Some writers on this topic affirm straightaway that since the retina is two-dimensional, the visual field must be two-dimensional. That argument is exasperatingly enthymematic. The optic nerve is effectively one-dimensional, but no one concludes from that alone that the visual field is one-dimensional. So what is the missing premise in the argument from the two-dimensionality of the retina? Not, one hopes, that retinal images are what we really perceive.

In Molyneux, the argument is this:

> Distance of itself, is not to be perceived; for 'tis a line (or a length) presented to our eye with its end toward us, which must therefore be only a *point*, and that is invisible. (Quoted in Daniels 1974:36 from Molyneux's *Dioptrics Nova* of 1692)

---

[19] The complications that arise when definitions in the D2b style are introduced can be illustrated by noting that the following set of propositions is inconsistent: (1) properties defined as second-order properties (like redness as defined in D2a) are dispositions; (2) if the property defined in D2a is a disposition, so is the property defined in D2b; (3) the property defined in D2b is co-intensive with the property defined in D3; (4) if one of two co-intensive properties is a disposition, so is the other; (5) the property defined in D3 is not a disposition, but the base of one. I suggest above that (2) is false. In correspondence with me, Maya Eddon and David Manley have suggested that (4) is also false.

But lines presented sideways-on to the eye, which Molyneux thinks we *can* perceive, are only one point thick. By this argument, lateral distance would be as unperceivable as outward distance.[20]

Berkeley makes better use of the premise that distance is a line presented endwise to the eye in the opening argument of the *New Theory of Vision*, sometimes called the "one-point argument:"

> It is, I think, agreed by all that distance, of itself and immediately, cannot be seen. For, distance being a line directed endwise to the eye, it projects only one point in the fund of the eye, which point remains invariably the same, whether the distance be longer or shorter. (NTV 2)

We need to furnish two premises unstated by Berkeley: (1) that a feature is perceivable only if our perceptual states vary with changes in that feature, and (2) that our perceptual states in vision are completely determined by retinal events. If we add these to Berkeley's premise (3) that retinal events do not vary with the outward distance of points perceived, we may validly conclude that distance is not perceived by sight.[21]

Each premise in this argument deserves comment.

Re (3): This premise is at best contingently true. Conceivably, closer points might "burn deeper" or affect the retina differently than remoter points. Also, what goes for points does not go for extended expanses (or volumes!), which are all we really see, and which *do* make different retinal patterns at different distances. But what Berkeley is relying on seems nonetheless to be true: retinal patterns do not uniquely determine the distance of what imprints them. It could be a small square close in or a larger one further out.[22]

Re (2): The assessment of this premise turns on the status of what Reid calls "acquired perception." Acquired perception, unlike original perception, is a function of past associations as well as current stimulation. We would need to settle the question, discussed in chapter 5, whether acquired perception qualifies as perception proper.

Re (1): This premise is appropriate if an epistemic sense of "perceive" (for which there is a requirement of reliability or sensitivity) is at issue. In other words, what the argument shows is that by sight alone we do not *know* whether objects are near or far. But is the

---

[20] For the same reason, it is an inconsistency in Abbott's *Flatland* that the women (who are line segments) can be seen broadside, but not end on. The law that they must wiggle when they walk to make themselves visible would accomplish nothing ([1884] 1984:27–29).

[21] My understanding of the argument is very nearly the same as John Stuart Mill's: "We can *see* nothing except so far as it is represented on our retina; and things which are represented on our retina exactly alike, will be seen alike. The distances of all objects from the eye, being lines directed endwise to the retina, can only project themselves upon it by single points, that is to say, exactly alike; therefore they are seen exactly alike" ([1842] 1973:116).

[22] Robert Schwartz denies that Berkeley's argument is (as I claim) an argument from underdetermination (1994:22). He says if degree of brightness varied unambiguously with distance, Berkeley would still maintain that distance is not immediately perceived. Yes; but even if Berkeley would not argue from not-P to not-C, he could still argue from P to C.

argument at all relevant to phenomenological issues, as I think it is meant to be?[23] I say no. I am quite convinced that objects *look* to me to be at various distances, and it is by no means clear that the argument dictates otherwise.[24]

The following consideration convinces me that there must be *something* wrong with Berkeley's argument: just as retinal patterns do not uniquely determine the *distance* of what imprints them, so they do not determine the *size* of what imprints them. As noted above, the same pattern could be caused by a small object nearby or large object of the same shape far away. Yet Berkeley does not conclude that there is no such thing as visible size; he holds that one line in a visual manifold can be visibly longer or shorter than another.

The same consideration arises more dramatically in the case of color. Retinal information does not uniquely determine the *color* of what produces it. Perhaps the same retinal pattern could be produced by an orange object close in or a red object farther away. (This is a made-up example of a genuine phenomenon, metamerism, under which different combinations of physical stimuli and circumstances produce the same color experiences.) Yet Berkeley is far from concluding that color is not immediately given to sight—that visual manifolds do not contain colors! On the contrary, light and colors are the only proper objects of vision (NTV 156 and 158).

So what exactly is wrong with the one-point argument? I think it may be faulted on two grounds. First, it is questionable whether underdetermination arguments show anything about the content of visual manifolds, or about how things look, as opposed to what can be known on the basis of them. Second, we now know that Berkeley's premise (3), the underdetermination premise, is false for creatures with two eyes. Perhaps the outward distance of x makes no pattern on eye 1 that unambiguously indicates the distance to x from eye 1, and similarly for eye 2; yet the outward distance of x *does* make a pattern on the joint system eye 1 + eye 2 that is different from the patterns produced by objects closer in or farther out. Such is the phenomenon of retinal disparity or stereopsis, discussed in appendix K.


# APPENDIX K

## Stereo Sue

The principles of stereo vision were discovered by Charles Wheatstone, inventor of the stereoscope, in 1838. ("Stereo" is from the Greek word for *solid*.) Wheatstone realized something that had somehow gone unnoticed by Euclid, Leonardo da Vinci, and Sir Isaac Newton: that the two eyes receive slightly different views of any object toward which both are directed, and that the amount of discrepancy between the views is a function of the distance to the

---

[23] *Pace* Atherton (1990:73–77), I take Berkeley to hold not merely that the eye cannot tell how far away things are (metric distance), but that there is no such thing as something's appearing through sight alone to be at any distance, however inexact. NTV 41 seems to me to leave little room for doubt on this score.

[24] On the other hand, Dretske makes a certain sort of covariation necessary not just for *knowledge*, but for *representation* (1995:2), and he goes on to maintain that an object *looks* F only if it is represented as being F. If he were right on both counts, we would have the materials for an argument for the NTV 2 thesis construed phenomenologically after all.

object. There is thus a way for our visual system to calculate the relative distances of objects. Moreover, there is a way our system can use this information to let us *perceive* the distance, as shown by the stereoscope. Wheatstone arranged mirrors so that each of the two eyes looking into his device saw slightly different flat images, which the viewer's brain then fused into a single object seen as a solid.

Reid understood some of the principles that are now used to explain stereo vision. He knew that when the retinal images from an object fall on corresponding regions of the retina, we see the object as single, and when they fall on noncorresponding regions, we typically see the object as double. He did not know that in a wide range of cases—those in which an object lies within Panum's fusion area, producing images on *nearly* corresponding regions—we see the object not as double, but as solid, with more than one plane of perceived depth.

It has been known since Hubel and Wiesel's experiments with cats and monkeys in the 1960s that there are binocular neurons, single neurons that respond to input from both eyes (Barry 2009:136–40). By registering retinal disparity, these neurons somehow enable us (perhaps by what Reid would have called "natural magic") to perceive depth.

"Stereo Sue" is Susan R. Barry, a professor of neurobiology at Mt. Holyoke College. Her story was first told in an article in *The New Yorker* by Oliver Sacks in 2006 and subsequently in her own book, *Fixing My Gaze*, in 2009. When Sue was three months old, she developed crossed eyes, a form of strabismus or what Reid called squint, which prevented her from fixating both eyes on the same object. Her eye alignment was subsequently corrected in surgeries at ages two, three, and seven, at least to the point where she looked normal. However, she did not have the habit of directing both eyes to the same object. She read by directing just one eye to the letters on a page and turning the other eye inward. Moreover, since she had lacked the ability to fixate the same object with both eyes during the so-called critical period in early life, it was believed that she had never developed the binocular neurons essential for stereo vision.

Sue could use monocular cues to tell how near or far things were from her. For example, she could tell that a door was turned inward because one vertical edge was longer than another, giving it a trapezoidal shape, and she could tell that a circular hollow was concave rather than convex by noting its pattern of shading. As she explains further,

> I knew that the student sitting in front of me was located between me and the blackboard because the student blocked my view of the blackboard. When I looked outside the classroom window, I knew which trees were located further away because they looked smaller than the closer ones. The footpath outside the window appeared to narrow as it extended out into the distance. (Barry 2009:3)

She did not know until learning about stereopsis in a college lecture at age twenty that she did not see in three dimensions like nearly everyone else.[25]

At age forty-seven, Sue began a course of vision therapy designed to enable her eyes to fixate the same object, conducted by behavioral optometrist Dr. Theresa Ruggiero. Sue undertook the therapy despite believing with scientific orthodoxy that since she had not developed the wherewithal for stereo vision during her critical period, she had no prospect of

---

[25] By the time she was in her forties, she knew all about the theory of stereo vision and taught it in her classes. If you substitute "depth" for "color," she was a real-life embodiment of Frank Jackson's Mary (Jackson 1986). Of course, whether there is a refutation of physicalism here is as debatable in her case as it is in Mary's.

doing so now. In one of her exercises, she practiced looking at a bead on a string stretching away from her nose until she could see the string as two strings crossing inside the bead—a sign that she was successfully directing both eyes to the same place.

Climbing into her car after a session with the string on the day after her forty-eighth birthday, Sue was startled to see the steering wheel pop out at her:

> The steering wheel was floating in its own space, with a palpable volume of empty space between the wheel and the dashboard. Curious and excited, I closed one eye and the position of the steering wheel looked "normal" again; that is, it lay flat just in front of the dashboard. I reopened the closed eye, and the steering wheel floated before me. (2009:95)

Sue had achieved stereopsis. Her case turned out not to be unique; after the Sacks article appeared, she received e-mails from hundreds of people reporting similar experiences.

Sue exulted in her new visual ability:

> Throughout the day, my stereovision would emerge—intermittently, fleetingly, unexpectedly—bringing me moments of absolute wonder and delight. The most ordinary objects looked so beautiful. A large sink faucet reached out toward me, and I thought I had never seen such a lovely arc as the arc of the faucet. The grape in my lunchtime salad was rounder and more solid than any grape I had ever seen before. I could see, not just infer, the volume of space between tree limbs, and I loved looking at, and even immersing myself in, those inviting pockets of space. (2009:95)

> The snow was falling lazily around me in large, wet flakes. I could see the space between each flake, and all the flakes together produced a beautiful three-dimensional dance. (Sacks 2006)

One thing I learned from Barry is that just as one who has never had stereo vision cannot imagine it, so a normal person cannot imagine how flat things are for the stereoblind. Closing one eye does not make things look flat: "when a normal binocular viewer closes one eye . . . he or she still uses a lifetime of past visual experiences to re-create the missing stereo information" (102). Binocular neurons are still firing even though there is input only from one eye.

The main message of Barry's book as far as she herself is concerned is that *the critical period is a myth*. There is evidence that binocular neurons are present at birth; they are quiescent rather than nonexistent in the absence of early co-ordination of the eyes, and they are revivable by appropriate exercise. But the main moral as far as I am concerned is that *Berkeley is wrong*. Everything Berkeley says is responsible for the perception of depth—all the traditional monocular cues and their association with tangible information—Sue already had before she acquired stereopsis.[26] She is a living refutation of Berkeley, who cannot account for the new dimension in Sue's life.[27]

[26] Admittedly, Sue did not have Berkeley's cue of convergence. But that is one of the least significant cues, operative only at quite near distances. It does nothing to contribute to the perceived voluminousness of the crown of the sycamore tree overhead.

[27] I venture to affirm as well that Sue is a living refutation of intentionalism, or what I am calling propositionalism. What new propositions did Sue come to be able to entertain for the first time after she achieved stereopsis?

## APPENDIX L

# Hyperbolic Claims About Hyperbolic Geometry

There is a tradition of experiment and theory in psychology (most associated with the name of R. K. Luneberg) according to which visual space is not spherical as Reid claimed, but hyperbolic. In hyperbolic geometry, a given line has many parallels through a given point rather than none, and a triangle has fewer than 180 degrees rather than more. What is to be said about the disagreement between Reid and Luneberg?

Luneberg's claims are based on a series of experiments of a type first performed by Blumenfeld in 1913. In this type of experiment, a subject sits in a darkened room with an array of tiny lights lying before him in the horizontal plane of his eyes, the two remotest lights being fixed at equal distances from the vertical median plane bisecting his field of view. He is given two tasks. In the first task, he is to arrange the lights in "parallel alleys"—two strings of lights extending toward him from the fixed lights and looking parallel. In the second task, he is to arrange the lights in such a way that they form "distance alleys"—two strings of lights in which the lights in each successively closer pair are equidistant from the median plane and just as far apart as the fixed pair. When the positions of the lights are measured afterward, it is usually found that the strings of lights the subject judged to be parallel, as well as the strings he judged to be equidistant, are actually divergent, curving outward as they get farther from where the subject was seated. Moreover, positions of the strings produced in the parallel alley task lie *inside* the positions of the strings produced in the distance alley task.

On the basis of experiments like this, Luneberg argued that the geometry of visual space is hyperbolic. The key feature of hyperbolic geometry for present purposes is this: in hyperbolic geometry, unlike Euclidean geometry, parallel lines are not everywhere equidistant— they get progressively farther apart. In other words, the properties of being parallel and being everywhere equidistant are not equivalent in hyperbolic geometry. The subject in a Blumenfeld experiment sees strings of light as parallel that he does not see as equidistant; lights he sees as forming parallel alleys would have to be rearranged for him to see them as forming distance alleys. Luneberg concluded that visual space is hyperbolic.

The hyperbolic character of visual space is not the only available explanation of Blumenfeld's results. In a chapter surveying work on this topic, Mark Wagner discusses several alternative explanations, including one I would like to report here: parallel alleys differ from distance alleys because the subjects are given different types of instruction for each task (2006, chapter 3).

In the parallel task, what is the subject asked to do? Is she asked to arrange the lights so they *look* parallel to her (regardless of their actual arrangement), or to arrange them so as to look the way they would look from her vantage point if they actually *were* parallel? (A suggestive phrase for the latter task might be "arrange them so they *look to be* parallel.") Psychologists call the former type of instruction *projective* and the latter *objective*.

(Incidentally, if subjects are given projective instructions, there is a natural explanation of why they produce divergent strings in the parallel task. When you look down railroad tracks, the rails appear to converge, and you know that in order to appear that way, they must actually be parallel. To appear parallel to you, they would actually have to diverge, the remoter ties being longer than the closer ties. Hence it is not surprising that in order to produce an arrangement in which the two lines of lights look parallel in the projective sense, the subject must set lights in remoter pairs farther apart from each other than lights in nearer pairs.)

Wagner notes that both for theoretical reasons and as confirmed by experiments designed specifically to test the effects of instructions, projective instructions should lead to alleys closer together than objective instructions. Moreover, in at least one of the Blumenfeld-type experiments (Indow and Watanabe 1984a, cited at Wagner:39), said to be typical in this regard, *projective instructions were given for the parallel alley task while objective instructions were given for the distance alley task.* This difference in instructions alone could account for the difference between the parallel and distance alleys. In a study in which instructions of the same type were used for each type of task, parallel alleys and distance alleys no longer differed (Higashiyama et al. 1990, cited at Wagner:40).

Wagner praises Luneberg's theory as an elegant and sophisticated piece of model-building, but his review makes clear that it has little going for it empirically. At most it applies to stimuli lying in a horizontal plane passing through the eyes and lying within arm's reach; even then, it is questionable in light of the alternative explanation of the data given above.

## APPENDIX M

# What Is Special About the Sphere?

In chapter 6, section 8, I advance the claim that what is special about the sphere as a surface of projection is this: among figures indistinguishable from a given visible figure, *spherical figures alone have their real angle magnitudes equal to the apparent magnitudes of the angles in the visible.* This turns out to be false, but for reasons that leave Reid's geometry of visibles unaffected. In this appendix, I explain both why it is false and why it does not matter.

Given that indistinguishable figures are alike in the apparent magnitudes of their corresponding angles, the claim I have italicized above would follow from the following proposition, once plausibly conjectured as a theorem by Gideon Yaffe:

> *Yaffe's conjecture*: If the visible magnitudes of angles in a figure f (as seen from e) are equal to the real magnitudes of angles in f, then f is a spherical figure. In particular, f is composed of segments of great circles of a sphere centered on e.

Yaffe's conjecture could be proved if we were entitled to use each of the following two lemmas:

*Lemma 1*: The real angles in a figure equal its apparent (or visible) angles (as seen from e) only when one is viewing each angle *head-on*—that is (roughly), only when the line of sight from e is orthogonal to the plane in which the angle is measured.[28]

---

[28] Here, more precisely, is what I mean by viewing an angle *head-on*: If the angle is composed of two straight lines AB and AC meeting at vertex A, then one's line of sight (i.e., the straight line connecting e with A) must be orthogonal to the plane containing AB and AC. If the angle is composed of two curved lines 1 and 2 meeting at vertex A, then one's line of sight must be orthogonal to the plane in which the angle is measured—i.e., the plane containing the straight lines tangent to 1 and 2 at A. (Recall what was said in the text about measuring angles between curved lines by the angles between their tangents.)

*Lemma 2*: One can view each of the angles in a figure head-on from a point of view e only if the figure is a spherical figure, composed of segments of great circles whose center is e.[29]

Together, these lemmas imply that if there is a point of view e such that the real angles in f equal the apparent angles in f as seen from e, then f is a spherical figure.

Unfortunately, however, both lemmas turn out to be false. Subsequent investigation has turned up counterexamples to each of them.[30]

As for Lemma 1, Yaffe has shown how to construct angles in which (surprisingly) the real magnitude and the visible magnitude as seen from e are the same even though the line from e to the plane of the angle is not orthogonal. The construction is too complex to present here, so I simply refer the reader to his article (Yaffe 2002).[31]

As for Lemma 2, figure M.1 provides a counterexample:[32]

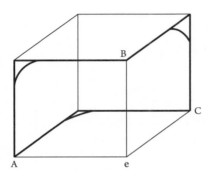

**Figure M.1**

---

There is an exception to Lemma 1 when we are dealing with right angles. Suppose I am viewing a planar angle whose real magnitude is 90 degrees, e.g., the angle between rail and tie. The apparent magnitude of this angle will equal 90 degrees just so long as my eye is either directly above the rail or directly above the tie, even if it is not directly above the point where they meet. So here the condition under which the real magnitude of the angle between AB and AC is equal to its apparent magnitude as seen from viewpoint e may be more relaxed than the head-on condition: e must lie outside the plane of AB and AC and in one of the planes erected upon either AB or AC and perpendicular to the plane containing them. This exception would not affect the use to be made of Lemma 1 provided the following were true: one can satisfy the more relaxed condition with respect to *all* the angles in a figure only if the figure is spherical.

[29] This lemma is clearly related to the fact that the following property is possessed by a surface S if and only if S is spherical: there is a point e (the center) such that the straight line from e to any point p on S is perpendicular to the tangent plane to S at p.

[30] I proposed Lemma 1 at the NEH Seminar on the Philosophy of Thomas Reid in August of 2000. On that occasion, Yaffe advanced his conjecture and suggested combining Lemma 1 with Lemma 2 to prove it. His attempts at proof led instead to counterexamples such as those reported in the text.

[31] Yaffe shows at 2002:617–18 how to find *single angles* in which real and visible magnitude are the same despite an oblique line of sight. He has suggested to me in correspondence that the same method will yield *complete figures* in which each angle as seen from e has the same visible magnitude as its real magnitude, despite not being viewed head-on.

[32] This is a variation on an example of Yaffe's in which the angles are all spherical angles (rather than flat angles as here) but there is deviation from a spherical triangle somewhere between the vertices.

In this diagram I have highlighted six edges of a cube to form a six-edged figure and then rounded off three of the corners to obtain a figure with three curved edges.[33] Imagine what this figure would look like to an eye placed at e. (To view the figure properly, assume that the face of the cube containing vertices A, B, and e is frontmost.) The eye would see visibly right angles to the left at A, to the right at C, and overhead at B. It would see the curved lines connecting A with B, B with C, and C with A as straight lines, since their curvature lies in the unseen outward dimension. Thus the Reidian eye would see the three-line system as a triangle. (It would also see the six-line system without rounded corners as a triangle.) Now the eye at e views each of the angles at A, B, and C head-on; yet the figure containing them is clearly not a spherical figure. So we have here a counterexample to Lemma 2.

The same figure serves as a counterexample to Yaffe's conjecture. The visible magnitudes of the angles at A, B, and C as seen from e are equal to the real magnitudes of these angles, which are right angles all around; yet the figure containing them is not spherical. The figure also serves as a counterexample to the claim in the first paragraph of this appendix, since it is a nonspherical figure having the same real angle magnitudes as the apparent magnitudes in a visible triangle indistinguishable from it.

Where does all this leave Reid?

First of all, even if the claim in the first paragraph is false, that does not harm Reid's case for the geometry of visibles. His case rests on the fact that spherical figures (seen from the center) enjoy equality of real and visible angle magnitudes, but it does not require that spherical figures be unique in this regard. If there are other figures that also enjoy this property (as in the counterexample), that is all right, provided the other figures have the same real angle magnitudes as the relevant spherical figure. And they do. The figure in the diagram is not a spherical figure, but it has the same angle sum—namely, 270 degrees—as the spherical figure Reid would use in assigning an angle sum to the visible figure presented to the eye.[34] So the counterexample leaves intact all of Reid's claims about the angle sums of visible figures. Nor does any other counterexample I know of jeopardize any of Reid's claims about the geometry of visibles. In short, even if some nonspherical figures represent visible figures as well as spherical figures do, the geometry of visibles is still the same as the geometry of sphericals.[35]

---

[33] Actually, neither the six straight lines nor the three rounded lines uniquely determine a figure; instead each set of lines forms the boundary of indefinitely many figures. But any of the figures bounded by these lines will do for my purposes.

[34] What about the six-edged figure that was there before we rounded three corners to get the figure in the diagram? That figure has an angle sum of 540 degrees rather than 270. This is not a problem. To reckon the angle sum of a visible, we do not sum all the angles in a representative of it; we sum only those of its angles that correspond to angles in the visible.

[35] See Yaffe 2002 for an argument that the geometry of visibles is in fact completely isomorphic to the geometry of the sphere.

What I am saying in this paragraph is that Reid's case for the geometry of visibles is not threatened by the difficulty I point out in chapter 6, section C, for the argument from indistinguishability. I criticize that argument on the ground that it would lead to the assignment of incompatible geometries to visible figures. In chapter 6, section H, I said that Reid gets around that problem by holding that we assign to visibles not the geometrical properties of *any* figures indistinguishable from them, but just those of figures that *represent* them (i.e., have real angle magnitudes equal to the apparent magnitudes of angles in the visible). Now it turns out that there are nonspherical figures that can represent visible figures. But that is all right, because using those representatives will not lead us to assign to visibles any properties incompatible with those of spherical geometry.

Second, although Reid does not claim (or need to claim) that the sphere is unique as a surface of projection for modeling the properties of visible figures, there may yet be a sense in which this is true. What the counterexamples in this appendix show is that for a given visible figure, we can find nonspherical *figures* that represent it. (Recall how we defined "figure x represents visible figure y" in chapter 6, section H: (i) x is indistinguishable from y, and (ii) the apparent magnitudes of angles in y are equal to the real magnitudes of corresponding angles in x.) Yet it may still be true that there is something special about the sphere as a *total surface* of representation. It may be, or so I conjecture, that the sphere is the only surface with the following property: *any* figure seen from a given point can be represented on it. In other words:

> *Further conjecture*: If S is a surface such that any figure seen from e can be represented by a figure on S, then S is a sphere centered on e.

If this conjecture is true, then although any visible figure may be represented by some nonspherical figure, that nonspherical figure will not lie on a surface on which *all* visible figures seen from e may be represented. The sphere alone will contain representatives of all figures seen from a given point of view. Reid says, "The whole surface of the sphere will represent the whole of visible space" (IHM 6.9:104). My conjecture is that no other surface does that.

## APPENDIX N

# Is Reid's Geometry Imaginable?

By this habit of giving so little attention to things every moment before our eyes, we become at last quite unacquainted with them; it is with great difficulty we can make them an object of thought & reflexion. Their most obvious properties surprize us & can hardly gain belief. (Thomas Reid, *1758 manuscript*[36])

If Reid is right, there are visible triangles containing three right angles. Such is the visible triangle that would be presented to the central eye by a spherical triangle composed of an arc of the equator running from due north on the horizon to due east and arcs of the lines of longitude running from those points up to the zenith. Yet I cannot imagine such a visible triangle—if I imagine the base angles as right angles, I cannot imagine the sides as meeting at all, let alone meeting at another right angle. Reid says, in effect, not to worry—we never see any triangle as large as the 90–90–90 triangle I have described. Any triangle small enough to be seen distinctly and in one view will depart only negligibly from a Euclidean triangle with an angle sum of 180 degrees. Yet I *do* worry, since even the small triangles must according to him have properties that I cannot imagine.[37]

---

[36] The quotation is from the manuscript of a discourse delivered before the Aberdeen Philosophical Society on June 14, 1758 (Brookes 276). The items whose properties surprise us are visible figures. This discourse contains the first extant fragment of the geometry of visibles (Brookes 274).
[37] I am using "imagination" as Reid does for "a conception of the appearance an object would make to the eye, if actually seen" (EIP 5.6:394; cf. 4.3:326).

If there are triangles with more than 180 degrees, there are rectangles with more than 360 degrees, so let me change my example. Reid's geometry of visibles forces us to reckon with the following inconsistent triad:

1. Some rectangles I see have four obtuse angles.
2. Whatever I see is something I can imagine.
3. I cannot imagine a rectangle with four obtuse angles.

Statement 1 must be true if Reid is right about the geometry of visibles. (For present purposes "rectangle" is to be defined as "equiangular quadrilateral." All quadrilaterals in Reid's geometry contain more than 360 degrees, so equiangular quadrilaterals must contain four obtuse angles.) Statement 2 is plausible in its own right. And statement 3 certainly seems to be true in my own case. Yet 1–3 are inconsistent, as is readily shown when they are symbolized as follows (using "Sx" for "I see x," "Rx" for "x is a rectangle," "Bx" for "x is bulgy," that is, x has four obtuse angles, and "Ix" for "I imagine x"):

1. $\exists x(Sx \& Rx \& Bx)$.
2. $(x)(Sx \to \Diamond Ix)$.
3. $(x)(Rx \& Bx \to \sim\Diamond Ix)$.

One of these three statements must be false—but which?

James Hopkins has suggested that imagination is indeterminate in a way that makes it incapable of passing verdicts on whether imagined figures are Euclidean or Riemannian (1973). If he is right, perhaps it is statement 3 that is false. Statement 3 is equivalent to "any rectangle I can imagine is nonbulgy," but if imagination is indeterminate, it may be that imagined rectangles are neither bulgy nor nonbulgy, in which case statement 3 would be false.

Another way out of the triad is suggested by Reid's observation that figures small enough to be seen in one view are not noticeably non-Euclidean. This suggests that our triad be rewritten thus:

1. Some rectangles I see have (unnoticeably) obtuse corners.
2. Whatever I see is something I can imagine.
3. I cannot imagine a rectangle with four (noticeably) obtuse corners.

Now the inconsistency has been removed. It will arise again, however, if statement 3 is true even without the parenthetical qualification—as I think it may well be. For I am inclined to think that as soon as I think of an angle that is the least bit obtuse, I see that four such angles cannot compose a rectangle.

"I see that four obtuse angles cannot compose a rectangle." In saying that bulgy rectangles are unimaginable in that sense, I am actually employing a sense of imaginability or unimaginability different from the one I started with. I began with an objectual sense in which the objects of imagination are phenomenal individuals, over which I quantified in symbolizing statements 2 and 3. The objectual sense contrasts with a sense of "imagine" in which the objects of imagination are propositional. To explicate the unimaginability of bulgy rectangles, we must move on to a propositional sense, because in the objectual sense, it is all too easily true that an individual that is both rectangular and bulgy "can be imagined by me,"[38] for the very individual that is both rectangular and bulgy might be imagined by me after it had morphed into another shape. To be sure, I cannot imagine x *while* it is rectangular and bulgy, but that suggests that the required sense of "imagine" must incorporate properties into its content—it must be a form of imagining *as* or imagining *that*.[39] There are two other reasons for moving on to a propositional sense. (i) When I imagine an F thing, is there an F thing that I imagine? On the objectual account, yes: $\exists x(Fx \& Ix)$. That is Berkeley's view—to imagine an F thing is to confront an F particular or have an F particular come before your mind. But this consequence does not go well with the indeterminacy of imagination contemplated above. Surely any actual individuals must be perfectly determinate. Berkeley insisted on just that, deriding the Lockean triangle that is neither equilateral, isosceles, nor scalene. (ii) On the objectual approach, statement 2 would imply that I can imagine specific objects in my environment—one of the very things I see (for instance, that tree over there) might be an object of my imagination. But when I imagine a tree, is it really the case that I am imagining one tree in the world as opposed to another?

Moving on, then, to a propositional sense, how shall we formalize the claim that I cannot imagine a rectangle with four obtuse corners? Here I shall use a distinction I have drawn elsewhere between strong and weak conceivability (Van Cleve 1983, developed further in Yablo 1993). To say that bulgy rectangles are inconceivable in the strong sense would be to say that I see that there cannot be items that are both rectangular and bulgy:

3. I see that $\sim\Diamond\exists x(Rx \& Bx)$.

If the "seeing" that figures in this version of 3 is veridical, 3 conflicts with 1 even without the aid of 2. Recall that 1 is

1. $\exists x(Sx \& Rx \& Bx)$.

To avoid the inconsistency, we would either have to repudiate Reid's geometry because it implies 1 or declare the "seeing" reported in 3 to be delusive.

Another possibility is that bulgy rectangles are inconceivable or unimaginable only in a weak sense—that I fail to see (even when I consider the matter) that they are possible, even though I do not positively see that they are impossible:

3. $\sim$I see that $\Diamond\exists x(Rx \& Bx)$.

Now there is no immediate conflict with 1.

Is there a formalization of 2 that still yields an inconsistent triad when combined with 1 and the most recent version of 3? The following will do: for any property F, if I see an F thing, then I see that Fs are possible. We may symbolize this as $(F)[\exists x(Sx \& Fx) \rightarrow$ I see

[38] That is, we can easily have $\exists x(Rx \& Bx \& \Diamond Ix)$, just as we can have $\exists x(Rx \& \Diamond\sim Rx)$, objects that are rectangular yet possibly not rectangular.

[39] Actually, it has occurred to me that an inconsistent triad might be formulated using objectual seeing and imagining exclusively as follows: (1) $\exists x(Sx \& Rx \& Bx)$; (2) $\exists x(Sx \& Rx \& Bx) \rightarrow \Diamond\exists x(Ix \& Rx \& Bx)$; (3) $\sim\Diamond\exists x(Ix \& Rx \& Bx)$. But there are still reasons (i) and (ii), given next in the text, for moving on to a propositional sense of imagining.

that ◊∃xFx)]. Taking "Rx & Bx" as an instance of "Fx," we would then obtain the following inconsistent triad:

1. ∃x(Sx & Rx & Bx).
2. ∃x(Sx & Rx & Bx) → I see that ◊∃x(Rx & Bx).
3. ~I see that ◊∃x(Rx & Bx).

In this version of the triad, I think we should deny statement 2. It may seem strange that we do not see the possibility of things that we see everyday, but on second thought it is not so strange. Suppose our universe contains God-knows-what unimaginable particles or extra dimensions posited by the physicists. When I see a tree, I would then see something composed of such particles and inhabiting such dimensions, yet I may not see that such things are possible.[40]

In a last attempt to generate an inconsistent triad, let us put a propositional kind of seeing in the antecedent of statement 2: if I see that there are Fs, then I see that Fs are possible. Plausible enough! But now there is no inconsistent triad unless we go propositional in statement 1 as well, saying I see that there are bulgy rectangles:

1. I see that ∃x(Rx & Bx).
2. I see that ∃x(Rx & Bx) → I see that ◊∃x(Rx & Bx).
3. ~I see that ◊∃x(Rx & Bx).

Reid would say that statement 1 is false of most people. But paradox still lurks, since Reid would have to say that he himself and those of his readers who have followed his case for the geometry of visibles do see that there are bulgy rectangles. So they had better also see that bulgy rectangles are possible—but do they? "Their most obvious properties surprise us & can hardly gain belief" (Brookes 276).

# APPENDIX O

# Forlorn Reflections

Lorne Falkenstein has mounted a severe challenge to Reid's geometry of visibles (Falkenstein, forthcoming). His challenge is based on the distinction between "viewed from the center of the sphere" and "more than that, viewed from the center of the sphere with the line of vision directed at the vertex of the angle." What is the difference between merely having a line of sight from the center and taking that line of sight? Falkenstein explains further that when one's line of vision is directed at a certain point, that point is in the axis of the eye and is in the center of the visual field of a normal subject. Let us say that such points are

---

[40] I am not saying that the "sees that" operator does not penetrate to the logical consequences of what it attaches to. Our latest statement 2 has objectual seeing in the antecedent and propositional seeing in the consequent, so there is no question about whether a propositional operator penetrates. (Thanks to Tamar Gendler for asking me to clarify this point.)

seen directly and others peripherally. He contends that some of Reid's key claims about how things appear when seen from the center of the sphere are not true when things are seen peripherally.

As a case in point, let us take Reid's claim that any segment of any great circle on a sphere will be seen by the central eye as a straight line. Suppose for the moment that the central eye has a 180-degree field of view and that it is directed at a point labeled N straight ahead on the equator. It will see the equator as a straight line running from a point W on the left to a point E on the right with N in the center. Reid claims that any other great circle segment will also be seen as straight. Consider, then, another equator, such as we would get by tilting the original equator up a bit (rotating it on the W-E axis). Let the eye rotate up so as to be directed at the midpoint of the W to E segment of this new equator. The new equator will appear straight, just as Reid says—but Falkenstein contends that the original equator will now appear curved. That is because the points W and E will remain where they were in the visual field, but the point N will now have dropped below the center of the visual field. The original equator will appear as a smile. It will not in general be possible to see each of two great circles as straight in a single view.[41]

Let us now consider the appearance to the eye of a spherical triangle formed from a segment of the equator running from N to E as base with legs running from N and E up to Z (the zenith or polar point). This spherical triangle will contain three right angles, and Reid claims that it will appear to the central eye as a triangle consisting of three straight lines and three right angles. Falkenstein claims that when the eye is directed at N, the lines NE and NZ will indeed appear as straight lines and the angle contained by them as a right angle. But he also contends, contrary to Reid, that if the eye remains directed at N, the third side, EZ, will *not* appear as straight, but as curved—for the same reason that the equator described in the previous paragraph appears as a smile when viewed peripherally.[42] If the eye rotated to fixate on E, EZ would *then* appear as straight—but NZ would no longer appear straight. Any line from E to Z that appeared as straight while NZ and NE also appeared straight and perpendicular to each other would have to meet them at visibly acute angles, or so Falkenstein avers.

If Falkenstein is right, one of the premises in the overall case for the geometry of visibles I attribute to Reid must be wrong. What would be false is the premise that *every visible triangle is indistinguishable from some spherical triangle*, as well as assumption A5 in the argument underlying it. What is true is only that for any visible triangle v, there is a spherical triangle s such that each angle in v, when viewed from the center directly, is indistinguishable from the corresponding angle of s when viewed from the center directly. But so long as the eye looks directly at just one angle, there will not be any spherical triangle with which the entire visible triangle is indistinguishable. One could put the point as follows: when the parts of a triangle are directly viewed in succession, they are indistinguishable part for part from the parts of a spherical triangle, but there is no spherical triangle from which the visible triangle

---

[41] There are exceptions—one can see the equator and a line of longitude both as straight when fixating on their intersection. But if one line of longitude appears straight, Falkenstein maintains, others will appear curved (unless one is fixating on a point where they intersect).

[42] Since the human field of view is actually less than 180 degrees, Falkenstein asks us to consider instead as E and Z points as far east and as far up as still appear in the visual field. Under this supposition, the reason for saying the third side will appear curved cannot be quite the same as in the "smily equator" case. I am not sure whether Falkenstein is right about this alternative case.

is indistinguishable as a whole. If Falkenstein is right, Reid makes the same mistake I charge against Angell and Lucas—he propounds a geometry of appearances that never appear in a single view.

Reid is not altogether in the same boat with Angell and Lucas. There remains a sense in which Reid's spherical geometry is the geometry of the single point of view (as I said in Van Cleve 2002 and chapter 6 above) and Lucas's is not. There is no one point from which each of the angles in Lucas's ceiling may be seen as it is (with the visible angles equal to the real angles), even if the eye at that point is allowed to rotate. There *is* a single point, namely the center of the sphere, from which each of the angles in a spherical figure may be seen as it is if the eye is allowed to rotate. But if the eye is *not* allowed to rotate—if we consider only what can be given in a single view—then (if Falkenstein is right) it is not the case that all the angles in a spherical figure can be seen as they are.[43]

So is Reid's case for a non-Euclidean geometry of visibles demolished? Not necessarily, for the following reason.

Falkenstein cannot take over Reid's definitions of visible figure and the kindred concepts of visible magnitude and visible position. Reid's definitions of these commodities make them a function of points in the object and one other point. Falkenstein's contentions implicitly make them all functions of points in the object and *two* other points. Let me explain.

Here is how Reid defines visible figure:

> As the real figure of a body consists in the situation of its several parts with regard to one another, so its visible figure consists in the position of its several parts with regard to the eye. (IHM 6.7:96).

Earlier on the same page, he says that the position of x with regard to the eye is given by a line from the center of the eye to x. I therefore gloss Reid's definition by saying that visible figure is given by the totality of directions from the center of the eye to points in the object. Let us now see why Falkenstein cannot adopt this definition and the related ones.

Visible figure: Recall the two great circle segments of the second paragraph of this appendix. As the eye rotates up and changes its fixation point to a point on the upper segment, Falkenstein says, the lower equatorial segment, which formerly appeared straight, will now appear curved. In other words, the visible figure of that segment will change. But its visible figure in Reid's sense has *not* changed: all the same lines still run in all the same directions from the center of the eye to points on the equator.

---

[43] In 2002, section 10, and chapter 6, section H, I claimed that Reid's geometry is the geometry of the single *point* of view, but not necessarily of the single *view*. I allowed that the eye may need to rotate in order to take in all the angles of some figures. But I did not question that Reid would be right about the visible properties of whatever angles did fit into the eye's field of view at once. That is to say, I did not anticipate the Falkensteinian objection that some angles would be seen only peripherally and therefore with properties different from what Reid claims.

In notes 34 of 2002 and 19 of chapter 6, I accused Reid of fallaciously inferring from the indistinguishability of the corresponding parts of two triangles to their having the same appearance as wholes. If Falkenstein is right, that inference is fallacious for a more damaging reason than the one I cited. I said the entire triangle might not appear at all, but did not question Reid's account of how it would appear if it did appear. Falkenstein says the entire triangle may appear, but some of it only in peripheral vision, in which case it will not have the appearance Reid says it would have.

Visible distance: If a line that formerly appeared straight now appears curved, some of its points must now appear to be closer together than before; the apparent or visible distance between them (along the straight line connecting them) must be less than before. But the visible distance between points in any pair on the equator according to Reid's definition of "visible distance" is the same as before. Reid measures the distance between two points by the size of the angle they subtend at the eye, and all these angles are the same as before, the lines enclosing them being the same. Reid makes the apparent distance from $a$ to $b$ a function just of the real locations of $a$, $b$, and the eye. Whatever it is that changes according to Falkenstein is a function of $a$, $b$, and *two* other points—the eye and the fixation point, the point from which the line of sight is directed and the point to which it is directed.

Visible location: There can be no change in the apparent distance of two points unless there is a change in the apparent location of at least one of them. If apparent distance changes with eye rotation, so must apparent location. Whereas the Reidian visible location of a point $p$ is a function only of $p$'s actual location and one other variable, the location of the eye, the visible location of $p$ for Falkenstein must be a function of $p$'s location and two other variables, the locations of the eye and the fixation point. Perhaps this was already obvious from the fact that when fixation changes, centrality changes.

For better or for worse, then, Falkenstein cannot accept Reid's definitions of the key geometrical concepts.[44] It remains an open possibility that Reid is right about the geometry of visible figures as he defines them—though how relevant his concepts are to the psychology of vision is subject to debate.

I close with one more suggestion about what Reid's geometry is the geometry *of*: it is the geometry of figures as seen by a Plotinian eye. By a Plotinian eye, I mean an eye that can see all the points in an object simultaneously, yet without peripheral distortion.[45] A Falkensteinian eye is not Plotinian, for it can see directly in only one direction at a time, all other directions being to some degree peripheral. I do not know whether a Plotinian eye is possible, but insofar as I cannot imagine the figures that would appear to such an eye (as explained in appendix N), I must have my doubts.

# APPENDIX P

# Ask Marilyn

In one of her weekly columns ("Ask Marilyn," *Parade* magazine, September 26, 1999), Marilyn Vos Savant describes an experiment that is highly relevant to the issues explored in chapter 7:

---

[44] Responding to this observation in the updated version of his conference paper (Falkenstein, forthcoming), Falkenstein says explicitly that he does not accept the Reidian definitions that make visible distance and visible figure functions of visible position alone. He finds in Helmholtz a more accurate account of the relations among these concepts.

[45] Plotinus is said to have argued from the unity of apperception to the simplicity of the soul: nothing but a single point can be a One seeing Many. What I mean by a Plotinian eye is not necessarily an eye that is punctiform in structure, but only an eye that sees all things as if from a single point, nothing but the location of that point mattering.

*I read in school that the eye sees everything upside down and that the brain turns it rightside up again. Is this true? How would one prove it?*
—*Ron Evangelista, Los Angeles, Calif.*

*It's true, and Hans G. Frommer, a reader from Mequon, Wisconsin, sent a simple proof: Go into a completely dark room with a little battery-operated cylindrical flashlight, switched off. Put the bulb end into your mouth and seal it with your lips. Then turn on the switch. Even though the flashlight is below your eyes, you will see light above your eyes. (The light penetrates some soft tissue areas above the mouth.)*

*I couldn't bring myself to try this experiment, so instead, I asked one of my assistants to do it, knowing that it would be difficult for him to say no. Hans and I were both right: Alex tried the experiment and was amazed. He also tried putting the bulb end of the flashlight directly against his forehead, closing his eyes, and then turning on the switch: he saw light below his eyes. (I don't want to think about why the light seemed to shine through his forehead.)*

* * *

Not so fastidious as Marilyn, I tried the experiment myself and got the same results as Alex: with the flashlight in my mouth, I saw a red glow above my eyes, and with the light held against my forehead, I saw a red glow below, seemingly wrapped around my chin. What does this show?

It does not show that the brain turns any images around—that we see objects erect with inverted images does not necessarily mean that. Flipping of images need not be the mechanism of seeing erect with inverted images.

The experiment does confirm Reid's "receive low, perceive high" law (and Alex's variant confirms "receive high, perceive low"). The light from the flashlight in one's mouth enters the eye cavity from below (not through the pupil) and strikes the lower portion of one's retina; thereupon it is seen as if from above.

The experiment does not decide between Reid and Berkeley$_2$. It remains to be determined whether receiving low makes us perceive high by virtue of a law of our constitution (as Reid maintains) or by virtue of past associations with touch (as Berkeley$_2$ maintains). To settle that, we should have to mix Marilyn with Molyneux, repeating the experiment on a man born blind and made to see.

## APPENDIX Q

## Stratton Overturned

In the century or so since Stratton's experiment (in which he was the only subject), there have been surprisingly few attempts to replicate his results; I know of only some half dozen. The most recent of these, published in 1999, proclaims the return of upright vision during adaptation to inverting spectacles to be a myth (Linden et al., 1999). I reproduce here the authors' abstract:

The adaptation to inverting prisms and mirror spectacles was studied in four subjects over periods of six to ten days. Subjects showed rapid adaptation of visuomotor functions, but did not report return of upright vision. The persistence of the transformed visual image was confirmed by the subjects' perception of shape from shading. No alteration of the retinotopy of early visual cortical areas was seen in the functional magnetic resonance images. These results are discussed in the context of previous claims of upright vision with inverting prisms and mirror spectacles.

The four subjects wore either inverting prisms or mirror spectacles. They rapidly achieved visuomotor adaptation, becoming able to ride bicycles, negotiate department stores, and the like. But none of them reported a return of upright vision. Moreover, the authors note that theirs is the only experiment to date in which the subjects' introspective judgments about the orientation of visual objects were tested independently—with reading and shape-from-shading tasks.

In the shape-from-shading tasks, subjects were presented with oval figures that could be seen either as eggs (convex) or cavities (concave), depending on the distribution of light and shadow. Inverting lenses reverse the light and shadows, making eggs appear as cavities and vice versa. If there is a return of upright vision for wearers of inverting lenses, the subjects should have come to judge eggs as eggs and cavities as cavities. Instead, three of the four subjects continued to make mistakes.

In the reading tasks, the subjects became better at reading "canonically presented" writing (which gave them inverted-from-normal retinal input), but did better yet with inverted writing (which gave them canonical retinal input). This confirms their reports that they continued to perceive canonically presented phrases to be oriented noncanonically (that is, turned upside down)—exactly as Reid's theory predicts.

## APPENDIX R

## A Clash Between Two Reidian Laws

When we look at a tree, two images of it are formed, one on each of our retinas. So why do we not see two trees? That question is reminiscent of another, discussed in chapter 7: given that the image formed by a tree on our retina is upside down, why do we not see the tree as upside down?

The eighteenth-century naturalist Comte de Buffon answered both questions in terms of touch and learning. Infants *do* see things double and upside down, he averred, until touch teaches them the correct number and orientation. Thereafter, they learn to interpret the inverted and doubled images as signifying erect and single objects (Wade 1998:254 and 324).

Reid gave a nativist answer to both questions. As discussed in chapter 7, he solved the inverted image problem by citing what we may call the *law of visual direction*:

> Every point of the object is seen in the direction of a right line passing from the picture of that point on the retina through the centre of the eye. (IHM 6.12:122–23)

This is the "receive low, perceive high" law. By this law, an object stimulating a point low in the retina will be perceived right from birth as high in the visual field—no learning or instruction by touch required. In similar fashion, he explained single vision with two eyes by another innate law, the *law of corresponding retinal points*. The foveae or central points of the two retinae are said to be corresponding, and so are two points of the two retinae lying in the same direction and distance from the foveae. (Corresponding points will coincide if one retina is superimposed on the other.) The law may formulated as follows:

> Now we find by experience that an object or point of an object appears single when its pictures fall upon corresponding points of the retinas, and double when they do not. (Wade 1998:266–67)

These words are actually those of Robert Smith, a writer on optics whose work Reid discusses, but Reid's own formulation is equivalent (Van Cleve 2008:2–3). The law explains the phenomenon of the finger and the candle, described at the beginning of chapter 3, section D, and portrayed in Figure R.1.

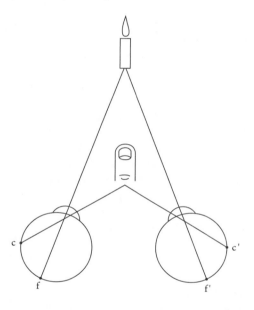

**Figure R.1**

When the eyes are focused on the candle, rays from it strike the two foveas, f and f,' which are corresponding points; hence the candle is seen as single. But rays from the finger, held up between face and candle, strike noncorresponding points, c and c', lying on opposite sides of the foveas; hence the finger is seen as double.

Each of the laws adduced by Reid does a fine job of explaining its target phenomena, but unfortunately there is an incompatibility between them. By the law of corresponding points, when we fixate a candle with both eyes, we shall see it as single. By the law of visual direction, we shall see the candle with the right eye as *over there* (on the left), while with the left eye we see it as *over there* (on the right). In other words, we shall see the candle in two different directions, or in two different places, and will therefore see it as two.[46] I first learned of this

---

[46] Reid is clear on the fact that seeing an object as single or double goes together with seeing it in one place or two: "The objects painted on those corresponding points are seen always in the same place, & so give one perception" (IHM 272; see also IHM 271, 330, and 331).

inconsistency from William James,[47] but subsequently learned from Grandi 2010 that the problem had already been pointed out in Reid's own day by William Charles Wells.[48]

What is to be done about the inconsistency? One might think to dispel it by saying that an object that is seen in two directions need not for that reason be seen in two places. One could say that an object that lies at the *intersection* of two lines of direction, one from each eye, will be seen in a single visual place; there will not be two copies of the object with visual separation between them. Wells points out, however, that to see an object as lying at the intersection of two lines of direction is in effect to see the outward distance of the object, which Reid says is not an original object of sight.[49] For Reid, the visual position of an object is given by direction alone, so an object lying in two visual directions would be seen in two places.

Wells notes another problem with the point-of-intersection resolution of the inconsistency. When we see an object through two holes in a sheet of cardboard, each eye seeing the object through its own hole, we see but one hole encircling the object.[50] If we explain our seeing the hole as single (or in one place) by the intersection strategy, we are committed to saying that we see the hole where we see the object, lying at the intersection of two lines of direction. But in fact, Wells says, we see the "united hole" as being *nearer* to us than the object.

Perhaps we should avoid the inconsistency by abandoning or revising the law of visual direction, at least in the binocular case. Wells himself proposes the following law: "Objects situated in the optic axis, do not appear to be in that line, but in the common axis" (Wade 2003:86). The common axis is the line connecting the point at which the optic axes intersect with the midpoint of the line connecting the two eyes; equivalently, it is the line bisecting the angle made by the optic axes at their intersection point. Wells's proposition implies that the candle of Figure R.1 will be seen not in two directions but one, that given by the line running from the midpoint of the line connecting the two eyes (the bridge of the nose, in effect) through the intersection of the two lines drawn from the foveae. A similar law was later advocated by Hering and Helmholtz (James 224).

Does revising the law of visual direction undermine Reid's solution to the problem of the inverted image? I believe not. An object stimulating the lower portions of the two retinae will still be seen in the upper portion of one's visual field—but fortunately in one compromise direction rather than in one upper leftward direction and another upper rightward direction.

---

[47] James discusses the law of corresponding points under the name "the theory of identical points" and the law of visual direction under the name "the projection theory" (James [1890] 1950, volume 2:222–31). He claims that the two theories are incompatible with each other, at least relative to the assumption that "the judgment of objective singleness and that of identical direction seem to hang necessarily together" (224).

[48] Wells's 1792 *An Essay upon Single Vision with Two Eyes* is reprinted in Wade 2003. Its bearing on Reid is well discussed in Grandi 2010.

[49] Wells does not explain how distance would be perceived in a phenomenological sense, but he is right in maintaining that if our visual system knew an object lay at the intersection of two lines of direction, it could compute our distance to the object.

[50] James describes a similar experiment with a pane of glass and two marks instead of a card with two holes (223).

## APPENDIX S

# Molyneux's Question Answered After 300 Years?

Although the experiments with Molyneux babies cited in chapter 8 are suggestive, it seems that nothing short of tests on adults or adolescents cured of congenital blindness would constitute direct tests of Molyneux's question. Such tests, with controls lacking in earlier and less systematic experiments, are now being conducted by Pawan Sinha and his collaborators in Project Prakash, a humanitarian and scientific project under way in India. Their first results were published in Held et al. 2011.

In India, unlike most Western countries, many children are born with curable blindness but not treated for it, owing to inadequate medical resources. Under the auspices of Project Prakash, such children are identified, operated on to cure their blindness, and (if they meet the screening requirements to be described next) recruited as subjects in Molyneux experiments. The patients are examined ophthalmologically before and after their operations, and only those are subsequently used as Molyneux subjects who (a) can see nothing more than light and dark before the operation and (b) who can discriminate visually presented shapes from each other after the operation. There is thus no question whether the subjects were sufficiently blind before the operation or whether any of them were "can't sees" afterward.

The tasks given to subjects who meet the screening requirements are as follows. They are given a Lego block of any of several shapes to hold in their hand; that object is taken away, and then it (the target) and another of a different shape (a distractor) are presented again to the subject's touch simultaneously. Can the subject say which of the two was felt previously? Next, the procedure is repeated for vision: first one shape is seen, then it and another are presented to the subject's vision simultaneously. Can the subject say which of the two was seen previously? Finally, the procedure is repeated with one initially felt Lego block (held under a sheet and out of sight) and two subsequently seen Lego blocks, one the same in shape as what was felt and the other different. Can the subject say which of the two seen objects is the same as the previously felt object? That is Sinha's version of the Molyneux question.

Concerning five subjects tested and reported on to date, the results are as follows: The subjects' success rate at matching one felt shape in a pair to a previously felt shape was very high (averaging 98 percent), as was their rate at matching one seen shape in a pair to a previously seen shape (averaging 92 percent). The fourth condition on Molyneux questions listed in chapter 8, section A, is therefore clearly satisfied: the subjects had the ability to discriminate and recognize visual shapes as well as tactual shapes. But their rate of success at matching one seen shape in a pair to a previously felt shape fell to a mean of 58 percent, which is statistically indistinguishable from chance. Sinha concludes:

> Our results suggest that the answer to Molyneux's question is likely negative. The newly sighted subjects did not exhibit an immediate transfer of their tactile shape knowledge to the visual domain. (2011:552).

He goes on to note, though, that the subjects' ability to make correct touch-to-vision transfer improved remarkably in a short period of time. I comment on the significance of this below.

I have one reservation to lodge about the significance of the Prakash results.[51] The targets and distractors used in their experiments to date are Lego blocks, which are three-dimensional objects—cubes, prisms, and other shapes with assorted projecting cylinders. As noted in chapter 8, Diderot proposed changing the Molyneux question from globe versus cube to circle versus square because he suspected that newly sighted subjects might not be able to see in three dimensions, and therefore might not be able to see any objects as having the three dimensions of objects they were familiar with by touch. This was probably the case with the Prakash subjects. The experimenters report that their tests were done within forty-eight hours of surgery *on the first eye.* Thus the subjects were presumably unable to see in depth; they lacked binocular vision, which is the most powerful mechanism of depth perception and one of the few that does not rely on cross-modal learning.

The Project Prakash experimenters tested three of the subjects again not long after the operation—five days in one case, seven days in another, and five months in the third. They found significant improvement in vision-to-touch matching, the success rate now averaging about 85 percent. Sinha mentions (but does not endorse) the possibility that the rapid improvement may be due to the subjects' acquiring the ability to construct three-dimensional visual representations. If so, that would confirm the conjecture that their initial failures to match seen and felt were due in large part to their inability to see in three dimensions,[52] and it would suggest all the more strongly the need for doing a two-dimensional variant of the experiment.

Of course, there are no strictly two-dimensional tangible objects. It may nonetheless be possible to conduct a Molyneux experiment with objects that are *effectively* two-dimensional—for example, circles and squares of fine wire that subjects are allowed to trace with their fingers. I hope the Prakash researchers conduct future experiments with two-dimensional targets and distractors. Until then, we have no direct empirical answer to Diderot's version of Molyneux's question.

# APPENDIX T

# Relative Identity

Those who believe in "relative identity" hold (i) that the question "Are x and y the same?" must always be short for "Are x and y the same F?" (where F is some appropriate sortal concept narrower than *entity* or *thing*) and (ii) that x and y can be the same F without being the same G, even though x and y are both Gs. Those who believe in absolute identity reject (i) and (ii), holding that "x and y are the same F" is simply short for "x and y are identical, period, and x is an F." Wiggins (1980) holds an in-between position—(i) without (ii).

---

[51] I ask several further questions about the experiments in Van Cleve 2014.

[52] In opposition to the conjecture, Sinha believes that the subjects still lack the ability to see in three dimensions when they do acquire the ability to match seen with felt (Held et al.:552).

An obviously bogus example of (ii), discussed in Perry 1970, would be this: pointing at a red Chevrolet and a red Ford, one says "This is the same color as that, but is not the same car." Here the first "is" probably expresses predication rather than identity; the first conjunct says that this and that *have* the same color, not that they *are* the same color. Suppose, however, that one does insist on taking the first conjunct as expressing identity. Then one is not taking "this" and "that" to refer to the same things in the two conjuncts; in the first conjunct, they refer to colors and in the second to cars. So we still do not have an example of (ii). To get a genuine example of (ii), it would have to be the selfsame x and y that are the same color according to the first conjunct but not the same car according to the second.

In other words, the item x that is the same color as y must be the same thing as the item x that is not the same car as y. It appears that we need an absolute notion of identity even to express what the relative identity theorist is trying to believe in.

In my opinion, other alleged examples of relative identity are no better at bottom than the bogus one.

Here is another difficulty for the doctrine of relative identity. Does "x is the same F as y" obey Leibniz's Law or not? That is, does x's being the same F as y guarantee that x and y have all their properties in common? If it does *not*, relative identity does not deserve the name of identity. If it *does*, claim (ii) above is demonstrably false.

Here is the demonstration, using "xSFy" as short for "x is the same F as y": Assume xSFy, Gx, and Gy. By reflexivity, xSGx. (Reflexivity is another property without which relative identity would not be identity.) Rewrite xSGx as (SGx)x, that is, x has the property of being the same G as x. (This is, in effect, Church's lambda notation.) Since xSFy and we are supposing relative identity to obey LL, y has every property x does; in particular, (SGx)y. In other words, xSGy. Q.E.D.

Since relative identity has the liabilities just noted, I do not like to attribute it to Locke. I think he disowns it himself when he says that in the case of the same oak that is not the same mass of matter, "*Identity* is not applied to the same thing" (2.27.3). I take "thing" here to mean individual, not sortal.

The price Locke must pay for eschewing relative identity is to abandon his principle at 2.27.1 that things of the same kind cannot be in the same place: the oak and the mass of matter of which it is temporarily composed are not identical, but they are of the same kind ("body") and they occupy the same place. Alternatively, he could expand his list of kinds to include not just God, finite intelligences, and bodies (2.27.2), but sortals like oak, horse, and thousands of others.

If Locke does eschew relative identity, it is inconsistent for him to say that persons are intelligent substances, yet you can have the same person where you do not have the same intelligent substance. Reid charges Locke with outright inconsistency on this point in the fourth paragraph of EIP 3.6. Hume makes the same charge of inconsistency (though not against Locke by name) in the appendix to the *Treatise*: "Is *self* the same with *substance*? If it be, how can that question have place, concerning the subsistence of self, under a change of substance?" (THN 635).

What Locke should have said (conformably to his memory theory of personal identity) is that a person is a construction out of diverse substances, but is never identical with whatever substance is its host at a given time.

# APPENDIX U

# Locke, Berkeley, Hume, and Reid on Abstract Ideas

Reid's view that the objects of conception may be nonexistent has an interesting application to the problem of abstract general ideas as discussed by Locke, Berkeley, and Hume.

It is a key tenet of Locke's philosophy that the mind has the power of forming abstract general ideas—abstract in the sense that they are not fully specific or determinate, but merely generic, and general in the sense that they are ideas of features that can be present in many things. Abstractness arguably goes along with generality at a certain level.[53] As Locke says in a famous passage,

> Does it not require some pains and skill to form the *general idea of a triangle* . . . for it must be neither oblique nor rectangle, neither equilateral, equicrural, nor scalenon, but all and none of these at once. (ECHU 4.7.9)

Berkeley ridiculed this passage in his polemic against abstract ideas. Believing it impossible that any triangle should fail to have a definite number of degrees in each of its angles (and more generally, that any existing thing could be less than fully determinate), he declared that we cannot really conceive of any such thing as a triangle in general. We can only conceive of particular triangles, which may nonetheless serve as representatives in our thinking of all triangles. In this he was followed by Hume.

On this issue, Reid writes, "Mr. Locke and his two antagonists have divided the truth between them" (EIP 5.6:394). Locke saw clearly "that the power of forming abstract and general conceptions is one of the most distinguishing powers of the human mind," but he did not see "that this power is perfectly irreconcileable to his doctrine concerning ideas" (395). Berkeley and Hume "saw this inconsistency; but instead of rejecting the hypothesis of ideas, they explain away the power of abstraction" (395).

To see how Locke and his critics "divided the truth between them," consider the following inconsistent triad of propositions:

1. We are sometimes aware in thought of the general and the abstract—in Reid's terminology, we have the power of forming abstract and general conceptions.
2. We can only be aware of what exists: "in all of the operations of the understanding, there must be an object of thought, which really exists while we think of it" (EIP 4.2:12).
3. General entities have no existence: "every thing that really exists is an individual" (EIP 5.6:393).

As Reid saw it, Locke accepted both 1 and 2 and was therefore driven to deny 3, despite his affirmation of it elsewhere. He posited "abstract general ideas," such as the infamous

---

[53] It is arguable, but not incontestable, that generality implies abstractness. If you believe that a description that is perfectly determinate in every respect must home in on just one object, you agree with (the contrapositive of) this implication, but otherwise you believe that a property could be general (multiply instantiable) without being abstract (indeterminate in some respect).

image of a triangle that is neither equilateral nor equicrural nor scalene, as merely generic entities existing in the mind. Berkeley and Hume, on the other hand, both accepted 2 and 3, and were led in consequence to reject 1. Not believing that entities such as Locke's merely generic triangle could exist even in the mind, they denied that we are ever aware of general entities. Thus were born their attempts to explain how we can think generally (for example, in proving propositions about all triangles) by means of ideas that are perfectly particular.

Reid's novelty is to deny proposition 2, which he castigates as one of the prejudices giving rise to the theory of ideas. It led all three of his predecessors in the British Empiricist tradition to affirm that the immediate object of awareness, in conception as well as in perception, must be an idea. By denying 2, Reid was enabled to uphold both 1 and 3, thus collecting together the truths his predecessors had divided between them.

## APPENDIX V

## The First Principles of Contingent Truths

I list below the twelve principles that Reid states in the chapter entitled "The First Principles of Contingent Truths" (EIP 6.5). A somewhat different but substantially overlapping list is given in "Principles Taken for Granted" (EIP 1.2).

One should not automatically assume, as many writers on Reid do, that the first principles of contingent truths are themselves contingent. Principle 2 below—that thoughts require a thinker—is pretty clearly necessary; indeed, it appears also in Reid's list of the first principles of necessary truths.[54] There is no contradiction in its appearing in both lists. "The first principles of necessary truths" are so called because they are axioms that are themselves necessary truths; "the first principles of contingent truths" are so called because they are principles that make knowledge of contingent truths possible, regardless of their own modal status.

1. First, then, I hold, as a first principle, the existence of every thing of which I am conscious.
2. Another first principle, I think, is, that the thoughts of which I am conscious, are the thoughts of a being which I call myself, my mind, my person.
3. Another first principle I take to be, that those things did really happen which I distinctly remember.
4. Another first principle is our own personal identity and continued existence, as far back as we remember any thing distinctly.
5. Another first principle is, that those things do really exist which we distinctly perceive by our senses, and are what we perceive them to be.

[54] Jack Lyons has called my attention to a subtle difference between the formulations of the principle I say occurs twice: in the principles of necessary truths, we have "the thoughts we are conscious of must have a subject, which we call mind" (EIP 6.6:495); in the principles of contingent truths, we have "the thoughts of which I am conscious, are the thoughts of a being which I call myself" (EIP 6.5:472). I doubt, however, that Reid really meant any difference between mind and myself, and if he did, I cannot see that it would make for any difference in modal status.

6. Another first principle, I think, is, that we have some degree of power over our actions, and the determinations of our will.

7. Another first principle is, that the natural faculties, by which we distinguish truth from error, are not fallacious.

8. Another first principle relating to existence, is, that there is life and intelligence in our fellow men with whom we converse.

9. Another first principle I take to be, that certain features of the countenance, sounds of the voice, and gestures of the body, indicate certain thoughts and dispositions of mind.

10. Another first principle, appears to me to be, that there is a certain regard due to human testimony in matters of fact, and even to human authority in matters of opinion.

11. There are many events depending upon the will of man, in which there is a self-evident probability, greater or less, according to circumstances.

12. The last principle of contingent truths I mention, is, that, in the phenomena of nature, what is to be, will probably be like to what has been in similar circumstances.

In EIP 6.5 he offers a companion list of the first principles of necessary truths, which belong to six different categories: grammar, logic, mathematics, taste, morals, and metaphysics.


## APPENDIX W

# Reid on the First Principle(s) of Descartes

In EIP 6.7, "Opinions Ancient and Modern about First Principles," Reid discusses the systems of Aristotle and Descartes. He tells us that Aristotle set the foundations of knowledge too wide, adopting as first principles many principles that were not properly such, whereas Descartes made the foundations too narrow, trying to get by with but a single first principle, regarding consciousness. It is clear that Reid takes the first principle he attributes to Descartes to be the same as his own principle about consciousness; he faults Descartes only for not admitting other first principles as well. In the hope that by paying close attention to what Reid says about Descartes's first principle we may learn more about how to understand his own, I offer here a commentary on Reid's discussion of Descartes, referring to selected paragraphs in EIP 6.7 by number. The results as they bear on the 1.1 reading of Reid's principle about consciousness versus the 1.2 reading are inconclusive, but instructive nonetheless.

Paragraph 21: Reid tells us that the first principle underlying Descartes's certainty in the premise of his famous enthymeme, *cogito ergo sum*, was this: "those doubts, and thoughts, and reasonings, of which he was conscious, did certainly exist, and that his consciousness put their existence beyond all doubt." That sounds like the 1.1 first principle, $(p)(Cp \rightarrow p)$,[55] but there is an important difference: the consequent of the principle attributes not just truth but *certainty*, an epistemic property. That is more in keeping with 1.2.

Paragraph 22: Reid says it might have been objected to Descartes's first principle, "How do you know that your consciousness cannot deceive you?" That sounds like an objection to

[55] What I mean by "the 1.1 first principle" is the principle that is a first principle *according to* 1.1, viz., $(p)(Cp \rightarrow p)$, rather than 1.1 itself.

the 1.1 first principle. It would be an objection to 1.2 only if being a first principle implies being true.

Paragraph 23: Reid says that the only reply to the foregoing objection is that "we find it impossible to doubt of things of which we are conscious." I take him to be saying that whenever we are conscious of some particular fact, we cannot doubt the truth of that fact. If indubitability is a mark of truth, what he says would support the 1.1 principle; if indubitability is a mark of first principles, it would support 1.2.

Paragraph 24: Descartes was justified "in assuming, as a first principle, the existence of thought, of which he was conscious." This formulation has the same ambiguity I have noted in Reid's formulation of his own Principle 1: it could be taken either as 1.1 or as 1.2.

Paragraph 25: Descartes believed that "upon this one first principle, he could support the whole fabric of human knowledge." If there is indeed only *one* first principle, it must be formulated as in 1.1—a single general principle rather than a battery of particular principles.

Paragraph 29: Descartes admitted "no other first principle of contingent truths besides that of consciousness." Here again we have the argument from uniqueness for 1.1: if 1.2 rather than 1.1 had been Reid's intended formulation, what he should have said is that Descartes admitted "no other first *principles* [plural] besides *those* of consciousness."

Paragraph 30: Reid says that Descartes was committed to holding that "even mathematical axioms require proof," since our knowledge of them depends on the nonfallaciousness of our faculties, which Descartes endeavored to prove by argument. Well, Reid himself would be committed to the same unpalatable result—that mathematical axioms are not really axioms—if the nonfallaciousness of our faculties were necessary as a premise we use in coming to know them. It would not matter whether the premise was immediately evident or itself in need of demonstration. So if Reid is to hold (as he does) that mathematical axioms are first principles, the principle that makes our knowledge of them possible had better be a principle of evidence, like 1.2, rather than a principle of truth, like the 1.1 principle. (Recall what was said about this distinction in sections E and H of chapter 11: principles of truth contribute to our knowledge only if they are themselves known, whereas principles of evidence contribute to our knowledge merely by being true.)

At the end of paragraph 30, Reid notes that Descartes's followers "agree in maintaining that knowledge of our own existence is the first and fundamental principle from which all knowledge must be deduced." "*The* first principle" suggests 1.1, but since the *content* of the principle ("our own existence") is singular, we also have a pointer toward 1.2.

Paragraph 31: Descartes "sought only one first principle as the foundation of all our knowledge"—here is another occasion for the argument from uniqueness for 1.1.

Paragraph 32: "This, therefore, may be considered as the spirit of modern philosophy, to allow of no first principles of contingent truths but this one, that the thoughts and operations of our own minds, of which we are conscious, are self-evidently real and true; but that every thing else that is contingent is to be proved by argument." Here again there is said to be just one principle, but note what it is: if we are conscious that p, then it is true *and self-evident* that p. Since self-evidence is the prime mark of a first principle, what we are really getting here is a single epistemic principle that specifies a multitude of first principles, in the style of 1.2. In further confirmation of the 1.2 reading, note that he is implying that for modern philosophy, propositions about the thoughts and operations that are taking place in our minds do not need proof—in other words, that particular propositions are first principles.

Paragraph 32 suggests the possibility that Reid may have envisioned a principle in which epistemic operators occur *twice*: it is a first principle (i.e., a self-evident truth) that all deliverances of consciousness are self-evident (i.e., are first principles). The question of 1.1 versus 1.2 is the question of where to place the epistemic operator "it is a first principle that" in relation to the formula "$(p)(Cp \rightarrow p)$"—in front of the entire formula or prefixed to its consequent. Dale Tuggy has suggested that it should go in *both* places, and paragraph 32 is one passage that bears him out. My main concern is to argue that the operator should go *at least* in the inside position—for that is what particularism requires—regardless of whether it also goes in the outside position.

Paragraph 33: "The existence of a material world, and of what we perceive by our senses, is not self-evident, according to this philosophy." Since Reid is marking a contrast between Descartes's philosophy and his own, he is saying here that *the existence of what we perceive by our senses is self-evident*. That formula has the crucial ambiguity again; it could be taken either as 5.1 or 5.2.

Paragraph 48: The existence of a material world "surely ought to be received as a first principle, if anything be, beyond what we are conscious of." "What we are conscious of" is of course a great many things, which suggests 1.2.

Paragraph 74: Reid cites as a first principle implicitly used by Locke, "That my feeling pain, or being conscious of pain, is a certain evidence of the real existence of that pain." Here an epistemic term occurs in the consequent of the principle, as happens in 1.2.

Paragraph 96: The Cartesians admit "no other first principle with regard to the existence of things but their own existence, and the existence of those operations of mind of which they are conscious." The second clause by itself is perhaps ambiguous as to whether the first principles are particular or general, but when we set it alongside the first, it seems likely that Reid has the Cartesians accepting many particular first principles, exactly as 1.2 would have it.

In summary, our attempt to decide between 1.1 and 1.2 using textual clues in EIP 6.7 has been inconclusive. Considerations that favor 1.1 (e.g., the singleness of Descartes's first principle) occur side by side and sometimes even in the same sentence with considerations that favor 1.2 (e.g., the occurrence of epistemic terms in the consequent of the principle). Perhaps Reid was not entirely clear in his own mind about the distinction. However, some of the points he makes against Descartes—for example, that Descartes implicitly denied that mathematical axioms are first principles—show that Reid *ought* to have favored the 1.2 style, even if he did not do so unequivocally.

## APPENDIX X

## Rowe's Regress

The infinite regress of exertions alleged against Reid by Rowe (1991:147–48) may be developed in a formal argument as follows:

1. S wills A freely (initial supposition).
2. Her so willing is an event—call it W.

3. Every event has a cause (Reidian causal principle).
4. Free willings (and other free doings) are caused by their agent (from Reid's account of freedom).
5. S causes W (from 1–4).
6. (X) (S causes X → S exerts her power to bring about X) (one of the conditions in Reid's account of agent causation).
7. S exerts her power to bring about W (from 5 and 6).
8. (X) (S exerts her power to bring about X → there is an event, call it EX, distinct from X, of S's exerting her power to bring about X) (premise).
9. There is an event, call it EW, ≠ W, of S's exerting her power to bring about W (from 7 and 8).
10. EW has a cause (from 9 and 3).
11. S caused EW (from 10, 4, and the unstated premise that EW is a free doing, which it presumably must be if W is free).
12. S exerts her power to bring about EW (from 11 and 6).
13. There is an event, call it EEW, ≠ EW, of S's exerting her power to bring about EW (from 12 and 8).
14. There is an event, call it EEEW, ≠ EEW, of S's exerting her power to bring about EEW (by reasoning similar to that in 9–13, which may now be repeated ad infinitum, assuming we rule out circles in the production of exertions).
15. Therefore, whenever S wills anything freely, there is an infinite series of exertions.

The responses discussed in chapter 15 may be classified according to which premise (if any) they deny.

> Accept the conclusion: Chisholm 1969 (in regard to "undertakings").
> Deny 3: Rowe 1991:154–59.
> Deny 6: Rowe (1987) 1995; Hoffman 2006.
> Deny 8 because EX is not an event: Rowe 1991:149–54 (nominally); O'Connor 2000.
> Deny 8 because EX is not always a *distinct* event: Yaffe 2004.

Premise 2 and premise 8 minus its distinctness clause are arguably implied by Reid's ontology of tropes. If when a sheet of paper is white, there is such a thing as the whiteness of the paper, then when S wills A, there should be such a thing as the willing of A by S—an event. (See EIP 5.3:367 on Reid's commitment to tropes and Bennett 2002 on the trope theory of events.).

In chapter 14, section D, I consider whether volitions (willings) should be considered as effects of exertions or identical with them, finding reason to favor the former. If instead willings were identified with exertings, the regress of exertions generated in the argument above would be a regress of willings. Something like the Hobbes-Locke-Edwards objection to libertarianism would be resurrected.

In chapter 15, section F, I propose to block the regress objection to agent causal theories in general by identifying an agent's causing of an event with his causing of his causing it. If we applied a similar strategy to the regress of exertions, we would deny the distinctness clause in premise 8, holding that exerting one's power to bring about an exertion is none other than the original exertion. We would not be falling in with Yaffe's view, however, because we would not be identifying willing to φ with trying to φ and successful trying with φ-ing.

# APPENDIX Y

# Volition and Undertaking

Roderick Chisholm (1969) has set forth a theory of action using the concepts of *undertaking* and *making happen*, which may be compared instructively with Reid's notions of volition and efficient causation.

Chisholm's fundamental undefined locution is 'He makes it happen that p in the endeavor that q,' which we may abbreviate as M(p,q). It is governed by the following axioms among others:

(A1)  M(p,q) → ∃p∃qM(p,q).

This tells us that we may quantify into the places filled by propositional variables.

(A2)  M(p,q) → p.

This tells us that if you make something happen in a certain endeavor, it does happen. The *object* of your endeavor need not happen, however; we do not have M(p,q) → q. We may be reminded here of Taylor's contention that *trying* is succeeding at one thing in the endeavor to achieve another.[56]

(A3)  M(p,q) → M(M(p,q),q).

This implies that whenever you make something happen, you also make it happen that you make it happen. Chisholm thus explicitly embraces something very like the regress of agent causation discussed in chapter 15, section F.

Other concepts may now be defined.

(D1)  He undertakes to make it happen that q (= Uq) = df ∃pM(p,q).
(D2)  He makes it happen that q (= Mq) = df ∃pM(q,p).

From these definitions, we learn that if there is something you undertake to make happen (∃qUq), there is something (though not necessarily the same thing) you make happen (∃qMq). Conversely, if there is something you make happen, there is something (though not necessarily the same thing) that you undertake to make happen. If you do either of these equivalent things, Chisholm says, you act and you are an agent cause.[57]

(D2) implies that all making happen is done in some endeavor or, in other words, that it has an object. This is a very Reidian point; it implies that we cannot say that a stone makes it happen that a window breaks. Note also that because all making happen is done in some

---

[56] Trying to bring it about that q would be symbolized as ∃pM(p,q), which implies p.
[57] This is not to say that M(p,q) implies that the agent is an agent cause of *p*. To be an agent cause of p, you must make p happen without making happen any other event that causes p to happen.

endeavor, it cannot be said that an agent's making something happen, even when it is uncaused by any further event, is capricious or inexplicable.

That making happen always has an object is a consequence of the fact that the operator "M(___, . . .)" is intentional in regard to its second place. I mean "intentional" in the sense of intentionality or object-directedness, not necessarily in the sense of intending or doing things intentionally. The latter concept is defined next:

(D3)  He intentionally makes it happen that p (= Ip) = df M(p,p).

Acting intentionally in this sense does not yet mean acting with a purpose, which receives a more complicated definition:

(D4)  He makes it happen that p for the purpose of making it happen that q = df M(p,[p & q & Up causes it to be the case that q]).

There is one major difference between Chisholm and Reid. Chisholm's operator "M(___, . . .)," though intentional in regard to its second place, is *not* intentional in regard to its first place. One can make p happen in the endeavor that q happen without entertaining or even being capable of entertaining the thought that p.[58] In other words, the concepts of causing and having an intentional object come apart; though combined in the same operator, they are separately targeted. For Reid, by contrast, being an efficient cause of X is willing X, and willing X requires conceiving X. There can be no causing of states of affairs you never entertain.

This difference allows Chisholm to give a response very different from Reid's to the puzzle of the unknown neural causes of our bodily motions. In chapter 14, section D, I aired the worry that Reid could not regard the motion of his limbs as anything he makes happen, since he is not the cause of the nerve impulses and muscle contractions leading up to it. The worry may actually be raised in a more extreme form as the worry that none of us ever makes *anything* happen, as follows:

1. If I make anything happen, there must be some things I make happen *directly*—that is, there must be some events or states of affairs I make happen without having first to make happen other events that cause them. (Otherwise, there would be a vicious infinite regress; I could never make anything happen without making something else happen first.) The things I make happen directly are the things of which I am the agent cause.
2. If I make anything happen directly, I must have some conception of that which I make happen directly.
3. In fact, I have *no* conception of the things I make happen directly.
4. Therefore, there is nothing I make happen (and nothing of which I am the agent cause).

---

[58] This obviates one objection to the infinite regress of agent causings discussed in chapter 15, section F. The agent would not need to entertain all of the successively more complicated states of affairs in the "makes it happen that ___" slot, but only the constant state of affairs in the "in the endeavor that . . ." slot.

Chisholm and Reid both accept the first premise and reject the conclusion. Reid avoids the conclusion by denying the third premise. As I represented him in chapter 14, section D, he allows that there are many events in the causal chain leading to the motion of my arm of which I am ignorant, but there is one event right at the head of the chain that I know well: a volition, happening prior to anything physical. That is what I directly cause, and I do have a conception of it.

Chisholm instead denies the second premise. He need not insert a special mental event at the head of the causal chain leading to my arm's going up, since he allows that the things I make happen in my various endeavors may be things of which I have no conception—neuron firings, sloshings of animal spirits, or what have you.[59]

Chisholm's "M" apparatus gives him the wherewithal for an ingenious solution to another problem as well. He formulates the problem thus:

> If [a man] has learned what the muscle motions are that cause his arm to go up and if he wishes to produce those motions, he can do so by raising his arm. But how can this be if they are what cause his arm to go up? (1969:216)

He answers as follows:

> The man who moves his muscles by raising his arm makes it happen that his arm goes up for the purpose of making it happen that his muscles move. This means that he under-takes to make it happen that his *endeavor* to make the arm go up will make it happen that the muscles move. (1969:216)

Expanding in accordance with D4, he makes his arm go up in the endeavor that (his arm goes up and his muscles move and his undertaking to make his arm go up causes his muscles to move). The man is exploiting a common cause of his muscles' moving and his arm's going up: his undertaking to make his arm go up.

I wonder if paradox lurks hereabouts. Presumably, there is a neurophysiological em-bodiment of undertaking to make your arm go up. Could you make *that* happen by raising your arm?

---

[59] Chisholm's own formulation of the argument 1–4 and his response to it are muddled, or at least confusing (1969:217). He states premise 1 by saying that if I make anything happen, there must be *basic* actions. That is an equivalent formulation of premise 1 in *one* sense of "basic action." He then faults the argument for assuming in a subsequent step that if an action is caused by physi-ological events, it cannot be basic. This assumption is false, he says, if "basic action" is defined as in his D7: roughly, as making something happen without undertaking to make anything else happen *for the purpose* of making the original thing happen. Yes; but that is not the sense of "basic" he uses in stating premise 1. Chisholm has changed the meaning of "basic" in midstream. If he keeps to the premise 1 sense of "basic," he should say what I say in the text: that I may directly make happen things of which I have no conception.

# APPENDIX Z

# Reid, Chisholm, Taylor, and Ginet

Table Z.1 below summarizes the views of Reid and three contemporary action theorists who have been significantly influenced by Reid—Roderick Chisholm, Richard Taylor, and Carl Ginet (Chisholm 1964 and 1969, Taylor 1966, Ginet 1990). A question mark indicates that the philosopher is officially agnostic.

**Table Z.1**

|  | *Reid* | *Chisholm* | *Taylor* | *Ginet* |
|---|---|---|---|---|
| Does every event have a cause— either an agent cause or an event cause? (Determinism$_1$) | Yes | Yes | ? | No |
| Are the same total antecedents always followed by the same total sequel? (Determinism$_2$) | No | No | ? | No |
| Are volitions ingredients in actions? | Yes | Yes | No | Yes |
| Is agent causation an ingredient in actions? | Yes | Yes | Yes | No |
| Are there any inanimate agents? | No | No | No | N.A. |
| Is freedom compatible with determinism$_2$? | No | No | No | No |
| May actions have external causes? | No | No | Yes | No |
| Are there anomic explanations of actions? | Yes | Yes | Yes | Yes |

I consider all three contemporary philosophers to be Reidians to some extent because all are incompatibilists and all find some place for the anomic explanation of action.

Chisholm agrees with Reid in finding both volition and agent causation to be ingredients in action. He does not use the language of volition, but his notion of undertaking plays much the same role as volition—it is a mental event with intentional content that serves as the cause or core of every action (see appendix Y).

Taylor and Ginet both split the difference with Reid, Taylor taking aboard the notion of agent causation as essential to action but repudiating volitions and Ginet doing the opposite.

Chisholm is the most thoroughgoing Reidian of all, agreeing with Reid on all eight questions.

# WORKS CITED

## 1. Works by Reid and Other Classical Authors through Mill

Works with well-known initials are cited by initials rather than dates, as indicated below.

Arnauld, Antoine. (1683) 1990. *On True and False Ideas*. Translated by Stephen Gaukroger. Manchester: Manchester University Press.

Berkeley, George. 1948–50. *The Works of George Berkeley*. Edited by A. Luce and T. Jessop. London: Nelson and Sons.

Berkeley, George. 1975. *Philosophical Works, including the Works on Vision*. Edited by M. R. Ayers. London: J. M. Dent. (Individual works by Berkeley are cited as follows: *Essay Towards a New Theory of Vision* as NTV, *The Theory of Vision, or Visual Language Vindicated and Explained* as TVV, *Principles Concerning Human Knowledge* as PHK, and *Three Dialogues Between Hylas and Philonous* as DHP.)

Condillac, Abbé de, Etienne Bonnot. (1754) 1982. *A Treatise on Sensations*. Translated by Franklin Philip. In *Philosophical Writings of Etienne Bonnot, Abbé de Condillac*. Two volumes. Hillsdale, NJ: Lawrence Erlbaum.

Descartes, René. 1911. *The Philosophical Works of Descartes*. Two volumes. Translated by Elizabeth S. Haldane and G. R. T. Ross. Cambridge: Cambridge University Press.

Descartes, René. 1984. *The Philosophical Writings of Descartes*, Vol. II. Translated by John Cottingham, Robert Stoothoff, and Dugald Murdoch. Cambridge: Cambridge University Press.

Descartes, René 1991. *The Philosophical Writings of Descartes*, Vol. III. Translated by John Cottingham, Robert Stoothoff, Dugald Murdoch, and Anthony Kenny. Cambridge: Cambridge University Press.

Edwards, Jonathan. (1754) 2012. *Freedom of the Will*. Mineola, NY: Dover.

Hobbes, Thomas. (1651) 1962. *Leviathan*. Edited by Michael Oakeshott. New York: Simon and Schuster.

Hobbes, Thomas. (1654) 1962. *Of Liberty and Necessity*. In *The English Works of Thomas Hobbes*, Vol. IV. Edited by Sir William Molesworth. Scienta Aalen (reprint of 1840 edition).

d'Holbach, Baron. (1770) 2008. "We Are Never Free: An Excerpt from *The System of Nature*." In *Metaphysics: The Big Questions*, 2nd edition. Edited by Peter van Inwagen and Dean W. Zimmerman, 413–19. Oxford: Blackwell.

Hume, David. (1739–40) 1978. *A Treatise of Human Nature*, 2nd edition. Edited by L. A. Selby-Bigge with notes by P. H. Nidditch. Oxford: Clarendon Press. Cited as THN.

Hume, David. (1748) 1975. *An Enquiry Concerning Human Understanding*. In *Enquiries Concerning Human Understanding and the Principles of Morals*, 3rd edition. Edited by L. A. Selby-Bigge with notes by P. H. Nidditch. Oxford: Clarendon Press. Cited as EHU.

Hume, David. (1751) 1975. *An Enquiry Concerning the Principles of Morals*. In the previous volume. Cited as EPM.

Kant, Immanuel. (1768) 2003. "Concerning the Ultimate Ground of the Differentiation of Directions in Space." In *Theoretical Philosophy, 1755–1770*. Edited by David Walford and Ralf Meerbote, 361–72. Cambridge: Cambridge University Press.

Kant, Immanuel. (1781 and 1787) 1929. *Critique of Pure Reason*. Translated by Norman Kemp Smith. London: Macmillan. Cited as CPR.

Kant, Immanuel. (1783) 1950. *Prolegomena to Any Future Metaphysics*. Translated by Lewis W. Beck. Indianapolis: Bobbs-Merrill.

Leibniz, G. W. (1765) 1981. *New Essays on Human Understanding*. Translated and edited by Peter Remnant and Jonathan Bennett. Cambridge: Cambridge University Press. (A draft of this work was complete in 1704.)

Locke, John. (1690, 1694) 1975. *An Essay Concerning Human Understanding*. Edited by Peter Nidditch. Oxford: Clarendon Press. Cited as ECHU.

Malebranche, Nicholas. (1674–75, 1680, 1688) 1992. *Philosophical Selections*. Edited by Steven Nadler. Indianapolis: Hackett.

Mill, John Stuart. (1842) 1973. "Bailey on Berkeley's Theory of Vision." In *Dissertations and Discussions*, 84–119. New York: Haskell House.

Mill, John Stuart. 1865. *An Examination of Sir William Hamilton's Philosophy*. Boston: W. V. Spencer.

Price, Richard. (1758) 1991. *A Review of the Principal Questions in Morals*. In *British Moralists 1650–1800*. Edited by D. D. Raphael, 132–98. Indianapolis: Hackett.

Priestley, Joseph. 1777. *The Doctrine of Philosophical Necessity Illustrated: being An Appendix to the Disquisitions Relating to Matter and Spirit*. London: J. Johnson.

Reid, Thomas. (1764) 1970. *An Inquiry into the Human Mind*. Edited with an introduction by Timothy Duggan. Chicago: University of Chicago Press.

Reid, Thomas. (1764) 1997. *An Inquiry into the Human Mind on the Principles of Common Sense*. Edited by Derek R. Brookes. Edinburgh: Edinburgh University Press. Cited as IHM. (References in the text to IHM without section numbers are references to supplementary materials included in the Brookes edition of the *Inquiry*, such as excerpts from Reid's unpublished manuscripts.)

Reid, Thomas. (1785) 1969. *Essays on the Intellectual Powers of Man*. Introduced by Baruch A. Brody. Cambridge, MA: MIT Press. Cited as Brody.

Reid, Thomas. (1785) 2002. *Essays on the Intellectual Powers of Man*. Edited by Derek R. Brookes. University Park: Pennsylvania State University Press. Cited as EIP.

Reid, Thomas. (1788) 2010. *Essays on the Active Powers of Man*. Edited by Knud Haakonssen and James A. Harris. University Park: Pennsylvania State University Press. Cited as EAP.

Reid, Thomas. (1792) 2001. "Of Power." *Philosophical Quarterly*, 51:3–12.

Reid, Thomas. 1895. *The Works of Thomas Reid, D.D. with Notes and Supplementary Dissertations by Sir William Hamilton*, 8th edition. Edinburgh: James Thin. Reprint edition by Georg Olms Verlag, Hildesheim, 1983. Cited as Hamilton.

Reid, Thomas. 1989. *The Philosophical Orations of Thomas Reid*. Edited by D. D. Todd. Carbondale: Southern Illinois University Press.

Reid, Thomas. 2002. *The Correspondence of Thomas Reid*. Edited by Paul Wood. University Park: Pennsylvania State University Press. Cited as COR.

Smith, Adam. (ca. 1745) 1980. "Of the External Senses." In *Essays on Philosophical Subjects*. Edited by W. P. D. Wightman and J. C. Bryce, 135–68. Oxford: Clarendon.

Wells. (1792) 2003. *An Essay upon Single Vision with Two Eyes*. Reprinted in *Destined for Distinguished Oblivion: The Scientific Vision of William Charles Wells (1757–1817)*, edited by Nicholas J. Wade,72–117. New York: Kluwer Academic/Plenum Publishers.

## 2. Works by More Recent Authors

Abbott, Edwin A. (1884) 1984. *Flatland*. New York: Signet Classics.

Ainslie, Donald. 2008. "Hume's Perceptions." Presented at the 35th Annual Hume Society Conference in Iceland in August 2008.

Alston, William P. 1971. "Varieties of Privileged Access." *American Philosophical Quarterly*, 8:223–41.

Alston, William P. 1985. "Thomas Reid on Epistemic Principles." *History of Philosophy Quarterly*, 2:435–52.

Alston, William P. 1986a. "Epistemic Circularity." *Philosophy and Phenomenological Research*, 47:1–30.

Alston, William P. 1986b. "Internalism and Externalism in Epistemology." *Philosophical Topics*, 14:179–221.

Alston, William P. 1989. "Reid on Perception and Conception." In *The Philosophy of Thomas Reid*. Edited by Melvin Dalgarno and Eric Matthews, 35–47. Dordrecht: Kluwer Academic.

Alston, William P. 1999. "Back to the Theory of Appearing." *Philosophical Perspectives*, 13:181–203.

Alvarez, Maria and John Hyman. 1998. "Agents and Their Actions." *Philosophy*, 73:219–45.

Angell, R. B. 1974. "The Geometry of Visibles." *Nous*, 8:87–117.

Anscombe, Elizabeth. 1957. *Intention*. Oxford: Blackwell.

Anscombe, Elizabeth. (1965) 1981. "The Intentionality of Sensation: A Grammatical Feature." In *Metaphysics and the Philosophy of Mind*, pp. 3–20. Reprinted from R. J. Butler (ed.), *Analytical Philosophy*, second series, Oxford University Press, 1965.

Armstrong, D. M. 1960. *Berkeley's Theory of Vision*. Melbourne: Melbourne University Press.

Armstrong, D. M. 1968. *A Materialist Theory of the Mind*. London: Routledge and Kegan Paul.

Armstrong, D. M. 1972. *Belief, Truth, and Knowledge*. Cambridge: Cambridge University Press.

Armstrong, D. M. 1980. *The Nature of Mind and Other Essays*. Ithaca, NY: Cornell University Press.

Armstrong, D. M. 1985. *What Is a Law of Nature?* Cambridge: Cambridge University Press.

Armstrong, D. M. (1968) 1988 "Perception and Belief." In *Perceptual Knowledge*. Edited by Jonathan Dancy, 127–44. Oxford: Oxford University Press.

Armstrong, D. M. 1996. "Dispositions as Categorical States." In *Dispositions: A Debate*. Edited by Tim Crane, 15–18. London: Routledge.

Armstrong, D. M. 1998. "Qualities: An Excerpt from *Consciousness* and *Causality*." In *Metaphysics: The Big Questions*, 2nd edition. Edited by Peter van Inwagen and Dean Zimmerman, 272–81. Oxford: Blackwell.

Atherton, Margaret. 1990. *Berkeley's Revolution in Vision*. Ithaca, NY: Cornell University Press.

Ayer, A. J. (1940) 1969. *The Foundations of Empirical Knowledge*. London: Macmillan.

Barry, Susan R. 2009. *Fixing My Gaze*. New York: Basic Books.

Beanblossom, Ronald. 1978. "Russell's Indebtedness to Reid." *The Monist*, 61:192–204.

Bennett, Jonathan. 1984. *A Study of Spinoza's Ethics*. Indianapolis: Hackett.

Bennett, Jonathan. 2002. "What Events Are." In *The Blackwell Guide to Metaphysics*, edited by Richard M. Gale, 43–65. Oxford: Blackwell.

Bergmann, Michael. 2004. "Epistemic Circularity: Malignant and Benign." *Philosophy and Phenomenological Research*, 69:708–26.

Bigelow, John. 1996. "Presentism and Properties." *Philosophical Perspectives*, 10:35–52.

Blackburn, Simon. 1984. *Spreading the Word*. Oxford: Clarendon Press.

Blackburn, Simon. 1990. "Filling in Space." *Analysis*, 50:62–65 Reprinted in Blackburn 1993.

Blackburn, Simon. 1993. *Essays in Quasi-Realism*. Oxford: Oxford University Press.

BonJour, Laurence. 2002. *Epistemology: Classical Problems and Contemporary Responses*. Lanham, MD: Rowman and Littlefield.

Boring, Edwin G. (1929) 1950. *A History of Experimental Psychology*. New York: Appleton-Century-Crofts.

Brentano, Franz. 1966. *The True and the Evident*. Edited and translated by R. M. Chisholm et al. New York: Humanities Press.

Brentano, Franz. (1874) 1973. *Psychology from an Empirical Standpoint*. Translated by A. C. Mancurello, D. B. Terrell, and L. L. McAlister. New York: Humanities Press.

Brentano, Franz. (1916) 1975. "Was an Reid zu Loben." *Grazer Philosophische Studien*, 1:1–18.

Broad, C. D. 1919. "Is There Knowledge by Acquaintance?" *Proceedings of the Aristotelian Society*, Sup. Vol. 2:206–20.

Broad, C. D. (1923) 1959. *Scientific Thought*. Paterson, N.J.: Littlefield, Adams. Reprint of 1923 edition by Kegan Paul. London: Kegan Paul, Trench, Trubner.

Broad, C. D. 1925. *The Mind and Its Place in Nature*. London: Routledge and Kegan Paul.

Broad, C. D. (1934) 1952. "Determinism, Indeterminism, and Libertarianism." In *Ethics and the History of Philosophy*, 195–217. London: Routledge and Kegan Paul.

Broad, C. D. 1945. "Some Reflections on Moral-Sense Theories in Ethics." *Proceedings of the Aristotelian Society*, 45:131–66.

Broadbent, D. 1958. *Perception and Communication*. London: Pergamon.

Broadie, Alexander. 1998. "Reid Making Sense of Moral Sense." *Reid Studies*, 1:5–16 Reprinted in *Reid on Ethics*. Edited by Sabine Roeser, 91–102. Houndmills: Palgrave Macmillan, 2010.

Buras, J. Todd. 2002. "The Problem with Reid's Direct Realism." *Philosophical Quarterly*, 52:457–77. Reprinted in *The Philosophy of Thomas Reid*. Edited by John Haldane and Stephen Read, 44–64. Oxford: Blackwell, 2003.

Buras, J. Todd. 2005. "The Nature of Sensations in Reid." *History of Philosophy Quarterly*, 22:221–38.

Buras, J. Todd. 2009. "An Argument against Causal Theories of Mental Content." *American Philosophical Quarterly*, 46:117–29.

Byrne, Alex. 2001. "Intentionalism Defended." *Philosophical Review*, 110:199–240.

Byrne, Alex and Heather Logue. 2008. "Either/Or." In *Disjunctivism: Perception, Action, Knowledge*. Edited by Adrian Haddock and Fiona Macpherson, 57–94. Oxford: Oxford University Press.

Campbell, John. 1994. "A Simple View of Colour." In *Reality, Representation, and Projection*. Edited by John Haldane and Crispin Wright, 257–69. Oxford: Clarendon Press.

Campbell, John. 1996. "Molyneux's Question." In *Philosophical Issues*, Vol. 7. Edited by Enrique Villanueva, 301–18. Atascadera, CA: Ridgeview.

Campbell, John. 2002a. "Berkeley's Puzzle." In *Conceivability and Possibility*. Edited by Tamar Szabo Gendler and John Hawthorne, 127–43. Oxford: Clarendon Press.

Campbell, John. 2002b. *Reference and Consciousness*. Oxford: Oxford University Press.

Chappell, Vere. 1989. "The Theory of Sensations." In *The Philosophy of Thomas Reid*. Edited by Melvin Dalgarno and Eric Matthews, 49–63. Dordrecht: Kluwer Academic.

Chisholm, Roderick M. 1957. *Perceiving*. Ithaca, NY: Cornell University Press.

Chisholm, Roderick M. (1964) 1982. "Human Freedom and the Self." In *Free Will*. Edited by Gary Watson, 24–35. Oxford: Oxford University Press. Originally published as the Lindley Lecture, 3–15, by the University of Kansas.

Chisholm, Roderick M. 1966. *Theory of Knowledge*. Englewood Cliffs, NJ: Prentice-Hall.

Chisholm, Roderick M. 1969. "Some Puzzles about Agency." In *The Logical Way of Doing Things*. Edited by Karel Lambert, 199–217. New Haven, CT: Yale University Press.

Chisholm, Roderick M. 1973. *The Problem of the Criterion*. (The Aquinas Lecture). Milwaukee: Marquette University Press.

Chisholm, Roderick M. 1976. *Person and Object*. La Salle, IL: Open Court.

Chisholm, Roderick M. 1977. *Theory of Knowledge*, 2nd edition. Englewood Cliffs, NJ: Prentice-Hall.

Chisholm, Roderick M. 1979. "Objects and Persons: Revisions and Replies." In *Essays on the Philosophy of Roderick M. Chisholm*. Edited by Ernest Sosa, 317–88. Amsterdam: Rodopi.

Chisholm, Roderick M. (1973) 1982. "Homeless Objects." In *Brentano and Meinong Studies*, 37–52. Amsterdam: Rodopi.

Chisholm, Roderick M. 1989. *Theory of Knowledge*, 3rd edition. Englewood Cliffs, NJ: Prentice-Hall.

Chislenko, Eugene. Forthcoming. "Moore's Paradox and Akratic Belief." *Philosophy and Phenomenological Research*.

Churchland, Paul. 1979. *Scientific Realism and the Plasticity of Mind*. Cambridge: Cambridge University Press.

Cockle, Sir James. 1888. "On the Confluences and Bifurcations of Certain Theories." Presidential Address delivered to the London Mathematical Society on November 8, 1888.

Cohen, Stewart. 2002. "Basic Knowledge and the Problem of Easy Knowledge." *Philosophical and Phenomenological Research*, 65:309–29.

Copenhaver, Rebecca. 2004. "A Realism for Reid: Mediated, but Direct." *British Journal for the History of Philosophy*, 12:61–74.

Copenhaver, Rebecca. 2006. "Thomas Reid's Theory of Memory." *History of Philosophy Quarterly*, 23:171–89.

Copenhaver, Rebecca. 2007. "Reid on Consciousness: HOP, HOT, or FOR?" *Philosophical Quarterly*, 57:613–34.

Copenhaver, Rebecca. 2009. "Reid on Memory and Personal Identity." *The Stanford Encyclopedia of Philosophy*. Edited by Edward N. Zalta. http://plato.stanford.edu/archives/spr2009/entries/reid-memory-identity/.

Copenhaver, Rebecca. 2010. "Thomas Reid on Acquired Perception." *Pacific Philosophical Quarterly*, 91:285–312.

Coventry, Angela and Uriah Kriegel. 2008. "Locke on Consciousness." *History of Philosophy Quarterly*, 25:221–42.

Craig, Edward. 1982. "Meaning, Use, and Privacy." *Mind*, 91:541–64.

Cummins, Phillip D. 1974. "Reid's Realism." *Journal of the History of Philosophy*, 12:317–40.

Cuneo, Terence. 2004. "Reid's Moral Philosophy." In *The Cambridge Companion to Reid*. Edited by Terence Cuneo and René van Woudenberg, 243–46. Cambridge: Cambridge University Press.

Cuneo, Terence. 2007. *The Normative Web*. Oxford: Oxford University Press.

Daniels, Norman. 1974. *Thomas Reid's "Inquiry": The Geometry of Visibles and the Case for Realism*. Stanford, CA: Stanford University Press.

David, Marian. 1985/86. "Nonexistence and Reid's Conception of Conceiving." *Grazer Philosophische Studien*, 25/26:585–99.

Davidson, Donaldson. (1963) 1980. "Actions, Reasons, and Causes." In *Essays on Actions and Events*, 3–19. Oxford: Clarendon.

Davidson, Donaldson. (1969) 1980. "The Individuation of Events." In *Essays on Actions and Events*, 163–80. Oxford: Clarendon.

De Bary, Philip. 2000. "Thomas Reid's Metaprinciple." *American Catholic Philosophical Quarterly*, 74:373–83.

De Bary, Philip. 2002. *Thomas Reid and Scepticism: His Reliabilist Response*. London: Routledge.

Degenaar, Marjolein. 1996. *Molyneux's Problem*. Dordrecht: Kluwer.

DeRose, Keith. 1989. "Reid's Anti-Sensationalism and His Realism." *Philosophical Review*, 98:313–48.

Desmurget, Michel, K. Reilly, N. Richard, A. Szathmari, C. Mottolese, and A. Sirigu. 2009. "Movement Intention after Parietal Cortex Stimulation in Humans." *Science*, 324:811–13.

Dokic, Jérôme. 2010. "Perception without Representation: The Case of Spatial Relations." Presented at a conference on spatial perception at Harvard University, November 2010.

Donagan, Alan. 1979. "Chisholm's Theory of Agency." In *Essays on the Philosophy of Roderick M.Chisholm*. Edited by Ernest Sosa, 215–29. Amsterdam: Rodopi.

Dretske, Fred. 1969. *Seeing and Knowing*. London: Routledge and Kegan Paul.

Dretske, Fred. 1981. *Knowledge and the Flow of Information*. Cambridge, MA: MIT Press.

Dretske, Fred. 1995. *Naturalizing the Mind*. Cambridge, MA: MIT Press.

Dretske, Fred. 2005. "The Case against Closure. In *Contemporary Debates in Epistemology*. Edited by Matthias Steup and Ernest Sosa, 13–26. Oxford: Blackwell.

Ducasse, C. J. 1942, 1952, and 1968. "Moore's 'The Refutation of Idealism.'" In *The Philosophy of G. E. Moore*. Edited by Paul Arthur Schilpp, 225–51. LaSalle, IL: Open Court.

Duggan, Timothy. 1976. "Active Power and the Liberty of Moral Agents." In *Thomas Reid: Critical Interpretations*. Edited by Stephen F. Barker and Tom L. Beauchamp, 103–12. Philadelphia: Philosophical Monographs

Earle, William. 1956. "Memory." *Review of Metaphysics*, 10:3–27.

Ekman, Paul, Richard E. Sorenson, and Wallace V. Friesen. 1969. "Pan-Cultural Elements in Facial Displays of Emotion." *Science*, NS 164:86–88.

Euclid. (ca. 300 B.C.) 1956. *The Thirteen Books of the Elements*. Translated by Sir Thomas L. Heath. New York: Dover.

Evans, Gareth. 1985a. "Molyneux's Question." In *Collected Papers*, 364–99. Oxford: Clarendon Press.

Evans, Gareth. (1979) 1985b. "Reference and Contingency." In *Collected Papers*, 178–213. Oxford: Clarendon Press.

Falkenstein, Lorne. 1994. "Intuition and Construction in Berkeley's Account of Visual Space." *Journal of the History of Philosophy*, 32:63–84.

Falkenstein, Lorne. 2000a. "Reid's Account of Localization." *Philosophy and Phenomenological Research*, 61:305–28.

Falkenstein, Lorne. 2000b. "Reid's Critique of Berkeley's Position on the Inverted Image." *Reid Studies*, 4:35–51.

Falkenstein, Lorne. 2004. "Nativism and the Nature of Thought in Reid's Account of Our Knowledge of the External World." In *The Cambridge Companion to Reid*. Edited by Terence Cuneo and René van Woudenberg, 156–79. Cambridge: Cambridge University Press.

Falkenstein, Lorne. Forthcoming. "Reid's Misappropriation of Spherical Geometry." Presented at a conference on the geometry of the visual field, Fribourg, Switzerland, October 2013. An updated version is forthcoming in *Topoi*.

Falkenstein, Lorne and Giovanni Grandi. 2003. "The Role of Material Impressions in Reid's Theory of Vision: A Critique of Gideon Yaffe's 'Reid on the Perception of Visible Figure.'" *Journal of Scottish Philosophy*, 1:117–33.

Ferreira, M. Jamie. 1986. *Scepticism and Reasonable Doubt: The British Naturalist Tradition in Wilkins, Hume, Reid, and Newman*. Oxford: Clarendon Press.

Firth, Roderick. 1949. "Sense-Data and the Percept Theory." *Mind*, 58:434–65 and 59:35–56.

Fischer, John Martin. 2002. "Frankfurt-type Counterexamples and Semi-Compatibilism." In *The Oxford Handbook of Free Will*. Edited by Robert Kane, 281–308. Oxford: Oxford University Press.

Fodor, Jerry. 1984: "Observation Reconsidered." *Philosophy of Science*, 51:23–43.

Folescu, Marina. 2013. *Thomas Reid on Singular Thought*. Ph.D. dissertation, University of Southern California.

Folescu, Marina. 2015. "Perceiving Bodies Immediately: Thomas Reid's Insight." Forthcoming in *History of Philosophy Quarterly*, 32.

Foster, John. 1982. *The Case for Idealism*. London: Routledge.

Frankfurt, Harry. 1969. "Alternate Possibilities and Moral Responsibility." *Journal of Philosophy*, 66:829–39.

Frova, A. and M. Marenzana, eds. 1998. *Thus Spoke Galileo*. Oxford: Oxford University Press.

Furlong, E. J. 1951. *A Study in Memory*. London: Thomas Nelson.

Gallie, Roger D. 1989. *Thomas Reid and "the Way of Ideas."* Dordrecht: Kluwer Academic.

Ganson, Todd Stuart. 2008. "Reid's Rejection of Intentionalism." *Oxford Studies in Early Modern Philosophy*, 4:245–63.

Gibson, J. J. 1966. *The Senses Considered as Perceptual Systems*. New York: Houghton Mifflin.

Ginet, Carl. 1990. *On Action*. Cambridge: Cambridge University Press.

Glenney, Brian. 2011. "Adam Smith and the Problem of the External World." *Journal of Scottish Philosophy*, 9:205–23.

Goldman, Alvin. 1979. "What Is Justified Belief?" In *Justification and Knowledge*. Edited by George S. Pappas, 1–23. Dordrecht: Reidel.

Grandi, Giovanni. 2003. *Thomas Reid's Theory of Vision*. Ph.D. dissertation, University of Western Ontario.

Grandi, Giovanni. 2005. "Thomas Reid's Geometry of Visibles and the Parallel Postulate." *Studies in History and Philosophy of Science*, 36:79–103.

Grandi, Giovanni. 2006. "Reid's Direct Realism about Vision." *History of Philosophy Quarterly*, 23:225–41.

Grandi, Giovanni. 2008a. "Reid on Ridicule and Common Sense." *Journal of Scottish Philosophy*, 6:71–90.

Grandi, Giovanni. 2008b. "Reid and Condillac on Sensation and Perception: A Thought Experiment on Sensory Deprivation." *Journal of the Southwestern Philosophical Society*, 24:191–200.

Grandi, Giovanni. 2010. "Reid and Wells on Single and Double Vision." *Journal of Scottish Thought*, 3:143–63.

Grandi, Giovanni. 2014. "The Extension of Color Sensations: Reid, Stewart, and Fearn." *Canadian Journal of Philosophy*, 41:50–79.

Grave, S.A. 1960. *The Scottish Philosophy of Common Sense*. Oxford: Clarendon Press.

Greco, John. 1995. "Reid's Critique of Berkeley and Hume: What's the Big Idea?" *Philosophy and Phenomenological Research*, 55:279–96.

Greco, John. 2004. "Reid's Reply to the Skeptic." In *The Cambridge Companion to Reid*. Edited by Terence Cuneo and René van Woudenberg, 134–55. Cambridge: Cambridge University Press.

Gregory, Richard L. 1997. *Eye and Brain*, 5th edition. Princeton, NJ: Princeton University Press.

Grice, H. P. (1941) 1975. "Personal Identity." In *Personal Identity*. Edited by John Perry, 73–95. Berkeley: University of California Press.

Hamilton, Andy. 2003. "'Scottish Commonsense' about Memory: A Defense of Thomas Reid's 'Direct Knowledge' Account." *Australasian Journal of Philosophy*, 81:229–45.

Harman, Gilbert. 1990. "The Intrinsic Quality of Experience." In *Philosophical Perspectives*. Edited by James Tomberlin, Vol. 4, 52–79. Atascadero, CA: Ridgeview. Reprinted in *The Nature of Consciousness*. Edited by Ned Block, Owen Flanagan, and Guven Guzeldere, 663–75. Cambridge, MA: MIT Press, 1997.

Harris, James. 2005. *Liberty and Necessity: The Free-Will Debate in Eighteenth-Century British Philosophy*. Oxford: Clarendon Press.

Hatfield, Gary. 1990. *The Natural and the Normative: Theories of Spatial Perception from Kant to Helmholtz*. Cambridge, MA: MIT Press.

Hawthorne, John. 2005. "The Case for Closure." In *Contemporary Debates in Epistemology*. Edited by Matthias Steup and Ernest Sosa, 26–43. Oxford: Blackwell.

Heck, Richard. 2000. "Nonconceptual Content and the 'Space of Reasons.'" *Philosophical Review*, 109:483–523.

Held, Richard, Yuri Ostrovsky, Beatrice de Gelder, Tapan Gandhi, Suma Ganesh, Umang Mathur, and Pawan Sinha. 2011. "The Newly Sighted Fail to Match Seen with Felt." *Nature Neuroscience*, 14:551–53.

Hempel, Carl. 1965. *Aspects of Scientific Explanation and Other Essays in the Philosophy of Science*. New York: Free Press.

Hill, Christopher. 2009. *Consciousness*. Cambridge: Cambridge University Press.

Hill, Christopher and David J. Bennett. 2008. "The Perception of Size and Shape." *Philosophical Issues*, 18:294–315.

Hochberg, Julian. 1978. *Perception*, 2nd edition. Englewood Cliffs, NJ: Prentice-Hall.

Hoffman, Paul. 2006. "Thomas Reid's Notion of Exertion." *Journal of the History of Philosophy*, 44:431–47.

Hopkins, James. 1973. "Visual Geometry." *Philosophical Review*, 82:3–34. Reprinted in *Kant on Pure Reason*. Edited by Ralph Walker, 41–65. Oxford: Oxford University Press, 1982.

Hopkins, Robert. 2005. "Thomas Reid on Molyneux's Question." *Pacific Philosophical Quarterly*, 86:340–64.

Hopp, Walter. 2011. *Perception and Knowledge: A Phenomenological Account*. Cambridge: Cambridge University Press.

Hossack, Keith. 2006. "Reid and Brentano on Consciousness." In *The Austrian Contribution to Analytic Philosophy*. Edited by Mark Textor, 36–63. London: Routledge.

Huemer, Michael. 1999. "The Problem of Memory Knowledge." *Pacific Philosophical Quarterly*, 80:346–57. Reprinted in *Epistemology: Contemporary Readings*. Edited by Michael Huemer, 113–23. London: Routledge, 2002.

Huemer, Michael. 2001. *Skepticism and the Veil of Perception*. Lanham, MD: Rowman and Littlefield.

Immerwahr, John. 1978. "The Development of Reid's Realism." *The Monist*, 61:245–56.

Jackson, Frank. 1977. *Perception*. Cambridge: Cambridge University Press.

Jackson, Frank. 1986. "What Mary Didn't Know." *Journal of Philosophy*, 83:291–95.

Jaeger, Robert A. 1973. "Action and Subtraction." *Philosophical Review*, 82:320–29.

James, William. (1890) 1950. *The Principles of Psychology*. Two volumes. New York: Dover Publications.

Jessop, T. E. 1966. "Berkeley as Religious Apologist." In *New Studies in Berkeley's Philosophy*. Edited by Warren E. Steinkraus, 98–109. New York: Holt, Rinehart, and Winston.

Johnston, Mark. 2004. "The Obscure Object of Hallucination." *Philosophical Studies*, 120:113–83.

Kelly, Sean. 2005. "The Puzzle of Temporal Experience." In *Cognition and the Brain: The Philosophy and Neuroscience Movement*. Edited by A. Brook and K. Akins, 208–38. Cambridge: Cambridge University Press.

Kim, Jaegwon. (1976) 1993. "Events as Property Exemplifications." In *Supervenience and Mind*, 33–52. Cambridge: Cambridge University Press.

Koch, Christof. 2004. *The Quest for Consciousness*. Englewood, CO: Roberts.

Kohler, Ivo. (1951) 1964. "The Formation and Transformation of the Perceptual World." *Psychological Issues*, 3:1–173.

Kriegel, Uriah. 2003. "Consciousness as Intransitive Self-Consciousness." *Canadian Journal of Philosophy*, 33:103–32.

Langton, Rae. 1998. *Kantian Humility: Our Ignorance of Things in Themselves*. Oxford: Clarendon Press.

Langton, Rae. 2000. "Locke's Relations and God's Good Pleasure." *Proceedings of the Aristotelian Society*, 100:75–91.

Lashley, Karl. 1950. "In Search of the Engram." *Society of Experimental Biology*, 4:454–82.

Lehrer, Keith. 1978. "Reid on Primary and Secondary Qualities." *The Monist*, 61:184–91.

Lehrer, Keith. 1980. "Preferences, Conditionals, and Freedom." In *Time and Cause*. Edited by Peter van Inwagen, 187–201. Dordrecht, Holland: D. Reidel.

Lehrer, Keith. 1985/86. "Reid on Conception and Nonbeing." *Grazer Philosophische Studien*, 25/26:573–83.

Lehrer, Keith. 1986. "Reid on Consciousness." *Reid Studies*, 1:1–9.

Lehrer, Keith. 1989. *Thomas Reid*. London: Routledge.

Lehrer, Keith. 1990. "Chisholm, Reid, and the Problem of the Epistemic Surd." *Philosophical Studies*, 60:39–45.

Lehrer, Keith. 1997. *Self-Trust*. Oxford: Clarendon Press.

Lehrer, Keith. 1998. "Reid, Hume, and Common Sense." *Reid Studies* 2:15–25.

Lehrer, Keith and John-Christian Smith. 1985. "Reid on Testimony and Perception." *Canadian Journal of Philosophy*. Supplementary Volume 11:21–38.

Le Morvan, Pierre. 2004. "Arguments against Direct Realism and How to Counter Them." *American Philosophical Quarterly*, 41:221–34.

Lemos, Noah. 2004. *Common Sense: A Contemporary Defense*. Cambridge: Cambridge University Press.

LePoidevin, Robin. 2011. "The Experience and Perception of Time." *The Stanford Encyclopedia of Philosophy*. Edited by Edward N. Zalta. http://plato.stanford.edu/archives/fall2011/entries/time-experience/.

Levin, Janet. 2008. "Molyneux's Question and the Individuation of Perceptual Concepts." *Philosophical Studies*, 139:1–28.

Lewis, David. 1966. "Percepts and Color Mosaics in Visual Experience." *Philosophical Review*, 75:357–68. Reprinted in *Papers in Metaphysics and Epistemology*, 359–72. Cambridge: Cambridge University Press.

Lewis, David. 1973. "Causation." *Journal of Philosophy*, 70:556–67. Reprinted in Lewis, *Philosophical Papers*. Vol. I, 159–72. Oxford: Oxford University Press, 1986.

Lewis, David. 1981. "Are We Free to Break the Laws?" *Theoria* 47:113–21. Reprinted in Lewis, *Philosophical Papers*. Vol. I, 291–98. Oxford: Oxford University Press, 1986.

Lewis, David. 1983. *Philosophical Papers*. Vol. I. Oxford: Oxford University Press.

Lewis, David. 1986a. *On the Plurality of Worlds*. Oxford: Blackwell.

Lewis, David. 1986b. *Philosophical Papers*. Vol. II. Oxford: Oxford University Press.

Lewis, David. (1994) 1999. "Humean Supervenience Debugged." In *Papers in Metaphysics and Epistemology*, 224–47. Cambridge: Cambridge University Press.

Linden, David E. J., and Ulrich Kallenbach, Armin Heinecke, Wolf Singer, and Rainer Goebel. 1999. "The Myth of Upright Vision: A Psychophysical and Functional Imaging Study of Adaptation to Inverting Spectacles." *Perception*, 28:469–81.

Loeb, Louis. 2007. "The Naturalisms of Reid and Hume." Romanell Lecture, given at the March 2007 meeting of the American Philosophical Association.

Lucas, J. R. 1969. "Euclides ab Omni Naevo Vindicatus." *British Journal for the Philosophy of Science*, 20:1–11.

Mack, Arien, and Irvin Rock. 1998. *Inattentional Blindness*. Cambridge, MA: MIT Press.

Mack, Arien. 2002. "Is the Visual World a Grand Illusion?" In *Is the Visual World a Grand Illusion?* Edited by Alva Noë, 102–10. Charlottesville, VA: Imprint Academic.

Mackie, J. L. 1976. *Problems from Locke*. Oxford: Oxford University Press.

Mackie, J. L. 1977. *Ethics: Inventing Right and Wrong*. London: Penguin Books.

Madden, E. H. 1982. "Commonsense and Agency Theory." *Review of Metaphysics*, 36:319–41.

Malcolm, Norman. 1963. "Three Forms of Memory." In *Knowledge and Certainty*, 203–21. Ithaca, NY: Cornell University Press.

Malcolm, Norman. 1976. "Memory as Direct Awareness of the Past." In *Impressions of Empiricism*. Edited by Godfrey Vesey, 1–22. New York: St. Martin's Press.

Martens, David. 2010. "Knowledge by Acquaintance/by Description." In *A Companion to Epistemology*, 2nd edition. Edited by Jonathan Dancy, Ernest Sosa, and Matthias Steup, 479–82. Oxford: Wiley-Blackwell.

Matthews, Gareth. 1980. *Philosophy and the Young Child*. Cambridge, MA: Harvard University Press.

Maund, Barry. 2008. "Color." *The Stanford Encyclopedia of Philosophy*, edited by Edward N. Zalta, forthcoming. http://plato.stanford.edu/archives/fall2008/entries/color/.

Maurer, Daphne, Christine L. Stager, and Catherine J. Mondloch. 1999. "Cross-Modal Transfer of Shape Is Difficult to Demonstrate in One-Month-Olds." *Child Development*, 70:1047–57.

McCann, Edwin. 1994. "Locke's Philosophy of Body." In *The Cambridge Companion to Locke*. Edited by Vere Chappell, 56–88. Cambridge: Cambridge University Press.

McCann, Hugh. 1975. "Trying, Paralysis, and Volition." *Review of Metaphysics*, 28:423–42.

McDermid, Douglas. 1999. "Thomas Reid on Moral Liberty and Common Sense." *British Journal for the History of Philosophy*, 7:275–303.

McDowell, John. (1982) 1988. "Criteria, Defeasibility, and Knowledge." In *Perceptual Knowledge*. Edited by Jonathan Dancy, 209–19. Oxford: Oxford University Press.

McDowell, John. (1985) 1977. "Values and Secondary Qualities." In *Moral Discourse and Practice: Some Philosophical Approaches*. Edited by Stephen Darwall, Allan Gibbard, and Peter Railton, 201–13. Oxford: Oxford University Press.

McDowell, John. 1994. *Mind and World*. Cambridge: Harvard University Press.

McGinn, Colin. 2004. "The Objects of Intentionality." In *The Externalist Challenge*. Edited by Richard Schantz, 495–512. Berlin: De Gruyter.

McKitrick, Jennifer. 2002. "Reid's Foundation for the Primary/Secondary Quality Distinction." In *The Philosophy of Thomas Reid*. Edited by John Haldane and Stephen Read, 65–81. Oxford: Blackwell, 2003.

Meinong, Alexis. (1904) 1960. "The Theory of Objects." In *Realism and the Background of Phenomenology*. Edited by R. M. Chisholm, 76–117. New York: Free Press.

Meinong, Alexis. (1886) 1973. "Toward an Epistemological Assessment of Memory." In *Empirical Knowledge*. Edited by R. M. Chisholm and R. J. Swartz, 253–70. Englewood Cliffs, NJ: Prentice-Hall.

Merleau-Ponty, Maurice. 1962. *Phenomenology of Perception*. Translated by Colin Smith. New York: Humanities Press.

Moore, G. E. (1903) 1922. "The Refutation of Idealism." In *Philosophical Studies*, 1–30. London: Kegan Paul.

Moore, G. E. (1912) 1965. *Ethics*. New York: Oxford University Press.

Moore, G. E. (1922) 1968. "The Conception of Intrinsic Value." In *Philosophical Studies*, 253–75. Totowa, New Jersey: Littlefield, Adams.

Moore, G. E. (1939) 1962. "Proof of an External World." In *Philosophical Papers*, 126–48. New York: Collier Books.

Moore, G. E. 1942, 1952, and 1968. "A Reply to My Critics: Analysis." In *The Philosophy of G. E. Moore*. Edited by Paul Arthur Schilpp, 660–67. LaSalle, IL: Open Court.

Morgan, Michael. 1977. *Molyneux's Question: Vision, Touch, and the Philosophy of Perception*. Cambridge: Cambridge University Press.

Nadler, Steven M. 1986. "Reid, Arnauld, and the Objects of Perception." *History of Philosophy Quarterly*, 3:165–73.

Nadler, Steven M. 1989. *Arnauld and the Cartesian Philosophy of Ideas*. Princeton, NJ: Princeton University Press.

Nerlich, Graham. 1994. *The Shape of Space*, 2nd edition. Cambridge: Cambridge University Press.

Nichols, Ryan. 2002. "Visible Figure and Reid's Theory of Visual Perception." *Hume Studies*, 28:49–82.

Nichols, Ryan. 2003. "Reid on Fictional Objects and the Way of Ideas." In *The Philosophy of Thomas Reid*. Edited by John Haldane and Stephen Read, 169–88. Oxford: Blackwell.

Nichols, Ryan. 2007. *Thomas Reid's Theory of Perception*. Oxford: Clarendon Press.

Noë, Alva. 2004. *Action in Experience*. Cambridge, MA: MIT Press.

O'Callaghan, Casey. 2007. *Sounds: A Philosophical Theory*. Oxford: Oxford University Press.

O'Connor, Timothy. 2000. *Persons and Causes: The Metaphysics of Free Will*. New York: Oxford University Press.

Owen, David. 2003. "Locke and Hume on Belief, Judgment and Assent." *Topoi*, 22:15–28.

Pappas, George S. 1989. "Sensation and Perception in Reid." *Nous*, 23:155–67.

Parsons, Terence. 1980. *Nonexistent Objects*. New Haven, CT: Yale University Press.

Pastore, Nicholas. 1971. *Selective History of Theories of Visual Perception 1650–1950*. Oxford: Oxford University Press.

Paton, H. J. (1929) 1951. "Self-Identity." In *In Defence of Reason*, 99–116. London: Hutchinson's University Library.

Peacocke, Christopher. 1983. *Sense and Content*. Oxford: Oxford University Press.

Peil, Timothy. 2006. "Survey of Geometry." web.mnstate.edu/peil/geometry/C2EuclidNon Euclid/7elliptic.htm

Pendlebury, Michael. 1990. "Sense Experiences and Their Contents: A Defence of the Propositional Account." *Inquiry*, 33:215–30.

Pendlebury, Michael. 1998. "In Defense of the Adverbial Theory of Experience." In *Thought, Language, and Ontology*, edited by F. Orilia and W. J. Rapaport, 95–106. The Netherlands: Kluwer.

Perry, John. 1970. "The Same F." *Philosophical Review*, 79:181–200.

Pitcher, George. 1971. *A Theory of Perception*. Princeton, NJ: Princeton University Press.

Pitcher, George. 1977. *Berkeley*. London: Routledge and Kegan Paul.

Plantinga, Alvin. 1983. "On Existentialism." *Philosophical Studies*, 44:1–20.

Plantinga, Alvin. 1993a. *Warrant: The Current Debate*. Oxford: Oxford University Press.

Plantinga, Alvin. 1993b. *Warrant and Proper Function*. Oxford: Oxford University Press.

Pollock, John L. 1974. *Knowledge and Justification*. Princeton, NJ: Princeton University Press.

Price, H. H. 1932. *Perception*. London: Methuen.

Price, H. H. 1940. *Hume's Theory of the External World*. Oxford: Clarendon Press.

Prichard, H. A. 1949. *Moral Obligation*. Oxford: Clarendon Press.

Prichard, H. A. 1950. *Knowledge and Perception*. Oxford: Clarendon Press.

Prior, Arthur N. (1962) 2003. "Changes in Events and Changes in Things." In *Papers on Time and Tense*. Edited by P. Hasle, P. Ohrstrom, T. Braüner, and J. Copeland, 7–20. Oxford: Oxford University Press.

Prior, Arthur N. (1968) 1976. "Intentionality and Intensionality." In *Papers in Logic and Ethics*. Edited by P. T. Geach and A. J. P. Kenny, 187–201. Amherst: University of Massachusetts Press

Prior, Arthur N. 1971. *Objects of Thought*. Oxford: Clarendon Press.

Prior, Elizabeth W., Robert Pargetter, and Frank Jackson. 1982. "Three Theses about Dispositions." *American Philosophical Quarterly*, 19:251–57.

Pruss, Alexander. 2006. *The Principle of Sufficient Reason: A Reassessment*. Cambridge: Cambridge University Press.

Pryor, James. 2000. "The Skeptic and the Dogmatist." *Nous*, 34:517–49.

Putnam, Hilary. 1981. *Reason, Truth, and History*. Cambridge: Cambridge University Press.

Putnam, Hilary. 1987. *The Many Faces of Realism*. La Salle, IL: Open Court.

Quilty-Dunn, Jake. 2013. "Was Reid a Direct Realist?" *British Journal for the History of Philosophy*, 21:302–23.

Quine, W. V. (1948). 1961. "On What There Is." In *From a Logical Point of View*, 2nd edition, 1–19. New York: Harper Torchbooks.

Quine, W. V. 1956. "Quantifiers and Propositional Attitudes." *Journal of Philosophy*, 53:177–87.

Quine, W. V. 1960. *Word and Object*. Cambridge, MA: MIT Press.

Quine, W. V. 1987. *Quiddities*. Cambridge, MA: Harvard University Press.

Quinton, Anthony. 1973. *The Nature of Things*. London: Routledge and Kegan Paul.

Ramachandran, V. S., and Sandra Blakeslee. 1999. *Phantoms in the Brain*. New York: Harper.

Rapaport, William J. 1979. "An Adverbial Meinongian Theory." *Analysis*, 39:75–81.

Raynor, David. 1980. "*Minima Visibilia* in Berkeley and Hume." *Dialogue*, 19:196–200.

Robinson, Howard. 1994. *Perception*. London: Routledge.

Rock, Irwin. 1975. *An Introduction to Perception*. New York: Macmillan.

Roeser, Sabine. 2009. "Reid and Moral Emotions." *Journal of Scottish Philosophy*, 7:177–92.

Rosenthal, David M. 1986. "Two Concepts of Consciousness." *Philosophical Studies*, 49:329–59.

Roskies, Adina. 2008. "A New Argument for Nonconceptual Content." *Philosophy and Phenomenological Research*, 76: 633–59.

Routley, Richard. 1966. "Some Things Do Not Exist." *Notre Dame Journal of Formal Logic*, 8:251–75.

Routley, Richard. 1980. *Exploring Meinong's Jungle and Beyond*. Canberra: Research School of Social Sciences, Philosophy Department.

Rowe, William. (1987) 1995. "Two Concepts of Freedom." In *Agents, Causes, and Events*. Edited by Timothy O'Connor, 151–71. New York: Oxford University Press. First published in the *Proceedings and Addresses of the American Philosophical Association*, 61:43–64.

Rowe, William. 1991. *Thomas Reid on Freedom and Morality*. Ithaca, NY: Cornell University Press.

Russell, Bertrand. 1903. *The Principles of Mathematics*. New York: W.W. Norton.

Russell, Bertrand. 1910. "Knowledge by Acquaintance and Knowledge by Description." *Proceedings of the Aristotelian Society*, 11:108–28. Reprinted in *Mysticism and Logic*, 209–32. London: Longmans, Green, 1921.

Russell, Bertrand. (1912) 1999. *The Problems of Philosophy*. Mineola, NY: Dover.

Russell, Bertrand. (1913) 1992. *Theory of Knowledge: The 1913 Manuscript*. Edited by Elizabeth Eames. London: Routledge. First published by Unwin in 1984.

Russell, Bertrand. 1921. *The Analysis of Mind*. London: Allen and Unwin. Excerpted in *Epistemology: Contemporary Readings*. Edited by Michael Huemer, 88–90. London: Routledge, 2002.

Russell, Bertrand. 1948. *Human Knowledge: Its Scope and Limits*. New York: Simon and Schuster.

Ryle, Gilbert. 1949. *The Concept of Mind*. London: Hutchinson University Press.

Rysiew, Patrick. 2005. "Reidian Evidence." *Journal of Scottish Philosophy*, 3:107–21.

Sacks, Oliver. 1995. *An Anthropologist on Mars*. New York: Alfred A. Knopf.

Sacks, Oliver. 2006. "Stereo Sue." *The New Yorker*, June 19, 2006, 64–73.

Salmon, Wesley. 1984. *Scientific Explanation and the Causal Structure of the World*. Princeton, NJ: Princeton University Press.

Schaffer, Jonathan. 2004. "Quiddistic Knowledge." In *Lewisian Themes*, edited by Frank Jackson and Graham Priest, 210–30. Oxford: Clarendon Press.

Schaffer, Jonathan. 2008. "The Metaphysics of Causation." *The Stanford Encyclopedia of Philosophy (Fall 2008 Edition)*. Edited by Edward N. Zalta. http://plato.stanford.edu/archives/fall2008/entries/causation-metaphysics/.

Schiffman, Harvey. 1976. *Sensation and Perception: An Integrated Approach*. New York: John Wiley.

Schwartz, Robert. 1994. *Vision*. Oxford: Blackwell.

Searle, John. 1983. *Intentionality*. Cambridge: Cambridge University Press.

Sellars, Wilfrid. 1963. "Empiricism and the Philosophy of Mind." In *Science, Perception, and Reality*, 127–96. London: Routledge and Kegan Paul.

Sellars, Wilfrid. 1969. "Metaphysics and the Concept of a Person." In *The Logical Way of Doing Things*. Edited by Karel Lambert, 219–52. New Haven, CT: Yale University Press.

Sidgwick, Henry. 1895. "The Philosophy of Common Sense." *Mind* 4:145–58.

Siegel, Susanna. 2006. "Which Properties Are Represented in Perception?" In *Perceptual Experience*. Edited by T. Gendler and J. Hawthorne, 481–503. Oxford: Clarendon Press.

Siegel, Susanna. 2010. "The Contents of Perception." *The Stanford Encyclopedia of Philosophy (Winter 2011 Edition)*, edited by Edward N. Zalta. http://plato.stanford.edu/archives/win2011/entries/perception-contents/.

Silins, Nico. 2008. "Basic Justification and the Moorean Response to the Skeptic." In *Oxford Studies in Epistemology*, Vol. 2. Edited by T. Gendler and J. Hawthorne, 108–142. Oxford: Oxford University Press.

Sinclair, W. A. (1944) 1973. "The Real World Is Astonishingly Rich and Complex." In *A Modern Introduction to Philosophy*, 3rd edition. Edited by Paul Edwards and Arthur Pap, 647–54. New York: Free Press.

Smart, J. J. C. 1959. "Sensations and Brain Processes." *Philosophical Review*, 68:141–56.

Smart, J. J. C. 1963. *Philosophy and Scientific Realism*. London: Routledge and Kegan Paul.

Smith, A. D. 2002. *The Problem of Perception*. Cambridge, MA: Harvard University Press.

Smith, Michael and Daniel Stoljar. 1998. "Global Response Dependence and Noumenal Realism." *The Monist*, 81:85–111.

Sorensen, Roy. 1992. "The Egg Came before the Chicken." *Mind*, 101:541–42.

Sorensen, Roy. 2008. *Seeing Dark Things*. Oxford: Oxford University Press.

Sosa, Ernest and James Van Cleve. 2001. "Thomas Reid." In *The Blackwell Guide to the Modern Philosophers from Descartes to Nietzsche*. Edited by Steven M. Emmanuel, 179–200. Oxford: Blackwell.

Sperling, George. 1960. "The Information Available in Brief Visual Presentations." *Psychological Monographs* 74:1–29.

Stang, Nick. Forthcoming. "Rationalist Responses to Skepticism: A New Puzzle." *Philosophical Imprints*.

Stewart, M. A. 2004. "Reid and Personal Identity: A Study in Sources." In *Thomas Reid: Context, Influence, Significance*. Edited by Joseph Houston, 9–28. Edinburgh: Dunedin Academic Press.

Stewart-Robinson, Charles. 1989. "Thomas Reid and Pneumatology." In *The Philosophy of Thomas Reid*. Edited by Melvin Dalgarno and Eric Matthews, 389–412. Dordrecht: Kluwer Academic.

Stratton, George M. 1896. "Some Preliminary Experiments on Vision without Inversion of the Retinal Image." *Psychological Review*, 3:611–17.

Stratton, George M. 1897. "Vision without Inversion of the Retinal Image." *Psychological Review*, 4:341–60 and 463–81.

Strawson, Galen. 1990. "What's So Good about Reid?" *London Review of Books*, February 22:14–16.

Strawson, P. F. 1966. *The Bounds of Sense*. London: Methuen.

Strawson, P. F. 1985. *Skepticism and Naturalism: Some Varieties*. New York: Columbia University Press.

Streri, Arlette and Edouard Gentaz. 2003. "Cross-Modal Recognition of Shape from Hand to Eye in Human Newborns." *Somatosensory and Motor Research*, 20:11–16.

Stroud, Barry. 1993. "'Gilding or Staining' the World with 'Sentiments' and 'Phantasms.'" *Hume Studies*, 19:253–72. Reprinted in *The New Hume Debate*. Edited by R. Read and K. Richman, 16–30. London: Routledge, 2000.

Šuster, Danilo. 2012. "Lehrer and the Consequence Argument." *Philosophical Studies*, 161:77–86.

Taylor, Richard and Timothy Duggan. 1958. "On Seeing Double." *Philosophical Quarterly*, 8:171–74.

Taylor, Richard. 1966. *Action and Purpose*. Englewood Cliffs, NJ: Prentice-Hall.

Thomson, Judith. 1974. "Molyneux's Problem." *Journal of Philosophy*, 71:637–50.

Thorp, John. 1980. *Free Will*. London: Routledge and Kegan Paul.

Thrane, Gary. 1977. "Berkeley's 'Proper Object of Vision.'" *Journal of the History of Ideas*, 38:243–60.

Tuggy, Dale. 2000. "Thomas Reid on Causation." *Reid Studies*, 3:3–27.

Turbayne, Colin M. 1955. "Berkeley and Molyneux on Retinal Images." *Journal of the History of Ideas*, 16:339–55.

Tye, Michael. 1984. "The Adverbial Approach to Visual Experience." *Philosophical Review*, 93:195–225.

Tye, Michael. 2006. "Nonconceptual Content, Richness, and Fineness of Grain." In *Perceptual Experience*. Edited by Tamar Gendler and John Hawthorne, 504–30. Oxford: Clarendon Press.

Unger, Peter. 2006. *All the Power in the World*. Oxford: Oxford University Press.

US National Institutes of Health. 2011. "Physiology of Volition Studied with Nerve Block." http://www.bioportfolio.com/resources/trial/63880/Physiology-Of-Volition-Studied-With-Nerve-Block.html.

Van Cleve, James. 1979. "Foundationalism, Epistemic Principles, and the Cartesian Circle." *Philosophical Review*, 88:55–91.

Van Cleve, James. 1983. "Conceivability and the Cartesian Argument for Dualism." *Pacific Philosophical Quarterly*, 64:35–45.

Van Cleve, James. 1984. "Reliability, Justification, and the Problem of Induction." In *Midwest Studies in Philosophy*, Vol. 9. Edited by Peter A. French, Theodore E. Uehling Jr., and Howard K. Wettstein, 555–67. Minneapolis: University of Minnesota Press.

Van Cleve, James. 1985. "Epistemic Supervenience and the Circle of Belief." *The Monist*, 68:90–104.

Van Cleve, James. 1987. "Right, Left, and the Fourth Dimension." *Philosophical Review*, 96:33–68.

Van Cleve, James. 1992. "Analyticity, Undeniability, and Truth." *Canadian Journal of Philosophy*, Supplementary Volume 18:89–111.

Van Cleve, James. 1994. "Predication without Universals? A Fling with Ostrich Nominalism." *Philosophy and Phenomenological Research*, 54:577–90.

Van Cleve, James. 1995. "Putnam, Kant, and Secondary Qualities." *Philosophical Papers*, 24:83–109.

Van Cleve, James. 1999. *Problems from Kant*. New York: Oxford University Press.

Van Cleve, James. 2002a. "Thomas Reid's Geometry of Visibles." *Philosophical Review*, 111:373–416.

Van Cleve, James. 2002b. "Receptivity and Our Knowledge of Intrinsic Properties." *Philosophy and Phenomenological Research*, 65:218–36.

Van Cleve, James. 2003a. "Is Knowledge Easy—Or Impossible? Externalism as the Only Alternative to Skepticism." In *The Skeptics: Contemporary Essays*. Edited by Stephen Luper, 45–59. Aldershot, UK: Ashgate.

Van Cleve, James. 2003b. "Reid versus Berkeley on the Inverted Retinal Image." *Philosophical Topics*. 31:425–55.

Van Cleve, James. 2004a. "Reid's Theory of Perception." In *The Cambridge Companion to Reid*. Edited by Terence Cuneo and René van Woudenberg, 101–33. Cambridge: Cambridge University Press.

Van Cleve, James. 2004b. "Externalism and Disjunctivism." In *The Externalist Challenge*. Edited by Richard Schantz, 481–92. Berlin: Walter de Gruyter.

Van Cleve, James. 2006a. "Touch, Sound, and Things without the Mind." *Metaphilosophy*, 37:162–82.

Van Cleve, James. 2006b. "Reid on the Credit of Human Testimony." In *The Epistemology of Testimony*. Edited by Jennifer Lackey and Ernest Sosa, 50–74. Oxford: Clarendon Press.

Van Cleve, James. 2007. "Reid's Answer to Molyneux's Question." *The Monist*, 90:251–70.

Van Cleve, James. 2008. "Reid on Single and Double Vision: Mechanics and Morals." *Journal of Scottish Philosophy*, 6:1–20.

Van Cleve, James. 2011. "Epistemic Humility and Causal Structuralism." In *Perception, Causation, and Objectivity*. Edited by J.Roessler, H. Lerman, and N. Eilan, 82–91. Oxford: Oxford University Press.

Van Cleve, James. 2012. "Defining and Defending Nonconceptual Content and States." In *Philosophical Perspectives*, Vol. 26. Edited by John Hawthorne and Jason Turner, 411–30. Oxford: Wiley-Blackwell.

Van Cleve, James. 2014 "Berkeley, Reid, and Sinha on Molyneux's Question." In *Sensory Integration and the Unity of Consciousness* Edited by Christopher Hill and David Bennett, 193–208. Cambridge, MA: MIT Press.

Van Cleve, James. 2015. "Troubles for Radical Transparency." In *Qualia and Mental Causation in a Physical World: Themes from the Philosophy of Jaegwon Kim*. Edited by T. Horgan, M. Sabates, and D. Sosa. Cambridge: Cambridge University Press.

Van Cleve, James. No date. "Does Suppositional Reasoning Solve the Bootstrapping Problem?"

Van Inwagen, Peter. 1975. "The Incompatibility of Freedom and Determinism." *Philosophical Studies*, 27:185–99.

Van Inwagen, Peter. 1983. *An Essay on Free Will*. Oxford: Clarendon Press.

Van Inwagen, Peter. 2002. "Free Will Remains a Mystery." In *The Oxford Handbook of Free Will*. Edited by Robert Kane, 158–77. Oxford: Oxford University Press.

Van Inwagen, Peter. 2008. "The Consequence Argument." In *Metaphysics: The Big Questions*, 2nd edition. Edited by Peter Van Inwagen and Dean Zimmerman, 450–56. Oxford: Blackwell.

Van Woudenberg, René. 2004. "Reid on Memory and the Identity of Persons." In *The Cambridge Companion to Reid*. Edited by Terence Cuneo and René van Woudenberg, 204–21. Cambridge: Cambridge University Press.

Vihvelin, Kadri. 2013. *Causes, Laws, and Free Will: Why Determinism Doesn't Matter*. Oxford: Oxford University Press.

Vogel, Jonathan. 1990. "Cartesian Skepticism and Inference to the Best Explanation." *Journal of Philosophy*, 87:658–66.

Vogel, Jonathan. 2000. "Reliabilism Leveled." *Journal of Philosophy*, 97:602–23.

Von Wright, G. H. 1963. *Norm and Action*. London: Routledge and Kegan Paul.

Von Wright, G. H. 1971. *Explanation and Understanding*. Ithaca, NY: Cornell University Press.

Vos Savant, Marilyn. 1999. "Ask Marilyn." *Parade* magazine, September 26, 1999.

Wade, Nicholas J. 1998. *A Natural History of Vision*. Cambridge, MA: MIT Press.

Wade, Nicholas J. 2003. *Destined for Distinguished Oblivion: The Scientific Vision of William Charles Wells (1757–1817)*. New York: Kluwer Academic/Plenum.

Wagner, Mark. 2006. *The Geometries of Visual Space*. Mahwah, NJ: Lawrence Erlbaum.

Weinstock, Jerome A. 1976. "Reid's Definition of Freedom." In *Thomas Reid: Critical Interpretations*. Edited by Stephen F. Barker and Tom L. Beauchamp, 95–102. Philadelphia: Philosophical Monographs, 1976.

White, Roger. 2006. "Problems for Dogmatism." *Philosophical Studies*, 131:525–57.

Whitehead, Alfred North. 1925. *Science and the Modern World*. New York: Macmillan.

Wiggins, David. 1980. *Sameness and Substance*. Oxford: Blackwell.

Wittgenstein, Ludwig. 1953, 1958, 2001. *Philosophical Investigations*. Translated by G. E. M. Anscombe. Oxford: Blackwell.

Wittgenstein, Ludwig. 1958. *The Blue and Brown Books*. Oxford: Basil Blackwell.

Wittgenstein, Ludwig. 1969. *On Certainty*. Edited by G. E. M. Anscombe and G. H. von Wright. Oxford: Blackwell.

Wolterstorff, Nicholas. 1980. *Worlds and Works of Art*. Oxford: Clarendon Press.

Wolterstorff, Nicholas. 2000. "Reid on Common Sense, with Wittgenstein's Assistance." *American Catholic Philosophical Quarterly*, 74:491–517.

Wolterstorff, Nicholas. 2001. *Thomas Reid and the Story of Epistemology*. New York: Cambridge University Press.

Wolterstorff, Nicholas. 2004. "Reid on Common Sense." In *The Cambridge Companion to Reid*. Edited by Terence Cuneo and René van Woudenberg, 77–100. Cambridge: Cambridge University Press.

Wood, Paul. 1998. "Reid, Parallel Lines, and the Geometry of Visibles." *Reid Studies*, 2: 27–41.

Wood, Paul. 2004. "Thomas Reid and the Culture of Science." In *The Cambridge Companion to Reid*. Edited by Terence Cuneo and René van Woudenberg, 53–76. Cambridge: Cambridge University Press.

Wright, Crispin. 1992. *Truth and Objectivity*. Cambridge, MA: Harvard University Press.

Wright, Crispin. 2004. "Warrant for Nothing (and Foundations for Free)?" *Proceedings of the Aristotelian Society, Supplementary Volumes,* 78:167–212.

Wright, John P. 1987. "Hume vs. Reid on Ideas: The New Hume Letter." *Mind,* 96:392–98.

Yablo, Stephen. 1993. "Is Conceivability a Guide to Possibility?" *Philosophy and Phenomenological Research,* 53:1–42.

Yaffe, Gideon. 2002. "Reconsidering Reid's Geometry of Visibles." *Philosophical Quarterly,* 52:602–20. Reprinted in *The Philosophy of Thomas Reid.* Edited by John Haldane and Stephen Read, 189–207. Oxford: Blackwell, 2003.

Yaffe, Gideon. 2003a. "Reid on the Perception of Visible Figure." *Journal of Scottish Philosophy,* 1:103–15.

Yaffe, Gideon. 2003b. "The Office of Introspectible Sensation: A Reply to Falkenstein and Grandi." *Journal of Scottish Philosophy,* 1:135–40.

Yaffe, Gideon. 2004. *Manifest Activity: Reid's Theory of Action.* Oxford: Oxford University Press.

Yaffe, Gideon. 2007. "Promises, Social Acts, and Reid's First Argument for Moral Liberty." *Journal of the History of Philosophy,* 45:267–89.

Yaffe, Gideon. 2008. "Thomas Reid." *The Stanford Encyclopedia of Philosophy.* Edited by Edward N. Zalta, forthcoming. http://plato.stanford.edu/archives/fall2008/entries/reid/.

Yaffe, Gideon. 2009. "Thomas Reid on Consciousness and Attention." *Canadian Journal of Philosophy,* 39:165–94.

Yaffe, Gideon. 2010. "Beyond the Brave Officer." In *Reid on Ethics,* edited by Sabine Roeser, 164–83. Hampshire, England: Palgrave Macmillan.

Yolton, John. 1956. *John Locke and the Way of Ideas.* Oxford: Oxford University Press.

Yolton, John. 1984. *Perceptual Acquaintance from Descartes to Reid.* Minneapolis: University of Minnesota Press.

# INDEX

Note: The letter 'n' following locators refers to notes

Aberdeen Philosophical Society, 1, 181n25
Abstraction, 283, 504–505
Acquaintance
  and conception, 16–19, 135–136
  and information sources, 93–94
  knowledge by, 16–17, 461–463
  and memory, 3, 239, 248–252
  and perception, 70, 83, 135–136,
    153–155, 298
  and perceptual direct realism, 96–98
  and presentational direct realism,
    90–94, 297
  principle of, 462
  and secondary qualities, 153–155
  and sensation, 12, 84–90, 96–97
Acquired perception, 127–157
  association model of, 129–130
  and color, 142–145
  and errors of the senses, 139–141
  and hypothetical reasoning, 151–152,
    152n35
  and immediacy, 132–134, 133n5, 134n7
  inconsistent tetrad of, 152–154
  inference model of, 129–130
  and localization, 142–143, 153
  mechanics of, 128–131
  and perceptual content, 145–149,
    151n35, 482
  and perceptual plasticity, 149–150
  of properties alone, 150–152
  and propositionalism, 138–139
  reality of, doubted, 131–141, 131n2
  and secondary qualities, 142–145
  and sensory modality jumping, 136–139
  upstairs wife counterexample, 134–136,
    135n9. *See also* Perception

Action, voluntary
  and agent causation, 391–400
  basic, 512n5
  and exertion, 393–395, 394n56, 395n57
  extension of, 395–400, 396n59, 397n60
  and external causation, 513
  and freedom, 416–417
  and non-cognitivism, 452–455
  and undertaking, 510–512
  and volition, 386–391, 393–395, 395n57,
    513. *See also* Active power; Freedom;
    Volition
Active power, 367–376
  and agent causation freedom, 413–415
  and conception, 370–371, 373
  defined, 367
  and disposition, 104
  an exception to empiricism, 368–370
  innateness of, 35–36, 372
  a primitive notion, 414
  and speculative power, 367
  two-pronged, 414
  and understanding, 373–374, 375n15
  and volition, 372–375, 391–400
  and williwig freedom, 409–410, 409n17,
    410n18, 411n20. *See also* Action,
    voluntary; Freedom; Volition
Adverbialism
  and hallucination, 287–288
  an intrinsic properties, 297–298
  and Meinongism, 276–283
  and perception, 276, 297–300
  and sensation, 10, 21, 25, 73–74, 79, 81,
    85, 276, 297–299
  and thinking, 276–283, 280n24,
    288, 289